Mike Holt's Illustrated Guide to

CHANGES TO
THE NATIONAL ELECTRICAL CODE®

Based on the 2017 NEC®

Mike Holt Enterprises

888.NEC.CODE (632.2633) • www.MikeHolt.com

NOTICE TO THE READER

The text and commentary in this book is the author's interpretation of the 2017 Edition of NFPA 70, the *National Electrical Code®*. It shall not be considered an endorsement of or the official position of the NFPA® or any of its committees, nor relied upon as a formal interpretation of the meaning or intent of any specific provision or provisions of the 2017 edition of NFPA 70, *National Electrical Code*.

The publisher does not warrant or guarantee any of the products described herein or perform any independent analysis in connection with any of the product information contained herein. The publisher does not assume, and expressly disclaims, any obligation to obtain and include information other than that provided to it by the manufacturer.

The reader is expressly warned to consider and adopt all safety precautions and applicable federal, state, and local laws and regulations. By following the instructions contained herein, the reader willingly assumes all risks in connection with such instructions.

Mike Holt Enterprises disclaims liability for any personal injury, property or other damages of any nature whatsoever, whether special, indirect, consequential or compensatory, directly or indirectly resulting from the use of this material. The reader is responsible for relying on his or her personal independent judgement in determining safety and appropriate actions in all circumstances.

The publisher makes no representation or warranties of any kind, including but not limited to, the warranties of fitness for particular purpose or merchantability, nor are any such representations implied with respect to the material set forth herein, and the publisher takes no responsibility with respect to such material. The publisher shall not be liable for any special, consequential, or exemplary damages resulting, in whole or part, from the reader's use of, or reliance upon, this material.

Mike Holt's Illustrated Guide to Changes to the National Electrical Code® Based on the 2017 NEC®

First Printing: October 2016

Author: Mike Holt
Technical Illustrator: Mike Culbreath
Cover Concept: Brian House
Cover Design: Bryan Burch
Layout Design and Typesetting: Cathleen Kwas

COPYRIGHT © 2016 Charles Michael Holt
ISBN 978-0-9863534-2-0

Produced and Printed in the USA

For more information, call 888.NEC.CODE (632.2633), or e-mail Info@MikeHolt.com.

NEC®, NFPA 70®, NFPA 70E® and National Electrical Code® are registered trademarks of the National Fire Protection Association.

This logo is a registered trademark of Mike Holt Enterprises, Inc.

If you are an instructor and would like to request an examination copy of this or other Mike Holt Publications:

Call: 888.NEC.CODE (632.2633) • Fax: 352.360.0983
E-mail: Info@MikeHolt.com • Visit: www.MikeHolt.com/Instructors

You can download a sample PDF of all our publications by visiting www.MikeHolt.com.

I dedicate this book to the
Lord Jesus Christ, *my mentor and teacher.*

Proverbs 16:3

Mike Holt
ENTERPRISES, INC.
888.NEC.CODE (632.2633)

We Care...

Since the day we started our business over 40 years ago, we have been working hard to produce products that get results, and to help individuals in their pursuit of learning more about this exciting industry. I have built my business on the idea that customers come first, and that everyone on my team will do everything they possibly can to take care of you. I want you to know that we value you, and are honored that you have chosen us to be your partner in electrical training.

I believe that you are the future of this industry and that it is you who will make the difference in years to come. My goal is to share with you everything that I know and to encourage you to pursue your education on a continuous basis. That not only will you learn theory, code, calculations or how to pass an exam, but that in the process you will become the expert in the field and the person who others know to trust.

We are dedicated to providing quality electrical training that will help you take your skills to the next level and we genuinely care about you. Thanks for choosing Mike Holt Enterprises for your electrical training needs.

God bless and much success,

Mike Holt

Exam Preparation | Continuing Education | Apprenticeship Products | In-House Training

"...as for me and my house, we will serve the Lord." [Joshua 24:15]

TABLE OF CONTENTS

ABOUT THIS TEXTBOOK

Mike Holt's Illustrated Guide to Changes to the National Electrical Code®, Based on the 2017 NEC®

Mike Holt's Illustrated Guide to Changes to the National Electrical Code®, Based on the 2017 NEC®, reviews the information necessary to understand the changes made for the *2017 National Electrical Code (NEC)*.

There were over 4,000 proposals submitted recommending changes to the 2014 *NEC*, and, as a result, there were hundreds of updates and five new articles.

The goal of this textbook is to review the significant changes and provide explanations and analyses to help you understand the rules, their impact, and their practical application.

Mike's writing style is intended to be informative, practical, easy to read, and applicable for today's electrical professional. Just like all of Mike Holt's textbooks, this one is built around hundreds of full-color illustrations that show the safety requirements of the *National Electrical Code* in practical use, helping you visualize *Code* rules as they're applied to electrical installations.

This illustrated textbook also contains cautions regarding possible conflicts or confusing *NEC* requirements, tips on proper electrical installations, and warnings of dangers related to improper electrical installations. It's possible that some rules may still seem unclear or need additional editorial improvement. We can't eliminate confusing, conflicting, or controversial *Code* requirements, but our goal is to put them into sharper focus to help you understand their intended purpose. Sometimes a requirement seems confusing and it might be hard to understand its actual application. When this occurs, this textbook will point the situation out in an upfront and straightforward manner. We apologize in advance if that ever seems disrespectful, but our intention is to help the industry understand the current *NEC* as best as possible, point out areas that need refinement, and encourage *Code* users to be a part of the change process that creates a better *NEC* for the future.

Keeping up with requirements of the *Code* should be the goal of everyone involved in electrical safety—whether you're an installer, contractor, inspector, engineer, or instructor. This textbook is the perfect tool to help you do that.

The Scope of this Textbook

This textbook, *Mike Holt's Illustrated Guide to Changes to the National Electrical Code, Based on the 2017 NEC*, covers those installation requirements that we consider to be of critical importance, excluding Article 690 (which is covered in a separate textbook, *Understanding NEC Requirements for Solar Photovoltaic Systems, Based on the 2017 NEC*), and is based on the following conditions:

1. Power Systems and Voltage. All power-supply systems are assumed to be one of the following, unless identified otherwise:

- 2-wire, single-phase, 120V
- 3-wire, single-phase, 120/240V
- 4-wire, three-phase, 120/240V Delta
- 4-wire, three-phase, 120/208V or 277/480V Wye

2. Electrical Calculations. Unless the question or example specifies three-phase, they're based on a single-phase power supply. In addition, all amperage calculations are rounded to the nearest ampere in accordance with Section 220.5(B).

3. Conductor Material. Conductors are considered copper, unless aluminum is identified or specified.

4. Conductor Sizing. Conductors are sized based on a THHN/THWN copper conductor terminating on a 75°C terminal in accordance with 110.14(C), unless the question or example indicates otherwise.

5. Overcurrent Device. The term "overcurrent device" refers to a molded-case circuit breaker, unless specified otherwise. Where a fuse is specified, it's a single-element type fuse, also known as a "onetime fuse," unless the text specifies otherwise.

How to Use this Textbook

This textbook is to be used along with the *NEC* and not as a replacement for it. Be sure to have a copy of the 2017 *National Electrical Code* handy. Compare what's being explained in this textbook to what the *Code* book says, and get with others who are knowledgeable about the *NEC* to discuss any topics that you find difficult to understand.

This textbook follows the *Code* format, but it doesn't cover every change or requirement. For example, it doesn't include every article, section, subsection, exception, or Informational Note. So don't be concerned if you see that the textbook contains Exception 1 and Exception 3, but not Exception 2.

Cross-References. *NEC* cross-references to other related *Code* requirements are included to help you develop a better understanding of how the *NEC* rules relate to one another. These cross-references are indicated by *Code* section numbers in brackets, an example of which is "[90.4]."

Informational Notes. Informational Notes contained in the *NEC* will be identified in this textbook as "Note."

Exceptions. Exceptions contained in this textbook will be identified as "Ex" and not spelled out.

We hope that as you read through this textbook, you'll allow sufficient time to review the text along with the outstanding graphics and examples, which will be invaluable to your understanding of the *NEC*.

Technical Questions

As you progress through this textbook, you might find that you don't understand every explanation, example, calculation, or comment. Don't become frustrated, and don't get down on yourself. Remember, this is the *National Electrical Code*, and sometimes the best attempt to explain a concept isn't enough to make it perfectly clear. If you're still confused, visit www.MikeHolt.com/forum, and post your question on our free *Code* Forum. The forum is a moderated community of electrical professionals.

Textbook Corrections

We're committed to providing you with the finest product with the fewest errors, and take great care to ensure our textbooks are correct. But we're realistic and know that errors might be found after printing. The last thing we want is for you to have problems finding, communicating, or accessing this information, so we list it on our website.

If you believe that there's an error of any kind (typographical, grammatical, technical, etc.) in this textbook or in the Answer Key, and it's not listed on the website, send an e-mail and be sure to include the textbook title, page number, and any other pertinent information.

To check for known errors, visit www.MikeHolt.com/corrections.
To report an error, email corrections@MikeHolt.com.

Textbook Format

The layout of this textbook incorporates special features and symbols designed not only to help you navigate easily through the material, but to also enhance your understanding.

A *Code* Rule icon signifies whether the rule is new, deleted, edited, reduced, clarified, expanded, reorganized, or moved.

CLARIFIED

Clarified—A change that clarifies the requirements of a rule that wasn't clear in the previous *Code* cycle.

EDITED

Edited—An editorial revision that doesn't change the requirement; but it gives us the opportunity to review the rule.

EXPANDED

Expanded—A change where a previous requirement(s) was expanded to cover additional applications.

NEW

New—A new requirement which could be an entirely new section, subsection, exception, table, and/or Informational Note.

REDUCED

Reduced—A change that's reduced the requirements from the previous edition of the *NEC*.

RELOCATED

Relocated—This identifies a rule that was relocated from one section of the *Code* to another without a change in the requirement(s).

REORGANIZED

Reorganized—A change made to place the existing requirements in a more logical order or list.

Danger, Caution and Warning icons highlight areas of concern.

Caution—Possible damage to property or equipment.

Warning—Severe property damage or personal injury.

Danger—Severe injury or death.

A QR Code under the article number can be scanned with a smartphone app to take you to a sample video clip to see Mike and the DVD panel discuss this rule.

Formulas are easily identifiable in green text on a gray bar.

Key Features

A summary of the *NEC* change is indicated in a gray box immediately under a black bar with the *Code* rule title.

Analysis of the rule in the yellow box provides the explanation and context for the change.

Detailed full-color educational graphics illustrate the change in a real-world application.

Author's comments provide additional information to help you understand the context.

Examples and practical application questions and answers are contained in framed yellow boxes.

Underlined text denotes changes to the *Code* for the 2017 *NEC*.

445.13 | Generators

445.13 Ampacity of Conductors

An allowance has been added for conductors to be tapped on the load side of generator overcurrent protective devices.

Analysis

EXPANDED Sometimes we discover that we've been doing things for years with no problems but it was never expressly allowed by the *NEC*. This is the case with tapping conductors from generators. Often several conductors are connected on the load side of the overcurrent protective device of a generator. This wasn't specifically allowed in the *Code*. An allowance has been added for these types of installations as long as they're done in accordance with 240.21(B).

445.13 Ampacity of Conductors

(A) General. The ampacity of the conductors from the generator winding output terminals to the first overcurrent protection device, typically on the generator, must have an ampacity of not less than 115 percent of the nameplate current rating of the generator. Figure 445–2

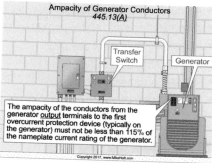

Ampacity of Generator Conductors
445.13(A)

The ampacity of the conductors from the generator <u>output</u> terminals to the first overcurrent protection device (typically on the generator) must not be less than 115% of the nameplate current rating of the generator.

Copyright 2017, www.MikeHolt.com

Figure 445–2

Author's Comment:

■ Since the overcurrent protection device is typically part of the generator, this rule applies to the generator manufacturer, not the field installer.

■ Conductors from the load side of the generator overcurrent protection device to the transfer switch are sized in accordance with 240.4.

Example: What size conductor is required from a 100A overcurrent protection device on a 20 kW, 120/240V single-phase generator to a 200A service rated transfer switch if the terminals are rated for 75°C conductor sizing? Figure 445–3

Solution: A 3 AWG conductor is required; Table 310.15(B)(16), rated 100A at 75°C [110.14(C)(1)(b)].

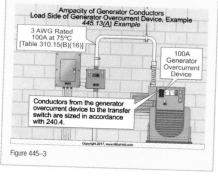

Ampacity of Generator Conductors
Load Side of Generator Overcurrent Device, Example
445.13(A) Example

3 AWG Rated
100A at 75°C
[Table 310.15(B)(16)]

100A
Generator
Overcurrent
Device

Conductors from the generator overcurrent device to the transfer switch are sized in accordance with 240.4.

Copyright 2017, www.MikeHolt.com

Figure 445–3

Generators that aren't a separately derived system must have the neutral conductor sized to carry the maximum unbalanced current as determined by 220.61, serve as part of the effective ground-fault current path, and be not smaller than required by 250.30. Figure 445–4

(B) Overcurrent Protection Provided. <u>Conductors can be tapped from the load side of the generator overcurrent protected device in accordance with 240.21(B).</u>

Additional Products to Help You Learn

Changes to the NEC 2017 DVDs

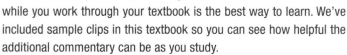

One of the best ways to get the most out of this textbook is to use it in conjunction with the companion DVDs. Mike Holt's DVDs provide a 360° view of each topic with specialized commentary from Mike and his panel of industry experts. Whether you're a visual or auditory learner, watching the DVDs while you work through your textbook is the best way to learn. We've included sample clips in this textbook so you can see how helpful the additional commentary can be as you study.

If you have not already purchased the DVDs for this title and would like to add them at a discounted price call our office at 888.632.2633.

Solar Photovoltaic Systems DVD Program

The 2017 *Code* includes major additions and changes to Article 690. The extent of these changes are beyond the scope of this textbook. As a result, we've incorporated all changes related to Solar Photovoltaic Systems into a separate textbook specifically created for this and related parts of the *Code*. That textbook *Understanding NEC Requirements for Solar Photovoltaic Systems, based on the 2017 NEC*, is required reading for everyone who works on solar installations, including designers, service contractors, installers, and inspectors. That textbook not only includes the 2017 changes related to Article 690, but it also provides a complete understanding of the major rules, changes, and supporting articles related to solar photovoltaic systems.

The program includes:

- *Understanding NEC Requirements for Solar Photovoltaic Systems* textbook
- *Understanding NEC Requirements for Solar Photovoltaic Systems DVDs (2)*

For more information visit www.mikeholt.com/17solar

Understanding the *NEC* Training Library

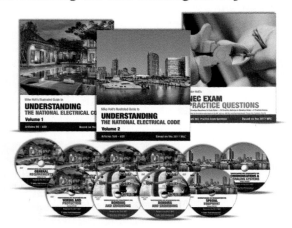

Do you want a comprehensive understanding of the *Code*? Then you need Mike's Understanding the *NEC* Training Library. This program takes you step-by-step through the *NEC*, in *Code* order with detailed illustrations, great practice questions, and in-depth DVD analysis. This library is perfect for engineers, electricians, contractors, and electrical inspectors.

- *Understanding the National Electrical Code—Volume 1* textbook
- *Understanding the National Electrical Code—Volume 2* textbook
- *NEC Exam Practice Questions* workbook
- *General Requirements DVD*
- *Bonding and Grounding DVDs (2)*
- *Wiring and Protection DVD*
- *Wiring Methods and Materials DVD*
- *Equipment for General Use DVD*
- *Special Occupancies DVD*
- *Special Equipment DVD*
- *Communications and Signaling Systems DVD*

2017 *Code* Book and Tabs

The easiest way to use your copy of the *NEC* correctly is to tab it for quick reference. Mike's best-selling tabs make organizing your *Code* book easy. Please note that if you're using it for an exam, confirm with your testing authority that a tabbed *Code* book is allowed into the exam room.

To order a *Code* product visit www.MikeHolt.com/17code, or call 1.888.NEC.CODE (632.2633).

HOW TO USE THE *NATIONAL ELECTRICAL CODE*

The purpose of the *Code* is the practical safeguarding of persons and property from hazards arising from the use of electricity. Now what could be a hazard? Electric shock or fires—and that's what drives the *NEC*. It isn't intended as a design specification or an instruction manual for untrained persons. In fact it's a standard that contains the minimum requirements for electrical installations. Learning to understand and use the *Code* is critical to you working safely, whether you're training to become an electrician, or are already an electrician, electrical contractor, inspector, engineer, designer, or instructor.

The original *NEC* document was developed in 1897 as a result of the united efforts of various insurance, electrical, architectural, and other allied interests. It was written for those who understand electrical terms, theory, safety procedures, and electrical trade practices. The National Fire Protection Association (NFPA®) has acted as sponsor of the *National Electrical Code* since 1911.

Learning to use the *National Electrical Code* is a lengthy process and can be frustrating if you don't approach it the right way. First of all, you'll need to understand electrical theory. If you don't have theory as a background when you get into the *NEC*, you're going to be struggling—so take one step back if you need to, and learn electrical theory. You must also understand the concepts and terms, and know your grammar and punctuation in order to understand the complex structure of the rules and their intended purpose(s). Our goal for the next few pages is to give you some guidelines and suggestions on using your *Code* book, to help you understand what you're trying to accomplish, and how to get there.

Language Considerations for the *NEC*

Terms and Concepts

The *NEC* contains many technical terms, so it's crucial for *Code* users to understand their meanings and applications. If you don't understand a term used in a rule, it will be impossible to properly apply the *NEC* requirement. Article 100 defines the terms that apply to two or more *Code* articles; for example, the term "Dwelling Unit" is found in many articles. If you don't know the *NEC* definition for a "dwelling unit" you can't properly identify the *Code* requirements for it.

Many articles have terms unique to that specific article, and the definitions of those terms are only applicable to that given article. These definitions are usually found in the beginning of the article. For example, Section 250.2 contains the definitions of terms that only apply to Article 250—Grounding and Bonding.

Small Words, Grammar, and Punctuation

It's not only the technical words that require close attention. Simple words can make a big difference to the application of a rule—was there a comma, was it "or," "and," "other than," "greater than," "smaller than." The word "or" can imply alternate choices for wiring methods. A word like "or" gives us choices while the word "and" can mean an additional requirement must be met. An example of these words being used in the *NEC* is found in 110.26(C)(2), where it says equipment containing overcurrent, switching, "or" control devices that are 1,200A or more "and" over 6 ft wide that require a means of egress at each end of the working space.

In 110.26(C)(2) the word "or" clarifies that equipment containing any of the three types of devices listed must follow this rule. The word "and" clarifies that 110.26(C)(2) only applies if the equipment is both 1,200A and over 6 ft wide.

Grammar and punctuation play an important role in establishing the meaning of a rule. The location of a comma can dramatically change the requirement of a rule such as in 250.28(A), where it says a main bonding jumper must be a wire, bus, screw or similar suitable conductor. If the comma between "bus" and "screw" was removed only a "bus screw" could be used. That comma makes a big change in the requirements of the rule.

Slang Terms or Technical Jargon

Trade-related professionals in different areas of the country often use local "slang" terms that aren't shared by all. This can make it difficult to communicate if it isn't clear what the meaning of those slang terms are. Use the proper terms by finding out what their definitions and applications are before you use them. For example, the term "pigtail" is often used to describe the short piece of conductor used to connect a device to a splice, but a "pigtail" is also a term used for a rubberized light socket with pre-terminated conductors. Although the term is the same, the meaning is very different and could cause confusion.

NEC Style and Layout

It's important to understand the structure and writing style of the *Code* if you want to use it effectively. The *National Electrical Code* is organized using eleven major components.

1. Table of Contents
2. Chapters—Chapters 1 through 9 (major categories)
3. Articles—Chapter subdivisions that cover specific subjects
4. Parts—Divisions used to organize article subject matter
5. Sections—Divisions used to further organize article subject matter
6. Tables and Figures—Represent the mandatory requirements of a rule
7. Exceptions—Alternatives to the main *Code* rule
8. Informational Notes—explanatory material for a specific rule (not a requirement)
9. Tables—Applicable as referenced in the *NEC*
10. Annexes—Additional explanatory information such as tables and references (not a requirement)
11. Index

1. Table of Contents. The Table of Contents displays the layout of the chapters, articles, and parts as well as the page numbers. It's an excellent resource and should be referred to periodically to observe the interrelationship of the various *NEC* components. When attempting to locate the rules for a particular situation, knowledgeable *Code* users often go first to the Table of Contents to quickly find the specific *NEC* Rule that applies.

2. Chapters. There are nine chapters, each of which is divided into articles. The articles fall into one of four groupings: General Requirements (Chapters 1 through 4), Specific Requirements (Chapters 5 through 7), Communications Systems (Chapter 8), and Tables (Chapter 9).

Chapter 1—General
Chapter 2—Wiring and Protection
Chapter 3—Wiring Methods and Materials
Chapter 4—Equipment for General Use
Chapter 5—Special Occupancies
Chapter 6—Special Equipment
Chapter 7—Special Conditions
Chapter 8— Communications Systems (Telephone, Data, Satellite, Cable TV and Broadband)
Chapter 9—Tables–Conductor and Raceway Specifications

3. Articles. The *NEC* contains approximately 140 articles, each of which covers a specific subject. The *NEC* begins with Article 90, the introduction to the *Code*. It contains the purpose of the *NEC*, what's covered and what isn't covered along with how the *Code* is arranged. It also gives information on enforcement and how mandatory and permissive rules are written and how explanatory material is included. Article 90 also includes information on formal interpretations, examination of equipment for safety, wiring planning, and information about formatting units of measurement. Here are some other examples of articles you will find in the *Code*:

Article 110—General Requirements
Article 250—Grounding and Bonding
Article 300—General Requirements for Wiring Methods and Materials
Article 430—Motors and Motor Controllers
Article 500—Hazardous (Classified) Locations
Article 680— Swimming Pools, Fountains, and Similar Installations
Article 725— Remote-Control, Signaling, and Power-Limited Circuits
Article 800—Communications Circuits

4. Parts. Larger articles are subdivided into parts. Because the parts of a *Code* article aren't included in the section numbers, we have a tendency to forget what "part" an *NEC* rule is relating to. For example, Table 110.34(A) contains working space clearances for electrical equipment. If we aren't careful, we might think this table applies to all electrical installations, but Table 110.34(A) is located in Part III, which only contains requirements for "Over 1000 Volts, Nominal" installations. The rules for working clearances for electrical equipment for systems 1000V, nominal, or less are contained in Table 110.26(A)(1), which is located in Part II—1000 Volts, Nominal, or Less.

5. Sections. Each *NEC* rule is called a "*Code* Section." A *Code* section may be broken down into subsections by letters in parentheses like (A), Numbers in parentheses like (1) and lowercase letters like (a), (b), and so on, further break the rule down to the second and third level. For example, the rule requiring all receptacles in a dwelling unit bathroom to be GFCI protected is contained in Section 210.8(A)(1). Section 210.8(A)(1) is located in Chapter 2, Article 210, Section 8, Subsection (A), Sub-subsection (1).

Many in the industry incorrectly use the term "Article" when referring to a *Code* section. For example, they say "Article 210.8," when they should say "Section 210.8." Section numbers in this textbook are shown without the word "Section," unless they begin a sentence. For example, Section 210.8(A) is shown as simply 210.8(A).

6. Tables and Figures. Many *NEC* requirements are contained within tables, which are lists of *Code* rules placed in a systematic arrangement. The titles of the tables are extremely important; you must read them carefully in order to understand the contents, applications and limitations of each table. Many times notes are provided in or below a table; be sure to read them as well since they're also part of the requirement. For example, Note 1 for Table 300.5 explains how to measure the cover when burying cables and raceways, and Note 5 explains what to do if solid rock is encountered.

7. Exceptions. Exceptions are *Code* requirements or permissions that provide an alternative method to a specific rule. There are two types of exceptions—mandatory and permissive. When a rule has several exceptions, those exceptions with mandatory requirements are listed before the permissive exceptions.

Mandatory Exceptions. A mandatory exception uses the words "shall" or "shall not." The word "shall" in an exception means that if you're using the exception, you're required to do it in a particular way. The phrase "shall not" means it isn't permitted.

Permissive Exceptions. A permissive exception uses words such as "shall be permitted," which means it's acceptable (but not mandatory) to do it in this way.

8. Informational Notes. An Informational Note contains explanatory material intended to clarify a rule or give assistance, but it isn't a *Code* requirement.

9. Tables. Chapter 9 consists of tables applicable as referenced in the *NEC*. The tables are used to calculate raceway sizing, conductor fill, the radius of raceway bends, and conductor voltage drop.

10. Annexes. Annexes aren't a part of the *NEC* requirements, and are included in the *Code* for informational purposes only.

Annex A. Product Safety Standards
Annex B. Application Information for Ampacity Calculation
Annex C. Raceway Fill Tables for Conductors and Fixture Wires of the Same Size
Annex D. Examples
Annex E. Types of Construction
Annex F. Critical Operations Power Systems (COPS)
Annex G. Supervisory Control and Data Acquisition (SCADA)
Annex H. Administration and Enforcement
Annex I. Recommended Tightening Torques
Annex J. ADA Standards for Accessible Design

11. Index. The Index at the back of the *Code* book is helpful in locating a specific rule.

Author's Comment:

■ Changes in the 2017 *Code* Book are indicated as follows:

♦ Changed rules are identified by shading the text that was changed since the previous edition.

♦ New rules aren't shaded like a change, instead they have a shaded "N" in the margin to the left of the section number.

♦ Relocated rules are treated like new rules with a shaded "N" in the left margin by the section number.

♦ Deleted rules are indicated by a bullet symbol "•" located in the left margin where the rule was in the previous edition.

How to Locate a Specific Requirement

How to go about finding what you're looking for in the *Code* book depends, to some degree, on your experience with the *NEC*. *Code* experts typically know the requirements so well that they just go to the correct rule. Very experienced people might only need the Table of Contents to locate the requirement they're looking for. On the other hand, average users should use all of the tools at their disposal, including the Table of Contents, the Index and the search feature on electronic versions of the *Code* book.

Table of Contents. Let's work through a simple example using the Table of Contents: What *NEC* rule specifies the maximum number of disconnects permitted for a service?

If you're an experienced *Code* user, you'll know Article 230 applies to "Services," and because this article is so large, it's divided up into multiple parts (actually eight parts). With this knowledge, you can quickly go to the Table of Contents and see it lists the Service Equipment Disconnecting Means requirements in Part VI.

Author's Comment:

- The number 70 precedes all page numbers because the *NEC* is NFPA Standard Number 70.

Index. If you use the Index, which lists subjects in alphabetical order, to look up the term "service disconnect," you'll see there's no listing. If you try "disconnecting means," then "services," you'll find that the Index indicates the rule is located in Article 230, Part VI. Because the *NEC* doesn't give a page number in the Index, you'll need to use the Table of Contents to find it, or flip through the *Code* book to Article 230, then continue to flip through pages until you find Part VI.

Many people complain that the *NEC* only confuses them by taking them in circles. As you gain experience in using the *Code* and deepen your understanding of words, terms, principles, and practices, you'll find the *NEC* much easier to understand and use than you originally thought.

Customizing Your *Code* Book

One way to increase your comfort level with the *Code* book is to customize it to meet your needs. You can do this by highlighting and underlining important *NEC* requirements. Preprinted adhesive tabs are also an excellent aid to quickly find important articles and sections that are regularly referenced. Be aware that if you're using your *Code* book to take an exam, some exam centers don't allow markings of any type.

Highlighting. As you read through textbooks or find answers to your questions, be sure you highlight those requirements in the *NEC* that are the most important or relevant to you. Use one color, like yellow, for general interest and a different one for important requirements you want to find quickly. Be sure to highlight terms in the Index and the Table of Contents as you use them.

Underlining. Underline or circle key words and phrases in the *Code* with a red or blue pen (not a lead pencil) using a short ruler or other straightedge to keep lines straight and neat. This is a very handy way to make important requirements stand out. A short ruler or other straightedge also comes in handy for locating the correct information in a table.

Different Interpretations

Industry professionals often enjoy the challenge of discussing the *NEC* requirements. This discussion is important to the process of better understanding the *Code* requirements and application(s). If you decide you're going to participate in one of these discussions, don't spout out what you think without having the actual *NEC* book in your hand. The professional way of discussing a *Code* requirement is by referring to a specific section, rather than talking in vague generalities. This will help everyone involved clearly understand the point and become better educated.

Become Involved in the *NEC* Process

The actual process of changing the *Code* takes about two years and involves hundreds of individuals making an effort to have the *NEC* as current and accurate as possible. As you study and learn how to use it, you'll find it very interesting, enjoy it more, and realize that you can also be a part of the process. Rather than sitting back and just reading it and learning it, you can participate by making proposals and being a part of its development. For the 2017 *Code*, there were 4,000 public inputs and 1,500 comments. Hundreds of updates and five new articles were added to keep the *NEC* up to date with new technologies, and pave the way to a safer and more efficient electrical future.

Let's review how this process works:

STEP 1—Public Input Stage

Public Input. The revision cycle begins with the acceptance of Public Input (PI): the public notice asking for anyone interested to submit input on an existing standard or a committee-approved new draft standard. Following the closing date, the Committee conducts a First Draft Meeting to respond to all public inputs.

First Draft (FD) Meeting. At the First Draft Meeting, the Technical Committee considers and provides a response to all Public Input. The Technical Committee may use the input to develop First Revisions to the standard. The First Draft documents consist of the initial meeting consensus of the committee by simple majority. However, the final position of the Technical Committee must be established by a ballot which follows.

Committee Ballot on First Draft. The First Draft developed at the First Draft Meeting is balloted: to appear in the First Draft, a revision must be approved by at least two-thirds of the Technical Committee.

First Draft Report Posted. First revisions which pass ballot are ultimately compiled and published as the First Draft Report on the document's NFPA web page. This report serves as documentation for the Input Stage and is published for review and comment. The public may review the First Draft Report to determine whether to submit Public Comments on the First Draft.

STEP 2—Public Comment Stage

Public Comment. Once the First Draft Report becomes available, there's a public comment period during which anyone can submit a Public Comment on the First Draft. After the Public Comment closing date, the Technical Committee conducts/holds their Second Draft Meeting.

Second Draft Meeting. After the Public Comment closing date, if Public Comments are received or the committee has additional proposed revisions, a Second Draft Meeting is held. At the Second Draft Meeting, the Technical Committee reviews the First Draft and may make additional revisions to the draft Standard. All Public Comments are considered, and the Technical Committee provides an action and response to each Public Comment. These actions result in the Second Draft.

Committee Ballot on Second Draft. The Second Revisions developed at the Second Draft Meeting are balloted. To appear in the Second Draft, a revision must be approved by at least two-thirds of the Technical Committee.

Second Draft Report Posted. Second Revisions which pass ballot are ultimately compiled and published as the Second Draft Report on the document's NFPA website. This report serves as documentation of the Comment Stage and is published for public review.

Once published, the public can review the Second Draft Report to decide whether to submit a Notice of Intent to Make a Motion (NITMAM) for further consideration.

STEP 3—NFPA Technical Meeting (Tech Session)

Following completion of the Public Input and Public Comment stages, there's further opportunity for debate and discussion of issues through the NFPA Technical Meeting that takes place at the NFPA Conference & Expo®. These motions are attempts to change the resulting final Standard from the committee's recommendations published as the Second Draft.

STEP 4—Council Appeals and Issuance of Standard

Issuance of Standards. When the Standards Council convenes to issue an NFPA standard, it also hears any related appeals. Appeals are an important part of assuring that all NFPA rules have been followed and that due process and fairness have continued throughout the standards development process. The Standards Council considers appeals based on the written record and by conducting live hearings during which all interested parties can participate. Appeals are decided on the entire record of the process, as well as all submissions and statements presented.

After deciding all appeals related to a standard, the Standards Council, if appropriate, proceeds to issue the Standard as an official NFPA Standard. The decision of the Standards Council is final subject only to limited review by the NFPA Board of Directors. The new NFPA standard becomes effective twenty days following the Standards Council's action of issuance.

Author's Comment:

- Proposals and comments can be submitted online at the NFPA website at www.nfpa.org/doc# (for NFPA 70, go to www.nfpa.org/70 for example). From the homepage, look for "Codes & Standards," then find "How the Process Works." Following the closing date, the Committee conducts a First Draft Meeting to respond to all public inputs. If you'd like to see something changed in the *Code*, you're encouraged to participate in the process.

ARTICLE 90

INTRODUCTION TO THE *NATIONAL ELECTRICAL CODE*

Introduction to Article 90—Introduction to the *National Electrical Code*

Many *NEC* violations and misunderstandings wouldn't occur if people doing the work simply understood Article 90. For example, many people see *Code* requirements as performance standards. In fact, the *NEC* requirements are bare minimums for safety. This is exactly the stance electrical inspectors, insurance companies, and courts take when making a decision regarding electrical design or installation.

Article 90 opens by saying the *NEC* isn't intended as a design specification or instruction manual. The *National Electrical Code* has one purpose only, and that's the "practical safeguarding of persons and property from hazards arising from the use of electricity." The necessity of carefully studying the *NEC* rules can't be overemphasized, and the role of textbooks such as this one is to help in that undertaking. Understanding where to find the rules in the *Code* that apply to the installation is invaluable. Rules in several different articles often apply to even a simple installation.

Article 90 then describes the scope and arrangement of the *NEC*. The balance of this article provides the reader with information essential to understanding the *Code* rules.

Typically, electrical work requires you to understand the first four chapters of the *NEC* which apply generally, plus have a working knowledge of the Chapter 9 tables. That understanding begins with Article 90. Chapters 5, 6, and 7 make up a large portion of the *Code*, but they apply to special occupancies, special equipment, or other special conditions. They build on, modify, or amend the rules in the first four chapters. Chapter 8 contains the requirements for communications systems, such as twisted pair conductors for telephone and data systems, satellite receivers, antenna systems, and coaxial cable wiring. Communications systems (twisted wire, antennas, and coaxial cable) aren't subject to the general requirements of Chapters 1 through 4, or the special requirements of Chapters 5 through 7, unless there's a specific reference in Chapter 8 to a rule in Chapters 1 through 7.

90.1 Purpose of the *NEC*

(A) Practical Safeguarding. The purpose of the *NEC* is to ensure that electrical systems are installed in a manner that protects people and property by minimizing the risks associated with the use of electricity. It isn't a design specification standard or instruction manual for the untrained and unqualified. Figure 90–1

Author's Comment:

- The *Code* is intended to be used by those skilled and knowledgeable in electrical theory, electrical systems, construction, and the installation and operation of electrical equipment.

Figure 90–1

(B) Adequacy. The *Code* contains requirements considered necessary for a safe electrical installation. If an electrical system is installed in compliance with the *NEC*, it'll be essentially free from electrical hazards. The *Code* is a safety standard, not a design guide.

NEC requirements aren't intended to ensure the electrical installation will be efficient, convenient, adequate for good service, or suitable for future expansion. Specific items of concern, such as electrical energy management, maintenance, and power quality issues aren't within the scope of the *Code*. Figure 90–2

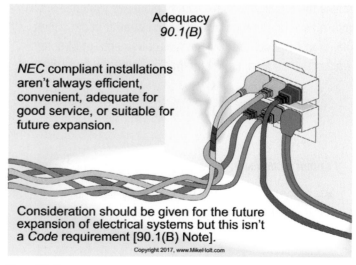

Figure 90–2

Note: Hazards in electrical systems often occur because circuits are overloaded or not properly installed in accordance with the *NEC*. These often occur if the initial wiring didn't provide reasonable provisions for system changes or for the increase in the use of electricity. Figure 90–3

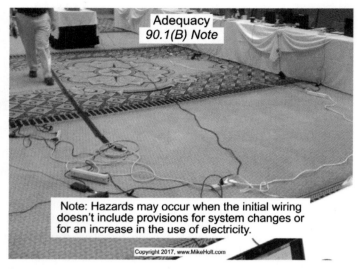

Figure 90–3

Author's Comment:

- See the definition of "Overload" in Article 100.

- The *NEC* doesn't require electrical systems to be designed or installed to accommodate future loads. However, the electrical designer (typically an electrical engineer) is concerned with not only ensuring electrical safety (*Code* compliance), but also with ensuring the system meets the customers' needs, both of today and in the near future. To satisfy customers' needs, electrical systems are often designed and installed above the minimum requirements contained in the *NEC*. But just remember, if you're taking an exam, licensing exams are based on your understanding of the minimum *Code* requirements.

(C) Relation to International Standards. The requirements of the *NEC* address the fundamental safety principles contained in the International Electrotechnical Commission (IEC) Standard, including protection against electric shock, adverse thermal effects, overcurrent, fault currents, and overvoltage. Figure 90–4

NEC Relation to International Standards
90.1(C) and Note

The *NEC* addresses the safety principles contained in the IEC Standard such as:
• Protection against electric shock
• Adverse thermal effects
• Overcurrent
• Fault currents
• Overvoltage

Copyright 2017, www.MikeHolt.com

Figure 90–4

Author's Comment:

■ The *NEC* is used in Chile, Ecuador, Peru, and the Philippines. It's also the *Electrical Code* for Colombia, Costa Rica, Mexico, Panama, Puerto Rico, and Venezuela. Because of these adoptions, it's available in Spanish from the National Fire Protection Association, 617.770.3000, or www.NFPA.org.

90.2 Scope of the *NEC*

Changes to this section include a new requirement for the removal of conductors, equipment, and raceways and clarification that utility energy storage equipment isn't covered by the *NEC*.

Analysis

NEW

Removal of Equipment. Although the *Code* is an installation standard, there are a few requirements that deal with the removal of electrical equipment, mainly limited-energy cables. Sections 640.6(B), 645.5(G), 725.25, 770.25, 800.25, and 820.25 require abandoned cables to be removed and 590.3(D) requires temporary wiring installations to be removed immediately upon the completion of the purpose for which they were installed. The scope of the previous edition of the *NEC* only discussed installation of the cables, not their removal. The 2017 edition of the *Code* corrected this oversight.

CLARIFIED

Utility Energy Storage Systems. The *NEC* now provides an exemption for utility energy storage systems that allow the utility to produce electricity at load demand, store it, and then provide it to customers when the demand is high. These energy storage systems are every bit as involved as the utility equipment that's already exempt from the *Code* (generation, transmission, distribution, and so forth) and therefore deserve exemption as well.

90.2 Scope of the *NEC*

(A) What Is Covered by the *NEC*. The *NEC* contains requirements necessary for the proper installation <u>and removal</u> of electrical conductors, equipment, cables, and raceways for power, signaling, fire alarm, optical cable, and communications systems (twisted wire, antennas, and coaxial cable) for: Figure 90–5

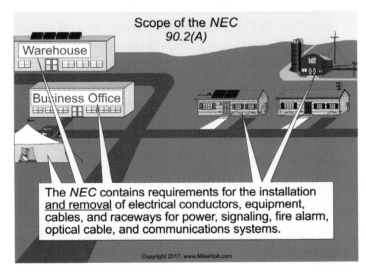

Scope of the *NEC*
90.2(A)

Warehouse

Business Office

The *NEC* contains requirements for the installation <u>and removal</u> of electrical conductors, equipment, cables, and raceways for power, signaling, fire alarm, optical cable, and communications systems.

Copyright 2017, www.MikeHolt.com

Figure 90–5

Author's Comment:

■ The *NEC* contains the following requirements on the removal of equipment and cables; temporary wiring 590.3 and abandoned cables for Audio [640.6(B)], Signaling [725.25], Fire Alarm [760.25], Optical Fiber [770.25], Twisted Pair [800.25], and Coaxial [820.25].

(1) Public and private premises, including buildings, mobile homes, recreational vehicles, and floating buildings. Figure 90–6

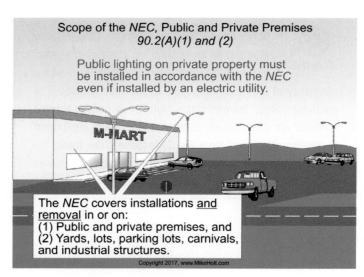

Figure 90–6

(2) Yards, lots, parking lots, carnivals, and industrial substations.

(3) Conductors and equipment connected to the electric utility supply.

(4) Installations used by an electric utility, such as office buildings, warehouses, garages, machine shops, recreational buildings, and other electric utility buildings that aren't an integral part of a utility's generating plant, substation, or control center. Figure 90–7

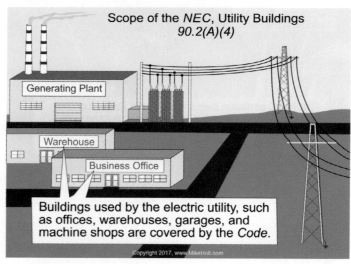

Figure 90–7

(B) What Isn't Covered by the *NEC*. The *NEC* doesn't apply to the installation of electrical or communications systems (twisted wire, antennas, and coaxial cable) for:

(1) Transportation Vehicles. The *NEC* doesn't apply to installations in cars, trucks, boats, ships and watercraft, planes, or electric trains.

(2) Mining Equipment. The *NEC* doesn't apply to installations underground in mines and self-propelled mobile surface mining machinery and its attendant electrical trailing cables.

(3) Railways. The *NEC* doesn't apply to railway power, signaling, energy storage, and communications wiring.

(4) Communications Utilities. If the installation is under the exclusive control of the communications utility, the installation requirements of the *NEC* don't apply to the communications (telephone) or network-powered broadband utility equipment located in building spaces used exclusively for these purposes, or located outdoors if the installation is under the exclusive control of the communications utility. Figure 90–8 and Figure 90–9

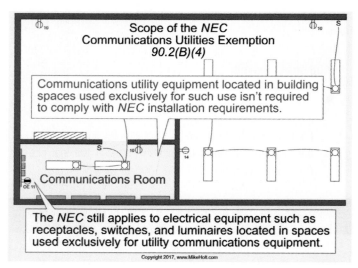

Figure 90–8

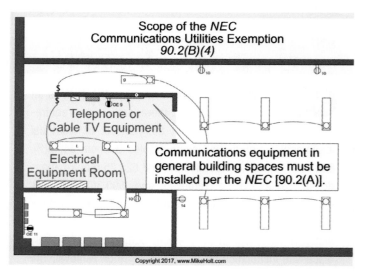

Figure 90–9

(5) Electric Utilities. The *NEC* doesn't apply to electrical installations under the exclusive control of an electric utility, where such installations:

a. Consist of electric utility installed service drops or service laterals under their exclusive control. Figure 90–10

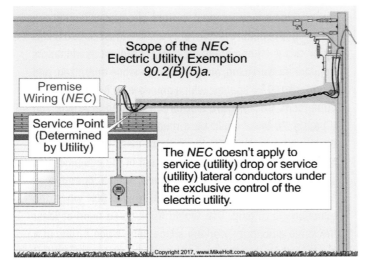

Figure 90–10

b. Are on property owned or leased by the electric utility for the purpose of generation, transformation, transmission, energy storage, distribution, or metering of electric energy. Figure 90–11

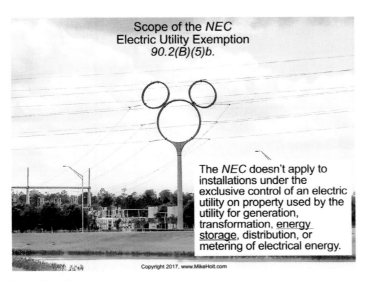

Figure 90–11

Author's Comment:

■ Luminaires located in legally established easements, or rights-of-way, such as at poles supporting transmission or distribution lines, are exempt from the *NEC*. However, if the electric utility provides site and public lighting on private property, then the installation must comply with the *Code* [90.2(A)(4)].

c. Are located on legally established easements or rights-of-way. Figure 90–12

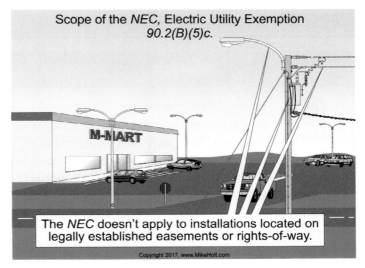

Figure 90–12

d. Are located by other written agreements either designated by or recognized by public service commissions, electric utility commissions, or other regulatory agencies having jurisdiction for such installations; limited to installations for the purpose of communications, metering, generation, control, transformation, transmission, energy storage, or distribution of electric energy where legally established easements or rights-of-way can't be obtained. These installations are limited to federal lands, Native American reservations through the U.S. Department of the Interior Bureau of Indian Affairs, military bases, lands controlled by port authorities and state agencies and departments, and lands owned by railroads.

Note to 90.2(B)(4) and (5): Utilities include entities that install, operate, and maintain communications systems (twisted wire, antennas, and coaxial cable) or electric supply (generation, transmission, or distribution systems) and are designated or recognized by governmental law or regulation by public service/utility commissions. Utilities may be subject to compliance with codes and standards covering their regulated activities as adopted under governmental law or regulation.

90.3 *Code* Arrangement

Editorial revisions to the arrangement of the *Code* clarify how the different chapters in the *NEC* apply, supplement or modify each other.

Analysis

CLARIFIED Many people skip over Article 90 because they want to dive into the meat and potatoes of the *Code* book. Most don't even realize this is a mistake until quite late in their career. Article 90 is the baseline of the *NEC* and tells you how the *Code* is laid out and how it works within itself.

Skipping this article is very much like doing electrical work without understanding theory—sure, you can run raceways and pull wire, but you don't really understand why you're doing what you're doing.

When you wire a doctor's office [Article 517], for example, you had better understand that everything in Chapters 1 through 4 apply to what you're doing, unless Article 517 specifically changes it, which it does. If you fail to read 517.13, which requires a special type of wiring method for patient care areas, you may find yourself ripping out all of the work you just did.

How about temporary installations? Temporary installations are covered in Chapter 5, specifically, Article 590. Do you think the rules for temporary installations are less restrictive or more restrictive than they are for a "normal" installation? They're more restrictive! That's because all of the rules in Chapters 1 through 4 apply, except as modified in Article 590. It doesn't modify much, but when it does, more rules are usually provided; not fewer.

When you install 12V landscape lighting near a pool, how far away from the nearest edge of the water must it be? The answer is 10 ft [411.5(B)] and this rule also applies

to swimming pools, spas, and fountains. This is another example how Chapters 1 through 4 apply to your electrical installations unless modified by Chapters 5 through 7. In this case Article 680 doesn't supplement or modify Article 411 so those requirements apply.

Here's a very strange example of how 90.3 works: What's the working space required in front of a power-limited fire alarm control panel that operates at 24V? Most *Code* experts agree this is equipment that's likely to require examination, adjustment, servicing, or maintenance while energized, and therefore 110.26 applies, which mandates 3 ft in front of the equipment. Because fire alarms are covered in Article 760 (Chapter 7), there could be a modification to this requirement within that article. Since there isn't, 110.26 applies. You need 3 ft of working space in front of the equipment.

Now consider a telephone board, which operates at about 50V to 60V, and goes up to around 90V when the telephone is ringing. One would think you'd need at least the same amount of working space here, since it runs at a higher voltage, but that isn't the case. Telephone equipment is covered in Article 800, which is in Chapter 8.

Remember that 90.3 tells us Chapter 8 is almost its own little *Code* book. Nothing in Chapters 1 through 7 applies to a Chapter 8 installation unless it says it does. So…what's the clearance? If there were a clearance requirement it would have to be located in Chapter 8, but there is none.

The change in the 2017 edition of the *NEC* is very subtle, but it clarifies that the rules in Chapters 5 through 7 sometimes modify each other. This should come in handy if you ever find yourself wiring a fire pump [Article 695] in a hospital [Article 517].

90.3 *Code* Arrangement

General Requirements. The *Code* is divided into an introduction and nine chapters followed by informational annexes. Chapters 1, 2, 3, and 4 are general conditions. Figure 90–13

Author's Comment:

- These first four chapters may be thought of as the foundation for the rest of the *Code*.

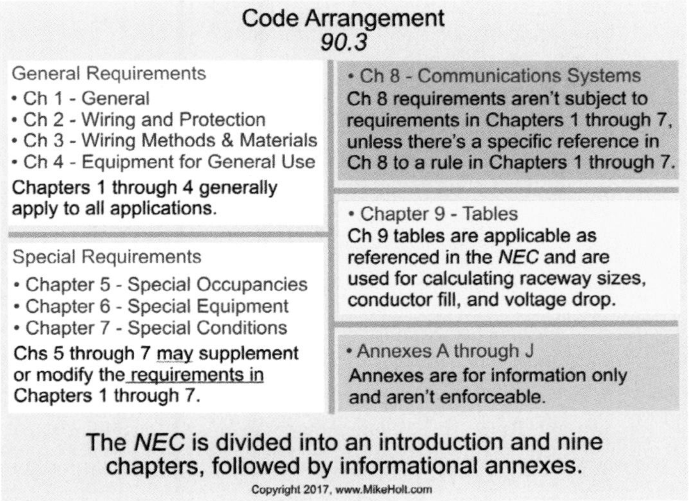

Code Arrangement
90.3

General Requirements
- Ch 1 - General
- Ch 2 - Wiring and Protection
- Ch 3 - Wiring Methods & Materials
- Ch 4 - Equipment for General Use

Chapters 1 through 4 generally apply to all applications.

Special Requirements
- Chapter 5 - Special Occupancies
- Chapter 6 - Special Equipment
- Chapter 7 - Special Conditions

Chs 5 through 7 <u>may</u> supplement or modify the <u>requirements in</u> Chapters 1 through 7.

- **Ch 8 - Communications Systems**
Ch 8 requirements aren't subject to requirements in Chapters 1 through 7, unless there's a specific reference in Ch 8 to a rule in Chapters 1 through 7.

- **Chapter 9 - Tables**
Ch 9 tables are applicable as referenced in the *NEC* and are used for calculating raceway sizes, conductor fill, and voltage drop.

- **Annexes A through J**
Annexes are for information only and aren't enforceable.

The *NEC* is divided into an introduction and nine chapters, followed by informational annexes.

Copyright 2017, www.MikeHolt.com

Figure 90–13

Special Requirements. The requirements contained in Chapters 5, 6, and 7 apply to special occupancies, special equipment, or other special conditions, which <u>may supplement</u> or modify the <u>requirements</u> contained in Chapters 1 through 7, but not Chapter 8.

Communications Systems. Chapter 8 contains the requirements for communications systems (twisted wire, antennas, and coaxial cable); which aren't subject to the general requirements of Chapters 1 through 4, or the special requirements of Chapters 5 through 7, unless there's a specific reference in Chapter 8 to a rule in Chapters 1 through 7.

Author's Comment:

- An example of how Chapter 8 works is in the rules for working space about equipment. The typical 3 ft working space isn't required in front of communications equipment, because Table 110.26(A)(1) isn't referenced in Chapter 8.

Tables. Chapter 9 consists of tables applicable as referenced in the *NEC*. The tables are used to calculate raceway sizing, conductor fill, the radius of raceway bends, and conductor voltage drop.

Annexes. Annexes aren't part of the *Code*, but are included for informational purposes. There are ten annexes:

- Annex A. Product Safety Standards
- Annex B. Application Information for Ampacity Calculation
- Annex C. Raceway Fill Tables for Conductors and Fixture Wires of the Same Size
- Annex D. Examples

- Annex E. Types of Construction
- Annex F. Critical Operations Power Systems (COPS)
- Annex G. Supervisory Control and Data Acquisition (SCADA)
- Annex H. Administration and Enforcement
- Annex I. Recommended Tightening Torques
- Annex J. ADA Standards for Accessible Design

90.7 Examination of Equipment for Product Safety

Edits were made to clarify that the listing of a product doesn't necessarily make it suitable for use.

Analysis

CLARIFIED In some cases a listed product may not be suitable for use because it doesn't meet the *NEC* requirements. Examples include "cheater plugs" and screw-shell receptacles, as well as LED lamps used in a retrofit application. While the lamp itself may be listed, 410.6 requires the lamp to be part of a UL 1598C listed retrofit conversion kit if it's used for a fixture conversion. This change clarifies that having a listing doesn't make a product suitable for an application unless the product's listing is compatible with the requirements of the *Code*.

90.7 Examination of Equipment for Product Safety

Product evaluation for safety is typically performed by a nationally recognized testing laboratory that's approved by the authority having jurisdiction. <u>The suitability of equipment use is determined by the application of product safety listing standards that are compatible with the *NEC*.</u>

Author's Comment:

- See Article 100 for the definition of "Approved."

Except to detect alterations or damage, listed factory-installed internal wiring and construction of equipment needn't be inspected at the time of installation [300.1(B)]. Figure 90–14

Figure 90–14

Note 1: See 110.3 on the required use of listed products.

Note 2: "Listed" is defined in Article 100.

Note 3: Annex A contains a list of product safety standards that comply with the NEC.

GENERAL RULES

Introduction to Chapter 1—General Rules

Before you can make sense of the *Code*, you must become familiar with a few basic rules, concepts, definitions, and requirements. As you study the *NEC*, you'll see that these are the foundation for a proper understanding of the *Code*.

Chapter 1 consists of two topics. Article 100 provides definitions so people can understand one another when trying to communicate about *Code*-related matters and Article 110 provides the general requirements needed to correctly apply the rest of the *NEC*.

Time spent learning this general material is a great investment. After understanding Chapter 1, some of the *Code* requirements that seem confusing to other people will become increasingly clear to you. The requirements will begin to make sense because you'll have the foundation from which to understand and apply them. When you read the *NEC* requirements in later chapters, you'll understand the principles upon which many of them are based, and not be surprised at all. You'll read them and feel like you already know them.

- **Article 100—Definitions.** Part I of Article 100 contains the definitions of terms used throughout the *Code* for systems that operate at 1,000V, nominal, or less. The definitions of terms in Part II apply to systems that operate at over 1,000V, nominal.

   Definitions of standard terms, such as volt, voltage drop, ampere, impedance, and resistance, aren't listed in Article 100. If the *NEC* doesn't define a term, then a dictionary suitable to the authority having jurisdiction should be consulted. A building code glossary might provide better definitions than a dictionary found at your home or school.

   Definitions located at the beginning of an article apply only to that specific article. For example, the definition of a "Pool" is contained in 680.2, because this term applies only to the requirements contained in Article 680—Swimming Pools, Fountains, and Similar Installations. As soon as a defined term is used in two or more articles, its definition should be included in Article 100.

- **Article 110—Requirements for Electrical Installations.** This article contains general requirements for electrical installations for the following:

   - Part I. General
   - Part II. 1,000V, Nominal, Or Less

ARTICLE
100 DEFINITIONS

Introduction to Article 100—Definitions

Have you ever had a conversation with someone, only to discover that what you said and what he or she heard were completely different? This often happens when people in a conversation don't understand the definitions of the words being used, and that's why the definitions of key terms are located right at the beginning of the *NEC* (Article 100), or at the beginning of each article. If we can all agree on important definitions, then we speak the same language and avoid misunderstandings. Because the *Code* exists to protect people and property, it's very important to know the definitions presented in Article 100.

Here are a few tips for learning the many definitions in the *NEC:*

- Break the task down. Study a few words at a time, rather than trying to learn them all at one sitting.
- Review the graphics in the textbook. These will help you see how a term is applied.
- Relate the definitions to your work. As you read a word, think about how it applies to the work you're doing. This will provide a natural reinforcement to the learning process.

Article 100—Definitions

Some definitions were relocated to Article 100, and the Code Making Panel responsible for each definition is now identified.

Analysis

This revision of the *Code* saw some definitions moved from specific articles to Article 100 to reduce confusion as they're used in other sections of the *NEC*. Few things are more frustrating than trying to find the definition of a term that isn't located in Article 100. In general, only those terms used in two or more articles are defined in here. Some terms, such as "Dust-Ignitionproof," Dusttight," "Hermetically Sealed [as applied to Hazardous (Classified) Locations]," "Information Technology Equipment (ITE)," and "Oil Immersion [as applied to Hazardous (Classified) Locations]" were relocated to Article 100 from other articles.

In order to identify the CMP (Code Making Panel) responsible for each definition, a short identifier was added. One example is the definition for "Bathroom" followed by (CMP-2) to identify Code Making Panel 2 as the one responsible for this definition.

> *Bathroom.* An area including a basin with one or more of the following: a toilet, a urinal, a tub, a shower, a bidet, or similar plumbing fixtures. (CMP-2)

Part I. General

100 Definitions

Scope. This article contains definitions essential to the application of this *Code*; it doesn't include general terms or technical terms from other codes and standards. In general, only those terms that are used in two or more articles are defined in Article 100.

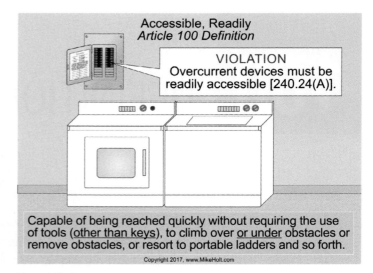

Figure 100-1

Note: Use of keys is a common practice under controlled or supervised conditions.

Accessible, Readily

This definition was editorially revised to clarify that having to climb under something makes it "not readily accessible" and the use of keys to gain access is "readily accessible." A new Informational Note was added as well.

Analysis

There are many rules in the *NEC* that required equipment to be readily accessible, such as circuit breakers and fuses [240.24(A)], GFCI devices [210.8], AFCI devices [210.12], building disconnects [225.32], service disconnects [230.70(A)(1)], and many others.

CLARIFIED

Use of Tools. New text about the use of "tools" was added in 2014. The *Code* added text stating that if a person needed to use a tool for access to a piece of equipment, then that equipment was no longer considered readily accessible. While this seems fine at first glance, it's actually quite problematic. Using an online dictionary to look up the definition of "tool," we find it's "a device or implement, especially one held in the hand, used to carry out a particular function."

Certainly a key meets that definition, but prohibiting the use of keys to gain access to electrical equipment such as panels, disconnects, and motor control centers (with locks or equipment in locked equipment rooms) would cause very serious safety implications! This was an unintended consequence of the 2014 process and is now fixed.

Accessible, Readily (Readily Accessible). Capable of being reached quickly for operation, renewal or inspections without requiring those to whom ready access is requisite to take actions such as the use tools (other than keys), to climb over or under, remove obstacles, or resort to portable ladders, and so forth. Figure 100-1

Building

Changes to this definition ensure that building codes, not the *NEC*, are the appropriate place to define a "building."

Analysis

The term "building" may not seem like something that needs to be defined in the *Code*, but it's actually an important concept. The most common application of this definition is as it relates to the number of services (or feeders) a building may have.

CLARIFIED

Building. One of the fundamental concepts of building codes is determining how large a building can be. This is determined by three main factors: What the building is used for (is it a dynamite factory or an office building), what it's built of (is it wood or concrete and steel), and how far away it is from property lines (if it's on fire, is it going to take the entire city down with it).

If a building larger than what the building code allows is needed, a "fire wall" through it can be built. There are now two buildings, each of which is within the size parameters allowed by the building code. This ensures that if a fire occurs, it will be confined to only one of them.

Be careful though because not all fire-resistance rated walls are really fire walls. There are also fire barriers, fire partitions, and other walls that aren't fire walls. This is something you need to discuss with the architect or, better still, the building official before you attempt to change a single structure into multiple buildings.

The change to this edition of the *Code* removes the language about fire doors as opening protective devices. Obviously the *NEC* isn't the right document to determine this, and even if it's accurate, changes may occur in the building codes that would render the *Code* inaccurate and therefore a potential source of conflict.

Building. A structure that stands alone or is <u>separated</u> from adjoining structures by fire <u>walls</u>. Figure 100–2

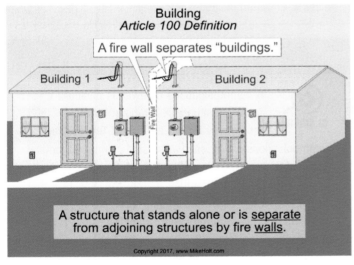

Figure 100–2

Cable Routing Assembly

The definition was editorially revised to broaden the application of the term.

Analysis

CLARIFIED The term "cable routing assembly" refers to a variety of devices used to organize cables between two points in a system. This definition was edited to clarify that a cable routing assembly is used for communication cables as well as a variety of other cable types.

Cable Routing Assembly. A channel or channels, with their fittings, that support and route communications wires and cables, optical fiber cables, data cables, <u>Class 2 and Class 3, and Type PLTC cables, and power-limited fire alarm cables in plenum, riser, and general-purpose applications.</u> Figure 100–3

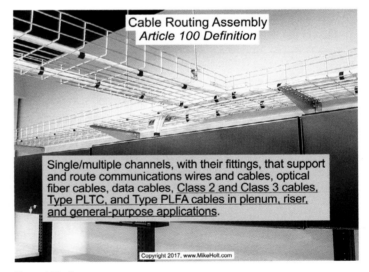

Figure 100–3

Author's Comment:

■ A cable routing assembly is typically a "U" shaped trough, with or without covers, designed to hold cables, and it isn't a raceway.

Communications Equipment

A note was added to clarify that routers, servers, and their powering equipment are part of communications equipment.

Analysis

CLARIFIED Communications equipment includes every piece of electrical equipment having to do solely with the communications of audio, video, and data. That includes telephone wiring, coaxial cables, and equipment like a router, telephone, or server. It doesn't include the 120V circuit and receptacle into which you plug your computer, but does include the computer itself.

Outside your house, the satellite dish on a roof, the grounding block for the coaxial cable, and the primary protector for telephone wiring are also considered communications equipment.

New to the 2017 *Code* is an Informational Note that clarifies, perhaps unnecessarily, that computers, routers, and servers are considered communications equipment, even though the definition itself is quite clear on the issue.

Communications Equipment. Electronic telecommunications equipment used for the transmission of audio, video, and data, including support equipment such as computers, as well as the conductors that are used solely for the operation of the equipment.

Note: Communications equipment includes computers, routers, and servers essential to the transmission of audio, video, and data. Figure 100–4

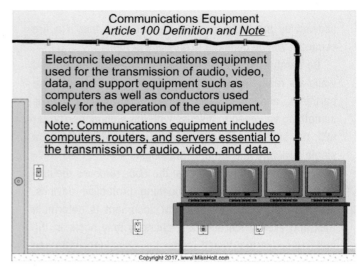

Communications Equipment
Article 100 Definition and Note

Electronic telecommunications equipment used for the transmission of audio, video, data, and support equipment such as computers as well as conductors used solely for the operation of the equipment.

Note: Communications equipment includes computers, routers, and servers essential to the transmission of audio, video, and data.

Copyright 2017, www.MikeHolt.com

Figure 100–4

Communications Raceway

The definition now indicates which cable types you're likely to see in a "Communications Raceway."

Analysis

CLARIFIED A communications raceway is basically electrical nonmetallic tubing [Article 362] (commonly known as "Smurf Tube") used for communications wiring, such as twisted pair cables, optical fiber cables, or coaxial cables. This raceway is typically orange in color to differentiate it from the blue ENT that electricians often use for lighting and power circuits. Installers of limited-energy systems find themselves having to replace wiring fairly often in order to keep up with the constantly evolving world of technology.

Changes to the definitions expanded the types of cables one is likely to install in a communications raceway. They include Class 2 and Class 3 cables for control and signaling [Article 725], power-limited fire alarm circuits [Article 760], optical fiber cables [Article 770], twisted pair cables [Article 800], and coaxial cables [Article 820].

Communications Raceway. An enclosed nonmetallic channel designed for holding communications wires and cables, optical fiber cables, data cables associated with information technology and communications equipment, Class 2, Class 3, and Type PLTC cables, and power-limited fire alarm cables in plenum spaces, risers, and general-purpose applications. Figure 100–5

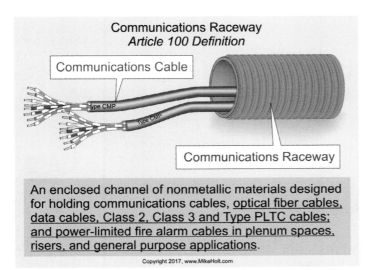

Communications Raceway
Article 100 Definition

Communications Cable

Communications Raceway

An enclosed channel of nonmetallic materials designed for holding communications cables, optical fiber cables, data cables, Class 2, Class 3 and Type PLTC cables; and power-limited fire alarm cables in plenum spaces, risers, and general purpose applications.

Copyright 2017, www.MikeHolt.com

Figure 100–5

Coordination, Selective (Selective Coordination)

The term "Coordination, (Selective)" is now "Coordination, Selective (Selective Coordination)" to reflect the common use of the term.

Analysis

EDITED Since "Selective Coordination" is the term people really use, this definition was revised to include it as a parenthetical reference.

You've probably heard of, or experienced, an event when the main breaker of a building tripped instead of a 20A breaker that should've done so. Speaking from experience, it's no fun when you're working in an office and you accidentally, and without warning, shut off power to the entire building. This can happen if the breakers (or fuses) aren't selectively coordinated.

Overcurrent protection devices function based on the concept of the "inverse-time" principal, which means the higher the current flow, the faster the device will open. Take for example a 400A main breaker and a ground-fault in a building on a 20A circuit. If that fault is, say, 1,000A, which breaker will trip? The answer is either of them could, but hopefully the 20A breaker trips before the 400A one does. That's the gist of selective coordination of overcurrent protection devices.

When the electrical system is being designed, the engineer (or other qualified person) will often look at the overcurrent protection devices and the available fault current at different locations to ensure that a single fault doesn't deenergize anything other than the circuit that has the fault. This is easier said than done; the coordination study could be hundreds of pages long!

While an unnecessary shutdown of a small office building because the overcurrent protection system wasn't selectively coordinated is certainly inconvenient, it often isn't going to be a major life safety issue. However, failure to selectively coordinate the overcurrent protection system for emergency wiring of a high-rise building could be a matter of life and death for the occupants.

Imagine a single ground fault of a 20A circuit opening the emergency generator overcurrent protection device resulting in the loss of all emergency means of egress lighting and exit signs! This is why the *NEC* requires selective coordination for emergency systems [700.28] and legally required standby systems [701.27].

It's important to note that selective coordination means that there's no way the upstream device opens before the downstream device...ever. That's the crux of the last sentence in the definition. There's no allowable overlap in the opening times of the devices in this definition, unlike the allowance of 0.10 seconds that's permitted in the essential electrical system of a hospital [517.31(G)]. That's right... the office building's emergency system is safer than the hospital's!

Coordination, _Selective_ (Selective _Coordination_). Localization of an overcurrent condition to restrict outages to the circuit or equipment affected, accomplished by the choice of overcurrent protective devices. Selective coordination includes all currents, from overloads to short circuits. Figure 100–6

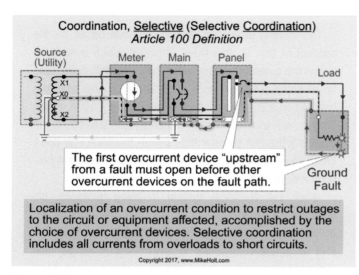

Figure 100–6

Author's Comment:

- Selective coordination means the overcurrent protection scheme confines the interruption to a particular area rather than to the whole system. For example, if someone plugs in a space heater and raises the total demand on a 20A circuit to 25A, or if a short circuit or ground fault occurs with selective coordination, the only breaker or fuse that will open is the one protecting just that branch circuit. Without selective coordination, an entire building can go dark!

Dusttight

Notes were added clarifying the types of enclosures suitable for use in dusttight applications.

Analysis

CLARIFIED
In the previous edition of the *Code*, dusttight simply stated that dust would not enter an enclosure under "specified test conditions"; this left a lot open to interpretation. A new informational note lists the types of enclosures that are considered suitable for use in dusttight applications. This should make it easier for both the installer and the AHJ to determine what is acceptable.

Dusttight. Enclosures constructed so that dust won't enter under specific test conditions. Figure 100–7

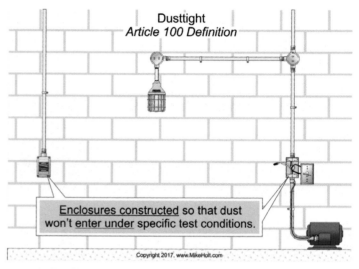

Figure 100–7

Note 1: Enclosure Types 3, 3S, 3SX, 4, 4X, 5, 6, 6P, 12, 12K, and 13, per NEMA 250, *Enclosures for Electrical Equipment*, are considered dusttight and suitable for use in unclassified locations and in Class II, Division 2, Class III hazardous (classified) locations.

Electric Sign

The definition of "electric sign" clarifies that the sign doesn't have to be Illuminated.

Analysis

CLARIFIED
It's hard to even contemplate our world without electric signage. In fact, electrical signs are so popular that the *Code* requires a circuit for them in every commercial building, and every commercial occupancy that's accessible to pedestrians [600.5(A)]. Electric signs are covered in Article 600, and include LED signs, neon tubing, section signs, and skeleton tubing.

The words "operated and/or" that were added should clarify that a sign doesn't need to be for illumination purposes only. Although most people think of a sign as something that says "open" or perhaps tells us the price of gas at a gas station, there are other signs that are quite subtle. For example, some signs aren't illuminated at all but are electrically operated. An example of this could be an unilluminated sign with a motor that moves parts on it to convey a message. According the UL standard, that's also an electric sign, and needs to be installed in accordance with Article 600. The added language to this definition now conveys that information.

Electric Sign [Article 600]. A fixed, stationary, or portable self-contained, electrically <u>operated and/or electrically</u> illuminated piece of equipment with words or symbols designed to convey information or attract attention.

Field Evaluation Body (FEB)

The term "Field Evaluation Body" was added.

Analysis

NEW

This new term identifies the organization that's permitted to evaluate equipment in the field and apply a field marking.

Field Evaluation Body (FEB). <u>An organization or part of an organization that performs field evaluations of electrical or other equipment.</u>

Field Labeled

The term "Field Labeled" was added.

Analysis

NEW

Field Labeled. Sometimes products or equipment that aren't listed or labeled must be used. Field evaluation bodies are authorized to evaluate this equipment so an inspector knows it complies with nationally accepted standards. They also provide the inspector with a test report that shows compliance.

Field Labeled (as applied to evaluated products). <u>Equipment or materials which have a label, symbol, or other identifying mark of an FEB indicating the equipment or materials were evaluated and found to comply with requirements as described in an accompanying field evaluation report.</u>

Interactive Inverter

This term used to be "Utility Interactive Inverter."

Analysis

CLARIFIED

An inverter changes direct-current power into alternating-current power. An interactive inverter allows the ac power from the inverter output to be in parallel with another ac power system. Of interest is to know that an interactive inverter will only provide ac power output when it's connected to another power system. If the other power system shuts down, then the interactive inverter stops providing ac power. This means that a dc system without an energy storage device (battery) can't be used for backup power.

An interactive inverter is permitted to be connected to a source of ac power other than the utility, although it would be unusual. By removing the word "utility" from the definition, we remove any argument about it.

Interactive Inverter. An inverter is used in parallel with an electric utility to supply common loads. Figure 100–8

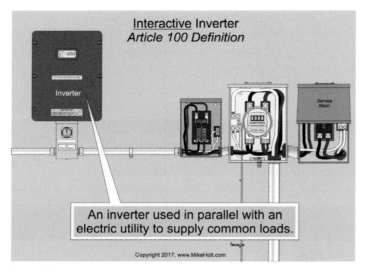

Figure 100–8

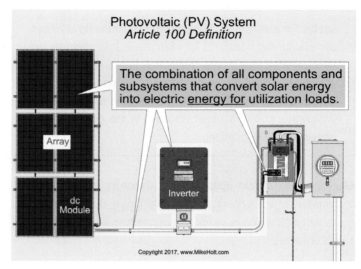

Figure 100–9

Photovoltaic (PV) System

A change to this definition removes any arguments about whether or not the energy created is "suitable" for connecting to a load.

Analysis

CLARIFIED

A PV system is made up of all of the equipment necessary to convert solar energy into electrical energy. The PV system includes the PV modules that capture and change solar energy into electrical energy, source circuits, output circuits, inverters, string combiners, batteries, charge controllers, and several other pieces of equipment; all of which are components of a PV system.

The electrical energy created by a PV system will be, hopefully, "suitable" for connecting to utilization loads. Who determines what's suitable and what isn't? Who cares…it's not part of the definition anymore.

Photovoltaic (PV) System. The combination of all components and subsystems that convert solar energy into electric energy for utilization loads. Figure 100–9

Raceway

The definition of "raceway" no longer contains construction specifications, such as "metallic" or "nonmetallic."

Analysis

CLARIFIED

Raceways include conduit, tubing, wireways, communications raceways, and obscure types like strut-type channel and cellular floor raceways. All of these raceways have the same purpose—to install conductors and cables and provide the ability to remove them.

All conduits are raceways, but not all raceways are conduits. For example, electrical metallic tubing (EMT) is a raceway, but it's not a conduit, it's a tubing (which is a raceway). A wireway isn't a conduit or a tubing, but it's still a raceway, and that's what's important. All of the raceways in the *Code* are discussed in their own article in Chapter 3. Be careful though, a common misconception is that cable tray systems are considered raceways; they aren't, they're a support system for cables and raceways [392.2].

In the 2014 *NEC*, the definition of a "raceway" specified they could be metallic or nonmetallic. That didn't exactly clear things up, did it? Because those words offered no real value, they're no longer in the *Code*. It may be a small change, but definitions work best when they're short and simple, so if we can remove some words, why not do so?

Raceway. An enclosed <u>channel designed</u> for the installation of conductors, cables, or busbars.

Author's Comment:

■ A cable tray system isn't a raceway; it's a support system for cables and raceways [392.2].

Receptacle

A small change was made in order to comply with the *NEC* style manual, and new text regarding a new type of receptacle was added.

Analysis

NEW

The receptacle is probably the most important component of an installation as it relates to convenience and usability, and due to that, everyone pretty much knows what one is. A duplex receptacle is constructed of two receptacles, a triplex receptacle is constructed of three receptacles, and a single pin and sleeve type of connection on a generator is also a single receptacle.

Another piece of equipment that you wouldn't think of as a receptacle is new device that allows for luminaires and paddle fans to be quickly installed, removed, or replaced. As can happen when a new rule is added in one part of the *NEC*, it might have a negative impact on other rules in the *Code*. For example, do all of the general receptacle rules in the *NEC* apply to this new type of "receptacle?" If it's installed in a residential garage, is it required to be GFCI protected in accordance with 210.8? One thing is sure, this is going to be an argument for many until the 2020 *Code* clears it up.

Receptacle [Article 406]. A contact device installed at an outlet for the connection of an attachment plug, <u>or for the direct connection of equipment designed to mate with the contact device</u> (SQL receptacle).
Figure 100–10

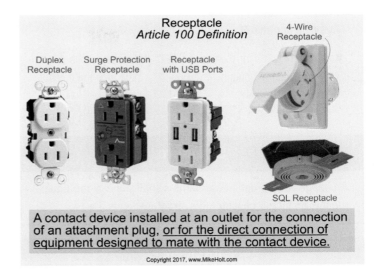

Figure 100–10

Author's Comment:

■ Outlet boxes are permitted to support listed locking support and mounting receptacles (SQL receptacles) used in combination with compatible attachment fittings [314.27(E)]. For additional information about listed locking, support, and mounting receptacles, visit http://www.safetyquicklight.com/.

A single receptacle contains one contact device on a yoke; a multiple receptacle has more than one contact device on the same yoke. Figure 100–11

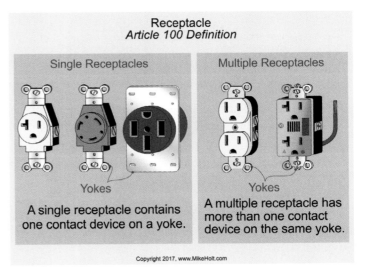

Figure 100–11

Author's Comment:

■ See 314.27(E) for the specific *NEC* application for the direct connection of equipment designed to mate with the contact device.

Structure

A change to this definition clarifies that stand-alone equipment is no longer considered a structure.

Analysis

CLARIFIED

The previous definition stated that a structure was "That which is built or constructed." This was a source of many, many debates in the electrical industry. Certainly buildings are structures, but the general statement that anything that's constructed was considered a structure was crazy! New to this edition of the *Code* is a clarification that "equipment" isn't considered a structure; so a free-standing switchboard, light pole, traffic signal, disconnect on a structure, or electric billboard sign isn't a structure.

Structure. That which is built or constructed, other than equipment. Figure 100–12

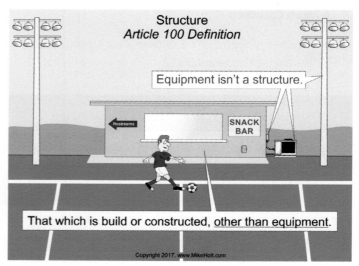

Figure 100–12

REQUIREMENTS FOR ELECTRICAL INSTALLATIONS

Introduction to Article 110—Requirements for Electrical Installations

Article 110 sets the stage for how you'll implement the rest of the *NEC*. This article contains a few of the most important and yet neglected parts of the *Code*. For example:

- How should conductors be terminated?
- What kinds of warnings, markings, and identification does a given installation require?
- What's the right working clearance for a given installation?
- What do the temperature limitations at terminals mean?
- What are the *NEC* requirements for dealing with flash protection?

It's critical that you master Article 110; as you read this article, you're building your foundation for correctly applying the *NEC*. In fact, this article itself is a foundation for much of the *Code*. The purpose for the *National Electrical Code* is to provide a safe installation, but Article 110 is perhaps focused a little more on providing an installation that's safe for the installer and maintenance electrician, so time spent in this article is time well spent.

Part I. General Requirements

110.1 Scope

Article 110 covers the general requirements for the examination and approval, installation and use, access to and spaces about electrical equipment; as well as general requirements for enclosures intended for personnel entry (manholes, vaults, and tunnels).

Note: See Annex J for information regarding ADA accessibility design.

Author's Comment:

- Requirements for people with disabilities include things like mounting heights for switches and receptacles, and requirements for the distance that objects such as wall sconces protrude from a wall.

110.3 Examination, Identification, Installation, Use, and Listing of Equipment

Changes to this section of the *Code* include addressing reconditioned, refurbished, or remanufactured equipment and providing rules for who may list electrical equipment.

Analysis

NEW

Remanufactured Equipment. In a perfect world all electrical equipment would be shiny and new; but that isn't reality. Sometimes older electrical equipment must continue to be used for many reasons, the most common is availability and cost. It would be nice if we could change all of the existing equipment in the world into new,

• • •

but since we can't we have to make do. This often includes installing electrical equipment that isn't new, but is reconditioned, refurbished, or remanufactured instead. This is commonly done with circuit breakers for obscure panels that haven't been manufactured in decades. A new Informational Note points out that the inspector shouldn't reject equipment based solely on the fact that it's remanufactured.

NEW **Listing.** A new subsection (C), covering listing, was added. Although the definition of "listed" in Article 100 states that a testing laboratory that tests and lists products must be acceptable to the AHJ, it does little else in terms of regulating the listing agency. This makes sense, because definitions aren't supposed to contain rules.

So, who does the testing and listing, and what do they use as their basis of acceptance? Can I open my own company, test a product in my backyard shop by plugging it in, put a sticker on it, and call it listed? With the revisions in the 2017 *NEC*, you can't. Testing laboratories must be recognized as being qualified and one source of finding out which ones are is OSHA, which lists Nationally Recognized Testing Laboratories (NRTLs).

110.3 Examination, <u>Identification, Installation, Use,</u> <u>and Product Listing (Certification)</u> of Equipment

(A) Guidelines for Approval. The authority having jurisdiction must approve equipment. In doing so, consideration must be given to the following:

(1) Suitability for installation and use in accordance with the *NEC*

Note 1: Equipment may be new, reconditioned, refurbished, or remanufactured.

Note 2: Suitability of equipment use may be identified by a description marked on, or provided with, a product to identify the suitability of the product for a specific purpose, environment, or application. Special conditions of use or other limitations may be marked on the equipment, in the product instructions, or appropriate listing and labeling information. Suitability of equipment may be evidenced by listing or labeling.

(2) Mechanical strength and durability

(3) Wire-bending and connection space

(4) Electrical insulation

(5) Heating effects under all conditions of use

(6) Arcing effects

(7) Classification by type, size, voltage, current capacity, and specific use

(8) Other factors contributing to the practical safeguarding of persons using or in contact with the equipment

(B) Installation and Use. Equipment must be installed and used in accordance with any instructions included in the listing or labeling requirements. Figure 110–1

Installation Instructions
110.3(B)

Equipment must be installed and used in accordance with instructions included in the listing or labeling.

Copyright 2017, www.MikeHolt.com

Figure 110–1

Author's Comment:

- See the definitions of "Labeling" and "Listing" in Article 100.
- Failure to follow product listing instructions, such as the torquing of terminals and the sizing of conductors, is a violation of this *Code* rule. Figure 110–2

(C) Product Listing (Certification). Product certification (testing, evaluation, and listing) must be performed by a recognized qualified testing laboratory in accordance with standards that achieve effective safety to comply with the *NEC*.

Note: OSHA recognizes qualified electrical testing laboratories that provide product certification that meets OSHA electrical standards.

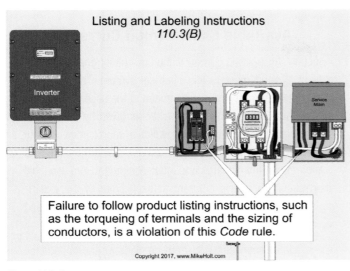

Listing and Labeling Instructions
110.3(B)

Inverter

Service Main

Failure to follow product listing instructions, such as the torqueing of terminals and the sizing of conductors, is a violation of this *Code* rule.

Copyright 2017, www.MikeHolt.com

Figure 110–2

110.5 Conductors

A change to this rule clarifies that conductors are to be copper or aluminum unless otherwise restricted by the *NEC*.

Analysis

CLARIFIED

This section used to stipulate that, where conductor material wasn't specified in the *Code* rule, copper conductors were to be used. This made for some strange interpretations of the *NEC*, none of which made sense or could be justified as necessary.

Aluminum conductors have the same negative stigma (for some) that they've had for decades, despite being made from different and far superior alloys than their predecessors. With the change to this section, there's no argument about the allowed conductor types. Aluminum can be used unless there's a specific requirement by the equipment listing or *Code* rule, such as 517.13(B)(1).

110.5 Conductors

Conductors are to be copper or aluminum unless otherwise provided in this *Code*; and when the conductor material isn't specified in a rule, the sizes given in the *Code* are based on a copper conductor.

110.9 Interrupting Overcurrent Protection Rating

A change to this very important rule creates enforceable language.

Analysis

CLARIFIED

Section 110.9 mandates that circuit breakers and fuses be capable of interrupting the circuit in the event of a ground fault without experiencing extensive damage. What's extensive damage?

When overcurrent protection devices are subjected to fault currents above their rating, they can literally explode, taking down everything in their path in the process. Because of this, it's critical to ensure that overcurrent protection devices be rated to handle the fault current on their line terminals.

Previous editions of the *NEC* stated that overcurrent protection devices must be "sufficient" for the available fault current. The word "sufficient" isn't a word that's used very often in the *Code*, because it lends itself to interpretation. What's "sufficient?" With the *NEC* now stating that the device rating must be "at least equal to" the available fault current, the opportunity for debate is closed.

110.9 Interrupting Overcurrent Protection Rating

Overcurrent protection devices such as circuit breakers and fuses are intended to interrupt the circuit, and they must have an interrupting rating at the nominal circuit voltage at least equal to the current available at the line terminals of the equipment. Figure 110–3

Author's Comment:

- See the definition of "Interrupting Rating" in Article 100.

- Ampere Interrupting Rating (AIR) is also described as "Ampere Interrupting Capacity" (AIC) by many in the industry.

- Unless marked otherwise, the ampere interrupting rating for circuit breakers is 5,000A [240.83(C)], and for fuses it's 10,000A [240.60(C)(3)]. Figure 110–4

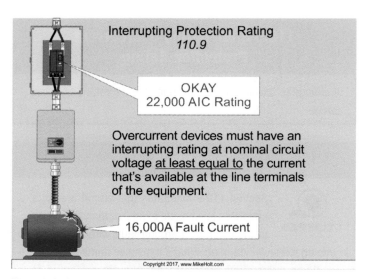

Figure 110–3

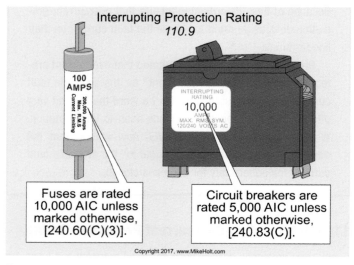

Figure 110–4

Available Short-Circuit Current

Available short-circuit current is the current, in amperes, available at a given point in the electrical system. This available short-circuit current is first determined at the secondary terminals of the electric utility transformer, as given by the electric utility engineer. Thereafter, the available short-circuit current is calculated at the terminals of service equipment, then at branch-circuit panelboards and other equipment. The available short-circuit current is different at each point of the electrical system. It's highest at the electric utility transformer and lowest at the branch-circuit load.

The available short-circuit current depends on the impedance of the circuit. The greater the circuit impedance (utility transformer and the additive impedances of the circuit conductors), the lower the available short-circuit current. Figure 110–5

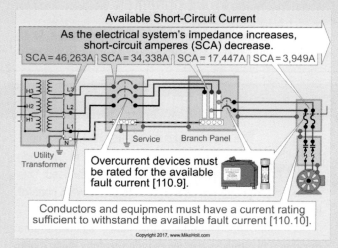

Figure 110–5

The factors that affect the available short-circuit current at the electric utility transformer include the system voltage, the transformer kVA rating, and the circuit impedance (expressed in a percentage on the equipment nameplate). Properties that have an impact on the impedance of the circuit include the conductor material (copper versus aluminum), conductor size, conductor length, and motor-operated equipment supplied by the circuit.

DANGER: *Extremely high values of current flow (caused by short circuits or ground faults) produce tremendously destructive thermal and magnetic forces. An overcurrent protection device not rated to interrupt the current at the available fault values at its listed voltage rating can explode while attempting to open the circuit overcurrent protection device from a short circuit or ground fault, which can cause serious injury or death, as well as property damage.* Figure 110–6

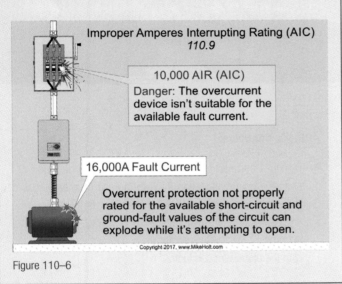

Figure 110–6

110.11 Deteriorating Agents

A new Informational Note intended to make *Code* users aware that there are minimum flood provisions contained in other building codes as they relate to electrical installations was added.

Analysis

NEW Typically, installing electrical equipment below the flood hazard level isn't allowed by the building code unless the equipment is suitable for the location. In some areas local rules require GFCI protection for equipment in flood zones, while in other areas, electrical equipment isn't permitted in the flood hazard zone at all. This new Informational Note should help designers and installers to be mindful of the building code requirements.

110.11 Deteriorating Agents

Electrical equipment and conductors must be suitable for the environment and conditions of use. Consideration must also be given to the presence of corrosive gases, fumes, vapors, liquids, or other substances that can have a deteriorating effect on the conductors or equipment. Figure 110–7

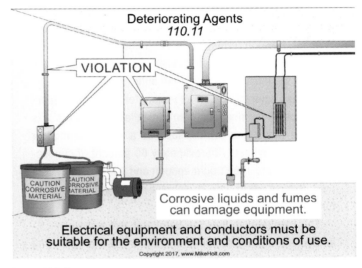

Figure 110–7

Author's Comment:

- Conductors aren't permitted to be exposed to ultraviolet rays from the sun unless identified for the purpose [310.10(D)].

Note 1: Raceways, cable trays, cablebus, cable armor, boxes, cable sheathing, cabinets, elbows, couplings, fittings, supports, and support hardware must be of materials that are suitable for the environment in which they're to be installed, in accordance with 300.6.

Note 2: Some cleaning and lubricating compounds contain chemicals that can cause deterioration of the plastic used for insulating and structural applications in equipment.

Equipment not identified for outdoor use and equipment identified only for indoor use must be protected against damage from the weather during construction.

Note 3: See Table 110.28 for NEMA enclosure-type designations.

Note 4: See the International Building Code (IBC) and the International Residential Code (IRC) for minimum flood provisions.

110.14 Conductor Termination and Splicing

A properly calibrated tool must be used when torquing terminal connections.

Analysis

NEW When electrical fires or failures occur, they usually do so at terminations, not in the middle of a cable or conductor. With that said, the rules in 110.14 are some of the most important in the entire *Code*.

Studies have found that approximately 75 to 80 percent of conductor terminations aren't installed correctly unless a torque measuring device, such as a torque wrench or screwdriver, is used. Approximately 60 percent of conductor terminations aren't tight enough and 20 percent are too tight, leaving about only 20 percent meeting the manufacturer's torquing requirements.

This new rule requires the installer to use a properly calibrated tool for conductor terminations when a tightening torque is specified by the manufacturer for the terminal.

Enforcement of this new rule will prove challenging. Does the electrical inspector need to be on site when the terminations are made so he or she can verify the tool being used? How will he or she know the tool is calibrated corrected? Has the tool been dropped since being calibrated and is now therefore inaccurate? Should the inspectors carry their own tools?

As with any new *Code* rule, this one might create growing pains, but we can all certainly agree on one thing; this rule is intended to increase safety by ensuring proper terminations. Let's not lose sight of the big picture—electrical safety.

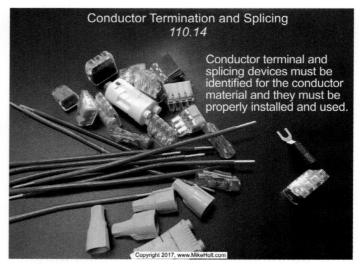

Conductor Termination and Splicing
110.14

Conductor terminal and splicing devices must be identified for the conductor material and they must be properly installed and used.

Copyright 2017, www.MikeHolt.com

Figure 110–8

Author's Comment:

- Switches and receptacles marked CO/ALR are designed to ensure a good connection through the use of a larger contact area and compatible materials. The terminal screws are plated with the element called "Indium." Indium is an extremely soft metal that forms a gas-sealed connection with the aluminum conductor.

Connectors and terminals for conductors more finely stranded than Class B and Class C, as shown in Table 10 of Chapter 9, must be identified for the use of finely stranded conductors. Figure 110–9

110.14 Conductor Termination and Splicing

Conductor terminal and splicing devices must be identified for the conductor material and they must be properly installed and used. Figure 110–8

Finely Stranded Flexible Conductor Termination
110.14

Connectors and terminations for conductors more finely stranded than Class B and Class C stranding must be identified for the conductor class [Chapter 9, Table 10].
Copyright 2017, www.MikeHolt.com

Figure 110–9

Author's Comment:

- According to UL Standard 486 A-B, a terminal/lug/connector must be listed and marked for use with other than Class B stranded conductors. With no marking or factory literature/instructions to the contrary, terminals may only be used with Class B stranded conductors.

- See the definition of "Identified" in Article 100.

- Conductor terminations must comply with the manufacturer's instructions as required by 110.3(B). For example, if the instructions for the device state "Suitable for 18-12 AWG Stranded," then only stranded conductors can be used with the terminating device. If the instructions state "Suitable for 18-12 AWG Solid," then only solid conductors are permitted, and if the instructions state "Suitable for 18-12 AWG," then either solid or stranded conductors can be used with the terminating device.

Copper and Aluminum Mixed. Copper and aluminum conductors must not make contact with each other in a device unless the device is listed and identified for this purpose.

Author's Comment:

- Few terminations are listed for the mixing of aluminum and copper conductors, but if they are, that will be marked on the product package or terminal device. The reason copper and aluminum shouldn't be in contact with each other is because corrosion develops between the two different metals due to galvanic action, resulting in increased contact resistance at the splicing device. This increased resistance can cause the splice to overheat and cause a fire.

(A) Terminations. Conductor terminals must ensure a good connection without damaging the conductors.

Terminals for more than one conductor and terminals used for aluminum conductors must be identified for this purpose, either within the equipment instructions or on the terminal itself. Figure 110–10

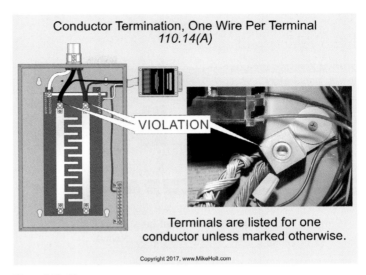

Figure 110–10

Author's Comment:

- Split-bolt connectors are commonly listed for only two conductors, although some are listed for three conductors. However, it's a common industry practice to terminate as many conductors as possible within a split-bolt connector, even though this violates the *NEC*. Figure 110–11

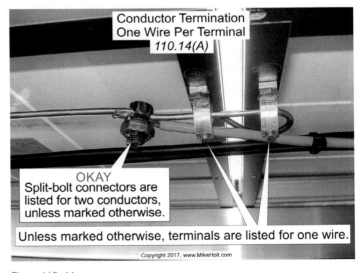

Figure 110–11

(B) Conductor Splices. Conductors must be spliced by a splicing device identified for the purpose or by exothermic welding. Figure 110–12

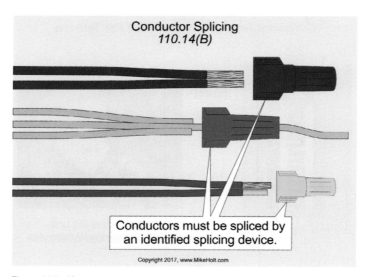

Conductor Splicing
110.14(B)

Conductors must be spliced by
an identified splicing device.

Figure 110–12

Author's Comment:

- Conductors aren't required to be twisted together prior to the installation of a twist-on wire connector, unless specifically required in the installation instructions. Figure 110–13

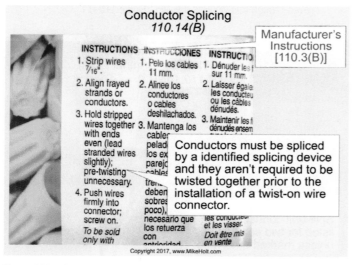

Conductor Splicing
110.14(B)

Figure 110–13

Unused circuit conductors aren't required to be removed. However, to prevent an electrical hazard, the free ends of the conductors must be insulated to prevent the exposed end of the conductor from touching energized parts. This requirement can be met by the use of an insulated twist-on or push-on wire connector. Figure 110–14

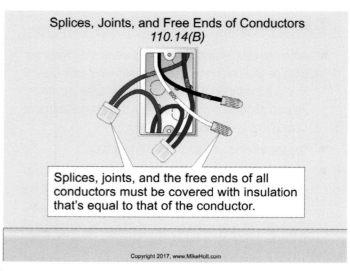

Splices, Joints, and Free Ends of Conductors
110.14(B)

Splices, joints, and the free ends of all
conductors must be covered with insulation
that's equal to that of the conductor.

Figure 110–14

Author's Comment:

- See the definition of "Energized" in Article 100.

Underground Splices:

Single Conductors. Single direct burial conductors of types UF or USE can be spliced underground without a junction box, but the conductors must be spliced with a device listed for direct burial [300.5(E) and 300.15(G)]. Figure 110–15

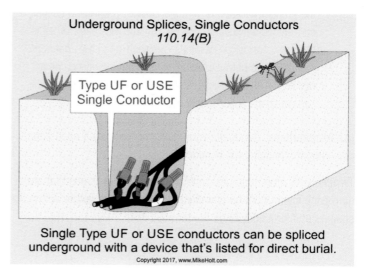

Underground Splices, Single Conductors
110.14(B)

Type UF or USE
Single Conductor

Single Type UF or USE conductors can be spliced
underground with a device that's listed for direct burial.

Figure 110–15

Multiconductor Cable. Multiconductor UF or USE cable can have the individual conductors spliced underground without a junction box as long as a listed splice kit that encapsulates the conductors as well as the cable jacket is used.

(C) Temperature Limitations (Conductor Size). Conductors are to be sized using their ampacity from the insulation temperature rating column of Table 310.15(B)(16) that corresponds to the lowest temperature rating of any terminal, device, or conductor of the circuit.

Conductors with insulation temperature ratings higher than the termination's temperature rating can be used for ampacity adjustment, correction, or both. Figure 110–16

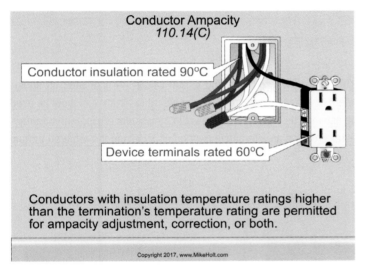

Figure 110–16

(1) Equipment Temperature Rating Provisions. Unless the equipment is listed and marked otherwise, conductor sizing for equipment terminations must be based on Table 310.15(B)(16) in accordance with (a) or (b):

(a) Equipment Rated 100A or Less.

(1) Conductors must be sized using the 60°C temperature column of Table 310.15(B)(16). Figure 110–17

(3) Conductors terminating on terminals rated 75°C are to be sized in accordance with the ampacities listed in the 75°C temperature column of Table 310.15(B)(16). Figure 110–18

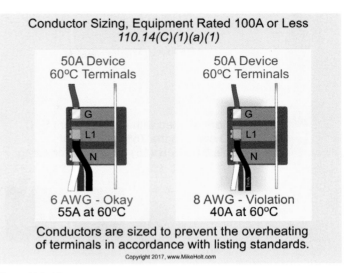

Figure 110–17

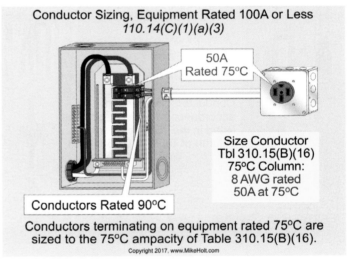

Figure 110–18

(4) For motors marked with design letters B, C, or D, conductors having an insulation rating of 75°C or higher can be used, provided the ampacity of such conductors doesn't exceed the 75°C ampacity. Figure 110–19

(b) Equipment Rated Over 100A.

(1) Conductors with an insulation temperature rating of 75°C must be sized to the 75°C temperature column of Table 310.15(B)(16). Figure 110–20

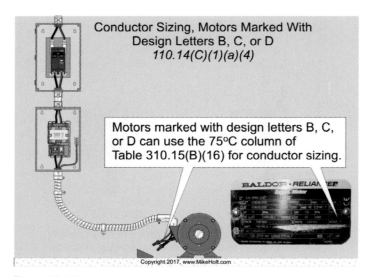

Figure 110-19

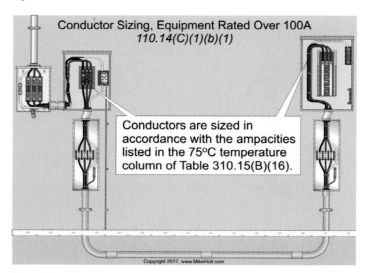

Figure 110-20

(2) Conductors with an insulation temperature rating of 90°C can be sized to the 75°C column of Table 310.15(B)(16).

(2) Separate Connector Provisions. Conductors can be sized to the 90°C column of Table 310.15(B)(16) if the conductors and pressure connectors are rated at least 90°C. Figure 110-21

Note: Equipment markings or listing information may restrict the sizing and temperature ratings of connected conductors.

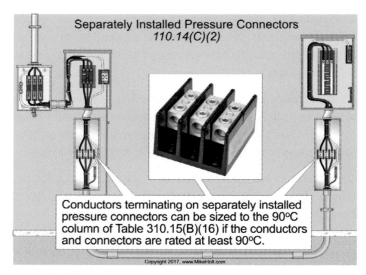

Figure 110-21

(D) Torque. Where tightening torque values are indicated on equipment or installation instructions, a calibrated torque tool must be used to achieve the indicated torque value, unless the equipment manufacturer provides an alternative method of achieving the required torque. Figure 110-22

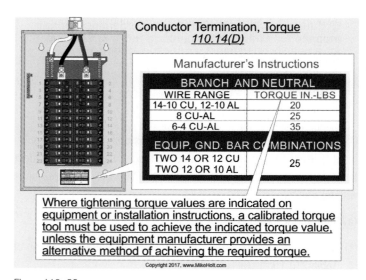

Figure 110-22

Author's Comment:

- Conductors must terminate in devices that have been properly tightened in accordance with the manufacturer's torque specifications included with equipment instructions. Failure to torque terminals can result in excessive heating of terminals or splicing devices due to a loose connection.

A loose connection can also lead to arcing which increases the heating effect and may also lead to a short circuit or ground fault. Any of these can result in a fire or other failure, including an arc-flash event. In addition, this is a violation of 110.3(B), which requires all equipment to be installed in accordance with listing or labeling instructions.

110.16 Arc-Flash Hazard Warning

The rules for warning qualified persons about arc-flash hazards have been increased, again.

Analysis

EXPANDED Since arc-flash hazard warnings rules were added in 2002, they've been revised every *Code* cycle like clockwork. There's no question that the continued revisions are due to the fact that electrical safety is taken more seriously than ever before.

Many people who are concerned with worker safety have tried to increase this rule to require information, such as restricted and prohibited approach boundaries, incident energy, arc rating of clothing, and other related information. While those requirements didn't make it into this edition of the *NEC* others did, but only for larger pieces of equipment.

The change is that for other than dwelling units, the arc-flash label must indicate the voltage of the system, the available fault current, the clearing time of the overcurrent protection device(s), and the date the label was installed. The available fault current can be obtained from the electric utility or be calculated with proper field information, and the clearing time can be obtained from the manufacturer of the fuse or circuit breaker.

An exception was added to allow arc-flash labels that are installed "in accordance with acceptable industry practice," and an Informational Note was added to explain what that means. Basically, if you follow the guidelines of NFPA 70E as they relate to labels, you'll meet the new *Code* requirement.

Proponents of this change claim this new rule will result in a safer environment for the electrical worker, but opponents claim these changes shouldn't be in the *NEC* at all, as it's intended to be an installation standard, not a workplace safety standard.

110.16 Arc-Flash Hazard Warning

(A) Arc-Flash Hazard Warning Label. Switchboards, switchgear, panelboards, industrial control panels, meter socket enclosures, and motor control centers in other than dwelling units must be marked to warn qualified persons of the danger associated with an arc flash from short circuits or ground faults. The arc-flash hazard warning marking must be permanently affixed, have sufficient durability to withstand the environment involved [110.21(B)], and be clearly visible to qualified persons before they examine, adjust, service, or perform maintenance on the equipment. Figure 110–23

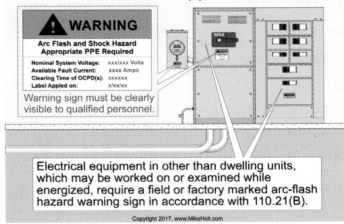

Figure 110–23

Author's Comment:

- See the definition of "Qualified Person" in Article 100.
- This rule is intended to warn qualified persons who work on energized electrical systems that an arc-flash hazard exists so they'll select proper personal protective equipment (PPE) in accordance with industry accepted safe work practice standards.

(B) Service Equipment Available Fault Current Label. Service equipment rated 1,200A or more must have a field or factory installed label containing the following details and have sufficient durability to withstand the environment: Figure 110–24

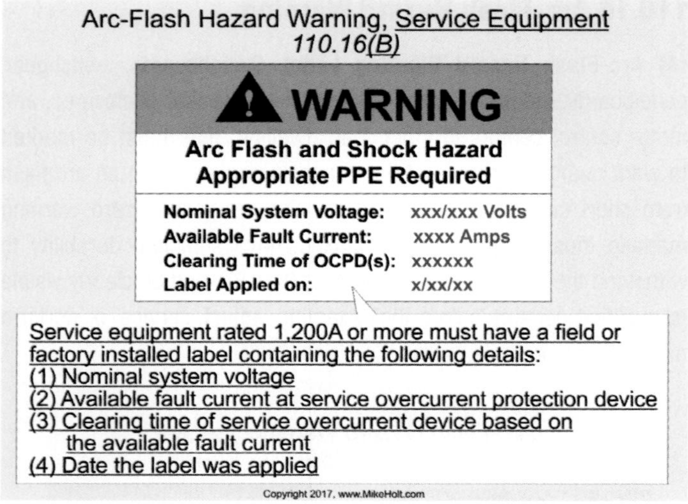

Arc-Flash Hazard Warning, <u>Service Equipment</u>
110.16<u>(B)</u>

⚠ WARNING

Arc Flash and Shock Hazard
Appropriate PPE Required

Nominal System Voltage:	xxx/xxx Volts
Available Fault Current:	xxxx Amps
Clearing Time of OCPD(s):	xxxxxx
Label Applied on:	x/xx/xx

Service equipment rated 1,200A or more must have a field or
factory installed label containing the following details:
(1) Nominal system voltage
(2) Available fault current at service overcurrent protection device
(3) Clearing time of service overcurrent device based on
    the available fault current
(4) Date the label was applied

Copyright 2017, www.MikeHolt.com

Figure 110–24

(1) Nominal system voltage

(2) Available fault current at the service overcurrent protection device

(3) Clearing time of the service overcurrent protection device based
    on the available fault current at the service equipment

(4) Date the service equipment available fault current label was
    installed

*Ex: Service equipment labeling isn't required if an arc-flash label
in accordance with NFPA 70E,* Standard for Electrical Safety in the
Workplac*e [see Note 3] is applied.*

Note 1: NFPA 70E, *Standard for Electrical Safety in the Workplace,* provides
guidance in determining the severity of potential exposure, planning safe work
practices, arc-flash labeling, and selecting personal protective equipment.

Note No. 3: NFPA 70E, *Standard for Electrical Safety in the Workplace* provides
specific criteria for developing arc-flash labels, such as nominal system voltage,
incident energy levels, arc-flash boundaries, and selecting personal protective
equipment.

110.21 Markings

New marking requirements for reconditioned equipment
have been added, and the warning signage requirements
have been editorially revised.

Analysis

NEW **Reconditioned Equipment.** While the thought of
"reconditioned" equipment may seem substandard
at first, sometimes it really is the only option. We all
long for a world where all of the electrical equipment in every
building is brand new, but when you find yourself living in that
world pinch yourself…because you're dreaming. In the real
world equipment isn't brand new, and some equipment isn't
even manufactured any more. When this is the case the only
options are complete removal and replacement of a system
or finding and using used or reconditioned equipment.

When reconditioned equipment is used, what are the
rules? This issue hasn't been addressed in the *Code* until
now. With these new changes, we now have requirements
for marking the equipment by the company responsible
for the reconditioning. This helps to ensure that a repu-
table company did the work. The date of refurbishing or
reconditioning must be included, which gives additional
information to the installer and to the AHJ, both of whom
need to use judgment when deciding on the suitability of
such a product.

CLARIFIED **Markings.** Section 110.21(B) was revised to
clarify that a combination of words, colors, and
symbols can (and probably should) be used for
caution, warning, or danger signs or labels. A literal reading
of the 2014 edition of 110.21(B) could be construed as
requiring words or colors or symbols, but not a combination
of those three. Obviously this isn't, and wasn't, the intent.

110.21 Markings

(A) <u>Equipment</u> Markings.

(1) General. The manufacturer's name, trademark, or other descriptive marking must be placed on all electrical equipment and, where
required by the *Code*, markings such as voltage, current, wattage, or
other ratings must be provided. Marking must have sufficient durability to withstand the environment involved.

(2) Reconditioned Equipment. Reconditioned equipment must be marked with the name, trademark, or other descriptive marking by the organization responsible for reconditioning the electrical equipment, along with the date of the reconditioning.

Reconditioned equipment must be identified as "reconditioned" and approval of the reconditioned equipment isn't based solely on the equipment's original listing.

Ex: Reconditioning markings aren't required in industrial occupancies, where conditions of maintenance and supervision ensure that only qualified persons service the equipment.

Note: Normal servicing of equipment isn't to be considered to be reconditioning equipment.

(B) Field-Applied Hazard Markings. Where caution, warning, or danger signs or labels are required, the labels must meet the following:

(1) The markings <u>must warn</u> of the <u>hazards</u> using effective words, colors, symbols, <u>or a combination of</u> words<u>, colors, and symbols</u>. Figure 110–25

Figure 110–25

Field-Applied Hazard Markings
110.21(B)(1)

CAUTION!
AREA IN FRONT OF ELECTRICAL EQUIPMENT SHALL BE KEPT CLEAR FOR DEPTH: _____ HEIGHT: _____

⚠ **WARNING**
Arc Flash Hazard
Appropriate PPE Required

⚡ **DANGER**
Electrical Hazard
Authorized Personel Only

The markings <u>must warn</u> of the <u>hazards</u> using effective words, colors, symbols, or a combination of words, <u>colors, and symbols</u>.

Copyright 2017, www.MikeHolt.com

Figure 110–25

Note: ANSI Z535.4, *Product Safety Signs and Labels*, provides guidelines for the design and durability of signs and labels.

(2) The label can't be handwritten, and it must be permanently affixed to the equipment. Figure 110–26

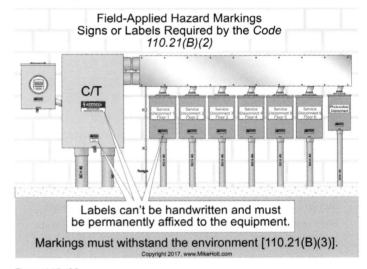

Field-Applied Hazard Markings
Signs or Labels Required by the *Code*
110.21(B)(2)

C/T

Labels can't be handwritten and must be permanently affixed to the equipment.
Markings must withstand the environment [110.21(B)(3)].
Copyright 2017, www.MikeHolt.com

Figure 110–26

Ex to (2): Labels that contain information that's likely to change can be handwritten, if it's legible.

Author's Comment:

■ A permanently affixed sign includes a sticker, but not a piece of paper taped to the equipment.

(3) The marking must be of sufficient durability to withstand the environment involved.

110.24 Available Fault Current

The available fault current calculation required by this section must now be made available upon request.

Analysis

EXPANDED

Using equipment that can handle the available fault current of an electrical system is one of the most important parts of a safe electrical installation. Determining the fault current rating of equipment for an installation can only be done after determining the available fault current at the line terminals of the equipment.

Calculating the available fault current at any given point in an electrical system is rather complicated and requires one to have knowledge and special training on this subject. Field marking of the maximum available fault current is an existing requirement. What's new to this edition of the *NEC*, is that the available fault current calculation must be made available upon request by the designer, installer, inspector, or those who operate or maintain the equipment.

Although the *Code* doesn't tell us how to make the information available, placing documentation in the equipment along with the panel schedule might not be a bad idea. This will ensure that not only the installer or inspector has access to it, but the future operator or maintenance personnel will as well.

110.24 Available Fault Current

(A) Field Marking. Service equipment, in other than dwelling units, must be field marked with the maximum available fault current, the date the fault current calculation was performed, and be of sufficient durability to withstand the environment involved. The available fault current calculation for the service equipment label must be documented and be available to those who are authorized to design, install, inspect, maintain, or operate the system. Figure 110–27

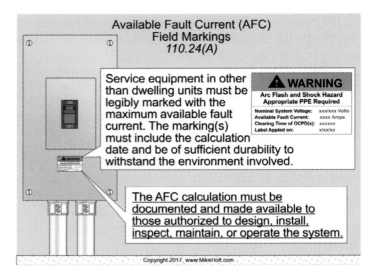

Figure 110–27

Note: The fault current markings required by this section are to ensure compliance with 110.9 and 110.10. They're not intended to be used for arc-flash analysis. Arc-flash hazard information is available in NFPA 70E, *Standard for Electrical Safety in the Workplace*.

(B) Modifications. When modifications to the electrical installation affect the maximum available fault current at the service, the maximum available fault current must be recalculated to ensure the service equipment ratings are sufficient for the maximum available fault current at the line terminals of the equipment. The required field marking(s) in 110.24(A) must be adjusted to reflect the new level of maximum available fault current.

Ex: Field markings aren't required for industrial installations where conditions of maintenance and supervision ensure that only qualified persons service the equipment.

110.26 Spaces About Electrical Equipment

Changes to 110.26 include a new Informational Note referring to NFPA 70E, *Standard for Electrical Safety in the Workplace*, new requirements for spaces with "limited access," and clarification to the outdoor dedicated space rules.

Analysis

NEW

Informational Note. Most of 110.26 is intended to provide safety for the electrical worker while working on energized equipment. This rule requires clear working space around equipment, it reminds people not to use the working space area for storage, provides rules on a viable escape route in case things go bad around large equipment, mandates illumination for equipment, and provides other safety provisions. Again, most of 110.26 relates to protecting the electrical worker who's working on energized equipment.

In this edition of the *NEC*, the new Informational Note tells the *Code* user to look to NFPA 70E to determine safe work practices, potential exposure, labeling of equipment, and the proper personal protective equipment. It's critical that the electrical the industry, electrician, inspector, contractor, and others follow the safe work practices identified in NFPA 70E as mandated by OSHA.

NEW

Above Suspended Ceilings. New to 2017 are rules for equipment that really can't meet the general working space requirements of 110.26. What do you do when a disconnect is located above a suspended ceiling and has to be there in order for it to be within sight of the equipment it supplies? It's impossible to get a 30 in. by 36 in. working space area in a ceiling grid that only has 24 in. by 48 in. openings. The 2017 change will allow the disconnect above the grid ceiling, but the equipment must be oriented so the depth of the working space required in Table 110.26(A) is satisfied.

This means that the disconnect needs to be mounted so that the 24-in. dimensions of the grid opening are to your left and right when facing the equipment, and the 48-in. dimensions must be in the front-to-back orientation. The equipment must be installed at the edge of the opening to ensure 36, 42, or 48 in. of space, as applicable.

NEW

Crawl Spaces. Installations in crawl spaces must have an access opening of 22 in. by 30 in., which happens to be the standard size of access to crawl spaces required by the International Building Code (IBC) and the International Residential Code (IRC). In addition to this access point, which only gets us into the crawlspace, we still need the required Table 110.26(A)(1) depth, but we don't have to meet the headroom requirements of 110.26(A)(3), which would typically be impossible.

CLARIFIED

Outdoor Equipment. The 2014 *NEC* created a new requirement for panelboards, switchboards, switchgear, and motor control centers installed outdoors to have dedicated electrical space, just like the indoor equipment requirements. As is usually the case, when you write a new rule you need to revise it and address the (sometimes embarrassingly) obvious things you didn't originally consider. This time it's the roof overhangs. Imagine installing a meter and service disconnect on a building, only to be told that you now need to cut out a space in the roof eaves so nothing is above your equipment. Well, you don't need to worry about that any longer.

Part II. 1,000V, Nominal, or Less

110.26 Spaces About Electrical Equipment

For the purpose of safe operation and maintenance of equipment, access and working space must be provided about all electrical equipment. Figure 110–28

(A) Working Space. Equipment that may need examination, adjustment, servicing, or maintenance while energized must have working space provided in accordance with 110.26(1), (2), (3), and (4):

Author's Comment:

- The phrase "while energized" is the root of many debates. As always, check with the AHJ to see what equipment he or she believes needs a clear working space.

Figure 110–28

Note: NFPA 70E, *Standard for Electrical Safety in the Workplace*, provides guidance in determining the severity of potential exposure, planning safe work practices, arc-flash labeling, and selecting personal protective equipment.

(1) Depth of Working Space. The working space, which is measured from the enclosure front, isn't permitted to be less than the distances contained in Table 110.26(A)(1). Figure 110–29

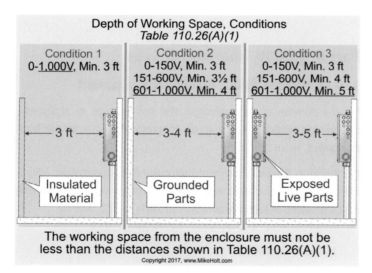

Figure 110–29

Table 110.26(A)(1) Working Space			
Voltage–to–Ground	Condition 1	Condition 2	Condition 3
0–150V	3 ft	3 ft	3 ft
151– 600V	3 ft	3½ft	4 ft
601– 1,000V	3 ft	4 ft	5 ft

(a) Rear and Sides. Working space isn't required for the back or sides of assemblies where all connections and all renewable or adjustable parts are accessible from the front. Figure 110–30

Figure 110–30

(b) Low Voltage. If special permission is granted in accordance with 90.4, working space for equipment that operates at not more than 30V ac or 60V dc can be less than the distance in Table 110.26(A)(1). Figure 110–31

Author's Comment:

■ See the definition of "Special Permission" in Article 100.

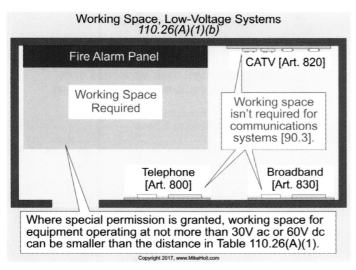

Figure 110–31

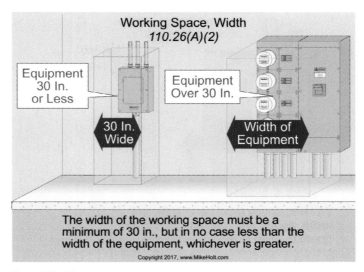

Figure 110–32

(c) Existing Buildings. If electrical equipment is being replaced, Condition 2 working space is permitted between dead-front switchboards, switchgear, panelboards, or motor control centers located across the aisle from each other where conditions of maintenance and supervision ensure that written procedures have been adopted to prohibit equipment on both sides of the aisle from being open at the same time, and only authorized, qualified persons will service the installation.

Author's Comment:

- The working space requirements of 110.26 don't apply to equipment included in Chapter 8—Communications Circuits [90.3].

(2) Width of Working Space. The width of the working space must be a minimum of 30 in., but in no case less than the width of the equipment. Figure 110–32

Author's Comment:

- The width of the working space can be measured from left-to-right, from right-to-left, or simply centered on the equipment, and can overlap the working space for other electrical equipment. Figure 110–33

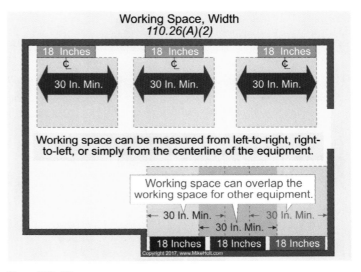

Figure 110–33

The working space must be of sufficient width, depth, and height to permit all equipment doors to open 90 degrees. Figure 110–34

(3) Height of Working Space (Headroom). The height of the working space in front of equipment isn't permitted to be less than 6½ ft, measured from the grade, floor, platform, or the equipment height, whichever is greater. Figure 110–35

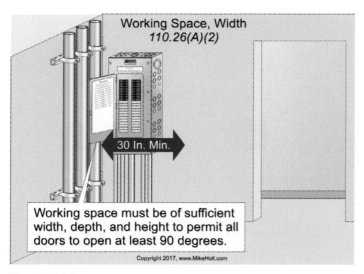

Figure 110–34

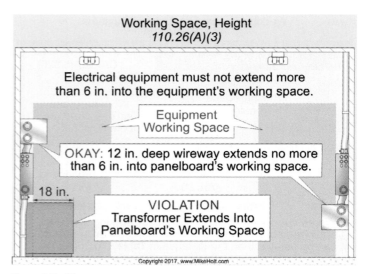

Figure 110–36

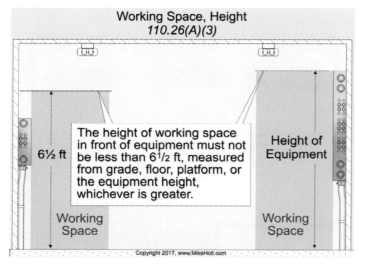

Figure 110–35

Equipment such as raceways, cables, wireways, cabinets, panels, and so on, can be located above or below electrical equipment, but must not extend more than 6 in. into the equipment's working space. Figure 110–36

Ex 1: The minimum headroom requirement doesn't apply to service equipment or panelboards rated 200A or less located in an existing dwelling unit.

Author's Comment:

■ See the definition of "Dwelling Unit" in Article 100.

Ex 2: Meters are permitted to extend beyond the other equipment.

Ex 3: For battery systems, see 480.10(D) for top clearance requirements.

(4) Limited Access. Where equipment is likely to require examination, adjustment, servicing, or maintenance while energized is located in a space with limited access, all of the following conditions apply:

(a)(1) Above Suspended Ceiling. Equipment installed above a suspended ceiling must have an access opening not smaller than 22 in. x 22 in.

(a)(2) Crawl Space. Equipment installed in a crawl space must have an accessible opening not smaller than 22 in. x 30 in.

(b) The width of the working space must be a minimum of 30 in., but in no case less than the width of the equipment.

(c) The working space must permit equipment doors to open 90 degrees.

(d) The working space in front of the equipment must comply with the depth requirements of Table 110.26(A)(1), and horizontal ceiling structural members are permitted in this space.

(B) Clear Working Space. The working space required by this section must be clear at all times. Therefore, this space isn't permitted for storage. Figure 110–37

When normally enclosed live parts are exposed for inspection or servicing, the working space, if in a passageway or open space, must be suitably guarded.

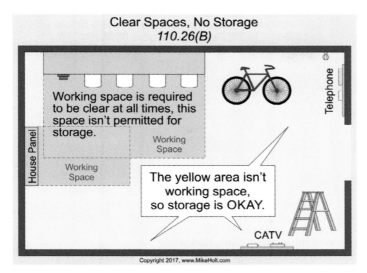

Figure 110–37

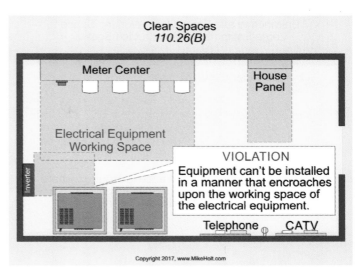

Figure 110–38

Author's Comment:

- When working in a passageway, the working space should be guarded from occupants using it. When working on electrical equipment in a passageway one must be mindful of a fire alarm evacuation with numerous occupants congregated and moving through the area.

⚠ **CAUTION:** *It's very dangerous to service energized parts in the first place, and it's unacceptable to be subjected to additional dangers by working around bicycles, boxes, crates, appliances, and other impediments.*

Author's Comment:

- Signaling and communications equipment aren't permitted to be installed in a manner that encroaches on the working space of the electrical equipment. Figure 110–38

(C) Entrance to and Egress from Working Space.

(1) Minimum Required. At least one entrance of sufficient area must provide access to and egress from the working space.

Author's Comment:

- Check to see what the authority having jurisdiction considers "Sufficient Area." Building codes contain minimum dimensions for doors and openings for personnel travel.

(2) Large Equipment. An entrance to and egress from each end of the working space of electrical equipment rated 1,200A or more that's over 6 ft wide is required. The opening must be a minimum of 24 in. wide and 6½ ft high. Figure 110–39

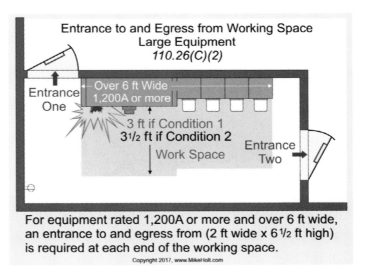

Figure 110–39

A single entrance to and egress from the required working space is permitted where either of the following conditions is met:

(a) Unobstructed Egress. Only one entrance is required where the location permits a continuous and unobstructed way of egress travel. Figure 110–40

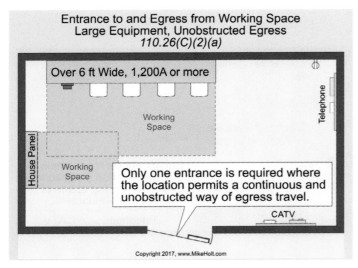

Figure 110–40

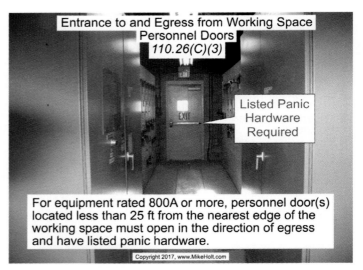

Figure 110–42

(b) Double Workspace. Only one entrance is required where the required working space depth is doubled, and the equipment is located so the edge of the entrance is no closer than the required working space distance. Figure 110–41

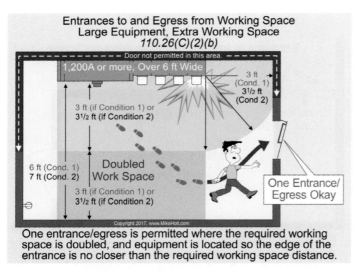

Figure 110–41

(3) Personnel Doors. If equipment with overcurrent or switching devices rated 800A or more is installed, personnel door(s) for entrance to and egress from the working space located less than 25 ft from the nearest edge of the working space must have the door(s) open in the direction of egress and be equipped with listed panic hardware. Figure 110–42

Author's Comment:

- History has shown that electricians who suffer burns on their hands in electrical arc-flash or arc-blast events often can't open doors equipped with knobs that must be turned.

- Since this requirement is in the *NEC*, the electrical contractor is responsible for ensuring that panic hardware is installed where required. Some are offended at being held liable for nonelectrical responsibilities, but this rule is designed to save the lives of electricians. For this and other reasons, many construction professionals routinely hold "pre-construction" or "pre-con" meetings to review potential opportunities for miscommunication—before the work begins.

(D) Illumination. Service equipment, switchboards, switchgear, and panelboards, as well as motor control centers located indoors must have illumination located indoors controlled by manual means; automatic control without manual control isn't permitted. Figure 110–43

Author's Comment:

- The *Code* doesn't provide the minimum foot-candles required to provide proper illumination. Proper illumination of electrical equipment rooms is essential for the safety of those qualified to work on such equipment.

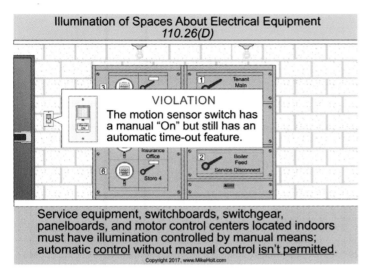

Figure 110–43

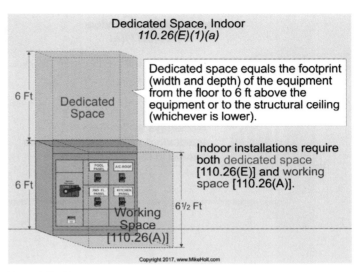

Figure 110–44

(E) Dedicated Equipment Space. Switchboards, switchgear, panelboards, and motor control centers must have dedicated equipment space and be protected from damage as follows:

(1) Indoors.

(a) Dedicated Electrical Space. The footprint space (width and depth of the equipment) extending from the floor to a height of 6 ft above the equipment or to the structural ceiling, whichever is lower, must be dedicated for the electrical installation. Figure 110–44

No piping, ducts, or other equipment foreign to the electrical installation can be installed in this dedicated footprint space. Figure 110–45

Ex: Suspended ceilings with removable panels can be within the dedicated footprint space [110.26(E)(1)(d)].

Author's Comment:

■ Electrical raceways and cables not associated with the dedicated space can be within the dedicated space. These aren't considered "equipment foreign to the electrical installation." Figure 110–46

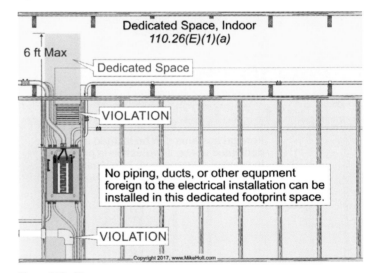

Figure 110–45

(b) Foreign Systems. Foreign systems can be located above the dedicated space if protection is installed to prevent damage to the electrical equipment from condensation, leaks, or breaks in the foreign systems, such protection can be as simple as a drip-pan. Figure 110–47

(c) Sprinkler Protection. Sprinkler protection piping isn't permitted in the dedicated space, but the *NEC* doesn't prohibit sprinklers from spraying water on electrical equipment.

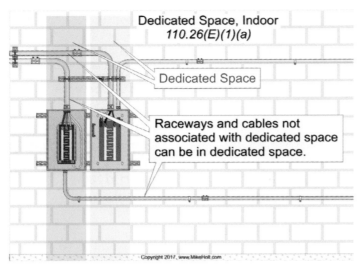

Figure 110–46

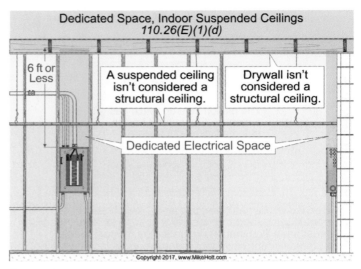

Figure 110–48

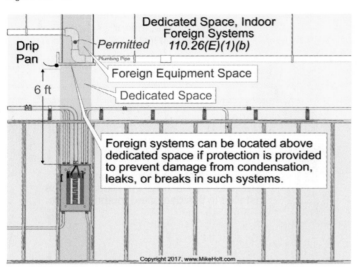

Figure 110–47

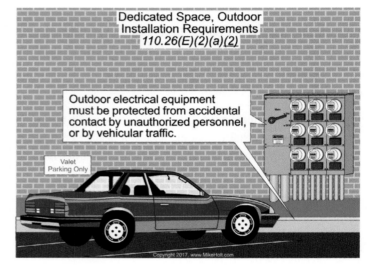

Figure 110–49

(d) Suspended Ceilings. A dropped, suspended, or similar ceiling isn't considered a structural ceiling. Figure 110–48

(2) Outdoor. Outdoor installations must comply with the following:

(a) Installation Requirements. Switchboards, switchgear, panelboards, and motor control centers installed outdoors must be:

(1) Installed in identified enclosures

(2) Protected from accidental contact by unauthorized personnel, or by vehicular traffic Figure 110–49

(3) Protected by accidental spillage or leakage from piping systems

(b) Work Space. Switchboards, switchgear, panelboards, and motor control centers installed outdoors must have sufficient working space clearance in accordance with 110.26(A). No architectural appurtenance or other equipment is permitted in the work space.

(c) Dedicated Equipment Space Outdoor. The footprint space (width and depth of the equipment) extending from grade to a height of 6 ft above the equipment must be dedicated for the electrical installation. No piping, ducts, or other equipment foreign to the electrical installation can be installed in this dedicated footprint space. Figure 110–50

Dedicated Equipment Space, Outdoor
110.26(E)(2)(c)

VIOLATION
No piping or other equipment foreign to the electrical installation can be located in this space.

Copyright 2017, www.MikeHolt.com

Figure 110–50

Author's Comment:

■ See the definition of "Accessible (as applied to equipment)" in Article 100.

(F) Locked Electrical Equipment Rooms or Enclosures. Electrical equipment rooms or enclosures containing electrical apparatus controlled by a lock(s) are considered accessible to qualified persons. Figure 110–51

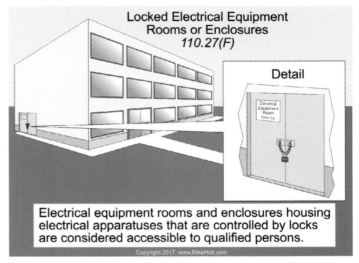

Locked Electrical Equipment
Rooms or Enclosures
110.27(F)

Detail

Electrical Equipment Room Keep Out

Electrical equipment rooms and enclosures housing electrical apparatuses that are controlled by locks are considered accessible to qualified persons.

Copyright 2017, www.MikeHolt.com

Figure 110–51

CHAPTER 2

WIRING AND PROTECTION

Introduction to Chapter 2—Wiring and Protection

Chapter 2 provides general rules for wiring and for the overcurrent protection of conductors. The rules in this chapter apply to all electrical installations covered by the *NEC*—except as modified in Chapters 5, 6, and 7 [90.3].

Communications systems (twisted wire, antennas, and coaxial cable) (Chapter 8 systems) aren't subject to the general requirements of Chapters 1 through 4, or the special requirements of Chapters 5 through 7, unless there's a specific reference in Chapter 8 to a rule in Chapters 1 through 7 [90.3].

As you go through Chapter 2, remember its purpose. It's primarily concerned with correctly sizing and protecting circuits. Every article in this chapter deals with a different aspect of this purpose. This differs from the purpose of Chapter 3, which is to correctly install the conductors that make up those circuits.

Chapter 1 introduced you to the *NEC* and provided a solid foundation for understanding the *Code*. Chapters 2 (Wiring and Protection) and 3 (Wiring Methods and Materials) continue building the foundation for applying the *NEC*. Chapter 4 applies the preceding chapters to general equipment. It's beneficial to learn the first four chapters of the *Code* in a sequential manner because each of the first four chapters builds on the one before it. Once you've become familiar with the first four chapters, you can learn the next four in any order you wish.

- **Article 200—Use and Identification of Grounded [Neutral] Conductors.** This article contains the requirements for the use and identification of the grounded conductor and its terminals.

  Author's Comment:

  - Throughout this textbook, we'll use the term "neutral" when referring to the grounded conductor when the application isn't related to PV systems or corner-grounded delta-connected systems.

- **Article 210—Branch Circuits.** Article 210 contains the requirements for branch circuits, such as conductor sizing, identification, and GFCI protection, as well as receptacle and lighting outlet requirements.

- **Article 215—Feeders.** This article covers the requirements for the installation and ampacity of feeders.

■ **Article 220—Branch-Circuit, Feeder, and Service Calculations.** Article 220 provides the requirements for calculating the minimum size for branch circuits, feeders, and services. This article also aids in determining related factors such as the number of receptacles on a circuit in nondwelling installations, and the minimum number of branch circuits required.

■ **Article 225—Outside Branch Circuits and Feeders.** This article covers the installation requirements for equipment, including branch circuits and feeders located outside (overhead and underground) that run on or between buildings, poles, and other structures on the premises.

■ **Article 230—Services.** Article 230 covers the installation requirements for service conductors and equipment. It's very important to know where the service begins and ends when applying Article 230.

Author's Comment:

■ Conductors from a battery, uninterruptible power supply, solar PV system, generator, or transformer aren't service conductors; they're feeder conductors.

■ **Article 240—Overcurrent Protection.** This article provides the requirements for overcurrent protection and overcurrent protection devices. Overcurrent protection for conductors and equipment is provided to open the circuit if the current reaches a value that will cause an excessive or dangerous temperature on the conductors or conductor insulation.

■ **Article 250—Grounding and Bonding.** Article 250 covers the grounding requirements for providing a path to the earth to reduce overvoltage from lightning, and the bonding requirements for a low-impedance fault current path necessary to facilitate the operation of overcurrent protection devices in the event of a ground fault.

■ **Article 285—Surge Protective Devices (SPDs).** This article covers the general, installation, and connection requirements for surge protective devices (SPDs) permanently installed on both the line side and load side of service equipment.

ARTICLE
210 BRANCH CIRCUITS

Introduction to Article 210—Branch Circuits

This article contains the requirements for branch circuits, such as conductor sizing and identification, GFCI protection, and receptacle and lighting outlet requirements. It consists of three parts:

- Part I. General Provisions
- Part II. Branch-Circuit Ratings
- Part III. Required Outlets

Table 210.3 of this article identifies specific-purpose branch circuits. The provisions for branch circuits that supply equipment listed in Table 210.3 amend or supplement the provisions given in Article 210 for branch circuits, so it's important to be aware of the contents of this table.

Mastering the branch-circuit requirements in Article 210 will give you a jump-start toward completing installations that are free of *Code* violations.

210.1 Scope

The scope of this article was clarified.

Analysis

CLARIFIED
The general requirements for all branch circuit installations are contained in chapters 1 through 4. Removing the reference to motors in this section clarifies that these are the general requirements that apply to all branch circuits unless modified elsewhere in the *NEC*.

Part I. General Provisions

210.1 Scope

Article 210 provides the general requirements for branch circuits such as, conductor sizing, overcurrent protection, identification, GFCI and AFCI protection, as well as receptacle outlets and lighting outlet requirements.

Author's Comment:

- Article 100 defines a "branch circuit" as the conductors between the final overcurrent protection device and the receptacle outlets, lighting outlets, or other outlets. Figure 210–1

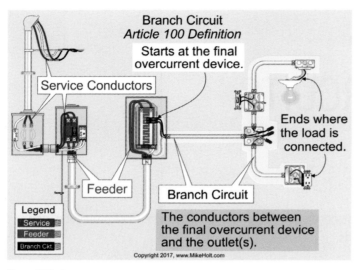

Branch Circuit
Article 100 Definition

Starts at the final overcurrent device.

Service Conductors

Ends where the load is connected.

Feeder

Branch Circuit

The conductors between the final overcurrent device and the outlet(s).

Legend
Service
Feeder
Branch Ckt.

Copyright 2017, www.MikeHolt.com

Figure 210–1

210.3 Other Articles

The section and corresponding table number were changed and the language was simplified for ease of use.

Analysis

CLARIFIED

This section was previously located in 210.2 with a corresponding table of the same number. Exactly what this section applied to and when it was modified was confusing. Now it clearly states what Article 210 applies to, references Table 210.3 for other general requirements not contained in this article, and reminds us that specific equipment referenced in Chapters 5 through 7 may amend this article.

210.3 Other Articles

Table 210.3 lists references for specific equipment and applications not located in Chapters 5, 6, and 7.

- Air-Conditioning and Refrigeration, 440.6, 440.31, and 440.32
- Central Heating Equipment, 422.12
- Electric Space-Heating Equipment, 424.3(B)
- Motors, 430.22

210.4 Multiwire Branch Circuits

The conductor grouping requirements for multiwire branch circuits now mirror similar rules contained in 200.4(B).

Analysis

EDITED

The *NEC* required the installer to group all circuit conductors (ungrounded and neutral conductors) of a shared neutral (multiwire) branch circuit in the panelboard. In 2014 a new rule was added in 200.4(B) that required all ungrounded and neutral circuit conductors (shared or otherwise) to be grouped together in not only the panel, but in every enclosure through which the circuit ran.

That rule made the requirements of 210.4(D) not only less stringent, but completely meaningless. Now the 2017 version of 210.4 requires compliance with 200.4(B), meaning that all ungrounded and neutral circuit conductors, shared or not shared, must be grouped in every enclosure by cable ties or similar means.

It's worth noting that the exception still remains, meaning that a raceway or cable with only one circuit doesn't need to meet this rule, as the circuitry is obvious.

210.4 Multiwire Branch Circuits

Author's Comment:

- A multiwire branch circuit consists of two or more ungrounded circuit conductors with a common neutral conductor. There must be a difference of voltage between the ungrounded conductors and an equal difference of voltage from each ungrounded conductor to the common neutral conductor. Figure 210–2

(A) General. A multiwire branch circuit can be considered a single circuit or a multiple circuit. To prevent inductive heating and to reduce conductor impedance for fault currents, all conductors of a multiwire branch circuit must originate from the same panelboard. Figure 210–3

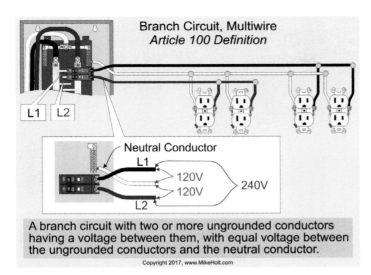

Figure 210–2

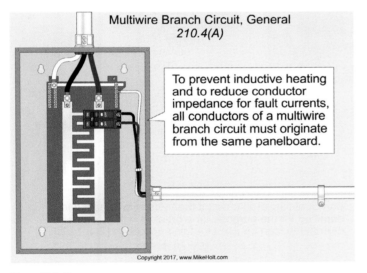

Figure 210–3

Author's Comment:

- For more information on the inductive heating of metal parts, see 300.3(B), 300.5(I), and 300.20.

Note 2: See 300.13(B) for the requirements relating to the continuity of the neutral conductor on multiwire branch circuits.

▶ **Hazard of Open Neutral**

Example: A 3-wire, single-phase, 120/240V multiwire circuit supplies a 1,200W, 120V hair dryer and a 600W, 120V television. Figure 210–4

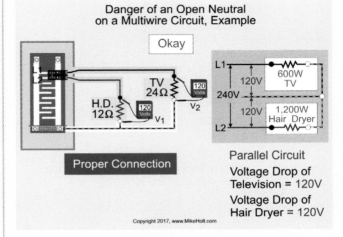

Figure 210–4

If the neutral conductor of the multiwire circuit is interrupted, it will cause the 120V television to operate at 160V and consume 1,067W of power (instead of 600W) for only a few seconds before it burns up. Figure 210–5

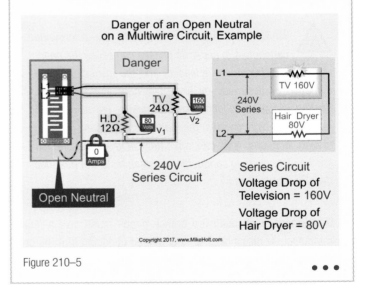

Figure 210–5

Step 1: *Determine the resistance of each appliance:*

$$R = E^2/P$$

R of the hair dryer = 120V²/1,200W

R of the hair dryer = 12 ohms

R of the television = 120V²/600W

R of the television = 24 ohms

Step 2: *Determine the current of the circuit:*

$$I = E/R$$

E = 240V

R = 36 ohms (12 ohms + 24 ohms)

I = 240V/36 ohms

I = 6.70A

Step 3: *Determine the operating voltage for each appliance:*

$$E = I \times R$$

I = 6.70A

R = 12 ohms for hair dryer and 24 ohms for TV

Voltage of hair dryer = 6.70A x 12 ohms

Voltage of hair dryer = 80V

Voltage of television = 6.70A x 24 ohms

Voltage of television = 160V

⚠ **WARNING:** *Failure to terminate the ungrounded conductors to separate phases can cause the neutral conductor to become overloaded, and the insulation can be damaged or destroyed by excessive heat. Conductor overheating is known to decrease the service life of insulating materials, which creates the potential for arcing faults in hidden locations, and can ultimately lead to fires. It isn't known just how long conductor insulation lasts, but heat does decrease its life span.*

(B) Disconnect. Each multiwire branch circuit must have a means to simultaneously disconnect all ungrounded conductors at the point where the branch circuit originates. Figure 210–6

Note: Individual single-pole circuit breakers with handle ties identified for the purpose can be used for this application [240.15(B)(1)]. Figure 210–7

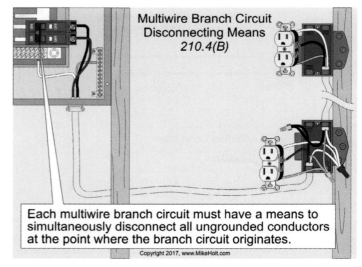

Multiwire Branch Circuit Disconnecting Means 210.4(B)

Each multiwire branch circuit must have a means to simultaneously disconnect all ungrounded conductors at the point where the branch circuit originates.

Copyright 2017, www.MikeHolt.com

Figure 210–6

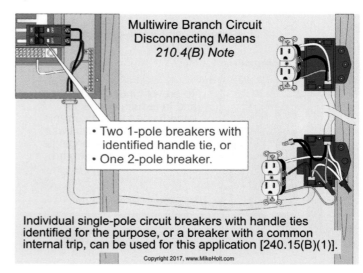

Multiwire Branch Circuit Disconnecting Means 210.4(B) Note

• Two 1-pole breakers with identified handle tie, or
• One 2-pole breaker.

Individual single-pole circuit breakers with handle ties identified for the purpose, or a breaker with a common internal trip, can be used for this application [240.15(B)(1)].

Copyright 2017, www.MikeHolt.com

Figure 210–7

⚠ **CAUTION:** *This rule is intended to prevent people from working on energized circuits they thought were disconnected.*

(C) Line-to-Neutral Loads. Multiwire branch circuits must supply only line-to-neutral loads.

Ex 1: A multiwire branch circuit can supply an individual piece of line-to-line utilization equipment, such as a range or dryer. Figure 210–8

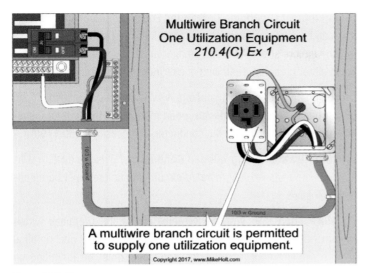

Figure 210–8

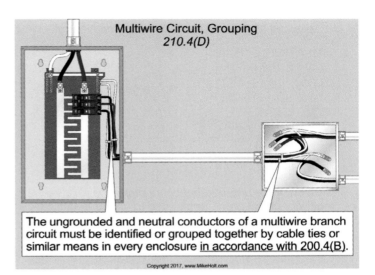

Figure 210–10

Ex 2: A multiwire branch circuit can supply both line-to-line and line-to-neutral loads if the circuit is protected by a device such as a multipole circuit breaker with a common internal trip that opens all ungrounded conductors of the multiwire branch circuit simultaneously under a fault condition. Figure 210–9

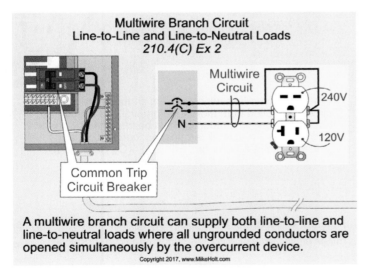

Figure 210–9

(D) Grouping. Ungrounded and neutral conductors of a multiple branch circuit must be identified or grouped together by cable ties or similar means in every enclosure in accordance with 200.4(B). Figure 210–10

Author's Comment:

- Grouping isn't required where the circuit conductors are contained in a single raceway or cable unique to that circuit that makes the grouping obvious [200.4(B) Ex 1].

- Grouping isn't required if the conductors pass through a box or conduit body without any splices or terminations, or if the conductors don't have a loop as described in 314.16(B)(1) [200.4(B) Ex 2].

- Grouping all associated conductors of a multiwire branch circuit together by cable ties or other means within the point of origination makes it easier to visually identify the conductors of the multiwire branch circuit. The grouping will assist in making sure that the correct neutral is used at junction points and in connecting multiwire branch-circuit conductors to circuit breakers correctly, particularly where twin breakers are used. If proper diligence isn't exercised when making these connections, two circuit conductors can be accidentally connected to the same phase or line.

⚠ **CAUTION:** *If the ungrounded conductors of a multiwire circuit aren't terminated to different phases or lines, the currents on the neutral conductor won't cancel, which can cause an overload on the neutral conductor.* Figure 210–11

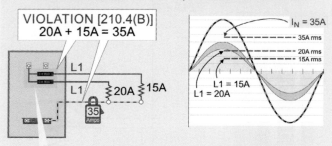

Miswired Multiwire Circuit, Overload on Neutral

VIOLATION [210.4(B)]
20A + 15A = 35A

I_N = 35A
35A rms
20A rms
15A rms
L1 = 15A
L1 = 20A

Caution: If the ungrounded conductors of a multiwire circuit aren't terminated to different phases or lines, the currents on the neutral conductor won't cancel, but will add, which can cause a dangerous overload on the neutral conductor.

Copyright 2017, www.MikeHolt.com

Figure 210–11

210.5 Identification for Branch Circuits

The identification and notification requirements were clarified for branch circuits and for existing wiring systems where a new system of a different voltage is added.

Analysis

CLARIFIED

When a building or structure contains two or more voltage systems, we need to come up with an identification system. Each ungrounded conductor must be identified by phase and system at all termination, connection, and splice points in order to differentiate the systems and phases of each. If we have a building with only one voltage system and we add a different voltage system, the new system needs to be identified and notification posted. We also need to inform people that this isn't the only voltage system on the premises, and that the other system isn't necessarily marked and posted.

210.5 Identification for Branch Circuits

(A) Neutral Conductor. The neutral conductor of a branch circuit must be identified in accordance with 200.6.

(B) Equipment Grounding Conductor. Equipment grounding conductors can be bare, covered, or insulated. Insulated equipment grounding conductors size 6 AWG and smaller must have a continuous outer finish either green or green with one or more yellow stripes [250.119].

On equipment grounding conductors 4 AWG and larger, insulation can be permanently reidentified with green marking at the time of installation at every point where the conductor is accessible [250.119(A)].

(C) Identification of Ungrounded Conductors. Where a system voltage is being installed, ungrounded circuit conductors must be identified as follows:

(1) More Than One Voltage System. Where the premises wiring system has branch circuits supplied from more than one nominal voltage system, each ungrounded conductor must be identified by phase and system at all termination, connection, and splice points as follows: Figure 210–12

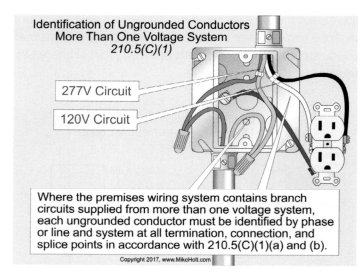

Identification of Ungrounded Conductors More Than One Voltage System
210.5(C)(1)

277V Circuit
120V Circuit

Where the premises wiring system contains branch circuits supplied from more than one voltage system, each ungrounded conductor must be identified by phase or line and system at all termination, connection, and splice points in accordance with 210.5(C)(1)(a) and (b).

Copyright 2017, www.MikeHolt.com

Figure 210–12

(a) Means of Identification. Color coding, marking tape, tagging, or other means approved by the authority having jurisdiction. Figure 210–13

(b) Posting of Branch Circuit Identification. The method of identification must be readily available or permanently posted at each branch-circuit panelboard, <u>not be handwritten, and be of sufficient durability to withstand the environment involved</u>. Figure 210–14

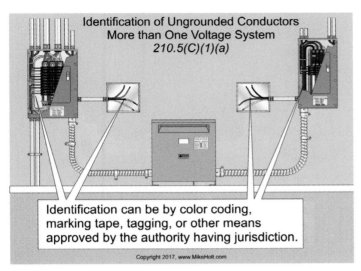

Figure 210–13

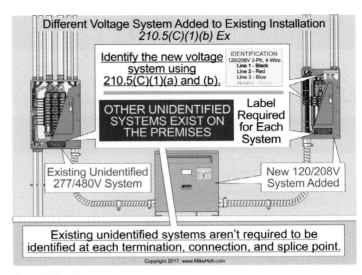

Figure 210–15

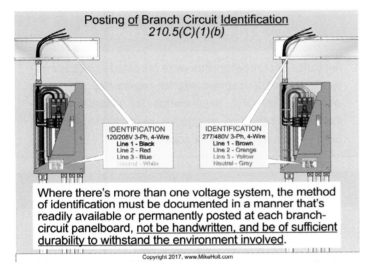

Figure 210–14

Ex: Where a different voltage system is added to an existing installation, branch circuit identification is required for the new voltage system. Existing unidentified systems aren't required to be identified at each termination, connection, and splice point in compliance with 210.5(C)(1)(a) and (b). Each voltage system distribution equipment must have a label with the words "other unidentified systems exist on the premises." Figure 210–15

Author's Comment:

■ When a premises has more than one voltage system supplying branch circuits, the ungrounded conductors must be identified by phase and system. This can be done by permanently posting an identification legend that describes the method used, such as color-coded marking tape or color-coded insulation.

■ Conductors with insulation that's green or green with one or more yellow stripes can't be used for an ungrounded or neutral conductor [250.119].

■ Although the *NEC* doesn't require a specific color code for ungrounded conductors, electricians often use the following color system for power and lighting conductor identification:

◆ 120/240V, single-phase—black, red, and white

◆ 120/208V, three-phase—black, red, blue, and white

◆ 120/240V, three-phase—black, orange, blue, and white

◆ 277/480V, three-phase—brown, orange, yellow, and gray; or, brown, purple, yellow, and gray

210.7 Multiple Branch Circuits

The rule requiring the simultaneous disconnect for multiple branch circuits was editorially revised.

Analysis

EDITED

The change made is editorial in nature to remove repetitious words.

210.7 Multiple Branch Circuits

If two or more branch circuits supply devices or equipment on the same yoke, a means to disconnect simultaneously all ungrounded <u>supply conductors</u> is required at the point where the branch circuit originates. Figure 210–16

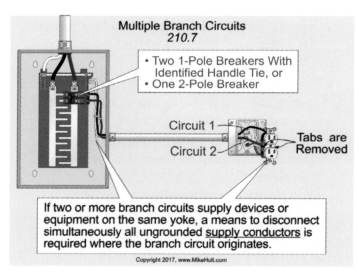

Multiple Branch Circuits
210.7

• Two 1-Pole Breakers With Identified Handle Tie, or
• One 2-Pole Breaker

Circuit 1
Circuit 2
Tabs are Removed

If two or more branch circuits supply devices or equipment on the same yoke, a means to disconnect simultaneously all ungrounded <u>supply conductors</u> is required where the branch circuit originates.

Copyright 2017, www.MikeHolt.com

Figure 210–16

Author's Comment:

- A yoke, also called a strap, is the metal mounting structure for such items as receptacles, switches, switches with pilot lights, and switch-receptacles to name a few. Figure 210–17

- Individual single-pole circuit breakers with handle ties identified for the purpose, or a circuit breaker with a common internal trip, can be used for this application [240.15(B)(1)].

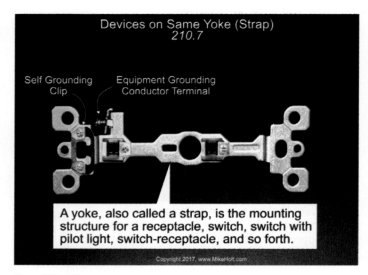

Devices on Same Yoke (Strap)
210.7

Self Grounding Clip   Equipment Grounding Conductor Terminal

A yoke, also called a strap, is the mounting structure for a receptacle, switch, switch with pilot light, switch-receptacle, and so forth.

Copyright 2017, www.MikeHolt.com

Figure 210–17

210.8 GFCI Protection

Appliance GFCI requirements were relocated to 422.5, measuring and GFCI requirements for receptacles near sinks were clarified, GFCI requirements for unfinished basement and nondwelling receptacles were clarified, and new requirements were added for crawl spaces.

Analysis

NEW

Informational Note. GFCI requirements have been added to the *NEC* every *Code* cycle since 1971, and this edition is no exception. A new Informational Note was added, alerting the user to the fact that GFCI protection requirements for appliances are now contained in 422.5 instead of 210.8.

CLARIFIED

Measurement of 6-Ft Rule. Where GFCI protection is required within 6 ft of a sink, how were we to measure the dimension? The change to this edition of the *NEC* makes it clear that it's measured as the path a cord would follow, without piercing a wall, door, window, or similar object.

CLARIFIED

Unfinished Basements. Revised GFCI requirements for receptacles in dwelling unit unfinished basements clarify that unfinished portions of basements require GFCI protection. This is hardly a new concept, but by removing the language specifying "storage areas, work areas, and the like" there's less room for interpretation and therefore less room for confusion. While this isn't much of a change, any opportunity to remove vagueness is worth at least considering, if not changing.

 CLARIFIED

Sinks. Receptacles within 6 ft of dwelling unit sinks require GFCI protection. How is this to be measured? The *Code* already clarified that it's the path a cord would take, but where do we begin the measurement? The *NEC* is now clear in that we begin at the inside edge of the bowl of the sink and measure 6 ft.

 EXPANDED

GFCI Protection. The 2017 *Code* now requires GFCI protection for single-phase receptacles rated 50A or less not exceeding 150V to ground and three-phase receptacles rated 100A or less not exceeding 150V to ground installed in nondwelling unit locations! Wow, that is amazing…

 NEW

Crawl Spaces. New to this edition of the *NEC* is the GFCI protection requirements for receptacles in crawl spaces and in unfinished basements of other than dwellings. While crawl spaces and unfinished basements are certainly more common in residential buildings, they do exist in commercial buildings as well. Because the GFCI rules are driven by location, it makes sense that the same locations requiring GFCI protection in a dwelling crawl space be mandated in commercial occupancies as well.

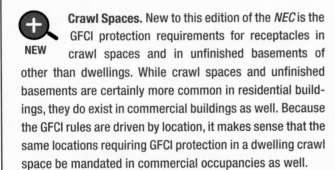 **NEW**

Lighting Outlet GFCI Protection. The 2017 *Code* now covers GFCI protection for lighting outlets in crawl spaces. It's easy to visualize a person crawling around under their house and having their back (or head) break a light in the crawl space, or to install a receptacle adapter in the screw shell of the lampholder. It doesn't take much more imagining to think of that person getting shocked. Add in a dirt floor and you really have a recipe for disaster. So adding GFCI protection for these lighting outlets is a great idea.

210.8 GFCI Protection

Ground-fault circuit interruption for personnel must be provided as required in 210.8(A) through (E). The GFCI device must be installed at a readily accessible location. Figure 210–18

Figure 210–18

Note 2: See 422.5 for GFCI requirements for automotive vacuum machines, drinking water coolers, high-pressure spray washing machines, tire inflation machines provided for public use, and vending machines.

Author's Comment:

- According to Article 100, "readily accessible" means capable of being reached quickly without having to climb over or remove obstacles, or resort to the use of portable ladders.

For the application of 210.8(A)(7), 210.8(A)(9), and 210.8(B)(5), distance is measured as the shortest path the flexible cord would follow without piercing a floor, wall, ceiling, or fixed barrier, or passing through a door, doorway, or window. Figure 210–19

(A) Dwelling Units. GFCI protection is required for 15A and 20A, 125V receptacles installed in the following locations:

Author's Comment:

- See the definitions of "GFCI" and "Dwelling Unit" in Article 100.

For the application of 210.8(A)(7), 210.8(A)(9), and 210.8(B)(5), distance is measured as the shortest path the flexible cord would follow without piercing a floor, wall, ceiling, or fixed barrier, or passing through a door, doorway, or window.

Figure 210–19

(1) Bathroom Area. GFCI protection is required for 15A and 20A, 125V receptacles in the bathroom area of a dwelling unit. Figure 210–20

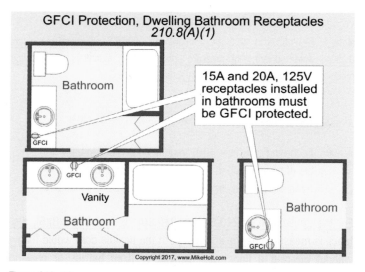

Figure 210–20

Author's Comment:

■ A bathroom is an area that includes a basin as well as one or more of the following: a toilet, urinal, tub, shower, bidet, or similar plumbing fixture [Article 100].

(2) Garages and Accessory Buildings. GFCI protection is required for 15A and 20A, 125V receptacles in garages, and in grade-level portions of accessory buildings used for storage or work areas of a dwelling unit. Figure 210–21 and Figure 210–22

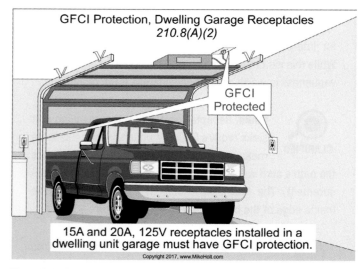

Figure 210–21

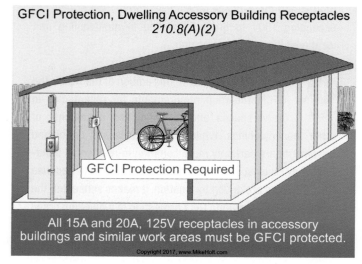

Figure 210–22

Author's Comment:

■ See the definition of "Garage" in Article 100.

■ A receptacle outlet is required in a dwelling unit attached garage [210.52(G)(1)], but a receptacle outlet isn't required in an accessory building or a detached garage without power. If a 15A or 20A, 125V receptacle is installed in an accessory building, it must be GFCI protected.

(3) Outdoors. GFCI protection is required for 15A and 20A, 125V receptacles located outdoors of dwelling units, including receptacles installed under the eaves of roofs. Figure 210–23

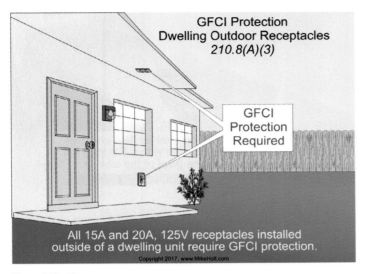

Figure 210–23

Ex: GFCI protection isn't required for a receptacle that's supplied by a branch circuit dedicated to fixed electric snow-melting, deicing or pipeline and vessel heating equipment, if the receptacle isn't readily accessible and the equipment or receptacle has ground-fault protection of equipment (GFPE) [426.28 and 427.22]. Figure 210–24

(4) Crawl Spaces at or Below Grade Level. GFCI protection is required for 15A and 20A, 125V receptacles installed in crawl spaces at or below grade. Figure 210–25

Figure 210–24

GFCI protection isn't required for a receptacle supplied by a branch circuit dedicated to fixed electric snow-melting or deicing or pipeline and vessel heating equipment, if the receptacle isn't readily accessible and the equipment or receptacle has GFPE [426.28 and 427.22].

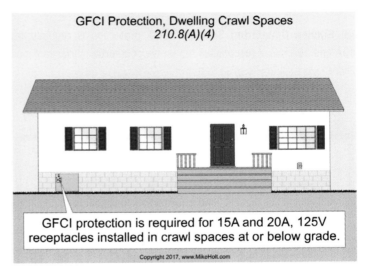

Figure 210–25

(5) Unfinished Portions of Basements. GFCI protection is required for 15A and 20A, 125V receptacles located in unfinished portions or areas of a basement not intended for habitable rooms. Figure 210–26

Ex: A receptacle supplying only a permanently installed fire alarm or burglar alarm system isn't required to be GFCI protected [760.41(B) and 760.121(B)].

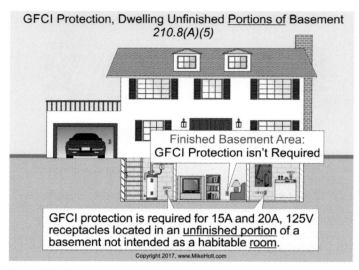

Figure 210–26

Figure 210–28

(6) Kitchen Countertop Surfaces. GFCI protection is required for 15A and 20A, 125V receptacles that serve countertop surfaces. Figure 210–27

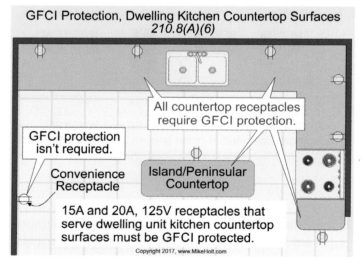

Figure 210–27

> **Author's Comment:**
>
> ■ See 210.52(C) for the location requirements of countertop receptacles.

(7) Sinks. GFCI protection is required for 15A and 20A, 125V receptacles located within 6 ft from the top inside edge of the bowl of the sink. Figure 210–28

(8) Boathouses. GFCI protection is required for 15A and 20A, 125V receptacles located in a dwelling unit boathouse. Figure 210–29

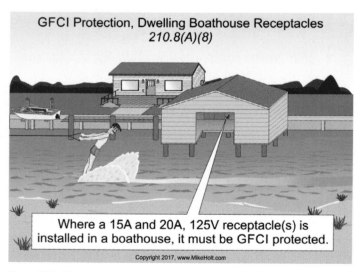

Figure 210–29

> **Author's Comment:**
>
> ■ The *Code* doesn't require a 15A or 20A, 125V receptacle to be installed in a boathouse, but if one is installed, it must be GFCI protected.

(9) Bathtubs or Shower Stalls. GFCI protection is required for 15A and 20A, 125V receptacles located within 6 ft of the outside edge of a bathtub or shower stall. Figure 210–30

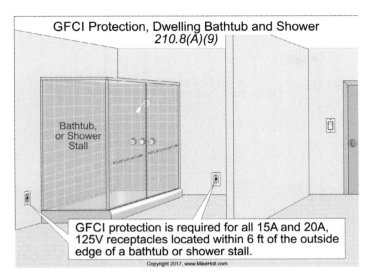

Figure 210–30

Figure 210–32

(10) Laundry Areas. GFCI protection is required for 15A and 20A, 125V receptacles installed in laundry areas. Figure 210–31

Figure 210–31

(B) Other than Dwelling Units. GFCI protection is required for single-phase receptacles rated 50A or less not exceeding 150V to ground and three-phase receptacles rated 100A or less not exceeding 150V to ground installed in the following locations:

(1) Bathrooms. GFCI protection is required for receptacles installed in bathrooms. Figure 210–32

Author's Comment:

■ A bathroom is an area that includes a basin as well as one or more of the following: a toilet, urinal, tub, shower, bidet, or similar plumbing fixture [Article 100].

(2) Kitchens. GFCI protection is required for receptacles installed in a kitchen. Figure 210–33

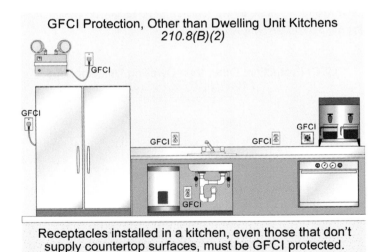

Figure 210–33

Author's Comment:

■ A kitchen is an area with a sink and permanent provisions for food preparation and cooking [Article 100].

(3) Rooftops. GFCI protection is required for receptacles installed on rooftops. Figure 210–34

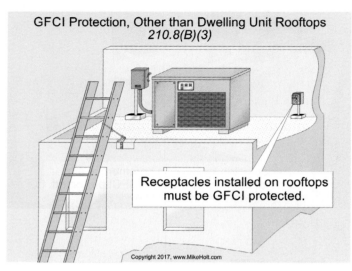

Figure 210–34

- A 15A or 20A, 125V receptacle outlet must be installed within 25 ft of heating, air-conditioning, and refrigeration equipment [210.63].

Ex 1: Rooftop receptacles are required to be readily accessible from the rooftop surface area. Figure 210–35

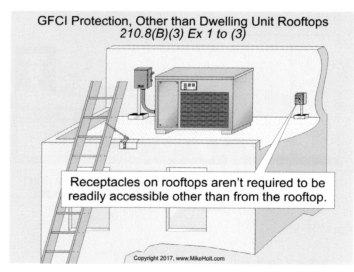

Figure 210–35

(4) Outdoors. GFCI protection is required for receptacles installed outdoors. Figure 210–36

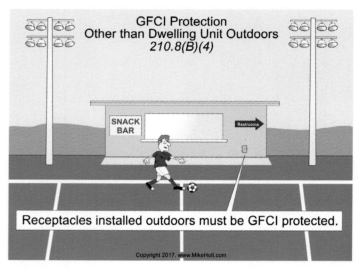

Figure 210–36

(5) Sinks. GFCI protection is required for receptacles installed within 6 ft <u>from</u> the <u>top inside</u> edge of the <u>bowl of the</u> sink. Figure 210–37

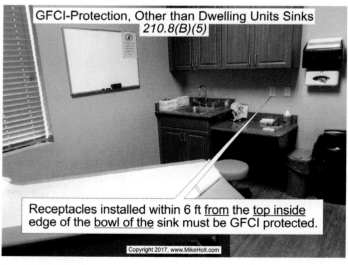

Figure 210–37

Ex 1: In industrial laboratories, receptacles used to supply equipment where removal of power would introduce a greater hazard aren't required to be GFCI protected.

(6) Indoor Wet Locations. GFCI protection is required for receptacles installed indoors in wet locations.

(7) Locker Rooms. GFCI protection is required for receptacles installed in locker rooms with associated showering facilities. Figure 210–38

Figure 210–38

(8) Garages. GFCI protection is required for receptacles installed in garages, service bays, and similar areas, other than show rooms and exhibition halls. Figure 210–39

Figure 210–39

(9) Crawl Space Receptacle Outlets. GFCI protection is required for receptacles in crawl spaces.

(10) Unfinished Portions of Basements. GFCI protection is required for receptacles located in the unfinished portions of a basement.

(C) Boat Hoist—Dwelling Unit. GFCI protection is required for boat hoist outlets not exceeding 240V at dwelling unit locations. Figure 210–40

Figure 210–40

(D) Dishwasher—Dwelling Unit. GFCI protection is required for outlets supplying dishwashers at a dwelling unit. Figure 210–41 and Figure 210–42

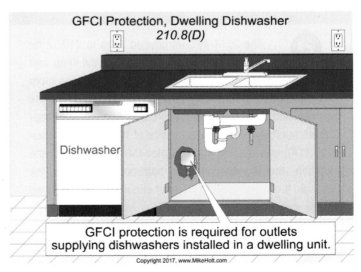

Figure 210–41

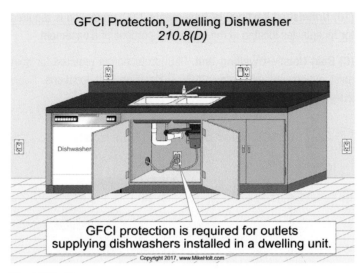

GFCI Protection, Dwelling Dishwasher
210.8(D)

GFCI protection is required for outlets
supplying dishwashers installed in a dwelling unit.

Copyright 2017, www.MikeHolt.com

Figure 210–42

(E) Crawl Space Lighting Outlets—Dwelling. GFCI protection is required for 120V lighting outlets in crawl spaces in dwelling units.

210.11 Branch Circuits Required

The rules for the circuiting of dwelling unit garages have been relocated and an exception was added.

Analysis

RELOCATED The 2014 *NEC* introduced rules in 210.52 for the circuiting requirements of dwelling unit garages. These rules included requiring more receptacle outlets, based on how many cars could fit in the garage, and stipulating that the circuit serving these receptacles must not serve loads outside of the garage. Section 210.11(C) is where we find the rules for how we circuit the kitchen, the laundry, and the bathroom—and now the garage. It makes sense to have all circuiting rules grouped in the same location of the *Code*.

NEW A new exception allows readily accessible receptacles outdoors to be on the dwelling unit garage circuit. This recognizes a very common installation practice that never seemed to result in any problems before, so there's no reason to think it would be unsafe now.

The original proposal was to allow for a receptacle located near a garage personnel door to be on this circuit, but the Code Making Panel decided to extended the allowance even further, to the delight of many electricians, I'm sure. Unfortunately, at least as of right now, the *NEC* doesn't allow lighting outlets on this circuit, which seems a bit odd.

210.11 Branch Circuits Required

(A) Number of Branch Circuits. The minimum number of general lighting and general-use receptacle branch circuits must be determined by dividing the total calculated load in amperes by the ampere rating of the circuits used.

Example: How many 15A or 20A, 120V circuits are required for the general lighting and general-use receptacles for a dwelling having a floor area of 1,500 ft^2, exclusive of an unfinished cellar not adaptable for future use [Example D1(a) in Annex D]? Figure 210–43

Solution: Three 15A or two 20A, 120V circuits.

Step 1: Determine the total VA load:

$$VA = 1,500 \text{ sq ft} \times 3 \text{ VA per sq ft [Table 220.12]}$$
$$VA = 4,500 \text{ VA}$$

Step 2: Determine the amperes:

$$I = VA/E$$
$$I = 4,500VA/120V$$
$$I = 38A$$

Step 3: Determine the number of circuits:

Number of 15A Circuits = 38A/15A
Number of 15A Circuits = Three

Number of 20A Circuits = 38A/20A
Number of 20A Circuits = Two

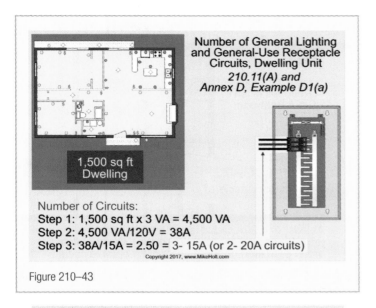

Figure 210–43

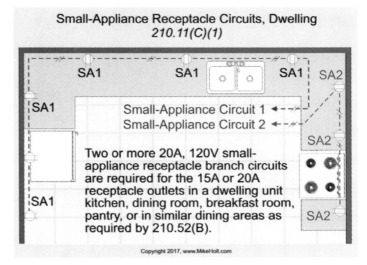

Figure 210–45

Author's Comment:

- There's no limit to the number of receptacles on a circuit in a dwelling unit.

(B) Load Evenly Proportioned Among Branch Circuits. If the load is calculated on the volt-amperes/square foot, the wiring system must be provided to serve the calculated load, with the loads evenly proportioned among multioutlet branch circuits within the panelboard. Figure 210–44

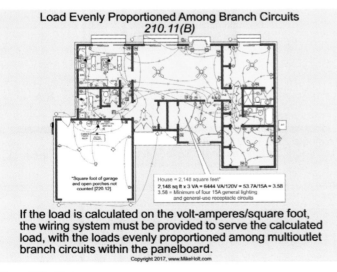

Figure 210–44

(C) Dwelling Unit.

(1) Small-Appliance Branch Circuits. At least two 20A, 120V small-appliance receptacle branch circuits are required to supply receptacle outlets in a dwelling unit kitchen, dining room, breakfast room, pantry, or similar dining areas as required by 210.52(B). Figure 210–45

Author's Comment:

- See the definition of "Receptacle Outlet" in Article 100.

- A 15A, 125V receptacle is rated for 20A feed-through, so it can be used for this purpose [210.21(B)(3)].

- Lighting outlets or receptacles located in other areas of a dwelling unit aren't permitted to be connected to the small-appliance branch circuit [210.52(B)(2)].

- The two 20A small-appliance branch circuits can be supplied by one 3-wire multiwire circuit or by two separate 120V circuits [210.4(A)].

(2) Laundry Branch Circuit. At least one 20A, 120V branch circuit is required to supply receptacle outlet(s) in the laundry area as required by 210.52(F). This circuit isn't permitted to serve any other outlets, such as the laundry room lighting or receptacles in other rooms. Figure 210–46

Author's Comment:

- The 20A laundry room receptacle circuit can supply more than one receptacle in the laundry room.

- The 20A, 120V laundry branch circuit is required, even if the laundry appliance installed is a 30A, 230V combination washer/dryer. Figure 210–47

- A 15A receptacle is rated for 20A feed-through, so it can be used for this purpose [210.21(B)(3)].

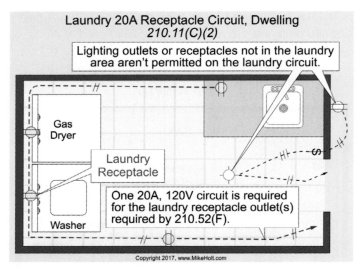

Figure 210–46

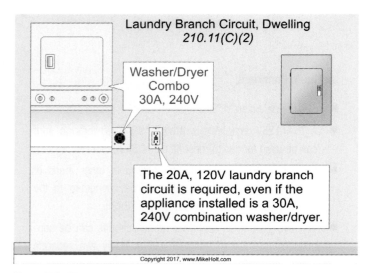

Figure 210–47

- GFCI protection is required for 15A and 20A, 125V receptacles located in a laundry room [210.8(A)(10)].

(3) Bathroom Branch Circuit. At least one 20A, 120V branch circuit is required to <u>supply the bathroom(s)</u> receptacle outlet(s) as required by 210.52(D). This circuit isn't permitted to serve any other outlet, such as bathroom lighting outlets or receptacles in other rooms. Figure 210–48

Author's Comment:

- A 15A, 125V receptacle is rated for 20A feed-through, so it can be used for this purpose [210.21(B)(3)].

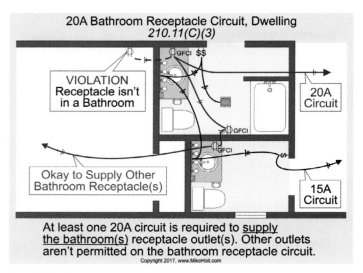

Figure 210–48

Ex: A single 20A, 120V branch circuit can supply all of the outlets in a single bathroom, as long as no single load fastened in place is rated more than 10A [210.23(A)]. Figure 210–49

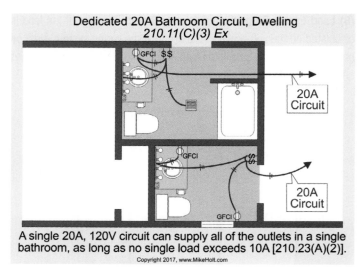

Figure 210–49

> **Example:** *Can a luminaire, ceiling fan, or bath fan be connected to the 20A, 120V branch circuit that supplies only one bathroom?*
>
> **Solution:** *Yes.*

(4) Garage Branch Circuits. At least one 20A, 120V branch circuit is required to supply the receptacle outlet(s) in attached garages and detached garages with electric power [210.52(G)]. This 20A, 120V branch circuit isn't permitted to serve any other outlet. Figure 210–50

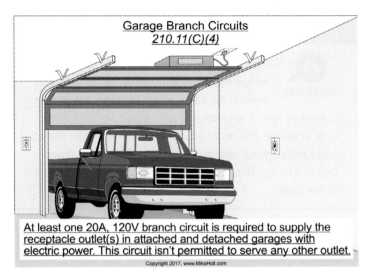

Garage Branch Circuits
210.11(C)(4)

At least one 20A, 120V branch circuit is required to supply the receptacle outlet(s) in attached and detached garages with electric power. This circuit isn't permitted to serve any other outlet.

Copyright 2017, www.MikeHolt.com

Figure 210–50

Ex: Readily accessible outdoor receptacle outlets (not lighting outlets) can be supplied by the 20A, 120V garage receptacle branch circuit. Figure 210–51

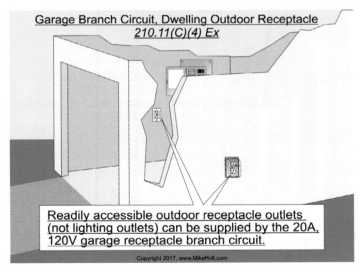

Garage Branch Circuit, Dwelling Outdoor Receptacle
210.11(C)(4) Ex

Readily accessible outdoor receptacle outlets (not lighting outlets) can be supplied by the 20A, 120V garage receptacle branch circuit.

Copyright 2017, www.MikeHolt.com

Figure 210–51

210.12 Arc-Fault Circuit-Interrupter Protection

The AFCI requirements have been greatly expanded.

Analysis

NEW AFCI protection is now required for guest rooms and suites of hotels and motels. This seems to be the progression of *Code* rules, such as the tamper-resistant receptacles required in 406.12. Because these areas are very similar in their use to dwelling units, this new rule was accepted.

The requirement for updating the electrical system when adding or modifying wiring was extended to dormitories. The *NEC* is often three years behind in making new allowances, and this will be the case as long as humans are responsible for the *Code*. Considering that there are typically 3,000 to 5,000 proposals (now called "public input") to change the *NEC*, things are going to slip through the cracks. Why not require the same rules and the same exception to all areas requiring AFCI protection?

210.12 Arc-Fault Circuit-Interrupter Protection

Arc-fault circuit-interrupter protection must be provided in accordance with 210.12(A), (B), and (C). AFCI devices must be installed in readily accessible locations.

(A) Required Locations. A listed combination AFCI breaker is required for all 15A or 20A, 120V branch circuits in dwelling units supplying outlets or devices in kitchens, family rooms, dining rooms, living rooms, parlors, libraries, dens, bedrooms, sunrooms, recreation rooms, closets, hallways, laundry areas, or similar rooms or areas. Figure 210–52

(B) Dormitory Units. A listed combination AFCI breaker is required for all 15A or 20A, 120V branch circuits for outlets and devices in dormitory unit bedrooms, living rooms, hallways, closets, bathrooms, and similar rooms in accordance with 210.12(A).

(C) Guest Rooms and Guest Suites. A listed combination AFCI breaker is required for all 15A or 20A, 120V branch circuits supplying outlets and devices in guest rooms and guest suites of hotels and motels. Figure 210–53

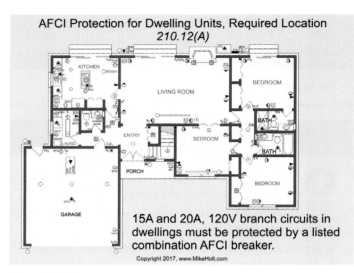

AFCI Protection for Dwelling Units, Required Location
210.12(A)

15A and 20A, 120V branch circuits in dwellings must be protected by a listed combination AFCI breaker.

Copyright 2017, www.MikeHolt.com

Figure 210–52

AFCI Protection, Guest Rooms and Guest Suites
210.12(C)

15A and 20A, 120V branch circuits in guest rooms and guest suites of hotels and motels must be protected by a listed combination AFCI breaker.

Copyright 2017, www.MikeHolt.com

Figure 210–53

(D) Branch-Circuit Extensions or Modifications in Dwelling Units and Dormitory Units. Where 15A or 20A, 120V branch-circuit wiring is modified, replaced, or extended in a dwelling unit or dormitory where AFCI protection is required [210.12(A)], the modified, replaced, or extended branch-circuit wiring must be AFCI protected by one of the following methods:

(1) A listed combination AFCI circuit breaker

(2) A listed AFCI receptacle located at the first receptacle outlet of the branch circuit

Ex: AFCI protection isn't required for extension wiring that's less than 6 ft in length if no outlets or devices are added.

210.18 Branch-Circuit Rating

This section was moved from 210.3 to this location.

Analysis

RELOCATED This is another common sense change that keeps important information about the same topic in the same place. Although this section is marked new, it was actually just moved from the beginning of Article 210 (in 210.3) to here. It was a little out of place before since ratings are discussed in Part II Branch-Circuit Ratings. This is another great change in this edition of the *Code*.

Part II. Branch-Circuit Ratings

210.18 Branch-Circuit Rating

The rating of a branch circuit is determined by the rating of the branch-circuit overcurrent protection device, not the conductor ampacity. Figure 210–54

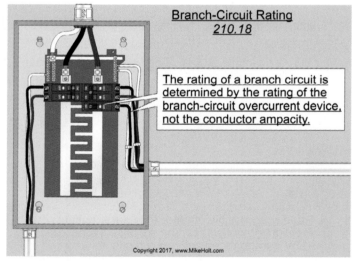

Branch-Circuit Rating
210.18

The rating of a branch circuit is determined by the rating of the branch-circuit overcurrent device, not the conductor ampacity.

Copyright 2017, www.MikeHolt.com

Figure 210–54

Author's Comment:

- For example, the branch-circuit rating of 10 THHN, rated 30A at 60ºC, protected by a 20A circuit breaker is 20A. Figure 210–55

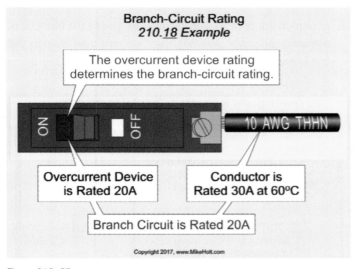

Figure 210–55

210.52 Dwelling Unit Receptacle Outlet Requirements

Many changes were made to dwelling unit receptacle location rules, most having to do with countertops and work surfaces.

Analysis

Wall Space. 210.52(A) provides the rules for the placement of receptacles at wall spaces. **CLARIFIED** Wall spaces don't include doorways and similar openings, fireplaces, and fixed cabinetry; unless, new to this edition, the cabinetry has a countertop. This results in the walls in rooms such as libraries, dens, and/or offices with built-in bookcases to not have receptacles installed in them since a bookcase is just a cabinet, not a wall. One area that's often missed is the installation of receptacles in an island or peninsula of a kitchen. This is certainly cabinetry, and as such, the back side of this cabinetry was exempt from the receptacle placement requirements for wall

spacing. Oftentimes a peninsula or island creates a wall of sorts, separating the kitchen from, say, the dining room. Because this cabinetry has a countertop it's now considered wall space, so a receptacle(s) will be required to be installed, which serves as a receptacle for the dining room.

Similar Work Space. Many changes were made throughout 210.52 to include "similar work **EDITED** spaces" wherever the word "countertop" was used. This clears up any disagreement about work spaces in kitchens that aren't necessarily countertops but are still likely to have appliances being used there.

Dedicated 15A Circuit. The receptacle for the kitchen refrigerator has long been allowed to **CLARIFIED** be installed on an individual 15A circuit instead of one of the two required small-appliance branch circuits. This makes sense, and, although it's an exception, it really makes for a better installation. With this said, why not allow the same exception for a trash compactor, garbage disposal, wine coolers, dishwasher, or a built-in microwave? If the refrigerator can have a dedicated 15A circuit, why not the other appliances in the kitchen?

Garages. The last change to 210.52 is found in (G) for garages. The 2014 *Code* added require- **CLARIFIED** ments for additional receptacle(s) in the garage based on its size and the 2017 *NEC* specifies that garage receptacles can't be installed above 5 ft 6 in. from the floor, otherwise they don't count as the required receptacle(s).

210.52 Dwelling Unit Receptacle Outlet Requirements

This section provides requirements for 15A and 20A, 125V receptacle outlets and are in addition to any receptacle that's:

(1) Part of a luminaire or appliance,

(2) Controlled by a wall switch in accordance with 210.70(A)(1), Ex 1. Figure 210–56

(3) Located within cabinets or cupboards, or

(4) Located more than 5½ ft above the floor.

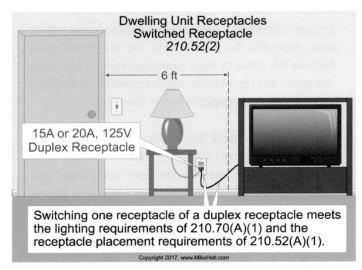

Figure 210–56

(A) General Requirements for Dwelling Unit Receptacle Outlets. A receptacle outlet must be installed in every kitchen, family room, dining room, living room, sunroom, parlor, library, den, bedroom, recreation room, and similar room or area in accordance with (1), (2), (3), and (4):

(1) Receptacle Placement. A receptacle outlet must be installed so that no point along the floor line of any wall is more than 6 ft, measured horizontally along the floor line, from a receptacle outlet. Figure 210–57

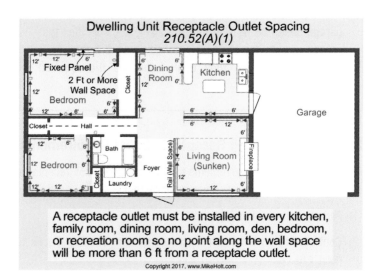

Figure 210–57

Author's Comment:

- The purpose of this rule is to ensure that a general-purpose receptacle is conveniently located to reduce the chance that an extension cord will be used.

(2) Definition of Wall Space for Placement of Receptacle Outlets.

(1) Any space 2 ft or more in width, unbroken along the floor line by doorways and similar openings, fireplaces, and fixed cabinets <u>that don't have countertops or similar work surfaces</u>. Figure 210–58

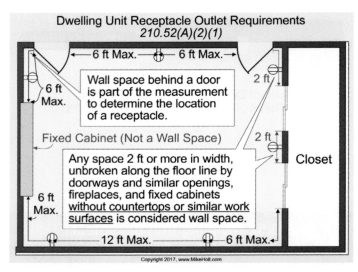

Figure 210–58

(2) The space occupied by fixed panels.

(3) The space occupied by fixed room dividers, such as freestanding bar-type counters or guard rails.

(3) Floor Receptacle Outlets. Floor receptacle outlets aren't counted as the required receptacle wall outlet if they're located more than 18 in. from the wall. Figure 210–59

(4) Countertop <u>and Similar Work Surface</u> Receptacle Outlets. Receptacles installed for countertop <u>and similar work</u> surfaces as required by 210.52(C), can't be used to meet the receptacle <u>outlet</u> requirements for wall space as required by 210.52(A). Figure 210–60

(B) Small-Appliance Circuits.

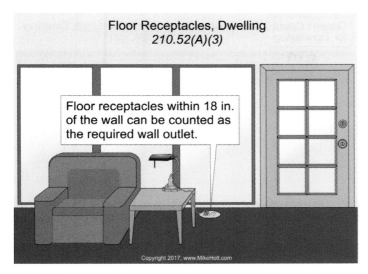

Figure 210–59

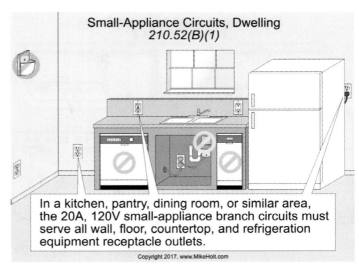

Figure 210–61

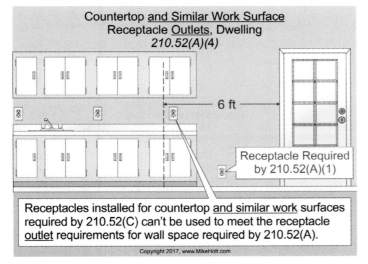

Figure 210–60

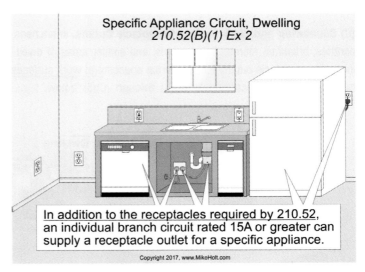

Figure 210–62

(1) Receptacle Outlets. The two or more 20A, 120V small-appliance branch circuits serving the kitchen, pantry, breakfast room, and dining room area of a dwelling unit [210.11(C)(1)] must serve all wall, floor and countertop receptacle outlets [210.52(C)], and the receptacle outlet for refrigeration equipment. Figure 210–61

Ex 2: In addition to the required receptacles specified by 210.52, an individual branch circuit rated 15A or greater can supply a receptacle outlet for a specific appliance, such as a refrigerator in the kitchen, pantry, breakfast room, or dining room area. Figure 210–62

(2) Not Supply Other Outlets. The 20A, 120V small-appliance circuits required by 210.11(C)(1) must not supply outlets for luminaires or appliances.

Ex 1: The 20A, 120V small-appliance branch circuit can be used to supply a receptacle for an electric clock.

Ex 2: A receptacle can be connected to the small-appliance branch circuit to supply a gas-fired range, oven, or counter-mounted cooking unit. Figure 210–63

Author's Comment:

- A range hood or over-the-range microwave listed as a range hood that's flexible cord-and-plug-connected must be supplied by an individual branch circuit [422.16(B)(4)(5)].

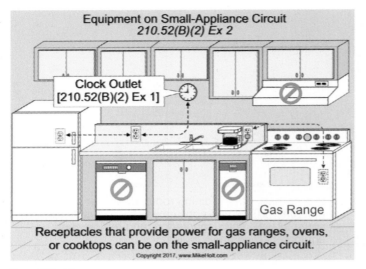

Figure 210–63

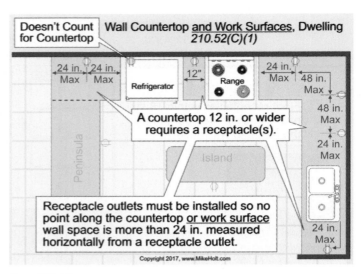

Figure 210–65

(C) Countertop and Work Surface Receptacle Outlets. In kitchens, pantries, breakfast rooms, dining rooms, and similar areas of dwelling units, receptacle outlets for countertop spaces and work surfaces must be installed according to (C)(1) through (C)(5) below. Figure 210–64

Figure 210–64

(1) Wall Countertop and Work Surfaces Receptacle Outlets. A receptacle outlet must be installed for each kitchen and dining area countertop wall space 1 ft or wider, and receptacle outlets must be placed so that no point along the countertop space or work surface wall space is more than 2 ft, measured horizontally, from a receptacle outlet. Figure 210–65

Ex: A receptacle outlet isn't required on a wall directly behind a range, counter-mounted cooking unit, or sink, in accordance with Figure 210.52(C)(1) in the NEC. Figure 210–66

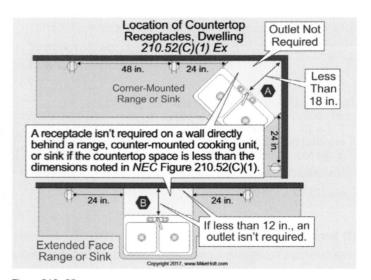

Figure 210–66

Author's Comment:

■ If the countertop space behind a range or sink is larger than the dimensions noted in Figure 210.52(C)(1) of the *NEC*, then a GFCI-protected receptacle must be installed in that space. This is because, for all practical purposes, if there's sufficient space for an appliance, an appliance will be placed there.

(2) Island Countertop Space Receptacle Outlets. At least one receptacle outlet must be installed at each island countertop space with a long dimension of 2 ft or more, and a short dimension of 1 ft or more. Figure 210–67

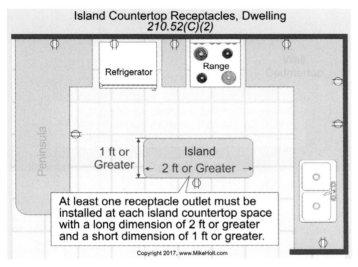

Figure 210–67

(3) Peninsular Countertop Space Receptacle Outlets. At least one receptacle outlet must be installed for each peninsular countertop long dimension space having a long dimension of 2 ft or greater, and a short dimension of 1 ft or greater. The peninsular countertop is measured from the connected peninsular wall. Figure 210–68

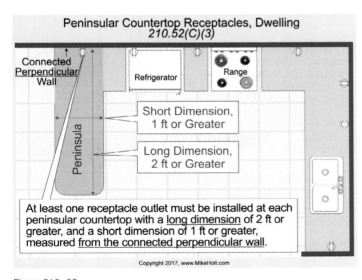

Figure 210–68

Author's Comment:

■ The *Code* doesn't require more than one receptacle outlet in an island or peninsular countertop space, regardless of the length of the countertop, unless the countertop is broken as described in 210.52(C)(4).

(4) Separate Countertop Spaces. When breaks occur in countertop spaces for rangetops, refrigerators, or sinks, each countertop space is considered as a separate countertop for determining receptacle placement. Figure 210–69

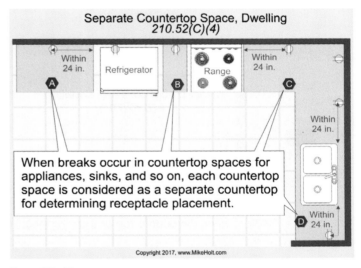

Figure 210–69

If a range, counter-mounted cooking unit, or sink is installed in an island or peninsular countertop, and the depth of the counter behind the range, counter-mounted cooking unit, or sink is less than 12 in., the countertop space is considered to be two separate countertop spaces. Figure 210–70

Author's Comment:

■ GFCI protection is required for all 15A and 20A, 125V receptacles that supply kitchen countertop surfaces [210.8(A)(6)].

(5) Receptacle Location. Receptacle outlets required by 210.52(C)(1) must be located on or above, but not more than 20 in. above, the countertop or work surface. Figure 210–71

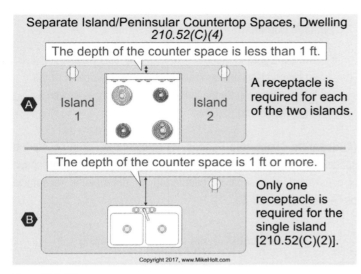

Figure 210–70

Figure 210–72

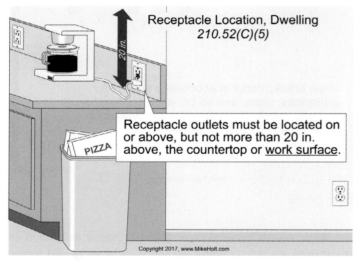

Figure 210–71

Receptacle outlet assemblies listed for use in countertops or work surfaces can be installed in countertops or work surfaces. Figure 210–72

Note: Receptacles aren't permitted to be installed in a face-up position in countertops [406.5(E) and 406.5(G)], nor are receptacles permitted face-up in work surfaces [406.5(F) and 406.5(G)].

Ex: Receptacle outlets are permitted to be mounted not more than 12 in. below the countertop or work surface, where the countertop or work surface doesn't extend more than 6 in. beyond its support base and the receptacle outlet (s) comply with the following conditions:

(1) The countertop or work surface is construction for the physically impaired

(2) The island and peninsular countertop or work surface is flat across its entire surface (no backsplashes, dividers, etc.) and there are no means to mount a receptacle within 20 in. above the countertop or work surface, such as an overhead cabinet. Figure 210–73

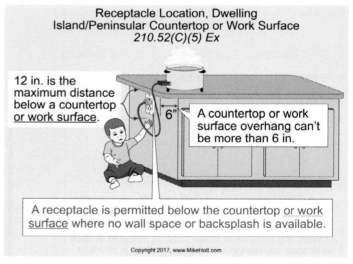

Figure 210–73

Receptacle outlets rendered not readily accessible by appliances fastened in place, located in an appliance garage, behind sinks, or rangetops [210.52(C)(1) Ex], or supplying appliances that occupy dedicated space don't count as the required countertop or work surface receptacles.

Author's Comment:

- An "appliance garage" is an enclosed area on the countertop where an appliance can be stored and hidden from view when not in use. If a receptacle is installed inside an appliance garage, it doesn't count as a required countertop receptacle outlet.

(D) Dwelling Unit Bathroom Receptacles. At least one 15A or 20A, 125V receptacle outlet must be installed within 3 ft from the outside edge of each bathroom basin. Figure 210–74

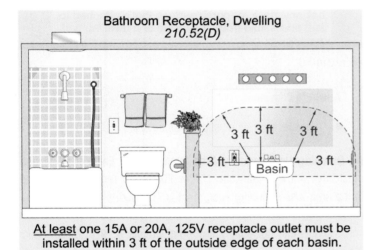

At least one 15A or 20A, 125V receptacle outlet must be installed within 3 ft of the outside edge of each basin.

Copyright 2017, www.MikeHolt.com

Figure 210–74

The receptacle outlet must be located on a wall or partition adjacent to the basin counter surface, or on the side or face of the basin cabinet. In no case can the receptacle be located more than 12 in. below the top of the basin or basin countertop. Figure 210–75

Note: See 406.5(E) and 406.5(G) for the installation of receptacles in countertops.

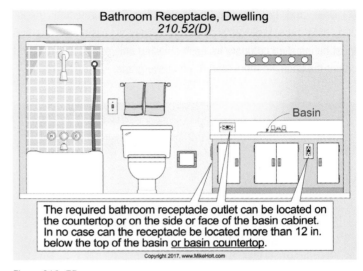

The required bathroom receptacle outlet can be located on the countertop or on the side or face of the basin cabinet. In no case can the receptacle be located more than 12 in. below the top of the basin or basin countertop.

Copyright 2017, www.MikeHolt.com

Figure 210–75

Author's Comment:

- One receptacle outlet can be located between two basins to meet this requirement, but only if it's located within 3 ft of the outside edge of each basin. Figure 210–76

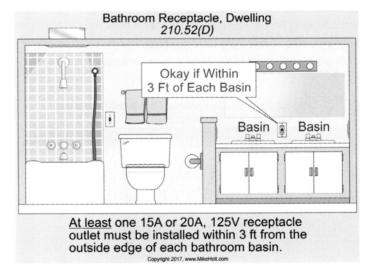

At least one 15A or 20A, 125V receptacle outlet must be installed within 3 ft from the outside edge of each bathroom basin.

Copyright 2017, www.MikeHolt.com

Figure 210–76

- Bathroom receptacles must be GFCI protected [210.8(A)(1)].

(E) Dwelling Unit Outdoor Receptacles. Outdoor receptacles must comply with the following:

Note: See 210.8(A)(3).

(1) One- and Two-Family Dwellings. Two GFCI-protected 15A or 20A, 125V receptacle outlets that are readily accessible from grade must be installed outdoors for each dwelling unit, one at the front and one at the back, no more than 6½ ft above grade. Figure 210–77

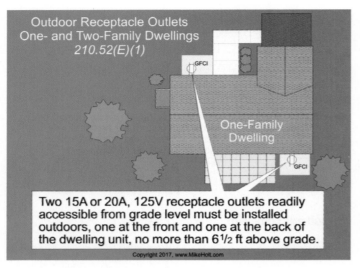

Figure 210–77

(2) Multifamily Dwelling. Each dwelling unit of a multifamily dwelling that has an individual entrance at grade level must have at least one GFCI-protected 15A or 20A, 125V receptacle outlet readily accessible from grade located not more than 6½ ft above grade. Figure 210–78

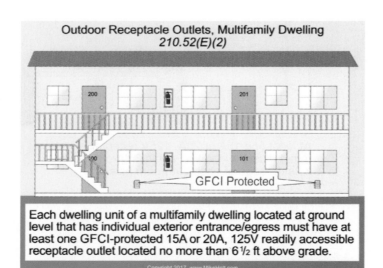

Figure 210–78

(3) Balconies, Decks, and Porches. At least one 15A or 20A, 125V receptacle outlet must be installed not more than 6½ ft above any balcony, deck, or porch surface that's attached to, and accessible from, the inside of a dwelling unit. The receptacle must be accessible from the deck, balcony, or porch surface. Figure 210–79

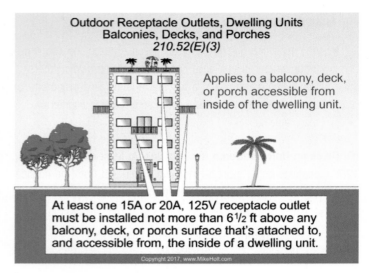

Figure 210–79

Author's Comment:

- These receptacles must be GFCI protected [210.8(A)(3)].

(F) Dwelling Unit Laundry Area Receptacles. Each dwelling unit must have not less than one 15A or 20A, 125V receptacle installed in the area where laundry equipment is intended to be installed. The receptacle(s) must be supplied by the 20A, 120V laundry branch circuit, which must not supply any other outlets [210.11(C)(2)]. Figure 210–80

Author's Comment:

- Receptacles located within 6 ft of a laundry room sink require GFCI protection [210.8(A)(7)].

Ex 1: A laundry receptacle outlet isn't required in a dwelling unit located in a multifamily dwelling unit with laundry facilities available to all occupants.

(G) Dwelling Unit Garage, Basement, and Accessory Building Receptacles. For one- and two-family dwellings, at least one receptacle must be installed in accordance with (1) through (3).

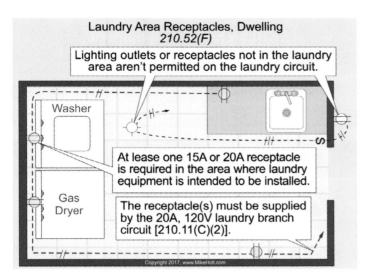

Laundry Area Receptacles, Dwelling
210.52(F)

Lighting outlets or receptacles not in the laundry area aren't permitted on the laundry circuit.

Washer

Gas Dryer

At lease one 15A or 20A receptacle is required in the area where laundry equipment is intended to be installed.

The receptacle(s) must be supplied by the 20A, 120V laundry branch circuit [210.11(C)(2)].

Copyright 2017, www.MikeHolt.com

Figure 210–80

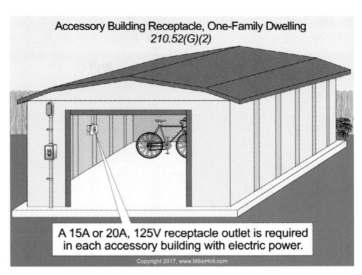

Accessory Building Receptacle, One-Family Dwelling
210.52(G)(2)

A 15A or 20A, 125V receptacle outlet is required in each accessory building with electric power.

Copyright 2017, www.MikeHolt.com

Figure 210–82

(1) Garages. At least one 15A or 20A, 125V receptacle outlet must be installed no higher than 5 ft 6 in. above the floor in each vehicle bay in each attached garage and in each detached garage with electric power. Figure 210–81

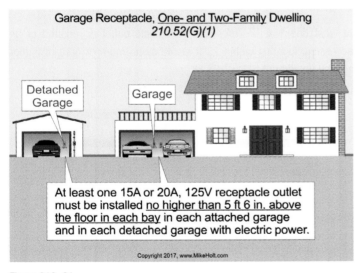

Garage Receptacle, One- and Two-Family Dwelling
210.52(G)(1)

Detached Garage

Garage

At least one 15A or 20A, 125V receptacle outlet must be installed no higher than 5 ft 6 in. above the floor in each bay in each attached garage and in each detached garage with electric power.

Copyright 2017, www.MikeHolt.com

Figure 210–81

(2) Accessory Buildings. A 15A or 20A, 125V receptacle is required in each accessory building with electric power. Figure 210–82

(3) Basements. Each unfinished portion of a basement must have a 15A or 20A, 125V receptacle outlet installed. Figure 210–83

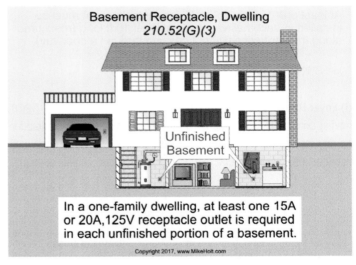

Basement Receptacle, Dwelling
210.52(G)(3)

Unfinished Basement

In a one-family dwelling, at least one 15A or 20A,125V receptacle outlet is required in each unfinished portion of a basement.

Copyright 2017, www.MikeHolt.com

Figure 210–83

Author's Comment:

■ One 15A or 20A, 125V receptacle outlet is required in a dwelling unit basement even if no portion has been finished into a habitable room.

■ The purpose of this requirement is to prevent an extension cord from a non-GFCI-protected receptacle from being used to supply power to loads in the unfinished portion of the basement.

■ GFCI protection is required for all 15A or 20A, 125V receptacles installed in unfinished basements [210.8(A)(5)], and detached garages and accessory buildings with electric power [210.8(A)(2)] of dwelling units.

(H) Dwelling Unit Hallway Receptacles. At least one 15A or 20A, 125V receptacle outlet must be installed in each hallway that's at least 10 ft long, measured along the centerline of the hallway without passing through a doorway. Figure 210–84

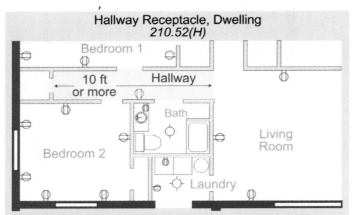

Hallway Receptacle, Dwelling
210.52(H)

At least one 15A or 20A, 125V receptacle outlet must be installed in each hallway that's at least 10 ft long (measured along the centerline without passing through a doorway).

Copyright 2017, www.MikeHolt.com

Figure 210–84

(I) Foyer Receptacles. Foyers that aren't part of a hallway [210.52(H)] having an area greater than 60 sq ft must have a receptacle located on any wall space 3 ft or more in width and unbroken by doorways, windows next to doors that extend to the floor, and similar openings. Figure 210–85

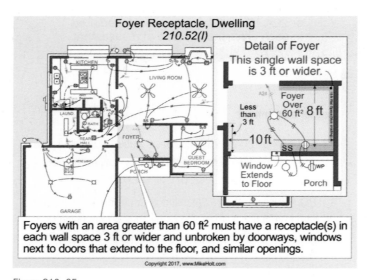

Foyer Receptacle, Dwelling
210.52(I)

Detail of Foyer
This single wall space is 3 ft or wider.

Foyers with an area greater than 60 ft² must have a receptacle(s) in each wall space 3 ft or wider and unbroken by doorways, windows next to doors that extend to the floor, and similar openings.

Copyright 2017, www.MikeHolt.com

Figure 210–85

210.64 Service Equipment Indoors—Receptacles

The rule requiring a convenience receptacle near the service disconnect was revised.

Analysis

EDITED

The 2014 *NEC* added 210.64 which requires a 15A or 20A, 125V receptacle within 50 ft of the service disconnect for other than one- and two-family dwellings. The 2017 edition changed this measurement to 25 ft, which allows a 25 ft extension cord to be used.

This rule now only applies to indoor service equipment, which eliminates a very large number of problems with the previous version of the requirement. For example, a service in the middle of a field now no longer requires a 125V receptacle, which I'm sure we can all agree is a good change.

210.64 Service Equipment Indoors—Receptacle

At least one 15A or 20A, 125V receptacle outlet is required <u>at an accessible location within 25 ft in the same room or area of indoor service equipment</u>. Figure 210–86

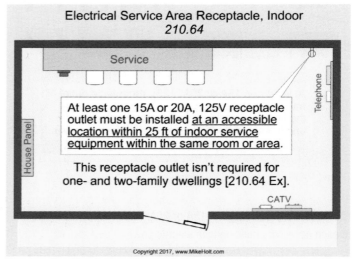

Electrical Service Area Receptacle, Indoor
210.64

At least one 15A or 20A, 125V receptacle outlet must be installed <u>at an accessible location within 25 ft of indoor service equipment within the same room or area</u>.

This receptacle outlet isn't required for one- and two-family dwellings [210.64 Ex].

Copyright 2017, www.MikeHolt.com

Figure 210–86

Ex: The service equipment receptacle outlet isn't required for one- and two-family dwellings.

210.70 Lighting Outlet Requirements

Requirements were clarified for lighting outlets in dwelling kitchens and stairways and there's a new requirement for switched lighting outlets in underfloor areas, attic areas, equipment spaces, and similar areas of other than dwelling units.

Analysis

CLARIFIED

Wall Switch Lighting Outlet. This rule has long required a wall switch-controlled outlet in habitable rooms and bathrooms, but never clearly required it for kitchens, even though the exception mentioned kitchens. With this change the *NEC* is now very clear that we need a wall switched lighting outlet for kitchens, which is already the common installation practice but was somehow absent from the actual rules.

CLARIFIED

Stairways. Stairways require a lighting outlet—the International Residential Code requires actual illumination, not just a box with a wire in it and a blank cover. This makes good sense, as falling down due to a lack of lighting is never fun, but it can be downright deadly when talking about a stairway. The *NEC* has required not only a lighting outlet in the stairway, but wall switches at each floor level for stairways containing six or more risers.

When installing dimmer switches, it's quite common to install only one dimmer in an area controlled by two three-way switches, meaning the other switch turns the lights on or off but doesn't change the level of illumination. This works well in a living space, but is a bad idea for stairways, as it has the potential of providing illumination for the stairs at a brightness that won't help anybody. In the 2017 *Code*, if we want dimmer control for stairway lighting, we must have a means of control at each wall switch that allows for the full range of illumination.

NEW

Storage Space. Section 210.70(C) requires wall switch-controlled lighting outlets for attics, under-floor areas, and basements if these areas are used for storage, or if they contain equipment that may need to be

worked on. The practice of installing pull chain fixtures is no longer acceptable. Most people agree that this isn't only reasonable but provides the safety we should all be granted. Why then does it apply only to residential occupancies? Well, it now applies to commercial occupancies as well.

210.70 Lighting Outlet Requirements

(A) Dwelling Unit Lighting Outlets. Lighting outlets must be installed in:

(1) Habitable Rooms. At least one wall switch-controlled lighting outlet must be installed in every habitable room, <u>kitchen,</u> and bathroom of a dwelling unit. Figure 210–87

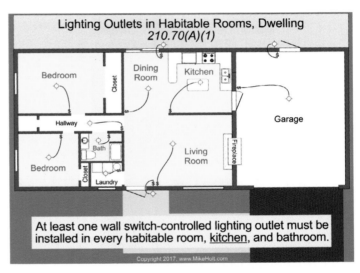

Figure 210–87

Author's Comment:

- See the definition of "Lighting Outlet" in Article 100.

Ex 1: In other than kitchens and bathrooms, a receptacle controlled by a wall switch can be used instead of a lighting outlet. Figure 210–88

Ex 2: Lighting outlets can be controlled by occupancy sensors equipped with a manual override that permits the sensor to function as a wall switch. Figure 210–89

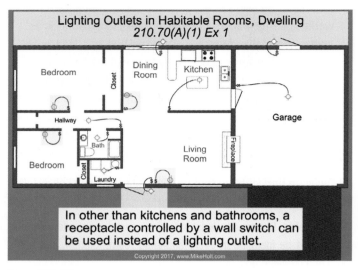

Figure 210–88

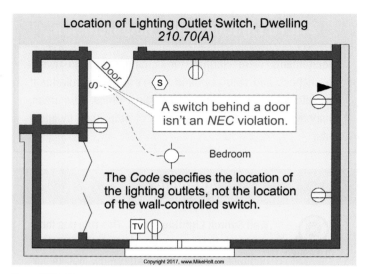

Figure 210–90

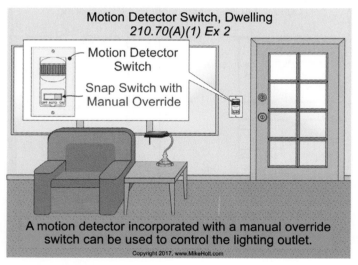

Figure 210–89

Author's Comment:

- The *Code* specifies the location of the wall switch-controlled lighting outlet, but it doesn't specify the switch location. Naturally, you wouldn't want to install a switch behind a door or other inconvenient location, but the *NEC* doesn't require you to relocate the switch to suit the swing of the door. When in doubt as to the best location to place a light switch, consult the job plans or ask the customer. Figure 210–90

(2) Other than Habitable Rooms

(1) Hallways, Stairways, and Garages. In dwelling units, not less than one wall switch-controlled lighting outlet must be installed in hallways, stairways, and attached and detached garages with electric power. Figure 210–91

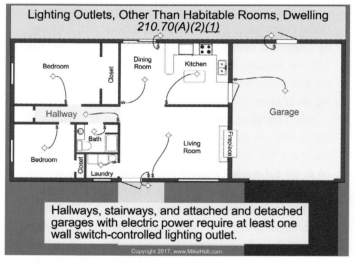

Figure 210–91

(2) Exterior Entrances. For dwelling units, attached garages, and detached garages with electric power, at least one wall switch-controlled lighting outlet must provide illumination on the exterior side of outdoor entrances or exits with grade-level access. Figure 210–92

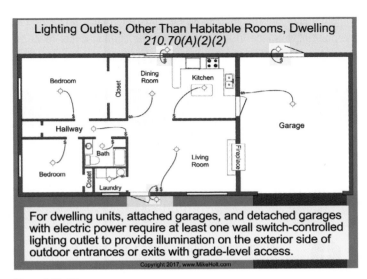

Figure 210–92

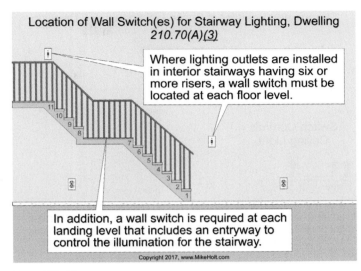

Figure 210–93

Author's Comment:

- A garage vehicle door isn't considered an outdoor entrance or exit.

- The *NEC* doesn't require a switch adjacent to each outdoor entrance or exit. The *Code* considers switch location a "design issue" which is beyond the purpose of the *NEC* [90.1(A)]. For this reason, proposals to mandate switch locations have been rejected.

- A lighting outlet isn't required to provide illumination on the exterior side of outdoor entrances or exits for a commercial or industrial occupancy.

(3) Stairway. Where lighting outlets are installed in interior stairways having six risers or more, a wall switch must be located at each floor level and at each landing level that includes an entryway to control the illumination for the stairway. Figure 210–93

Ex to (A)(2)(1), (A)(2)(2), and (A)(2)(3): Lighting outlets for hallways, stairways, and outdoor entrances can be switched by a remote, central, or automatic control device. Figure 210–94

(4) Dimmer Control. Lighting outlets located in stairways [210.70(A)(2)(3)] can be controlled by dimmer switches where there's a full range of dimming control at each switch location in accordance with 210.70(A)(2)(3).

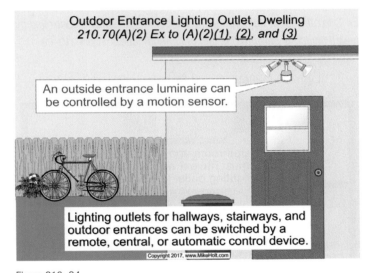

Figure 210–94

(3) Storage and Equipment Rooms. At least one lighting outlet that contains a switch or is controlled by a wall switch must be installed in attics, underfloor spaces, utility rooms, and basements used for storage or containing equipment that requires servicing. The switch must be located at the usual point of entrance to these spaces, and the lighting outlet must be located at or near the equipment that requires servicing. Figure 210–95

(B) Guest Rooms or Guest Suites. At least one wall switch-controlled lighting outlet must be installed in every habitable room and bathroom of a guest room or guest suite of hotels, motels, and similar occupancies.

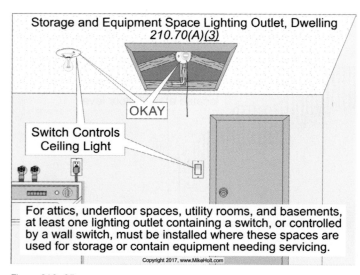

Figure 210–95

Ex 1: In other than bathrooms and kitchens, a receptacle controlled by a wall switch is permitted in lieu of lighting outlets. Figure 210–96

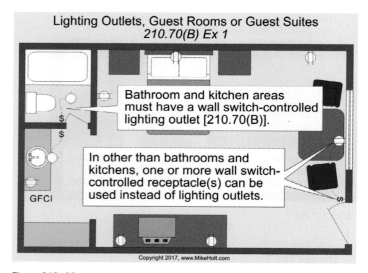

Figure 210–96

Ex 2: Lighting outlets can be controlled by occupancy sensors equipped with a manual override that permits the sensor to function as a wall switch.

(C) Other Than Dwelling Units and Guest Rooms or Guest Suites.
For attics and underfloor spaces, utility rooms, and basements, at least one lighting outlet containing a switch or controlled by a wall switch must be installed where these spaces are used for storage or

contain equipment requiring servicing. The switch must be located at the point of entrance to the spaces and the lighting outlet must be located at or near the equipment requiring servicing.

210.71 Meeting Rooms

New rules require receptacle outlets for meeting rooms in commercial occupancies.

Analysis

NEW

Meeting rooms are breeding grounds for cord usage; we all know that! When teaching a seminar, I always need an extension cord to reach my laptop and projector. There are often people in the audience who have laptops and no way of plugging them in, short of running a 25 ft extension cord right across a walkway.

During other types of meetings, every participant usually has and needs a laptop as well. It's not uncommon to see extension cords and daisy-chained relocatable power taps (plug strips) all over the floor.

This requirement was added proactively, as there haven't been any injuries or fires reported...yet. With this new rule we'll hopefully never have any such reports.

Of course, there are also other arguments to discuss as well. I've personally seen people step on cords that were being used at floor receptacles (including my own laptop cord). When this happens the person can trip or roll their ankle, and the attachment plug on the cord can be damaged.

This new requirement only applies to spaces not exceeding 1,000 sq ft. What's magical about 1,000 sq ft? If this is a problem for smaller meeting rooms, why isn't it a problem for larger ones as well?

There are concerns about what is and what isn't a meeting room, hence the inclusion of two Informational Notes. Meeting rooms are where people have meetings. Meeting rooms aren't where people meet, like a coffee shop. Trust me—this rule is going to cause lots of unintended problems...

210.71 Meeting Rooms

(A) General. Meeting rooms not larger than 1,000 sq ft must have receptacle outlets for 15A or 20A, 125V receptacles in accordance with 210.71(B) through (E).

Where a room or space is provided with a movable partition(s), the room size must be determined with the partition in the position that results in the smallest size meeting room.

Note 1: Meeting rooms are typically designed or intended for the gathering of seated occupants for conferences, deliberations, or similar purposes, where portable electronic equipment such as computers, projectors, or similar equipment is likely to be used.

Note 2: Examples of rooms that aren't meeting rooms within the scope of 210.70 include auditoriums, school rooms, and coffee shops.

(B) Number of Receptacle Outlets Required. Meeting room receptacle outlets are located by the designer or building owner and the number of receptacle outlets are determined in accordance with (B)(1) and (2) as follows. Figure 210–97

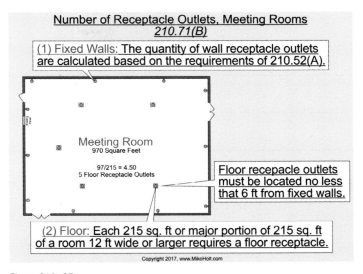

Figure 210–97

(1) Fixed Walls. The quantity of wall receptacle outlets is calculated on the basis of a receptacle outlet installed so that no point along the floor line is more than 6 ft, measured horizontally from a receptacle outlet in accordance with 210.52(A).

(2) Floor. A floor receptacle outlet is required for each 215 sq ft or major portion of a 215 sq ft meeting room space having a width of 12 ft or more. The floor receptacle outlets must be located no less than 6 ft from fixed walls.

Note 1: Receptacle floor boxes must be listed for the purpose [314.27(B)].

Note 2: See Article 518 for assembly occupancies designed for 100 or more persons.

Introduction to Article 215—Feeders

Article 215 covers the rules for the installation and ampacity of feeders. The requirements for feeders have some similarities to those for branch circuits, but in some ways, feeders bear a resemblance to service conductors. It's important to understand the distinct differences between these three types of circuits in order to correctly apply the *Code* requirements.

Feeders are the conductors between the service equipment, the separately derived system, or other supply source, and the final branch-circuit overcurrent protection device. Conductors past the final overcurrent protection device protecting the circuit and the outlet are branch-circuit conductors and fall within the scope of Article 210 [Article 100 Definitions].

Service conductors are the conductors from the service point to the service disconnect. [Article 100 Definition]. If there's no serving utility, and the electrical power is derived from a generator or other on-site electric power source, then the conductors from the supply source are defined as feeders and there are no service conductors.

It's easy to be confused between feeder, branch circuit, and service conductors, so it's important to evaluate each installation carefully using the Article 100 Definitions to be sure the correct *NEC* rules are followed.

215.1 Scope

Article 215 covers the installation, conductor sizing, and overcurrent protection requirements for feeder conductors.

Author's Comment:

■ Article 100 defines feeders as the conductors between service equipment, a separately derived system, or other power supply, and the final branch-circuit overcurrent protection device. Figure 215–1 and Figure 215–2

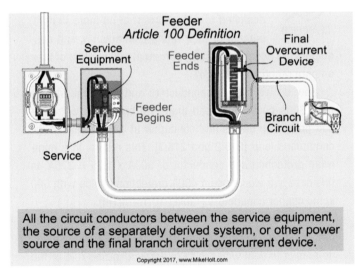

All the circuit conductors between the service equipment, the source of a separately derived system, or other power source and the final branch circuit overcurrent device.

Copyright 2017, www.MikeHolt.com

Figure 215–1

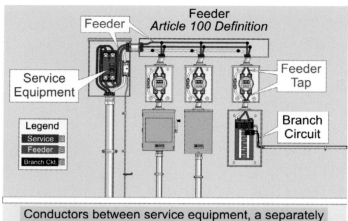

Conductors between service equipment, a separately derived system, or other power supply, and the final branch-circuit overcurrent device.

Copyright 2017, www.MikeHolt.com

Figure 215–2

215.2 Minimum Rating

A new rule clarifies the application of smaller feeder conductor sizing when using separate 90ºC terminations in accordance with 110.14(C)(2).

Analysis

CLARIFIED Circuit breakers and fuses are typically designed to carry current at no more than 80 percent of their rating continuously, and conductors are designed to carry current at 100 percent of their ampere rating continuously.

How do we size the conductors and protection device for a 300A continuous load then? We have to size the circuit protection device and conductor at 125 percent of the continuous load [215.2 and 215.3]. This results in a minimum protection and conductor of 300A x 1.25 = 375A. In this case, we would use a 400A protection device with 500 kcmil copper conductors [Table 310.15(B)(16)].

What if our conductors aren't terminating on an overcurrent protection device or equipment terminal? Then there's no reason to deal with the "125 percent" sizing rule or the 75°C ampacity limiter. For example, a 300A continuous load requires 500 kcmil conductors on the load and supply equipment, but if we install an enclosure next to the equipment, we can downsize the conductors between the supply

and load ends by taking advantage of the 90ºC column of Table 310.15(B)(16). In this case, we can install 400 kcmil conductors between the 500 kcmil conductors via 90°C terminal splices and still be *Code* compliant.

215.2 Minimum Rating

Scan this QR code for a video of Mike explaining this topic; it's a sample from the DVDs that accompany this textbook.

(A) Feeder Conductor Size.

(1) General. Feeder conductors must be sized to carry the larger of (a) or (b):

(a) The feeder conductor must have an ampacity before ampacity correction and adjustment of not less than 125 percent of the continuous load, plus 100 percent of the noncontinuous load, based on the terminal temperature rating ampacities as listed in Table 310.15(B)(16) [110.14(C)(1)]. Figure 215–3

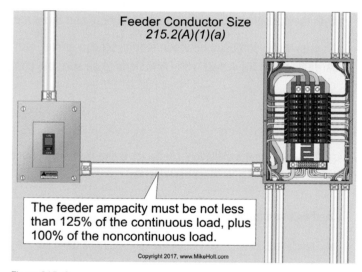

Feeder Conductor Size
215.2(A)(1)(a)

The feeder ampacity must be not less than 125% of the continuous load, plus 100% of the noncontinuous load.

Copyright 2017, www.MikeHolt.com

Figure 215–3

Example: *What size feeder conductors are required for a 200A continuous load if the terminals are rated 75°C?* Figure 215–4

Solution: *250 kcmil ungrounded conductors are required.*

Since the load is 200A continuous, the feeder conductors must have an ampacity of not less than 250A (200A x 1.25). According to the 75°C column of Table 310.15(B)(16) [110.14(C)(1)(b)], 250 kcmil has an ampacity of 255A.

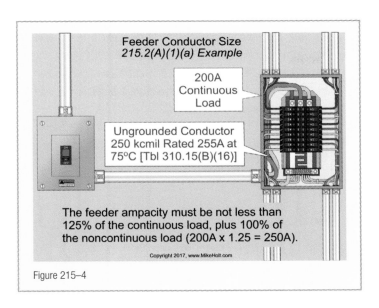

Figure 215–4

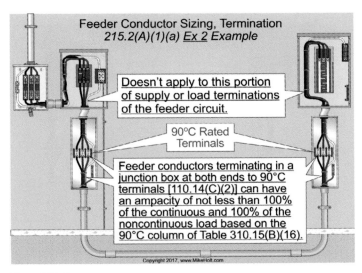

Figure 215–5

Ex 1: If the assembly and the overcurrent protection device are both listed for operation at 100 percent of their rating, the conductors can be sized at 100 percent of the continuous and noncontinuous load.

Author's Comment:

■ Equipment suitable for 100 percent continuous loading is rarely available in ratings under 400A.

Ex 2: A section of feeder conductors that terminates in a junction box at both ends to 90°C terminals in accordance with 110.14(C)(2) are permitted to have an ampacity of not less than 100 percent of the continuous and 100 percent of the noncontinuous load based on the 90°C column of Table 310.15(B)(16) for 90°C conductor insulation. The 100 percent at 90°C feeder conductors aren't permitted to extend into the supply or the load terminations to the feeder circuit. Figure 215–5

Author's Comment:

■ Equipment Terminals Rated 75°C. Feeder circuits must be sized to 125% of the continuous load [215.2(A)(1)(a)] for circuits over 100A. The conductors must be sized to the 75°C ampacity listed on Table 310.15(B)(16) [110.14(C)(1)(b)]. Circuits rated not over 800A can have overcurrent protection sized in accordance with 240.4(B), and for circuits rated over 800A, overcurrent must be in accordance with 240.4(C). The neural conductor is sized to 100% of the

continuous load [215.2(A)(1) Ex 3] to the 75°C ampacity listed on Table 310.15(B)(16) [110.14(C)(1)(b)], based on the maximum unbalanced load in accordance with 220.61, and not smaller than required by 250.122 for equipment grounding conductor.

▶ **75°C Equipment Terminals**

Example: *What size feeder conductor is required for a 300A continuous load, having a neutral load of 50A?* Figure 215–6

Solution: *Feeder 500 kcmil, rated 380A at 75°C, Neutral 3 AWG, rated 100A at 75°C, and equipment grounding conductor of 3 AWG*

Feeder conductor must have an ampacity of at least 375A (125% of the 300 A continuous load) [215.2(A)(1)(a)]; 500 kcmil, rated 380A at 75°C in accordance with Table 310.15(B)(16) is suitable [110.14(C)(1)(b). The 500 kcmil conductor, rated 375A at 75°C is permitted to be protected by a 400A protection device [240.4(B)]. The neutral conductor must be sized to carry 50A continuously, which can be 6 AWG, rated 50A [100 Ampacity, 110.14(C)(1)(b), 215.2(A), and 220.61], but it can't be smaller than 3 AWG based on the 400A overcurrent protection device size in accordance with Table 250.122.

● ● ●

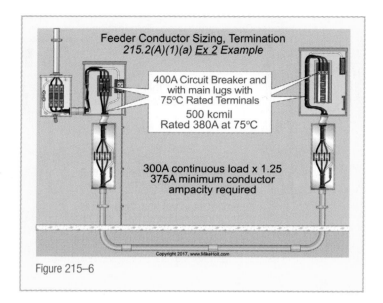

Figure 215–6

Author's Comment:

■ Equipment Terminals Rated 90°C. Feeder circuits can be sized to 100% of the continuous load based [215.2(A)(1)(a) Ex 1] according to the 90°C ampacity listed on Table 310.15(B)(16) [110.14(C)(2)]. Circuits rated not over 800A can have overcurrent protection sized in accordance with 240.4(B), and for circuits rated over 800A feeder, overcurrent must be in accordance with 240.4(C). The neural conductor is sized to 100% of the continuous load [215.2(A)(1) Ex 3] to the 75°C ampacity listed on Table 310.15(B)(16) [110.14(C)(1)(b)], based on the maximum unbalanced load in accordance with 220.61, and not smaller than required by 250.122 for equipment grounding conductor.

▶ 75°C Equipment Terminals

Example: *What size feeder conductor is required for a 300A continuous load?* Figure 215–7

Solution: *Feeder 400 kcmil, rated 380A at 75°C, Neutral 3 AWG, rated 100A at 75°C, and equipment grounding conductor of 3 AWG*

Feeder conductor must have an ampacity of at least 300A (100% of the 300A continuous load) [215.2(A)(1)(a) Ex 1]; 400 kcmil, rated 380A at 90°C in accordance with Table 310.15(B)(16) is suitable [110.14(C)(1)(b). The 400 kcmil conductor, rated 380A at 90°C is permitted to be protected by a 400A protection device

[240.4(B)]. The neutral conductor must be sized to carry 50A continuously, which can be 6 AWG, rated 50A [100 Ampacity, 110.14(C)(1)(b), 215.2(A), and 220.61], but it can't be smaller than 3 AWG based on the 400A overcurrent protection device size in accordance with Table 250.122.

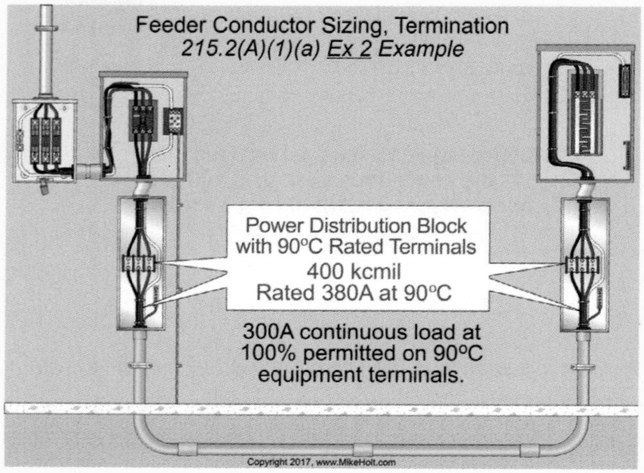

Figure 215–7

Ex 3: Neutral conductors must have an ampacity of not less than 100 percent of the continuous and noncontinuous load.

Example: *What size feeder conductors are required for a 200A continuous load if the terminals are rated 75°C?* Figure 215–8

Solution: *250 kcmil AWG ungrounded conductors and a 3/0 AWG neutral conductor are required.*

Since the load is 200A continuous, the feeder conductors must have an ampacity of not less than 250A (200A x 1.25). According to the 75°C column of Table 310.15(B)(16) [110.14(C)(1)(b)], 250 kcmil has an ampacity of 255A. The neutral conductor is sized to the 200A continuous load (100%). According to the 75°C column of Table 310.15(B)(16) [110.14(C)(1)(b)], 3/0 has an ampacity of 200A.

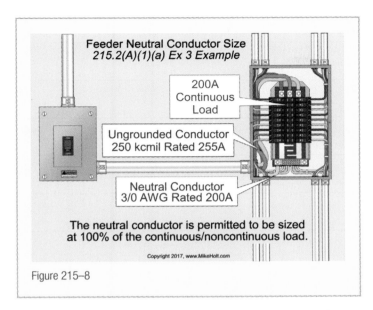

Figure 215–8

(b) The feeder conductor must have an ampacity after ampacity correction and adjustment of not less than the load to be served. Figure 215–9

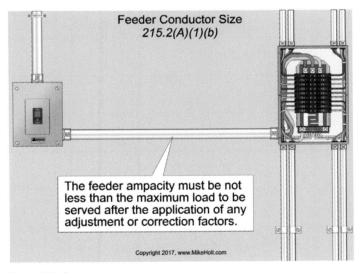

Figure 215–9

Author's Comment:

■ See 215.3 for the feeder overcurrent protection device sizing requirements for continuous and noncontinuous loads.

Note 2: To provide reasonable efficiency of operation of electrical equipment, feeder conductors should be sized to prevent a voltage drop not to exceed 3 percent. In addition, the maximum total voltage drop on both feeders and branch circuits shouldn't exceed 5 percent.

Note 3: See 210.19(A), Note 4, for voltage drop for branch circuits.

(2) Neutral Conductor Size. The feeder neutral conductor must be sized to carry the maximum unbalanced load in accordance with 220.61, and isn't permitted to be smaller than listed in 250.122, based on the rating of the feeder overcurrent protection device.

Example: What size neutral conductor is required for a feeder consisting of 250 kcmil ungrounded conductors and one neutral conductor protected by a 250A overcurrent protection device, where the unbalanced load is only 50A, with 75°C terminals? Figure 215–10

Solution: A 4 AWG neutral conductor is required [based on Table 250.122].

Table 310.15(B)(16) and 220.61 permit an 8 AWG neutral conductor rated 50A at 75°C to carry the 50A unbalanced load, but the neutral conductor isn't permitted to be smaller than 4 AWG, as listed in Table 250.122, based on the 250A overcurrent protection device.

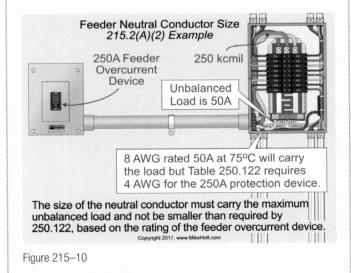

Figure 215–10

Mike Holt's Illustrated Guide to Changes to the National Electrical Code 2017

BRANCH-CIRCUIT, FEEDER, AND SERVICE LOAD CALCULATIONS

Introduction to Article 220—Branch-Circuit, Feeder, and Service Load Calculations

This five-part article focuses on the requirements for calculating the minimum size of branch circuit, feeder, and service conductors.

Part I describes the layout of Article 220 and provides a table of where other types of load calculations can be found in the *NEC*. Part II provides requirements for branch-circuit calculations and for specific types of branch circuits. Part III covers the requirements for feeder and service calculations, using what's commonly called the "standard method of calculation." Part IV provides optional calculations that can be used in place of the standard calculations provided in Parts II and III—if your installation meets certain requirements. Farm Load Calculations are discussed in Part V of the article.

In many cases, either the standard method (Part III) or the optional method (Part IV) can be used; however, these two methods don't yield identical results. In fact, sometimes these two answers may be diverse enough to call for different service sizes. There's nothing to say that either answer is right or wrong. If taking an exam, read the instructions carefully to be sure which method the test wants you to use. As you work through Article 220, be sure to study the illustrations to help you fully understand it. Also be sure to review the examples in Annex D of the *NEC* to provide more practice with these calculations.

Part I. General

220.1 Scope

This article contains the requirements necessary for calculating the load for branch circuits, feeders, and services.

Note 2: See NEC Figure 220.1 for information on the organization of Article 220. Figure 220–1

Author's Comment:

- Article 220 also is used to determine the number of receptacles on a circuit and the number of general-purpose branch circuits required.

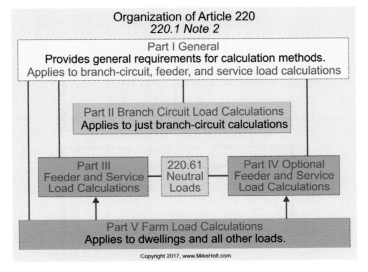

Figure 220–1

220.12 General Lighting

A new exception for calculating lighting loads might result in designers dancing in the streets.

Analysis

NEW In most areas of the country, an energy code is adopted and it's often the International Energy Conservation Code (IECC). This code regulates not only how much insulation you need in building walls and ceilings, but also how much electricity you can use.

For example, the IECC at times limits some buildings to no more than 1 VA per sq ft for general lighting. If that's the case, why do I have to design the electrical system with 3.50 VA per sq ft per the *NEC*? That's a tremendous amount of extra capacity, and it can result in more panelboards, more transformers, bigger services, and additional costs to the end user.

Part II. Branch-Circuit Load Calculations

220.12 General Lighting

The general lighting load specified in Table 220.12 must be calculated from the outside dimensions of the building or area involved. Figure 220–2

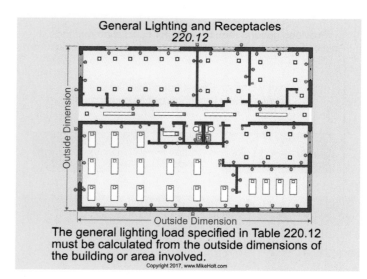

General Lighting and Receptacles 220.12

The general lighting load specified in Table 220.12 must be calculated from the outside dimensions of the building or area involved.

Copyright 2017, www.MikeHolt.com

Figure 220–2

Table 220.12 General Lighting VA per Square Foot

Occupancy	VA/Sq Ft
Armories and auditoriums	1
Assembly halls and auditoriums	1
Banks	3½[b]
Barber shops and beauty parlors	3
Churches	1
Clubs	2
Courtrooms	2
Dwelling units[a]	3
Garages—commercial (storage)	½
Halls, corridors, closets, stairways	½
Hospitals	2
Hotels and motels without cooking facilities	2
Industrial commercial (loft buildings)	2
Lodge rooms	1½
Office buildings	3½[b]
Restaurants	2
Schools	3
Storage spaces	¼
Stores	3
Warehouses (storage)	¼

Table Note a: *The VA load for general-use receptacles, bathroom receptacles [220.14(J)(1) and 210.11(C)(3)], outside receptacles, as well as garage, basement receptacles [220.14(J)(2), 210.52(E) and (G)], and lighting outlets [220.14(J)(3), 210.70(A) and (B)] in a dwelling unit are included in the 3 VA per-square-foot general lighting [220.14(J)].*

Table Note b: *The receptacle calculated load for banks and office buildings is the largest calculation of either (1) or (2) [220.14(K)].*

For dwelling units, the calculated floor area doesn't include open porches, garages, or unused or unfinished spaces not adaptable for future use. Figure 220–3

Ex 1: Where the adopted energy code requires a smaller value for lighting loads, the energy code values can be used if the following requirements are met:

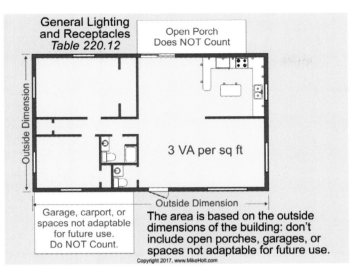

Figure 220–3

(1) A power monitoring system that provides continuous information on the lighting load of the building must be installed.

(2) The power monitoring system must have an alarm that alerts the building owner or manager if the lighting load exceeds the values set by the energy code.

(3) The lighting load demand factors in 220.42 can't be used.

Ex 2: Where a building is designed and constructed to comply with an energy code (efficient lighting), that's adopted by the local authority, specifying an overall lighting density of less than 1.20 VA per 1.20 sq ft, the unit lighting loads in Table 220.12 for office and bank areas within the building can be reduced by 1 VA per sq ft.

220.87 Determining Existing Loads

It was clarified that real world data can be used for load calculations on existing installations.

Analysis

CLARIFIED Some of us know that the load calculations in Article 220 are significantly higher than reality. This is particularly true when talking about dwelling units. If your service load calculation for a dwelling unit is 200A, there's a very real chance that the actual load will be no more than 50A at any given moment in time.

When adding a load to an existing building we need to ensure that the new load won't overload the existing premises wiring system, so we do a load calculation. This makes sense. What doesn't make sense is finding out that you need to do a service change to this 200A service despite the fact that the load isn't even 60A or so.

For this reason, the *NEC* allows the use of an alternative method to determine the load for an existing installation. It's simple; just use the actual power usage data for one year. If you can't get the data from the utility, and you often can't, you can use a recording ammeter for 30 days and use that data instead.

When using the recording ammeter method for 30 days, the *Code* makes it clear that we must use the highest average current over a 15-minute period during those 30 days, not the lowest average and not the peak instantaneous current value. We'll always have spike current usage, for example, when the air conditioner starts ups, but that spike value is very brief and isn't part of the 15-minute highest average current value.

220.87 Determining Existing Loads

The calculation of a feeder or service load for existing dwelling unit can use the actual maximum demand of the existing dwelling unit as follows:

(1) The maximum demand data for a 1-year period.

Ex: If the maximum demand data for one year isn't available, the calculated service load can be based on the highest average kW maintained for a 15-minute period, over a recorded period of 30 days.
Figure 220–4

(2) When adding loads to an existing dwelling unit, the feeder or service demand load isn't permitted to be less than 125 percent of the new loads and maximum demand load [220.87(1)].

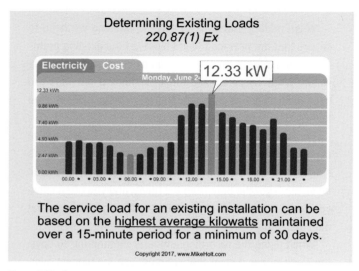

Figure 220–4

ARTICLE 225

OUTSIDE BRANCH CIRCUITS AND FEEDERS

Introduction to Article 225—Outside Branch Circuits and Feeders

This article covers the installation requirements for equipment, including branch circuit and feeder conductors (overhead and underground), located outdoors on or between buildings, poles, and other structures on the premises. Conductors installed outdoors can serve many purposes such as area lighting, power for outdoor equipment, or providing power to a separate building or structure. It's important to remember that the power supply for buildings isn't always a service conductor, but in many cases may be feeders or branch-circuit conductors originating in another building. Be careful not to assume that the conductors supplying power to a building are service conductors until you've identified where the service point is [Article 100] and reviewed the Article 100 Definitions for feeders, branch circuits, and service conductors. If they're service conductors, use Article 230. For outside branch-circuit and feeder conductors, whatever they feed, use this article.

Table 225.3 shows other articles that may furnish additional requirements, then Part I of Article 225 goes on to address installation methods intended to provide a secure installation of outside conductors while providing sufficient conductor size, support, attachment means, and maintaining safe clearances.

Part II of this article limits the number of supplies (branch circuits or feeders) permitted to a building or structure and provides rules regarding disconnects for them. These rules include the disconnect rating, construction characteristics, labeling, and where to locate the disconnect and the grouping of multiple disconnects.

Outside branch circuits and feeders over 1,000V are the focus of Part III of Article 225.

Part I. General

225.1 Scope

Article 225 contains the installation requirements for outside branch circuits and feeders installed on or between buildings, structures, or poles. Figure 225–1

Author's Comment:

- Review the following definitions in Article 100:
  - "Branch Circuit"
  - "Building"
  - "Feeder"
  - "Structure"

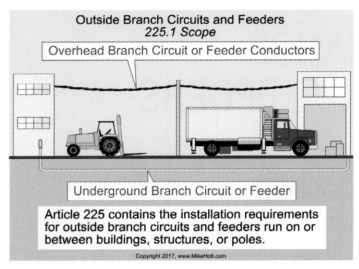

Figure 225–1

225.17 Masts as Supports

The rules for overhead masts were editorially revised.

Analysis

EDITED The 2014 *NEC* added some desperately needed guidance to this section. The previous editions of the *Code* simply stated that masts had to be strong enough to support the conductors, or they needed guys wires or bracing. In addition, the 2014 *NEC* added rules about the location of couplings in relation to the last point of support. While these were great rules, they weren't particularly well written. Revisions to this edition of the *Code* leave the same requirements and intent, but the text is easier to read and understand.

225.17 Masts as Supports

Masts for the support of overhead conductors must be installed as follows:

Author's Comment:

- Aerial cables and antennas for radio and TV equipment aren't permitted to be attached to the feeder or branch-circuit mast [810.12]. In addition, 800.133(B) prohibits communications cables from being attached to raceways, including a mast for power conductors.

(A) Strength. The mast must <u>have</u> adequate mechanical strength, braces, or guy wires to <u>safely withstand</u> the strain caused by the conductors. Figure 225–2

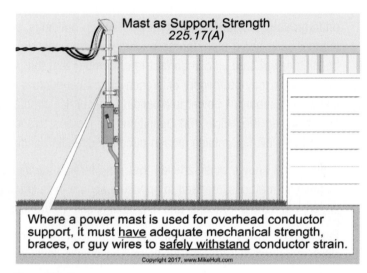

Figure 225–2

(B) Attachment. Overhead conductors can't be attached to a mast <u>where the conductor attachment is</u> located between a weatherhead and a coupling located above the last point of securement to the building or structure, <u>or where the coupling</u> is located above the roof or structure. Figure 225–3

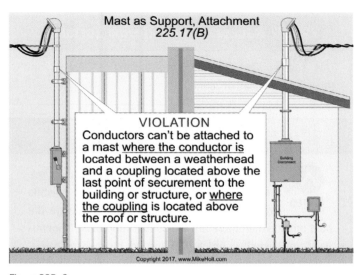

Mast as Support, Attachment
225.17(B)

VIOLATION
Conductors can't be attached to a mast <u>where the conductor is</u> located between a weatherhead and a coupling located above the last point of securement to the building or structure, or <u>where the coupling</u> is located above the roof or structure.

Copyright 2017, www.MikeHolt.com

Figure 225–3

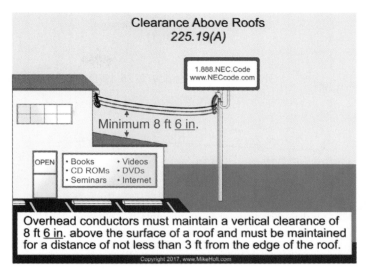

Clearance Above Roofs
225.19(A)

1.888.NEC.Code
www.NECcode.com

Minimum 8 ft <u>6 in.</u>

OPEN • Books • Videos
• CD ROMs • DVDs
• Seminars • Internet

Overhead conductors must maintain a vertical clearance of 8 ft <u>6 in.</u> above the surface of a roof and must be maintained for a distance of not less than 3 ft from the edge of the roof.

Copyright 2017, www.MikeHolt.com

Figure 225–4

225.19 Clearances from Buildings

The vertical clearance requirement for conductors located over a roof was increased.

Analysis

EXPANDED

The change here is subtle and could easily go unnoticed, causing a lot of stress on inspection day. The 2014 *NEC* required 8 ft of clearance for conductors over rooftops. It's now been increased to 8 ft 6 in.

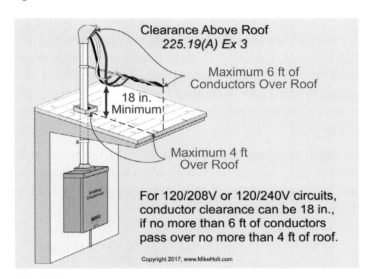

Clearance Above Roof
225.19(A) Ex 3

Maximum 6 ft of Conductors Over Roof

18 in. Minimum

Maximum 4 ft Over Roof

For 120/208V or 120/240V circuits, conductor clearance can be 18 in., if no more than 6 ft of conductors pass over no more than 4 ft of roof.

Copyright 2017, www.MikeHolt.com

Figure 225–5

225.19 Clearances from Buildings

(A) Above Roofs. Overhead conductors must maintain a vertical clearance of 8 ft <u>6 in.</u> above the surface of a roof and must be maintained for a distance of at least 3 ft from the edge of the roof. Figure 225–4

Ex 2: The overhead conductor clearances from the roof can be reduced to 3 ft if the slope of the roof meets or exceeds 4 in. of vertical rise for every 12 in. of horizontal run.

Ex 3: For 120/208V or 120/240V circuits, the conductor clearance over the roof overhang can be reduced to 18 in., if no more than 6 ft of conductor passes over no more than 4 ft of roof. Figure 225–5

Ex 4: The 3-ft clearance from the roof edge doesn't apply when the point of attachment is on the side of the building below the roof.

(B) From Other Structures. Overhead conductors must maintain a clearance of at least 3 ft from signs, chimneys, radio and television antennas, tanks, and other nonbuilding or nonbridge structures.

(D) Final Span Clearance.

(1) Clearance from Windows. Overhead conductors must maintain a clearance of 3 ft from windows that open, doors, porches, balconies, ladders, stairs, fire escapes, or similar locations. Figure 225–6

Ex: Overhead conductors installed above a window aren't required to maintain the 3-ft distance from the window.

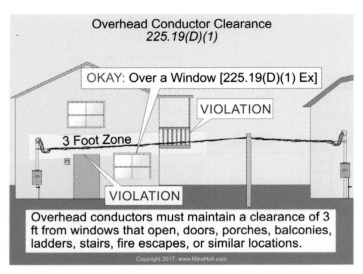

Overhead Conductor Clearance
225.19(D)(1)

OKAY: Over a Window [225.19(D)(1) Ex]

VIOLATION

3 Foot Zone

VIOLATION

Overhead conductors must maintain a clearance of 3 ft from windows that open, doors, porches, balconies, ladders, stairs, fire escapes, or similar locations.

Copyright 2017, www.MikeHolt.com

Figure 225–6

(2) Vertical Clearance. Overhead conductors must maintain a vertical clearance of at least 10 ft above platforms, projections, or surfaces that permit personal contact in accordance with 225.18. This vertical clearance must be maintained for 3 ft, measured horizontally from the platforms, projections, or surfaces from which they might be reached.

(3) Below Openings. Overhead conductors aren't permitted to be installed under an opening through which materials might pass, and they're not permitted to be installed where they'll obstruct an entrance to these openings. Figure 225–7

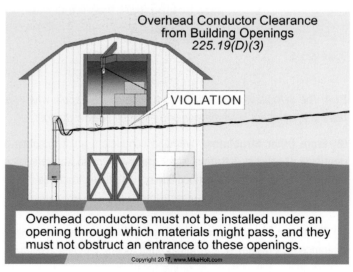

Overhead Conductor Clearance
from Building Openings
225.19(D)(3)

VIOLATION

Overhead conductors must not be installed under an opening through which materials might pass, and they must not obstruct an entrance to these openings.

Copyright 2017, www.MikeHolt.com

Figure 225–7

225.22 Raceways on Exterior Surfaces

This section was revised using the terms "listed" and "approved" instead of "suitable."

Analysis

EDITED Pretty much everyone will agree that the *Code* needs to be written using clear and specific words. Words like "suitable" aren't always the best option when there are words like "approved," "identified," and "listed" in Article 100 that can be used instead.

Previous editions of this rule stated that raceways on exterior surfaces needed to be arranged to drain and needed to be "suitable" for a wet location. Listed raceways and fittings or even approved raceways and fittings are probably suitable, but why leave room for interpretation? Using the words "listed" and "approved" instead of "suitable" makes it a better rule.

225.22 Raceways on Exterior Surfaces

Raceways on exterior surfaces must be arranged to drain and be listed or approved for use in wet locations. Figure 225–8

Raceways on Exterior Surfaces
225.22

Raceways on exterior surfaces must be arranged to drain and be listed or approved for use in wet locations.

Copyright 2017, www.MikeHolt.com

Figure 225–8

- A "Wet Location" is an area subject to saturation with water and unprotected locations exposed to weather [Article 100].

225.27 Raceway Seals

The rules regarding the sealing of underground raceways entering a building have been expanded to include all raceways entering buildings.

Analysis

EXPANDED

Anytime a raceway can transmit moisture it needs to be sealed. While this most often happens in underground locations, it isn't limited to them. Even aboveground raceways can convey moisture, although previous editions of the *NEC* were silent about the issue.

Two changes were made in this edition of the *Code*. First, the language regarding underground wiring was removed, thereby expanding the sealing requirements to all outdoor raceways entering a building or structure. Equally, or perhaps more, importantly the reference to 300.5(G), which requires the sealing of raceways when moisture could contact energized live parts was removed. With the removal of this reference it's now clear that the *NEC* wants all raceways entering buildings or structures sealed, with no exceptions.

225.27 Raceway Seals

Raceways (used or unused) entering buildings from <u>outside</u> must be sealed with a sealant identified for use with the conductor or cable insulation. Figure 225–9

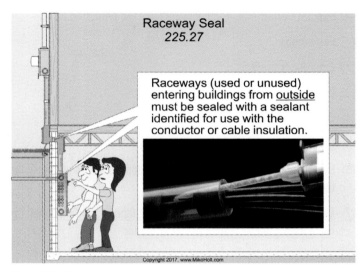

Raceway Seal
225.27

Raceways (used or unused) entering buildings from <u>outside</u> must be sealed with a sealant identified for use with the conductor or cable insulation.

Copyright 2017, www.MikeHolt.com

Figure 225–9

225.30 Number of Feeder Supplies

An additional branch circuit or feeder supply is now allowed for electric vehicle (EV) charging systems.

Analysis

NEW

Buildings are only allowed to have one source of power supply, unless one of a dozen or so allowances apply. These allowances include an additional supply for fire pumps, emergency systems, standby systems, capacity requirements, the physical size of the building, different characteristics, and now electric vehicle chargers.

225.30 Number of Feeder Supplies

If more than one building or other structure is on the same property, each building must be served by no more than one feeder or single or multiwire branch circuit, except for the following conditions;

- Article 100 defines a "Structure" as, "That which is built or constructed, other than equipment."

(A) Special Conditions. Additional supplies are permitted for:

(1) Fire pumps

(2) Emergency systems

(3) Legally required standby systems

(4) Optional standby systems

(5) Parallel power production systems

(6) Systems designed for connection to multiple sources of supply for the purpose of enhanced reliability

(7) <u>Electric vehicle charging systems listed, labeled, and identified for more than a single branch circuit or feeder</u>

Author's Comment:

- To minimize the possibility of simultaneous interruption, the disconnecting means for the fire pump or standby power must be located remotely away from the normal power disconnecting means [225.34(B)].

(B) Special Occupancies. By special permission, additional supplies are permitted for:

(1) Multiple-occupancy buildings where there's no available space for supply equipment accessible to all occupants, or

(2) A building so large that two or more supplies are necessary.

(C) Capacity Requirements. Additional supplies are permitted for a building where the capacity requirements exceed 2,000A.

(D) Different Characteristics. Additional supplies are permitted for different voltages, frequencies, or uses, such as control of outside lighting from multiple locations.

(E) Documented Switching Procedures. Additional supplies are permitted where documented safe switching procedures are established and maintained for disconnection.

225.36 Type of Disconnecting Means

The title of this section was changed.

Analysis

EDITED

The subject of this section wasn't apparent at first glance. Adding "disconnecting means" to the title makes it clear that this section is about the acceptable types of disconnecting means for a building.

225.36 Type <u>of Disconnecting Means</u>

The building disconnecting means can be comprised of a circuit breaker, molded case switch, general-use switch, snap switch, or other approved means. If an existing building uses the neutral conductor for the bonding of metal parts as permitted by 250.32(B) Ex, the disconnect must be listed for use as service equipment. Figure 225–10

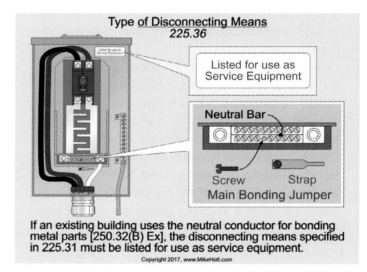

Figure 225–10

Author's Comment:

- "Suitable for use as service equipment" means, among other things, that the service disconnect is supplied with a main bonding jumper so a neutral-to-case connection can be made, as required in 250.24(C) and 250.142(A).

ARTICLE
230 | SERVICES

Introduction to Article 230—Services

This article covers the installation requirements for service conductors and service equipment. The requirements for service conductors differ from those for other conductors. For one thing, service conductors for one building can't pass through the interior of another building or structure [230.3], and you apply different rules depending on whether a service conductor is inside or outside a building. When are they "outside" as opposed to "inside?" The answer may seem obvious, but 230.6 should be consulted before making this decision.

Let's review the following definitions in Article 100 to understand when the requirements of Article 230 apply:

■ **Service Point.** The point of connection between the serving electric utility and the premises wiring.

■ **Service Conductors.** The conductors from the service point to the service disconnecting means. Service-entrance conductors can either be overhead or underground.

■ **Service Equipment.** The necessary equipment, usually consisting of circuit breakers or switches and fuses and their accessories, connected to the load end of service conductors at a building or other structure, and intended to constitute the main control and cutoff of the electrical supply. Service equipment doesn't include individual meter socket enclosures [230.66].

After reviewing these definitions, you should understand that service conductors originate at the serving electric utility (service point) and terminate on the line side of the service disconnect. Conductors and equipment on the load side of service equipment are considered feeder conductors or branch circuits, and must be installed in accordance with Articles 210 and 215. They must also comply with Article 225 if they're outside branch circuits and feeders, such as the supply to a building. Feeder conductors include: Figure 230–1 and Figure 230–2

– Secondary conductors from customer-owned transformers,
– Conductors from generators, UPS systems, or PV systems, and
– Conductors to remote buildings

Article 230 consists of seven parts:
– Part I. General
– Part II. Overhead Service Conductors
– Part III. Underground Service Conductors
– Part IV. Service-Entrance Conductors
– Part V. Service Equipment
– Part VI. Disconnecting Means
– Part VIII. Overcurrent Protection

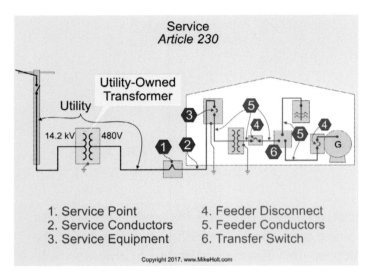

Figure 230–1

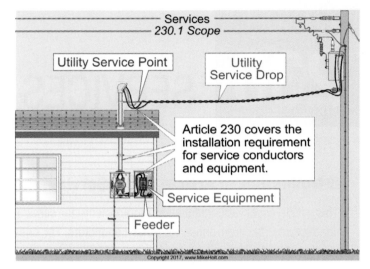

Figure 230–3

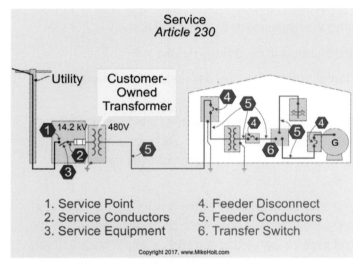

Figure 230–2

Part I. General

230.1 Scope

Article 230 covers the installation requirements for service conductors and service equipment. Figure 230–3

230.7 Service Conductors Separate from Other Conductors

The permitted uses of a service raceway were clarified.

Analysis

CLARIFIED There must have been some confusion about the exact meaning of this section so it's now been clarified. The use of a service raceway for other than service conductors seemed to be a violation. It's now been clarified that the raceway isn't the issue but rather what's in it. We can install branch circuit and feeder conductors in a service raceway unless it contains service conductors. The exceptions were also edited for clarification.

230.7 Service Conductors Separate from Other Conductors

Feeder and branch-circuit conductors aren't permitted to be installed in a service raceway containing service conductors. Figure 230–4

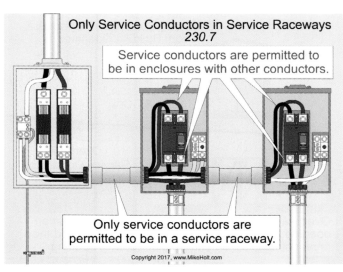

Figure 230–4

Ex 1: *Grounding electrode conductors or supply-side bonding jumpers are permitted in a service raceway with service conductors.*

Ex 2: *Conductors used for load management with overcurrent protection are permitted in service raceways with service conductors.*

⚠ **WARNING:** *Overcurrent protection for the feeder or branch-circuit conductors can be bypassed if service conductors are mixed with feeder or branch-circuit conductors in the same raceway and a fault occurs between the service and feeder or branch-circuit conductors.* Figure 230–5

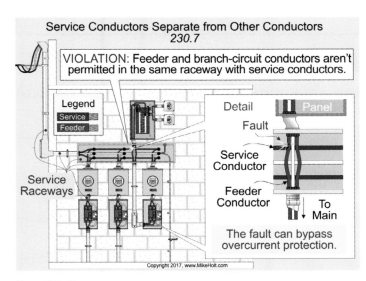

Figure 230–5

- This rule doesn't prohibit the mixing of service, feeder, and branch-circuit conductors in the same service equipment enclosure.

- This requirement may be the root of the misconception that "line" and "load" conductors aren't permitted to be installed in the same raceway. It's true that service conductors aren't permitted to be installed in the same raceway with feeder or branch-circuit conductors, but line and load conductors for feeders and branch circuits can be in the same raceway or enclosure. Figure 230–6

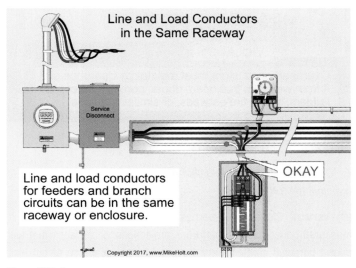

Figure 230–6

230.9 Clearance from Building Openings

Language was added to this section to clarify the requirements for vertical clearance from a building.

Analysis

CLARIFIED There are applications where the final span of conductors over a building or structure may pose a risk to people who might reach, or otherwise come in contact with them. This section clarified that 230.24 must be applied if personal contact is possible.

230.9 Clearance from Building Openings

(A) Clearance. Overhead service conductors must maintain a clearance of 3 ft from windows that open, doors, porches, balconies, ladders, stairs, fire escapes, or similar locations. Figure 230–7

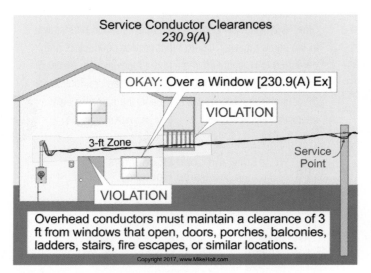

Figure 230–7

Ex: Overhead conductors installed above a window aren't required to maintain the 3 ft distance.

(B) Vertical Clearance. Overhead service conductors within 3 ft measured horizontally of platforms, projections, or surfaces <u>that will permit personal contact</u>, must have a vertical clearance of not less than 10 ft above the platforms, projections, or surfaces in accordance with 230.24(B).

(C) Below Openings. Service conductors aren't permitted to be installed under an opening through which materials might pass, and they're not permitted to be installed where they'll obstruct entrance to building openings. Figure 230–8

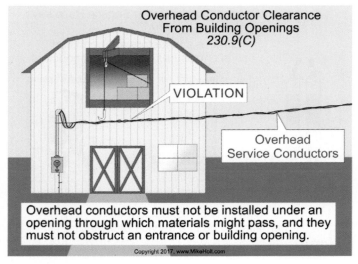

Figure 230–8

230.10 Vegetation as Support

Trees are no longer allowed to support service equipment.

Analysis

NEW

Have you ever seen a tree with a luminaire mounted to it and then years later noticed the luminaire is falling off the tree because it grew? Now imagine if the luminaire was a service disconnect. It was never a good idea and now it's an illegal installation. About time...

230.10 Vegetation as Support

Trees or other vegetation aren't permitted to be used for the support of overhead service conductor spans <u>or service equipment</u>. Figure 230–9

Author's Comment:

■ Service-drop conductors installed by the electric utility must comply with the *National Electrical Safety Code* (NESC), not the *National Electrical Code* [90.2(B)(5)]. Overhead service conductors that aren't under the exclusive control of the electric utility must be installed in accordance with the *NEC*.

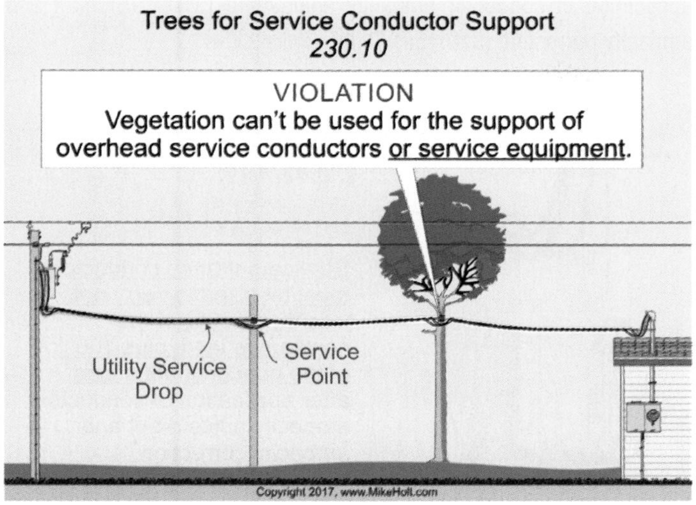

Trees for Service Conductor Support
230.10

VIOLATION
Vegetation can't be used for the support of overhead service conductors <u>or service equipment</u>.

Utility Service Drop

Service Point

Copyright 2017, www.MikeHolt.com

Figure 230–9

230.29 Supports over Buildings

A new requirement for overhead conductor support above buildings was added.

Analysis

NEW When overhead service conductors are installed by an electrician rather than the utility, this rule provides a requirement to use "substantial structures" (whatever that might mean). If these "substantial structures" are metallic, we must bond them to the grounded overhead service conductor. This bonding jumper is called a "supply-side bonding jumper" (SSBJ), and should therefore be sized in accordance with 250.102(C).

In the event of this "substantial structure" becoming energized by one of the overhead ungrounded conductors, the supply-side bonding jumper will hopefully aid in the opening of the utility's primary overcurrent protection device. While this might not happen even with the bonding jumper installed, it will certainly never happen without it.

230.29 Supports over Buildings

Service conductors over a roof must be securely supported by substantial structures. <u>Where the support structure is metal, it must be</u>

bonded to the grounded overhead service conductor with a supply-side bonding conductor, sized in accordance with 250.102(C)(1), based on the size of the ungrounded service conductors. Where practicable, overhead service conductor support must be independent of the building.

Author's Comment

- This rule doesn't apply to utility overhead service drop conductors, which are beyond the scope of the *NEC* [90.2(B)(5)].

230.42 Size and Rating

The sizing requirements for service conductors were revised to be consistent with similar rules elsewhere in the *NEC*.

Analysis

EDITED It's easy to become frustrated when *Code* rules that should say the same thing as other similar rules don't. It's important to remember that there are 19 Code Making Panels (CMPs) made up of individuals who are experts and are passionate about the *NEC*—and they aren't even paid to do this!

Why don't the rules for conductor sizing in 210.19, 215.2, and 230.42 use similar *Code* language to say the same thing? Because rules in Articles 210 and 215 are covered by CMP-2, and CMP-4 covers the ones in Article 230. While there's certainly no animosity between the two groups, it's tough to make that many people agree on what the best language is for a given rule. Changes to this section still don't result in mirror images of the similar rules, but it's closer now than it's been in a long time.

230.42 Size and Rating

(A) General. Service-entrance <u>conductors</u> must be sized to carry not less than the largest of the following:

(1) Before Ampacity Adjustment and Correction. <u>Service-entrance conductors must be sized to carry not less than</u> 100 percent of the noncontinuous load(s), plus 125 percent of the continuous load(s). Figure 230–10

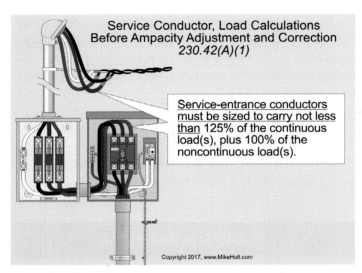

Figure 230–10

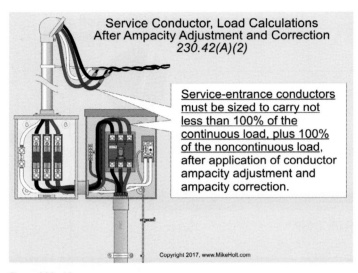

application of conductor ampacity adjustment [310.15(B)(3)(a)] and ampacity correction [310.15(B)(2)(a)]. Figure 230–12

Figure 230–12

Example: *What size service-entrance conductors are required for a 200A continuous three-phase load, where the four conductors are considered current carrying?* Figure 230–11

Solution: *250 kcmil service-entrance conductors are required.*

Since the load is 200A continuous, the service-entrance conductors must have an ampacity not less than 250A (200A x 1.25). According to the 75ºC column of Table 310.15(B)(16), 250 kcmil conductors are suitable because they have an ampere rating of 255A.

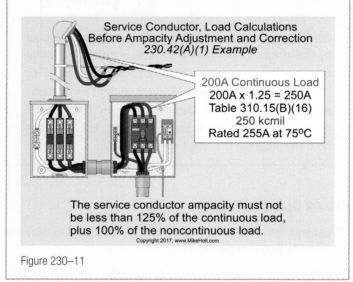

Figure 230–11

(2) After Ampacity Adjustment and Correction. Service-entrance conductors must be sized to carry not less than 100 percent of the noncontinuous load plus 100 percent of the continuous load, after the

Example: *What size service-entrance conductors are required for a 200A continuous three-phase load, where the four conductors are considered current carrying?* Figure 230–13

Solution: *250 kcmil service-entrance conductors are required.*

Since the load is 200A continuous, the service-entrance conductors must have an ampacity not less than 200A after conductor adjustment of 80 percent [310.15(B)(3)(a)]. According to the 90ºC column of Table 310.15(B)(16), 250 kcmil conductors have an ampere rating of 290A before adjustment and 232A (255A x 0.80) after adjustment.

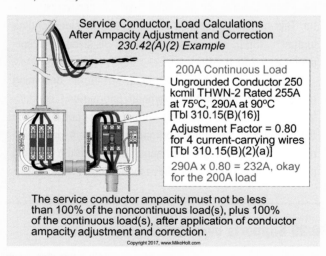

Figure 230–13

(C) Neutral Conductor Size. The service neutral conductor must be sized to carry the maximum unbalanced load in accordance with 220.61, and isn't permitted to be sized smaller than required by 250.24(C).

> **WARNING:** *In all cases the service neutral conductor size must not be smaller than required by 250.24(C) to ensure that it has sufficiently low impedance and current-carrying capacity to safely carry fault current in order to facilitate the operation of the overcurrent protection device.*

230.53 Raceways to Drain

This section was revised to use the terms "listed" and "approved" instead of "suitable."

Analysis

CLARIFIED Pretty much everyone will agree that the *Code* needs to be written with clear and specific words. Words like "suitable" aren't always the best option when there others like "approved," "identified," and "listed" in Article 100 that can be used instead.

Previous editions of this rule stated that raceways on exterior surfaces needed to be arranged to drain and needed to be "suitable" for a wet location. Listed raceways and fittings or even approved raceways and fittings are probably suitable, but why leave room for interpretation? Using the words "listed" and "approved" instead of "suitable" makes it a better rule.

230.53 Raceways to Drain

Raceways on exterior surfaces of buildings or other structures must be arranged to drain, and be listed or approved for use in wet locations.

230.54 Overhead Service Locations

The rules on service heads were clarified.

Analysis

 CLARIFIED The point of attachment is the point where the utility conductors are secured to the structure (or mast). The service head (or gooseneck) must be installed higher than the point of attachment because water can (will) track down the inside and outside conductors and enter into the raceway or equipment.

Previous editions of the *NEC* didn't address this fact because it only talked about service heads on service cables, not raceways. Water inside the raceway is just as bad (or worse) than water inside the cable, so it makes sense for the weatherhead on a raceway to be installed above the point of attachment.

230.54 Overhead Service Locations

(A) Service Head. Raceways for overhead service drops or overhead service conductors must have a weatherhead listed for wet locations.

(B) Service-Entrance Cable. Service-entrance cables must be equipped with a weatherhead listed for wet locations.

(C) Above the Point of Attachment. Service heads on raceways or service-entrance cables, must be located above the point of attachment [230.26] for service-drop or overhead service conductors. Figure 230–14

Ex: If it's impractical to locate the service head above the point of attachment, it must be located within 2 ft of the point of attachment.

(D) Secured. Service-entrance cables must be held securely in place.

(E) Opposite Polarity Through Separately Bushed Holes. Service heads must provide a bushed opening, and ungrounded conductors must be in separate openings.

(F) Drip Loops. Drip loop conductors must be connected to the service-drop or overhead service conductors below the service head or termination of the service-entrance cable sheath. Figure 230–15

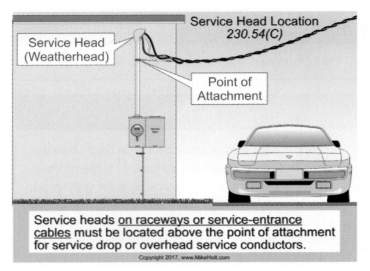

Service heads on raceways or service-entrance cables must be located above the point of attachment for service drop or overhead service conductors.

Figure 230–14

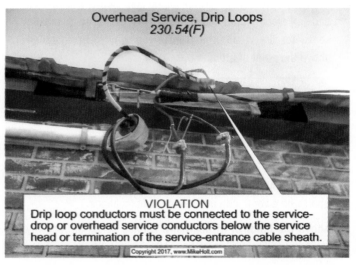

VIOLATION
Drip loop conductors must be connected to the service-drop or overhead service conductors below the service head or termination of the service-entrance cable sheath.

Figure 230–15

(G) Arranged So Water Won't Enter. Service entrance and overhead service conductors must be arranged to prevent water from entering service equipment.

230.66 Marking for Service Equipment

A new requirement allows service equipment to be field labeled and requires meter socket enclosures to be listed.

Analysis

NEW Service equipment (service disconnects) must be listed as "suitable for use as service equipment" among other requirements. This means that there must be a way to bond the frame of the enclosure to the utility-supplied neutral conductor.

New to this version of the *NEC* is to allow for the field labeling of service equipment by a qualified testing facility. The testing laboratory visits the site, analyzes the equipment, and determines the suitability. This was probably acceptable to most inspectors before as well, but now it's *Code*.

This section has long stated that meter socket enclosures aren't considered to be service equipment, and that's still the case. However, the 2017 *NEC* is now requiring meter socket enclosures to be listed if the electrician provides and installs them. If the utility provides the meter socket enclosure, then it isn't required to be listed or field labeled since this falls outside of the scope of the *Code* [90.2(B)(5)].

230.66 Marking for Service Equipment

The service disconnect must be listed or field labeled as service equipment. Figure 230–16

The service disconnect must be listed or field labeled for use as service equipment.

Figure 230–16

Author's Comment

■ "Listed or field labeled for use as service equipment" means, among other things, that the service disconnect is supplied with a main bonding jumper so a neutral-to-case connection can be made, as required in 250.24(C) and 250.142(A). Figure 230–17

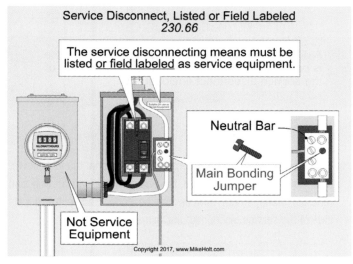

Figure 230–17

Individual meter socket enclosures aren't considered service equipment, but they <u>must be listed and rated for the voltage and ampacity of the service.</u> Figure 230–18

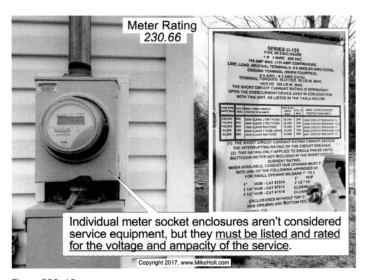

Figure 230–18

Ex: Meter socket enclosures supplied by and under the exclusive control of an electric utility aren't required to be listed.

230.82 Connected on Supply Side of the Service Disconnect

Wind and energy storage systems can now be installed on the supply side of the service disconnect.

Analysis

CLARIFIED This section provides a general statement that no electrical equipment can be installed on the supply side of the service disconnect. This is for good reason, as supply-side equipment can't be shut off by the service disconnect and it doesn't have overcurrent protection. The *NEC* does, however, permit a long list of products to be installed on the supply side of the service disconnect. Solar PV equipment was allowed, so it makes sense for wind or energy storage systems to also be permitted on the supply side.

230.82 Connected on Supply Side of the Service Disconnect

Electrical equipment isn't permitted to be connected to the supply side of the service disconnect enclosure, except for: Figure 230–19

(2) Meter sockets can be connected to the supply side of the service disconnect enclosure.

(3) Meter disconnect switches are permitted to be connected to the supply side of the service disconnect, and they must be legibly field marked on the exterior in a manner suitable for the environment as follows: Figure 230–20

**METER DISCONNECT
NOT SERVICE EQUIPMENT**

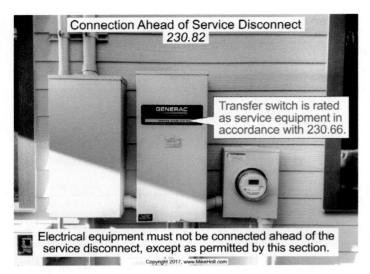

Figure 230–19

Figure 230–20

Author's Comment:

■ Some electric utilities require a disconnect switch ahead of the meter enclosure for 277/480V services for the purpose of enhancing safety for electric utility personnel when they install or remove a meter socket.

(4) Type 1 surge protective devices can be connected to the supply side of the service disconnect enclosure. Figure 230–21

Author's Comment:

■ A Type 1 surge protective device is listed to be permanently connected on the line side of service equipment [285.23].

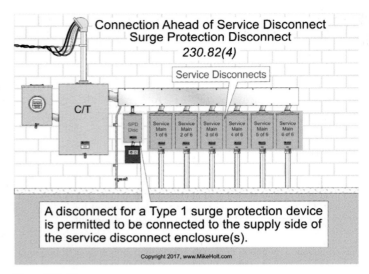

Figure 230–21

(5) Taps used to supply legally required and optional standby power systems, fire pump equipment, fire and sprinkler alarms, and load (energy) management devices can be connected to the supply side of the service disconnect enclosure.

Author's Comment:

■ Emergency standby power isn't permitted to be supplied by a connection ahead of service equipment [700.12]. Figure 230–22

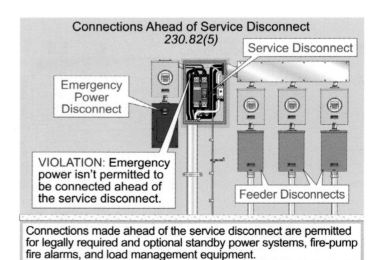

Figure 230–22

(6) Solar PV systems, <u>wind electric systems, energy storage systems,</u> or interconnected electric power production sources can be connected to the supply side of the service disconnect enclosure in accordance with 705.12(A). Figure 230–23

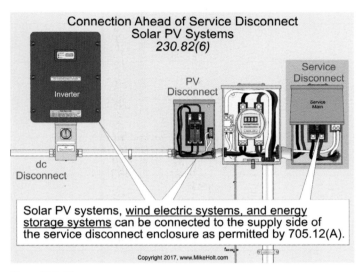

Connection Ahead of Service Disconnect Solar PV Systems 230.82(6)

Solar PV systems, <u>wind electric systems, and energy storage systems</u> can be connected to the supply side of the service disconnect enclosure as permitted by 705.12(A).

Copyright 2017, www.MikeHolt.com

Figure 230–23

Author's Comment:

■ Transfer switches for generators aren't permitted ahead of the service disconnecting means unless they're rated as the service disconnect in accordance with 230.66.

230.91 Location

A new requirement for fused disconnects was added.

Analysis

NEW Although it's probably a "no brainer," we need to be able to change fuses when they aren't energized. Previous versions of the *Code* didn't address this clearly, so it would have been possible for a person to back-feed the service disconnect such that the fuses were energized with the switch open. This is no longer an option, and, to tell the truth, it was probably never intended to be one.

230.91 Location

Where circuit breakers are used for service overcurrent protection, they must be integral with or located immediately adjacent to the service disconnect. <u>Where fuses are used for service overcurrent protection, the service disconnect must be placed on the supply side of the fuses.</u> Figure 230–24

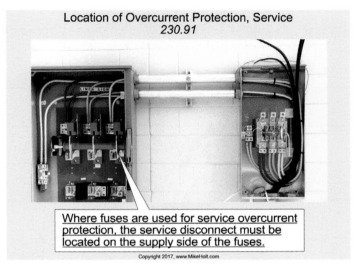

Location of Overcurrent Protection, Service 230.91

Where fuses are used for service overcurrent protection, the service disconnect must be located on the supply side of the fuses.

Copyright 2017, www.MikeHolt.com

Figure 230–24

ARTICLE
240 OVERCURRENT PROTECTION

Introduction to Article 240—Overcurrent Protection

This article provides the requirements for selecting and installing overcurrent protection devices. Overcurrent exists when current exceeds the rating of equipment or the ampacity of a conductor due to an overload, short circuit, or ground fault [Article 100].

- **Overload.** An overload is a condition where equipment or conductors carry current exceeding their current rating [Article 100]. A fault, such as a short circuit or ground fault, isn't an overload. An example of an overload is plugging two 12.50A (1,500W) hair dryers into a 20A branch circuit.

- **Short Circuit.** A short circuit is the unintentional electrical connection between any two normally current-carrying conductors of an electrical circuit, either line-to-line or line-to-neutral.

- **Ground Fault.** A ground fault is an unintentional, electrically conducting connection between an ungrounded conductor of an electrical circuit and the normally noncurrent-carrying conductors, metallic enclosures, metal raceways, metallic equipment, or the earth [Article 100]. During the period of a ground fault, dangerous voltages will be present on metal parts until the circuit overcurrent protection device opens.

Overcurrent protection devices protect conductors and equipment. Selecting the proper overcurrent protection for a specific circuit can become more complicated than it sounds. The general rule for overcurrent protection is that conductors must be protected in accordance with their ampacities at the point where they receive their supply [240.4 and 240.21]. There are many special cases that deviate from this basic rule, such as the overcurrent protection limitations for small conductors [240.4(D)] and the rules for specific conductor applications found in other articles, as listed in Table 240.4(G). There are also a number of rules allowing tap conductors in specific situations [240.21(B)]. Article 240 even has limits on where overcurrent protection devices are allowed to be located [240.24].

An overcurrent protection device must be capable of opening a circuit when an overcurrent situation occurs, and must also have an interrupting rating sufficient to avoid damage in fault conditions [110.9]. Carefully study this article to be sure you provide sufficient overcurrent protection in the correct location.

Part I. General

240.1 Scope

Article 240 covers the general requirements for overcurrent protection and the installation requirements of overcurrent protection devices. Figure 240–1

Author's Comment:

- Overcurrent is a condition where the current exceeds the rating of equipment or ampacity of a conductor due to overload, short circuit, or ground fault [Article 100]. Figure 240–2

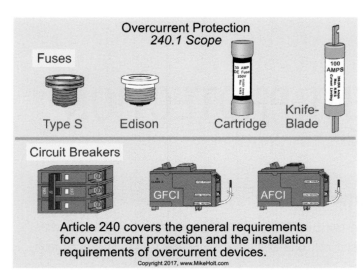

Figure 240–1

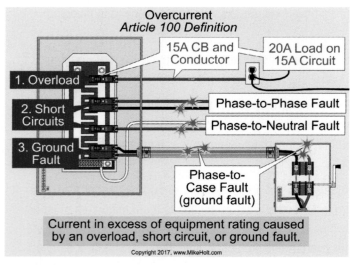

Figure 240–2

Note: An overcurrent protection device protects the circuit by opening the device when the current reaches a value that will cause excessive or dangerous temperature rise (overheating) in conductors. Overcurrent protection devices must have an interrupting rating sufficient for the maximum possible fault current available on the line-side terminals of the equipment [110.9]. Electrical equipment must have a short-circuit current rating that permits the circuit's overcurrent protection device to clear short circuits or ground faults without extensive damage to the circuit's electrical components [110.10].

240.6 Standard Ampere Ratings

The standard ratings for fuses and circuit breakers were put into a table.

Analysis

EDITED

This section was always a chore to reference. In this edition of the *Code* it's been reorganized into a table making it easier to use.

240.6 Standard Ampere Ratings

(A) Fuses and Fixed-Trip Circuit Breakers. The standard ratings in amperes for fuses and inverse time breakers are shown in Table 240.6(A). The use of fuses and inverse time circuit breakers with non-standard ampere ratings are permitted. Figure 240–3

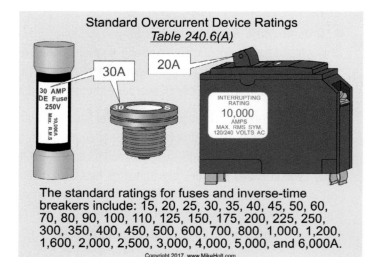

Figure 240–3

Additional standard ampere ratings for fuses include 1, 3, 6, 10, and 601.

- Fuses rated less than 15A are sometimes required for the overcurrent protection of fractional horsepower motor circuits [430.52], motor control circuits [430.72], small transformers [450.3(B)], and remote-control circuit conductors [725.43].

(B) Adjustable Circuit Breakers. The ampere rating of an adjustable circuit breaker is equal to its maximum long-time pickup current setting.

(C) Restricted Access, Adjustable-Trip Circuit Breakers. The ampere rating of adjustable-trip circuit breakers that have restricted access to the adjusting means is equal to their adjusted long-time pickup current settings.

240.24 Location of Overcurrent Protection Devices

The accessibility of overcurrent protection devices was clarified.

Analysis

CLARIFIED

Article 240 covers overcurrent protection devices, which means that Article 240 makes the rules on the accessibility of them. Section 240.24(A) has a long-standing requirement that overcurrent protection devices must be readily accessible. Are the fuses themselves required to be ready accessible too, or is it the switch containing the fuses?

Since 110.27 requires live parts of 50V or more to be guarded, changes were made to this rule to clarify that the fuse itself isn't the issue, it's the switch on the enclosure containing the fuses to which we need ready access.

240.24 Location of Overcurrent Protection Devices

(A) Readily Accessible. Circuit breakers and switches containing fuses must be readily accessible and installed so the center of the grip of the operating handle of the circuit breaker or switch, when in its highest position, isn't more than 6 ft 7 in. above the floor or working platform, except for: Figure 240–4

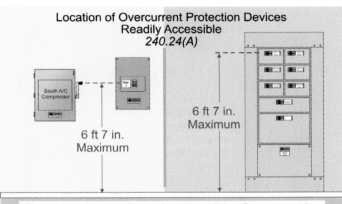

Figure 240–4

(1) Busways, as provided in 368.17(C).

(2) Supplementary overcurrent protection devices [240.10]. Figure 240–5

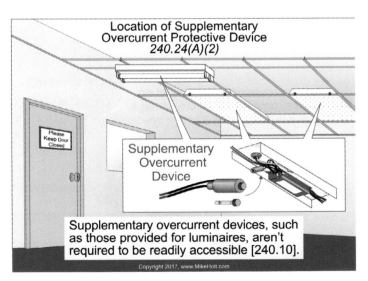

Figure 240–5

(3) For overcurrent protection devices, as described in 225.40 and 230.92.

(4) Circuit breakers and switches for fuses are permitted above 6 ft 7 in. where located next to equipment if accessible by portable means [404.8(A) Ex 2]. Figure 240–6

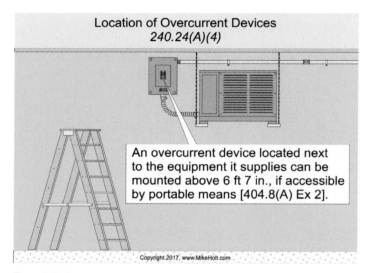

Figure 240–6

Ex. The use of a tool is permitted to access overcurrent protection devices located within listed industrial control panels or similar enclosures.

(C) Not Exposed to Physical Damage. Overcurrent protection devices aren't permitted to be exposed to physical damage. Figure 240–7

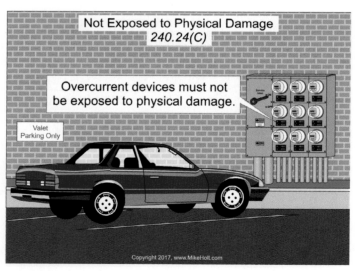

Figure 240–7

Note: Electrical equipment must be suitable for the environment, and consideration must be given to the presence of corrosive gases, fumes, vapors, liquids, or chemicals that have a deteriorating effect on conductors or equipment [110.11]. Figure 240–8

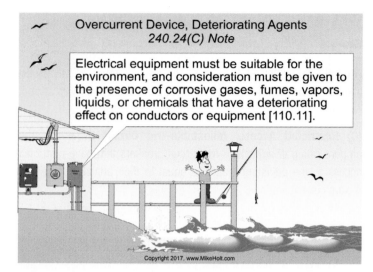

Figure 240–8

(D) Not in Vicinity of Easily Ignitible Material. Overcurrent protection devices aren't permitted to be located near easily ignitible material, such as in clothes closets. Figure 240–9

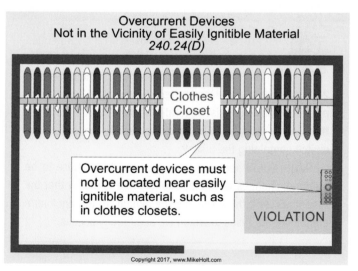

Figure 240–9

(E) Not in Bathrooms. Overcurrent protection devices aren't permitted to be located in the bathrooms of dwelling units, dormitories, or guest rooms or guest suites of hotels or motels. Figure 240–10

Figure 240–10

Author's Comment:

- The service disconnect switch isn't permitted to be located in a bathroom, even in commercial or industrial facilities [230.70(A)(2)].

(F) Over Steps. Overcurrent protection devices aren't permitted to be located over the steps of a stairway. Figure 240–11

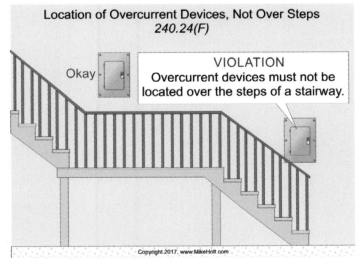

Figure 240–11

Author's Comment:

- Clearly, it's difficult for electricians to safely work on electrical equipment that's located on uneven surfaces such as over stairways.

240.87 Arc Energy Reduction

New language was added to this article to address arc energy reduction options.

Analysis

EXPANDED The requirements of NFPA 70E must be addressed for personnel to safely operate and maintain electrical equipment. One of the hardest parts of meeting these requirements is that of knowing what protective equipment is required to work safely. This section was expanded to allow additional methods to reduce arc energy in the case of an arc flash incident.

240.87 Arc Energy Reduction

Arc Energy Reduction. Where the highest continuous current trip setting for which the overcurrent protection device in a circuit breaker is rated or can be adjusted to 1,200A or higher, 240.87(A) and (B) applies.

(A) Documentation. Documentation must be available to those authorized to design, install, operate, or inspect the installation as to the location of the arc energy reduction circuit breaker(s).

(B) Method to Reduce Clearing Time. One of the following means must be used so as to reduce the overcurrent clearing times, resulting in reduced arc energy:

(1) Zone-selective interlocking

(2) Differential relaying

(3) Energy-reducing maintenance switching with local status indicator

(4) Energy-reducing active arc flash mitigation system

(5) An instantaneous trip setting that's less than the available arcing current

(6) An instantaneous override that's less than the available arcing current

(7) An approved equivalent means

Note 1: An energy-reducing maintenance switch [240.87(B)(3)] allows a worker to set a circuit breaker trip unit to "no intentional delay" to reduce the clearing time while the worker is working within an arc-flash boundary as defined in NFPA 70E, *Standard for Electrical Safety in the Workplace*, and then to set the trip unit back to a normal setting after the potentially hazardous work is complete.

Note 2: An energy-reducing active arc flash mitigation system [240.87(B)(4)] helps in reducing arcing duration in the electrical distribution system. No change in the circuit breaker or the settings of other devices is required during maintenance when a worker is working within an arc flash boundary as defined in NFPA 70E, *Standard for Electrical Safety in the Workplace.*

Note 3: An instantaneous trip [240.87(B)(5)] is a function that causes a circuit breaker to trip with no intentional delay when currents exceed the instantaneous trip setting or current level. If arcing currents are above the instantaneous trip level, the circuit breaker will trip in the minimum possible time.

Note 4: IEEE 1584, *IEEE Guide for Performing Arc Flash Hazard Calculations*, is one of the available methods that provides guidance in determining arcing current.

ARTICLE
250 | GROUNDING AND BONDING

Introduction to Article 250—Grounding and Bonding

No other article can match Article 250 for misapplication, violation, and misinterpretation. Terminology used in this article has been a source for much confusion, but that's improved during the last few *NEC* revisions. It's very important to understand the difference between grounding and bonding in order to correctly apply the provisions of Article 250. Pay careful attention to the definitions that apply to grounding and bonding both here and in Article 100 as you begin the study of this important article. Article 250 covers the grounding requirements for providing a path to the earth to reduce overvoltage from lightning, and the bonding requirements for a low-impedance fault current path back to the source of the electrical supply to facilitate the operation of overcurrent protection devices in the event of a ground fault.

Over the past several *Code* cycles, this article was extensively revised to organize it better and make it easier to understand and implement. It's arranged in a logical manner, so it's a good idea to just read through Article 250 to get a big picture view—after you review the definitions. Next, study the article closely so you understand the details. The illustrations will help you understand the key points.

Part I. General

250.1 Scope

Article 250 contains the following grounding and bonding requirements:

(1) What systems and equipment are required to be grounded.

(3) Location of grounding connections.

(4) Types of electrodes and sizes of grounding and bonding conductors.

(5) Methods of grounding and bonding.

250.4 Performance Requirements for Grounding and Bonding

New Informational Notes were added to inform *Code* users of NFPA 780, *Standard for the Installation of Lightning Protection Systems*.

Analysis

NEW The reason we earth ground systems to the earth is to reduce overvoltage, from lightning induced energy, and other events, on the conductors and electrical components (such as transformer and motor windings) of the installation.

Adding an Informational Note referencing NFPA 780 *Standard for the Installation of Lightning Protection Systems* makes no sense, since a lightning protection system won't assist in reducing overvoltage on systems addressed by 250.4. But the Code Making Panel apparently thinks it does...

250.4 Performance Requirements for Grounding and Bonding

(A) Solidly Grounded Systems.

(1) Electrical System Grounding. Electrical power systems are grounded (connected to the earth) to limit the voltage induced by lightning, line surges, or unintentional contact by higher-voltage lines. Figure 250–1

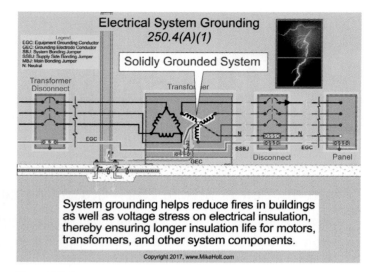

Figure 250–2

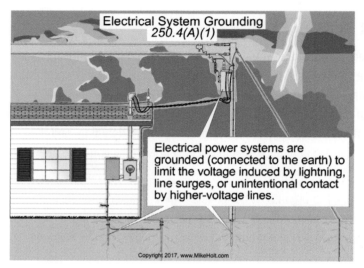

Figure 250–1

Author's Comment:

■ System grounding helps reduce fires in buildings as well as voltage stress on electrical insulation, thereby ensuring longer insulation life for motors, transformers, and other system components. Figure 250–2

Note 1: To limit imposed voltage, the grounding electrode conductors shouldn't be any longer than necessary and unnecessary bends and loops should be avoided. Figure 250–3

Note 2: See NFPA 780, *Standard for the Installation of Lightning Protection Systems* for grounding and bonding of lightning protection systems.

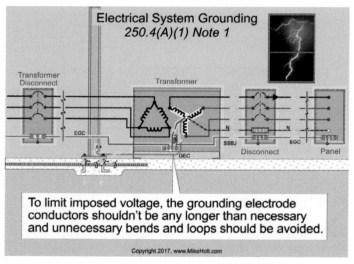

Figure 250–3

(2) Equipment Grounding. Metal parts of electrical equipment are grounded to reduce arcing within the buildings/structures from induced voltage from indirect lightning strikes. Figure 250–4

⚡ **DANGER:** *Failure to ground metal parts to earth can result in induced voltage on metal parts from an indirect lightning strike seeking a path to the earth within the building—possibly resulting in a fire and/or electric shock from a side flash.* Figure 250–5

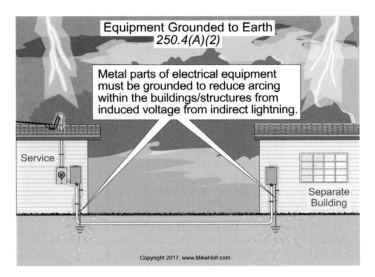

Figure 250-4

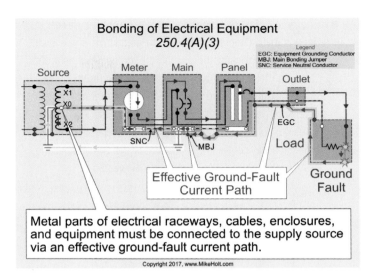

Figure 250-6

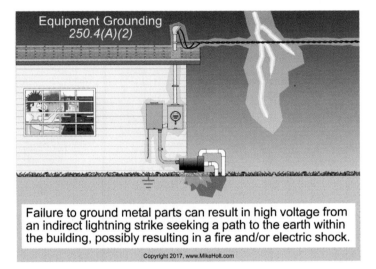

Figure 250-5

Author's Comment:

■ Grounding metal parts helps drain off static electricity charges before flashover potential is reached. Static grounding is often used in areas where the discharge (arcing) of the voltage buildup (static) can cause dangerous or undesirable conditions [500.4 Note 3].

(3) Equipment Bonding. Metal parts of electrical raceways, cables, enclosures, and equipment must be connected to the supply source via an effective ground-fault current path. Figure 250-6

Author's Comment:

■ To quickly remove dangerous voltage on metal parts from a ground fault, the effective ground-fault current path must have sufficiently low impedance to the source so fault current will quickly rise to a level that will open the branch-circuit overcurrent protection device. Figure 250-7

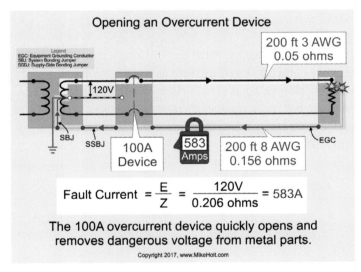

The 100A overcurrent device quickly opens and removes dangerous voltage from metal parts.

Figure 250-7

■ The time it takes for an overcurrent protection device to open is inversely proportional to the magnitude of the fault current. This means the higher the ground-fault current value, the less time it will take for the overcurrent protection device to open and clear the fault. For example, a 20A circuit with an overload of 40A (two times the 20A rating) takes 25 to 150 seconds to open the circuit overcurrent protection device. At 100A (five times the 20A rating) the 20A breaker trips in 5 to 20 seconds. Figure 250–8

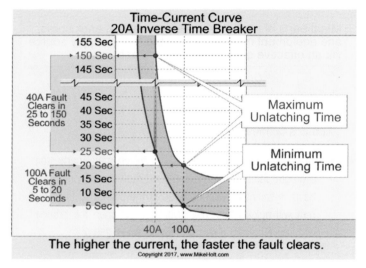

Figure 250–8

(4) Bonding Conductive Materials. Electrically conductive materials likely to become energized, such as metal water piping systems, metal sprinkler piping, metal gas piping, and other metal-piping systems, as well as exposed structural steel members, must be connected to the supply source via an effective ground-fault current path. Figure 250–9

Author's Comment:

■ The phrase "likely to become energized" is subject to interpretation by the authority having jurisdiction.

(5) Effective Ground-Fault Current Path. Metal parts of electrical raceways, cables, enclosures, or equipment must be bonded together and to the supply source in a manner that creates a low-impedance path for ground-fault current that facilitates the operation of the circuit overcurrent protection device. Figure 250–10

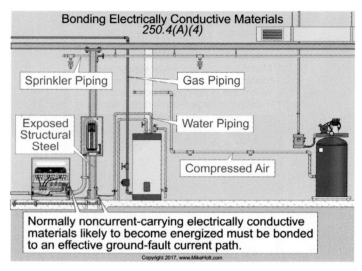

Figure 250–9

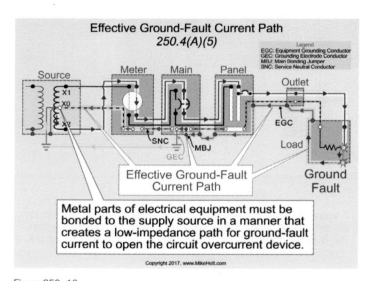

Figure 250–10

Author's Comment:

■ To ensure a low-impedance ground-fault current path, all circuit conductors must be grouped together in the same raceway, cable, or trench [300.3(B), 300.5(I), and 300.20(A)]. Figure 250–11

Because the earth isn't a low impedance path for fault current, it isn't suitable to serve as the required effective ground-fault current path, therefore an equipment grounding conductor of a type recognized in 250.118 is required to be installed with all circuits. Figure 250–12

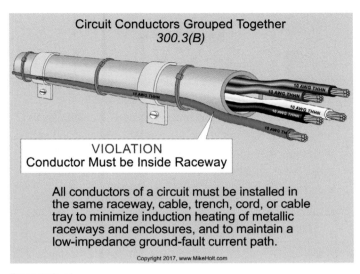

Circuit Conductors Grouped Together
300.3(B)

VIOLATION
Conductor Must be Inside Raceway

All conductors of a circuit must be installed in the same raceway, cable, trench, cord, or cable tray to minimize induction heating of metallic raceways and enclosures, and to maintain a low-impedance ground-fault current path.

Copyright 2017, www.MikeHolt.com

Figure 250–11

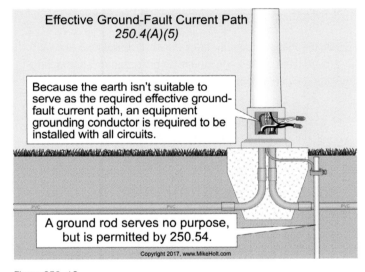

Effective Ground-Fault Current Path
250.4(A)(5)

Because the earth isn't suitable to serve as the required effective ground-fault current path, an equipment grounding conductor is required to be installed with all circuits.

A ground rod serves no purpose, but is permitted by 250.54.

Copyright 2017, www.MikeHolt.com

Figure 250–12

Example: *What's the maximum fault current that can flow through the earth to the power supply from a 120V ground fault to metal parts of a light pole without an equipment grounding conductor that's grounded (connected to the earth) via a rod having a contact resistance to the earth of 25 ohms?* Figure 250–13

Solution: *4.80A.*

$I = E/R$

$I = 120V/25$ ohms

$I = 4.80A$

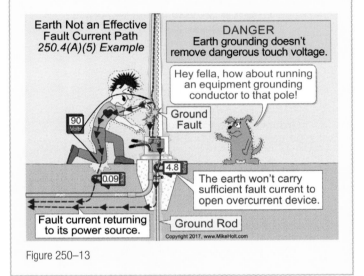

Earth Not an Effective Fault Current Path
250.4(A)(5) Example

DANGER
Earth grounding doesn't remove dangerous touch voltage.

Hey fella, how about running an equipment grounding conductor to that pole!

90 Volts

Ground Fault

4.8

0.09

The earth won't carry sufficient fault current to open overcurrent device.

Fault current returning to its power source.

Ground Rod

Copyright 2017, www.MikeHolt.com

Figure 250–13

⚡ **DANGER:** *Because the contact resistance of an electrode to the earth is so high, very little fault current returns to the power supply if the earth is the only fault current return path.* Figure 250–14

Result—the circuit overcurrent protection device won't open and all metal parts associated with the electrical installation, metal piping, and structural building steel will become and remain energized. Figure 250–15

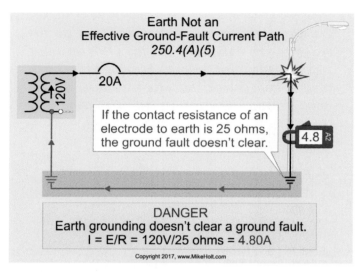

Figure 250–14

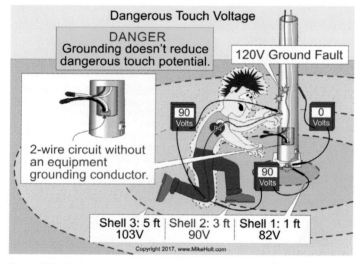

Figure 250–15

Earth Shells

According to ANSI/IEEE 142, *Recommended Practice for Grounding of Industrial and Commercial Power Systems* (Green Book) [4.1.1], the resistance of the soil outward from a rod is equal to the sum of the series resistances of the earth shells. The shell nearest the rod has the highest resistance and each successive shell has progressively larger areas and progressively lower resistances. Don't be concerned if you don't understand this statement; just review the table below.

Distance from Rod	Soil Contact Resistance
1 ft (Shell 1)	68% of total contact resistance
3 ft (Shells 1 and 2)	75% of total contact resistance
5 ft (Shells 1, 2, and 3)	86% of total contact resistance

Since voltage is directly proportional to resistance, the voltage gradient of the earth around an energized rod, assuming a 120V ground fault, will be as follows: Figure 250–16

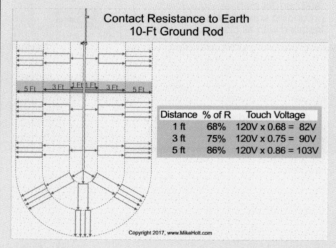

Figure 250–16

Distance from Rod	Soil Contact Resistance	Voltage Gradient
1 ft (Shell 1)	68%	82V
3 ft (Shells 1 and 2)	75%	90V
5 ft (Shells 1, 2, and 3)	86%	103V

(B) Ungrounded Systems.

Author's Comment:

- Ungrounded systems are those systems with no connection to the ground or to a conductive body that extends the ground connection [Article 100]. Figure 250–17

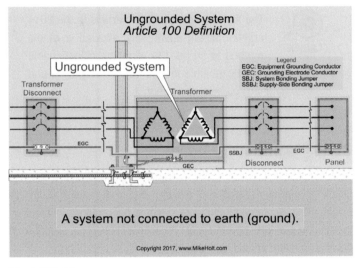

Figure 250–17

(1) Equipment Grounding. Metal parts of electrical equipment are grounded (connected to the earth) to reduce induced voltage on metal parts from lightning so as to prevent fires from an arc within the buildings. Figure 250–18

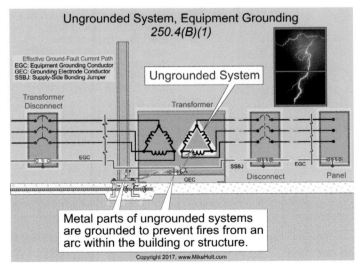

Figure 250–18

Note 2: See NFPA 780, *Standard for the Installation of Lightning Protection Systems* for grounding and bonding of lightning protection systems.

Author's Comment:

- Grounding metal parts helps drain off static electricity charges before an electric arc takes place (flashover potential). Static grounding is often used in areas where the discharge (arcing) of the voltage buildup (static) can cause dangerous or undesirable conditions [500.4 Note 3].

⚡ **CAUTION:** *Connecting metal parts to the earth (grounding) serves no purpose in electrical shock protection.*

(2) Equipment Bonding. Metal parts of electrical raceways, cables, enclosures, or equipment must be bonded together in a manner that creates a low-impedance path for ground-fault current to facilitate the operation of the circuit overcurrent protection device.

The fault current path must be capable of safely carrying the maximum ground-fault current likely to be imposed on it from any point on the wiring system should a ground fault occur to the electrical supply source.

(3) Bonding Conductive Materials. Conductive materials such as metal water piping systems, metal sprinkler piping, metal gas piping, and other metal-piping systems, as well as exposed structural steel members likely to become energized must be bonded together in a manner that creates a low-impedance fault current path that's capable of carrying the maximum fault current likely to be imposed on it. Figure 250–19

Author's Comment:

- The phrase "likely to become energized" is subject to interpretation by the authority having jurisdiction.

(4) Fault Current Path. Electrical equipment, wiring, and other electrically conductive material likely to become energized must be installed in a manner that creates a low-impedance fault current path to facilitate the operation of overcurrent protection devices should a second ground fault from a different phase occur. Figure 250–20

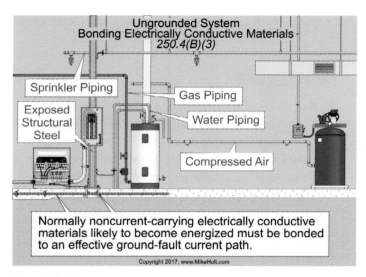

Ungrounded System
Bonding Electrically Conductive Materials
250.4(B)(3)

Sprinkler Piping
Gas Piping
Exposed Structural Steel
Water Piping
Compressed Air

Normally noncurrent-carrying electrically conductive materials likely to become energized must be bonded to an effective ground-fault current path.

Copyright 2017, www.MikeHolt.com

Figure 250–19

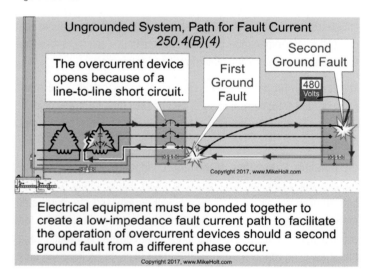

Ungrounded System, Path for Fault Current
250.4(B)(4)

The overcurrent device opens because of a line-to-line short circuit.

First Ground Fault

Second Ground Fault

 480 Volts

Copyright 2017, www.MikeHolt.com

Electrical equipment must be bonded together to create a low-impedance fault current path to facilitate the operation of overcurrent devices should a second ground fault from a different phase occur.

Copyright 2017, www.MikeHolt.com

Figure 250–20

Author's Comment:

■ A single ground fault can't be cleared on an ungrounded system because there's no low-impedance fault current path to the electric power source. The first ground fault simply grounds the system and initiates the ground detector. However, a second ground fault on a different phase results in a line-to-line short circuit between the two ground faults. The conductive path, between the ground faults, provides the low-impedance fault current path necessary so the overcurrent protection device will open.

250.6 Objectionable Current

This section was clarified to allow the use of multiple means to avoid objectionable current.

Analysis

CLARIFIED The literal language of this article in the 2014 edition of the *Code* only allowed a single method to be used to eliminate objectionable current. In actuality, multiple means may be employed and the new language clarifies the intent.

250.6 Objectionable Current

(A) Preventing Objectionable Current. To prevent a fire, electric shock, or improper operation of circuit overcurrent protection devices or electronic equipment, electrical systems and equipment must be installed in a manner that prevents objectionable neutral current from flowing on metal parts. Figure 250–21

Objectionable Current
250.6(A)

To prevent a fire, electric shock, or improper operation of circuit overcurrent devices or electronic equipment, electrical systems and equipment must be installed in a manner that prevents objectionable neutral current from flowing on metal parts.

Copyright 2017, www.MikeHolt.com

Figure 250–21

(B) Stopping Objectionable Current. If the use of multiple grounding connections results in objectionable current and the requirements of 250.4(A)(5) or (B)(4) are met, <u>one or more of the following alterations are permitted:</u>

(1) Discontinue one or more but not all of such grounding connections.

(2) Change the locations of the grounding connections.

(3) Interrupt the continuity of the conductor or conductive path causing the objectionable current.

(4) Take other suitable remedial and approved action.

(C) Temporary Currents Not Classified as Objectionable Currents. Temporary currents from abnormal conditions, such as ground faults, aren't to be classified as objectionable current. Figure 250–22

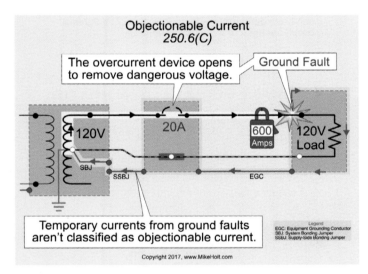

Figure 250–22

(D) Limitations to Permissible Alterations. Currents that introduce noise or data errors in electronic equipment aren't considered objectionable currents for the purposes of this section. Circuits that supply electronic equipment must be connected to an equipment grounding conductor.

Objectionable Current

Objectionable neutral current occurs because of improper neutral-to-case connections or wiring errors that violate 250.142(B).

Improper Neutral-to-Case Connection [250.142]

Panelboards. Objectionable neutral current will flow on metal parts and the equipment grounding conductor when the neutral conductor is connected to the metal case of a panelboard on the load side of service equipment. Figure 250–23

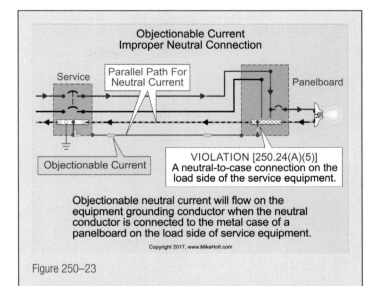

Figure 250–23

Separately Derived Systems. Objectionable neutral current will flow on metal parts if the neutral conductor is connected to the circuit equipment grounding conductor on the load side of the system bonding jumper for a separately derived system. Figure 250–24

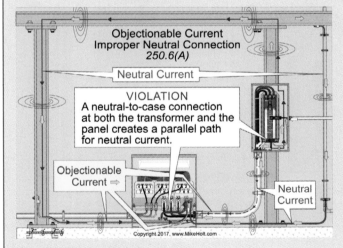

Figure 250–24

Generator. Objectionable neutral current will flow on metal parts and the equipment grounding conductor if a generator is connected to a transfer switch with a solidly connected neutral and a neutral-to-case connection is made at the generator. Figure 250–25

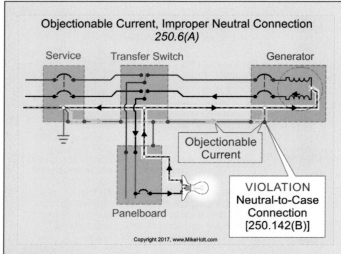

Figure 250–25

Disconnects. Objectionable neutral current will flow on metal parts and the equipment grounding conductor when the neutral conductor is connected to the metal case of a disconnect that's not part of the service equipment. Figure 250–26

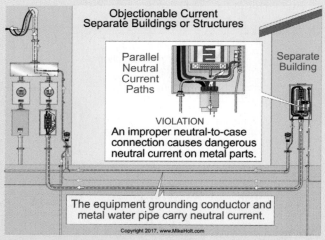

Figure 250–26

Wiring Errors. Objectionable neutral current will flow on metal parts and equipment grounding conductors when the neutral conductor from one system is used as the neutral conductor for a different system. Figure 250–27

Objectionable neutral current will flow on the equipment grounding conductor when the circuit equipment grounding conductor is used as a neutral conductor such as where:

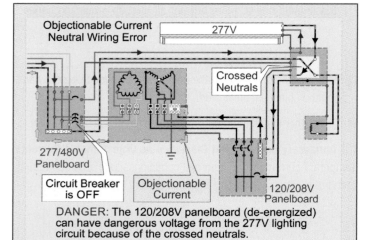

Figure 250–27

- A 230V time-clock motor is replaced with a 115V time-clock motor, and the circuit equipment grounding conductor is used for neutral return current.

- A 115V water filter is wired to a 240V well-pump motor circuit, and the circuit equipment grounding conductor is used for neutral return current. Figure 250–28

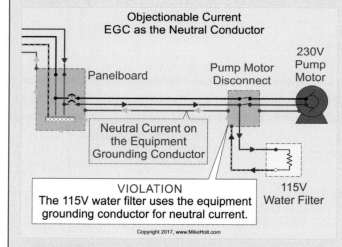

Figure 250–28

- The circuit equipment grounding conductor is used for neutral return current. Figure 250–29

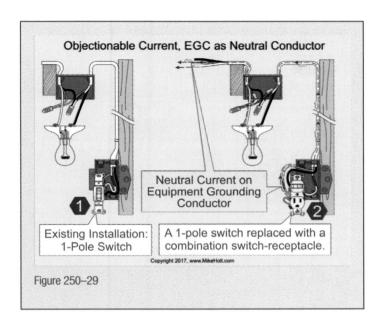

Figure 250–29

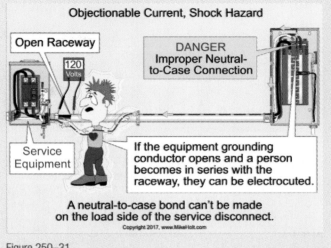

Figure 250–31

Fire Hazard. When objectionable neutral current flows on metal parts, a fire can ignite adjacent combustible material. Heat is generated whenever current flows, particularly over high-resistance parts. In addition, arcing at loose connections is especially dangerous in areas containing easily ignitible and explosive gases, vapors, or dust. Figure 250–32

Dangers of Objectionable Current

Objectionable neutral current on metal parts can cause electric shock, fires, and improper operation of electronic equipment and overcurrent protection devices such as GFPs, GFCIs, and AFCIs.

Shock Hazard. When objectionable neutral current flows on metal parts or the equipment grounding conductor, electric shock and even death can occur from the elevated voltage on those metal parts. Figure 250–30 and Figure 250–31

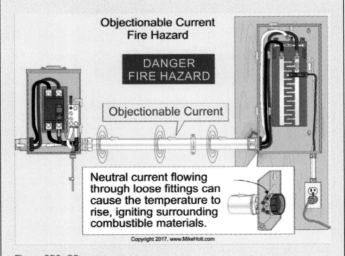

Figure 250–32

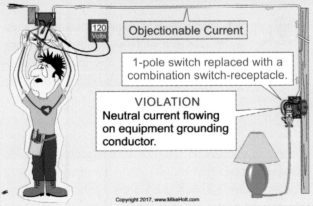

Figure 250–30

Improper Operation of Electronic Equipment. Objectionable neutral current flowing on metal parts of electrical equipment and building parts can cause electromagnetic fields which negatively affect the performance of electronic devices, particularly medical equipment. Figure 250–33

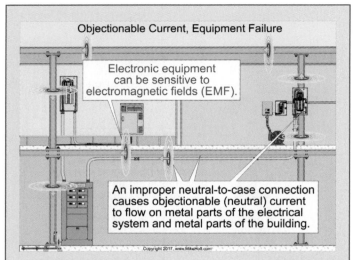

Figure 250–33

For more information, visit www.MikeHolt.com, click on the "Technical" link, and then on "Power Quality."

When a solidly grounded system is properly bonded, the voltage of all metal parts to the earth and to each other will be zero. Figure 250–34

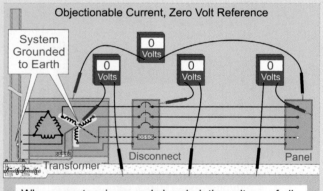

Figure 250–34

When objectionable neutral current travels on metal parts and equipment grounding conductors because of the improper bonding of the neutral to metal parts, a difference of voltage will exist between all metal parts. This situation can cause some electronic equipment to operate improperly. Figure 250–35

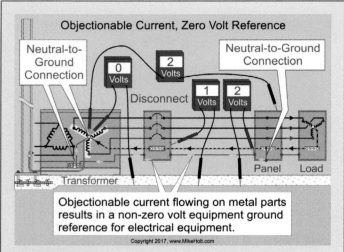

Figure 250–35

Operation of Overcurrent Protection Devices. When objectionable neutral current travels on metal parts, tripping of electronic overcurrent protection devices equipped with ground-fault protection can occur because some neutral current flows on the circuit equipment grounding conductor instead of the neutral conductor.

250.24 Service Equipment— Grounding and Bonding

Clarification that the sizing requirements for service neutral conductors apply to cable-type wiring methods was made.

Analysis

CLARIFIED

I've always liked to visualize the utility neutral conductor as a white wire with green stripes on it. That's really what it is; the service neutral wire carries the unbalanced return (white) and it's the fault-clearing conductor on the supply side of the service (green stripe).

Because the service neutral conductor serves the role of carrying unbalanced current and is intended to provide a low-impedance fault return path to the utility secondary winding, it must be sized to carry the neutral load and the fault current back to the source in the event of a ground fault.

Think about it, if we have a 400A three-phase service supplying only three-phase motors and one 20A line-to-neutral lighting circuit, what size neutral wire do we need?

A 12 AWG conductor will certainly carry the lighting circuit neutral load, but what about the fault current? Have you ever seen a 500 kcmil phase conductor collide with a 12AWG equipment grounding conductor? I haven't either, but I can guess that there wouldn't be anything left of the 12AWG conductor, other than copper vapor floating around in the air, should it happen.

To ensure a safe installation, the *Code* requires the service neutral conductor to be sized in accordance with Table 250.102(C)(1). In our 400 kcmil example, this would be a 1/0 AWG copper neutral. That kind of mass can carry the fault carry current without any problem.

Since none of this is actually new to the *NEC*, what changed? The 2014 *Code* was clear when it came to sizing the neutral conductor in a raceway, but it was dead silent when it came to sizing the neutral conductor in a cable assembly. It's now clear that the service neutral conductor must be sized in accordance with 250.61 and 250.102(C)(1), whether the installation is a raceway or a cable.

250.24 Service Equipment—Grounding and Bonding

(A) Grounded System. Service equipment supplied from a grounded system must have the grounding electrode conductor terminate in accordance with (1) through (5).

(1) Grounding Location. A grounding electrode conductor must connect the service neutral conductor to the grounding electrode at any accessible location, from the load end of the overhead service conductors, service drop, underground service conductors, or service lateral, up to and including the service disconnect. Figure 250–36

Author's Comment:

- Some inspectors require the service neutral conductor to be grounded (connected to the earth) from the meter socket enclosure, while other inspectors insist that it be grounded (connected to the earth) only from the service disconnect. Grounding at either location complies with this rule.

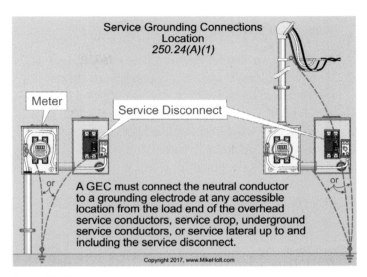

Figure 250–36

(4) Grounding Termination. When the service neutral conductor is connected to the service disconnect [250.24(B)] by a wire or busbar [250.28], the grounding electrode conductor can terminate to either the neutral terminal or the equipment grounding terminal within the service disconnect.

(5) Neutral-to-Case Connection. A neutral-to-case connection isn't permitted on the load side of service equipment, except as permitted by 250.142(B). Figure 250–37

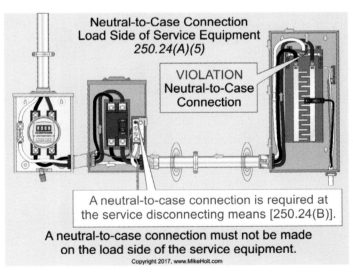

Figure 250–37

Author's Comment:

- If a neutral-to-case connection is made on the load side of service equipment, dangerous objectionable neutral current will flow on conductive metal parts of electrical equipment [250.6(A)]. Objectionable neutral current on metal parts of electrical equipment can cause electric shock and even death from ventricular fibrillation, as well as a fire. Figure 250–38 and Figure 250–39

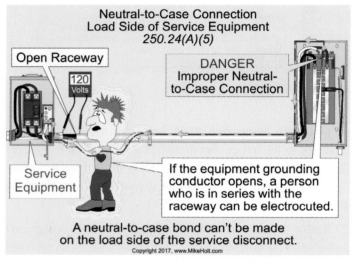

Figure 250–38

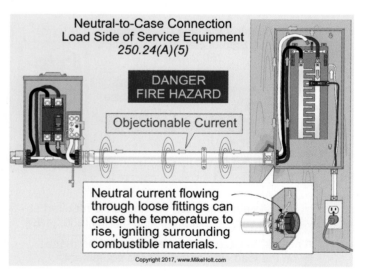

Figure 250–39

(B) Main Bonding Jumper. A main bonding jumper [250.28] is required to connect the neutral conductor to the equipment grounding conductor within the service disconnect. Figure 250–40 and Figure 250–41

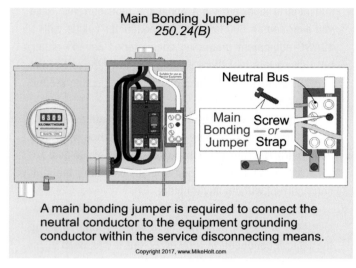

Figure 250–40

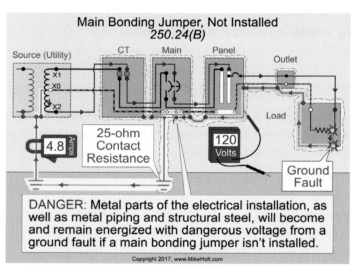

Figure 250–41

(C) Neutral Conductor Brought to Service Equipment. A service neutral conductor must be run from the electric utility power supply with the ungrounded conductors and terminate to the service disconnect neutral terminal. A main bonding jumper [250.24(B)] must be installed between the service neutral terminal and the service disconnect enclosure [250.28]. Figure 250–42 and Figure 250–43

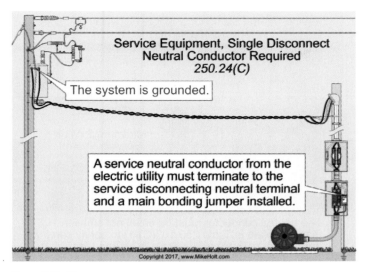

Figure 250–42

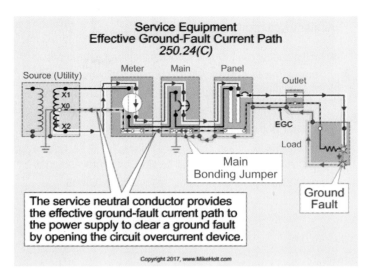

Figure 250–44

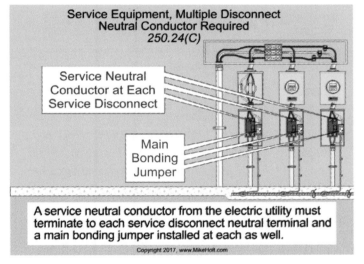

Figure 250–43

Author's Comment:

- The service neutral conductor provides the effective ground-fault current path to the power supply to ensure that dangerous voltage from a ground fault will be quickly removed by opening the overcurrent protection device [250.4(A)(3) and 250.4(A)(5)]. Figure 250–44

DANGER: *Dangerous voltage from a ground fault won't be removed from metal parts, metal piping, and structural steel if the service disconnect enclosure isn't connected to the service neutral conductor. This is because the contact resistance of a grounding electrode to the earth is so great that insufficient fault current returns to the power supply if the earth is the only fault current return path to open the circuit overcurrent protection device.* Figure 250–45

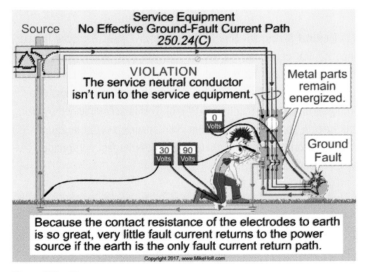

Figure 250–45

Author's Comment:

- If the neutral conductor is opened, dangerous voltage will be present on metal parts under normal conditions, providing the potential for electric shock. If the earth's ground resistance is 25 ohms and the load's resistance is 25 ohms, the voltage drop across each of these resistors will be half of the voltage source. Since the neutral is connected to the service disconnect, all metal parts will be elevated to 60V above the earth's voltage for a 120/240V system. Figure 250–46

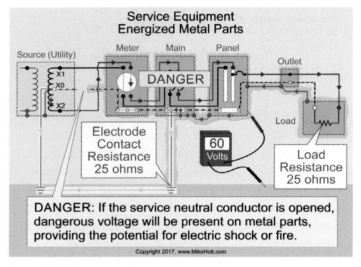

Figure 250–46

(1) Neutral Sizing for Single Raceway or Cable. Because the service neutral conductor serves as the effective ground-fault current path to the source for ground faults, the neutral conductor must be sized so it can safely carry the maximum fault current likely to be imposed on it [110.10 and 250.4(A)(5)]. This is accomplished by sizing the neutral conductor not smaller than specified in Table 250.102(C)(1), based on the cross-sectional area of the largest ungrounded service conductor. Figure 250–47

Author's Comment:

- In addition, the neutral conductors must have the capacity to carry the maximum unbalanced neutral current in accordance with 220.61.

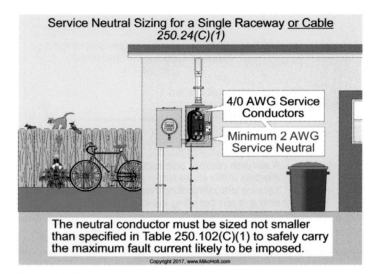

Figure 250–47

Example: What's the minimum size service neutral conductor required where the ungrounded service conductors are 350 kcmil and the maximum unbalanced load is 100A? Figure 250–48

Solution: 2 AWG is the minimum size service neutral conductor required [Table 250.102(C)(1)].

The unbalanced load of 100A requires a 3 AWG service neutral conductor, which is rated 100A at 75ºC in accordance with Table 310.15(B)(16) [220.61], but the neutral conductor can't be smaller than 2 AWG to carry fault current, based on the 350 kcmil ungrounded conductors in accordance with Table 250.102(C)(1).

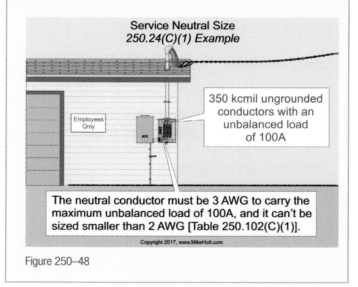

Figure 250–48

(2) Neutral Sizing for Parallel Conductors in Two or More Raceways or Cables. If service conductors are paralleled in two or more raceways or cables, a neutral conductor must be installed in each of the parallel raceways or cables. The size of the neutral conductor in each raceway or cable isn't permitted to be smaller than specified in Table 250.102(C)(1), based on the cross-sectional area of the largest ungrounded service conductor in each raceway or cable. In no case can the neutral conductor in each parallel set be sized smaller than 1/0 AWG [310.10(H)(1)].

Author's Comment:

■ In addition, the neutral conductors must have the capacity to carry the maximum unbalanced neutral current in accordance with 220.61.

Example: *What's the minimum size service neutral conductor required for each of two raceways, where the ungrounded service conductors in each of the raceways are 350 kcmil and the maximum unbalanced load is 100A?* Figure 250–49

Solution: *The minimum size service neutral conductor required is 1/0 AWG per raceway [Table 250.102(C)(1) and 310.10(H)].*

The unbalanced load of 50A in each raceway requires an 8 AWG service neutral conductor, which is rated 50A at 75°C in accordance with Table 310.15(B)(16) [220.61]. Also, Table 250.102(C)(1) requires a minimum of 2 AWG in each raceway, however, 1/0 AWG is the smallest conductor permitted to be paralleled [310.10(H) and Table 310.15(B)(16)].

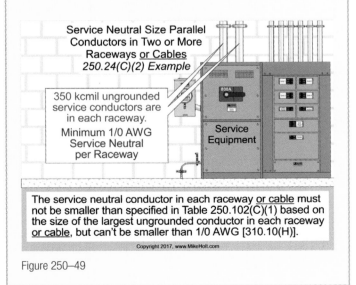

Service Neutral Size Parallel Conductors in Two or More Raceways or Cables 250.24(C)(2) Example

350 kcmil ungrounded service conductors are in each raceway.

Minimum 1/0 AWG Service Neutral per Raceway

Service Equipment

The service neutral conductor in each raceway or cable must not be smaller than specified in Table 250.102(C)(1) based on the size of the largest ungrounded conductor in each raceway or cable, but can't be smaller than 1/0 AWG [310.10(H)].

Copyright 2017, www.MikeHolt.com

Figure 250–49

(D) Grounding Electrode Conductor. A grounding electrode conductor, sized in accordance with 250.66 based on the area of the ungrounded service conductor, must connect the neutral conductor and metal parts of service equipment enclosures to a grounding electrode in accordance with Part III of Article 250.

Example: *What's the minimum size grounding electrode conductor for a 400A service where the ungrounded service conductors are sized at 500 kcmil?* Figure 250–50

Solution: *1/0 AWG is the minimum size grounding electrode conductor [Table 250.66].*

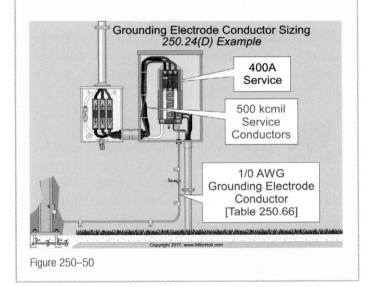

Grounding Electrode Conductor Sizing 250.24(D) Example

400A Service

500 kcmil Service Conductors

1/0 AWG Grounding Electrode Conductor [Table 250.66]

Copyright 2017, www.MikeHolt.com

Figure 250–50

Author's Comment:

■ If the grounding electrode conductor or bonding jumper connects to one or more ground rods [250.52(A)(5)] and doesn't connect to any another type of electrode, the grounding electrode conductor isn't required to be larger than 6 AWG copper.

■ If the grounding electrode conductor or bonding jumper is connected to one or more concrete-encased electrodes [250.52(A)(3)] and doesn't connect to another type of electrode that requires a larger size conductor, the grounding electrode conductor isn't required to be larger than 4 AWG copper.

250.30 Separately Derived Systems—Grounding and Bonding

The requirement to use either structural metal or water piping as the preferred grounding electrodes was removed. Metal water piping can now be used for multiple separately derived systems, and the dimensions of the busbar used to splice grounding electrode conductors was clarified.

Analysis

The past few *Code* cycles have seen many revisions to 250.30 and 250.68 to clarify what items can and can't be called a grounding electrode. These revisions have had varying amounts of success. This cycle includes a change that definitely makes things easier.

EXPANDED

Grounding Electrode. When grounding a separately derived system, we need to connect the neutral point to the building's grounding electrode system. Previous editions of the *NEC* stipulated that the separately derived system needed to be connected to the structural metal or water pipe, and if those weren't present we could then seek other types of electrodes. Now in 2017, the *Code* simply requires us to connect the separately derived system to the building's grounding electrode system.

CLARIFIED

Multiple Separately Derived Systems. When grounding multiple separately derived systems, we've had the option of terminating grounding electrode taps to a common 3/0 AWG copper grounding electrode conductor or to structural metal. Why shouldn't we be allowed to terminate to interior metal water piping? Now we can.

CLARIFIED

Busbar Terminations. Lastly, the dimensions of the busbar that can be used to splice the common grounding electrode conductor and the taps have been clarified. The busbar must be ¼ in. thick by 2 in. wide, and whatever length is necessary to accommodate the terminations.

250.30 Separately Derived Systems—Grounding and Bonding

Note 1: An alternate alternating-current power source such as an on-site generator isn't a separately derived system if the neutral conductor is solidly interconnected to a service-supplied system neutral conductor. An example is a generator provided with a transfer switch that includes a neutral conductor that's not switched. Figure 250–51

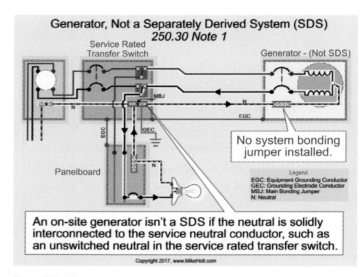

Figure 250–51

Author's Comment:

- According to Article 100, a separately derived system is a wiring system whose power is derived from a source, other than the electric utility, where there's no direct electrical connection to the supply conductors of another system, other than through grounding and bonding connections.

- Transformers are separately derived when the primary conductors have no direct electrical connection from circuit conductors of one system to circuit conductors of another system, other than connections through grounding and bonding connections. Figure 250–52

- A generator having transfer equipment that switches the neutral conductor, or one that has no neutral conductor at all, is a separately derived system and must be grounded and bonded in accordance with 250.30(A). Figure 250–53

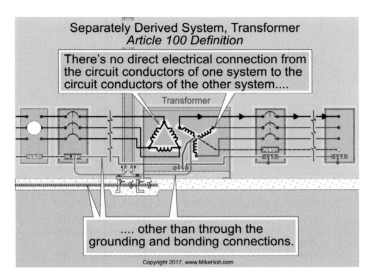

Figure 250–52

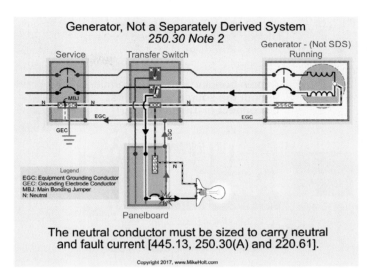

Figure 250–54

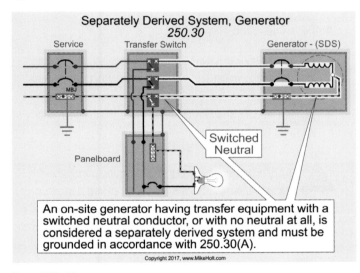

Figure 250–53

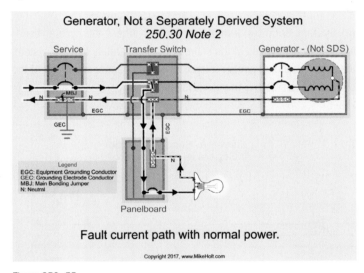

Figure 250–55

Note 2: For nonseparately derived systems, see 445.13 for the minimum size neutral conductors necessary to carry fault current. Figure 250–54 and Figure 250–55

(A) Grounded Systems. Separately derived systems must be grounded and bonded in accordance with (A)(1) through (A)(8). A neutral-to-case connection isn't permitted to be made on the load side of the system bonding jumper, except as permitted by 250.142(B).

(1) System Bonding Jumper. A system bonding jumper must be installed at the same location where the grounding electrode conductor terminates to the neutral terminal of the separately derived system; either at the separately derived system or the system disconnect, but not at both locations [250.30(A)(5)].

If the separately derived source is located outside the building or structure supplied, a system bonding jumper must be installed at the grounding electrode connection in accordance with 250.30(C).

Ex. 2: If a building or structure is supplied by a feeder from an out-door separately derived system, a system bonding jumper at both the source and the first disconnect is permitted. The grounded conductor isn't permitted to be smaller than the size specified for the system bonding jumper, but it's not required to be larger than the ungrounded conductor(s). Figure 250–56

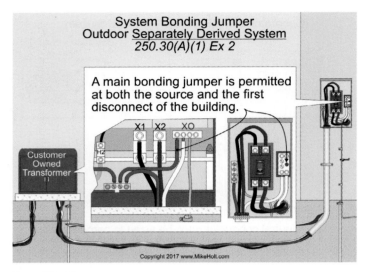

Figure 250–56

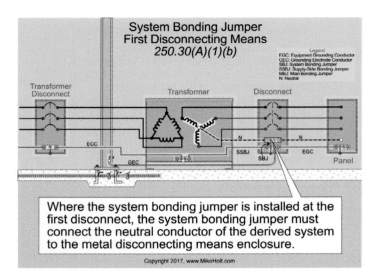

Figure 250–58

(a) System Bonding Jumper at Source. Where the system bonding jumper is installed at the source of the separately derived system, the system bonding jumper must connect the neutral conductor of the derived system to the metal enclosure of the derived system. Figure 250–57

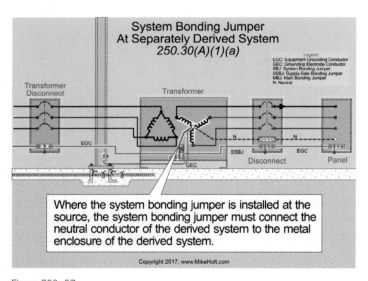

Figure 250–57

(b) System Bonding Jumper at Disconnect. Where the system bonding jumper is installed at the first disconnect of a separately derived system, the system bonding jumper must connect the neutral conductor of the derived system to the metal disconnect enclosure. Figure 250–58

Author's Comment:

- A system bonding jumper is a conductor, screw, or strap that bonds the metal parts of a separately derived system to the system neutral point [Article 100 Bonding Jumper, System], and it's sized to Table 250.102(C)(1) in accordance with 250.28(D).

DANGER: *During a ground fault, metal parts of electrical equipment, as well as metal piping and structural steel, will become and remain energized providing the potential for electric shock and fire if the system bonding jumper isn't installed.* Figure 250–59

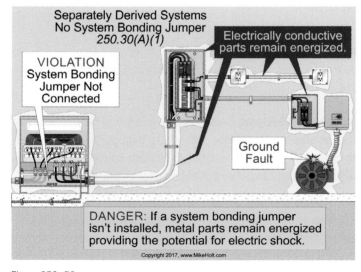

Figure 250–59

⚡ **CAUTION:** *Dangerous objectionable neutral current will flow on conductive metal parts of electrical equipment as well as metal piping and structural steel, in violation of 250.6(A), if more than one system bonding jumper is installed, or if it's not located where the grounding electrode conductor terminates to the neutral conductor.* Figure 250–60

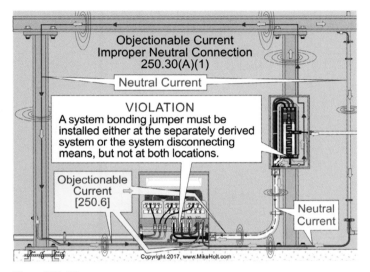

Figure 250–60

(2) Supply-Side Bonding Jumper to Disconnect. A supply-side bonding jumper (nonflexible metal raceway or wire) must be run from the derived system to the derived system disconnect.

(a) If the supply-side bonding jumper is of the wire type, it must be sized in accordance with Table 250.102(C)(1), based on the area of the largest ungrounded derived system conductor in the raceway or cable.

> ***Example:*** *What size supply-side bonding jumper is required for flexible metal conduit containing 300 kcmil secondary conductors?* Figure 250–61
>
> ***Solution:*** *2 AWG [Table 250.102(C)(1)].*

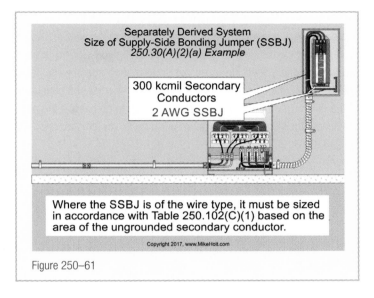

Figure 250–61

(3) System Bonding Jumper at Disconnect—Neutral Conductor Size. If the system bonding jumper is installed at the disconnect instead of at the source, the following requirements apply:

(a) Sizing for Single Raceway. The neutral conductor must be routed with the ungrounded conductors of the derived system to the disconnect and be sized not smaller than specified in Table 250.102(C)(1), based on the area of the ungrounded conductor of the derived system. Figure 250–62

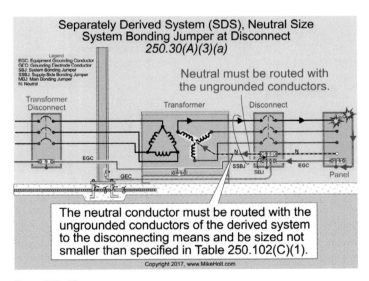

Figure 250–62

(b) Parallel Conductors in Two or More Raceways. If the conductors from the derived system are installed in parallel in two or more raceways, the neutral conductor of the derived system in each raceway or cable must be sized not smaller than specified in Table 250.102(C)(1), based on the area of the largest ungrounded conductor of the derived system in the raceway or cable. In no case is the neutral conductor of the derived system permitted to be smaller than 1/0 AWG [310.10(H)].

Author's Comment:

- If the system bonding jumper is installed at the disconnect instead of at the source, a supply-side bonding jumper must connect the metal parts of the separately derived system to the neutral conductor at the disconnect [250.30(A)(2)].

(4) Grounding Electrode. Indoor separately derived systems must use the building or structure grounding electrode; outdoor separately derived systems must be grounded in accordance with 250.30(C). Figure 250–63

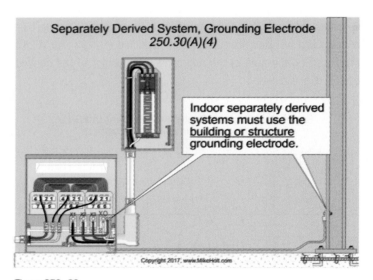

Figure 250–63

Note 1: Interior metal water piping in the area served by separately derived systems must be bonded to the separately derived system in accordance with 250.104(D).

Note 2: See 250.50 and 250.58 for requirements for bonding all electrodes together if located at the same building or structure.

(5) Grounding Electrode Conductor, Single Separately Derived System. The grounding electrode conductor for the separately derived system is sized in accordance with 250.66 and it must terminate to the grounding electrode in accordance with 250.30(A)(4).

The grounding electrode conductor is required to terminate to the neutral conductor at the same point on the separately derived system where the system bonding jumper is connected. Figure 250–64

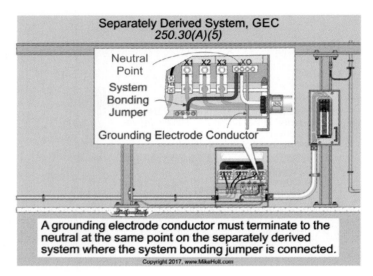

Figure 250–64

Author's Comment:

- System grounding helps reduce fires in buildings as well as voltage stress on electrical insulation, thereby ensuring longer insulation life for motors, transformers, and other system components. Figure 250–65

- To prevent objectionable neutral current from flowing [250.6] onto metal parts, the grounding electrode conductor must originate at the same point on the separately derived system where the system bonding jumper is connected [250.30(A)(1)].

Ex 1: If the system bonding jumper [250.30(A)(1)] is a wire or busbar, the grounding electrode conductor is permitted to terminate to the equipment grounding terminal, bar, or bus. Figure 250–66

Ex 3: Separately derived systems rated 1 kVA or less aren't required to be grounded (connected to the earth).

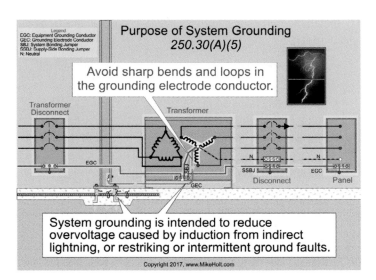

Figure 250–65

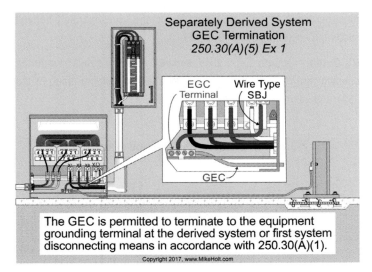

Figure 250–66

(6) Grounding Electrode Conductor, Multiple Separately Derived Systems. Where there are multiple separately derived systems, a grounding electrode conductor tap from each separately derived system to a common grounding electrode conductor is permitted. This connection is to be made at the same point on the separately derived system where the system bonding jumper is connected [250.30(A)(1)]. Figure 250–67

Ex 1: If the system bonding jumper is a wire or busbar, the grounding electrode conductor tap can terminate to either the neutral terminal or the equipment grounding terminal, bar, or bus in accordance with 250.30(A)(1).

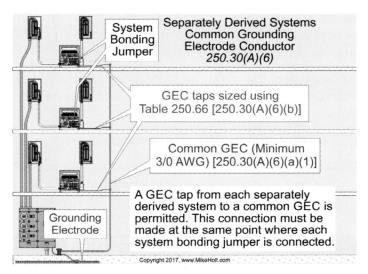

Figure 250–67

Ex 2: Separately derived systems rated 1 kVA or less aren't required to be grounded (connected to the earth).

(a) Common Grounding Electrode Conductor. The common grounding electrode conductor can be any of the following:

(1) A conductor not smaller than 3/0 AWG copper or 250 kcmil aluminum.

(2) Interior metal water pipe located not more than 5 ft from the point of entrance to the building [250.68(C)(1)].

(3) The metal frame of the building or structure that complies with 250.68(C)(2) or is connected to the grounding electrode system by a conductor not smaller than 3/0 AWG copper or 250 kcmil aluminum. Figure 250–68

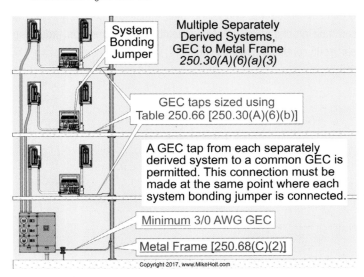

Figure 250–68

(b) Tap Conductor Size. Grounding electrode conductor taps must be sized in accordance with Table 250.66, based on the area of the largest ungrounded conductor of the given derived system.

(c) Connections. Tap connections to the common grounding electrode conductor must be made at an accessible location by any of the following methods:

(1) A connector listed as grounding and bonding equipment.

(2) Listed connections to aluminum or copper busbars not less than ¼ in. thick x 2 in. wide, and of sufficient length to accommodate the terminations necessary for the installation. Figure 250–69

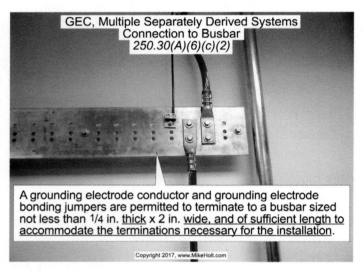

Figure 250–69

(3) Exothermic welding.

Grounding electrode conductor taps must be connected to the common grounding electrode conductor so the common grounding electrode conductor isn't spliced.

(7) Installation. The grounding electrode conductor must comply with the following:

- Be of copper where within 18 in. of the surface of the earth [250.64(A)].
- Be securely fastened to the surface on which it's carried [250.64(B)].
- Be adequately protected if exposed to physical damage [250.64(B)].
- Metal enclosures enclosing a grounding electrode conductor must be made electrically continuous from the point of attachment to cabinets or equipment to the grounding electrode [250.64(E)].

(8) Structural Steel and Metal Piping. To ensure dangerous voltage on metal parts from a ground fault is removed quickly, structural steel and metal piping in the area served by a separately derived system must be connected to the neutral conductor at the separately derived system in accordance with 250.104(D).

(C) Outdoor Source. Separately derived systems located outside the building must have the grounding electrode connection made at the separately derived system location. Figure 250–70

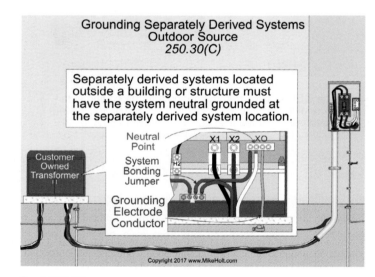

Figure 250–70

250.52 Grounding Electrode Types

Changes to this section clarified that structural metal is allowed to be an electrode and added a requirement prohibiting the use of swimming pool steel as an electrode.

Analysis

CLARIFIED

Structural Metal Electrode. Over the last several *Code* cycles changes have been made attempting to try to clearly indicate when the structural metal of a building is considered a grounding electrode. For years the *NEC* didn't really say anything at all, and it was just assumed by most that the structural metal was a grounding electrode.

The *Code* then clarified that the structural metal of a building can be used as a conductor, but it wasn't necessarily a grounding electrode, unless it's in the earth, or if we connected a wire to it from an object that is in the earth (like a water pipe or a concrete-encased electrode). This makes sense, since grounding electrodes are supposed to be in the earth, after all.

We've now come a full 180 degrees from where we started. The structural metal is now called "metal in-ground support structure(s)." The metal of a building isn't a grounding electrode unless it's actually in the earth for ten vertical feet, hence the name "metal in-ground support structure(s)."

Structural metal that isn't an electrode (because it isn't in the earth for ten feet) can still be used to interconnect electrodes [250.68(C)(2)], so when you get right down to it, this change is really a change to the language.

NEW

Swimming Pool Steel as Electrode. I have no idea why a person would use the rebar in a swimming pool as a grounding electrode, but if you were doing that, then you need to stop. It isn't allowed anymore!

250.52 Grounding Electrode Types

(A) Electrodes Permitted for Grounding.

(1) Underground Metal Water Pipe Electrode. Underground metal water pipe in direct contact with the earth for 10 ft or more can serve as a grounding electrode. Figure 250–71

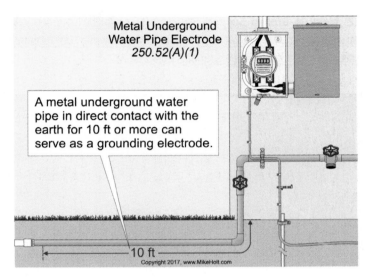

Figure 250–71

Author's Comment:

- Controversy about using metal underground water piping as a grounding electrode has existed since the early 1900s. The water industry believes that neutral current flowing on water piping corrodes the metal. For more information, contact the American Water Works Association about their report—*Effects of Electrical Grounding on Pipe Integrity and Shock Hazard*, Catalog No. 90702, 1.800.926.7337. Figure 250–72

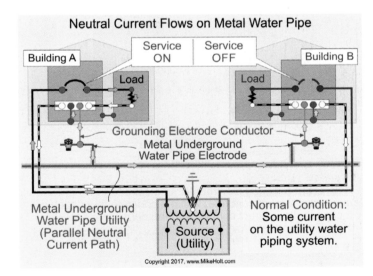

Figure 250–72

(2) Metal In-Ground Support Structure(s). Metal building support structure(s) in direct contact with the earth vertically for 10 ft or more can serve as a grounding electrode. Figure 250–73

Figure 250–73

Note: Metal in-ground support structures include, but aren't limited to, pilings, casings, and other structural metal.

(3) Concrete-Encased Electrode. Figure 250–74

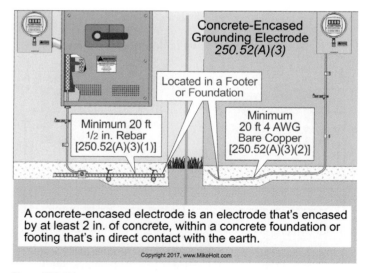

Figure 250–74

(1) One or more electrically conductive steel reinforcing bars of not less than ½ in. diameter, mechanically connected together by steel tie wires, or other effective means to create a 20 ft or greater length can serve as a grounding electrode. Figure 250–75

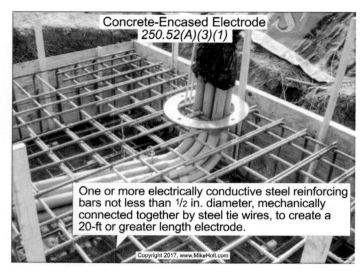

Figure 250–75

(2) Bare copper conductor not smaller than 4 AWG of 20 ft or greater length.

The reinforcing bars or bare copper conductor must be encased by at least 2 in. of concrete located horizontally within a concrete footing or vertically within a concrete foundation that's in direct contact with the earth can serve as a grounding electrode.

Where multiple concrete-encased electrodes are present at a building, only one is required to serve as a grounding electrode. Figure 250–76

Note: Concrete separated from the earth because of insulation, vapor barriers, or similar items isn't considered to be in direct contact with the earth. Figure 250–77

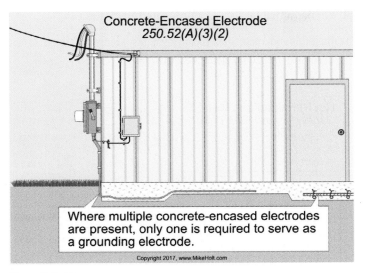

Figure 250–76

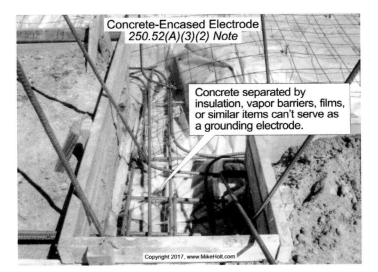

Figure 250–77

Author's Comment:

- The grounding electrode conductor to a concrete-encased grounding electrode isn't required to be larger than 4 AWG copper [250.66(B)].

- The concrete-encased grounding electrode is also called a "Ufer Ground," named after a consultant working for the U.S. Army during World War II. The technique Mr. Ufer came up with was necessary because the site needing grounding had no underground water table and little rainfall. The desert site was a series of bomb storage vaults in the area of Flagstaff, Arizona. This type of grounding electrode generally offers the lowest ground resistance for the cost.

(4) Ground Ring Electrode. A ground ring consisting of at least 20 ft of bare copper conductor not smaller than 2 AWG buried in the earth encircling a building, can serve as a grounding electrode. Figure 250–78

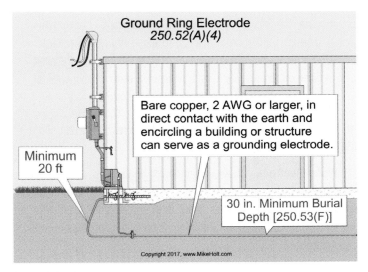

Figure 250–78

(5) Rod Electrode. Rod electrodes must have at less 8 ft in length in contact with the earth [250.53(G)].

(b) Rod-type electrodes must have a diameter of at least ⅝ in., unless listed. Figure 250–79

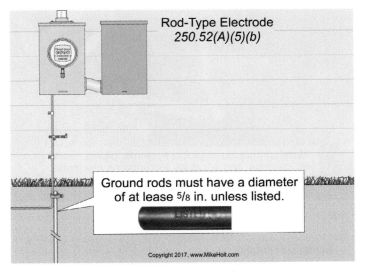

Figure 250–79

- The grounding electrode conductor, if it's the sole connection to the rod(s), isn't required to be larger than 6 AWG copper [250.66(A)].

- The diameter of a rod has an insignificant effect on the contact resistance of a rod(s) to the earth. However, larger diameter rods (¾ in. and 1 in.) are sometimes installed where mechanical strength is desired, or to compensate for the loss of the electrode's metal due to corrosion.

(6) Listed Electrode. Other listed grounding electrodes can serve as a grounding electrode.

(7) Plate Electrode. Bare or <u>electrically conductive</u> coated iron or steel plate with not less than ¼ in. of thickness, or a solid uncoated copper metal plate not less than 0.06 in. of thickness, with an exposed surface area of not less than 2 sq ft can serve as a grounding electrode.

(8) Metal Underground Systems. Metal underground systems, piping, and well casings can serve as a grounding electrode. Figure 250–80

Figure 250–80

- The grounding electrode conductor to the metal underground system must be sized in accordance with Table 250.66.

(B) Not Permitted for Use as a Grounding Electrode.

(1) Underground metal gas-piping systems aren't permitted to be used as a grounding electrode. Figure 250–81

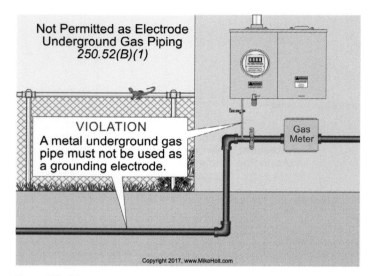

Figure 250–81

(2) Aluminum isn't permitted to be used as a grounding electrode.

(3) <u>Swimming pool reinforcing steel for equipotential bonding in accordance with 680.26(B)(1) and 680.26(B)(2) isn't permitted to be used as a grounding electrode.</u> Figure 250–82

Figure 250–82

(3) The service neutral conductor

(4) A nonflexible metal service raceway

(5) The service disconnect

Ex: A single rod electrode having a contact resistance to the earth of 25 ohms or less isn't required to have a supplemental electrode.
Figure 250–84

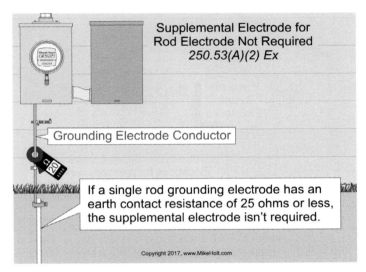

Figure 250–84

(3) Spacing. The supplemental electrode for a rod electrode must be installed not less than 6 ft from the rod electrode. Figure 250–85

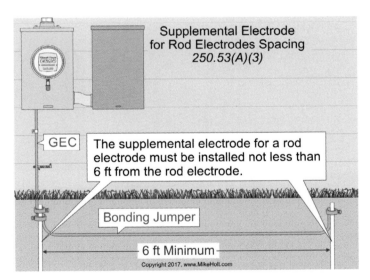

Figure 250–85

250.53 Grounding Electrode Installation Requirements

The installation requirements for ground ring electrodes were revised for consistency with other rules.

Analysis

EDITED

Instead of "burying" a ground ring, we now "install" a ground ring. Clear enough?

250.53 Grounding Electrode Installation Requirements

(A) Rod Electrodes.

(1) Below Permanent Moisture Level. If practicable, pipe electrodes must be embedded below the permanent moisture level and be free from nonconductive coatings such as paint or enamel.

(2) Supplemental Electrode. A rod electrode must be supplemented by an additional electrode that's bonded to: Figure 250–83

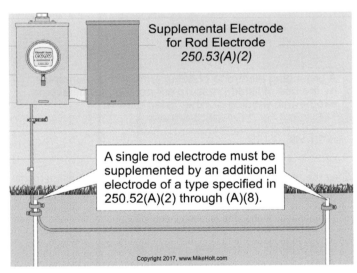

Figure 250–83

(1) Another rod electrode

(2) The grounding electrode conductor

(B) Electrode Spacing. Electrodes for premises systems must be located no closer than 6 ft from lightning protection system grounding electrodes. Two or more grounding electrodes that are bonded together are considered a single grounding electrode system. Figure 250–86

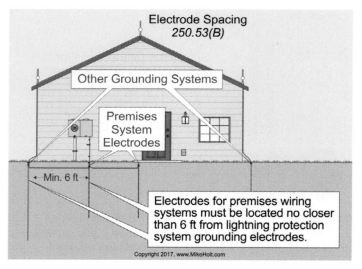

Figure 250–86

(C) Grounding Electrode Bonding Jumper. Grounding electrode bonding jumpers must be copper when within 18 in. of the earth [250.64(A)], be securely fastened to the surface, and be protected from physical damage [250.64(B)]. The bonding jumper to each electrode must be sized in accordance with 250.66. Figure 250–87

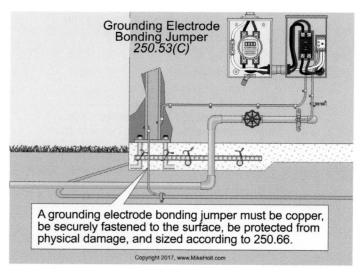

Figure 250–87

Author's Comment:

- The grounding electrode bonding jumpers must terminate by any of the following means in accordance with 250.8(A): Figure 250–88
  - ◆ Listed pressure connectors
  - ◆ Terminal bars
  - ◆ Pressure connectors listed as grounding and bonding equipment
  - ◆ Exothermic welding
  - ◆ Machine screw-type fasteners that engage not less than two threads or are secured with a nut
  - ◆ Thread-forming machine screws that engage not less than two threads in the enclosure
  - ◆ Connections that are part of a listed assembly
  - ◆ Other listed means

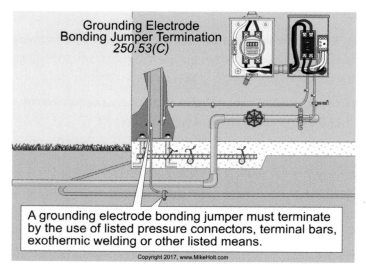

Figure 250–88

When the termination is encased in concrete or buried, the termination fittings must be listed for this purpose [250.70].

(D) Underground Metal Water Pipe Electrode.

(1) Interior Metal Water Piping. The bonding connection for the interior metal water piping system, as required by 250.104(A), isn't permitted to be dependent on water meters, filtering devices, or similar equipment likely to be disconnected for repairs or replacement. When necessary, a bonding jumper must be installed around insulated joints and equipment likely to be disconnected for repairs or replacement. Figure 250–89

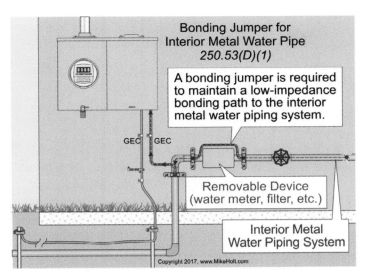

Figure 250–89

(2) Underground Metal Water Pipe Supplemental Electrode. When an underground metal water pipe grounding electrode is present, it must be used as part of the grounding electrode system [250.52(A)(1)], and it must be supplemented by any of the following electrodes:

- Metal frame of the building electrode [250.52(A)(2)]
- Concrete-encased electrode [250.52(A)(3)] Figure 250–90
- Rod electrode [250.52(A)(5)]
- Other listed electrode [250.52(A)(6)]
- Metal underground piping electrode [250.52(A)(8)]

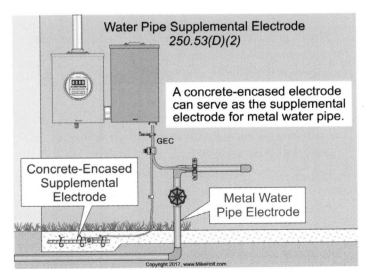

Figure 250–90

The supplemental grounding electrode conductor must terminate to any of the following: Figure 250–91

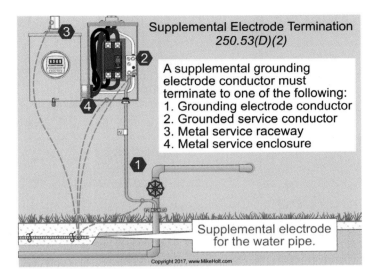

Figure 250–91

(1) Grounding electrode conductor

(2) Service neutral conductor

(3) Metal service raceway

(4) Service equipment enclosure

Ex: The supplemental electrode can be bonded to interior metal water piping located not more than 5 ft from the point of entrance to the building [250.68(C)(1)].

(E) Supplemental Rod Electrode. The grounding electrode conductor to a rod(s) that serves as a supplemental electrode isn't required to be larger than 6 AWG copper.

(F) Ground Ring. A bare 2 AWG or larger copper conductor <u>installed</u> not less than 30 in. <u>below the surface of the earth</u> encircling the building [250.52(A)(4)]. Figure 250–92

(G) Rod Electrodes. Rod electrodes must be installed so that not less than 8 ft of length is in contact with the soil. If rock bottom is encountered, the rod must be driven at an angle not to exceed 45 degrees from vertical. If rock bottom is encountered at an angle up to 45 degrees from vertical, the rod can be buried in a minimum 30 in. below the surface of the earth. Figure 250–93

The upper end of the rod must be flush with or underground unless the grounding electrode conductor attachment is protected against physical damage as specified in 250.10.

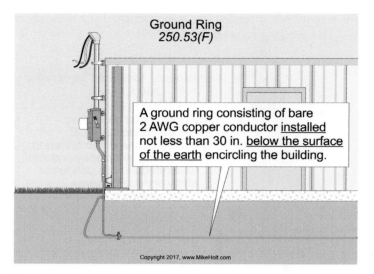

Figure 250–92

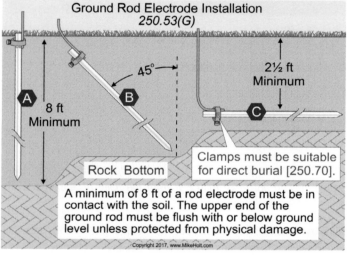

Figure 250–93

Author's Comment:

■ When the grounding electrode attachment fitting is located underground, it must be listed for direct soil burial [250.68(A) Ex 1 and 250.70].

Measuring the Ground Resistance

A ground resistance clamp meter, or a three-point fall of potential ground resistance meter, can be used to measure the contact resistance of a grounding electrode to the earth.

Ground Clamp Meter. The ground resistance clamp meter measures the contact resistance of the grounding electrode system to the earth by injecting a high-frequency signal via the service neutral conductor to the electric utility grounding connection, and then measuring the strength of the return signal through the earth to the grounding electrode being measured. Figure 250–94

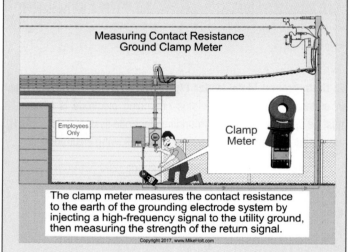

Figure 250–94

Fall of Potential Ground Resistance Meter. The three-point fall of potential ground resistance meter determines the contact resistance of a single grounding electrode to the earth by using Ohm's Law: R=E/I. Figure 250–95

This meter divides the voltage difference between the electrode to be measured and a driven voltage test stake (P) by the current flowing between the electrode to be measured and a driven current test stake (C). The test stakes are typically made of ¼ in. diameter steel rods, 24 in. long, driven two-thirds of their length into the earth.

The distance and alignment between the voltage and current test stakes, and the electrode, is extremely important to the validity of the earth contact resistance measurements. For an 8-ft rod, the accepted practice is to space the current test stake (C) 80 ft from the electrode to be measured.

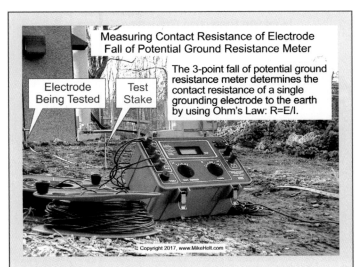

Figure 250–95

The voltage test stake (P) is positioned in a straight line between the electrode to be measured and the current test stake (C). The voltage test stake should be located at approximately 62 percent of the distance the current test stake is located from the electrode. Since the current test stake (C) for an 8-ft rod is located 80 ft from the grounding electrode, the voltage test stake (P) will be about 50 ft from the electrode to be measured.

Example: *If the voltage between the rod and the voltage test stake (P) is 3V and the current between the rod and the current test stake (C) is 0.20A, what will be the earth contact resistance of the electrode to the earth? Figure 250–96*

Solution: *The earth contact resistance of the electrode to the earth will be 15 ohms.*

Resistance = Voltage/Current
E (Voltage) = 3V
I (Current) = 0.20A

R = E/I
Resistance = 3V/0.20A
Resistance = 15 ohms

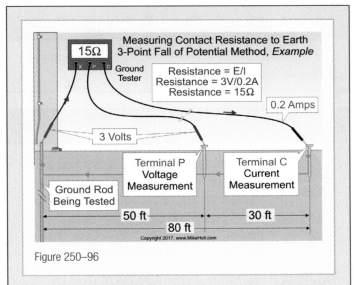

Figure 250–96

Author's Comment:

■ The three-point fall of potential meter should only be used to measure the contact resistance of one electrode to the earth at a time, and this electrode must be independent and not connected to any part of the electrical system. The contact resistance of two electrodes bonded together must not be measured until they've been separated. The contact resistance of two separate electrodes to the earth can be thought of as two resistors in parallel, if they're outside each other's sphere of influence.

Soil Resistivity

The earth's ground resistance is directly impacted by soil resistivity, which varies throughout the world. Soil resistivity is influenced by electrolytes, which consist of moisture, minerals, and dissolved salts. Because soil resistivity changes with moisture content, the resistance of any grounding system varies with the seasons of the year. Since moisture is stable at greater distances below the surface of the earth, grounding systems are generally more effective if the grounding electrode can reach the water table. In addition, placing the grounding electrode below the frost line helps to ensure less deviation in the system's contact resistance to the earth year round.

The contact resistance to the earth can be lowered by chemically treating the earth around the grounding electrodes with electrolytes designed for this purpose.

250.60 Lightning Protection Electrode

The Informational Notes regarding lightning protection electrodes were both revised.

Analysis

CLARIFIED Although lightning protection systems aren't within the scope of the *NEC*, when they are installed it's a good practice to do so in accordance with NFPA 780, the *Standard for the Installation of Lightning Protection Systems*. NFPA 70E includes requirements such as bonding and separation of lighting protection components from premises wiring equipment.

Note 1 revisions clarify that there could be rules for all sorts of lightning protection equipment, and not just strike termination devices (formerly known as "air terminals" or "lightning rods").

Note 2 was revised to clarify that the potential difference discussed in Note 2 relates to voltage. Perhaps by calling them "potential differences," as was done in previous *Code* versions, people were thinking that the differences were differences of opinion and not voltage. I'm really not sure…

250.60 Lightning Protection Electrode

A lightning protection system installed in accordance with NFPA 780 is intended to protect the structure from lighting damage. Figure 250–97

The lightning protection electrode isn't permitted to be used for the building or structure grounding electrode system required for service equipment [250.24] and remote building feeder disconnecting means [250.32(A)]. Figure 250–98

Note 1: See 250.106 for the bonding requirements of the lightning protection system to the building or structure grounding electrode system.

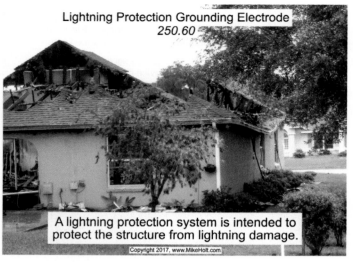

A lightning protection system is intended to protect the structure from lightning damage.

Figure 250–97

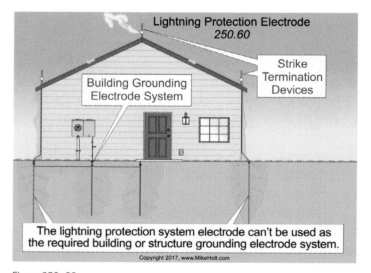

The lightning protection system electrode can't be used as the required building or structure grounding electrode system.

Figure 250–98

Note 2: If a lightning protection system is installed, the lightning protection system must be bonded to the building grounding electrode system so as to limit voltage differences between it and the electrical system wiring in accordance with 250.106. Figure 250–99

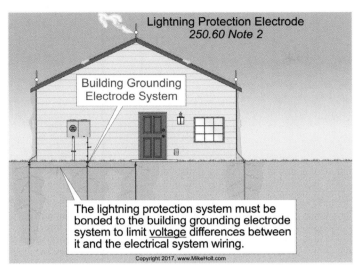

Figure 250–99

250.64 Grounding Electrode Conductor Installation

This section was revised into a list format to make it easier to use.

Analysis

CLARIFIED This *Code* cycle the Code Making Panels have made an effort, throughout all of *NEC*, to improve its ease of usage, and this section is no exception. The requirements were reorganized into a list so they're easier to read and understand.

250.64 Grounding Electrode Conductor Installation

Grounding electrode conductors must be installed as specified in (A) through (F).

(A) Aluminum Conductors. Bare or covered aluminum grounding electrode conductors aren't permitted to be in contact with masonry, the earth, or subject to corrosive conditions. Where used outside, aluminum grounding electrode conductors aren't permitted within 18 in. of the earth.

(B) Conductor Protection. Where exposed, a grounding electrode conductor or its enclosure must be securely fastened to the surface on which it's carried.

(1) Not Exposed to Physical Damage. Grounding electrode conductors 6 AWG and larger can be installed exposed along the surface of the building if securely fastened and <u>not</u> exposed to physical <u>damage</u>. Figure 250–100

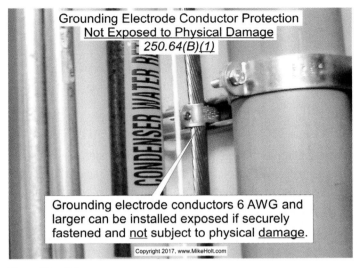

Figure 250–100

(2) Exposed to Physical Damage. Grounding electrode conductors 6 AWG and larger subject to physical damage must be installed in rigid metal conduit, intermediate metal conduit, rigid polyvinyl chloride conduit, <u>Type XW</u> reinforced thermosetting resin conduit (RTRC-XW), electrical metallic tubing, or cable armor. Figure 250–101

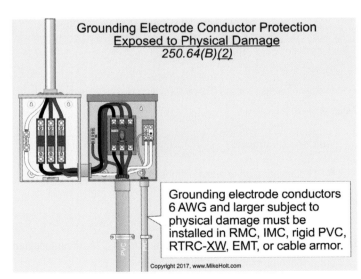

Figure 250–101

(3) Smaller than 6 AWG. Grounding electrode conductors sized 8 AWG must be protected by installing them in rigid metal conduit, intermediate metal conduit, PVC conduit, electrical metallic tubing, Type XW reinforced thermosetting resin conduit (RTRC-XW), or cable armor.

Author's Comment:

■ A ferrous metal raceway containing a grounding electrode conductor must be made electrically continuous by bonding each end of the raceway to the grounding electrode conductor [250.64(E)], so it's best to use nonmetallic conduit.

(4) In Contact with the Earth. Grounding electrode conductors and bonding jumpers in contact with the earth aren't required to comply with the cover requirements of 300.5, <u>but must be protected if subject to physical damage.</u> Figure 250–102

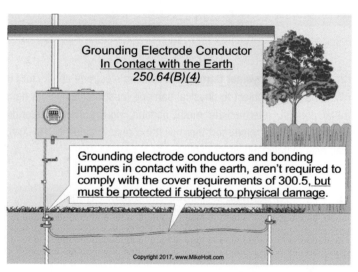

Figure 250–102

Author's Comment:

■ Grounding and bonding fittings must be protected from physical damage by enclosing the fittings in metal, wood, or an equivalent protective covering [250.10].

(C) Continuous. Grounding electrode conductor(s) must be installed without a splice or joint except by: Figure 250–103

(1) Irreversible compression-type connectors or exothermic welding.

(2) Busbars connected together.

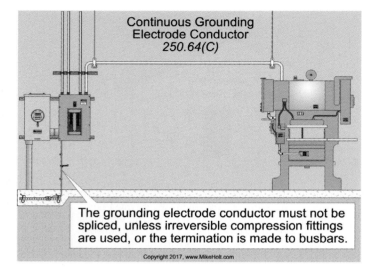

Figure 250–103

(3) Bolted, riveted, or welded connections of structural metal frames of buildings.

(4) Threaded, welded, brazed, soldered, or bolted-flange connections of metal water piping.

(D) Grounding Electrode Conductor for Multiple Building or Structure Disconnects. <u>If a building or structure contains</u> two or more building disconnects in separate enclosures, the grounding electrode connections must be made in any of the following methods:

(1) Common Grounding Electrode Conductor and Taps. A grounding electrode conductor tap must extend to the inside of each disconnect enclosure.

The common grounding electrode conductor must be sized in accordance with 250.66, based on the sum of the circular mil area of the largest ungrounded conductor supplying the equipment. Figure 250–104

A grounding electrode conductor must extend from each disconnect, sized no smaller than specified in Table 250.66, based on the area of the largest ungrounded conductor for each disconnect.

The grounding electrode tap conductors must be connected to the common grounding electrode conductor, without splicing the common grounding electrode conductor, by any of the following methods:

(1) Exothermic welding.

(2) Connectors listed as grounding and bonding equipment.

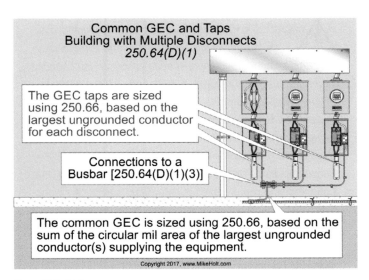

Figure 250–104

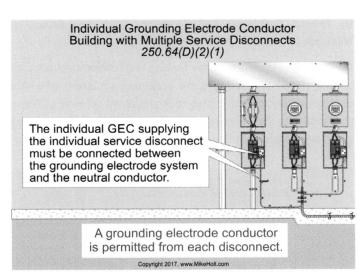

Figure 250–106

(3) Connections to a busbar of sufficient length and not less than ¼ in. thick × 2 in. wide that's securely fastened and installed in an accessible location. Figure 250–105

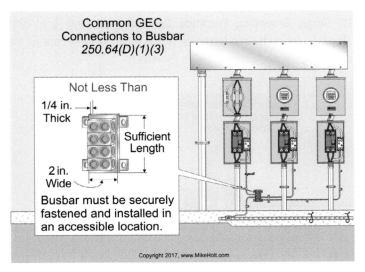

Figure 250–105

(2) Individual Grounding Electrode Conductors. A grounding electrode conductor, sized in accordance with 250.66 based on the ungrounded conductor(s) supplying the individual disconnect, must be connected between the grounding electrode system and one or more of the following:

(1) The service neutral conductor Figure 250–106

(2) The equipment grounding conductor of the feeder circuit

(3) The supply-side bonding jumper

(3) Common Grounding Electrode Conductor Location. A grounding electrode conductor can be connected from an accessible enclosure on the supply side of the disconnect to one or more of the following locations:

(1) The service neutral conductor Figure 250–107

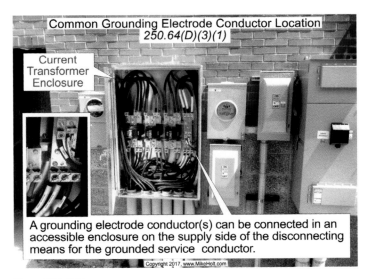

Figure 250–107

(2) The equipment grounding conductor of the feeder circuit

(3) The supply-side bonding jumper

(E) Ferrous Enclosures and Raceways Containing Grounding Electrode Conductor.

(1) General. To prevent inductive choking of grounding electrode conductors, metal steel raceways and enclosures containing grounding electrode conductors must have each end of the raceway or enclosure bonded to the grounding electrode conductor <u>so as to create an electrically parallel path.</u> Figure 250–108

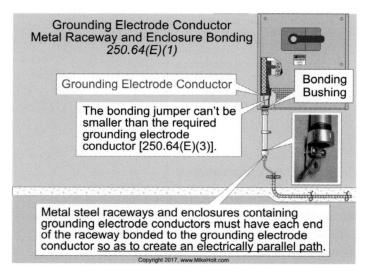

Figure 250–108

(2) Methods. Bonding must be done by one of the methods discussed in 250.92(B)(2) through (B)(4).

(3) Size. Bonding jumpers must be the same size or larger than the required size of the grounding electrode conductor in the raceway or other enclosure.

Author's Comment:

- Nonferrous metal raceways, such as aluminum rigid metal conduit, enclosing the grounding electrode conductor aren't required to meet the "bonding each end of the raceway to the grounding electrode conductor" provisions of this section.

CAUTION: *The effectiveness of a grounding electrode is significantly reduced if a ferrous metal raceway containing a grounding electrode conductor isn't bonded to the ferrous metal raceway at both ends. This is because a single conductor carrying high-frequency induced lightning current in a ferrous raceway causes the raceway to act as an inductor, which severely limits (chokes) the current flow through the grounding electrode conductor. ANSI/IEEE 142— Recommended Practice for Grounding of Industrial and Commercial Power Systems (Green Book) states: "An inductive choke can reduce the current flow by 97 percent."*

Author's Comment:

- To save a lot of time and effort, install the grounding electrode conductor exposed if it's not subject to physical damage [250.64(B)], or enclose it in nonmetallic conduit suitable for the application [352.10(F)].

(F) Termination to Grounding Electrode.

(1) Single Grounding Electrode Conductor. A single grounding electrode conductor can terminate to any grounding electrode of the grounding electrode system. Figure 250–109

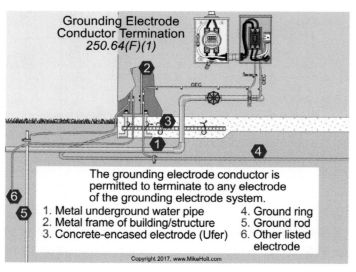

Figure 250–109

(2) Multiple Grounding Electrode Conductors. When multiple grounding electrode conductors are installed [250.64(D)(2)], each grounding electrode conductor can terminate to any grounding electrode of the grounding electrode system. Figure 250–110

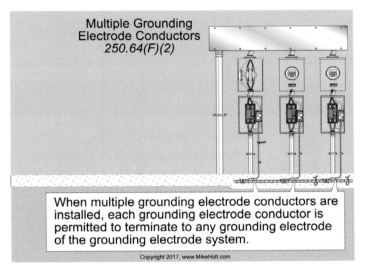

When multiple grounding electrode conductors are installed, each grounding electrode conductor is permitted to terminate to any grounding electrode of the grounding electrode system.

Figure 250–110

(3) Termination to Busbar. Grounding electrode conductors and grounding electrode bonding jumpers are permitted to terminate to a busbar not less than ¼ in. thick x 2 in. wide, and of sufficient length to accommodate the terminations necessary for the installation. The busbar must be securely fastened and be installed an accessible location. Figure 250–111

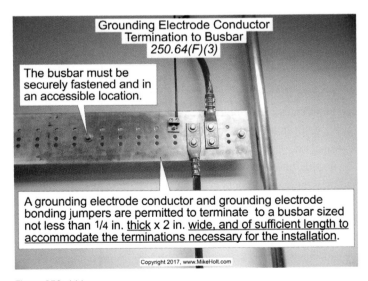

Grounding Electrode Conductor Termination to Busbar 250.64(F)(3)

The busbar must be securely fastened and in an accessible location.

A grounding electrode conductor and grounding electrode bonding jumpers are permitted to terminate to a busbar sized not less than 1/4 in. thick x 2 in. wide, and of sufficient length to accommodate the terminations necessary for the installation.

Figure 250–111

250.66 Sizing Grounding Electrode Conductor

The text of "sole connection" for rods, pipes, rings, and concrete-encased electrodes was clarified.

Analysis

CLARIFIED Although many people don't read the rules in 250.66, they allow for smaller grounding electrode conductors for driven rods, concrete-encased electrodes, and ground rings than those in Table 250.66.

These smaller grounding electrode conductors, as compared to Table 250.66, can only be used when the grounding electrode conductor is the "sole connection" to these electrodes.

What exactly does "sole connection" mean? In this edition of the *Code* we won't be asking this question any longer because that language was replaced. We can use the smaller grounding electrode conductors if they don't also connect to an electrode requiring a larger grounding electrode conductor.

This was the intent all along, and you could easily argue that the *NEC* was already clear on this, but now it's even more so, and that's always worth the effort.

250.66 Sizing Grounding Electrode Conductor

Except as permitted in (A) through (C), the grounding electrode conductor must be sized in accordance with Table 250.66.

(A) Rod. If the grounding electrode conductor or bonding jumper connects to one or more ground rods [250.52(A)(5)] and doesn't connect to another type of electrode that requires a larger conductor, the grounding electrode conductor isn't required to be larger than 6 AWG copper. Figure 250–112

(B) Concrete-Encased Grounding Electrode. If the grounding electrode conductor or bonding jumper is connected to one or more concrete-encased electrodes [250.52(A)(3)] and doesn't connect to another type of electrode that requires a larger size conductor, the grounding electrode conductor isn't required to be larger than 4 AWG copper. Figure 250–113

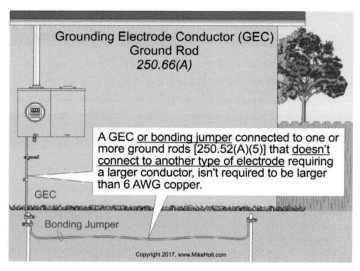

Grounding Electrode Conductor (GEC)
Ground Rod
250.66(A)

A GEC <u>or bonding jumper</u> connected to one or more ground rods [250.52(A)(5)] that <u>doesn't connect to another type of electrode</u> requiring a larger conductor, isn't required to be larger than 6 AWG copper.

GEC

Bonding Jumper

Copyright 2017, www.MikeHolt.com

Figure 250–112

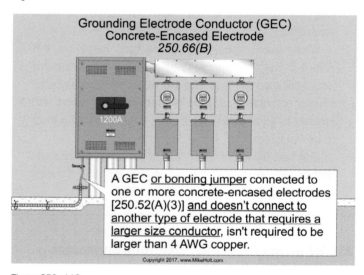

Grounding Electrode Conductor (GEC)
Concrete-Encased Electrode
250.66(B)

1200A

A GEC <u>or bonding jumper</u> connected to one or more concrete-encased electrodes [250.52(A)(3)] <u>and doesn't connect to another type of electrode that requires a larger size conductor,</u> isn't required to be larger than 4 AWG copper.

Copyright 2017, www.MikeHolt.com

Figure 250–113

Table 250.66 Sizing Grounding Electrode Conductor

Conductor or Area of Parallel Conductors	Copper Grounding Electrode Conductor
12 through 2 AWG	8 AWG
1 or 1/0 AWG	6 AWG
2/0 or 3/0 AWG	4 AWG
Over 3/0 through 350 kcmil	2 AWG
Over 350 through 600 kcmil	1/0 AWG
Over 600 through 1,100 kcmil	2/0 AWG
Over 1,100 kcmil	3/0 AWG

250.68 Termination to the Grounding Electrode

Requirements were clarified for a grounding electrode conductor connection to a metal underground water pipe, building steel that's a grounding electrode conductor, and rebar electrodes that extend vertically through a slab.

Analysis

CLARIFIED

Underground Metal Water Pipe. The 2017 *Code* has cleared up what we all thought was a requirement in the 2014 *NEC*. For quite some time now we've had to connect to the underground metal piping system for grounding the electrical equipment. Because of the very real concern of interior metal piping being replaced with nonmetallic varieties, the *Code* has required that we make the grounding electrode connection within five ft of where the metal underground water pipe enters the building. This makes a lot of sense and has merit, as we're seeing less and less copper, and more and more plastics.

Search through the previous editions of the *NEC* and you'll have a hard time finding this rule; it was accidentally changed to permissive language during some of the (rather extensive) editing of this section in the past. The issue is resolved now by making it mandatory text once again.

CLARIFIED

Building Steel. As was discussed in 250.52(A) (2), the structural metal of a building isn't always a grounding electrode. In fact, it seldom is. We can use it as a conductor, however, and it makes a great one with all of the cross-sectional area that it has.

If we connect the structural metal to a concrete-encased electrode it doesn't magically become an electrode (it still doesn't have ten ft of steel vertically in the earth), but it can now be used to connect, say, the underground water pipe to the concrete-encased electrode. How do we connect the concrete-encased electrode to the metal? We do so by connecting the bolts for the metal that are in the footings to the rebar (concrete-encased electrode) in the footings. On the other hand, we could just run a piece of wire and call it done, but that might prove too easy!

CLARIFIED

Rebar Electrode. The practice of continuing a piece of rebar vertically through the top of a foundation wall and connecting a grounding electrode conductor to it isn't new. It's been done for decades, and proven effective. In the 2014 *Code* it was made clear that this practice is acceptable. In 2017, it's also being made clear that this is only permitted if the exposed rebar isn't subject to corrosion and if it doesn't make contact with the earth, as that would cause corrosion.

250.68 Termination to the Grounding Electrode

(A) Accessibility. The mechanical elements used to terminate a grounding electrode conductor or bonding jumper to a grounding electrode must be accessible. Figure 250–114

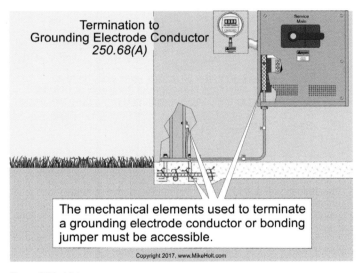

Figure 250–114

Ex 1: The termination isn't required to be accessible if the termination to the electrode is encased in concrete or buried in the earth. Figure 250–115

Author's Comment:

■ If the grounding electrode attachment fitting is encased in concrete or buried in the earth, it must be listed for direct soil burial or concrete encasement [250.70].

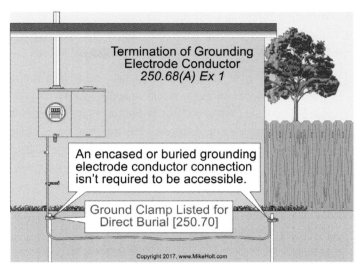

Figure 250–115

Ex 2: Exothermic or irreversible compression connections, together with the mechanical means used to attach to fireproofed structural metal, aren't required to be accessible.

(B) Integrity of Underground Metal Water Pipe Electrode. A bonding jumper must be installed around insulated joints and equipment likely to be disconnected for repairs or replacement for an underground metal water piping system used as a grounding electrode. The bonding jumper must be of sufficient length to allow the removal of such equipment while retaining the integrity of the grounding path. Figure 250–116

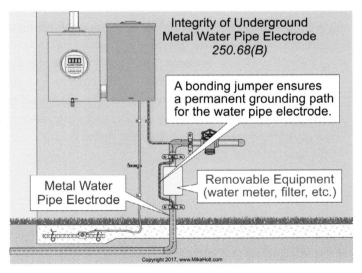

Figure 250–116

(C) Grounding Electrode Conductor Connections. Grounding electrode conductors and bonding jumpers are permitted to terminate and use the following to extend the connection to another electrode(s):

(1) Interior metal water piping that's electrically continuous with a metal underground water pipe electrode and is located not more than 5 ft from the point of entrance to the building can be used to extend the connection to electrodes. Interior metal water piping located more than 5 ft from the point of entrance to the building isn't permitted to be used as a conductor to interconnect electrodes of the grounding electrode system. Figure 250–117

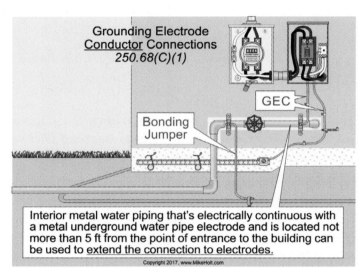

Figure 250–117

(2) The metal structural frame of a building can be used as a conductor to interconnect electrodes, or as a grounding electrode conductor. Hold-down bolts securing the structural steel column to a concrete-encased electrode [250.52(A)(3)] can connect the metal structural frame of a building to the concrete-encased grounding electrode. The hold-down bolts must be connected to the concrete-encased electrode by welding, exothermic welding, the usual steel tie wires, or other approved means. Figure 250–118 and Figure 250–119

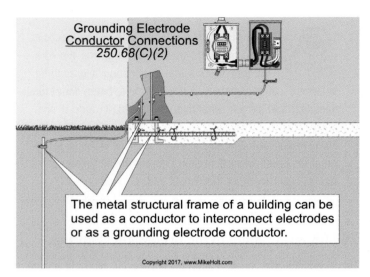

Figure 250–118

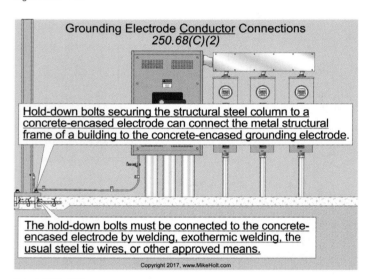

Figure 250–119

(3) A rebar-type concrete-encased electrode [250.52(A)(3)] with an additional rebar section to an accessible location above the concrete, where not in contact with the earth or subject to corrosion, can be used for the connection of the grounding electrode conductors and bonding jumpers. Figure 250–120

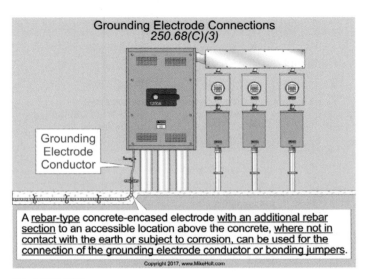

Grounding Electrode Connections
250.68(C)(3)

Grounding Electrode Conductor

A rebar-type concrete-encased electrode with an additional rebar section to an accessible location above the concrete, where not in contact with the earth or subject to corrosion, can be used for the connection of the grounding electrode conductor or bonding jumpers.

Copyright 2017, www.MikeHolt.com

Figure 250–120

250.80 Service Raceways and Enclosures

The items that aren't required to be bonded in underground service raceways have been expanded.

Analysis

CLARIFIED Connecting isolated metal electrical components is one of the most important safety requirements in the entire *Code* book. Section 250.4(A)(3) and perhaps even 300.10 say it best; you need to able to read continuity between any two metal objects in which there are conductors. This is a simple statement, but it's critically important.

You should be able to read continuity between the metal parts of any luminaire to the grounding terminal of any receptacle in a building, or any metal part of the electrical system. By doing so, you're satisfying the real goal; ensuring a low-impedance path of continuity between all metal electrical parts to the power supply—typically the utility neutral.

There are some exceptions; Ex 1 to 300.10 says that a short sleeve of metal raceway that's just protecting a cable like Type NM from physical damage doesn't need to be bonded to the electrical system. This makes sense, as the likelihood of a raceway that short becoming energized is quite small.

Another object that doesn't require connection to the electrical system is a metal elbow buried 18 in. deep in an underground installation of a nonmetallic raceway containing service conductors. If that elbow was to become energized due to a ground fault (which is highly unlikely to begin with), there would be very little risk of electrical shock due to its burial depth, and there would be no risk of fire.

Changes in the 2017 *NEC* now address other underground components that have 18 in. of cover. This might include a rigid coupling, for example, as the risk is no greater with a coupling than it is with a metal elbow.

250.80 Service Raceways and Enclosures

Metal enclosures and raceways containing service conductors must be bonded to the neutral conductor at service equipment if the electrical system is grounded, or to the grounding electrode conductor for electrical systems that aren't grounded.

Ex: Metal components installed in a run of an underground nonmetallic raceway having a minimum cover of 18 in. isn't required to be bonded to the service neutral, supply-side bonding jumper, or grounding electrode conductor. Figure 250–121

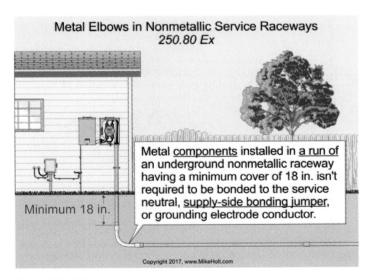

Metal Elbows in Nonmetallic Service Raceways
250.80 Ex

Minimum 18 in.

Metal components installed in a run of an underground nonmetallic raceway having a minimum cover of 18 in. isn't required to be bonded to the service neutral, supply-side bonding jumper, or grounding electrode conductor.

Copyright 2017, www.MikeHolt.com

Figure 250–121

250.86 Other Enclosures

The items that aren't required to be bonded in underground raceways containing branch circuits and feeders have been expanded beyond just metal elbows.

Analysis

EXPANDED It seems there was a question about which small metal parts installed as part of a nonmetallic raceway system needed to be bonded. Metal elbows were previously an exception to this requirement as long as they were isolated from possible contact by a minimum cover of 18 in. The exception has been expanded to any small metal components that are isolated from possible contact—not just elbows.

250.86 Other Enclosures

Metal raceways and enclosures containing electrical conductors operating at 50V or more [250.20(A)] must be connected to the circuit equipment grounding conductor. Figure 250–122

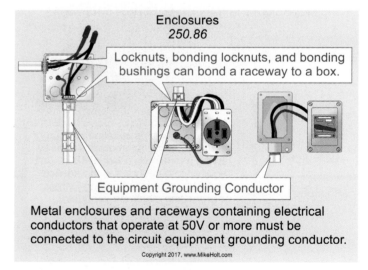

Enclosures
250.86

Locknuts, bonding locknuts, and bonding bushings can bond a raceway to a box.

Equipment Grounding Conductor

Metal enclosures and raceways containing electrical conductors that operate at 50V or more must be connected to the circuit equipment grounding conductor.

Copyright 2017, www.MikeHolt.com

Figure 250–122

Ex 2: Short sections of metal raceways used for the support or physical protection of cables aren't required to be connected to the circuit equipment grounding conductor. Figure 250–123

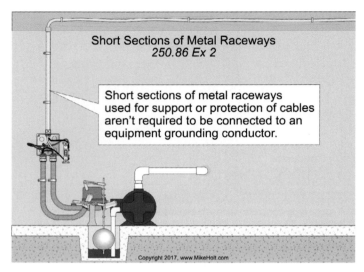

Short Sections of Metal Raceways
250.86 Ex 2

Short sections of metal raceways used for support or protection of cables aren't required to be connected to an equipment grounding conductor.

Copyright 2017, www.MikeHolt.com

Figure 250–123

Ex 3: *Metal components* aren't required to be connected to the circuit equipment grounding conductor *or supply-side bonding jumper where either of the following conditions exist*:

(1) *The metal components are* installed in a run of an underground nonmetallic raceway *and isolated* from possible contact by a minimum cover of 18 in. to any part of the metal components. Figure 250–124

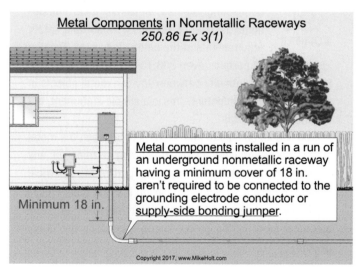

Metal Components in Nonmetallic Raceways
250.86 Ex 3(1)

Minimum 18 in.

Metal components installed in a run of an underground nonmetallic raceway having a minimum cover of 18 in. aren't required to be connected to the grounding electrode conductor or supply-side bonding jumper.

Copyright 2017, www.MikeHolt.com

Figure 250–124

(2) *The metal components are part of an installation of nonmetallic raceway(s) and are isolated from possible contact to any part of the metal components by being* enclosed in not less than 2 in. of concrete.

250.94 Bonding for Communications Systems

The title of this section was revised, options for bonding communications systems to the electrical system were clarified, and an exception for buildings or structures unlikely to need communications systems and a note addressing "electrical noise" were added.

Analysis

CLARIFIED
Communications systems need to be electrically connected together and to the premises wiring system. For twisted pair circuits see 800.100, antennas see 810.21, and coaxial cables see 820.100.

Oftentimes it's the satellite or cable TV installer who makes this bonding connection, and we obviously can't expect them to open and work on an energized panel to connect the metal parts of their system to premises wiring.

Several *Code* cycles ago this rule only required an exposed, nonflexible metallic service conductor raceway for bonding purposes. The communications contractors bonded their systems to the electrical system by installing a bonding conductor to a bonding strap, which is listed for indoor locations only, onto the service raceway. Since metal service raceways for underground services are becoming extinct, the 2008 *NEC* required terminals for this application and called them an "intersystem bonding termination."

In some commercial installations, a busbar is commonly used to bond communications and premises systems together. Since there's no safety reason not to allow a busbar for bonding purposes, it's recognized as a permitted option in the 2017 *NEC*.

NEW
A new exception to the communications bonding rule addresses buildings or structures supplied with electricity that are unlikely to need any communications systems. A chicken coop or a detached storage building come to mind immediately, although stand-alone equipment like a temporary power pedestal is less obvious but equally deserving of this allowance.

NEW
A new Informational Note alerts the *Code* user that "electrical noise" can be reduced on communications systems by bonding all communications systems to the premises system via an intersystem bonding termination. The term "electrical noise" isn't defined, and there are plenty of people who would argue that using an intersystem bonding termination actually adds "noise," so it's still a bit unclear about how valuable this note will prove to be.

250.94 Bonding <u>Communications</u> Systems

Where communications systems (twisted wire, antennas, and coaxial cable) are likely to be used in a building or structure, <u>communications system bonding terminations must be provided in accordance with (A) or (B)</u> at service equipment or building disconnects supplied by a feeder.

(A) Intersystem Bonding Termination Device. Where an intersystem bonding termination device is required, it must meet the following requirements:

(1) Be accessible for connection and inspection. Figure 250–125

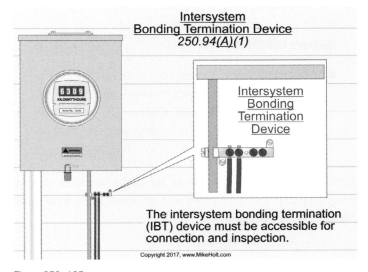

Figure 250–125

(2) Have a capacity for connection of at least three intersystem bonding conductors.

(3) Installed so that it doesn't interfere with opening any enclosure.

(4) Be securely mounted and electrically connected to the service equipment or meter enclosure, or grounding electrode conductor with a minimum 6 AWG copper conductor. Figure 250–126

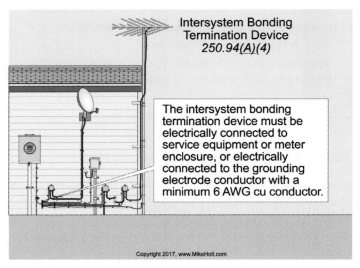

The intersystem bonding termination device must be electrically connected to service equipment or meter enclosure, or electrically connected to the grounding electrode conductor with a minimum 6 AWG cu conductor.

Figure 250–126

(5) Be securely mounted and electrically connected to the building's disconnect, or grounding electrode conductor with a minimum 6 AWG copper conductor.

(6) The terminals are listed as grounding and bonding equipment.

Author's Comment:

■ According to Article 100, an intersystem bonding termination is a device that provides a means to connect communications systems (twisted wire, antennas, and coaxial cable) bonding conductors to the building grounding electrode system.

Ex: At existing buildings, an external accessible means for bonding communications systems (twisted wire, antennas, and coaxial cable) together can be by the use of a:

(1) Nonflexible metallic raceway,

(2) Grounding electrode conductor, or

(3) Connection approved by the authority having jurisdiction.

Note 2: Communications systems (twisted wire, antennas, and coaxial cable) must be bonded to the intersystem bonding termination in accordance with the following requirements: Figure 250–127

- Antennas/Satellite Dishes, 810.15 and 810.21
- Coaxial Circuits, 820.100
- Telephone Circuits, 800.100

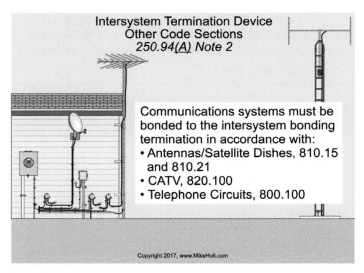

Communications systems must be bonded to the intersystem bonding termination in accordance with:
• Antennas/Satellite Dishes, 810.15 and 810.21
• CATV, 820.100
• Telephone Circuits, 800.100

Figure 250–127

Author's Comment:

■ External communications systems (twisted wire, antennas, and coaxial cable) must be connected to the intersystem bonding termination to minimize the damage to them from induced voltage differences between the systems from a lightning event. Figure 250–128

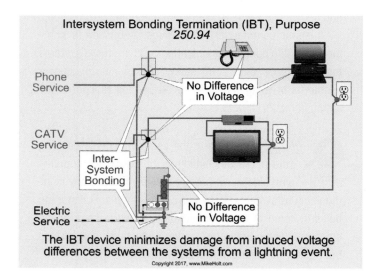

The IBT device minimizes damage from induced voltage differences between the systems from a lightning event.

Figure 250–128

(B) Other Means. A busbar securely fastened at an accessible location sized not less than ¼ in. thick × 2 in. wide, and of sufficient length to accommodate at least three terminations for communications systems in addition to other connections. Figure 250–129

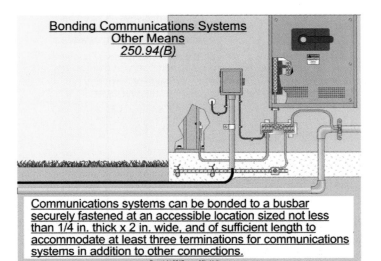

Bonding Communications Systems
Other Means
250.94(B)

Communications systems can be bonded to a busbar securely fastened at an accessible location sized not less than 1/4 in. thick x 2 in. wide, and of sufficient length to accommodate at least three terminations for communications systems in addition to other connections.

Copyright 2017, www.MikeHolt.com

Figure 250–129

Ex to (A) and (B): An intersystem bonding termination device isn't required where communications systems (twisted wire, antennas, and coaxial cable) aren't likely to be used.

250.102 Grounded Conductor, Bonding Conductors, and Jumpers

The title was revised for accuracy, the allowance of aluminum as a bonding conductor was clarified, and the titles of 250.102 250.102(C)(2) were revised.

Analysis

EDITED Because this section is referenced by numerous requirements in the *Code*, its title was edited to clearly include the "grounded" or neutral conductors.

For example, a 400A service that only feeds three-phase motors and one lighting circuit might only need a 12 AWG neutral conductor for the unbalanced load [220.61]; but 250.24(C) refers us to Table 250.102(C)(1) to size the grounded/neutral conductor to carry the fault current.

Aluminum Bonding Conductor. Section 250.102(A) tells us that the types of materials **CLARIFIED** permitted for an equipment bonding jumper are copper or other corrosion-resistant material. Contrary to popular belief, aluminum is corrosion resistant, so mentioning just copper here might make you think aluminum can't be used. This isn't the case, and the intent of this rule has been clarified.

Cable in Raceway. Sizing a bonding jumper on the supply side of a service must be done when a **NEW** metal raceway is used for service conductors [250.92]. Previous editions of the *NEC* had requirements for single and parallel conductors installed in metal service raceways. Although it's not common, cables might also be installed in a metal service raceway rather than insulated conductors. If this is done, we would probably size the bonding jumper exactly the same way, but the *Code* didn't mention this. It was an oversight, probably caught by very few, that's now been addressed.

250.102 Grounded Conductor, Bonding Conductors, and Jumpers

(A) Material. Equipment bonding jumpers can be of copper, aluminum, or other corrosion-resistant material.

(B) Termination. Equipment bonding jumpers must terminate by any of the following means in accordance with 250.8(A):

- Listed pressure connectors
- Terminal bars
- Pressure connectors listed as grounding and bonding equipment
- Exothermic welding
- Machine screw-type fasteners that engage not less than two threads or are secured with a nut
- Thread-forming machine screws that engage not less than two threads in the enclosure
- Connections that are part of a listed assembly
- Other listed means

(C) Supply-Side Bonding Jumper Sizing.

(1) Single Raceway or Cable Installations. The supply-side bonding jumper is sized in accordance with Table 250.102(C)(1), based on the largest ungrounded conductor within the raceway or cable. Figure 250–130

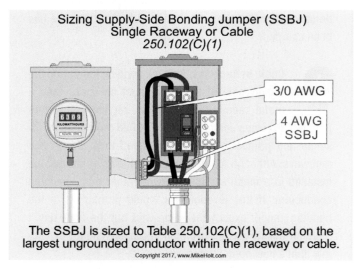

Figure 250–130

(2) Parallel Conductor Installations in Two or More Raceways or Cables. If the ungrounded supply conductors are paralleled in two or more raceways or cables, the size of the supply-side bonding jumper for each raceway or cable is sized in accordance with Table 250.102(C)(1), based on the size of the largest ungrounded conductors in each raceway or cable.

> **Example:** What size single supply-side bonding jumper is required for three metal raceways, each containing 400 kcmil service conductors? Figure 250–131
>
> **Solution:** A single supply-side 1/0 AWG bonding jumper is required [Table 250.102(C)(1)].

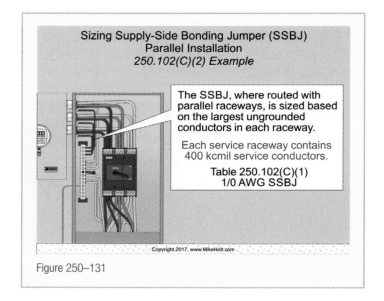

Figure 250–131

Note 1: The term "supply conductors" includes ungrounded conductors that don't have overcurrent protection on their supply side and terminate at service equipment or the first disconnect of a separately derived system.

Note 2: See Chapter 9, Table 8, for the circular mil area of conductors 18 AWG through 4/0 AWG.

Table 250.102(C)(1) Grounded Conductor, Main Bonding Jumper, System Bonding Jumper, and Supply-Side Bonding Jumper

Size of Largest Ungrounded Conductor Per Raceway or Equivalent Area for Parallel Conductors		Size of Bonding Jumper or Grounded Conductor
Copper	Aluminum or Copper-Clad Aluminum	Copper-Aluminum
2 or smaller	1/0 or smaller	8—6
1 or 1/0	2/0 or 3/0	6—4
2/0 or 3/0	Over 3/0 250 kcmil	4—2
Over 3/0 through 350 kcmil	Over 250 through 500 kcmil	2—1/0
Over 350 through 600 kcmil	Over 500 through 900 kcmil	1/0—3/0

(D) Load Side Bonding Jumper Sizing. Bonding jumpers on the load side of feeder and branch-circuit overcurrent protection devices are sized in accordance with 250.122, based on the rating of the circuit overcurrent protection device.

> **Question:** *What size equipment bonding jumper is required for each metal raceway where the circuit conductors are protected by a 1,200A overcurrent protection device?* Figure 250–132
>
> **Solution:** *A 3/0 AWG equipment bonding jumper is required [Table 250.122].* Figure 250–133

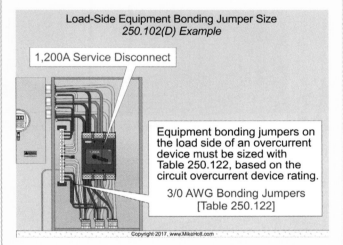

Figure 250–132

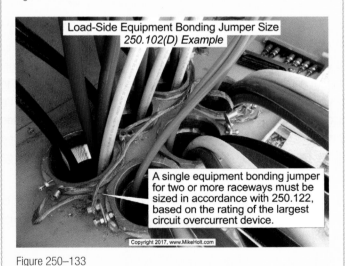

Figure 250–133

If a single bonding jumper is used to bond two or more raceways, it must be sized in accordance with 250.122, based on the rating of the largest circuit overcurrent protection device.

(E) Installation of Bonding Jumpers.

(1) Inside Raceway. Bonding jumpers installed inside a raceway must be identified in accordance with 250.119 and must terminate to the enclosure in accordance with 250.148.

(2) Outside Raceway. Bonding jumpers installed outside a raceway must be routed with the raceway and can't exceed 6 ft in length. Figure 250–134

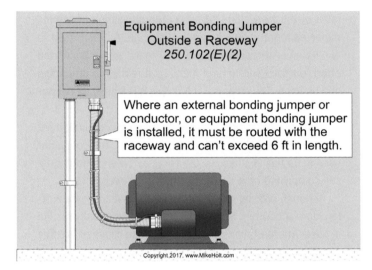

Figure 250–134

250.104 Bonding of Piping Systems and Exposed Structural Metal

The requirements for bonding piping systems and structural metal have been editorially revised.

Analysis

REORGANIZED At first glance, it looks like the text in this section of the *NEC* was drastically revised. Further examination, however, shows that most of the work done here was reorganization and some minor editorial changes to the language. As discussed in 250.52, over the past *Code* cycles, there was a concerted effort to address structural metal as it relates to grounding and bonding. The changes in this rule are simply a continuation of that effort.

You still have to bond the structural metal of a building if it's exposed and likely to become energized. The conductor used to do this is still sized the same as before, and it must still comply with the same installation requirements.

Although nothing really changed in this section, it's written more accurately. More accurate language usually results in fewer interpretations and arguments, so changes like this are still worthwhile.

250.104 Bonding of Piping Systems and Exposed Structural Metal

Author's Comment:

- To remove dangerous voltage on metal parts from a ground fault, electrically conductive metal water piping systems, metal sprinkler piping, metal gas piping, as well as exposed structural metal members likely to become energized, must be connected to an effective ground-fault current path [250.4(A)(4)].

(A) Metal Water Piping System. Metal water piping systems that are interconnected to form a mechanically and electrically continuous system must be bonded in accordance with 250.104(A)(1), (A)(2), or (A)(3).

(1) Buildings Supplied by a Service. The metal water piping system, including the metal sprinkler water piping system, of a building supplied with service conductors must be bonded to <u>any of the following</u>: Figure 250–135

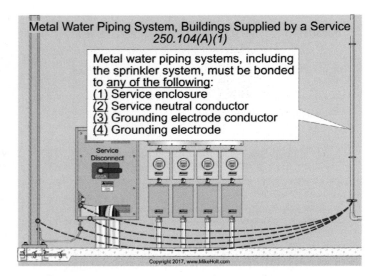

Figure 250–135

(1) Service equipment enclosure,

(2) Neutral at service equipment,

(3) Grounding electrode conductor if of sufficient size, or

(4) One of the grounding electrodes of the grounding electrode system if the grounding electrode conductor or bonding jumper to the electrode is of sufficient size.

<u>The bonding jumper must be copper where within 18 in. of the surface of earth [250.64(A)], must be adequately protected if exposed to physical damage [250.64(B)], and all points of attachment must be accessible. A ferrous metal raceway containing a grounding electrode conductor must be made electrically continuous by bonding each end of the raceway to the grounding electrode conductor [250.64(E)], so it's best to use nonmetallic conduit.</u>

<u>The metal water piping system bonding jumper must be sized in accordance with Table 250.102(C)(1), based on the cross-sectional area of the ungrounded service conductors.</u>

Example: *What size bonding jumper is required for a metal water piping system, if the 300 kcmil service conductors are paralleled in two raceways?* Figure 250–136

Solution: *A 1/0 AWG bonding jumper is required, based on 600 kcmil conductors, in accordance with 250.102(C)(1).*

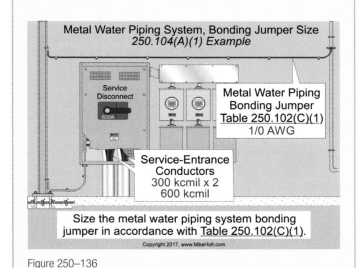

Metal Water Piping System, Bonding Jumper Size 250.104(A)(1) Example

Service Disconnect
600A

Metal Water Piping Bonding Jumper Table 250.102(C)(1) 1/0 AWG

Service-Entrance Conductors 300 kcmil x 2 600 kcmil

Size the metal water piping system bonding jumper in accordance with Table 250.102(C)(1).

Copyright 2017, www.MikeHolt.com

Figure 250–136

Author's Comment:

- If hot and cold metal water pipes are electrically connected, only one bonding jumper is required, either to the cold or hot water pipe. Bonding isn't required for isolated sections of metal water piping connected to a nonmetallic water piping system. Figure 250–137

(2) Multiple Occupancy Building. When a metal water piping system in an individual occupancy is metallically isolated from other occupancies, the metal water piping system for that occupancy can be bonded to the <u>equipment</u> grounding terminal of the occupancy's switchgear, switchboard, or panelboard. <u>The bonding</u> jumper must be sized in accordance with <u>250.102(D)</u>, based on the cross-sectional area of the feeder conductor. Figure 250–138

(3) Buildings Supplied by a Feeder. The metal water piping system of a building supplied by a feeder must be bonded to one of the following:

<u>(a)</u> The equipment grounding terminal of the building disconnect enclosure,

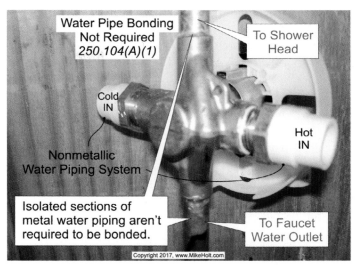

Water Pipe Bonding Not Required 250.104(A)(1)

To Shower Head

Cold IN

Hot IN

Nonmetallic Water Piping System

Isolated sections of metal water piping aren't required to be bonded.

To Faucet Water Outlet

Copyright 2017, www.MikeHolt.com

Figure 250–137

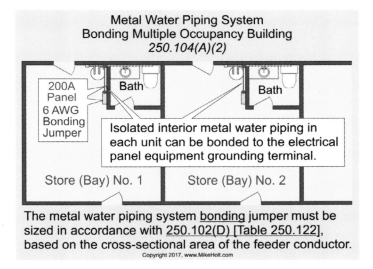

Metal Water Piping System Bonding Multiple Occupancy Building 250.104(A)(2)

200A Panel 6 AWG Bonding Jumper

Bath

Bath

Isolated interior metal water piping in each unit can be bonded to the electrical panel equipment grounding terminal.

Store (Bay) No. 1

Store (Bay) No. 2

The metal water piping system <u>bonding</u> jumper must be sized in accordance with <u>250.102(D) [Table 250.122]</u>, based on the cross-sectional area of the feeder conductor.

Copyright 2017, www.MikeHolt.com

Figure 250–138

<u>(b)</u> The feeder <u>equipment</u> grounding conductor, or

<u>(c)</u> One of the building <u>grounding electrodes</u> of the grounding electrode system <u>if the grounding electrode or bonding jumper to the electrode is of sufficient size</u>.

The bonding jumper is sized to Table 250.102(C)(1), based on the cross-sectional area of the feeder conductor.

(B) Other Metal-Piping Systems. Metal-piping systems in or attached to a building that's likely to become energized must be bonded to one of the following:

(1) Equipment grounding conductor for the circuit that's likely to energize the piping system Figure 250–139

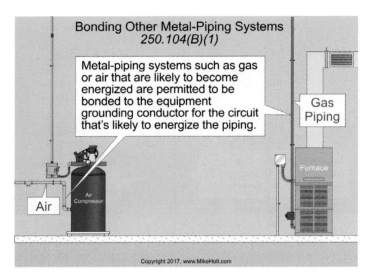

Figure 250–139

(2) Service equipment enclosure

(3) Neutral conductor at the service equipment

(4) Grounding electrode conductor, if of sufficient size

(5) One of the grounding electrodes of the grounding electrode system <u>if the grounding electrode conductor or bonding jumper to the electrode is of sufficient size</u>.

The bonding jumper is sized to Table 250.122, based on the cross-sectional area of the feeder conductor, and equipment grounding conductors are sized to Table 250.122 using the rating of the circuit that's likely to energize the piping system(s). The points of attachment of the bonding jumper(s) must be accessible.

Note 1: Bonding all piping and metal air ducts within the premises will provide additional safety. Figure 250–140

Note 2: The *National Fuel Gas Code*, NFPA 54, Section 7.13 contains further information about bonding gas piping. Figure 250–141

Author's Comment

- Informational Notes in the *NEC* are for information purposes only and aren't enforceable as a requirement of the *Code* [90.5(C)].

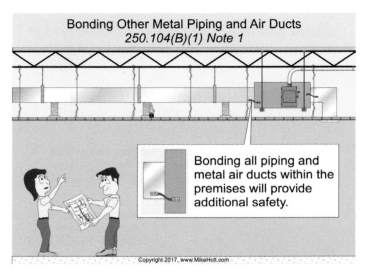

Figure 250–140

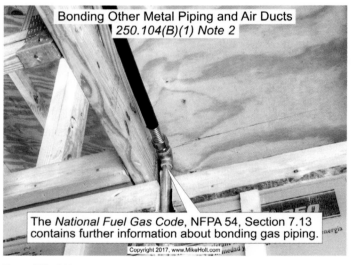

Figure 250–141

(C) Structural Metal. Exposed structural metal that's interconnected to form a metal building frame and is likely to become energized must be bonded <u>to any of the following</u>: Figure 250–142

(1) The service equipment enclosure,

(2) The neutral at the service equipment,

(3) The building disconnect enclosure for buildings supplied by a feeder,

(4) The grounding electrode conductor where of sufficient size, or

(5) One of the grounding electrodes of the grounding electrode system <u>if the grounding electrode conductor or bonding jumper to the electrode is of sufficient size</u>.

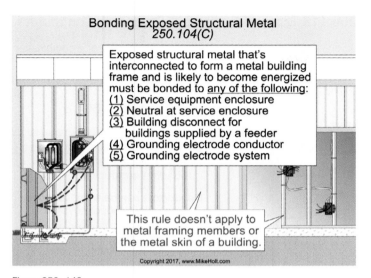

Figure 250–142

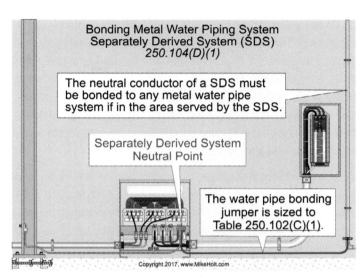

Figure 250–143

The structural metal bonding <u>conductor or</u> jumper must be sized in accordance with Table <u>250.102(C)(1)</u>, based on the area of the ungrounded supply conductors. The bonding jumper must be copper where within 18 in. of the surface of the earth [250.64(A)], be securely fastened to the surface on which it's carried [250.64(B)], and be adequately protected if exposed to physical damage [250.64(B)]. In addition, all points of attachment must be accessible, except as permitted in 250.68(A) Ex.

Author's Comment:

■ This rule doesn't require the bonding of sheet metal framing members (studs) or the metal skin of a wood-frame building.

(D) Separately Derived Systems. Metal water piping systems and structural metal that's interconnected to form a building frame <u>must be bonded to the separately derived system</u> in accordance with 250.104(D)(1) through (D)(3).

(1) Metal Water Pipe. If metal water piping systems exists in the area served by a separately derived system, it must be bonded to the neutral point of the separately derived system where the grounding electrode conductor is connected. Figure 250–143

The bonding jumper must be sized in accordance with <u>Table 250.102(C)(1)</u>, based on the area of the ungrounded conductor of the derived system.

Ex 2: The metal water piping system can be bonded to the structural metal building frame if it serves as the grounding electrode [250.52(A)(1)] for the separately derived system. Figure 250–144

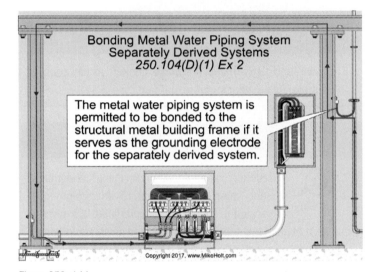

Figure 250–144

(2) Structural Metal. <u>Exposed structural metal</u> that's interconnected to form the building frame located in the area served by a separately derived system must be bonded to the neutral conductor where the grounding electrode conductor is connected at the separately derived system.

The bonding jumper must be sized in accordance with Table 250.102(C)(1), based on the largest ungrounded conductor of the separately derived system.

Ex 1: Bonding to the separately derived system isn't required <u>if</u> the metal serves as the grounding electrode [250.52(A)(2)] for the separately derived system.

(3) Common Grounding Electrode Conductor. If a common grounding electrode conductor is installed for multiple separately derived systems as permitted by 250.30(A)(6), and exposed structural metal that's interconnected to form the building frame or interior metal piping exists in the area served by the separately derived system, the metal piping and the structural metal member can be bonded to the common grounding electrode conductor in the area served by the separately derived system.

Ex: A separate bonding jumper from each derived system to metal water piping and to structural metal members isn't required if the metal water piping and the structural metal members in the area served by the separately derived system are bonded to the common grounding electrode conductor.

250.118 Types of Equipment Grounding Conductors

The permitted uses of flexible metal conduit as an equipment grounding conductor were clarified.

Analysis

CLARIFIED
Generally speaking, all metal electrical equipment must be connected to an equipment grounding conductor. Section 250.118 gives us a list of all of the items that can be used as an equipment grounding conductor, including EMT, RMC, IMC, flexible metal conduit, and several others.

The use of flexible metal conduit as the equipment grounding conductor has restrictions because it's inherently limited in how much fault current it can carry due to its higher resistance/impedance as compared to nonflexible metallic raceways.

Flexible metal conduit can be used as an equipment grounding conductor in lengths not exceeding 6 ft, containing 15A and/or 20A branch circuits, where flexibility after the installation isn't required, and now for the 2017 *NEC,* only in sizes up to and including trade size 1¼.

Compliance with this change will probably be automatic, given that it's pretty rare to see a raceway that large used for 15A or 20A circuits.

250.118 Types of Equipment Grounding Conductors

An equipment grounding conductor can be any one or a combination of the following: Figure 250–145

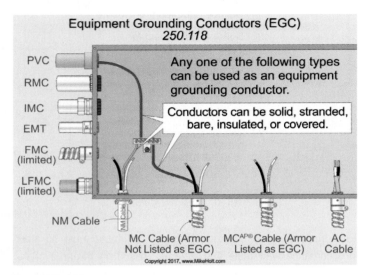

Figure 250–145

Note: The equipment grounding conductor is intended to serve as part of the effective ground-fault current path. See 250.2. **Figure 250–146**

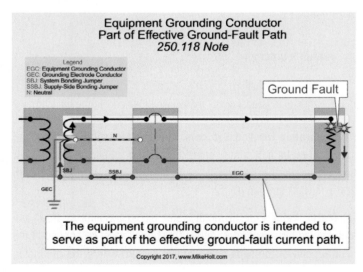

Figure 250–146

Author's Comment:

- The effective ground-fault path is an intentionally constructed low-impedance conductive path designed to carry fault current from the point of a ground fault on a wiring system to the electrical supply source. Its purpose is to quickly remove dangerous voltage from a ground fault by opening the circuit overcurrent protection device [250.2]. Figure 250–147

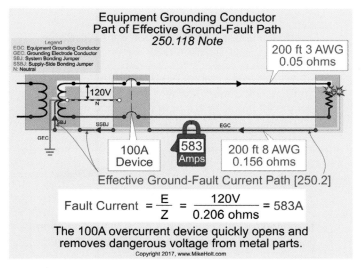

Figure 250–147

(1) An equipment grounding conductor of the wire type can be a bare or insulated copper or aluminum conductor. Figure 250–148

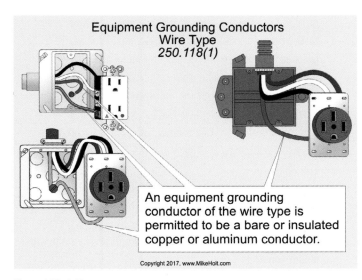

Figure 250–148

(2) Rigid metal conduit can serve as an equipment grounding conductor.

(3) Intermediate metal conduit can serve as an equipment grounding conductor.

(4) Electrical metallic tubing can serve as an equipment grounding conductor.

(5) Listed flexible metal conduit (FMC) can serve as an equipment grounding conductor where: Figure 250–149

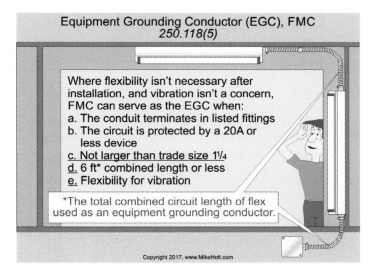

Figure 250–149

a. The raceway terminates in listed fittings.

b. The circuit conductors are protected by an overcurrent protection device rated 20A or less.

c. The size of the flexible metal conduit doesn't exceed trade size 1¼.

d. The combined length of the flexible conduit in the same ground-fault current path doesn't exceed 6 ft.

e. If flexibility is required to minimize the transmission of vibration from equipment or to provide flexibility for equipment that requires movement after installation, an equipment grounding conductor of the wire type must be installed with the circuit conductors in accordance with 250.102(E), and it must be sized in accordance with 250.122, based on the rating of the circuit overcurrent protection device. Figure 250–150

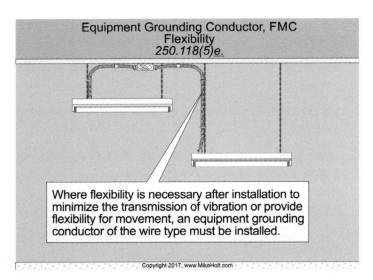

Figure 250–150

(6) Listed liquidtight flexible metal conduit (LFMC) can serve as an equipment grounding conductor where: Figure 250–151

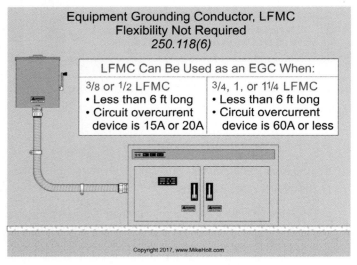

Figure 250–151

a. The raceway terminates in listed fittings.

b. For ⅜ in. through ½ in., the circuit conductors are protected by an overcurrent protection device rated 20A or less.

c. For ¾ in. through 1¼ in., the circuit conductors are protected by an overcurrent protection device rated 60A or less.

d. The combined length of the flexible conduit in the same ground-fault current path doesn't exceed 6 ft.

e. If flexibility is required to minimize the transmission of vibration from equipment or to provide flexibility for equipment that requires movement after installation, an equipment grounding conductor of the wire type must be installed with the circuit conductors in accordance with 250.102(E), and it must be sized in accordance with 250.122, based on the rating of the circuit overcurrent protection device.

(8) The sheath of Type AC cable containing an aluminum bonding strip can serve as an equipment grounding conductor. Figure 250–152

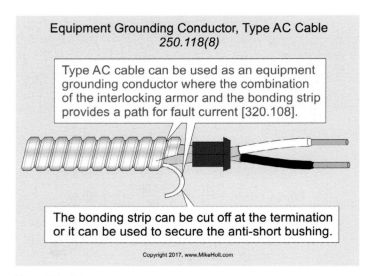

Figure 250–152

Author's Comment:

■ The internal aluminum bonding strip isn't an equipment grounding conductor, but it allows the interlocked armor to serve as an equipment grounding conductor because it reduces the impedance of the armored spirals to ensure that a ground fault will be cleared. It's the aluminum bonding strip in combination with the cable armor that creates the circuit equipment grounding conductor. Once the bonding strip exits the cable, it can be cut off because it no longer serves any purpose.

■ The effective ground-fault current path must be maintained by the use of fittings specifically listed for Type AC cable [320.40]. See 300.12, 300.15, and 320.100.

(9) The copper sheath of Type MI cable can serve as an equipment grounding conductor.

(10) Type MC cable

a. The interlock type cable that contains an insulated or uninsulated equipment grounding conductor in accordance with 250.118(1) can serve as an equipment grounding conductor. Figure 250–153

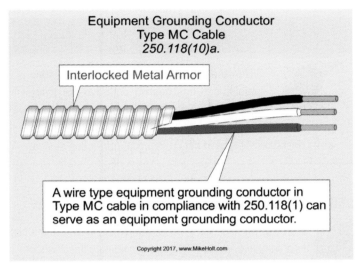

Figure 250–153

b. The combined metallic sheath and uninsulated equipment grounding/bonding conductor of interlocked metal that's listed and identified as an equipment grounding conductor can serve as an equipment grounding conductor. Figure 250–154

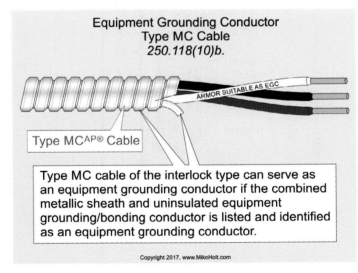

Figure 250–154

■ Once the bare aluminum grounding/bonding conductor exits the cable, it can be cut off because it no longer serves any purpose. The effective ground-fault current path must be maintained by the use of fittings specifically listed for Type MC^{AP®} cable [330.40]. See 300.12, 300.15, and 330.100. Figure 250–155

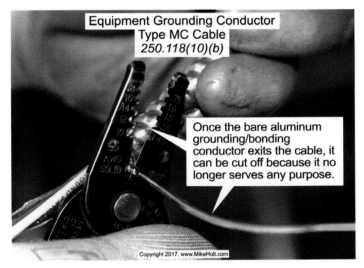

Figure 250–155

c. The metallic sheath of the smooth or corrugated tube-type MC cable that's listed and identified as an equipment grounding conductor can serve as an equipment grounding conductor.

(11) Metallic cable trays can serve as an equipment grounding conductor if continuous maintenance and supervision ensure only qualified persons will service the cable tray, with cable tray and fittings identified for grounding and the cable tray, fittings [392.10], and raceways are bonded together using bolted mechanical connectors or bonding jumpers sized and installed in accordance with 250.102 [392.60]. Figure 250–156

(13) Listed electrically continuous metal raceways, such as metal wireways [Article 376] or strut-type channel raceways [384.60] can serve as an equipment grounding conductor. Figure 250–157

(14) Surface metal raceways listed for grounding [Article 386] can serve as an equipment grounding conductor.

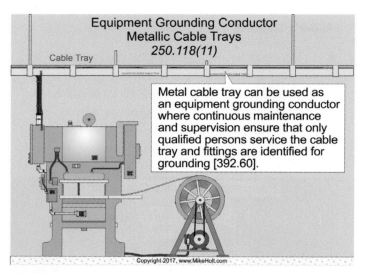

Equipment Grounding Conductor
Metallic Cable Trays
250.118(11)

Cable Tray

Metal cable tray can be used as an equipment grounding conductor where continuous maintenance and supervision ensure that only qualified persons service the cable tray and fittings are identified for grounding [392.60].

Figure 250–156

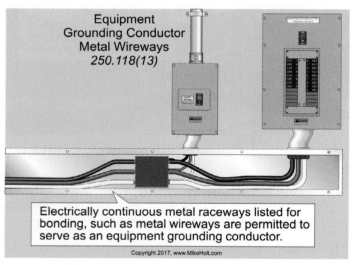

Equipment
Grounding Conductor
Metal Wireways
250.118(13)

Electrically continuous metal raceways listed for bonding, such as metal wireways are permitted to serve as an equipment grounding conductor.

Figure 250–157

250.122 Sizing Equipment Grounding Conductor

The requirements for sizing EGCs for voltage drop and for feeder circuits have been expanded.

Analysis

EXPANDED Sizing the EGC for parallel raceway or cable installations has been a controversial issue for decades, and now the 2017 *NEC* revisions have solved this problem! The EGC is now required to be sized based on the size of the overcurrent protection device.

250.122 Sizing Equipment Grounding Conductor

 Scan this QR code for a video of Mike explaining this topic; it's a sample from the DVDs that accompany this textbook.

(A) General. Equipment grounding conductors of the wire type must be sized not smaller than shown in Table 250.122, based on the rating of the circuit overcurrent protection device; however, the circuit equipment grounding conductor isn't required to be larger than the circuit conductors. Figure 250–158

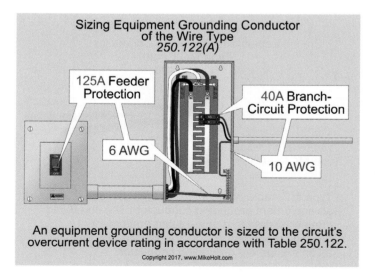

Sizing Equipment Grounding Conductor
of the Wire Type
250.122(A)

125A Feeder Protection

40A Branch-Circuit Protection

6 AWG

10 AWG

An equipment grounding conductor is sized to the circuit's overcurrent device rating in accordance with Table 250.122.

Figure 250–158

Table 250.122 Sizing Equipment Grounding Conductor

Overcurrent protection device Rating	Copper Conductor
15A	14 AWG
20A	12 AWG
25A—60A	10 AWG
70A—100A	8 AWG
110A—200A	6 AWG
225A—300A	4 AWG
350A—400A	3 AWG
450A—500A	2 AWG
600A	1 AWG
700A—800A	1/0 AWG
1,000A	2/0 AWG
1,200A	3/0 AWG

(B) Increased in Size. If ungrounded conductors are increased in size for any reason from the minimum size that has sufficient ampacity for the intended installation before the application of any adjustment or correction factor(s), wire-type equipment grounding conductors must be at least proportionately increased in size according to the circular mil area of the ungrounded conductors.

Author's Comment:

- Ungrounded conductors are sometimes increased in size to accommodate conductor voltage drop, harmonic current heating, short-circuit rating, or simply for future capacity.

Example: If the ungrounded conductors for a 40A circuit (with 75ºC terminals) are increased in size from 8 AWG to 6 AWG due to voltage drop, the circuit equipment grounding conductor must be increased in size from 10 AWG to what size? Figure 250–159

Solution: The circuit equipment grounding conductor must be increased to size 8 AWG.

The circular mil area of 6 AWG is 59 percent more than 8 AWG (26,240 Cmil/16,510 Cmil) [Chapter 9, Table 8].

According to Table 250.122, the circuit equipment grounding conductor for a 40A overcurrent protection device will be 10 AWG (10,380 Cmil), but the circuit equipment grounding conductor for this circuit must be increased in size by a multiplier of 1.59.

Conductor Size = 10,380 Cmil x 1.59
Conductor Size = 16,504 Cmil
Conductor Size = 8 AWG, Chapter 9, Table 8

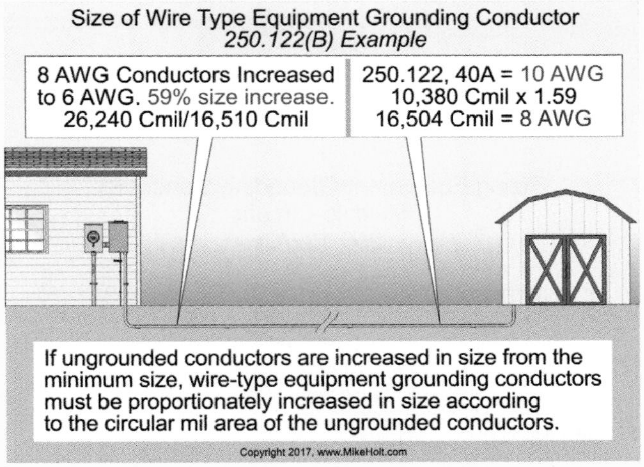

Size of Wire Type Equipment Grounding Conductor 250.122(B) Example

8 AWG Conductors Increased to 6 AWG. 59% size increase. 26,240 Cmil/16,510 Cmil	250.122, 40A = 10 AWG 10,380 Cmil x 1.59 16,504 Cmil = 8 AWG

If ungrounded conductors are increased in size from the minimum size, wire-type equipment grounding conductors must be proportionately increased in size according to the circular mil area of the ungrounded conductors.

Copyright 2017, www.MikeHolt.com

Figure 250–159

(C) Multiple Circuits. When multiple circuits are installed in the same raceway, cable, or cable tray, one equipment grounding conductor sized in accordance with 250.122, based on the rating of the largest circuit overcurrent protection device is sufficient. Figure 250–160 and Figure 250–161

(D) Motor Branch Circuits.

(1) General. The equipment grounding conductor of the wire type must be sized in accordance with Table 250.122, based on the rating of the motor circuit branch-circuit short-circuit and ground-fault overcurrent protection device, but this conductor isn't required to be larger than the circuit conductors [250.122(A)].

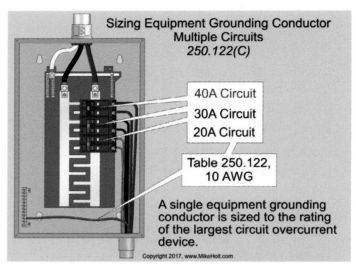

Figure 250–160

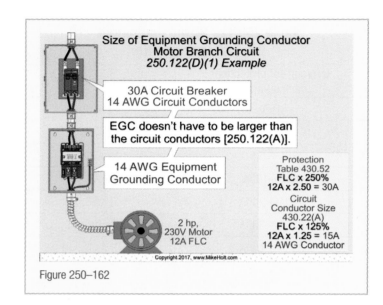

Figure 250–162

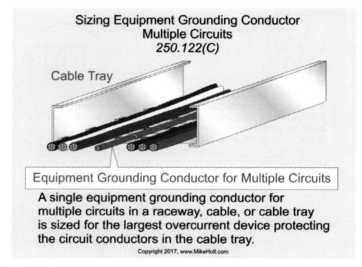

Figure 250–161

Example: *What size equipment grounding conductor of the wire type is required for a 14 AWG motor branch circuit [430.22], protected with a 2-pole, 30A circuit breaker in accordance with 430.22 and 430.52(C)(1)?* Figure 250–162

Solution: *The equipment grounding conductor isn't required to be larger than the 14 AWG motor branch circuit conductors [250.122(D)(1) and 250.122(A)].*

(F) Parallel Runs. If circuit conductors are installed in parallel as permitted by 310.10(H), an equipment grounding conductor must be installed for each parallel conductor set in accordance with the following:

(1) Raceways or Cable Trays.

(a) Parallel Feeder Runs in a Single Raceway or Cable Tray. The single wire-type equipment grounding conductor is required in each raceway or cable tray. It must be sized in accordance with Table 250.122, based on the rating of the circuit overcurrent protection device. Figure 250–163 and Figure 250–164

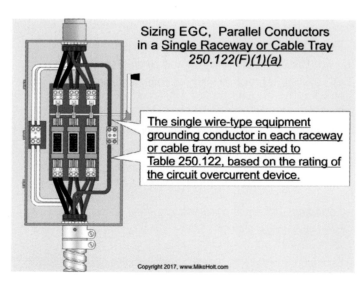

Figure 250–163

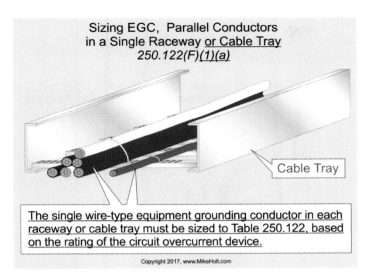

Figure 250–164

(b) Parallel Feeder Runs in Multiple Raceways. The equipment grounding conductor in each parallel run raceway must be sized in accordance with Table 250.122, based on the rating of the feeder overcurrent protection device. Figure 250–165

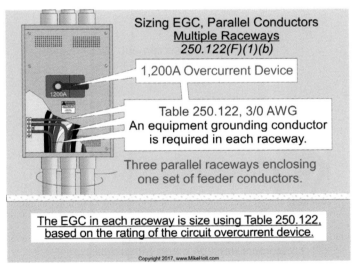

Figure 250–165

(2) Parallel Feeder Runs Using Multiconductor Cables

(a) Multiconductor cables used in parallel must have the equipment grounding conductors of all cables electrically paralleled with each other.

(b) Parallel multiconductor cables in a single raceway or cable tray are permitted to have a single equipment grounding conductor connected to the equipment grounding conductors within the multiconductor cables. This single equipment grounding conductor must be sized in accordance with 250.122, based on the rating of the feeder overcurrent protection device.

(c) Equipment grounding conductors installed in cable trays must comply with 392.10(B)(1)(c).

(d) Parallel multiconductor cables not installed in a raceway or cable tray must have an equipment grounding conductor of the wire type in each cable sized in accordance with 250.122, based on the rating of the circuit overcurrent protection device.

(G) Feeder Tap Conductors. Equipment grounding conductors for feeder taps must be sized in accordance with Table 250.122, based on the ampere rating of the overcurrent protection device ahead of the feeder, but in no case is it required to be larger than the feeder tap conductors. Figure 250–166

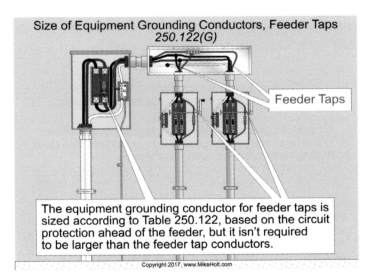

Figure 250–166

250.148 Continuity and Attachment of Equipment Grounding Conductors to Boxes

This section was edited to require all equipment grounding conductors in the same enclosure to be connected together.

Analysis

EDITED It's very common to have multiple circuit conductors spliced or terminated on equipment within a box. For safety reasons, it's imperative that the equipment grounding conductors for these circuits be spliced together and to the metal box. The revision changes the word "any" to "all," clarifying that all of the equipment grounds in a given enclosure must be spliced together and not in separate groups.

250.148 Continuity and Attachment of Equipment Grounding Conductors in Metal Boxes

If circuit conductors are spliced or terminated on equipment within a box, all equipment grounding conductor associated with any of the spliced or terminated circuits must be connected together or to the metal box in accordance (A) through (E). Figure 250–167

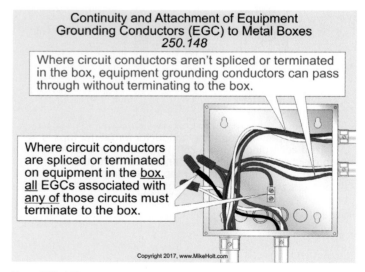

Continuity and Attachment of Equipment Grounding Conductors (EGC) to Metal Boxes
250.148

Where circuit conductors aren't spliced or terminated in the box, equipment grounding conductors can pass through without terminating to the box.

Where circuit conductors are spliced or terminated on equipment in the box, all EGCs associated with any of those circuits must terminate to the box.

Figure 250–167

Ex: The circuit equipment grounding conductor for an isolated ground receptacle installed in accordance with 250.146(D) isn't required to terminate to a metal box. Figure 250–168

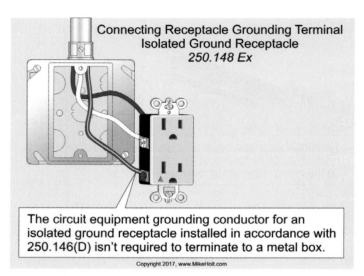

Connecting Receptacle Grounding Terminal Isolated Ground Receptacle
250.148 Ex

The circuit equipment grounding conductor for an isolated ground receptacle installed in accordance with 250.146(D) isn't required to terminate to a metal box.

Figure 250–168

(A) Splicing. Equipment grounding conductors must be spliced together with a device listed for the purpose [110.14(B)]. Figure 250–169

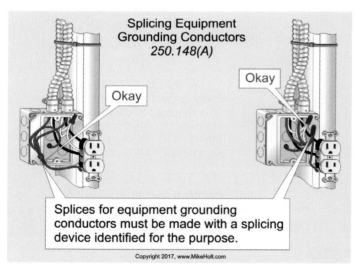

Splicing Equipment Grounding Conductors
250.148(A)

Okay

Okay

Splices for equipment grounding conductors must be made with a splicing device identified for the purpose.

Figure 250–169

Author's Comment:

- Wire connectors of any color can be used with equipment grounding conductor splices, but green wire connectors can only be used with equipment grounding conductors since they're only tested for that application.

(B) Grounding Continuity. Equipment grounding conductors must terminate in a manner such that the disconnection or the removal of a receptacle, luminaire, or other device won't interrupt the grounding continuity. Figure 250–170

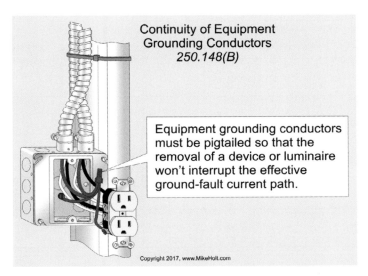

Continuity of Equipment Grounding Conductors 250.148(B)

Equipment grounding conductors must be pigtailed so that the removal of a device or luminaire won't interrupt the effective ground-fault current path.

Figure 250–170

(C) Metal Boxes. Terminating equipment grounding conductors within metal boxes must be with a grounding screw that's not used for any other purpose, a fitting listed for grounding, or a listed grounding device such as a ground clip. Figure 250–171

Author's Comment:

■ Equipment grounding conductors aren't permitted to terminate to a screw that secures a plaster ring. Figure 250–172

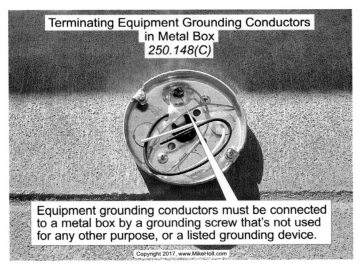

Terminating Equipment Grounding Conductors in Metal Box 250.148(C)

Equipment grounding conductors must be connected to a metal box by a grounding screw that's not used for any other purpose, or a listed grounding device.

Figure 250–171

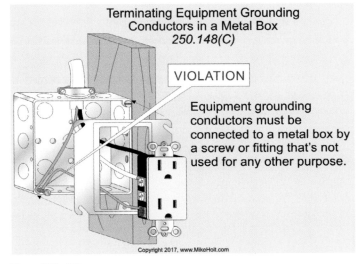

Terminating Equipment Grounding Conductors in a Metal Box 250.148(C)

VIOLATION

Equipment grounding conductors must be connected to a metal box by a screw or fitting that's not used for any other purpose.

Figure 250–172

CHAPTER 3

WIRING METHODS AND MATERIALS

Chapter 3—Wiring Methods and Materials

Chapter 3 covers wiring methods and materials, and provides some very specific installation requirements for conductors, cables, boxes, raceways, and fittings. This chapter includes detailed information about the installation and restrictions involved with wiring methods.

It may be because of those details that many people incorrectly apply the rules from this chapter. Be sure to pay careful attention to the details, and be sure you make your installation comply with the rules in the *NEC*, not just completing it in the manner you may have been taught or because "it's always been done that way." This is especially true when it comes to applying the Tables.

Violations of the rules for wiring methods found in Chapter 3 can result in problems with power quality and can lead to fire, shock, and other hazards.

The type of wiring method you'll use depends on several factors; job specifications, *Code* requirements, the environment, need, and cost are among them.

Chapter 3 begins with rules that are common to most wiring methods [Article 300]. It then covers conductors [Article 310] and enclosures [Articles 312 and 314]. The articles that follow become more specific and deal more in-depth with individual wiring methods such as specific types of cables [Articles 320 through 340] and various raceways [Articles 342 through 390]. The chapter winds up with Article 392, a support system, and the final articles [Articles 394 through 398] for open wiring.

Notice as you read through the various wiring methods that the *Code* attempts to use similar subsection numbering for similar topics from one article to the next, using the same digits after the decimal point in the section number for the same topic. This makes it easier to locate specific requirements in a particular article. For example, the rules for securing and supporting can be found in the section that ends with .30 of each article. In addition to this, you'll find a "uses permitted" and "uses not permitted" section in nearly every article.

Wiring Method Articles

- **Article 300—General Requirements for Wiring Methods and Materials.** Article 300 contains the general requirements for all wiring methods included in the *NEC*, except for signaling and communications systems (twisted wire, antennas, and coaxial cable), which are covered in Chapters 7 and 8.

- **Article 310—Conductors for General Wiring.** This article contains the general requirements for conductors, such as insulation markings, ampacity ratings, and conductor use. Article 310 doesn't apply to conductors that are part of flexible cords, fixture wires, or conductors that are an integral part of equipment [90.6 and 300.1(B)].

- **Article 312—Cabinets, Cutout Boxes, and Meter Socket Enclosures.** Article 312 covers the installation and construction specifications for cabinets, cutout boxes, and meter socket enclosures.

- **Article 314—Outlet, Device, Pull, and Junction Boxes, Conduit Bodies, Fittings, and Handhole Enclosures.** Installation requirements for outlet boxes, pull and junction boxes, as well as conduit bodies, and handhole enclosures are contained in this article.

Cable Articles

Articles 320 through 340 address specific types of cables. If you take the time to become familiar with the various types of cables, you'll:

- Understand what's available for doing the work.
- Recognize cable types that have special *NEC* requirements.
- Avoid buying cable that you can't install due to *Code* requirements you can't meet with that particular wiring method.

Here's a brief overview of each one:

- **Article 320—Armored Cable (Type AC).** Armored cable is an assembly of insulated conductors, 14 AWG through 1 AWG, individually wrapped with waxed paper. The conductors are contained within a flexible spiral metal (steel or aluminum) sheath that interlocks at the edges. Armored cable looks like flexible metal conduit. Many electricians call this metal cable "BX®."

- **Article 330—Metal-Clad Cable (Type MC).** Metal-clad cable encloses insulated conductors in a metal sheath of either corrugated or smooth copper or aluminum tubing, or spiral interlocked steel or aluminum. The physical characteristics of Type MC cable make it a versatile wiring method permitted in almost any location and for almost any application. The most commonly used Type MC cable is the interlocking kind, which looks similar to armored cable or flexible metal conduit.

- **Article 334—Nonmetallic-Sheathed Cable (Type NM).** Nonmetallic-sheathed cable encloses two, three, or four insulated conductors, 14 AWG through 2 AWG, within a nonmetallic outer jacket. Because this cable is nonmetallic, it contains a separate equipment grounding conductor. Nonmetallic-sheathed cable is a common wiring method used for residential and commercial branch circuits. Many electricians call this plastic-sheathed cable "Romex®."

- **Article 336—Power and Control Tray Cable (Type TC).** Power and Control Tray Cable is flexible, inexpensive, and easily installed. It provides very limited physical protection for the conductors, so the installation restrictions are strict. Its low cost and relative ease of installation make it a common wiring method for industrial applications.

- **Article 338—Service-Entrance Cable (Types SE and USE).** Service-entrance cable can be a single-conductor or a multiconductor assembly within an overall nonmetallic covering. This cable is used primarily for services not over 1,000V, but is also permitted for feeders and branch circuits.

■ **Article 340—Underground Feeder and Branch-Circuit Cable (Type UF).** Underground feeder cable is a moisture-, fungus-, and corrosion-resistant cable suitable for direct burial in the earth, and it comes in sizes 14 AWG through 4/0 AWG [340.104]. Multiconductor UF cable is covered in molded plastic that surrounds the insulated conductors.

Raceway Articles

Articles 342 through 390 address specific types of raceways. Refer to Article 100 for the definition of a raceway. If you take the time to become familiar with the various types of raceways, you'll:

– Understand what's available for doing the work.
– Recognize raceway types that have special *Code* requirements.
– Avoid buying a raceway that you can't install due to *NEC* requirements you can't meet with that particular wiring method.

Here's a brief overview of each one:

■ **Article 342—Intermediate Metal Conduit (Type IMC).** Intermediate metal conduit is a circular metal raceway with the same outside diameter as rigid metal conduit. The wall thickness of intermediate metal conduit is less than that of rigid metal conduit, so it's a greater interior cross-sectional area for holding conductors. Intermediate metal conduit is lighter and less expensive than rigid metal conduit, but it's permitted in all the same locations as rigid metal conduit. Intermediate metal conduit also uses a different steel alloy, which makes it stronger than rigid metal conduit, even though the walls are thinner.

■ **Article 344—Rigid Metal Conduit (Type RMC).** Rigid metal conduit is similar to intermediate metal conduit, except the wall thickness is greater, so it's a smaller interior cross-sectional area. Rigid metal conduit is heavier than intermediate metal conduit and it's permitted to be installed in any location, just like intermediate metal conduit.

■ **Article 348—Flexible Metal Conduit (Type FMC).** Flexible metal conduit is a raceway of circular cross section made of a helically wound, interlocked metal strip of either steel or aluminum. It's commonly called "Greenfield" or "Flex."

■ **Article 350—Liquidtight Flexible Metal Conduit (Type LFMC).** Liquidtight flexible metal conduit is a raceway of circular cross section with an outer liquidtight, nonmetallic, sunlight-resistant jacket over an inner flexible metal core, with associated couplings, connectors, and fittings. It's listed for the installation of electrical conductors. Liquidtight flexible metal conduit is commonly called "Sealtite®" or simply "liquidtight." Liquidtight flexible metal conduit is of similar construction to flexible metal conduit, but it's an outer thermoplastic covering.

■ **Article 352—Rigid Polyvinyl Chloride Conduit (Type PVC).** Rigid polyvinyl chloride conduit is a nonmetallic raceway of circular cross section with integral or associated couplings, connectors, and fittings. It's listed for the installation of electrical conductors.

■ **Article 356—Liquidtight Flexible Nonmetallic Conduit (Type LFNC).** Liquidtight flexible nonmetallic conduit is a raceway of circular cross section with an outer liquidtight, nonmetallic, sunlight-resistant jacket over an inner flexible core, with associated couplings, connectors, and fittings.

- **Article 358—Electrical Metallic Tubing (EMT).** Electrical metallic tubing is a nonthreaded thinwall raceway of circular cross section designed for the physical protection and routing of conductors and cables. Compared to rigid metal conduit and intermediate metal conduit, electrical metallic tubing is relatively easy to bend, cut, and ream. EMT isn't threaded, so all connectors and couplings are of the threadless type. Today, it's available in a range of colors, such as red and blue.

- **Article 362—Electrical Nonmetallic Tubing (ENT).** Electrical nonmetallic tubing is a pliable, corrugated, circular raceway made of PVC. It's often called "Smurf Pipe" or "Smurf Tube," because it was available only in blue when it came out and at the time the children's cartoon characters "The Smurfs" were popular. It's now available in multiple colors such as red and yellow as well as blue.

- **Article 376—Metal Wireways.** A metal wireway is a sheet metal trough with hinged or removable covers for housing and protecting electrical conductors and cable, in which conductors are placed after the wireway has been installed as a complete system.

- **Article 380—Multioutlet Assemblies.** A multioutlet assembly is a surface, flush, or freestanding raceway designed to hold conductors and receptacles. It's assembled in the field or at the factory.

- **Article 386—Surface Metal Raceways.** A surface metal raceway is a metal raceway intended to be mounted to the surface with associated accessories, in which conductors are placed after the raceway has been installed as a complete system.

Cable Tray

- **Article 392—Cable Trays.** A cable tray system is a unit or assembly of units or sections with associated fittings that form a structural system used to securely fasten or support cables and raceways. A cable tray isn't a raceway; it's a support system for raceways, cables, and enclosures.

GENERAL REQUIREMENTS FOR WIRING METHODS AND MATERIALS

Introduction to Article 300—General Requirements for Wiring Methods and Materials

Article 300 contains the general requirements for all wiring methods included in the *NEC*. However, the article doesn't apply to communications systems (twisted wire, antennas, and coaxial cable), which are covered in Chapter 8, except when Article 300 is specifically referenced in Chapter 8.

This article is primarily concerned with how to install, route, splice, protect, and secure conductors and raceways. How well you conform to the requirements of Article 300 will generally be evident in the finished work, because many of the requirements tend to determine the appearance of the installation. Because of this, it's often easy to spot Article 300 problems if you're looking for *Code* violations. For example, you can easily see when someone runs an equipment grounding conductor outside a raceway instead of grouping all conductors of a circuit together, as required by 300.3(B).

A good understanding of Article 300 will start you on the path to correctly installing the wiring methods included in Chapter 3. Be sure to carefully consider the accompanying illustrations, and refer to the definitions in Article 100 as needed.

Part I. General

300.1 Scope

(A) Wiring Installations. Article 300 contains the general requirements for wiring methods and materials for power and lighting.

> **Author's Comment:**
>
> - The requirements contained in Article 300 don't apply to the wiring methods for Class 2 and 3 circuits, fire alarm circuits, and communications systems (twisted wire, antennas, and coaxial cable), except where there's a specific reference in Chapter 7 or 8 to a rule in Article 300.
>   - ◆ Class 2 and 3 Remote Control and Signaling, 725.3
>   - ◆ Communications Cables and Raceways, 800.133(A)(2)
>   - ◆ Coaxial Circuits, 820.3
>   - ◆ Fire Alarm Circuits, 760.3

(B) Integral Parts of Equipment. The requirements contained in Article 300 don't apply to the internal parts of electrical equipment. Figure 300–1

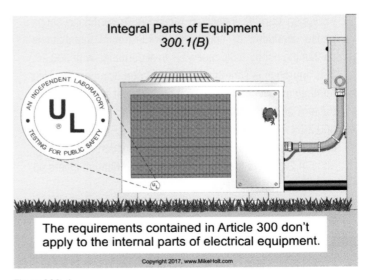

Figure 300–1

(C) Trade Sizes. Designators for raceway trade sizes are given in Table 300.1(C).

Author's Comment:

- Industry practice is to describe raceways using inch sizes, such as ½ in., 2 in., and so on; however, the proper reference is to use "Trade Size ½," or "Trade Size 2." In this textbook we use the term "Trade Size."

300.3 Conductors

The exception allowing for parallel isolated phase installations was clarified.

Analysis

CLARIFIED Section 300.3 contains some of the most fundamental, yet important rules in the entire *NEC*. Section 300.3(A), for example, requires that conductors be installed in a *Code*-compliant wiring method, meaning that a person can't just install individual conductors through the walls and ceilings of a building.

Section 300.3(B) requires all conductors of a circuit (ungrounded, neutral, and equipment grounding conductors) to be installed in the same raceway, cable tray, or trench. This is a principle that's been in the *Code* for about 80 years to address "inductive heating," which occurs any time individual conductors are installed in ferrous (steel) raceways. The exception permits individual raceways to contain a single phase conductor or neutral for underground installations containing nonmetallic raceways in accordance with 300.20. This approach is sometimes used in large occupancies with multiple parallel sets to make it easier to terminate the conductors and still comply with 310.10(H)(2). The change to 300.3(B)(1) Ex clarifies that the "neutral" conductor can be installed isolated, not just the phase conductors. Although 300.5(I) Ex 2 says the same thing, this clarification clears up what was construed as a conflict by some.

300.3 Conductors

(A) Conductors. Single conductors must be installed within a Chapter 3 wiring method, such as a raceway, cable, or enclosure. Figure 300–2

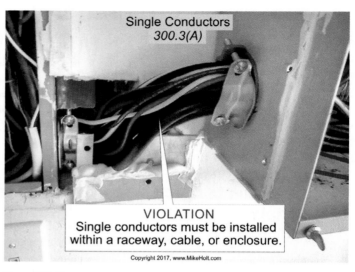

Figure 300–2

Ex: Overhead conductors can be installed in accordance with 225.6.

(B) Circuit Conductors Grouped Together. Conductors of a circuit and, where used, the neutral and equipment grounding and bonding conductors must be installed in the same raceway, cable, trench, cord, or cable tray, except as permitted by (1) through (4). Figure 300–3

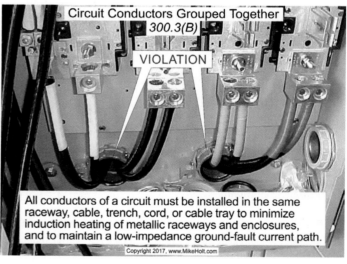

Figure 300–3

(1) Paralleled Installations. Conductors installed in parallel in accordance with 310.10(H) must have all circuit conductors within the same raceway, cable tray, trench, or cable. Figure 300–4

Ex: Parallel phase and neutral conductors can be installed in individual underground nonmetallic raceways (Phase A in raceway 1, Phase B in raceway 2, and so forth) as permitted by 300.5(I) Ex 2, if the installation complies with 300.20(B). Figure 300–5

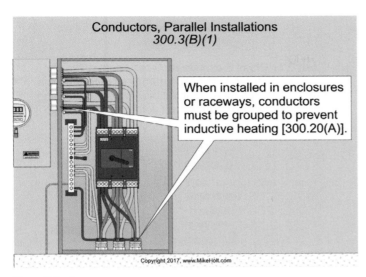

Conductors, Parallel Installations
300.3(B)(1)

When installed in enclosures or raceways, conductors must be grouped to prevent inductive heating [300.20(A)].

Figure 300–4

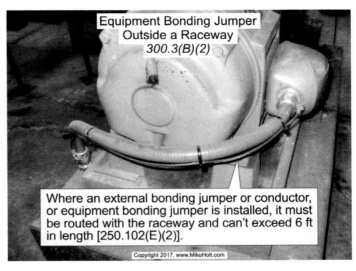

Equipment Bonding Jumper Outside a Raceway
300.3(B)(2)

Where an external bonding jumper or conductor, or equipment bonding jumper is installed, it must be routed with the raceway and can't exceed 6 ft in length [250.102(E)(2)].

Figure 300–6

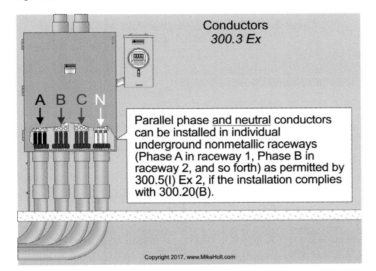

Conductors
300.3 Ex

A B C N

Parallel phase and neutral conductors can be installed in individual underground nonmetallic raceways (Phase A in raceway 1, Phase B in raceway 2, and so forth) as permitted by 300.5(I) Ex 2, if the installation complies with 300.20(B).

Figure 300–5

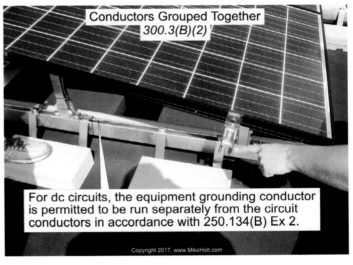

Conductors Grouped Together
300.3(B)(2)

For dc circuits, the equipment grounding conductor is permitted to be run separately from the circuit conductors in accordance with 250.134(B) Ex 2.

Figure 300–7

(2) Outside a Raceway or an Enclosure. Equipment grounding jumpers can be located outside of a flexible raceway if the bonding jumper is installed in accordance with 250.102(E)(2). Figure 300–6

For dc circuits, the equipment grounding conductor can be run separately from the circuit conductors in accordance with 250.134(B) Ex 2. Figure 300–7

(3) Nonferrous Wiring Methods. Circuit conductors can be installed in different raceways (Phase A in raceway 1, Phase B in raceway 2, and so on) if, in order to reduce or eliminate inductive heating, the raceway is nonmetallic or nonmagnetic and the installation complies with 300.20(B). See 300.3(B)(1) and 300.5(I) Ex 2.

(C) Conductors of Different Systems.

(1) Mixing. Power conductors of alternating-current and direct-current systems rated 1,000V or less can occupy the same raceway, cable, or enclosure if all conductors have an insulation voltage rating not less than the maximum circuit voltage. Figure 300–8

Author's Comment:

■ Control, signal, and communications wiring must be separated from power and lighting circuits so the higher-voltage conductors don't accidentally energize the control, signal, or communications wiring: Figure 300–9
  ◆ Class 1 control circuits, 725.48
  ◆ Class 2 and Class 3 Control Circuits, 725.136(A)
  ◆ Communications Circuits, 800.133(A)(1)(c)

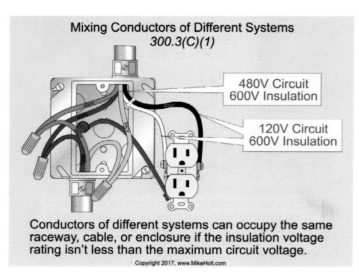

Figure 300–8

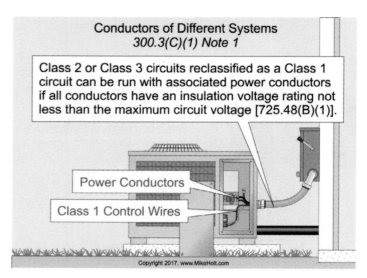

Figure 300–10

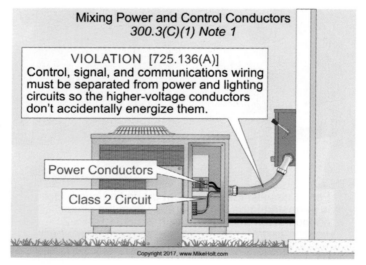

Figure 300–9

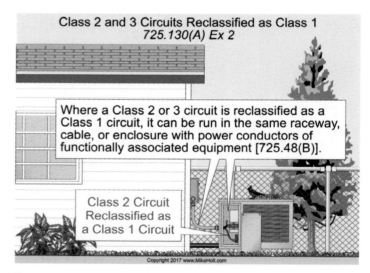

Figure 300–11

- ◆ Coaxial Cable, 820.133(A)
- ◆ Fire Alarm Circuits, 760.136(A)
- ◆ Sound Circuits, 640.9(C)

■ Class 1 circuit conductors can be installed with associated power conductors [725.48(B)(1)] if all conductors have an insulation voltage rating not less than the maximum circuit voltage [300.3(C)(1)]. Figure 300–10

■ A Class 2 circuit that's been reclassified as a Class 1 circuit [725.130(A) Ex 2] can be installed with associated power conductors [725.48(B)(1)] if all conductors have an insulation voltage rating not less than the maximum circuit voltage [300.3(C)(1)]. Figure 300–11

Note 2: PV system conductors, both direct current and alternating current, are permitted to be installed in the same raceways, outlet and junction boxes, or similar fittings with each other, but they must be kept entirely independent of all other non-PV system wiring [690.31(B)]. Figure 300–12

300.5 Underground Installations

Several changes have been made to the rules for underground installations including added footnotes in table 300.5, clarifications to requirements for parallel conductors, burial warning ribbons, sealing underground raceways, and backfill materials.

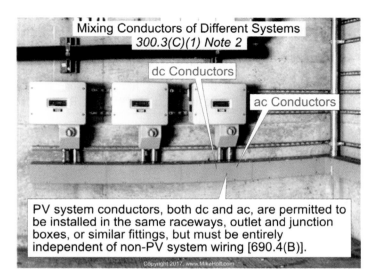

Mixing Conductors of Different Systems
300.3(C)(1) Note 2

dc Conductors

ac Conductors

PV system conductors, both dc and ac, are permitted to be installed in the same raceways, outlet and junction boxes, or similar fittings, but must be entirely independent of non-PV system wiring [690.4(B)].

Copyright 2017, www.MikeHolt.com

Figure 300–12

Analysis

Table 300.5 consumes most of this section. It's enormous and gives the "cover" requirements for underground installations (cover being measured from the top of the wiring method to the finished grade, in accordance with Note 1 of the table).

NEW

Table 300.5. New to the table are a couple of footnotes. It's worth mentioning here that Informational Notes aren't enforceable parts of the *Code* [90.5(C)] but table notes are. There was a conflict with UL 1838, *Standard for Safety for Low Voltage Landscape Lighting Systems* and Table 300.5, and 110.3(B). UL 1838 permits wiring for low-voltage wiring that isn't intended for direct burial and the instructions are required to include this information for the installer if the wiring can't be buried. 110.3(B) requires the instructions to be followed and 300.5 now has a new footnote that allows a lesser depth where specified in the instructions. The new table notes clear up the conflicting codes, UL listing, and Table.

Table 300.5 Footnote "a" was added to column 5, which addresses circuits for low-voltage lighting systems (30V or less). Generally speaking, a cover of only six in. is required for these systems. While that may seem rather shallow, a 30V installation is very unlikely to cause a fatal electric shock. It's perhaps impossible for there to be a 30V fatal shock in a dry location, and improbable in a wet one. If a

Class 2 transformer supplies the lighting system, the threat of a fatal shock disappears completely. With the increasing use of LED lighting, these power supplies are becoming more and more popular, so why not allow less cover if permitted by the instructions? While the *NEC* doesn't necessarily limit this to Class 2 power-supplied low-voltage lighting systems, it seems that it will probably be the most common application of this allowance.

NEW

A new Table 300.5 Footnote "b" addresses low-voltage lighting systems for swimming pools, with the same justification as other low-voltage lighting systems.

EDITED

Suitable for Wet Locations. Section 300.3(B) contains a rule requiring underground conductors and cables, including those in underground raceways, to be suitable for wet locations in accordance with 310.10(C). The previous edition of the *Code* required underground splices to be listed for wet locations; but this text was removed from this section of *NEC* because it's already covered in 110.14(B).

CLARIFIED

Physical Damage. The rules for direct-buried conductors and cables are in 300.5(D). They include the requirement for installing a warning ribbon for direct-buried service conductors [300.5(D)(3)], but most of the rules are concerned with protecting the cables or conductors when they emerge from underground. Section 300.5(D)(4) provides a list of raceways that can be used to protect these conductors and cables, but interestingly, the list has never included EMT.

The fact that the conductors are subject to physical damage doesn't mean that a raceway surrounding them is, because physical damage is relative to the material being used. The things that can damage UF cable won't necessarily damage RMC, PVC, or even EMT.

CLARIFIED

Sealing of Underground Raceways. The sealing of underground raceways is a concept that's seen a number of changes over the last few *Code* cycles. Section 225.27 was added a few years ago to require underground raceways entering buildings to be

• • •

sealed, and was then revised to require that the sealing material not damage the conductors or cables in the raceway. This is ensured by using a product that's identified for the application. The text in 300.5(G) now follows the lead of 225.27 which requires the compound to be identified for use with the cable or conductor insulation.

CLARIFIED

Backfill. The requirements for backfill material surrounding underground installations [300.5(F)] have long required that the backfill doesn't damage the underground cables. This prohibits large rocks or construction debris from being used for, or mixed with, backfill. Sometimes we can have an *NEC* rule with a massive loophole for decades without anyone ever noticing it; such is the case here. Why are we worried about damaging direct-buried cables but not direct-buried conductors? Well, that loophole has been closed since conductors are now also subject to these rules. A similar change was made to the note in 300.5(J) regarding earth movement; it also now mentions both conductors and cables.

300.5 Underground Installations

(A) Minimum Burial Depths. When cables or raceways are installed underground, they must have a minimum "cover" in accordance with Table 300.5. Figure 300–13

Table 300.5 Minimum Cover Requirements in Inches

Location	Column 1 Buried Cables	Column 2 RMC or IMC	Column 3 Nonmetallic Raceway
Under Building	0	0	0
Dwelling Unit	24/12*	6	18
Dwelling Unit Driveway	18/12*	6	18/12*
Under Roadway	24	24	24
Other Locations	24	6	18

Residential branch circuits rated 120V or less with GFCI protection and maximum protection of 20A.

See the table in the NEC for full details.

a. Lesser depth is permitted where specified in the installation instructions of a listed low-voltage lighting system.

b. A depth of 6 in. is permitted for pool, spa, and fountain lighting wiring installed in a nonmetallic raceway, where part of a listed 30V lighting system.

Note 1 to Table 300.5 defines "Cover" as the distance from the top of the underground cable or raceway to the top surface of finished grade. Figure 300–14

Underground Installations, Minimum Cover Depths
Table 300.5

	UF or USE Cables or Conductors	RMC or IMC	PVC not Encased in Concrete	Residential 15A & 20A GFCI 120V Branch Ckts
Dwelling Unit	24 in.	6 in.	18 in.	12 in.
Dwelling Unit Driveway and Parking Area	18 in.	18 in.	18 in.	12 in.
Under Roadway Driveway Parking Lot	24 in.	24 in.	24 in.	24 in.
Other Locations	24 in.	6 in.	18 in.	12 in.

Copyright 2017, www.MikeHolt.com

Figure 300–13

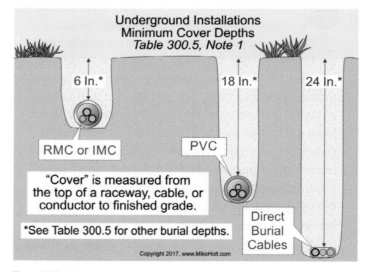

Figure 300–14

- The cover requirements contained in 300.5 don't apply to signaling, communications, and other power-limited wiring systems: Figure 300–15
  - ◆ Class 2 and 3 Circuits, 725.3
  - ◆ Communications Cables and Raceways, 90.3
  - ◆ Coaxial Cable, 90.3
  - ◆ Fire Alarm Circuits, 760.3
  - ◆ Optical Fiber Cables and Raceways, 770.3

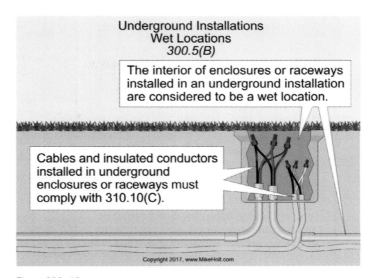

Figure 300–16

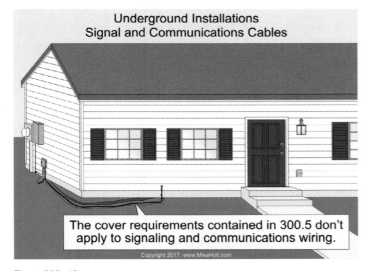

The cover requirements contained in 300.5 don't apply to signaling and communications wiring.

Figure 300–15

(B) Wet Locations. The interior of enclosures or raceways installed in an underground installation are considered to be a wet location. Cables and insulated conductors installed in underground enclosures or raceways must comply with 310.10(C). Figure 300–16

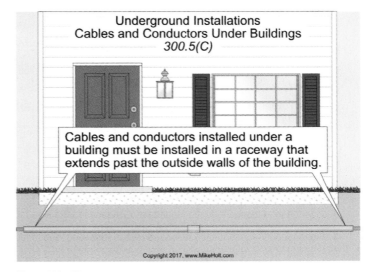

Figure 300–17

Author's Comment:

- The definition of a "Wet Location" as contained in Article 100, includes installations underground, in concrete slabs in direct contact with the earth, locations subject to saturation with water, and unprotected locations exposed to weather. If raceways are installed in wet locations above grade, the interior of these raceways is also considered to be a wet location [300.9].

(C) Cables and Conductors Under Buildings. Cables and conductors installed under a building must be installed within a raceway that extends past the outside walls of the building. Figure 300–17

Ex 2: Type MC Cable listed for direct burial is permitted under a building without installation within a raceway [330.10(A)(5)]. Figure 300–18

(D) Protecting Underground Cables and Conductors. Direct-buried conductors and cables such as Types MC, UF, and USE installed underground must be protected from damage in accordance with (1) through (4).

(1) Emerging from Grade. Direct-buried cables or conductors that emerge from grade must be installed in an enclosure or raceway to protect against physical damage. Protection isn't required to extend more than 18 in. below grade, and protection above ground must extend to a height of not less than 8 ft. Figure 300–19

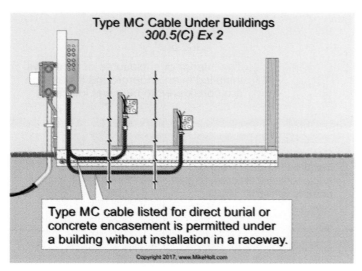

Figure 300–18

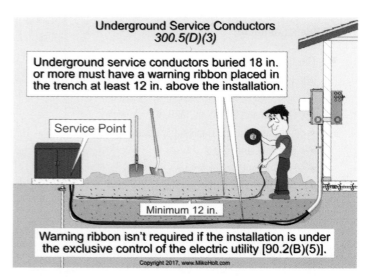

Figure 300–20

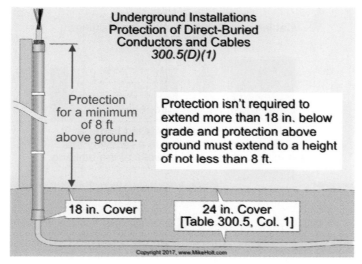

Figure 300–19

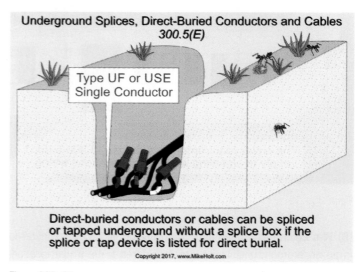

Figure 300–21

(2) Conductors Entering Buildings. Underground conductors and cables that enter a building must be protected to the point of entrance.

(3) Service Conductors. Underground service conductors must have their location identified by a warning ribbon placed in the trench at least 12 in. above the underground conductor installation. Figure 300–20

(4) Raceway Damage. Where a raceway is subject to physical damage, the conductors must be installed in EMT, RMC, IMC, RTRC-XW, or Schedule 80 PVC conduit.

(E) Underground Splices and Taps. Direct-buried conductors or cables can be spliced or tapped underground without a splice box [300.15(G)], if the splice or tap is made in accordance with 110.14(B). Figure 300–21

(F) Backfill. Backfill material for underground wiring must not damage underground raceways, cables, or conductors. Figure 300–22

Author's Comment:

- Large rocks, chunks of concrete, steel rods, mesh, and other sharp-edged objects aren't permitted to be used for backfill material, because they can damage the underground conductors, cables, or raceways.

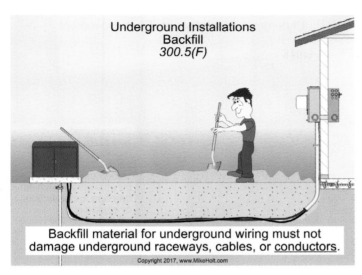

Figure 300–22

(G) Raceway Seals. If moisture could contact energized live parts from an underground raceway, including spare raceways, a seal identified for use with the cable or conductor insulation must be installed at either or both ends of the raceway [225.27 and 230.8]. Figure 300–23

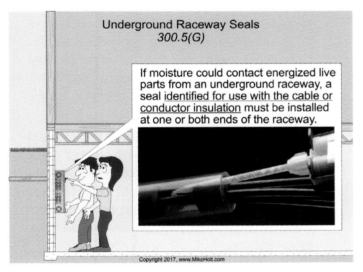

Figure 300–23

Author's Comment:

■ This is a common problem for equipment located downhill from the supply, or in underground equipment rooms. See 230.8 for service raceway seals and 300.7(A) for different temperature area seals.

Note: Hazardous explosive gases or vapors make it necessary to seal underground raceways that enter the building in accordance with 501.15.

Author's Comment:

■ It isn't the intent of this Note to imply that sealing fittings of the types required in hazardous locations be installed in unclassified locations, except as required in Chapter 5. This also doesn't imply that the sealing material provides a watertight seal, but only that it prevents moisture from entering the raceways.

(H) Bushing. Raceways that terminate underground must have a bushing or fitting at the end of the raceway to protect emerging cables or conductors.

(I) Conductors Grouped Together. Underground conductors of the same circuit, including the equipment grounding conductor, must be inside the same raceway, or in close proximity to each other in the same trench. See 300.3(B). Figure 300–24

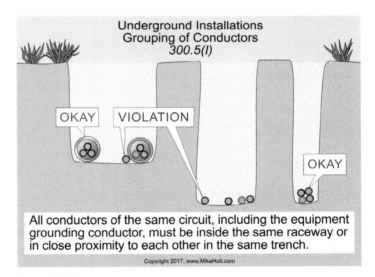

Figure 300–24

Ex 1: Conductors can be installed in parallel in raceways, multiconductor cables, or direct-buried single-conductor cables. Each raceway or multiconductor cable must contain all conductors of the same circuit including the equipment grounding conductor. Each direct-buried single-conductor cable must be located in close proximity in the trench to the other single-conductors cables in the same parallel set of conductors, including equipment grounding conductors.

Ex 2: Parallel circuit conductors installed in accordance with 310.10(H) of the same phase or neutral can be installed in underground PVC conduits, if inductive heating at raceway terminations is reduced by the use of aluminum locknuts and cutting a slot between the individual holes through which the conductors pass as required by 300.20(B). Figure 300–25

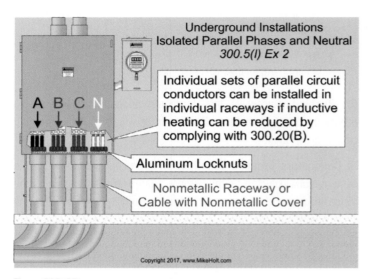

Figure 300–25

Author's Comment:

- Installing ungrounded and neutral conductors in different PVC conduits makes it easier to terminate larger parallel sets of conductors, but it will result in higher levels of electromagnetic fields (EMF).

(J) Earth Movement. Direct-buried conductors, cables, or raceways that are subject to movement by settlement or frost must be arranged to prevent damage to conductors or equipment connected to the wiring. Figure 300–26

Note: "S" loops in underground direct burial <u>cables and conductors</u>, raceway expansion fittings, and flexible connections to equipment can serve this purpose.

(K) Directional Boring. Cables or raceways installed using directional boring equipment must be approved by the authority having jurisdiction for this purpose.

Figure 300–26

Author's Comment:

- Directional boring technology uses a directional drill, which is steered continuously from point "A" to point "B." When the drill head comes out of the earth at point "B," it's replaced with a back-reamer and the duct or raceway being installed is attached to it. The size of the boring rig (hp, torque, and pull-back power) comes into play, along with the types of soil, in determining the type of raceways required. For telecommunications work, multiple poly innerducts are pulled in at one time. At major crossings, such as expressways, railroads, or rivers, outerduct may be installed to create a permanent sleeve for the innerducts.

- "Innerduct" and "outerduct" are terms usually associated with optical fiber cable installations, while "unitduct" comes with factory installed conductors. Galvanized rigid metal conduit, Schedule 40 and Schedule 80 PVC, HDPE conduit and nonmetallic underground conduit with conductors (NUCC) are common wiring methods used with directional boring installations.

300.7 Raceways Exposed to Different Temperatures

This section was revised to clarify that the requirements for raceway expansion fittings also apply to deflection fittings.

Analysis

CLARIFIED

I'll never forget teaching a seminar on Article 300 and watching an audience member cringe when I brought up the rules for expansion joints in raceways. He's a good electrician, and I've known him for years, but like everyone else in the world (including me) he doesn't know every single rule in the *Code*. He didn't know about expansion fittings, but he learned all about them after installing a run of exposed PVC conduit over 1,000 ft! Take a look the next time you drive behind a shopping center and you're sure to see this for yourself.

Thermal expansion isn't the only time we need to compensate for raceway movement, and expansion fittings aren't the only method of dealing with it. For example, structures that flex or vibrate, such as bridges, deal with this variable by installing a deflection fitting. The *NEC* now makes specific mention of these products, and a quick search on the Internet will yield plenty of results for the products available for these applications.

300.7 Raceways Exposed to Different Temperatures

(A) Sealing. If a raceway is subjected to different temperatures, and where condensation is known to be a problem, the raceway must be filled with a material approved by the authority having jurisdiction that will prevent the circulation of warm air to a colder section of the raceway. An explosionproof seal isn't required for this purpose. Figure 300–27

(B) Expansion, Expansion-Deflection, and Deflection Fittings. Raceways must be provided with expansion, expansion-deflection, and deflection fittings where necessary to compensate for thermal expansion, deflection, and contraction. Figure 300–28

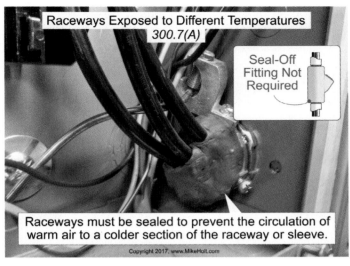

Figure 300–27

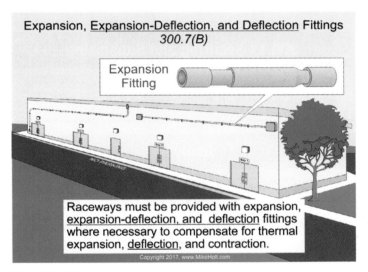

Figure 300–28

Note: Table 352.44 provides the expansion characteristics for PVC conduit. The expansion characteristics for steel conduit are determined by multiplying the values from Table 352.44 by 0.20, and the expansion characteristics for aluminum raceways are determined by multiplying the values from Table 352.44 by 0.40. Table 354.44 provides the expansion characteristics for reinforced thermosetting resin conduit (RTRC). Figure 300–29

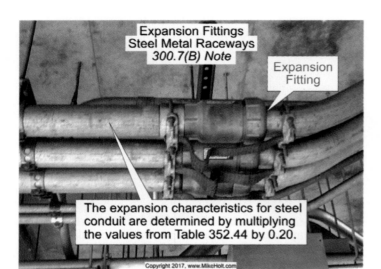

Expansion Fittings
Steel Metal Raceways
300.7(B) Note

Expansion Fitting

The expansion characteristics for steel conduit are determined by multiplying the values from Table 352.44 by 0.20.

Copyright 2017, www.MikeHolt.com

Figure 300–29

300.11 Securing and Supporting

The rules for securing and supporting wiring methods were editorially revised to clarify it's a general rule.

Analysis

CLARIFIED

The 2014 *Code* was a bit unclear about how this rule applies. Did 300.11(A) pertain only to suspended ceilings? It starts with a general statement indicating that raceways, cables, boxes, and so forth must be secured in place. This seems like a stand-alone general requirement to all installations. But then the next few sentences talk about ceiling grid wires, and then we immediately go into subsections (1) and (2) which are definitely talking about ceiling grids. From there we go to 300.11(B) and (C), which don't seem to be talking about ceiling grids at all.

The change to 300.11(A) is very simple, but it helps in a major way. The first sentence of this rule is clear that it's a general rule that applies in general; electrical equipment must be secured in place. Then we have the other subsection pertaining to ceiling grids and other issues. The remaining subsections were renumbered accordingly, without any text changes.

300.11 Securing and Supporting

(A) Secured in Place. Raceways, cable assemblies, and enclosures must be securely fastened in place. Figure 300–30

Securing and Supporting
Secured in Place
300.11(A)

Raceways, cable assemblies, boxes, cabinets, and fittings nust be securely fastened in place.

Copyright 2017, www.MikeHolt.com

Figure 300–30

(B) Wiring Systems Installed Above Suspended Ceilings. The ceiling-support wires or ceiling grid aren't permitted to be used to support raceways and cables (power, signaling, or communications). However, independent support wires that are secured at both ends and provide secure support are permitted. Figure 300–31

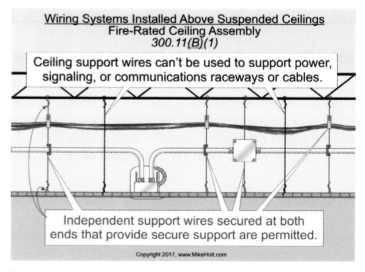

Wiring Systems Installed Above Suspended Ceilings
Fire-Rated Ceiling Assembly
300.11(B)(1)

Ceiling support wires can't be used to support power, signaling, or communications raceways or cables.

Independent support wires secured at both ends that provide secure support are permitted.

Copyright 2017, www.MikeHolt.com

Figure 300–31

- Outlet boxes [314.23(D)] and luminaires can be secured to the suspended-ceiling grid if securely fastened to the ceiling-framing members by mechanical means such as bolts, screws, or rivets, or by the use of clips or other securing means identified for use with the type of ceiling-framing member(s) used [410.36(B)].

(1) Fire-Rated Ceiling Assembly. Electrical wiring within the cavity of a fire-rated floor-ceiling or roof-ceiling assembly can be supported by independent support wires attached to the ceiling assembly. The independent support wires must be distinguishable from the suspended-ceiling support wires by color, tagging, or other effective means.

(2) Nonfire-Rated Ceiling Assembly. Wiring in a nonfire-rated floor-ceiling or roof-ceiling assembly can be supported by independent support wires attached to the ceiling assembly. The independent support wires must be distinguishable from the suspended-ceiling support wires by color, tagging, or other effective means. Figure 300–32

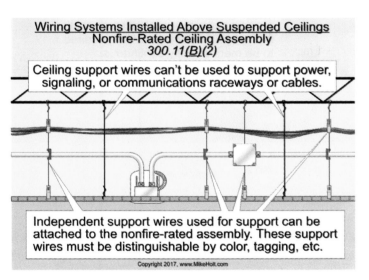

Figure 300–32

(C) Raceways Used for Support. Raceways aren't permitted to be used as a means of support for other raceways, cables, or nonelectrical equipment, except as permitted in (1) through (3). Figure 300–33

(1) Identified. If the raceway or means of support is identified as a means of support.

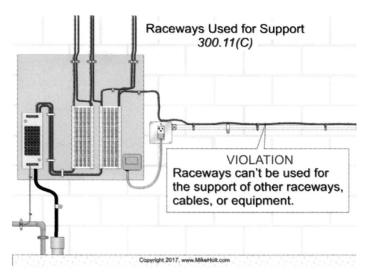

Figure 300–33

(2) Class 2 and 3 Circuits. Class 2 and 3 cables can be supported by the raceway that supplies power to the equipment controlled by the Class 2 or 3 circuit. Figure 300–34

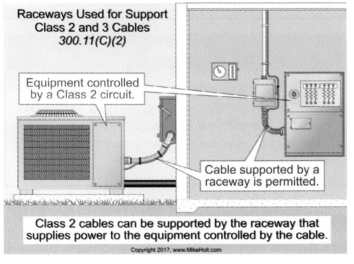

Figure 300–34

(3) Boxes Supported by Raceways. Raceways are permitted as a means of support for threaded boxes and conduit bodies in accordance with 314.23(E) and (F), or to support luminaires in accordance with 410.36(E).

(D) Cables Not Used as Means of Support. Cables aren't permitted to be used to support other cables, raceways, or nonelectrical equipment. Figure 300–35

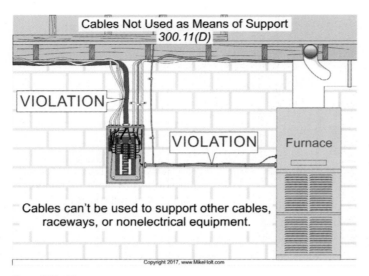

Figure 300–35

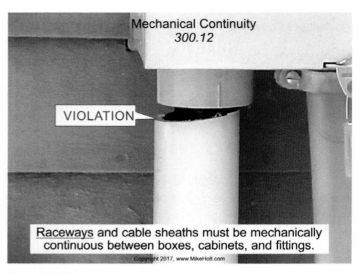

Figure 300–36

300.12 Mechanical Continuity

The text about "metallic and nonmetallic" raceways was removed from the rule relating to mechanical continuity.

Analysis

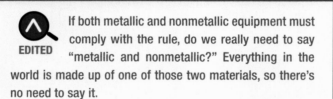

EDITED If both metallic and nonmetallic equipment must comply with the rule, do we really need to say "metallic and nonmetallic?" Everything in the world is made up of one of those two materials, so there's no need to say it.

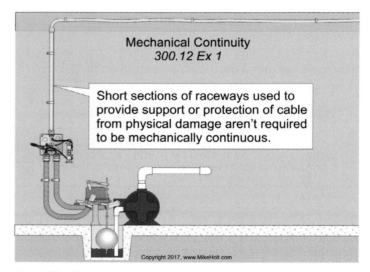

Figure 300–37

300.12 Mechanical Continuity

Raceways and cable sheaths must be mechanically continuous between boxes, cabinets, and fittings. Figure 300–36

Ex 1: Short sections of raceways used to provide protection of cable from physical damage aren't required to be mechanically continuous [250.86 Ex 2 and 300.10 Ex 1]. Figure 300–37

Ex 2: Raceways at the bottom of open-bottom equipment, such as switchboards, motor control centers, and transformers, aren't required to be mechanically secured to the equipment. Figure 300–38

Author's Comment:

■ When raceways are stubbed into an open-bottom switchboard, the raceway, including the end fitting, can't rise more than 3 in. above the bottom of the switchboard enclosure [408.5].

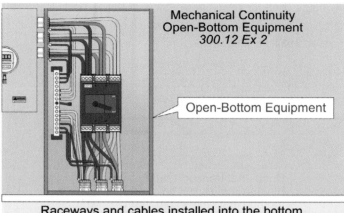

Mechanical Continuity
Open-Bottom Equipment
300.12 Ex 2

Open-Bottom Equipment

Raceways and cables installed into the bottom
of open-bottom equipment aren't required to be
mechanically secured to the equipment.

Copyright 2017, www.MikeHolt.com

Figure 300–38

300.19 Supporting Conductors in Vertical Raceways

The rule about supporting conductors in vertical installations
was clarified.

Analysis

CLARIFIED

If you've worked in a high-rise building you've
probably had to deal with securing conductors
inside a raceway. The idea of pulling wires in a
raceway only to have them disappear back into it and fall all
the way to the ground floor is sort of funny when thinking
about a couple of 12 AWG wires, but not so much if you visualize 4/0 AWG conductors flooding the panel room, wrecking
everything and injuring everyone in their path.

The changes made state that at least one support
method must be used; implying different methods could be
used where multiple supports are installed.

300.19 Supporting Conductors in Vertical Raceways

(A) Spacing Intervals. If the vertical rise of a raceway exceeds the
values of Table 300.19(A), <u>each conductor</u> must be supported at the
top, or as close to the top as practical. Intermediate support must
also be provided in increments that don't exceed the values of Table
300.19(A). Figure 300–39

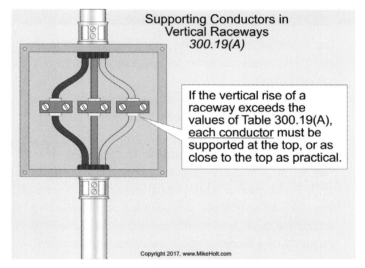

Supporting Conductors in
Vertical Raceways
300.19(A)

If the vertical rise of a
raceway exceeds the
values of Table 300.19(A),
<u>each conductor</u> must be
supported at the top, or as
close to the top as practical.

Copyright 2017, www.MikeHolt.com

Figure 300–39

Author's Comment:

■ The weight of long vertical runs of conductors can cause the
conductors to actually drop out of the raceway if they aren't
properly secured. There have been many cases where conductors in a vertical raceway were released from the pulling
"basket" or "grip" (at the top) without being secured, and the
conductors fell down and out of the raceway, injuring those
at the bottom of the installation.

300.22 Wiring in Ducts and Plenums Spaces

A new exception provides options for installing wiring in ducts, and the requirements for equipment and associated wiring used in air handling spaces were clarified.

Analysis

The requirements for installing wiring methods inside air ducts and plenum spaces are fairly simple, yet remain very misunderstood.

Section 300.22(A) is very easy—you can't have any wiring in a duct used for dust collection or similar purposes.

 NEW Section 300.22(B) applies to physically constructed ducts (typically metallic ducts, but ducts of drywall or other material are included). You can only have wiring in these ducts if it's a permitted wiring method and needs to be there to sense or act upon the air in the duct. A new exception now allows other wiring methods and cable systems, that are permitted in plenum spaces, to be installed in these ducts if lengths don't exceed 4 ft.

 CLARIFIED Section 300.22(C) applies to equipment and associated wiring used in air handling spaces such as closets, areas above suspended ceilings, and areas beneath raised floors. If a space is used for air handling, you must use only wiring methods that have low smoke and heat release properties. This rule and the corresponding note were edited to clarify that equipment and its associated wiring used in these spaces must also meet these requirements.

300.22 Wiring in Ducts and Plenums Spaces

This section applies to the installation and uses of electrical wiring and equipment in ducts used for dust, loose stock, or vapor removal; ducts specifically fabricated for environmental air, and plenum spaces used for environmental air.

(A) Ducts Used for Dust, Loose Stock, or Vapor. Ducts that transport dust, loose stock, or vapors must not have any wiring method installed within them. Figure 300–40

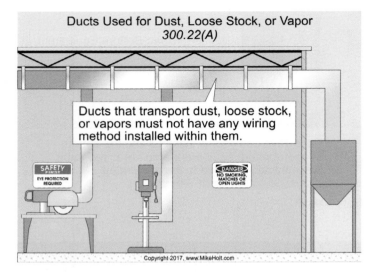

Figure 300–40

(B) Ducts Specifically Fabricated for Environmental Air. If necessary for direct action upon, or sensing of, the contained air, Type MC cable that has a smooth or corrugated impervious metal sheath without an overall nonmetallic covering, electrical metallic tubing, flexible metallic tubing, intermediate metal conduit, or rigid metal conduit without an overall nonmetallic covering can be installed in ducts specifically fabricated to transport environmental air. Flexible metal conduit in lengths not exceeding 4 ft can be used to connect physically adjustable equipment and devices within the fabricated duct.

Equipment is only permitted within the duct specifically fabricated to transport environmental air if necessary for the direct action upon, or sensing of, the contained air. Equipment, devices, and/or illumination are only permitted to be installed in the duct if necessary to facilitate maintenance and repair. Figure 300–41

Ex: Wiring methods and cables listed for plenum space can be installed in ducts specifically fabricated for environmental air-handling purposes under the following conditions:

(1) The wiring method or cabling is necessary to connect to equipment or devices associated with the direct action upon or sensing of the contained air, and

(2) The total length of such wiring method or cabling doesn't exceed 4 ft.

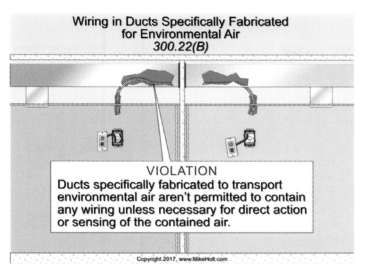

Figure 300–41

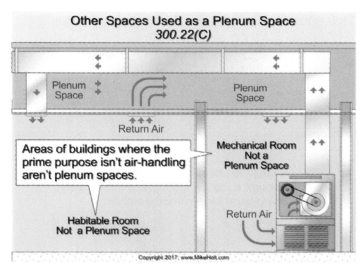

Figure 300–42

Author's Comment:

- Class 2 and Class 3 cables selected in accordance with Table 725.154 and installed in accordance with 725.135(B) are permitted to be installed in ducts specifically fabricated for environmental air [725.3(C) Ex. 1].

- Power-limited fire alarm cables selected in accordance with Table 760.154 and installed in accordance with 760.135(B) are permitted to be installed in ducts specifically fabricated for environmental air [760.3(C) Ex. 1].

(C) Plenum Space for Environmental Air. This subsection applies only to plenum space (space above a suspended ceiling or below a raised floor used for environmental air), it doesn't apply to habitable rooms or areas of buildings, the prime purpose of which isn't air handling. Figure 300–42

Note 1: The spaces above a suspended ceiling or below a raised floor used for environmental air are examples of the type of plenum space to which this section applies. Figure 300–43

Ex: In a dwelling unit, this section doesn't apply to the space between joists or studs where the wiring passes through that space perpendicular to the long dimension of that space. Figure 300–44

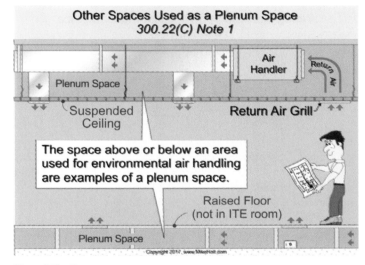

Figure 300–43

(1) Wiring Methods. Electrical metallic tubing, rigid metal conduit, intermediate metal conduit, armored cable, metal-clad cable without a nonmetallic cover, and flexible metal conduit can be installed in a plenum space. Surface metal raceways or metal wireways with metal covers can be installed in a plenum space. Figure 300–45

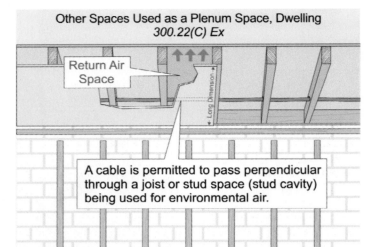

Other Spaces Used as a Plenum Space, Dwelling
300.22(C) Ex

Return Air Space

Long Dimension

A cable is permitted to pass perpendicular through a joist or stud space (stud cavity) being used for environmental air.

Copyright 2017, www.MikeHolt.com

Figure 300–44

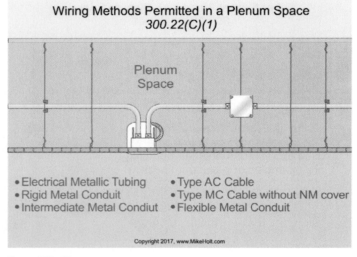

Wiring Methods Permitted in a Plenum Space
300.22(C)(1)

Plenum Space

• Electrical Metallic Tubing
• Rigid Metal Conduit
• Intermediate Metal Condiut
• Type AC Cable
• Type MC Cable without NM cover
• Flexible Metal Conduit

Copyright 2017, www.MikeHolt.com

Figure 300–45

Cable ties for securing and supporting must be listed for for use in a plenum space. Figure 300–46

Author's Comment:

■ PVC conduit [Article 352], electrical nonmetallic tubing [Article 362], liquidtight flexible conduit, and nonmetallic cables aren't permitted to be installed in plenum spaces because they give off deadly toxic fumes when burned or superheated.

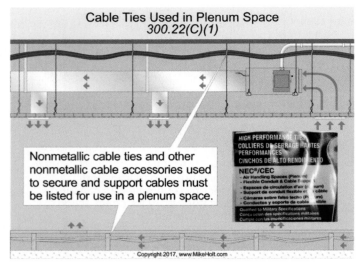

Cable Ties Used in Plenum Space
300.22(C)(1)

Nonmetallic cable ties and other nonmetallic cable accessories used to secure and support cables must be listed for use in a plenum space.

HIGH PERFORMANCE TIES
COLLIERS DE SERRAGE HAUTES PERFORMANCES
CINCHOS DE ALTO RENDIMIENTO
NEC®/CEC
- Air Handling Spaces (Plenum)
- Flexible Conduit & Cable Support
- Espaces de circulation d'air (plenum)
- Support de conduit flexible et câble
- Cámaras sobre falso techo (Plenum)
- Conductos y soporte de cable flexible
Qualified to Military Specifications

Copyright 2017, www.MikeHolt.com

Figure 300–46

■ Plenum-rated control, signaling, and communications cables and raceways are permitted in plenum spaces according to the following:
  ◆ Communications, Table 800.154(a)
  ◆ Control and Signaling, 725.3(C) Ex. 2
  ◆ Coaxial Cable, Table 820.154(a)
  ◆ Fire Alarm, Table 760.3(C) Ex. 2
  ◆ Optical Fiber Cables and Raceways, Table 770.154(a)
  ◆ Sound Systems, 640.9(C) and Table 725.154

■ Any wiring method suitable for the condition can be used in a space not used for environmental air-handling purposes. Figure 300–47

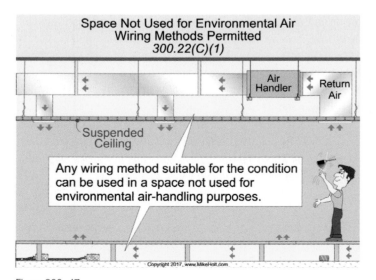

Space Not Used for Environmental Air
Wiring Methods Permitted
300.22(C)(1)

Air Handler
Return Air

Suspended Ceiling

Any wiring method suitable for the condition can be used in a space not used for environmental air-handling purposes.

Copyright 2017, www.MikeHolt.com

Figure 300–47

(2) Cable Tray Systems.

(a) Metal Cable Tray Systems. Metal cable tray systems can be installed to support the wiring methods and equipment permitted to be installed in a plenum space. Figure 300–48

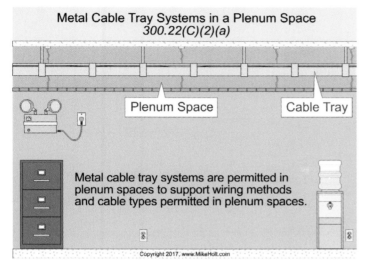

Figure 300–48

(3) Equipment. Electrical equipment with a metal enclosure can be installed in a plenum space. Figure 300–49

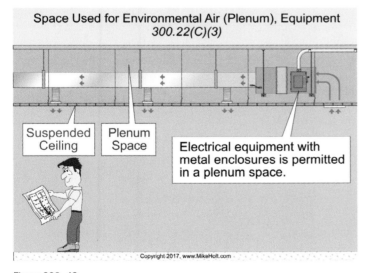

Figure 300–49

Author's Comment:

■ Examples of electrical equipment permitted in plenum spaces are air-handlers, junction boxes, and dry-type transformers; however, transformers must not be rated over 50 kVA when located in hollow spaces [450.13(B)]. Figure 300–50

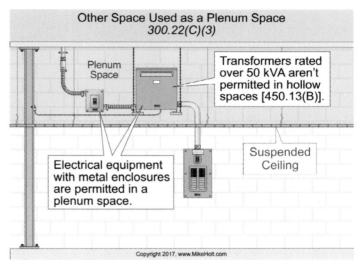

Figure 300–50

(D) Information Technology Equipment. Wiring methods beneath raised floors for information technology equipment can be installed as permitted in Article 645. Figure 300–51

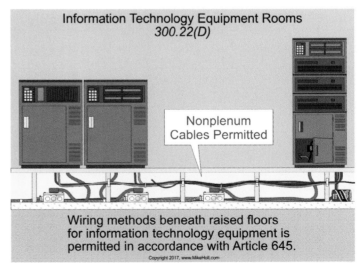

Figure 300–51

ARTICLE 310

CONDUCTORS FOR GENERAL WIRING

Introduction to Article 310—Conductors for General Wiring

This article contains the general requirements for conductors, such as insulation markings, ampacity ratings, and conditions of use. Article 310 doesn't apply to conductors that are part of flexible cords, fixture wires, or to conductors that are an integral part of equipment [90.7 and 300.1(B)].

People often make mistakes in applying the ampacity tables contained in Article 310. If you study the explanations carefully, you'll avoid common errors such as applying Table 310.15(B)(17) when you should be applying Table 310.15(B)(16).

Why so many tables? Why does Table 310.15(B)(17) list the ampacity of 6 THHN as 105A, while Table 310.15(B)(16) lists the same conductor as having an ampacity of only 75A? To answer that, go back to Article 100 and review the definition of ampacity. Notice the phrase "conditions of use." These tables set a maximum current value at which premature failure of the conductor insulation shouldn't occur during normal use, under the conditions described in the tables.

The designations THHN, THHW, RHH, and so on, are insulation types. Every type of insulation has a limit as to how much heat it can withstand. When current flows through a conductor, it creates heat. How well the insulation around a conductor can dissipate that heat depends on factors such as whether that conductor is in free air or not. Think about what happens when you put on a sweater, a jacket, and then a coat—all at the same time. You heat up. Your skin can't dissipate heat with all that clothing on nearly as well as it dissipates heat in free air. The same principal applies to conductors.

Conductor insulation also fails with age. That's why we conduct cable testing and take other measures to predict failure and replace certain conductors (for example, feeders or critical equipment conductors) while they're still within design specifications. But conductor insulation failure takes decades under normal use—and it's a maintenance issue. However, if a conductor is forced to exceed the ampacity listed in the appropriate table, and as a result its design temperature is exceeded, insulation failure happens much more rapidly—often catastrophically. Consequently, exceeding the allowable ampacity of a conductor is a serious safety issue.

Part I. General

310.1 Scope

(A) Installations. Article 310 contains the general requirements for conductors, such as insulation markings, ampacity ratings, and their use.

(B) Integral Parts of Equipment. This article doesn't apply to conductors that are an integral part of equipment [90.7 and 300.1(B)]. Figure 310–1

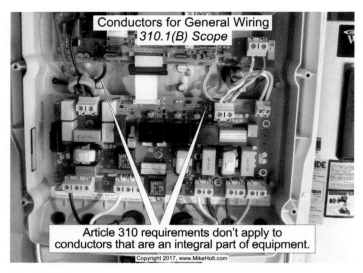

Figure 310–1

310.10 Uses Permitted

The word "bonding" has been replaced with the word "grounding" for technical accuracy.

Analysis

EDITED As time has passed, the Code Making Panels have made a huge effort to change the language that we use to describe grounding and bonding so it accurately describes what we're doing. In this case "equipment bonding conductor," which isn't defined in Article 100, was replaced with the term "equipment grounding conductor" which is. The purpose of this conductor is to clear a fault as explained in the definition of equipment grounding conductor in Article 100.

310.10 Uses Permitted

(B) Dry and Damp Locations. Insulated conductors typically used in dry and damp locations include THHN, THHW, THWN, or THWN-2.

Author's Comment:

■ Refer to Table 310.104 for a complete list of conductors that may be installed in dry or damp locations.

(C) Wet Locations. Insulated conductors typically used in wet locations include:

(2) Types THHW, THWN, THWN-2, XHHW, or XHHW-2

Author's Comment:

■ Refer to Table 310.104 for a complete list of conductors that may be installed in wet locations.

(D) Locations Exposed to Direct Sunlight. Insulated conductors and cables exposed to the direct rays of the sun must be:

(1) Listed as sunlight resistant or marked as being sunlight resistant. Figure 310–2

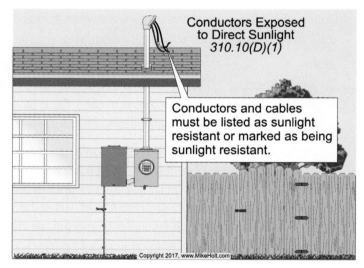

Figure 310–2

Author's Comment:

■ SE cable and the conductors contained in the cable are listed as sunlight resistant. However, according to the UL listing standard, the conductors contained in SE cable aren't required to be marked as sunlight resistant.

(2) Covered with insulating material, such as tape or sleeving materials that are listed as being sunlight resistant or marked as being sunlight resistant.

(G) Corrosive Conditions. Conductor insulation must be suitable for any substance to which it may be exposed that may have a detrimental effect on the conductor's insulation, such as oil, grease, vapor, gases, fumes, liquids, or other substances. See 110.11.

(H) Conductors in Parallel.

(1) General. Ungrounded and neutral conductors can be connected in parallel, only in sizes 1/0 AWG and larger where installed in accordance with (H)(2) through (H)(6). Figure 310–3

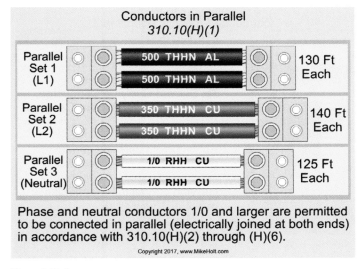

Figure 310–3

(2) Conductor and Installation Characteristics. When circuit conductors are installed in parallel, the conductors must be connected so that the current will be evenly distributed between the individual parallel conductors by requiring all circuit conductors within each parallel set to: Figure 310–4

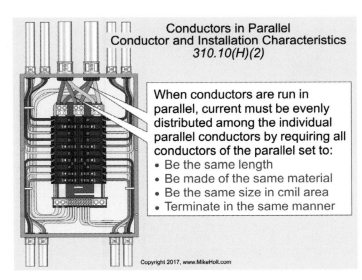

Figure 310–4

(1) Be the same length.

(2) Consist of the same conductor material (copper/aluminum).

(3) Be the same size in circular mil area (minimum 1/0 AWG).

(4) Have the same type of insulation (like THHN).

(5) Terminate in the same method (set screw versus compression).

Author's Comment:

■ Conductors aren't required to have the same physical characteristics as those of another ungrounded or neutral conductor to achieve balance. Figure 310–5

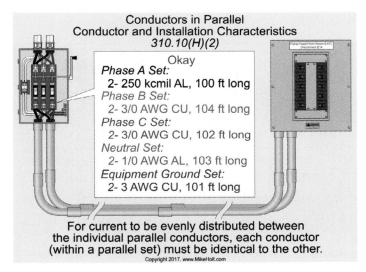

Figure 310–5

■ When installed in raceways or enclosures, paralleled conductors must be grouped to prevent inductive heating. Figure 310–6

(3) Separate Raceways or Cables. Raceways or cables containing parallel conductors must have the same electrical characteristics. Figure 310–7

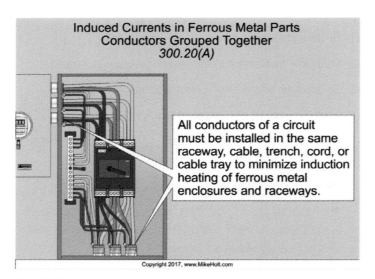

Figure 310–6

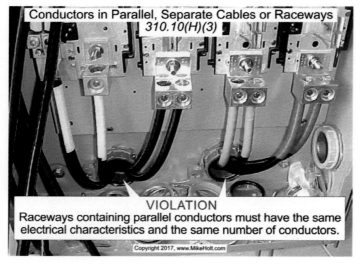

Figure 310–7

Author's Comment:

- If one set of parallel conductors is installed in a metal raceway and the other conductors are installed in PVC conduit, the conductors in the metal raceway will have an increased opposition to current flow (impedance) as compared to the conductors in the nonmetallic raceway. This results in an unbalanced distribution of current between the parallel conductors.

- Parallel conductor sets must have all circuit conductors within the same raceway [300.3(B)(1)].

Parallel sets of conductors aren't required to have the same physical characteristics as those of another set to achieve balance.

(4) Conductor Ampacity Adjustment. Each current-carrying conductor of a paralleled set of conductors must be counted as a current-carrying conductor for the purpose of conductor ampacity adjustment, in accordance with Table 310.15(B)(3)(a). Figure 310–8

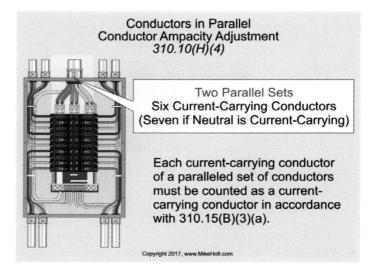

Figure 310–8

(5) Equipment Grounding Conductors. The equipment grounding conductors for circuits in parallel must be sized in accordance with 250.122(F). Sectioned equipment grounding conductors smaller than 1/0 AWG are permitted in multiconductor cables, if the combined circular mil area of the sectioned equipment grounding conductors in each cable complies with 250.122. Figure 310–9

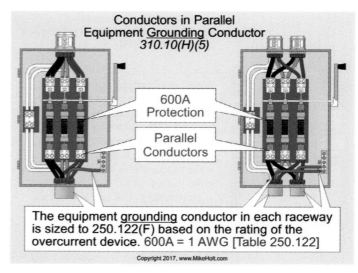

Figure 310–9

Author's Comment:

- The minimum 1/0 AWG parallel conductor size rule of 310.10(H) doesn't apply to equipment grounding conductors.

(6) Bonding Jumpers. Equipment bonding jumpers and supply-side bonding jumpers are sized in accordance with 250.102.

Author's Comment:

- The equipment bonding jumper isn't required to be larger than the largest ungrounded circuit conductors supplying the equipment.

310.15 Conductor Ampacity

As always, many changes to the rules for establishing conductor ampacities have been made, including requirements for cable bundling, rooftop temperature correction, and dwelling service conductor sizing.

Analysis

EDITED

Bundling of Cables. There's been an allowance to ignore ampacity adjustments for up to twenty 12 AWG three-conductor Type MC or AC cables without a nonmetallic outer covering for a long time. One of the factors that allows for this permission is that these cables have ridges from the spiral interlocking metal armor, which means that when the cables are touching each other there's actually space between them. This permissive allowance is still in place but was rewritten as an exception, without changing any of the technical requirements or allowances.

NEW

Rooftop Wiring Methods. Of much greater interest is a change made to 310.15(B)(3)(c) for cables and raceways on rooftops. Since its inclusion in the 2011 *NEC*, few rules have been more controversial than this one. Temperatures on a rooftop are higher than they are at grade level; nobody denies this. However, if this is a real issue in the world of electrical installations, why haven't any buildings burned down because of conductor failures from excessive ambient heat? If there were actual incidents of failures there would be interested parties telling us all about it, mainly to require larger conductors. Think about it. If you were a conductor manufacturer, wouldn't you be on the lookout for points of failure so you could lobby for rules mandating larger wires? Of course you would.

Well…there have never been fires on rooftops that were caused by excessive ambient heat. This requirement was poorly substantiated from the start, and now it's pretty much gone. Instead of having to apply a correction temperature adder for wiring on a rooftop, we only have to deal with this if the wiring method is within ⅞ of an inch from the roof. This should be very easy to work around.

NEW

Dwelling Unit Conductor Sizing. Section 310.15(B)(7) has seen a tremendous number of changes over the last few *Code* cycles. The allowance for smaller service and feeder conductors for dwellings has never been present for 120/208V systems; until now.

In a 120/240V system, when a circuit consists of two ungrounded conductors and a shared neutral, the neutral will carry the difference in current between the ungrounded conductors. For example, 80A on line 1 and 60A on line 2 will result in 20A on the neutral; or, 80A on each phase will result in zero current on the neutral conductor.

This isn't the case for a 120/208V system. With two ungrounded conductors and a shared neutral, the neutral will carry a substantial amount of current. If we have 80A on line 1 and 80A on line 2, the neutral will carry 80A! This was the reason 120/208V systems weren't permitted to take advantage of the reduced sizing allowances of this section. In this cycle, this requirement was relaxed. We'll see how it turns out, but I have a feeling it will be just fine. The *NEC* load calculations for dwellings are still much higher than the actual consumption of power, so it seems there's probably enough safety already factored into the design.

Author's Comment:

- According to Article 100, "ampacity" means the maximum current, in amperes, a conductor can carry continuously, where the temperature of the conductor won't be raised in excess of its insulation temperature rating. Figure 310–10

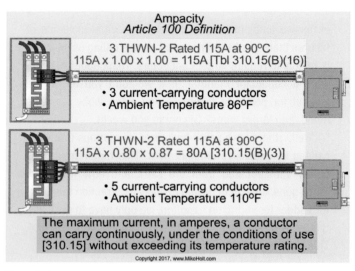

Figure 310–10

310.15 Conductor Ampacity

(A) General Requirements.

(1) Tables for Engineering Supervision. The ampacity of a conductor can be determined either by using the tables in accordance with 310.15(B), or under engineering supervision as provided in 310.15(C).

Note 1: Ampacities provided by this section don't take voltage drop into consideration. See 210.19(A) Note 4, for branch circuits and 215.2(D) Note 2, for feeders.

(2) Conductor Ampacity—Lower Rating. Where more than one ampacity applies for a given circuit length, the lowest ampacity value is to be used for the circuit. Figure 310–11

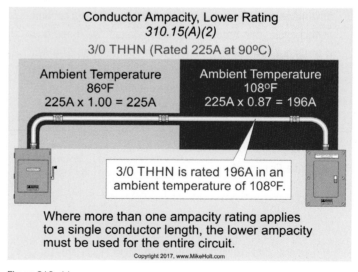

Figure 310–11

Ex: When different ampacities apply *to a length* of conductor because of temperature correction [310.15(B)(2)(a)] or conductor bundling [310.15(B)(3)(a)], the higher ampacity can apply for the entire circuit *if length of the corrected or adjusted ampacity doesn't exceed the lesser of* 10 ft or 10 percent of the length of the *total circuit*. Figure 310–12 and Figure 310–13

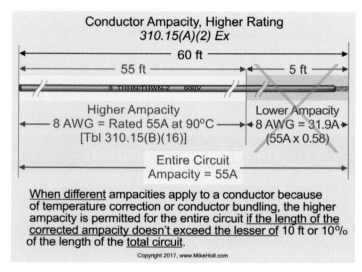

Figure 310–12

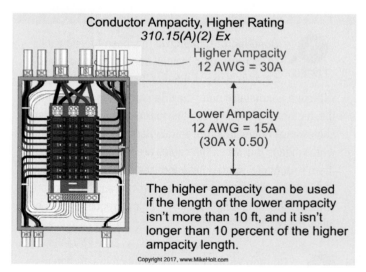

Figure 310–13

(3) Insulation Temperature Limitation. Conductors aren't permitted to be used where the operating temperature exceeds that designated for the type of insulated conductor involved.

Note 1: The insulation temperature rating of a conductor [Table 310.104(A)] is the maximum temperature a conductor can withstand over a prolonged time period without serious degradation. The main factors to consider for conductor operating temperature include:

(1) Ambient temperature may vary along the conductor length as well as from time to time [Table 310.15(B)(2)(a)].

(2) Heat generated internally in the conductor—load current flow.

(3) The rate at which generated heat dissipates into the ambient medium.

(4) Adjacent load-carrying conductors have the effect of raising the ambient temperature and impeding heat dissipation [Table 310.15(B)(3)(a)].

Note 2: See 110.14(C)(1) for the temperature limitation of terminations.

(B) Ampacity Table. The allowable conductor ampacities listed in Table 310.15(B)(16) are based on conditions where the ambient temperature isn't over 86°F, and no more than three current-carrying conductors are bundled together. Figure 310–14

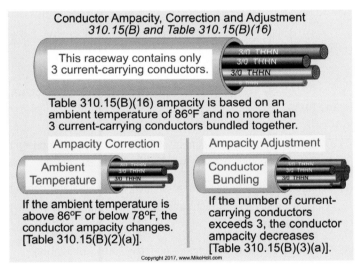

Figure 310–14

The temperature correction [310.15(B)(2)(a)] and adjustment factors [310.15(B)(3)(a)] apply to the conductor ampacity, based on the temperature rating of the conductor insulation in accordance with Table 310.15(B)(16).

(2) Conductor Ampacity Ambient Temperature Correction. When conductors are installed in an ambient temperature other than 78°F to 86°F, the ampacities listed in Table 310.15(B)(16) must be corrected in accordance with the multipliers listed in Table 310.15(B)(2) (a). Figure 310–15

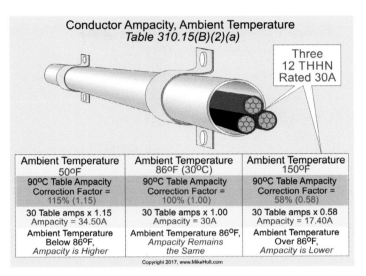

Figure 310–15

Table 310.15(B)(2)(a) Ambient Temperature Correction			
Ambient Temperature °F	Ambient Temperature °C	Correction Factor 75°C Conductors	Correction Factor 90°C Conductors
50 or less	10 or less	1.20	1.15
51–59°F	11–15°C	1.15	1.12
60–68°F	16–20°C	1.11	1.08
69–77°F	21–25°C	1.05	1.04
78–86°F	26–30°C	1.00	1.00
87–95°F	31–35°C	0.94	0.96
96–104°F	36–40°C	0.88	0.91
105–113°F	41–45°C	0.82	0.87
114–122°F	46–50°C	0.75	0.82
123–131°F	51–55°C	0.67	0.76
132–140°F	56–60°C	0.58	0.71
141–149°F	61–65°C	0.47	0.65
150–158°F	66–70°C	0.33	0.58
159–167°F	71–75°C	0.00	0.50
168–176°F	76–80°C	0.00	0.41
177–185°F	81–85°C	0.00	0.29

Example 1: *What's the corrected ampacity of 3/0 THHN conductors if the ambient temperature is 108°F?*

Solution: *The corrected ampacity of 3/0 THHN conductors is 196A.*

Conductor Ampacity [90°C] = 225A
Correction Factor [Table 310.15(B)(2)(a)] = 0.87

Corrected Ampacity = 225A x 0.87
Corrected Ampacity = 196A

Example 2: *What's the corrected ampacity of 3/0 THWN conductors if the ambient temperature is 108°F?*

Solution: *The corrected ampacity of 3/0 THWN conductors is 164A.*

Conductor Ampacity [75°C] = 200A
Correction Factor [Table 310.15(B)(2)(a)] = 0.82

Corrected Ampacity = 200A x 0.82
Corrected Ampacity = 164A

(3) Conductor Ampacity Adjustment.

(a) Four or More Current-Carrying Conductors. Where four or more current-carrying power conductors are within a raceway longer than 24 in. [310.15(B)(3)(a)(3)], or where cables are bundled for a length longer than 24 in., the ampacity of each conductor must be reduced in accordance with Table 310.15(B)(3)(a).

Table 310.15(B)(3)(a) Conductor Ampacity Adjustment for More Than Three Current–Carrying Conductors

Number of Conductors[1]	Adjustment
4–6	0.80 or 80%
7–9	0.70 or 70%
10–20	0.50 or 50%
21–30	0.45 or 45%
31–40	0.40 or 40%
41 and above	0.35 or 35%

[1]Number of conductors is the total number of conductors, including spare conductors, adjusted in accordance with 310.15(B)(5) and (B)(6). It doesn't include conductors that can't be energized at the same time.

Author's Comment:

■ Conductor ampacity reduction is required when four or more current-carrying conductors are bundled together because heat generated by current flow isn't able to dissipate as quickly as when there are three or fewer current-carry conductors. Figure 310–16

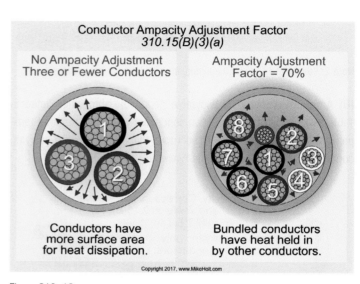

Conductor Ampacity Adjustment Factor
310.15(B)(3)(a)

No Ampacity Adjustment
Three or Fewer Conductors

Ampacity Adjustment
Factor = 70%

Conductors have
more surface area
for heat dissipation.

Bundled conductors
have heat held in
by other conductors.

Copyright 2017, www.MikeHolt.com

Figure 310–16

(1) Conductor ampacity adjustment of Table 310.15(B)(3)(a) doesn't apply to conductors installed in cable trays, 392.80 applies.

(2) Conductor ampacity adjustment of Table 310.15(B)(3)(a) doesn't apply to conductors in raceways having a length not exceeding 24 in. Figure 310–17

(4) Conductor ampacity adjustment of Table 310.15(B)(3)(a) doesn't apply to conductors within Type AC or Type MC cable under the following conditions: Figure 310–18

  a. The cables don't have an outer jacket,

  b. Each cable has no more than three current-carrying conductors,

  c. The conductors are 12 AWG copper, and

  d. No more than 20 current-carrying conductors (ten 2-wire cables or six 3-wire cables) are installed without maintaining spacing for a continuous length longer than 24 in.

Ex to (4): A 60 percent adjustment factor applies if the number of current-carrying conductors in these cables that are stacked or bundled longer than 24 in. without maintaining spacing exceeds 20.

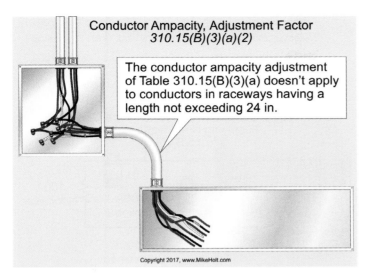

Figure 310–17

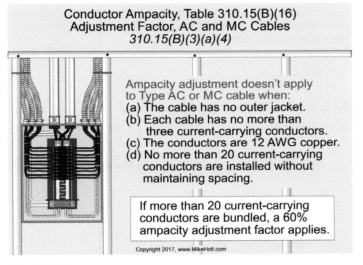

Figure 310–18

(c) Raceways and Cables Exposed to Sunlight on Rooftops. Where raceways or cables are exposed to direct sunlight <u>and located less than ⅞ in. above the roof, a temperature adder of 60°F/33°C</u> is to be added to the outdoor ambient temperature to determine the ambient temperature for the application of the ampacity correction in accordance with Table 310.15(B)(2)(a). Figure 310–19

Ex: Type XHHW-2 insulated conductors aren't subject to the <u>temperature adder of 60°F/33°C</u>.

Note 1: See the *ASHRAE Handbook—Fundamentals* (www.ashrae.org) as a source for the ambient temperatures in various locations.

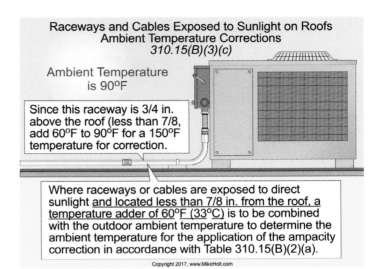

Figure 310–19

■ This rule requires the ambient temperature used for ampacity correction to be adjusted where conductors or cables are installed within a raceway or cable on or above a rooftop and the raceway is exposed to direct sunlight. The reasoning is that the air inside raceways and cables that are in direct sunlight is significantly hotter than the surrounding air, and appropriate ampacity corrections must be made in order to comply with 310.10.

(5) Neutral Conductors.

(a) The neutral conductor of a 3-wire, single-phase, 120/240V system, or 4-wire, three-phase, 120/208V or 277/480V wye-connected system, isn't considered a current-carrying conductor for conductor ampacity adjustment of 310.15(B)(3)(a). Figure 310–20

(b) The neutral conductor of a 3-wire circuit from a 4-wire, three-phase, 120/208V or 277/480V wye-connected system is considered a current-carrying conductor for conductor ampacity adjustment of 310.15(B)(3)(a).

■ When a 3-wire circuit is supplied from a 4-wire, three-phase, 120/208V or 277/480V wye-connected system, the neutral conductor carries approximately the same current as the ungrounded conductors. Figure 310–21

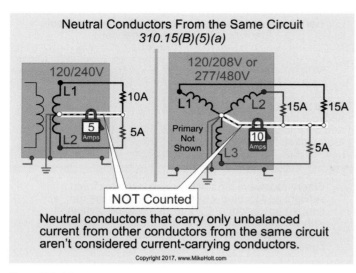

Figure 310–20

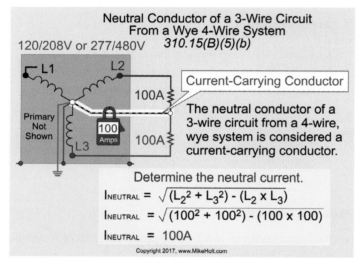

Figure 310–21

(c) The neutral conductor of a 4-wire, three-phase, 120/208V or 277/480V wye-connected system is considered a current-carrying conductor for conductor ampacity adjustment of 310.15(B)(3)(a) if more than 50 percent of the neutral load consists of nonlinear loads.

Author's Comment:

■ Nonlinear loads supplied by a 4-wire, three-phase, 120/208V or 277/480V wye-connected system can produce unwanted and potentially hazardous odd triplen harmonic currents (3rd, 9th, 15th, and so on) that can add on the neutral conductor. To prevent fire or equipment damage from excessive harmonic neutral current, the designer should consider increasing the size of the neutral conductor or installing a separate neutral for each phase. For more information, visit www. MikeHolt.com, click on the "Technical" link, then the "Power Quality" link. Also see 210.4(A) Note, 220.61 Note 2, and 450.3 Note 2. Figure 310–22

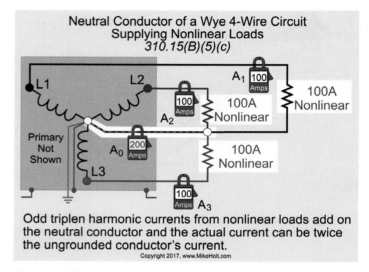

Figure 310–22

(6) Grounding Conductors. Grounding and bonding conductors aren't considered current carrying. Figure 310–23

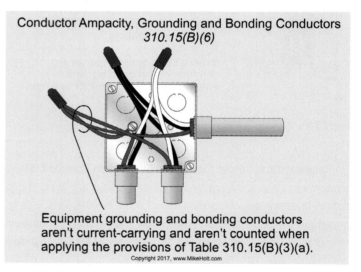

Figure 310–23

(7) Single-Phase Dwelling Services and Feeders.

120/240V System. For dwelling units, service and feeder conductors supplied by a single-phase, 120/240V system can be sized in accordance with the requirements contained in 310.15(B)(7)(1) through (4). Figure 310–24

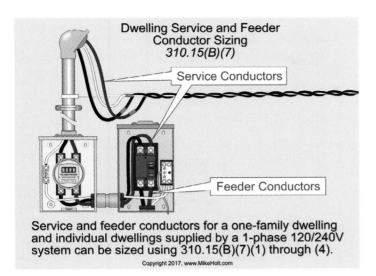

Figure 310–24

120/208V System. For dwelling units, service and feeder conductors supplied by a single-phase, 120/208V system can be sized in accordance with the requirements contained in 310.15(B)(7)(1) through (3).

(1) **Service Conductors.** Ungrounded service conductors supplying the entire load of a one-family dwelling or an individual dwelling unit in a two-family or multifamily dwelling can have the conductor ampacity sized to 83 percent of the service overcurrent protection device rating. Figure 310–25

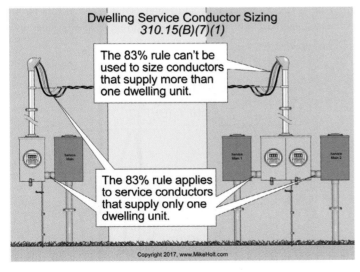

Figure 310–25

Example: _What size service conductors are required if the calculated load for a dwelling unit equals 195A, and the service disconnect is rated 200A?_ Figure 310–26

Solution: _2/0 AWG service conductors are required._

Service Conductor: 2/0 AWG rated 175A at 75°C [Table 310.15(B)(16)] (200A rated circuit breaker multiplied by 83% = 166A).

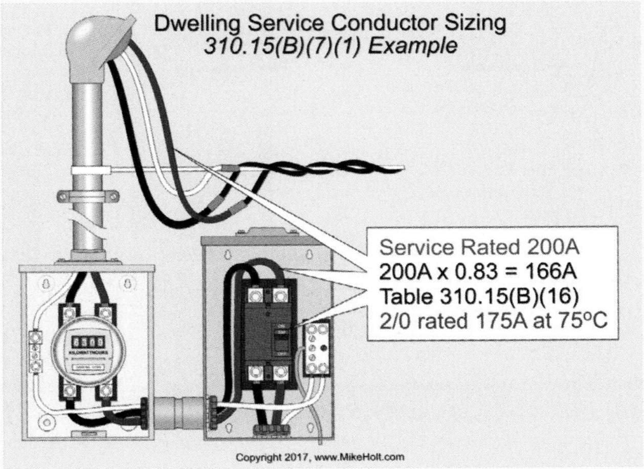

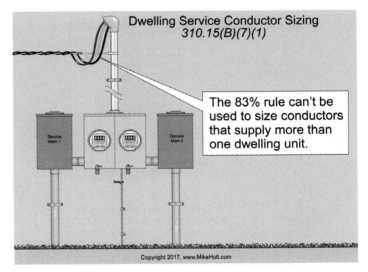

Figure 310–26

Author's Comment:

■ 310.15(B)(7) can't be used for service conductors for two-family or multifamily dwelling buildings. Figure 310–27

Figure 310–27

(2) Feeder Conductors. Ungrounded feeder conductors not over 400A supplying the entire load of a one-family dwelling, or an individual dwelling unit in a two-family or multifamily dwelling, can have the ungrounded feeder conductors sized to 83 percent of the feeder overcurrent protection device rating. Figure 310–28

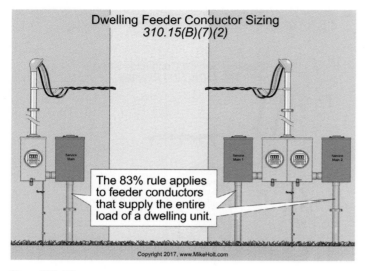

Figure 310–28

Author's Comment:

- Section 310.15(B)(7)(2) can't be used to size feeder conductors where a feeder doesn't carry the entire load of the dwelling unit, except as permitted in 310.15(B)(7)(3). Figure 310–29

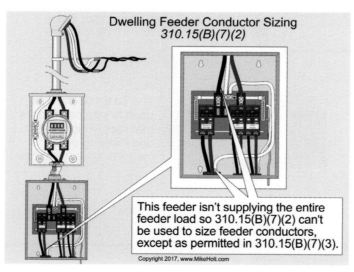

Figure 310–29

Example: What size feeder conductors are required if the calculated load for a dwelling unit equals 195A, the service disconnect is rated 200A, and the feeder conductors carry the entire load of the dwelling unit? Figure 310–30

Solution: 2/0 AWG feeder conductors are required.

Feeder Conductor: 2/0 AWG rated 175A at 75°C [Table 310.15(B)(16)] (200A rated circuit breaker multiplied by 83% = 166A).

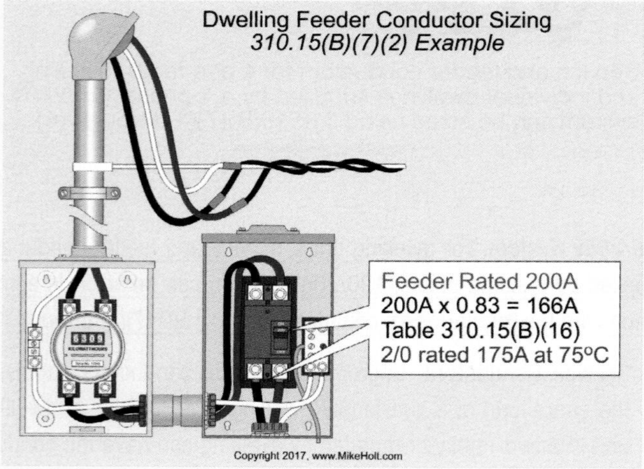

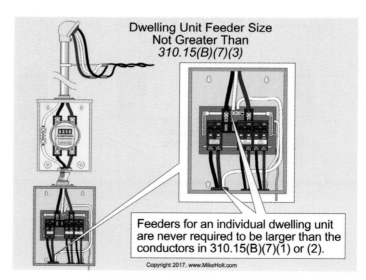

Figure 310–30

(3) Feeder Conductors Not Greater Than. Feeders conductors for an individual dwelling unit aren't required to be larger than the service conductors. Figure 310–31

Figure 310–31

(4) Neutral Conductors. For one-family dwellings and individual dwelling units of two-family and multifamily dwellings, service and feeder neutral conductors supplied by a single-phase, 120/240V system can be smaller than the ungrounded conductors, provided that the requirements of 220.61 and 230.42 for services and 220.61 and 215.2 for feeders are met. Figure 310–32

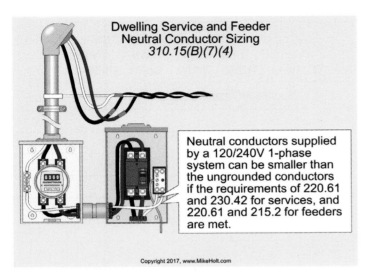

Dwelling Service and Feeder
Neutral Conductor Sizing
310.15(B)(7)(4)

Neutral conductors supplied by a 120/240V 1-phase system can be smaller than the ungrounded conductors if the requirements of 220.61 and 230.42 for services, and 220.61 and 215.2 for feeders are met.

Copyright 2017, www.MikeHolt.com

Figure 310–32

CAUTION: *Because the service neutral conductor is required to serve as the effective ground-fault current path, it must be sized so it can safely carry the maximum fault current likely to be imposed on it [110.10 and 250.4(A) (5)]. This is accomplished by sizing the neutral conductor in accordance with Table 250.102(C), based on the area of the largest ungrounded service conductor [250.24(C)(1)].*

Example: *What size neutral conductor is required if the calculated load for a dwelling unit equals 195A, the maximum unbalanced load is 100A, and the service disconnect is rated 200A with 2/0 AWG conductors?* Figure 310–33

Solution: *A 3 AWG neutral conductor is required.*

Neutral Conductor: 3 AWG is rated 100A at 75°C in accordance with Table 310.15(B)(16), and 310.15(B)(7)(3) doesn't allow for the 83 percent deduction for neutral conductors. In addition, 250.24(C) requires the neutral conductor to be sized no smaller than 4 AWG based on 2/0 AWG service conductors in accordance with Table 250.102(C).

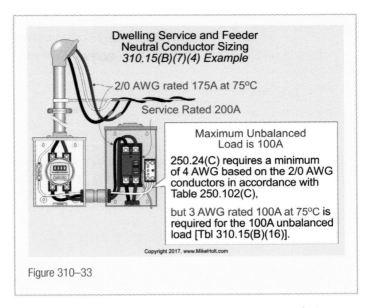

Dwelling Service and Feeder
Neutral Conductor Sizing
310.15(B)(7)(4) Example

2/0 AWG rated 175A at 75°C

Service Rated 200A

Maximum Unbalanced Load is 100A

250.24(C) requires a minimum of 4 AWG based on the 2/0 AWG conductors in accordance with Table 250.102(C),

but 3 AWG rated 100A at 75°C is required for the 100A unbalanced load [Tbl 310.15(B)(16)].

Copyright 2017. www.MikeHolt.com

Figure 310–33

Where conductor ampacity correction or adjustment factors are required by 310.15(B)(2) or (3), we're to use the ampacity associated with the temperature rating of the conductor in accordance with Table 310.15(B)(16).

Note 1: The service or feeder ratings addressed by this section are based on the standard ampacity ratings from 240.6(A).

Size	60°C (140°F)	75°C (167°F)	90°C (194°F)	60°C (140°F)	75°C (167°F)	90°C (194°F)	Size
		RHW THHW THW THWN XHHW USE	RHH RHW-2 THHN THHW THW-2 THWN-2 USE-2 XHHW XHHW-2		THHN THW THWN XHHW	THHN THW-2 THWN-2 THHW XHHW XHHW-2	
AWG kcmil	TW UF			TW UF			AWG kcmil
	Copper			Aluminum/Copper–Clad Aluminum			
14*	15	20	25				14*
12*	20	25	30	15	20	25	12*
10*	30	35	40	25	30	35	10*
8	40	50	55	35	40	45	8
6	55	65	75	40	50	55	6
4	70	85	95	55	65	75	4
3	85	100	115	65	75	85	3
2	95	115	130	75	90	100	2
1	110	130	145	85	100	115	1
1/0	125	150	170	100	120	135	1/0
2/0	145	175	195	115	135	150	2/0
3/0	165	200	225	130	155	175	3/0
4/0	195	230	260	150	180	205	4/0
250	215	255	290	170	205	230	250
300	240	285	320	195	230	260	300
350	260	310	350	210	250	280	350
400	280	335	380	225	270	305	400
500	320	380	430	260	310	350	500

Table 310.15(B)(16) Allowable Ampacities of Insulated Conductors Based on Not More Than Three Current–Carrying Conductors and Ambient Temperature of 30°C (86°F)*

*See 240.4(D)

ARTICLE 312

CABINETS, CUTOUT BOXES, AND METER SOCKET ENCLOSURES

Introduction to Article 312—Cabinets, Cutout Boxes, and Meter Socket Enclosures

This article addresses the installation and construction specifications for the items mentioned in its title. In Article 310, we observed that the conditions of use have an effect on the ampacity of a conductor. Likewise, the conditions of use have an effect on the selection and application of cabinets. For example, you can't use just any enclosure in a wet location or in a hazardous location. The conditions of use impose special requirements for these situations.

For all such enclosures, certain requirements apply—regardless of the use. For example, you must cover any openings, protect conductors from abrasion, and allow sufficient bending room for conductors.

Notice that Article 408 covers switchboards and panelboards, with primary emphasis on the interior, or "guts," while the cabinet that would be used to enclose a panelboard is covered here in Article 312. Therefore, you'll find that some important considerations such as wire-bending space at terminals of panelboards are included in this article.

Part I. Scope and Installation

312.1 Scope

Article 312 covers the installation and construction specifications for cabinets, cutout boxes, and meter socket enclosures. Figure 312–1

> **Author's Comment:**
> - A cabinet is an enclosure for either surface mounting or flush mounting and provided with a frame in which a door may be hung.

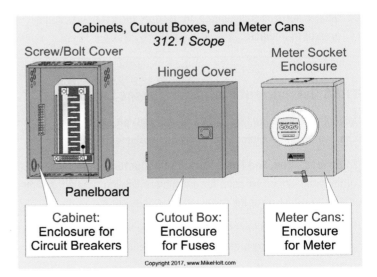

Figure 312–1

312.8 Overcurrent Protection Device Enclosures

The rules for sufficient conductor space within cabinets have been revised to deal with power monitoring equipment.

Analysis

NEW

As technology evolves so too must the *NEC*. Energy management and power monitoring systems are becoming more popular in today's modern buildings, and the *Code* has a bit of catching up to do. This section has long given requirements on enclosures containing splices and feed-through conductors, and it even made mention of "other equipment" in the enclosure.

Now the "other equipment" being discussed is clear and has clear rules. Power monitoring equipment can be, and often is, installed in a cabinet containing overcurrent protection devices. According to the 2017 *NEC*, when this is the case, the equipment must be identified as a field-installable accessory or it must be listed for installation in a switch or overcurrent protection device enclosure. The total area consumed by the equipment and its associated wiring, splices, and so forth is still limited to 75% of the cross-sectional area of that space.

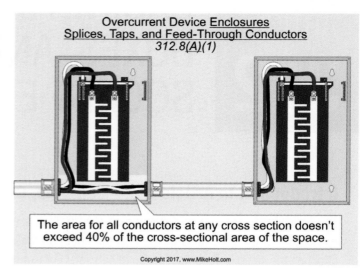

The area for all conductors at any cross section doesn't exceed 40% of the cross-sectional area of the space.

Copyright 2017, www.MikeHolt.com

Figure 312–2

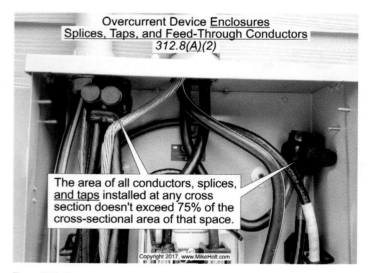

The area of all conductors, splices, and taps installed at any cross section doesn't exceed 75% of the cross-sectional area of that space.

Copyright 2017, www.MikeHolt.com

Figure 312–3

312.8 Overcurrent Protection Device Enclosures

Cabinets are permitted to contain overcurrent protection devices and other wiring and equipment as provided in (A) and (B).

(A) Splices, Taps, and Feed-Through Conductors. The wiring space within cabinets can be used for conductors feeding through, spliced, or tapping where all of the following conditions are met:

(1) The area of conductors at any cross section doesn't exceed 40 percent of the cross-sectional area of the space. Figure 312–2

(2) The area of conductors, splices, and taps installed at any cross section doesn't exceed 75 percent of the cross-sectional area of that space. Figure 312–3

(3) A permanently affixed warning label having sufficient durability to withstand the environment involved and comply with 110.21(B), must be applied on the cabinet to identify the location of the disconnecting means for the feed-through conductors. Figure 312–4

(B) Power Monitoring Equipment. The wiring space within cabinets can contain power monitoring equipment where all of the following conditions are met:

(1) The power monitoring equipment is identified as a field installable accessory as part of listed equipment, or a listed kit for field installation in the overcurrent protection device enclosures. Figure 312–5

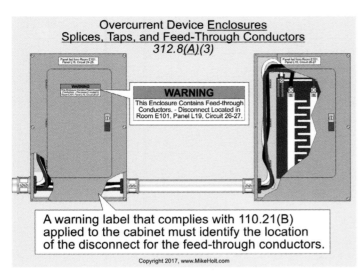

Figure 312–4

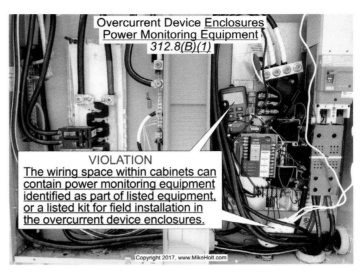

Figure 312–5

(2) The area of all conductors, splices, taps, and equipment at any cross section doesn't exceed 75 percent of the cross-sectional area of that space.

OUTLET, DEVICE, PULL, AND JUNCTION BOXES; CONDUIT BODIES; AND HANDHOLE ENCLOSURES

Introduction to Article 314—Outlet, Device, Pull, and Junction Boxes; Conduit Bodies; and Handhole Enclosures

Article 314 contains installation requirements for outlet boxes, pull and junction boxes, conduit bodies, and handhole enclosures. As with the cabinets covered in Article 312, the conditions of use have a bearing on the type of material and equipment selected for a particular installation. If a raceway is installed in a wet location, for example, the correct fittings and the proper installation methods must be used.

The information here will help you size an outlet box using the proper cubic-inch capacity as well as calculating the minimum dimensions for larger pull boxes. There are limits on the amount of weight that can be supported by an outlet box and rules on how to support a device or outlet box to various surfaces. Article 314 will help you understand these types of rules so that your installation will be compliant with the *NEC*. As always, the clear illustrations in this article will help you visualize the finished installation.

Part I. Scope and General

314.1 Scope

Article 314 contains the installation requirements for outlet boxes, conduit bodies, pull and junction boxes, and handhole enclosures. Figure 314–1

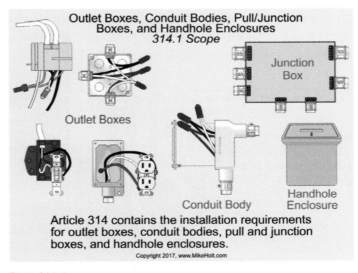

Figure 314–1

314.15 Damp or Wet Locations

Field-installed drainage holes now have a minimum size of ⅛ in.

Analysis

CLARIFIED Although electricians have been making field-installed drainage openings (drilling holes) in enclosures for decades, the practice wasn't specifically recognized in the *Code* until 2014. That edition of the *NEC* added an allowance for drilling holes in enclosures for drainage, provided the hole wasn't larger than ¼ in., unless it was for an actual drainage fitting.

The 2017 *Code* has added a new minimum diameter dimension of ⅛ in. to ensure the hole doesn't become blocked or clogged, thereby defeating the purpose of the drilled hole altogether. The word "diameter" was added to clarify that the opening must be round and not rectangular, or some other shape.

314.15 Damp or Wet Locations

Boxes, conduit bodies, and fittings in damp or wet locations must be listed for wet locations and prevent moisture or water from entering or accumulating within the enclosure. Figure 314–2

Boxes, conduit bodies, and fittings in damp or wet locations must be listed for wet locations and prevent moisture or water from entering or accumulating within the enclosure.

Figure 314–2

Approved drainage openings can be created in the field if they aren't smaller than ⅛ in. in diameter and not larger than ¼ in. in diameter. Figure 314–3

Drainage openings can be field installed if not smaller than 1/8 in. and not larger that 1/4 in. in diameter.

Figure 314–3

Author's Comment:

- If handhole enclosures without bottoms are installed, all enclosed conductors and any splices or terminations must be listed as suitable for wet locations [314.30(C)].

314.16 Number of Conductors in Boxes and Conduit Bodies

The conductor fill calculation for boxes with a barrier is now addressed.

Analysis

CLARIFIED It's not uncommon to see a two-gang box with a barrier in the middle of it. This barrier can be for multiple reasons, such as limiting 300V between adjacent switches [404.8(B)] or receptacles [406.5(H)], or separating line voltage conductors from power-limited circuits such as Class 2 circuits or twisted pair communications or coaxial cables. When a gas fireplace is installed, it's quite common to have a 120V circuit for the fan and a Class 2 circuit for the ignitor in the same two-gang switch box. This would require a divider.

Although it may seem obvious, the *NEC* has never explained how to deal with box fill when this type of situation is encountered. With the addition of this language it's now clearly addressed.

314.16 Number of Conductors in Boxes and Conduit Bodies

Boxes containing 6 AWG and smaller conductors must be sized in an approved manner to provide free space for all conductors, devices, and fittings. In no case can the volume of the box, as calculated in 314.16(A), be less than the volume requirement as calculated in 314.16(B).

Conduit bodies must be sized in accordance with 314.16(C).

Author's Comment:

- The requirements for sizing boxes and conduit bodies containing conductors 4 AWG and larger are contained in 314.28. The requirements for sizing handhole enclosures are contained in 314.30(A).

(A) Box Volume Calculations. The volume of a box includes plaster rings, extension rings, and domed covers that are either marked with their volume in cubic inches (cu in.), or are made from boxes listed in Table 314.16(A). Figure 314–4

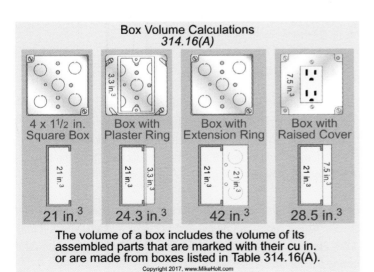

Figure 314–4

Where a box is divided by a barrier, the volume for each section of the box is calculated at ½ cu in. the volume of the enclosure. Figure 314–5

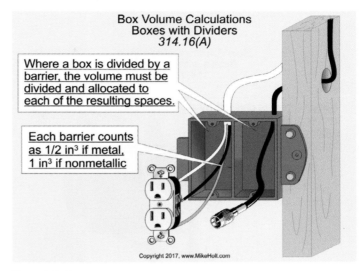

Figure 314–5

(B) Box Fill Calculations. The calculated conductor volume as determined by 314.16(B)(1) through (5) and Table 314.16(B) determine the total volume of the conductors, devices, and fittings. Raceway and cable fittings, including locknuts and bushings, aren't counted for box fill calculations. Figure 314–6

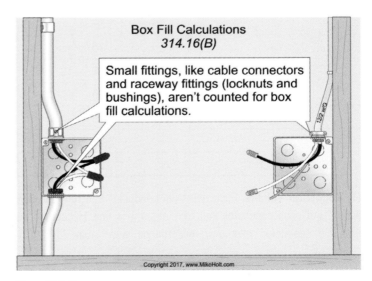

Figure 314–6

Where a box is divided by a barrier, the volume must be apportioned to each of the resulting spaces. Each nonmarked volume barrier is considered to take up ½ cu in. if of metal, and 1 cu in. if nonmetallic. Figure 314–7

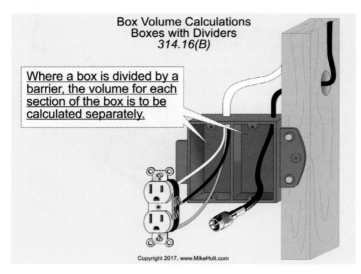

Box Volume Calculations
Boxes with Dividers
314.16(B)

Where a box is divided by a barrier, the volume for each section of the box is to be calculated separately.

Copyright 2017, www.MikeHolt.com

Figure 314–7

Table 314.16(B) Volume Allowance Required per Conductor	
Conductor AWG	Volume cu in.
18	1.50
16	1.75
14	2.00
12	2.25
10	2.50
8	3.00
6	5.00

(1) Conductor Volume. Each unbroken conductor that runs through a box, and each conductor that terminates in a box, is counted as a single conductor volume in accordance with Table 314.16(B). Figure 314–8

Each loop or coil of unbroken conductor having a length of at least twice the minimum length required for free conductors in 300.14 must be counted as two conductor volumes. Conductors that originate and terminate within the box, such as pigtails, aren't counted at all. Figure 314–9

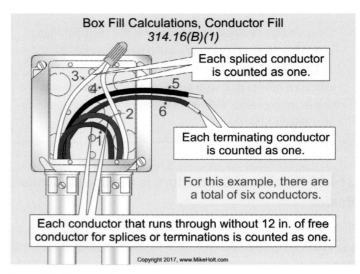

Box Fill Calculations, Conductor Fill
314.16(B)(1)

Each spliced conductor is counted as one.

Each terminating conductor is counted as one.

For this example, there are a total of six conductors.

Each conductor that runs through without 12 in. of free conductor for splices or terminations is counted as one.

Copyright 2017, www.MikeHolt.com

Figure 314–8

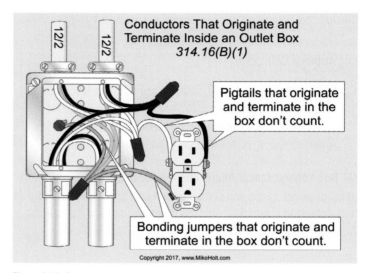

Conductors That Originate and Terminate Inside an Outlet Box
314.16(B)(1)

Pigtails that originate and terminate in the box don't count.

Bonding jumpers that originate and terminate in the box don't count.

Copyright 2017, www.MikeHolt.com

Figure 314–9

Author's Comment:

■ According to 300.14, boxes that have openings less than 8 in. in any dimension, must have at least 6 in. of free conductor, measured from the point where the conductors enter the box, and at least 3 in. of free conductor outside the box opening. Figure 314–10

Ex: Equipment grounding conductors, and up to four 16 AWG and smaller fixture wires, can be omitted from box fill calculations if they enter the box from a domed luminaire or similar canopy, such as a ceiling paddle fan canopy. Figure 314–11

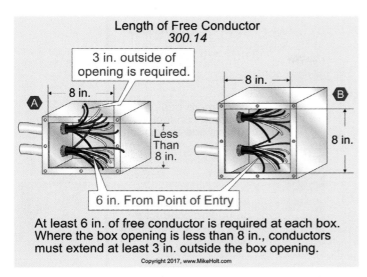

Figure 314–10

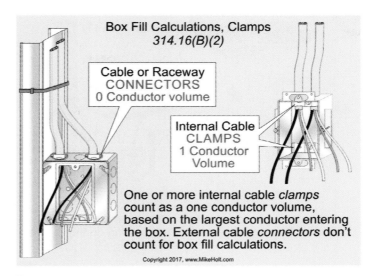

Figure 314–12

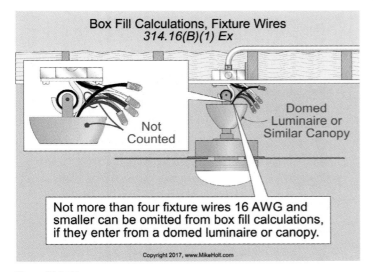

Figure 314–11

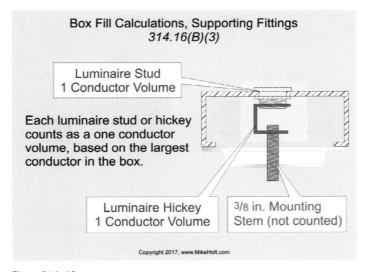

Figure 314–13

(2) Cable Clamp Volume. One or more internal cable clamps count as a single conductor volume in accordance with Table 314.16(B), based on the largest conductor that enters the box. Cable connectors that have their clamping mechanism outside of the box aren't counted. Figure 314–12

(3) Support Fitting Volume. Each luminaire stud or luminaire hickey counts as a single conductor volume in accordance with Table 314.16(B), based on the largest conductor that enters the box. Figure 314–13

Author's Comment:

- Luminaire stems don't need to be counted as a conductor volume.

(4) Device Yoke Volume. Each single-gang device yoke (regardless of the ampere rating of the device) counts as two conductor volumes, based on the largest conductor that terminates on the device in accordance with Table 314.16(B). Figure 314–14

Each multigang-device yoke counts as two conductor volumes for each gang, based on the largest conductor that terminates on the device in accordance with Table 314.16(B). Figure 314–15

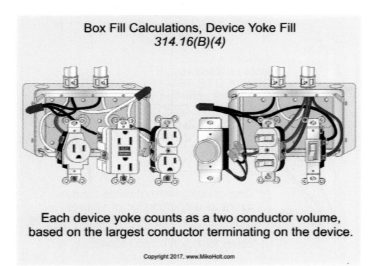

Box Fill Calculations, Device Yoke Fill
314.16(B)(4)

Each device yoke counts as a two conductor volume,
based on the largest conductor terminating on the device.

Copyright 2017, www.MikeHolt.com

Figure 314–14

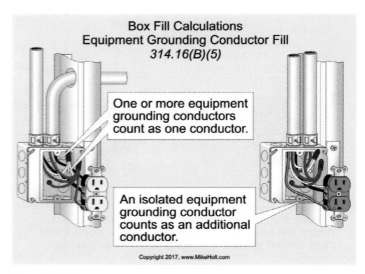

Box Fill Calculations
Equipment Grounding Conductor Fill
314.16(B)(5)

One or more equipment
grounding conductors
count as one conductor.

An isolated equipment
grounding conductor
counts as an additional
conductor.

Copyright 2017, www.MikeHolt.com

Figure 314–16

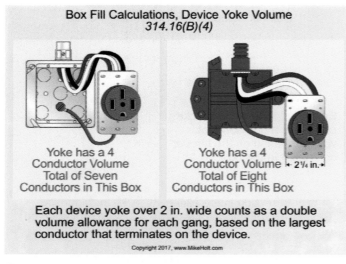

Box Fill Calculations, Device Yoke Volume
314.16(B)(4)

Yoke has a 4
Conductor Volume
Total of Seven
Conductors in This Box

Yoke has a 4
Conductor Volume
Total of Eight
Conductors in This Box

←— 2¼ in. —→

Each device yoke over 2 in. wide counts as a double
volume allowance for each gang, based on the largest
conductor that terminates on the device.

Copyright 2017, www.MikeHolt.com

Figure 314–15

Author's Comment:

- A device that's too wide for mounting in a single-gang box, as described in Table 314.16(A), is counted based on the number of gangs required for the device.

(5) Equipment Grounding Conductor Volume. Equipment grounding conductors in a box count as a single conductor volume in accordance with Table 314.16(B), based on the largest equipment grounding conductor that enters the box. Insulated equipment grounding conductors for receptacles having insulated grounding terminals (isolated ground receptacles) [250.146(D)], count as a single conductor volume in accordance with Table 314.16(B). Figure 314–16

Author's Comment:

- Conductor insulation isn't a factor that's considered when determining box volume calculations.

Example: How many 14 AWG conductors can be pulled through a 4 in. square x 2⅛ in. deep box with a plaster ring with a marking of 3.60 cu in.? The box contains two receptacles, five 12 AWG conductors, and two 12 AWG equipment grounding conductors.

Solution: Five 14 AWG conductors can be pulled through.

Step 1: Determine the volume of the box assembly [314.16(A)]:
Box 30.30 cu in. + 3.60 cu in. plaster ring = 33.90 cu in.
A 4 x 4 x 2⅛ in. box has a volume of 30.30 cu in., as listed in Table 314.16(A).

Step 2: Determine the volume of the devices and conductors in the box:

Two—receptacles		4—12 AWG
Five—12 AWG		5—12 AWG
Two—12 AWG Grounds		1—12 AWG
Total Ten—12 AWG x 2.25 cu in. = 22.50 cu in.		

Step 3: Determine the remaining volume permitted for the 14 AWG conductors (volume of box less volume of conductors):
33.90 cu in. – 22.50 cu in. = 11.40 cu in.

Step 4: *Determine the number of 14 AWG conductors (at 2.00 cu in. each) permitted in the remaining volume of 11.40 cu in:*

14 AWG = 2.00 cu in. each [Table 314.16(B)]
11.40 cu in./2.00 cu in. = 5 conductors

(C) Conduit Bodies.

(2) Splices. Splices are permitted in conduit bodies that are legibly marked by the manufacturer with their volume, and the maximum number of conductors permitted in a conduit body is limited in accordance with 314.16(B).

Example: *How many 12 AWG conductors can be spliced in a 15 cu in. conduit body?* Figure 314–17

Solution: *Six 12 AWG conductors (15 cu in./2.25 cu in.).*

12 AWG = 2.25 cu in. [Table 314.16(B)]
15 cu in./2.25 cu in. = 6 conductors

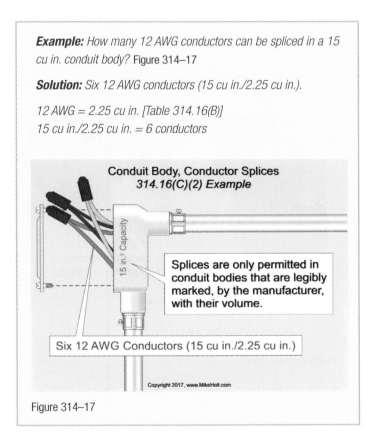

Conduit Body, Conductor Splices
314.16(C)(2) Example

15 in.³ Capacity

Splices are only permitted in conduit bodies that are legibly marked, by the manufacturer, with their volume.

Six 12 AWG Conductors (15 cu in./2.25 cu in.)

Copyright 2017, www.MikeHolt.com

Figure 314–17

(3) Short-Radius Conduit Bodies. Capped elbows, handy ells, and service-entrance elbows aren't permitted to contain any splices. Figure 314–18

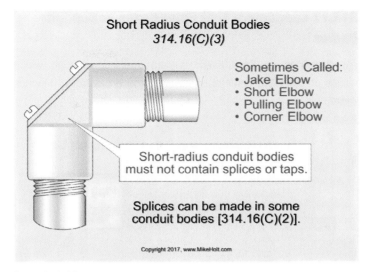

Short Radius Conduit Bodies
314.16(C)(3)

Sometimes Called:
• Jake Elbow
• Short Elbow
• Pulling Elbow
• Corner Elbow

Short-radius conduit bodies must not contain splices or taps.

Splices can be made in some conduit bodies [314.16(C)(2)].

Copyright 2017, www.MikeHolt.com

Figure 314–18

314.17 Conductors That Enter Boxes or Conduit Bodies

Nonmetallic-sheathed cables installed in metal boxes must now meet the ¼ in. cable sheath rule.

Analysis

CLARIFIED Nonmetallic-sheathed cables entering nonmetallic boxes need to have at least ¼ in. of cable sheath in the box. This ensures that we don't have open conductors outside the box in the wall or ceiling framing, and to make sure a cable clamp doesn't clamp onto the actual conductors, which could result in a ground fault from damaged conductor insulation.

This concept is hardly new, but interestingly enough, it was only required for nonmetallic boxes, not metal ones! You're not the only who thought this was already covered in the *Code*...I did too!

314.17 Conductors That Enter Boxes or Conduit Bodies

(A) Openings to Be Closed. Unused openings through which cables or raceways enter must be closed in an approved manner. Figure 314–19

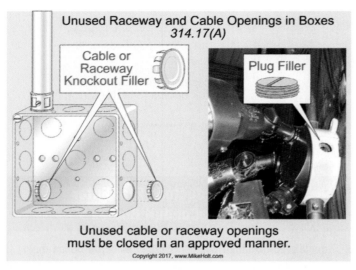

Figure 314–19

Author's Comment:

- Unused cable or raceway openings in electrical equipment must be effectively closed by fittings that provide protection substantially equivalent to the wall of the equipment [110.12(A)].

(B) Metal Boxes. Nonmetallic-sheathed cable and multiconductor Type UF cable must extend at least ¼ in. inside the box. Figure 314–20

(C) Nonmetallic Boxes and Conduit Bodies. Raceways and cables must be securely fastened to nonmetallic boxes or conduit bodies by fittings designed for the wiring method [300.12 and 300.15]. Figure 314–21

The sheath of type NM cable must extend not less than ¼ in. into the nonmetallic box.

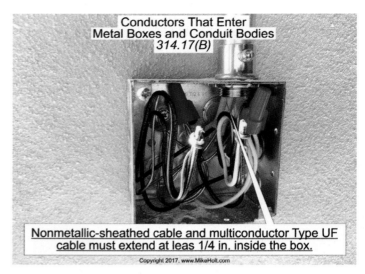

Figure 314–20

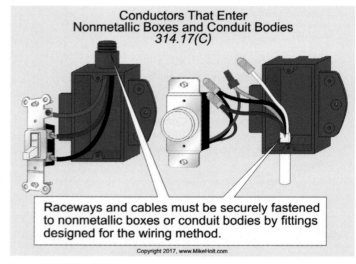

Figure 314–21

Author's Comment:

- Two Type NM cables can terminate in a single cable clamp, if the clamp is listed for this purpose.

Ex: Type NM cable terminating to a single-gang (2¼ x 4 in.) device box isn't required to be secured to the box if the cable is securely fastened within 8 in. of the box. Figure 314–22

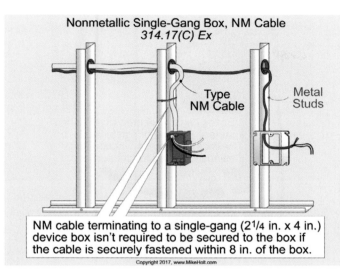

NM cable terminating to a single-gang (2¼ in. x 4 in.) device box isn't required to be secured to the box if the cable is securely fastened within 8 in. of the box.

Copyright 2017, www.MikeHolt.com

Figure 314–22

314.20 Flush-Mounted Box Installations

The rules for flush-mounted boxes have been expanded and clarified to cover all installations.

Analysis

CLARIFIED

Outlet boxes installed inside a wall or ceiling must comply with this section, but what if the box is installed in something that isn't a wall or ceiling, like a post? The *NEC* was silent on the issue, although most would argue that the same rule would apply since the same hazard exists. This change removes the argument altogether, and provides consistency with 314.27, which was changed in a similar manner in 2014.

314.20 Flush-Mounted Box Installations

Installation within or behind walls or ceilings that are constructed of noncombustible material must have the front edge of the flush-mounted box, plaster ring, extension ring, or listed extender set back no more than ¼ in. from the finished surface. Figure 314–23

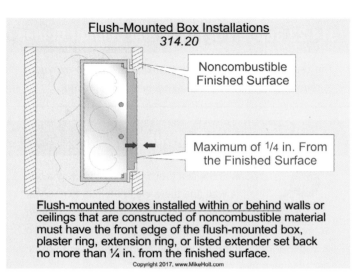

Flush-mounted boxes installed within or behind walls or ceilings that are constructed of noncombustible material must have the front edge of the flush-mounted box, plaster ring, extension ring, or listed extender set back no more than ¼ in. from the finished surface.

Copyright 2017, www.MikeHolt.com

Figure 314–23

Installation within or behind walls or ceilings constructed of wood or other combustible material must have the front edge of the flush-mounted box, plaster ring, extension ring, or listed extender extend to the finished surface or project out from the finished surface. Figure 314–24

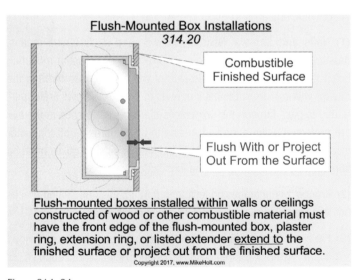

Flush-mounted boxes installed within walls or ceilings constructed of wood or other combustible material must have the front edge of the flush-mounted box, plaster ring, extension ring, or listed extender extend to the finished surface or project out from the finished surface.

Copyright 2017, www.MikeHolt.com

Figure 314–24

Author's Comment:

- Plaster rings and extension rings are available in a variety of depths to meet the above requirements.

314.23 Support of Boxes and Conduit Bodies

The requirements for mounting boxes have been expanded to require field-made mounting holes to be approved.

Analysis

EXPANDED

Think of the last time you went to screw a box to the wall and there wasn't a hole where you needed it. Usually I just use a self drilling screw and make my own. Apparently there must have been a problem with where people were drilling holes in boxes, because now they need to be approved.

314.23 Support of Boxes and Conduit Bodies

(A) Surface. Boxes can be fastened to any surface that provides adequate support.

(B) Structural Mounting. Boxes can be supported from any structural member, or they can be supported from grade by a metal, plastic, or wood brace.

(1) Nails and Screws. Nails or screws used as fastening means, must <u>secure</u> boxes by using outside brackets or by using mounting holes in the back or in a single side of the box, or pass through the interior within ¼ in. of the back or ends of the box. Screws aren't permitted to pass through the box unless the exposed threads in the box are protected using approved means to avoid abrasion of conductor insulation. <u>Mounting holes made in the field to support boxes must be approved by the authority having jurisdiction.</u>

(2) Braces. Metal braces no less than 0.02 in. thick and wood braces not less than a nominal 1 in. x 2 in. can support a box.

(C) Finished Surface Support. Boxes can be secured to a finished surface (drywall or plaster walls, or ceilings) by clamps, anchors, or fittings identified for the purpose. Figure 314–25

(D) Suspended-Ceiling Support. Outlet boxes can be supported to the structural or supporting elements of a suspended ceiling, if securely fastened by any of the following methods:

(1) Ceiling-Framing Members. An outlet box can be secured to suspended-ceiling framing members by bolts, screws, rivets, clips, or other means identified for the suspended-ceiling framing member(s). Figure 314–26

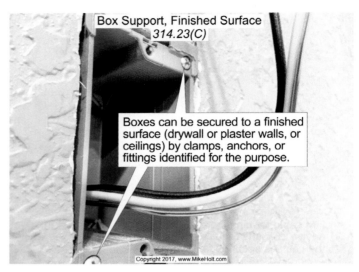

Box Support, Finished Surface
314.23(C)

Boxes can be secured to a finished surface (drywall or plaster walls, or ceilings) by clamps, anchors, or fittings identified for the purpose.

Copyright 2017, www.MikeHolt.com

Figure 314–25

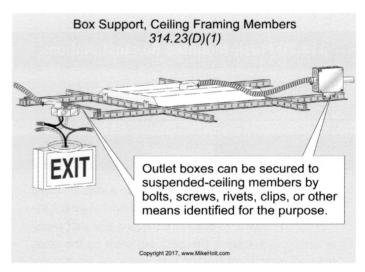

Box Support, Ceiling Framing Members
314.23(D)(1)

EXIT

Outlet boxes can be secured to suspended-ceiling members by bolts, screws, rivets, clips, or other means identified for the purpose.

Copyright 2017, www.MikeHolt.com

Figure 314–26

Author's Comment:

■ If framing members of suspended-ceiling systems are used to support luminaires, they must be securely fastened to each other and must be securely attached to the building structure at appropriate intervals. In addition, luminaires must be attached to the suspended-ceiling framing members with screws, bolts, rivets, or clips listed and identified for such use [410.36(B)].

(2) Independent Support Wires. Outlet boxes can be secured with identified fittings to the ceiling-support wires. If independent support wires are used for outlet box support, they must be taunt and secured at both ends [300.11(B)]. Figure 314–27

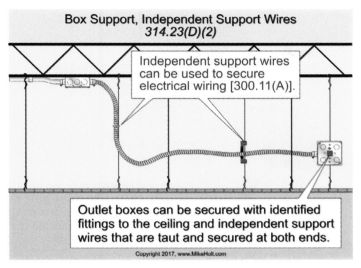

Figure 314–27

Author's Comment:

- See 300.11(B) on the use of independent support wires to support raceways and cables.

(E) Raceways—Boxes and Conduit Bodies Without Devices or Luminaires. Two intermediate metal or rigid metal conduits, threaded wrenchtight into the enclosure, can be used to support an outlet box that doesn't contain a device or luminaire, if each raceway is supported within 36 in. of the box or within 18 in. of the box if all conduit entries are on the same side. Figure 314–28

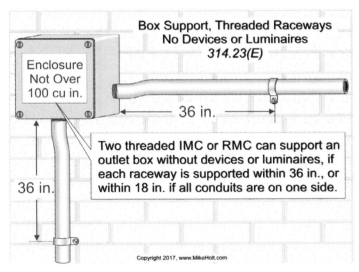

Figure 314–28

Ex: *Conduit bodies are permitted to be supported by any of the following wiring methods:* Figure 314–29

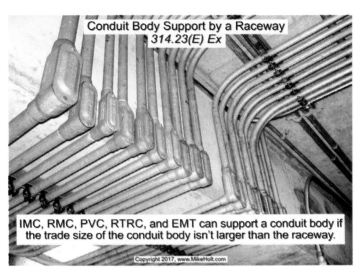

Figure 314–29

(1) Intermediate metal conduit, Type IMC

(2) Rigid metal conduit, Type RMC

(3) Rigid polyvinyl chloride conduit, Type PVC

(4) Reinforced thermosetting resin conduit, Type RTRC

(5) Electrical metallic tubing, Type EMT

(F) Raceways—Boxes and Conduit Bodies with Devices or Luminaires. Two intermediate metal or rigid metal conduits, threaded wrenchtight into the enclosure, can be used to support an outlet box containing devices or luminaires, if each raceway is supported within 18 in. of the box. Figure 314–30 and Figure 314–31

(H) Pendant Boxes.

(1) Flexible Cord. Boxes containing a hub can be supported from a flexible cord connected to fittings that prevent tension from being transmitted to joints or terminals [400.10]. Figure 314–32

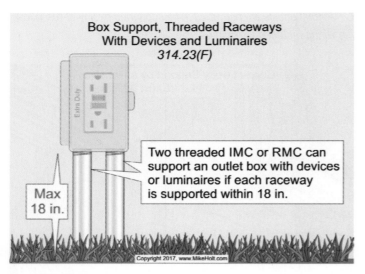

Box Support, Threaded Raceways
With Devices and Luminaires
314.23(F)

Two threaded IMC or RMC can
support an outlet box with devices
or luminaires if each raceway
is supported within 18 in.

Max
18 in.

Figure 314–30

Box Support, Threaded Raceways
With Devices and Luminaires
314.23(F)

VIOLATION
A free-standing outlet
box with a device(s)
or luminaire(s) must
be supported by two
threaded IMC or RMC
raceways within 18 in.
of the box.

Figure 314–31

Pendant Boxes, Flexible Cord
314.23(H)(1)

Boxes containing a hub can be
supported from a flexible cord
connected to fittings that prevent
tension from being transmitted to
joints or terminals [400.10].

Figure 314–32

314.27 Outlet Box

New text addresses "receptacles" that support stuff...like
luminaires and paddle fans.

Analysis

NEW

When new technologies emerge, new *Code* rules
soon follow. Sometimes the new technology is so
bizarre, esoteric, or just plain unique, that the new
rule makes no sense unless you know exactly which product it addresses. This is certainly the case here.

A new product (a listed locking support and mounting
receptacle) is available that can be mounted to a ceiling
outlet box and allows a person to mount a luminaire or a
paddle fan in about 10 seconds by pushing it onto the device
then twisting and locking it into place. This technology is
very interesting and I'm looking forward to seeing what the
future holds for it and what the future adjustments to the
NEC might be.

314.27 Outlet Box

(A) Boxes at Luminaire Outlets.

(1) Luminaire Outlets in or on Vertical Surfaces. Boxes or fittings designed for the support of luminaires in or on a wall or other vertical surface must be identified and marked on the interior of the box to indicate the maximum weight of the luminaire if other than 50 lb. Figure 314–33

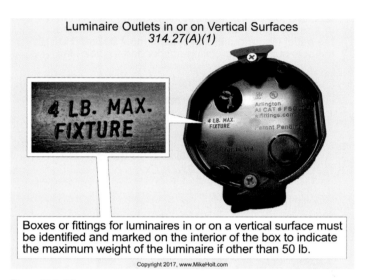

Figure 314–33

Ex: A vertically mounted luminaire weighing no more than 6 lb can be supported to a device box or plaster ring secured to a device box. Figure 314–34

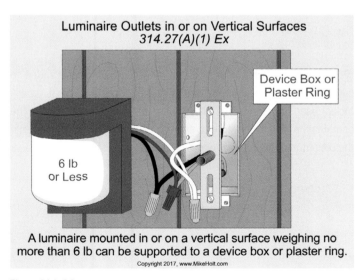

Figure 314–34

(2) Luminaire Outlets in the Ceiling. Boxes for ceiling luminaires must be listed and marked to support a luminaire weighing a minimum of 50 lb. Luminaires weighing more than 50 lb must be supported independently of the outlet box unless the outlet box is listed and <u>marked</u> on the interior of the box <u>by the manufacturer for the maximum weight the box can support.</u> Figure 314–35

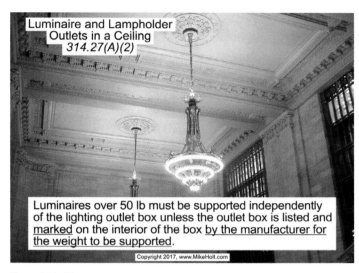

Figure 314–35

(B) Floor Box. Floor boxes must be specifically listed for the purpose. Figure 314–36

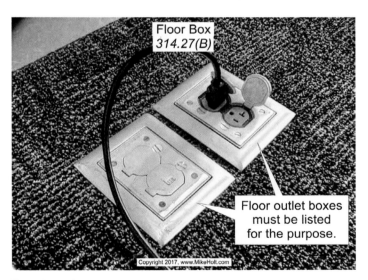

Figure 314–36

(C) Ceiling Paddle Fan Box. Outlet boxes for a ceiling paddle fan must be listed and marked as suitable for the purpose, and must not support a fan weighing more than 70 lb. Outlet boxes for a ceiling paddle fan that weighs more than 35 lb must include the maximum weight to be supported in the required marking. Figure 314–37

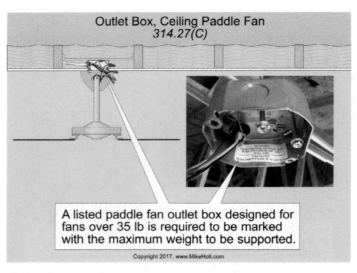

Outlet Box, Ceiling Paddle Fan
314.27(C)

A listed paddle fan outlet box designed for fans over 35 lb is required to be marked with the maximum weight to be supported.

Copyright 2017, www.MikeHolt.com

Figure 314–37

Author's Comment:

■ If the maximum weight isn't marked on the box, and the fan weighs over 35 lb, it must be supported independently of the outlet box. Ceiling paddle fans over 70 lb must be supported independently of the outlet box.

Where spare, separately switched, ungrounded conductors are provided to a ceiling-mounted outlet box, in a location acceptable for a ceiling-suspended (paddle) fan in one-family, two-family, or multifamily dwellings, the outlet box or outlet box system must be listed for the support of a ceiling-suspended (paddle) fan. Figure 314–38

(D) Utilization Equipment. Boxes used for the support of utilization equipment must be designed to support equipment that weighs a minimum of 50 lb [314.27(A)].

Ex: Utilization equipment weighing 6 lb or less can be supported by any box or plaster ring secured to a box, provided the equipment is secured with no fewer than two No. 6 or larger screws. Figure 314–39

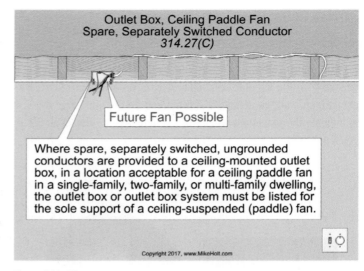

Outlet Box, Ceiling Paddle Fan
Spare, Separately Switched Conductor
314.27(C)

Future Fan Possible

Where spare, separately switched, ungrounded conductors are provided to a ceiling-mounted outlet box, in a location acceptable for a ceiling paddle fan in a single-family, two-family, or multi-family dwelling, the outlet box or outlet box system must be listed for the sole support of a ceiling-suspended (paddle) fan.

Copyright 2017, www.MikeHolt.com

Figure 314–38

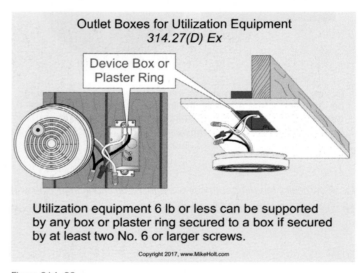

Outlet Boxes for Utilization Equipment
314.27(D) Ex

Device Box or Plaster Ring

Utilization equipment 6 lb or less can be supported by any box or plaster ring secured to a box if secured by at least two No. 6 or larger screws.

Copyright 2017, www.MikeHolt.com

Figure 314–39

(E) Separable Attachment Fittings. Outlet boxes are permitted to support listed locking, support, and mounting receptacles (SQL receptacles) used in combination with compatible attachment fittings. The combination must be identified for the support of equipment within the weight and mounting orientation limits of the listing. Figure 314–40

Author's Comment:

■ See the Article 100 definition of a receptacle and visit http://www.safetyquicklight.com/ for additional information on SQL receptacles.

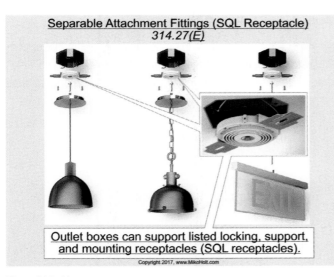

Separable Attachment Fittings (SQL Receptacle)
314.27(E)

Outlet boxes can support listed locking, support, and mounting receptacles (SQL receptacles).

Copyright 2017, www.MikeHolt.com

Figure 314–40

314.28 Sizing Boxes and Conduit Bodies— Conductors 4 AWG and Larger

The allowance for using conduit bodies smaller than generally required was clarified, and power distribution blocks on the supply side of the service are now allowed if listed for the location.

Analysis

CLARIFIED

Conduit Body. When it comes to sizing conduit bodies, the general rule is that they must comply with the requirements of pull junction boxes, like a length of six times the diameter of the raceway entry. However, the *Code* permits conduit bodies to be smaller than those dimensions when marked to accommodate a specific size and number of conductors. This makes sense, until you consider the fact that not all conductors have the same outside diameter because not all of them have the same insulation. Revised text provides guidance on how to manage this application. The 2017 *NEC* requires the conduit body size to be based on XHHW insulation, which is one of the thicker insulations in use today.

NEW **Power Distribution Blocks.** When power distribution blocks are installed on the supply side of the service disconnect, they must be marked that they're suitable for that application. While that might sound like a strange rule, consider the fact that they weren't allowed on the supply side at all until now!

314.28 Sizing Boxes and Conduit Bodies— Conductors 4 AWG and Larger

 Scan this QR code for a video of Mike explaining this topic; it's a sample from the DVDs that accompany this textbook.

Boxes and conduit bodies containing conductors 4 AWG and larger that are required to be insulated must be sized so the conductor insulation won't be damaged. Figure 314–41

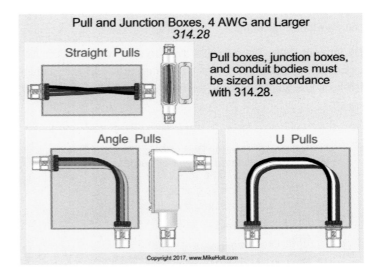

Pull and Junction Boxes, 4 AWG and Larger
314.28

Straight Pulls

Angle Pulls

U Pulls

Pull boxes, junction boxes, and conduit bodies must be sized in accordance with 314.28.

Copyright 2017, www.MikeHolt.com

Figure 314–41

Author's Comment:

- The requirements for sizing boxes and conduit bodies containing conductors 6 AWG and smaller are contained in 314.16.

- If conductors 4 AWG and larger enter a box or other enclosure, a fitting that provides a smooth, rounded, insulating surface, such as a bushing or adapter, is required to protect the conductors from abrasion during and after installation [300.4(G)]. Figure 314–42

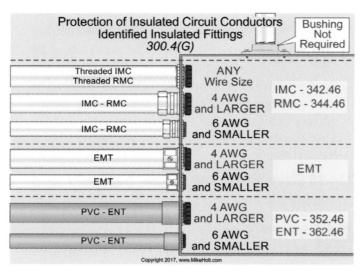

Figure 314–42

(A) Minimum Size. For raceways containing conductors 4 AWG and larger, the minimum dimensions of boxes and conduit bodies must comply with the following:

(1) Straight Pulls. The minimum distance from where the conductors enter the box or conduit body to the opposite wall isn't permitted to be less than eight times the trade size of the largest raceway. Figure 314–43

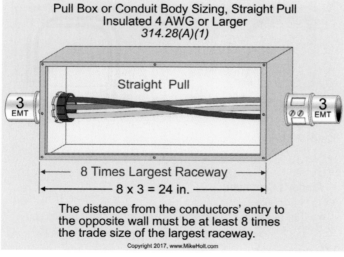

Figure 314–43

(2) Angle Pulls, U Pulls, or Splices.

Angle Pulls. The distance from the raceway entry of the box or conduit body to the opposite wall isn't permitted to be less than six times the trade size of the largest raceway, plus the sum of the trade sizes of the remaining raceways on the same wall and row. Figure 314–44

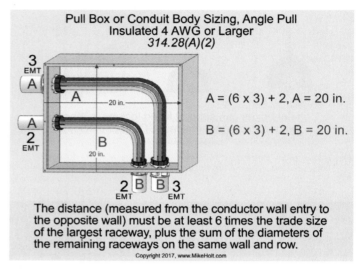

Figure 314–44

U Pulls. When a conductor enters and leaves from the same wall of the box, the distance from where the raceways enter to the opposite wall isn't permitted to be less than six times the trade size of the largest raceway, plus the sum of the trade sizes of the remaining raceways on the same wall and row. Figure 314–45

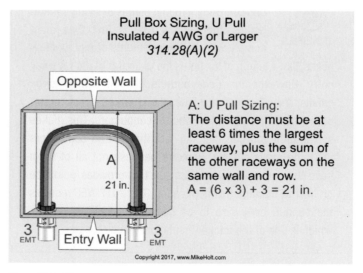

Figure 314–45

Splices. When conductors are spliced, the distance from where the raceways enter to the opposite wall isn't permitted to be less than six times the trade size of the largest raceway, plus the sum of the trade sizes of the remaining raceways on the same wall and row. Figure 314–46

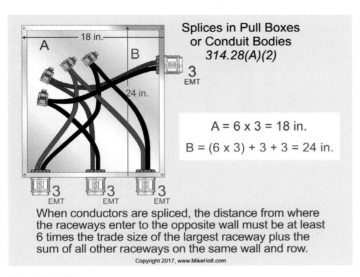

Splices in Pull Boxes or Conduit Bodies
314.28(A)(2)

A = 6 x 3 = 18 in.

B = (6 x 3) + 3 + 3 = 24 in.

When conductors are spliced, the distance from where the raceways enter to the opposite wall must be at least 6 times the trade size of the largest raceway plus the sum of all other raceways on the same wall and row.

Copyright 2017, www.MikeHolt.com

Figure 314–46

Rows. If there are multiple rows of raceway entries, each row is calculated individually and the row with the largest distance must be used. Figure 314–47

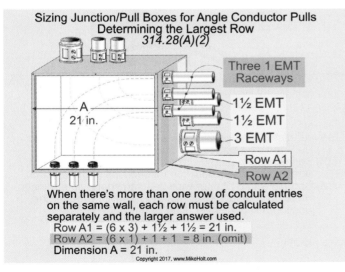

Sizing Junction/Pull Boxes for Angle Conductor Pulls
Determining the Largest Row
314.28(A)(2)

Three 1 EMT Raceways

1½ EMT
1½ EMT
3 EMT

Row A1
Row A2

When there's more than one row of conduit entries on the same wall, each row must be calculated separately and the larger answer used.
Row A1 = (6 x 3) + 1½ + 1½ = 21 in.
Row A2 = (6 x 1) + 1 + 1 = 8 in. (omit)
Dimension A = 21 in.

Copyright 2017, www.MikeHolt.com

Figure 314–47

Distance Between Raceways. The distance between raceways enclosing the same conductor isn't permitted to be less than six times the trade size of the largest raceway, measured from the raceways' nearest edge-to-nearest edge. Figure 314–48 and Figure 314–49

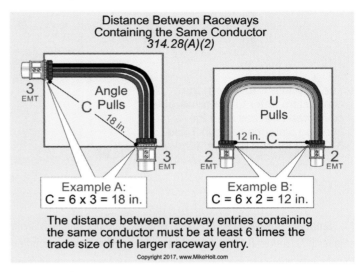

Distance Between Raceways Containing the Same Conductor
314.28(A)(2)

Angle Pulls
C

U Pulls
C

Example A:
C = 6 x 3 = 18 in.

Example B:
C = 6 x 2 = 12 in.

The distance between raceway entries containing the same conductor must be at least 6 times the trade size of the larger raceway entry.

Copyright 2017, www.MikeHolt.com

Figure 314–48

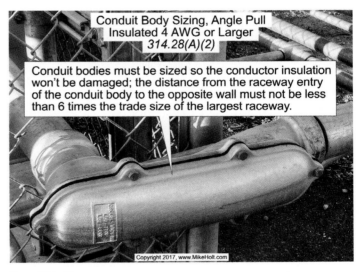

Conduit Body Sizing, Angle Pull Insulated 4 AWG or Larger
314.28(A)(2)

Conduit bodies must be sized so the conductor insulation won't be damaged; the distance from the raceway entry of the conduit body to the opposite wall must not be less than 6 times the trade size of the largest raceway.

Copyright 2017, www.MikeHolt.com

Figure 314–49

Ex: When conductors enter an enclosure with a removable cover, the distance from where the conductors enter to the removable cover isn't permitted to be less than the bending distance as listed in Table 312.6(A) for one conductor per terminal. Figure 314–50

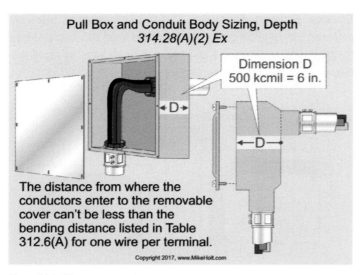

Figure 314–50

(3) Smaller Dimensions Conduit Bodies. Conduit bodies sized smaller than required by 314.28(A)(1) and 314.28(A)(2) are permitted to be used <u>if the cross-sectional area of the conductors installed don't exceed the cross-sectional area of the number of conductors and size of conductors marked on the conduit body.</u> Figure 314–51

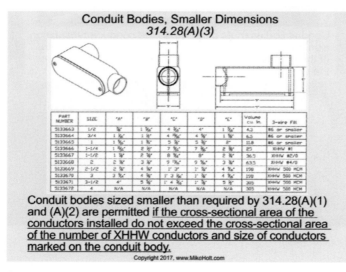

Figure 314–51

Note: Unless otherwise specified, the fill markings on the conduit body are based on conductors with Type XHHW insulation.

(B) Conductors in Pull or Junction Boxes. Pull boxes or junction boxes with any dimension over 6 ft must have all conductors cabled or racked in an approved manner.

(C) Covers. Pull boxes, junction boxes, and conduit bodies must have a cover suitable for the conditions. Metal covers must be connected to an equipment grounding conductor of a type recognized in 250.118, in accordance with 250.110 [250.4(A)(3)]. Figure 314–52

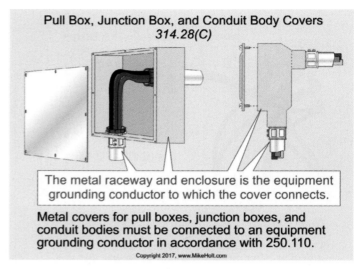

Figure 314–52

(E) Power Distribution Block. Power distribution blocks must comply with the following: Figure 314–53

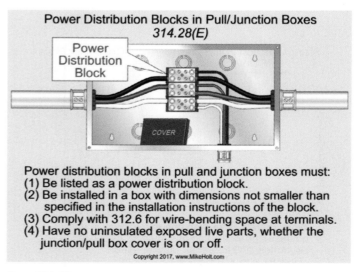

Figure 314–53

(1) Installation. Power distribution blocks must be listed; if <u>installed on the line side of the service equipment, power distribution blocks must be listed and marked "suitable for use on the line side of service equipment" or equivalent.</u> Figure 314–54

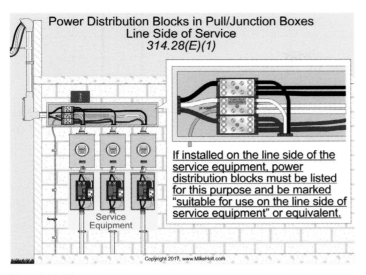

Power Distribution Blocks in Pull/Junction Boxes
Line Side of Service
314.28(E)(1)

If installed on the line side of the service equipment, power distribution blocks must be listed for this purpose and be marked "suitable for use on the line side of service equipment" or equivalent.

Service Equipment

Copyright 2017, www.MikeHolt.com

Figure 314–54

(2) Size. Be installed in a box not smaller than required by the installation instructions of the power distribution block.

(3) Wire-Bending Space. The junction box is sized so that the wire-bending space requirements of 312.6 can be met.

(4) Live Parts. Exposed live parts on the power distribution block aren't present when the junction box cover is removed.

(5) Through Conductors. Where the junction box has conductors that don't terminate on the power distribution block(s), the through conductors must be arranged so the power distribution block terminals are unobstructed following installation.

320 ARMORED CABLE (TYPE AC)

Introduction to Article 320—Armored Cable (Type AC)

Armored cable is an assembly of insulated conductors, 14 AWG through 1 AWG, individually wrapped within waxed paper and contained within a flexible spiral metal sheath. The outside appearance of armored cable looks like flexible metal conduit as well as metal-clad cable to the casual observer. This cable has been referred to as "BX®" cable over the years and used in residential wiring in some areas of the country.

Part I. General

320.1 Scope

This article covers the use, installation, and construction specifications of armored cable, Type AC. Figure 320–1

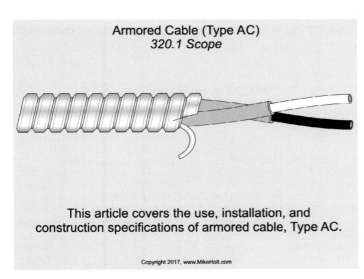

Armored Cable (Type AC)
320.1 Scope

This article covers the use, installation, and construction specifications of armored cable, Type AC.

Copyright 2017, www.MikeHolt.com

Figure 320–1

320.6 Listing Requirements

Type AC Cable and its associated fittings must now be listed.

Analysis

NEW Testing and subsequent listing of products ensures that a product is safe. This concept is well over 100 years old. It's such a well understood and accepted concept that not one single comment was made to reject this new requirement. In fact, many people probably thought it was already a *Code* rule, as a listing requirement for products, especially wiring methods, is something that we've just come to expect.

320.6 Listing Requirements

Listing and Labeling. Type AC cable and associated fittings must be listed.

320.30 Securing and Supporting

Cable ties for securing and supporting must now be listed.

Analysis

NEW Many of the products mentioned in the *NEC* don't have to be listed. Often the reason is that there simply isn't a product standard by which they can be tested and then listed. In June of 2014, UL 62275 became effective; now that we have a product standard for cable ties, we have a *Code* requirement.

320.30 Securing and Supporting

(A) General. Type AC cable must be supported and secured by staples, cable ties listed and identified for securing and supporting; straps, hangers, or similar fittings, or other approved means designed and installed so as not to damage the cable. Figure 320–2

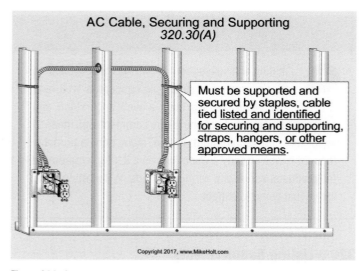

AC Cable, Securing and Supporting
320.30(A)

Must be supported and secured by staples, cable tied listed and identified for securing and supporting, straps, hangers, or other approved means.

Figure 320–2

(B) Securing. Type AC cable must be secured within 12 in. of every outlet box, junction box, cabinet, or fitting, and at intervals not exceeding 4½ ft. Figure 320–3

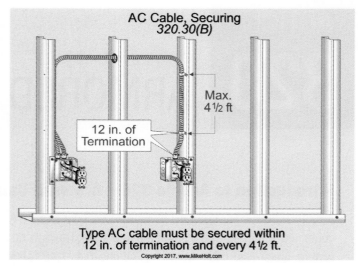

AC Cable, Securing
320.30(B)

Max. 4½ ft

12 in. of Termination

Type AC cable must be secured within 12 in. of termination and every 4½ ft.

Figure 320–3

Author's Comment:

- Type AC cable is considered secured when installed horizontally through openings in wooden or metal framing members [320.30(C)].

(C) Supporting. Type AC cable must be supported at intervals not exceeding 4½ ft. Cables installed horizontally through wooden or metal framing members are considered supported if support doesn't exceed 4½ ft. Figure 320–4

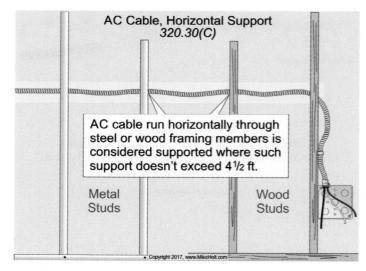

AC Cable, Horizontal Support
320.30(C)

AC cable run horizontally through steel or wood framing members is considered supported where such support doesn't exceed 4½ ft.

Metal Studs

Wood Studs

Figure 320–4

(D) Unsupported Cables. Type AC cable can be unsupported <u>and unsecured</u> where:

(1) Fished through concealed spaces

(2) Not more than 2 ft long at terminals where flexibility is necessary

(3) Not more than 6 ft long from the last point of cable support or Type AC cable fitting to the point of connection to a luminaire or electrical equipment within an accessible ceiling. Figure 320–5

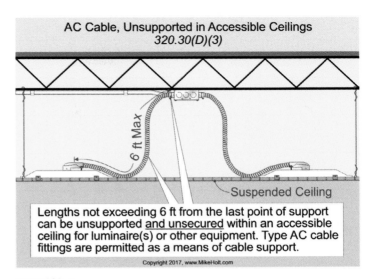

AC Cable, Unsupported in Accessible Ceilings
320.30(D)(3)

6 ft Max

Suspended Ceiling

Lengths not exceeding 6 ft from the last point of support can be unsupported <u>and unsecured</u> within an accessible ceiling for luminaire(s) or other equipment. Type AC cable fittings are permitted as a means of cable support.

Copyright 2017, www.MikeHolt.com

Figure 320–5

Introduction to Article 330—Metal-Clad Cable (Type MC)

Metal-clad cable encloses insulated conductors in a metal sheath of either corrugated or smooth copper or aluminum tubing, or spiral interlocked steel or aluminum. The physical characteristics of Type MC cable make it a versatile wiring method that you can use in almost any location, and for almost any application. The most commonly used Type MC cable is the interlocking kind, which looks similar to armored cable or flexible metal conduit. Traditional interlocked Type MC cable isn't permitted to serve as an equipment grounding conductor, therefore this cable must contain an equipment grounding conductor in accordance with 250.118(1). There's a fairly new product available called interlocked Type MC^AP cable that contains a bare aluminum grounding/bonding conductor running just below the metal armor, which allows the sheath to serve as an equipment grounding conductor [250.118(10)(b)].

Part I. General

330.1 Scope

Article 330 covers the use, installation, and construction specifications of metal-clad cable. Figure 330–1

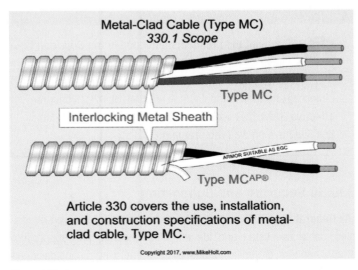

Metal-Clad Cable (Type MC)
330.1 Scope

Type MC

Interlocking Metal Sheath

ARMOR SUITABLE AS EGC

Type MC^AP®

Article 330 covers the use, installation, and construction specifications of metal-clad cable, Type MC.

Copyright 2017, www.MikeHolt.com

Figure 330–1

330.6 Listing Requirements

Type MC cable and fittings must be listed and the fittings must be identified for the use.

Analysis

NEW Testing and subsequent listing of products ensures that the product is safe. This concept is well over 100 years old. It's such a well understood and accepted concept that not one single comment was made to reject this new requirement. In fact, many people probably thought it was already an *NEC* rule, as a listing requirement for products, especially wiring methods, is something that we've just come to expect.

330.6 Listing Requirements

Type MC cable must be listed and the fittings must be listed and identified for the use. Figure 330–2

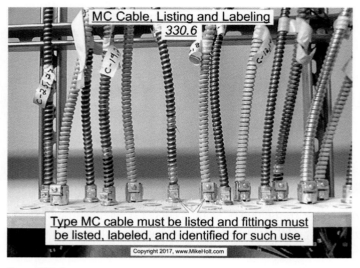

Figure 330–2

Author's Comment:

- The *NEC* doesn't require anti-short bushings (red heads) at the termination of Type MC cable, but if they're supplied it's considered by many to be a good practice to use them.

330.15 Exposed Work

New requirements for the installation of exposed Type MC cable have been added.

Analysis

EDITED

There are a number of small changes that improve the *NEC* but go unnoticed by the casual user. One of them is the concept of parallel numbering between *Code* articles. If you look at the rules for cables in Articles 320 through 340, you'll notice that the "dot 1" section is the scope, "dot 2" is a definition, "dot 6" is listing, "dot 10" is uses permitted, and so forth.

This makes good sense, and the Code Making Panels involved should be applauded for their efforts, as every little thing that improves the *NEC* is worth doing. It's rather strange, but most of the cable articles have a "dot 15" section addressing exposed cables. Article 330 didn't have one before, but now it does. As you might expect, it says the same thing as the other cable articles, as it should. Why should the rules on exposed Types MC cable and AC cable be different? They aren't anymore.

330.15 Exposed Work

Exposed runs of Type MC cable must closely follow the surface of the building finish or running boards. Type MC cable installed on the bottom of floor or ceiling joists must be secured at every joist and not be subject to physical damage. Figure 330–3

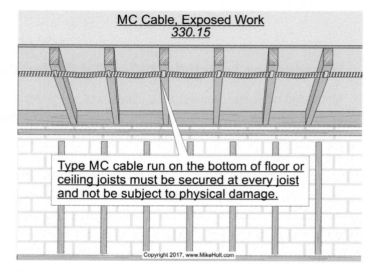

Figure 330–3

330.30 Securing and Supporting

Cable ties for securing and supporting must now be listed.

Analysis

NEW

Many of the products mentioned in the *Code* don't have to be listed. Often the reason is that there simply isn't a product standard by which they can be tested and then listed. In June of 2014, UL 62275 became effective. Now that we have a product standard for cable ties, we have an *NEC* requirement.

330.30 Securing and Supporting

(A) General. Type MC cable must be supported and secured by staples, cable ties listed and identified for securing and supporting; straps, hangers, or similar fittings, or other approved means designed and installed so as not to damage the cable. Figure 330–4 and Figure 330–5

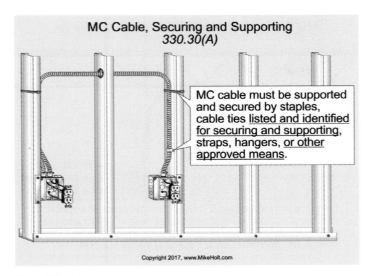

Figure 330–4

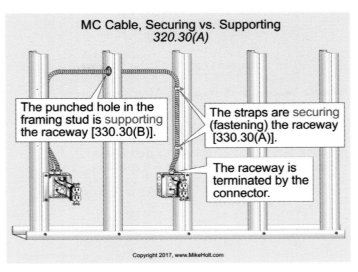

Figure 330–6

Figure 330–5

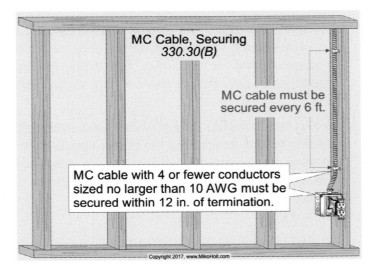

Figure 330–7

Author's Comment:

■ Secured is "fastened" such as with a strap or tie wrap; supported is "held" such as a hanger or through a hole in a stud, joist, or rafter. Figure 330–6

(B) Securing. Type MC cable with four or less conductors sized no larger than 10 AWG, must be secured within 12 in. of every outlet box, junction box, cabinet, or fitting and at intervals not exceeding 6 ft. Figure 330–7

Listed cables with ungrounded conductors 250 kcmil and larger can be secured at 10-ft intervals when installed vertically.

(C) Supporting. Type MC cable must be supported at intervals not exceeding 6 ft. Cables installed horizontally through wooden or metal framing members are considered secured and supported if such support doesn't exceed 6-ft intervals. Figure 330–8

(D) Unsupported Cables. Type MC cable can be unsupported and unsecured where:

(1) Fished through concealed spaces

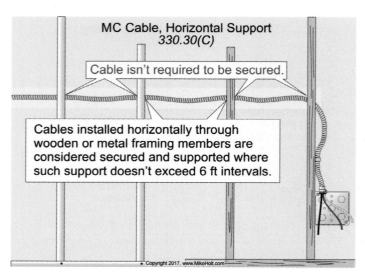

Figure 330–8

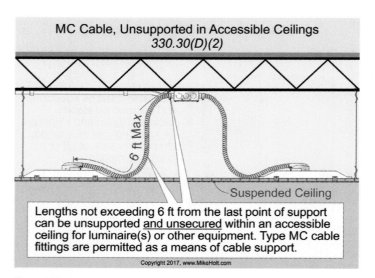

Figure 330–9

(2) Not more than 6 ft long from the last point of cable support to the point of connection to a luminaire or electrical equipment within an accessible ceiling. For the purposes of this section, Type MC cable fittings are permitted as a means of cable support. Figure 330–9

(3) Not more than 3 ft from the last point where it's securely fastened to provide flexibility for equipment that requires movement after installation, or to connect equipment where flexibility is necessary to minimize the transmission of vibration from the equipment. Figure 330–10

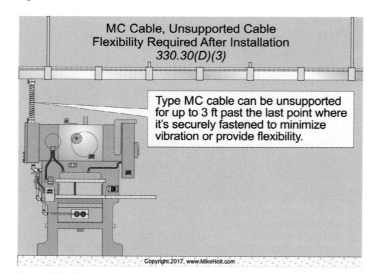

Figure 330–10

Introduction to Article 334—Nonmetallic-Sheathed Cable (Types NM and NMC)

Nonmetallic-sheathed cable is flexible, inexpensive, and easily installed. It provides very limited physical protection for the conductors, so the installation restrictions are strict. Its low cost and relative ease of installation make it a common wiring method for residential and commercial branch circuits. In the field, Type NM cable is typically referred to as "Romex®."

Part I. General

334.1 Scope

Article 334 covers the use, installation, and construction specifications of nonmetallic-sheathed cable. Figure 334–1

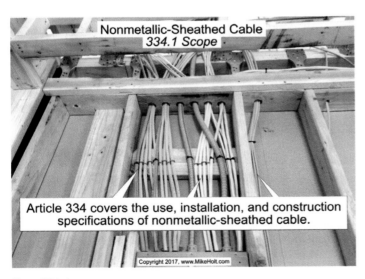

Figure 334–1

334.6 Listing Requirements

Type NM Cable fittings must now be listed.

Analysis

NEW Previous editions of the *NEC* required that the cable itself be listed, but didn't have the same requirement for the fittings. In order to create harmony with the rest of Chapter 3, this change was made and was met with no resistance at all during the *Code*-change process.

334.6 Listing Requirements

Type NM cable <u>and associated fittings</u> must be listed. Figure 334–2

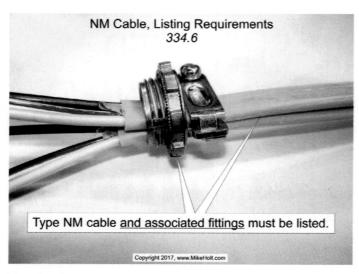

Figure 334–2

334.12 Uses Not Permitted

An editorial change was made to the language regarding ceilings.

Analysis

EDITED Up until the 1999 edition of the *NEC*, the number of stories in a building limited the use of Type NM cable. When this was removed from the *Code* in 2002, tradeoffs were made. One of those was that we could use Type NM cable in a building of any height provided the building wasn't required to be noncombustible (Types I and II Construction) and that the cable wouldn't be in a suspended ceiling. You can't possibly put a cable in a ceiling; you can only put it above one. Okay, fine; now the rule is clear, you can't put a cable above a suspended ceiling.

334.12 Uses Not Permitted

(A) Types NM and NMC. Types NM and NMC cables aren't permitted.

(1) In any dwelling or structure not specifically permitted in 334.10(1), (2), (3), and (5).

(2) Exposed <u>within a dropped</u> or suspended <u>ceiling cavity</u> in other than one- and two-family, and multifamily dwellings. Figure 334–3

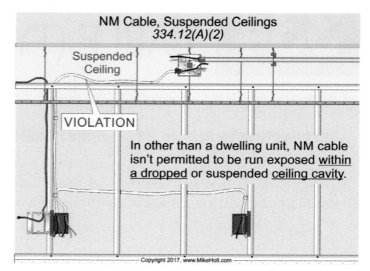

Figure 334–3

(3) As service-entrance cable.

(4) In commercial garages having hazardous locations, as defined in 511.3.

(5) In theaters and similar locations, except where permitted in 518.4(B).

(6) In motion picture studios.

(7) In storage battery rooms.

(8) In hoistways, or on elevators or escalators.

(9) Embedded in poured cement, concrete, or aggregate.

(10) In any hazardous location, except where permitted by other sections in the *Code*.

(B) Type NM. Type NM cables aren't permitted to be used under the following conditions, or in the following locations:

(1) If exposed to corrosive fumes or vapors.

(2) If embedded in masonry, concrete, adobe, fill, or plaster.

(3) In a shallow chase in masonry, concrete, or adobe and covered with plaster, adobe, or similar finish.

(4) In wet or damp locations. Figure 334–4

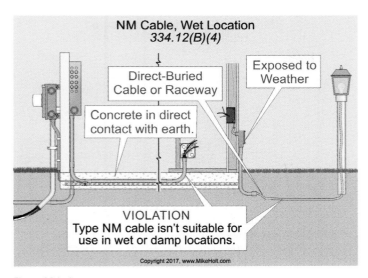

Figure 334–4

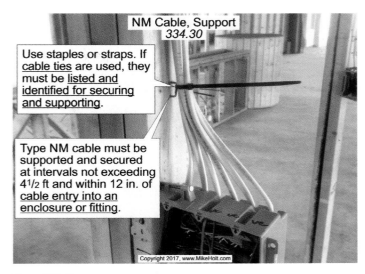

Figure 334–5

Author's Comment:

■ Type NM cable isn't permitted in ducts or plenum spaces [300.22], or for wiring in patient care spaces [517.13].

334.30 Securing and Supporting

Cable ties for securing and supporting must now be listed.

Analysis

NEW Many of the products mentioned in the *NEC* don't have to be listed. Often the reason is that there simply isn't a product standard by which they can be tested and then listed. In June of 2014, UL 62275 became effective. Now that we have a product standard for cables ties, we have a *Code* requirement.

334.30 Securing and Supporting

Nonmetallic-sheathed cable must be supported and secured by staples, straps, cable ties listed and identified for securing and supporting; hangers, or similar fittings, at intervals not exceeding 4½ ft and within 12 in. of the cable entry into enclosures or fittings. Figure 334–5 and Figure 334–6

Figure 334–6

Two-wire (flat) Type NM cable isn't permitted to be stapled on edge. Figure 334–7

Type NM cable installed within a raceway isn't required to be secured within the raceway. Figure 334–8

(A) Horizontal Runs. Type NM cable installed horizontally in bored or punched holes in wood or metal framing members, or notches in wooden members is considered secured and supported, but the cable must be secured within 1 ft of termination. Figure 334–9

Note: See 314.17(C) for support where nonmetallic boxes are used.

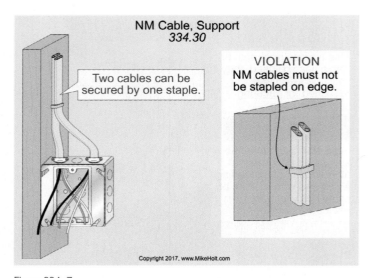

Figure 334–7

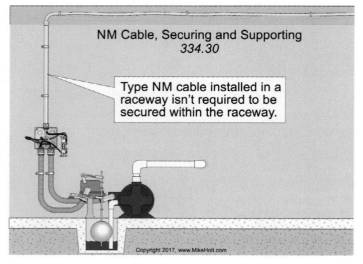

Figure 334–8

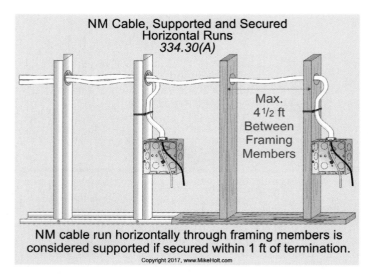

Figure 334–9

(B) Unsupported. Type NM cable can be unsupported in the following situations:

(1) If Type NM cable is fished between concealed access points in finished buildings, and support is impracticable.

(2) Not more than 4½ ft of unsupported cable is permitted from the last point of support within an accessible ceiling for the connection of luminaires or equipment in one-, two-, or multifamily dwellings.

Author's Comment:

- Type NM cable isn't permitted as a wiring method above accessible ceilings, except in dwellings [334.12(A)(2)].

POWER AND CONTROL TRAY CABLE (TYPE TC)

Introduction to Article 336—Power and Control Tray Cable (Type TC)

Power and Control Tray Cable is flexible, inexpensive, and easily installed. It provides very limited physical protection for the conductors, so the installation restrictions are strict. Its low cost and relative ease of installation make it a common wiring method for industrial applications.

Part I. General

336.1 Scope

This article covers the use and installation for power and control tray cable, Type TC.

336.6 Listing Requirements

Type TC cable and associated fittings must now be listed.

Analysis

NEW

Previous editions of the *NEC* didn't require TC cable or fittings to be listed. They're now required to be listed.

336.6 Listing Requirements

Type TC cables and associated fittings must be listed. Figure 336–1

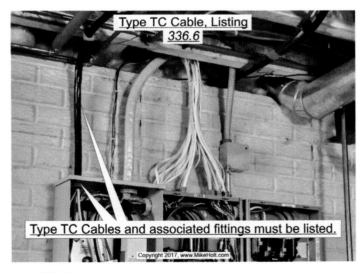

Figure 336–1

336.10 Uses Permitted

The allowable uses of Type TC cable were expanded to allow it to be used in trays with discontinuous segments and to be installed in dwelling units.

Analysis

EXPANDED

As the use of optional standby systems has increased in the last 10 years, the need for installation options have also grown. A new type TC cable marked TC-ER-JP recently became available making it easier to install the feeder and control conductors for generators. Because Type TC cable wasn't previously allowed in dwelling units this cable wasn't permitted. This section has now been expanded to permit this.

Part II. Installation

336.10 Uses Permitted

(1) Power, lighting, control, and signal circuits.

(2) In cable trays including those with mechanically discontinuous segments up to 1 ft.

(3) In raceways.

(4) Outdoor locations supported by a messenger wire.

(5) Class 1 circuits as permitted in Parts II and III of Article 725.

(6) Non-power-limited fire alarm circuits in accordance with if 760.49.

(7) Industrial establishments where the conditions of maintenance and supervision ensure that only qualified persons service the installation.

(8) In wet locations where the cable is resistant to moisture and corrosive agents.

(9) In one- and two-family dwellings, Type TC-ER cable is permitted in accordance with Part II of Article 334.

Author's Comment:

■ The "ER" marking on Type TC-ER cable identifies that the cable is suitable for exposed run use in accordance with UL 1277.

Ex: Where Type TC cable is used to connect a generator and its associated equipment, the cable ampacity limitations of 334.80 don't apply.

Note 1: Type TC cable that's suitable for pulling through structural members of a dwelling unit will be marked TC-ER-JP. Figure 336–2

Type TC Cable, Uses Permitted
336.10(9) *Note 1*

Type TC cable that's suitable for pulling through structural members of a dwelling unit must be marked TC-ER-JP.

Copyright 2017, www.MikeHolt.com

Figure 336–2

Author's Comment:

■ The "JP" marking on Type TC-ER-JP cable identifies that the cable is suitable to be pulled through wood framing members because the cable has met the joist pull testing requirements of UL 1277.

Note 2: Control and Class 1 power conductors within the same Type TC cable are only permitted where the conductors are functionally associated with each other in accordance with 725.136.

(10) Direct buried where identified for direct burial.

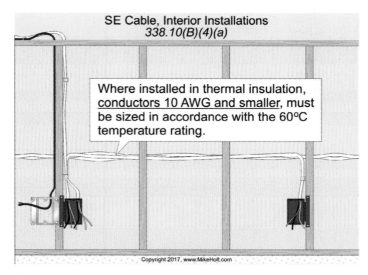

SE Cable, Interior Installations
338.10(B)(4)(a)

Where installed in thermal insulation, conductors 10 AWG and smaller, must be sized in accordance with the 60°C temperature rating.

Copyright 2017, www.MikeHolt.com

Figure 338–4

 CAUTION: *Underground service-entrance cable (USE) isn't permitted for interior wiring because it doesn't have a flame-retardant insulation. It would only be permitted in interior wiring when listed as both a cable (USE) and a conductor, such as RHH, in accordance with Table 310.104.*

(b) Exterior Installations. The cable must be supported in accordance with 334.30 and where run underground the cable must comply with Part II of Article 340.

UNDERGROUND FEEDER AND BRANCH-CIRCUIT CABLE (TYPE UF)

Introduction to Article 340—Underground Feeder and Branch-Circuit Cable (Type UF)

UF cable is a moisture-, fungus-, and corrosion-resistant cable suitable for direct burial in the earth.

Part I. General

340.1 Scope

Article 340 covers the use, installation, and construction specifications of underground feeder and branch-circuit cable, Type UF. Figure 340–1

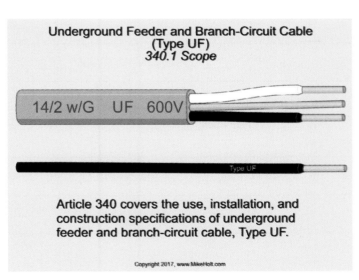

Underground Feeder and Branch-Circuit Cable (Type UF) 340.1 Scope

14/2 w/G   UF   600V

Type UF

Article 340 covers the use, installation, and construction specifications of underground feeder and branch-circuit cable, Type UF.

Copyright 2017, www.MikeHolt.com

Figure 340–1

340.6 Listing Requirements

Type UF Cable fittings must now be listed.

Analysis

NEW Previous editions of the *NEC* required UF cable itself be listed, but didn't require the same of the fittings. In order to create harmony with the rest of Chapter 3, this change was made and was met with no resistance at all during the *Code*-change process.

340.6 Listing Requirements

Type UF cable <u>and associated fittings</u> must be listed.

INTERMEDIATE METAL CONDUIT (TYPE IMC)

Introduction to Article 342—Intermediate Metal Conduit (Type IMC)

Intermediate metal conduit is a circular metal raceway with an outside diameter equal to that of rigid metal conduit. The wall thickness of intermediate metal conduit is less than that of rigid metal conduit, so it has a greater interior cross-sectional area for containing conductors. Intermediate metal conduit is lighter and less expensive than rigid metal conduit, but it can be used in all of the same locations as rigid metal conduit. Intermediate metal conduit also uses a different steel alloy that makes it stronger than rigid metal conduit, even though the walls are thinner. Intermediate metal conduit is manufactured in both galvanized steel and aluminum; the steel type is much more common.

Part I. General

342.1 Scope

Article 342 covers the use, installation, and construction specifications of intermediate metal conduit and associated fittings. Figure 342–1

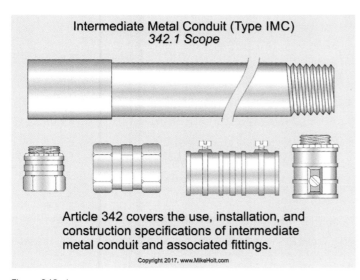

Intermediate Metal Conduit (Type IMC)
342.1 Scope

Article 342 covers the use, installation, and construction specifications of intermediate metal conduit and associated fittings.

Copyright 2017, www.MikeHolt.com

Figure 342–1

342.10 Uses Permitted

IMC in corrosive environments must now be approved for the location.

Analysis

CLARIFIED

Whenever possible, the *Code* should use the terms defined in Article 100. Previous editions of this rule stated that IMC installed in severely corrosive areas needed to have supplementary corrosion protection and the protection had to be judged as "suitable." Who's supposed to do the judging? If it's the manufacturer it should say "identified." If it's the testing laboratory it should say "listed." If it's the inspector it should say "approved." Now the 2017 *NEC* says it must be "approved." Good! Now we know who's supposed to make the determination.

342.10 Uses Permitted

(A) Atmospheric Conditions and Occupancies. Intermediate metal conduit is permitted in all atmospheric conditions and occupancies.

(B) Corrosive Environments. Intermediate metal conduit, elbows, couplings, and fittings can be installed in concrete, in direct contact with the earth, or in areas subject to severe corrosive influences if provided with supplementary corrosion protection approved for the condition.

> **Author's Comment:**
>
> ■ See 300.6 for additional details.

(D) Wet Locations. Support fittings, such as screws, straps, and so forth, installed in a wet location must be made of corrosion-resistant material, or be protected by corrosion-resistant coatings in accordance with 300.6.

⚠ **CAUTION:** *Supplementary coatings for corrosion protection haven't been investigated by a product testing and listing agency, and these coatings are known to cause cancer in laboratory animals. There's a documented case where an electrician was taken to the hospital for lead poisoning after using a supplemental coating product (asphalted paint) in a poorly ventilated area. As with all products, be sure to read and follow all product instructions, including material data safety sheets, particularly when petroleum-based chemicals (volatile organic compounds) may be in the material.*

RIGID METAL CONDUIT (TYPE RMC)

Introduction to Article 344—Rigid Metal Conduit (Type RMC)

Rigid metal conduit, commonly called "rigid," has long been the standard raceway for providing protection from physical impact and from difficult environments. The outside diameter of rigid metal conduit is the same as intermediate metal conduit. However, the wall thickness of rigid metal conduit is greater than intermediate metal conduit; therefore the interior cross-sectional area is smaller. Rigid metal conduit is heavier and more expensive than intermediate metal conduit, and it can be used in any location. Rigid metal conduit is manufactured in both galvanized steel and aluminum; the steel type is much more common.

Part I. General

344.1 Scope

Article 344 covers the use, installation, and construction specifications of rigid metal conduit and associated fittings. Figure 344–1

Rigid Metal Conduit (Type RMC)
344.1 Scope

Article 344 covers the use, installation, and construction specifications of rigid metal conduit and associated fittings.

Copyright 2017, www.MikeHolt.com

Figure 344–1

344.10 Uses Permitted

RMC in corrosive environments must now be approved for the location.

Analysis

CLARIFIED Whenever possible, the *Code* should use the terms defined in Article 100. Previous editions of this rule stated that aluminum RMC installed in earth or concrete needed to have supplementary corrosion protection and the protection had to be judged as "suitable." Who's supposed to do the judging? If it's the manufacturer it should say "identified." If it's the testing laboratory it should say "listed." If it's the inspector it should say "approved." Now the 2017 *NEC* says it must be "approved." Excellent! Now we know who's supposed to make the determination.

344.10 Uses Permitted

(A) Atmospheric Conditions and Occupancies.

(1) Galvanized Steel and Stainless Steel. Galvanized steel and stainless steel rigid metal conduit is permitted in all atmospheric conditions and occupancies.

(2) Red Brass. Red brass rigid metal conduit is permitted for direct burial and swimming pool applications.

(3) Aluminum. Rigid aluminum conduit is permitted if <u>approved</u> for the environment.

(B) Corrosive Environments.

(1) Galvanized Steel and Stainless Steel. Rigid metal conduit fittings, elbows, and couplings can be installed in concrete, in direct contact with the earth, or in areas subject to severe corrosive influences if <u>approved</u> for the condition.

(2) Aluminum. Rigid aluminum conduit must be provided with supplementary corrosion protection approved by the authority having jurisdiction if encased in concrete or in direct contact with the earth.

(D) Wet Locations. Support fittings, such as screws, straps, and so forth, installed in a wet location must be made of corrosion-resistant material or protected by corrosion-resistant coatings in accordance with 300.6.

> ⚠ **CAUTION:** *Supplementary coatings (asphalted paint) for corrosion protection haven't been investigated by a product testing and listing agency, and these coatings are known to cause cancer in laboratory animals.*

The rules for using fittings of metal dissimilar to that of the metal raceway have been clarified.

Analysis

CLARIFIED

Although galvanized steel is far and away the most common type of rigid metal conduit being used, red brass, aluminum, and stainless steel rigid metal conduits exist as well. Aluminum fittings are permitted to be used on galvanized steel rigid metal conduit. This change clarifies the fact that aluminum fittings can't be used on stainless steel rigid metal conduit.

344.14 Dissimilar Metals

If practical, contact with dissimilar metals should be avoided to prevent the deterioration of the metal because of galvanic action. Aluminum fittings and enclosures are permitted to be used with <u>galvanized</u> steel intermediate metal conduit where not subject to severe corrosive influences.

FLEXIBLE METAL CONDUIT (TYPE FMC)

Introduction to Article 348—Flexible Metal Conduit (Type FMC)

Flexible metal conduit (FMC), commonly called "Greenfield" or "flex," is a raceway of an interlocked metal strip of either steel or aluminum. It's primarily used for the final 6 ft or less of raceways between a more rigid raceway system and equipment that moves, shakes, or vibrates. Examples of such equipment include pump motors and industrial machinery.

Part I. General

348.1 Scope

Article 348 covers the use, installation, and construction specifications for flexible metal conduit and associated fittings. Figure 348–1

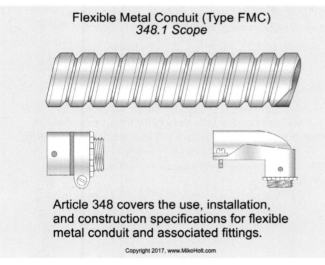

Flexible Metal Conduit (Type FMC)
348.1 Scope

Article 348 covers the use, installation, and construction specifications for flexible metal conduit and associated fittings.

Copyright 2017, www.MikeHolt.com

Figure 348–1

348.30 Securing and Supporting

Cable ties for securing and supporting must now be listed.

Analysis

NEW Many of the products mentioned in the *Code* don't have to be listed. Often the reason is that there simply isn't a product standard by which they can be tested and then listed. In June of 2014, UL 62275 became effective. Now that we have a product standard for cable ties, we have an *NEC* requirement.

348.30 Securing and Supporting

(A) Securely Fastened. Flexible metal conduit must be securely fastened by a means approved by the authority having jurisdiction within 1 ft of termination, and it must be secured and supported at intervals not exceeding 4½ ft. Figure 348–2

Where cable ties are to be used to secure and support flexible metal conduit, cable ties must be listed and identified for securing and supporting.

Ex 1: Flexible metal conduit isn't required to be securely fastened or supported where fished between access points through concealed spaces and supporting is impracticable.

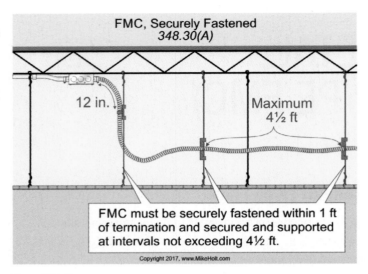

Figure 348–2

Ex 2: If flexibility is necessary after installation, unsecured lengths from the last point the raceway is securely fastened must not exceed: Figure 348–3

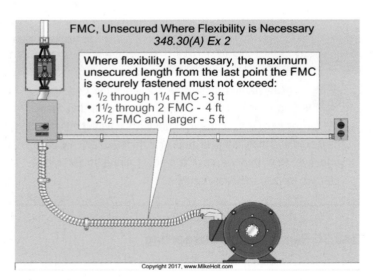

Figure 348–3

(1) 3 ft for trade sizes ½ through 1¼

(2) 4 ft for trade sizes 1½ through 2

(3) 5 ft for trade sizes 2½ and larger

Ex 4: Lengths not exceeding 6 ft from the last point where the raceway is securely fastened can be unsecured within an accessible ceiling for luminaire(s) or other equipment. For the purposes of this exception, listed fittings are considered a means of securement and support. Figure 348–4

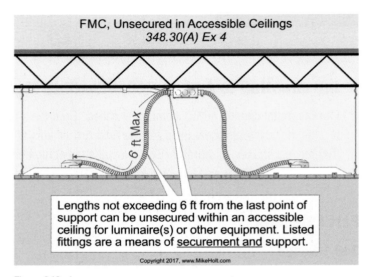

Figure 348–4

(B) Horizontal Runs. Flexible metal conduit installed horizontally in bored or punched holes in wood or metal framing members, or notches in wooden members, is considered supported, but the raceway must be secured within 1 ft of terminations. Figure 348–5

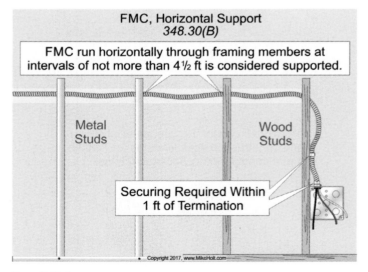

Figure 348–5

LIQUIDTIGHT FLEXIBLE METAL CONDUIT (TYPE LFMC)

Introduction to Article 350—Liquidtight Flexible Metal Conduit (Type LFMC)

Liquidtight flexible metal conduit (LFMC), with its associated connectors and fittings, is a flexible raceway commonly used for connections to equipment that vibrates or is required to move occasionally. Liquidtight flexible metal conduit is commonly called "Sealtight®" or "liquidtight." Liquidtight flexible metal conduit is of similar construction to flexible metal conduit, but it also has an outer liquidtight thermoplastic covering. It has the same primary purpose as flexible metal conduit, but it also provides protection from moisture and some corrosive effects.

Part I. General

350.1 Scope

Article 350 covers the use, installation, and construction specifications of liquidtight flexible metal conduit and associated fittings. Figure 350–1

Liquidtight Flexible Metal Conduit (Type LFMC)
350.1 Scope

Listed Liquidtight

Article 350 covers the use, installation, and construction specifications of liquidtight flexible metal conduit and associated fittings.

Copyright 2017, www.MikeHolt.com

Figure 350–1

350.28 Trimming

A new rule requires the cut edges of liquidtight flexible metal conduit to be trimmed.

Analysis

NEW We have to deburr and ream the cut ends of flexible metal conduit [348.28], so why wouldn't we have to do the same thing with liquidtight flexible metal conduit? It's the same stuff, only there's a nonmetallic covering on one versus the other. It's worth noting that trimming isn't really required if the termination fittings thread into the metal portion of the conduit, since any sharp edges wouldn't be in contact with the contained conductors.

350.28 Trimming

Cut ends of liquidtight flexible metal conduit must be trimmed both inside and outside the raceway to remove rough edges from the cut ends.

350.30 Securing and Supporting

Cable ties for securing and supporting must now be listed.

Analysis

NEW Many of the products mentioned in the *Code* don't have to be listed. Often the reason is that there simply isn't a product standard by which they can be tested and then listed. In June of 2014, UL 62275 became effective. Now that we have a product standard for cable ties, we have an *NEC* requirement.

350.30 Securing and Supporting

Liquidtight flexible metal conduit must be securely fastened in place and supported in accordance with (A) and (B).

(A) Securely Fastened. Liquidtight flexible metal conduit must be securely fastened by a means approved by the authority having jurisdiction within 1 ft of termination, and must be secured and supported at intervals not exceeding 4½ ft. Figure 350–2

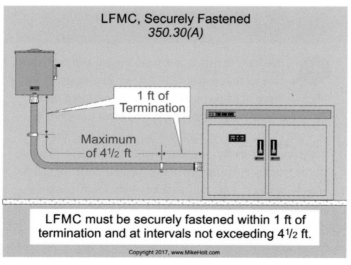

Figure 350–2

Where cable ties are used for securing liquidtight flexible metal conduit, the cable ties must be listed and identified for securement and support.

Ex 1: Liquidtight flexible metal conduit isn't required to be securely fastened or supported where fished between access points through concealed spaces and supporting is impracticable.

Ex 2: If flexibility is necessary after installation, unsecured lengths from the last point where the raceway is securely fastened must not exceed: Figure 350–3

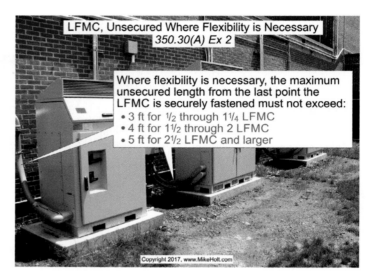

Figure 350–3

(1) 3 ft for trade sizes ½ through 1¼

(2) 4 ft for trade sizes 1½ through 2

(3) 5 ft for trade sizes 2½ and larger

Ex 4: Lengths not exceeding 6 ft from the last point where the raceway is securely fastened can be unsecured within an accessible ceiling for luminaire(s) or other equipment. For the purposes of this exception, listed fittings are considered a means of securement and support. Figure 350–4

(B) Horizontal Runs. Liquidtight flexible metal conduit installed horizontally in bored or punched holes in wood or metal framing members, or notches in wooden members, is considered supported, but the raceway must be secured within 1 ft of termination.

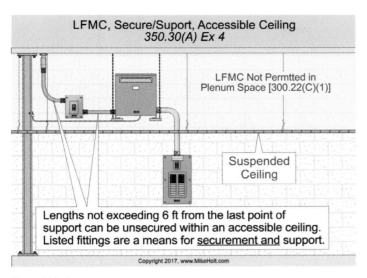

LFMC, Secure/Suport, Accessible Ceiling
350.30(A) Ex 4

LFMC Not Permtted in Plenum Space [300.22(C)(1)]

Suspended Ceiling

Lengths not exceeding 6 ft from the last point of support can be unsecured within an accessible ceiling. Listed fittings are a means for <u>securement and</u> support.

Copyright 2017, www.MikeHolt.com

Figure 350–4

LIQUIDTIGHT FLEXIBLE NONMETALLIC CONDUIT (TYPE LFNC)

Introduction to Article 356—Liquidtight Flexible Nonmetallic Conduit (Type LFNC)

Liquidtight flexible nonmetallic conduit (LFNC) is a listed raceway of circular cross section having an outer liquidtight, nonmetallic, sunlight-resistant jacket over an inner flexible core with associated couplings, connectors, and fittings.

Part I. General

356.1 Scope

Article 356 covers the use, installation, and construction specifications of liquidtight flexible nonmetallic conduit and associated fittings. Figure 356–1

Liquidtight Flexible Nonmetallic Conduit (Type LFNC)
356.1 Scope

Listed Liquidtight

Article 356 covers the use, installation, and construction specifications of liquidtight flexible nonmetallic conduit and associated fittings.

Copyright 2017, www.MikeHolt.com

Figure 356–1

356.30 Securing and Supporting

Cable ties for securing and supporting must now be listed.

Analysis

NEW

Many of the products mentioned in the *Code* don't have to be listed. Often the reason is that there simply isn't a product standard by which they can be tested and then listed. In June of 2014, UL 62275 became effective. Now that we have a product standard for cable ties, we have an *NEC* requirement.

356.30 Securing and Supporting

LFNC (gray color) must be securely fastened and supported in accordance with any of the following:

(1) The conduit must be securely fastened at intervals not exceeding 3 ft, and within 1 ft of termination when installed in lengths longer than 6 ft. Figure 356–2

Where cable ties are to be used to secure and support LFNC, they must be listed as suitable for the application and for securing and supporting.

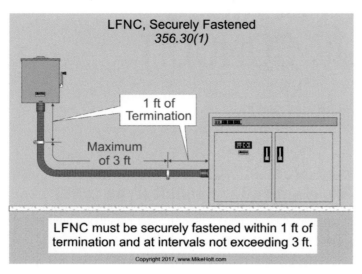

Figure 356–2

(2) Securing or supporting isn't required if it's fished, installed in lengths not exceeding 3 ft at terminals if flexibility is required, or installed in lengths not exceeding 6 ft for tap conductors to luminaires, as permitted in 410.117(C).

(3) Horizontal runs of liquidtight flexible nonmetallic conduit installed horizontally in bored or punched holes in wood or metal framing members, or notches in wooden members, are considered supported, but the raceway must be secured within 1 ft of termination.

(4) Securing or supporting of LFNC (gray color) isn't required if installed in lengths not exceeding 6 ft from the last point where the raceway is securely fastened for connections within an accessible ceiling to luminaire(s) or other equipment. For the purposes of this allowance, listed fittings are considered support. Figure 356–3

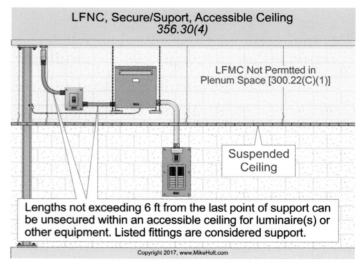

Figure 356–3

ARTICLE 358

ELECTRICAL METALLIC TUBING (TYPE EMT)

Introduction to Article 358—Electrical Metallic Tubing (Type EMT)

Electrical metallic tubing is a lightweight raceway that's relatively easy to bend, cut, and ream. Because it isn't threaded, all connectors and couplings are of the threadless type and provide quick, easy, and inexpensive installation when compared to other metallic conduit systems, which makes it very popular. Electrical metallic tubing is manufactured in both galvanized steel and aluminum; the steel type is used the most.

Part I. General

358.1 Scope

Article 358 covers the use, installation, and construction specifications of electrical metallic tubing and associated fittings. Figure 358–1

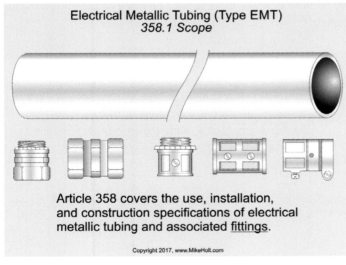

Electrical Metallic Tubing (Type EMT)
358.1 Scope

Article 358 covers the use, installation, and construction specifications of electrical metallic tubing and associated fittings.

Copyright 2017, www.MikeHolt.com

Figure 358–1

358.10 Uses Permitted

The permitted uses list for electrical metallic tubing (EMT) was greatly expanded.

Analysis

EXPANDED The uses permitted and uses not permitted rules are present in all wiring method articles. The "uses not permitted" is simple enough— these are the locations in which you can't use the wiring method.

The "uses permitted" isn't intended to be an all-inclusive list, it just helps with some of the grayer areas, or some of the lesser understood areas of the *NEC*. Sometimes this helps, and sometimes it creates confusion. For example, 358.10(C) discussed wet locations, but nothing in 358.10 said anything about dry and damp locations. Does that mean EMT can only be installed in wet locations? Of course it doesn't. Now there are more permitted uses listed in this section, but because of this it doesn't really give any requirements (just clarifications and information found elsewhere, like product standards and other *Code* sections), this change is somewhat meaningless.

358.10 Uses Permitted

(A) Exposed and Concealed. Electrical metallic tubing is permitted exposed or concealed <u>for the following applications:</u> Figure 358–2

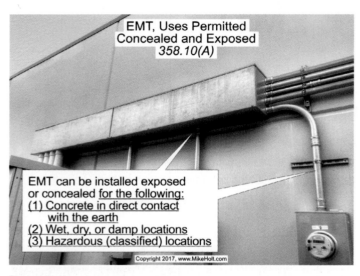

Figure 358–2

(1) <u>Concrete in direct contact with the earth in accordance with 358.10(B).</u>

(2) <u>In wet, dry, or damp locations.</u>

(3) <u>In any hazardous (classified) location as permitted by other articles in this *Code*.</u>

(B) Corrosive Environments.

(1) Galvanized Steel. Electrical metallic tubing, elbows and fittings can be installed in concrete, in direct contact with the earth, or in areas subject to severe corrosive influences if protected by corrosion protection and approved as suitable for the condition [300.6(A)].

■ Galvanized steel EMT installed in concrete on grade or above requires no supplementary corrosion protection. Galvanized steel EMT in contact with soil requires supplementary corrosion protection. Figure 358–3

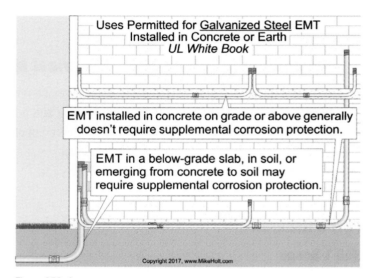

Figure 358–3

(D) Wet Locations. Support fittings, such as screws, straps, and so on, installed in a wet location must be made of corrosion-resistant material.

■ If installed in wet locations, fittings for EMT must be listed for use in wet locations and prevent moisture or water from entering or accumulating within the enclosure in accordance with 314.15 [358.42].

ELECTRICAL NONMETALLIC TUBING (TYPE ENT)

Introduction to Article 362—Electrical Nonmetallic Tubing (Type ENT)

Electrical nonmetallic tubing (ENT) is a pliable, corrugated, circular raceway made of polyvinyl chloride. In some parts of the country, the field name for electrical nonmetallic tubing is "Smurf Pipe" or "Smurf Tube," because it was only available in blue when it originally came out at the time the children's cartoon characters "The Smurfs" were most popular. Today, the raceway is available in many colors such as white, yellow, red, green, and orange, and is sold in both fixed lengths and on reels.

Part I. General

362.1 Scope

Article 362 covers the use, installation, and construction specifications of electrical nonmetallic tubing and associated fittings. Figure 362–1

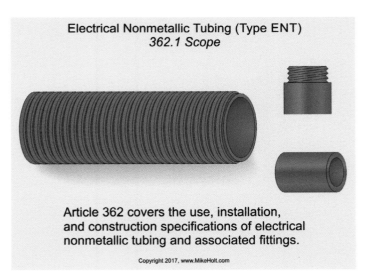

Electrical Nonmetallic Tubing (Type ENT)
362.1 Scope

Article 362 covers the use, installation, and construction specifications of electrical nonmetallic tubing and associated fittings.

Copyright 2017, www.MikeHolt.com

Figure 362–1

362.30 Securing and Supporting

Cable ties for securing and supporting must now be listed.

Analysis

NEW

Many of the products mentioned in the *NEC* don't have to be listed. Often the reason is that there simply isn't a product standard by which they can be tested and then listed. In June of 2014, UL 62275 became effective. Now that we have a product standard for cable ties, we have a *Code* requirement.

362.30 Securing and Supporting

Electrical nonmetallic tubing must be installed as a complete system in accordance with 300.18 [300.10 and 300.12], and it must be securely fastened in place by an approved means and supported in accordance with (A) and (B).

(A) Securely Fastened. Electrical nonmetallic tubing must be secured within 3 ft of every box, cabinet, or termination fitting, such as a conduit body, and at intervals not exceeding 3 ft. Figure 362–2

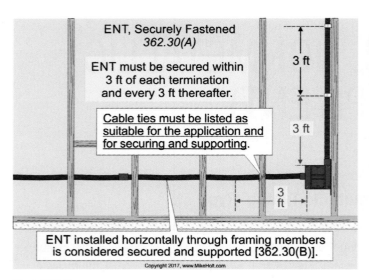

Figure 362–2

Figure 362–3

Where cable ties are to be used to secure and support electrical nonmetallic tubing, they must be listed as suitable for the application and for securing and supporting. Figure 362–3

Ex 2: Lengths not exceeding 6 ft from the last point if the raceway is securely fastened within an accessible ceiling to luminaire(s) or other equipment.

Ex 3: If fished between access points through concealed spaces and supporting is impractical.

(B) Horizontal Runs. Electrical nonmetallic tubing installed horizontally in bored or punched holes in wood or metal framing members, or notches in wooden members, is considered supported, but the raceway must be secured within 3 ft of terminations.

ARTICLE
376 METAL WIREWAYS

Introduction to Article 376—Metal Wireways

Metal wireways are commonly used where access to the conductors within a raceway is required to make terminations, splices, or taps to several devices at a single location. High cost precludes their use for other than short distances, except in some commercial or industrial occupancies where the wiring is frequently revised.

Author's Comment:

- Both metal wireways and nonmetallic wireways are often incorrectly called "troughs," "auxiliary gutters," "auxiliary wireways," or "gutters" in the field.

Part I. General

376.1 Scope

Article 376 covers the use, installation, and construction specifications of metal wireways and associated fittings. Figure 376–1

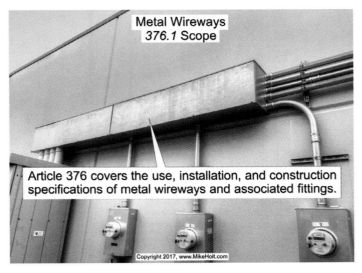

Article 376 covers the use, installation, and construction specifications of metal wireways and associated fittings.

Figure 376–1

376.20 Conductors Connected in Parallel

A new requirement for grouping parallel conductors was added.

Analysis

NEW The concept of grouping the ungrounded and grounded conductors of a circuit together has been in the *NEC* for about 80 years. It's repeated multiple times throughout the *Code*, including three separate occurrences in Article 300 alone! It really is that important.

The requirement for grouping parallel conductors in wireways was added during this cycle. According to Code Making Panel 8, there've been documented conductor failures in metal wireways because parallel conductors weren't grouped together.

376.20 Conductors Connected in Parallel

Where conductors are installed in parallel as permitted in 310.10(H), the parallel conductor sets must be installed in groups consisting of not more than one conductor per phase, or neutral conductor to prevent current imbalance in the paralleled conductors due to inductive reactance. Figure 376–2

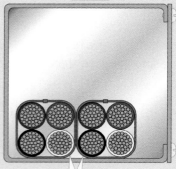

Metal Wireways, Conductors Connected in Parallel
376.20

Parallel conductor sets must be installed in groups of not more than one conductor per phase, neutral, or grounded conductor to prevent current imbalance due to inductive reactance.

Copyright 2017, www.MikeHolt.com

Figure 376–2

376.22 Number of Conductors and Ampacity

The conductor fill rules for wireway sizing now include requirements for cables installed in wireways.

Analysis

CLARIFIED

Although it goes without saying, the number of conductors in a wireway needs to be limited. This concept for cables wasn't addressed before but now it is, and that loophole is closed.

376.22 Number of Conductors and Ampacity

(A) Number of Conductors. The maximum number of conductors or cables permitted in a wireway is limited to 20 percent of the cross-sectional area of the wireway. Figure 376–3

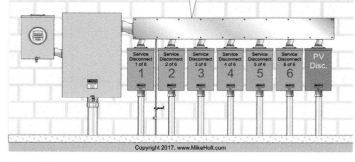

Metal Wireways, Number of Conductors
376.22(A)

The maximum number of conductors or cables permitted in a wireway is limited to 20 percent of the cross-sectional area of the wireway.

Copyright 2017, www.MikeHolt.com

Figure 376–3

Author's Comment:

- Splices and taps must not fill more than 75 percent of the wiring space at any cross section [376.56].

(B) Conductor Ampacity Adjustment Factors. When more than 30 current-carrying conductors are installed in any cross-sectional area of the wireway, the conductor ampacity, as listed in Table 310.15(B)(16), must be adjusted in accordance with Table 310.15(B)(3)(a). Figure 376–4

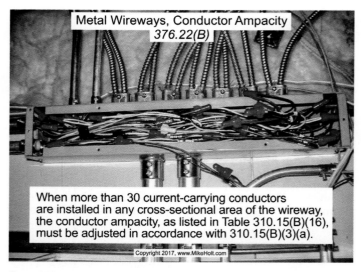

Metal Wireways, Conductor Ampacity
376.22(B)

When more than 30 current-carrying conductors are installed in any cross-sectional area of the wireway, the conductor ampacity, as listed in Table 310.15(B)(16), must be adjusted in accordance with 310.15(B)(3)(a).

Copyright 2017, www.MikeHolt.com

Figure 376–4

Signaling and motor-control conductors between a motor and its starter used only for starting duty aren't considered current carrying for conductor ampacity adjustment.

376.56 Splices, Taps, and Power Distribution Blocks

An allowance has been added for the use of power distribution blocks on the supply side of the service disconnect.

Analysis

NEW When power distribution blocks are installed on the supply side of the service disconnect they must be marked as suitable for the application. Few would disagree that a power distribution block provides a better and safer installation than a split bolt, especially since split bolts are frequently not insulated per the manufacturer's instructions when they're installed. Power distribution blocks are much easier to install properly and should be allowed. Now they are, if they're marked as suitable for the supply side of service disconnect use.

376.56 Splices, Taps, and Power Distribution Blocks

(A) Splices and Taps. Splices and taps in metal wireways must be accessible, and they must not fill the wireway to more than 75 percent of its cross-sectional area. Figure 376–5

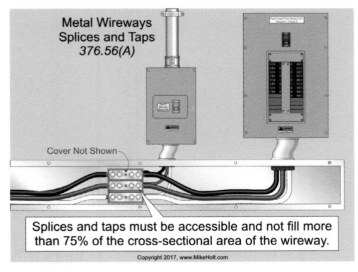

Splices and taps must be accessible and not fill more than 75% of the cross-sectional area of the wireway.

Figure 376–5

Author's Comment:

- The maximum number of conductors permitted in a metal wireway is limited to 20 percent of its cross-sectional area at any point [376.22(A)].

(B) Power Distribution Blocks.

(1) Installation. Power distribution blocks installed in wireways must be listed; if installed on the supply side of the service disconnect, they must be marked "suitable for use on the line side of service equipment" or equivalent. Figure 376–6

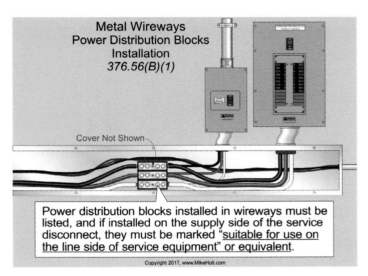

Metal Wireways
Power Distribution Blocks
Installation
376.56(B)(1)

Cover Not Shown

Power distribution blocks installed in wireways must be listed, and if installed on the supply side of the service disconnect, they must be marked "suitable for use on the line side of service equipment" or equivalent.

Figure 376–6

(2) Size of Enclosure. In addition to the wiring space requirements [376.56(A)], the power distribution block must be installed in a metal wireway not smaller than specified in the installation instructions of the power distribution block.

(3) Wire-Bending Space. Wire-bending space at the terminals of power distribution blocks must comply with 312.6(B).

(4) Live Parts. Power distribution blocks must not have uninsulated exposed live parts in the metal wireway after installation, whether or not the wireway cover is installed. Figure 376–7

(5) Conductors. Conductors must be installed so that the terminals of the power distribution block aren't obstructed. Figure 376–8

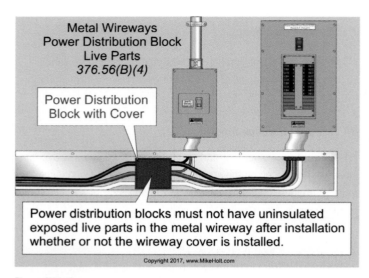

Figure 376–7

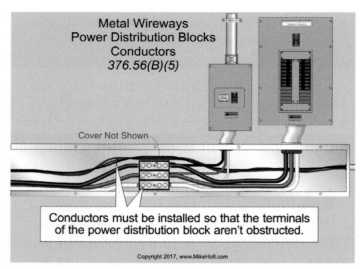

Figure 376–8

Introduction to Article 392—Cable Trays

A cable tray system is a unit or an assembly of units or sections with associated fittings that forms a structural system used to securely fasten or support cables and raceways. A cable tray isn't a raceway.

Cable tray systems include ladder, ventilated trough, ventilated channel, solid bottom, and other similar structures. Cable trays are manufactured in many forms, from a simple hanger or wire mesh to a substantial, rigid, steel support system. Cable trays are designed and manufactured to support specific wiring methods, as identified in 392.10(A).

Part I. General

392.1 Scope

Article 392 covers cable tray systems, including ladder, ventilated trough, ventilated channel, solid bottom, and other similar structures. Figure 392–1

Cable Trays
392.1 Scope

Article 392 covers cable tray systems, including ladder, ventilated, trough, ventilated channel, solid bottom and other similar structures.

Copyright 2017, www.MikeHolt.com

Figure 392–1

392.22 Number of Conductors or Cables

The cable tray conductor fill sizing calculations have been clarified.

Analysis

CLARIFIED Cable trays often contain more than just individual conductors or cables for lighting and power. They can also contain limited-energy cables, such as twisted pair, coaxial, Class 2 or Class 3 cables, as well as optical fiber cables. When individual conductors are installed with limited-energy circuits, a barrier must be installed between the power and limited-energy circuits, as required by 725.136, 800.136, and 820.136.

Sizing the cable tray for conductor and cable fill must be based on the area of the compartment separated by the barrier, not on the entire area of the tray.

392.22 Number of Conductors or Cables

(A) Number of Multiconductor Cables in Cable Trays. The number of multiconductor cables, rated 2,000V or less, permitted in a single cable tray must not exceed the requirements of this section. The conductor sizes herein apply to both aluminum and copper conductors. Where dividers are used, fill calculations apply to each divided section of the cable tray.

(1) Any Mixture of Cables. If ladder or ventilated trough cable trays contain multiconductor power or lighting cables, the maximum number of cables must conform to the following:

(a) If all of the cables are 4/0 AWG and larger, the sum of the diameters of all cables must not exceed the cable tray width, and the cables must be installed in a single layer.

4

EQUIPMENT FOR GENERAL USE

Introduction to Chapter 4—Equipment for General Use

With the first three chapters behind you, the final chapter in the *NEC* necessary for building a solid foundation in general work is Chapter 4. This chapter helps you apply the first three to installations involving general equipment. These first four chapters follow a natural sequential progression. Each of the next four chapters—5, 6, 7, and 8—build upon the first four, but in no particular order. You need to understand all of the first four chapters to properly apply any of the next ones.

As in the preceding chapters, Chapter 4 is also arranged logically. Here are the groupings:

- Flexible cords and flexible cables, and fixture wires.
- Switches and receptacles.
- Switchboards, switchgear, and panelboards.
- Lamps and luminaires.
- Appliances and space heaters.
- Motors, refrigeration equipment, generators, and transformers.
- Batteries, capacitors, and other components.

This logical arrangement of the *NEC* is something to keep in mind when you're searching for a particular item. You know, for example, that transformers are general equipment. So you'll find the *Code* requirements for them in Chapter 4. You know they're wound devices, so you'll find transformer requirements located somewhere near motor requirements.

- **Article 400—Flexible Cords and Flexible Cables.** Article 400 covers the general requirements, applications, and construction specifications for flexible cords and flexible cables.

- **Article 402—Fixture Wires.** This article covers the general requirements and construction specifications for fixture wires.

- **Article 404—Switches.** The requirements of Article 404 apply to switches of all types. These include snap (toggle) switches, dimmer switches, fan switches, knife switches, circuit breakers used as switches, and automatic switches such as time clocks, timers, and switches and circuit breakers used for disconnecting means.

- **Article 406—Receptacles, Cord Connectors, and Attachment Plugs (Caps).** This article covers the rating, type, and installation of receptacles, cord connectors, and attachment plugs (cord caps). It also covers flanged surface inlets.

- **Article 408—Switchboards, Switchgear, and Panelboards.** Article 408 covers specific requirements for switchboards, panelboards, switchgear, and distribution boards that supply lighting and power circuits.

Author's Comment:

- See Article 100 for the definitions of "Panelboard," "Switchboard," and "Switchgear."

- **Article 410—Luminaires, Lampholders, and Lamps.** This article contains the requirements for luminaires, lampholders, and lamps. Because of the many types and applications of luminaires, manufacturer's instructions are very important and helpful for proper installation. Underwriters Laboratories produces a pamphlet called the *Luminaire Marking Guide*, which provides information for properly installing common types of incandescent, fluorescent, and high-intensity discharge (HID) luminaires.

- **Article 411—Low-Voltage Lighting.** Article 411 covers lighting systems, and their associated components, that operate at no more than 30V alternating current, or 60V direct current.

- **Article 422—Appliances.** This article covers electric appliances used in any occupancy.

- **Article 424—Fixed Electric Space-Heating Equipment.** Article 424 covers fixed electric equipment used for space heating. For the purpose of this article, heating equipment includes heating cable, unit heaters, boilers, central systems, and other fixed electric space-heating equipment. Article 424 doesn't apply to process heating and room air-conditioning.

- **Article 430—Motors, Motor Circuits, and Controllers.** This article contains the specific requirements for conductor sizing, overcurrent protection, control circuit conductors, motor controllers, and disconnecting means. The installation requirements for motor control centers are covered in Article 430, Part VIII.

- **Article 440—Air-Conditioning and Refrigeration Equipment.** Article 440 applies to electrically driven air-conditioning and refrigeration equipment with a motorized hermetic refrigerant compressor. The requirements in this article are in addition to, or amend, the requirements in Article 430 and others.

- **Article 445—Generators.** Article 445 contains the electrical installation requirements for generators and other requirements, such as where they can be installed, nameplate markings, conductor ampacity, and disconnecting means.

- **Article 450—Transformers.** This article covers the installation of transformers.

- **Article 480—Batteries.** Article 480 covers stationary installations of storage batteries.

FLEXIBLE CORDS AND FLEXIBLE CABLES

Introduction to Article 400—Flexible Cords and Flexible Cables

This article covers the general requirements, applications, and construction specifications for flexible cords. The *NEC* doesn't consider flexible cords to be wiring methods like those defined in Chapter 3.

Always use a flexible cord (and fittings) identified for the application. Table 400.4 will help you in that regard. For example, use cords listed for a wet location if you're using them outdoors. The jacket material of any flexible cord is tested to maintain its insulation properties and other characteristics in the environments for which it's been listed. Tables 400.5(A)(1) and 400.5(A)(2) are also important tables to turn to when looking for the ampacity of flexible cords.

Article 400—Flexible Cords and Flexible Cables

The title of this article was changed to more clearly address its application.

Analysis

CLARIFIED

While this article has always applied to flexible cords and flexible cables, the title of the article was "Flexible Cords and Cables." This was a point of confusion for many *Code* users over the years. The term "cables" includes the wiring methods discussed in Articles 320 through 340, and limited-energy cables like twisted pair and coaxial cable. However, none of these cables are regulated by article 400, because they aren't the flexible cables addressed in Table 400.4, and they aren't the ones addressed by UL 62. This change will (hopefully) clear up the issue.

400.1 Scope

A new Informational Note was added to try to clear up the scope of Article 400.

Analysis

CLARIFIED

Flexible cords and flexible cables are manufactured in accordance with UL 62, *Flexible Cords and Cables*. It seems logical that this article wouldn't apply to anything that isn't covered by UL 62. The question in the field was "did Article 400 cover extension cords or power supply cords?" The new Informational Note makes it clear that it covers them both.

What does this change mean to the *Code* user? Does it mean that the cord on my band saw needs to comply with Article 400? No, because the *NEC* covers electrical installations [90.2(A)], not the use of electrical products. When I vacuum my bedroom, I often have the power-supply cord plugged into the receptacle in the hallway. That means the cord is going through a doorway, which would violate

• • •

400.12(3), right? Wrong. Me vacuuming my floor isn't an electrical installation of a product, it's the use of a product.

What about the power-supply cord on a projector that's attached to a ceiling? That's an installation of electrical equipment and I need to follow the related *Code* rules. That cord on the projector is a power-supply cord, and because they're now within the scope of Article 400, there might be prohibitions on their installations, such as placing them in a ceiling.

Extension cords are also subject to the requirements contained in Article 400, but the same principal applies. Do I apply the *NEC* when it comes to running an extension cord in my garage to plug in my leaf blower? Of course not. Can I wire a projector or stage lighting in the ceiling of a church building or restaurant using extension cords? No, I'm afraid not.

400.1 Scope

Article 400 covers the general requirements, applications, and construction specifications for flexible cords as contained in Table 400.4. Figure 400–1

Article 400 covers the general requirements, applications, and construction specifications for flexible cords and flexible cables as contained in Table 400.4.

Figure 400–1

Note: Extension cords and power supply cords are restricted in use by the requirements contained in Article 400.

400.12 Uses Not Permitted

Changes attempt to clarify the restriction on cord use above a suspended ceiling; but unfortunately the attempt failed.

Analysis

CLARIFIED Cords above a suspended ceiling have been the bane of inspectors and electricians alike ever since the invention of the projector. Nearly every office building and every school has a projector (or dozens of them) installed above a suspended ceiling.

In previous editions of the *Code*, it wasn't clear that the power-supply cord for a projector had to follow the restrictions on its use above and through a suspended ceiling. The 2017 *NEC* allows a power supply above a suspended ceiling if installed in a metal enclosure. Before you get too excited, this is for a very specific type of equipment enclosure, not a metal raceway.

The problem with the 2017 changes to this section is that now it doesn't apply to "flexible cords," it only applies to extension cords and power-supply cords.

The renumbering of this section, from 400.8 and 400.10 uses permitted and uses not permitted, is also worth noting as they've now been changed to 400.10 and 400.12 to mirror Chapter 3's uses permitted and uses not permitted sections.

400.12 Uses Not Permitted

Unless specifically permitted in 400.10, flexible cords sets (extension cords) and power-supply cords aren't permitted for the following:

(1) Flexible cords sets (extension cords) and power-supply cords aren't permitted to be a substitute for the fixed wiring of a structure. Figure 400–2

(2) Flexible cords sets (extension cords) and power-supply cords aren't permitted to be run through holes in walls, structural ceilings, suspended or dropped ceilings, or floors. Figure 400–3

Figure 400–2

Figure 400–4

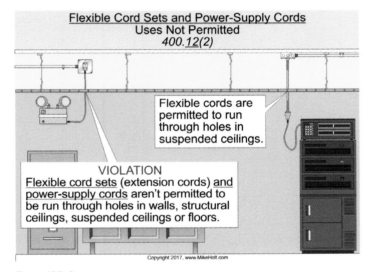

Figure 400–3

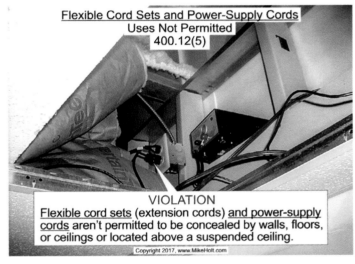

Figure 400–5

(3) Flexible cords sets (extension cords) and power-supply cords aren't permitted to be run through doorways, windows, or similar openings. Figure 400–4

(4) Flexible cords sets (extension cords) and power-supply cords aren't permitted to be attached to building surfaces.

(5) Flexible cords sets (extension cords) and power-supply cords aren't permitted to be concealed by walls, floors, or ceilings, or located above suspended or dropped ceilings. Figure 400–5

Ex: Flexible cords can be located above suspended or dropped ceilings if installed in a metal enclosure in accordance with 300.22(C)(3).

(6) Flexible cords sets (extension cords) and power-supply cords aren't permitted to be installed in raceways, except as permitted by 400.17 for industrial establishments where the conditions of maintenance and supervision ensure that only qualified persons will service the installation.

(7) Flexible cords sets (extension cords) and power-supply cords aren't permitted to be where subject to physical damage.

Author's Comment:

- Even cords listed as "extra-hard usage" must not be used where subject to physical damage.

ARTICLE
404 SWITCHES

Introduction to Article 404—Switches

The requirements of Article 404 apply to switches of all types, including snap (toggle) switches, dimmer switches, fan switches, knife switches, circuit breakers used as switches, and automatic switches, such as time clocks and timers.

404.1 Scope

The requirements of Article 404 apply to all types of switches, switching devices, and circuit breakers used as switches. Figure 404–1

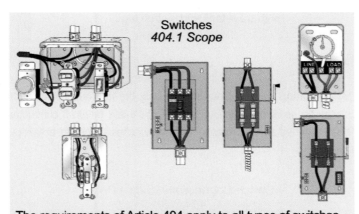

Switches
404.1 Scope

The requirements of Article 404 apply to all types of switches, such as snap (toggle) switches, knife switches, circuit breakers used as switches, and automatic switches such as time clocks.

Copyright 2017, www.MikeHolt.com

Figure 404–1

404.2 Switch Connections

An attempt was made to clarify when a neutral is required at a switch.

Analysis

CLARIFIED Ever since this rule was added in the 2011 *NEC*, it's been hotly debated. Before getting upset at the *Code* language, challenge yourself to write a rule that addresses this issue, and that's clear, concise, and not subject to interpretation. It isn't easy at all.

The concept is that we need a neutral at switch locations for line-to-neutral lighting loads, such as 120V or 277V lighting. This ensures we have a neutral if we install an electronic switch that requires one for proper operation. Everyone will agree that switches are becoming more complex as technology evolves. Yesterday's light switch turned the lights on and off, but today's switch dims the lights, checks for movement, and sometimes does things like turn on computers, raise and lower projector screens, and all sorts of other things.

Smart electronic switches need a return path to the source for proper operation. In the past, the *NEC* permitted the equipment grounding conductor to be used for the return path.

• • •

> Changes to this edition of the *Code* clarify that if line-to-neutral lighting is controlled by multiple switch locations (like a set of three-way switches) the neutral is only required at one switch location. In 2014 it wasn't required at all!
>
> The 2014 *NEC* included a major error by requiring the neutral at switches to be located in "habitable space," which meant that no commercial buildings needed to comply with this rule. To address this issue, the *Code* now says that we need a neutral in areas "suitable for habitation or occupancy." Problem solved.

404.2 Switch Connections

(A) Three-Way and Four-Way Switches. Wiring for 3-way and 4-way switching must be done so that only the ungrounded conductors are switched. Figure 404–2

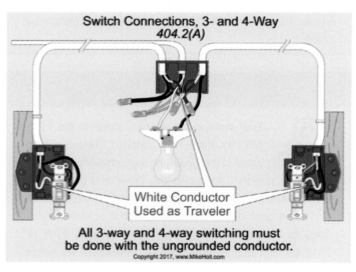

Figure 404–2

Author's Comment:

- In other words, the neutral conductor must not be switched. The white insulated conductor within a cable assembly can be used for single-pole, 3-way, or 4-way switch loops if it's permanently reidentified to indicate its use as an ungrounded conductor at each location where the conductor is visible and accessible [200.7(C)(2)].

If a metal raceway or metal-clad cable contains the ungrounded conductors for switches, the wiring must be arranged to avoid heating the surrounding metal by induction. This is accomplished by installing all circuit conductors in the same raceway in accordance with 300.3(B) and 300.20(A), or ensuring that they're all within the same cable.

Ex: A neutral conductor isn't required in the same raceway or cable with travelers and switch leg (switch loop) conductors. Figure 404–3

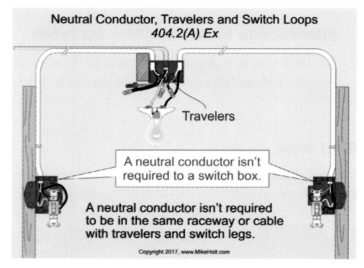

Figure 404–3

(B) Switching Neutral Conductors. Only the ungrounded conductor can be used for switching, and the grounded [neutral] conductor isn't permitted to be disconnected by switches or circuit breakers. Figure 404–4

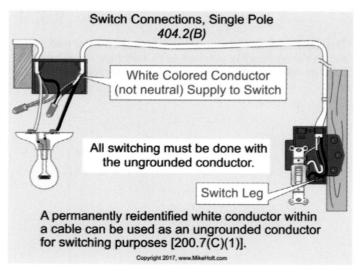

Figure 404–4

Ex: A switch or circuit breaker can disconnect a grounded circuit conductor where it disconnects all circuit conductors simultaneously.

(C) Switches Controlling Lighting Loads. Switches controlling line-to-neutral lighting loads must have a neutral conductor <u>installed</u> at a switch serving <u>bathrooms, hallways, stairways, or rooms suitable for human habitation or occupancy as defined in the applicable building code.</u> Figure 404–5

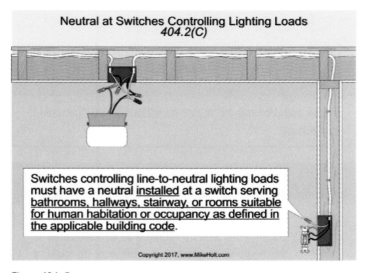

Figure 404–5

<u>Where 3-way and 4-way switches are visible in a room, only one of the switches requires a neutral conductor.</u> Figure 404–6

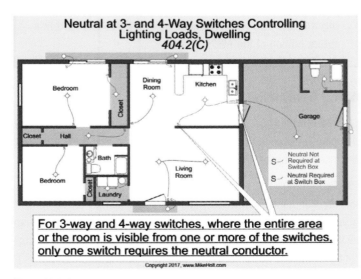

Figure 404–6

A neutral conductor isn't required under any of the following conditions:

(1) Where conductors enter the box through a raceway with sufficient cross-sectional area to accommodate a neutral conductor. Figure 404–7

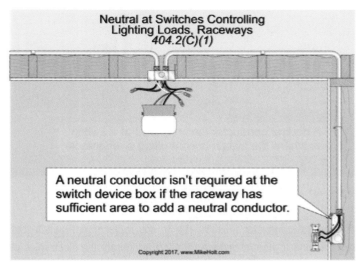

Figure 404–7

(2) Where the switch box can be accessed to add or replace a cable without damaging the building finish. Figure 404–8

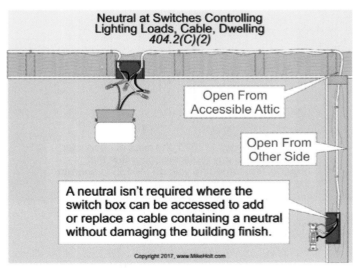

Figure 404–8

(3) Snap switches with integral enclosures [300.15(E)].

(4) Where the lighting is controlled by automatic means.

(5) Switches controlling receptacles. Figure 404–9

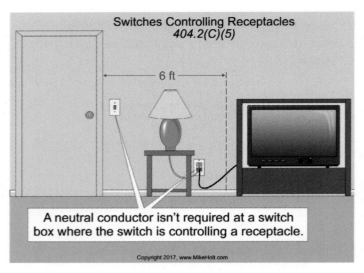

Figure 404–9

The neutral conductor must be run to any replacement switch that requires line-to-neutral voltage [404.22] to operate the electronics of the switch in the standby mode. Figure 404–10

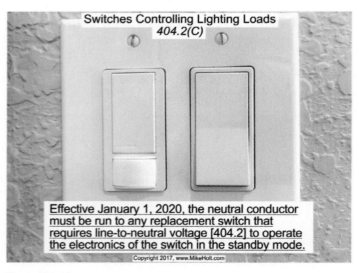

Figure 404–10

Ex: A neutral conductor isn't required for replacement switches installed in locations wired prior to the adoption of 404.2(C) where the neutral conductor can't be extended without removing finish materials. The number of electronic lighting control switches without a neutral conductor on a branch circuit must not exceed five switches, and the number connected to any feeder must not exceed twenty-five switches.

Note: The purpose of the neutral conductor at a switch is to complete a circuit path for electronic lighting control devices that require a neutral conductor.

404.9 Switch Faceplates

A new requirement for metal faceplates to be "grounded" was added.

Analysis

NEW Isn't this already in the *Code*? Yes, and no! Switch plates were already required to be connected to the equipment grounding conductor to clear a fault, but now it appears they want us to connect them to the earth as well. Using the term "grounded" here adds confusion to what we're really trying to accomplish. It appears the intent of this change was to make metal switch plates safer in the case of contact with an energized conductor. Connecting metal parts to the earth won't do that, but bonding it to the EGC will. I suspect we'll see this changed in a future edition of the *NEC*.

404.9 Switch Faceplates

(A) Mounting. Faceplates for switches must be installed so they completely cover the outlet box opening and, where flush mounted, the faceplate must seat against the wall surface.

(B) Grounding. The metal mounting yokes for switches, dimmers, and similar control switches must be connected to an equipment grounding conductor. Metal faceplates must be grounded. Snap switches are considered to be part of an effective ground-fault current path if either of the following conditions is met:

(1) Metal Boxes. The switch is mounted with metal screws to a metal box or a metal cover that's connected to an equipment grounding conductor in accordance with 250.148. Figure 404–11

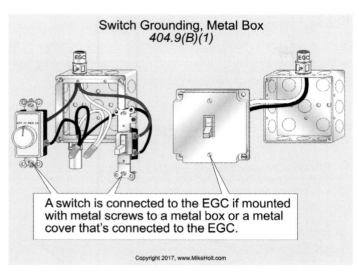

Figure 404–11

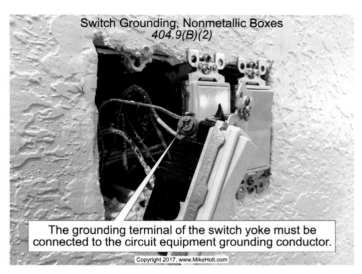

The grounding terminal of the switch yoke must be connected to the circuit equipment grounding conductor.

Figure 404–13

Author's Comment:

■ Direct metal-to-metal contact between the device yoke of a switch and the box isn't required. Figure 404–12

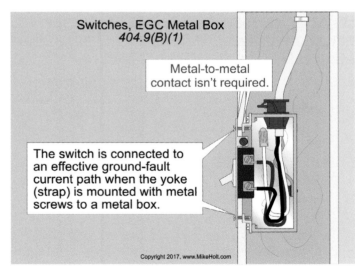

Figure 404–12

(2) Nonmetallic Boxes. The grounding terminal of the switch yoke must be connected to the circuit equipment grounding conductor. Figure 404–13

Ex 1: The metal mounting yoke of a replacement switch isn't required to be connected to an equipment grounding conductor if the wiring at the existing switch doesn't contain an equipment grounding conductor and the switch faceplate is nonmetallic with nonmetallic screws, or the replacement switch is GFCI protected.

Ex 2: Listed assemblies aren't required to be connected to an equipment grounding conductor if all of the following conditions are met:

(1) The device is provided with a nonmetallic faceplate that can't be installed on any other type of device,

(2) The device doesn't have mounting means to accept other configurations of faceplates,

(3) The device is equipped with a nonmetallic yoke, and

(4) Parts of the device that are accessible after installation of the faceplate are manufactured of nonmetallic material.

Ex 3: A snap switch with an integral nonmetallic enclosure complying with 300.15(E).

404.22 Electronic Lighting Switches

A new rule requires electronic switch manufacturers to use a neutral for return current, not the equipment grounding conductor.

Analysis

NEW As discussed in 404.2(C), using the equipment grounding conductor as a return path is a practice that we've been trying to eliminate for over half a century. This new requirement carries an effective date of January 1, 2020. Electricians shouldn't really be caught off guard by this rule, as 404.2(C) requires a neutral at most switch locations for this very reason.

404.22 Electronic Lighting Switches

Effective January 1, 2020, electronic lighting control switches must be listed to not introduce current on the equipment grounding conductor during normal operation. Figure 404–14

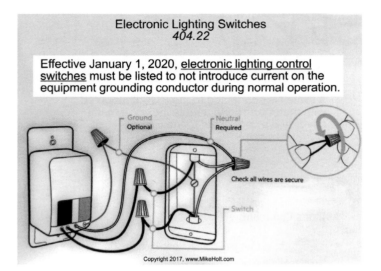

Electronic Lighting Switches
404.22

Effective January 1, 2020, electronic lighting control switches must be listed to not introduce current on the equipment grounding conductor during normal operation.

Ground Optional

Neutral Required

Check all wires are secure

Switch

Copyright 2017, www.MikeHolt.com

Figure 404–14

Ex: Electronic lighting control switches that put current on the equipment grounding conductor [404.2(C) Ex] must be listed and marked for use only for replacement or retrofit applications.

RECEPTACLES, CORD CONNECTORS, AND ATTACHMENT PLUGS (CAPS)

Introduction to Article 406—Receptacles, Cord Connectors, and Attachment Plugs (Caps)

This article covers the rating, type, and installation of receptacles, flexible cord connectors, and attachment plugs (cord caps). It also addresses their grounding requirements. Some key points to remember include:

- Following the grounding requirements of the specific type of device you're using.
- Providing GFCI protection where specified by 406.4(D)(3).
- Mounting receptacles according to the requirements of 406.5.

406.1 Scope

Article 406 covers the rating, type, and installation of receptacles, flexible cord connectors, and attachment plugs (cord caps). Figure 406–1

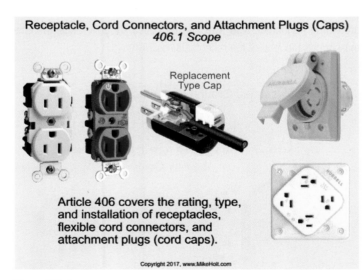

Receptacle, Cord Connectors, and Attachment Plugs (Caps)
406.1 Scope

Replacement Type Cap

Article 406 covers the rating, type, and installation of receptacles, flexible cord connectors, and attachment plugs (cord caps).

Copyright 2017, www.MikeHolt.com

Figure 406–1

406.2 Definitions

A new definition for "outlet box hoods" was added.

Analysis

NEW Section 406.9(B) requires most receptacles installed in a wet location to have an outlet box hood that's listed and identified for "extra duty." That's fine, but what's an outlet box hood? Most people call it an "in-use cover," or a "bubble cover."

406.2 Definitions

Child Care Facility. A building or portions thereof used for educational, supervision, or personal care services for five or more children seven years in age or less.

Outlet Box Hood. A housing shield (hood) over a faceplate for flush-mounted wiring devices, or an integral component of an outlet box or of a faceplate for flush-mounted wiring devices, commonly known as a "bubble cover." Figure 406–2

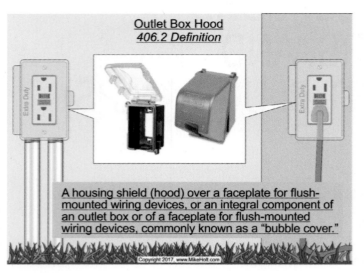

Outlet Box Hood
406.2 Definition

A housing shield (hood) over a faceplate for flush-mounted wiring devices, or an integral component of an outlet box or of a faceplate for flush-mounted wiring devices, commonly known as a "bubble cover."

Figure 406–2

406.3 Receptacle Rating and Type

The rules on automatically controlled receptacles have been revised, and new text regarding receptacles with USB outlets was added.

Analysis

EDITED

Automatically Controlled Receptacles. The 2014 *NEC* added a requirement for marking receptacles that are automatically controlled. Few things can be more upsetting than working on your computer in an office and having it shut down automatically before you have a chance to save your work. In order to prevent this, the *Code* required that the receptacle or its cover plate be marked with the power symbol to identify it as automatically controlled.

The problem is, who knows what that the power symbol is supposed to mean? New to the 2017 *Code*, the receptacle, not its cover plate, must have the word "controlled" on it along with the power symbol. This will (hopefully) do more to tell the user that the receptacle is automatically controlled. Instead of plugging their computer into it perhaps they'll plug a desk lamp in there instead, since controlling lighting is the intent of this whole concept.

NEW

USB Receptacles. Receptacles with USB chargers are being installed at an incredibly increasing rate as we've come to depend more and more on USBs for powering or charging many mechanisms (like lighting) as well as portable devices.

It's not uncommon in new construction to see them installed in the kitchen and in the master bedroom at a minimum. Doing so in every bedroom is becoming more popular. With demand comes new creative products, some of which are a bit too creative. These receptacles must now be listed, which helps to ensure the safety of the product.

406.3 Receptacle Rating and Type

(C) Receptacles for Aluminum Conductors. Receptacles rated 20A or less for use with aluminum conductors must be marked CO/ALR.

Author's Comment:

■ According to UL listing requirements, aluminum conductors must not terminate in screwless (push-in) terminals of a receptacle (UL White Book, *Guide Information for Electrical Equipment,* www.ul.com/regulators/2008_WhiteBook.pdf).

(D) Isolated Ground Receptacles. Receptacles of the isolated grounding conductor type must be identified by an orange triangle marking on the face of the receptacle. Figure 406–3

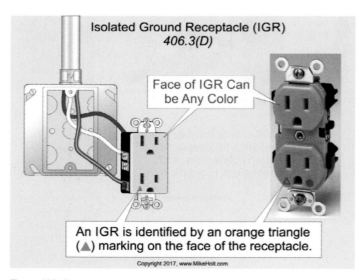

Isolated Ground Receptacle (IGR)
406.3(D)

Face of IGR Can be Any Color

An IGR is identified by an orange triangle (▲) marking on the face of the receptacle.

Figure 406–3

(1) Isolated ground receptacles must have the grounding contact connected to an insulated equipment grounding conductor installed with the circuit conductors, in accordance with 250.146(D). Figure 406–4

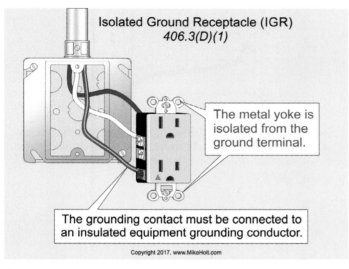

Isolated Ground Receptacle (IGR)
406.3(D)(1)

The metal yoke is isolated from the ground terminal.

The grounding contact must be connected to an insulated equipment grounding conductor.

Copyright 2017, www.MikeHolt.com

Figure 406–4

(E) Controlled Receptacle Marking. Nonlocking, 15A or 20A, 125V receptacles that are automatically controlled to remove power for energy management or building automation must be permanently marked with the word "controlled" and have a visible power symbol on the receptacle after installation. Figure 406–5

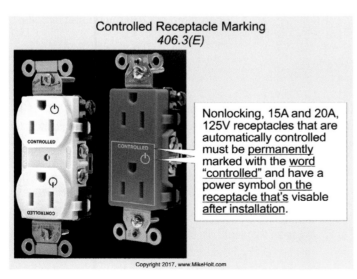

Controlled Receptacle Marking
406.3(E)

Nonlocking, 15A and 20A, 125V receptacles that are automatically controlled must be permanently marked with the word "controlled" and have a power symbol on the receptacle that's visable after installation.

Copyright 2017, www.MikeHolt.com

Figure 406–5

Ex: The marking isn't required for wall switch-controlled receptacles used for lighting in a dwelling [210.70(A)(1) Ex 2].

(F) Receptacle with USB Charger. A 125V, 15A or 20A receptacle that provides Class 2 power must be listed and constructed such that the Class 2 circuitry is integral with the receptacle. Figure 406–6

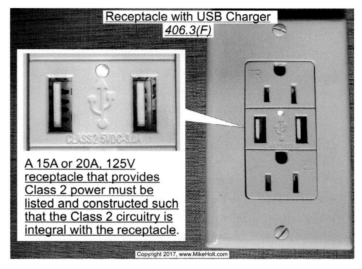

Receptacle with USB Charger
406.3(F)

A 15A or 20A, 125V receptacle that provides Class 2 power must be listed and constructed such that the Class 2 circuitry is integral with the receptacle.

Copyright 2017, www.MikeHolt.com

Figure 406–6

406.4 General Installation Requirements

Two Informational Notes about replacing nongrounding type receptacles have been added, and a new exception addresses the required AFCI protection of replacement receptacles.

Analysis

NEW **Nongrounding Receptacles (GFCI Required).** When replacing nongrounding (two-wire) receptacles we have a few options. We can replace the receptacle with another nongrounding-type receptacle, install an equipment grounding conductor to a grounding-type receptacle, or install a grounding-type receptacle that's GFCI protected. Because of the difficulty in adding an equipment grounding conductor in most existing buildings, the option of providing GFCI protection is far and away the most common practice.

• • •

The instructions for equipment that must be plugged into a receptacle might require an equipment grounding conductor. If the product is listed, then 110.3(B) requires us to follow those listing instructions. In addition, 250.114 contains a list of equipment required to be connected to an equipment grounding conductor if supplied by a receptacle. These include washing machines, refrigerators, kitchen waste disposals, and others. Under these conditions, you can't replace a nongrounding-type receptacle with another nongrounding-type receptacle; the receptacle must be of the grounding type that's either connected to an equipment grounding conductor or GFCI protected.

Nongrounding Receptacles (AFCI Required). When replacing nongrounding (two-wire) receptacles with a grounding type we have to be aware that in addition to required GCFI protection, AFCI protection may also be required by 210.12. In most cases replacing the circuit breaker with an AFCI device will satisfy this requirement and still allow you to replace the 2-wire receptacle with a GFCI-type receptacle. If the panel is older and an AFCI breaker isn't an option, a dual rated AFCI/GFCI receptacle is permitted. An exception was added exempting dormitory receptacles from this requirement.

406.4 General Installation Requirements

(A) Grounding Type. Receptacles installed on 15A and 20A branch circuits must be of the grounding type, unless used for replacements as permitted in (D)(2). Figure 406–7

Receptacles must be installed on circuits for which they're rated, except as permitted in Table 210.21(B)(2) and Table 210.21(B)(3). Figure 406–8

Table 210.21(B)(3) Receptacle Ratings

Circuit Rating	Receptacle Rating
15A	15A
20A	15A or 20A
30A	30A
40A	40A or 50A
50A	50A

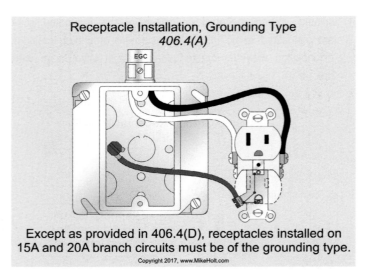

Receptacle Installation, Grounding Type
406.4(A)

Except as provided in 406.4(D), receptacles installed on 15A and 20A branch circuits must be of the grounding type.

Figure 406–7

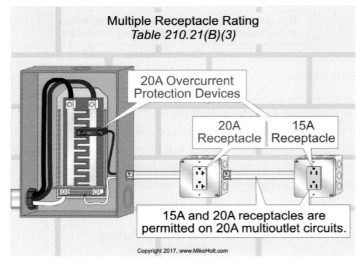

Multiple Receptacle Rating
Table 210.21(B)(3)

20A Overcurrent Protection Devices

20A Receptacle   15A Receptacle

15A and 20A receptacles are permitted on 20A multioutlet circuits.

Figure 406–8

(C) Methods of Equipment Grounding. The grounding contacts for receptacles must be connected to an equipment grounding conductor supplied with the branch-circuit wiring. Figure 406–9

Author's Comment:

■ See 250.146 for the specific requirements on connecting the grounding terminals of receptacles to the circuit equipment grounding conductor.

(D) Receptacle Replacement. Arc-fault circuit-interrupter type and ground-fault circuit interrupter type receptacles must be installed at a readily accessible location.

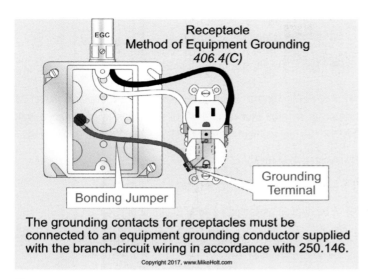

Figure 406–9

(1) Grounding-Type Receptacles. If an equipment grounding conductor exists, grounding-type receptacles must replace nongrounding-type receptacles and the receptacle's grounding terminal must be connected to the circuit equipment grounding conductor in accordance with 250.130(C) or 406.4(C).

(2) Nongrounding-Type Receptacles. If an equipment grounding conductor doesn't exist in the outlet box, the existing nongrounding-type receptacles can be replaced with:

(a) A nongrounding-type receptacle.

(b) A GFCI-type receptacle with the receptacle or cover plate marked "No Equipment Ground." Figure 406–10

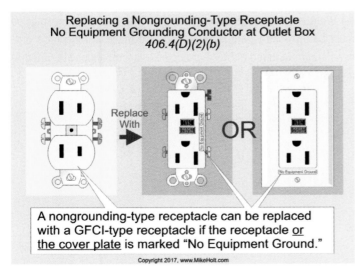

Figure 406–10

(c) A GFCI-protected grounding-type receptacle with the receptacle or cover plate marked "GFCI Protected" and "No Equipment Ground" and be visible after installation. Figure 406–11

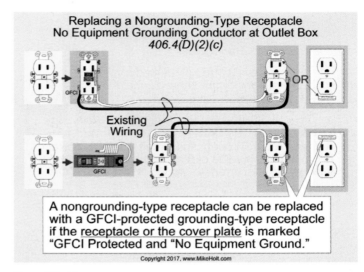

Figure 406–11

Note 1: Where equipment instructions require an equipment grounding conductor, a nongrounding type receptacle isn't permitted

Note 2: Where an equipment grounding conductor is required by 250.114, a nongrounding type receptacle isn't permitted.

Author's Comment:

■ GFCI protection functions properly on a 2-wire circuit without an equipment grounding conductor because the circuit equipment grounding conductor serves no role in the operation of the GFCI-protection device. See the definition of "Ground-Fault Circuit Interrupter" for more information. Figure 406–12

⚡ **CAUTION:** *The permission to replace nongrounding-type receptacles with GFCI-protected grounding-type receptacles doesn't apply to new receptacle outlets that extend from an existing outlet box that's not connected to an equipment grounding conductor. Once you add a receptacle outlet (branch-circuit extension), the receptacle must be of the grounding type and it must have its grounding terminal connected to an equipment grounding conductor of a type recognized in 250.118, in accordance with 250.130(C).* Figure 406–13

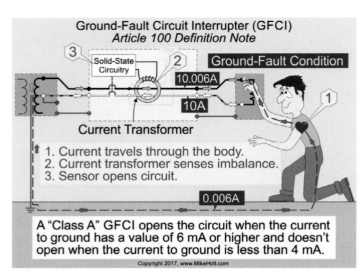

Figure 406–12

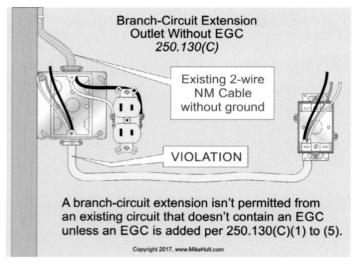

Figure 406–13

(3) GFCI protection Required. When existing receptacles are replaced in locations where GFCI protection is currently required, the replacement receptacles must be GFCI protected.

Ex: Where receptacle replacement is impracticable, such as where the outlet box size won't permit the installation of the GFCI receptacle, a GFCI-protected grounding-type receptacle marked "GFCI Protected" and "No Equipment Ground" is permitted.

Author's Comment:

■ See 210.8 for specific GFCI-protection requirements.

(4) Arc-Fault Circuit Interrupters. Where a receptacle outlet is located in an area that requires AFCI protection in accordance with 210.12, the replacement receptacle(s) must be one of the following:

(1) A listed AFCI receptacle.

(2) A receptacle protected by a listed AFCI receptacle.

(3) A receptacle protected by an AFCI circuit breaker.

Ex 1: AFCI protection for receptacles isn't required where all of the following conditions apply:

(1) The replacement receptacle is of the GFCI type in accordance with 406.4(D)(2)(b).

(2) It's impracticable to provide an equipment grounding conductor as provided by 250.130(C).

(3) A listed combination type AFCI circuit breaker isn't commercially available for the panelboard.

(4) A listed dual function GFCI/AFCI receptacle isn't commercially available.

(5) Tamper-Resistant Receptacles. Listed tamper-resistant receptacles must be provided where replacements are made at receptacle outlets that are required to be tamper resistant in accordance with 406.12 for dwelling units, guest rooms and guest suites, and child care facilities, except where a nongrounding-type receptacle is being replaced by another nongrounding-type receptacle.

(6) Weather-Resistant Receptacles. Weather-resistant receptacles must be provided where replacements are made at receptacle outlets that are required to be so protected in accordance with 406.9(A) and (B).

406.5 Receptacle Mounting

The rules governing the installation of receptacles in countertops and work surfaces have been clarified.

Analysis

CLARIFIED

In the 2014 *Code*, rules were added about receptacles in countertops and work surfaces, stating that if the receptacle is oriented in the face-up position, it had to be listed for use in a countertop. This meant that if the receptacle was facing any direction other than up it didn't have to be listed for the application. Revisions to this section in 2017 require a receptacle assembly to be listed for countertop use regardless of the orientation, and if it's installed in a work surface that isn't a countertop, it can be listed for use in a countertop or listed for use in a work surface. If the receptacle assembly is installed face-up, it must be listed for countertop assembly use.

406.5 Receptacle Mounting

Receptacles must be installed in identified outlet boxes that are securely fastened in place in accordance with 314.23.

Author's Comment:

▪ Boxes containing a hub can be supported from a flexible cord connected to fittings that prevent tension from being transmitted to joints or terminals [400.14 and 314.23(H)(1)]. Figure 406–14

Screws for attaching receptacles to a box must be machine screws matching the thread gauge or size of the holes in the box, or must be part of a listed assembly. Figure 406–15

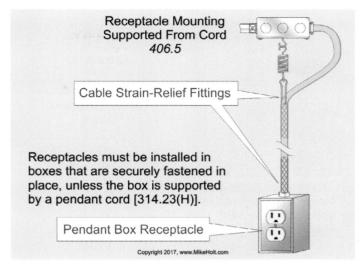

Receptacle Mounting Supported From Cord
406.5

Cable Strain-Relief Fittings

Receptacles must be installed in boxes that are securely fastened in place, unless the box is supported by a pendant cord [314.23(H)].

Pendant Box Receptacle

Copyright 2017, www.MikeHolt.com

Figure 406–14

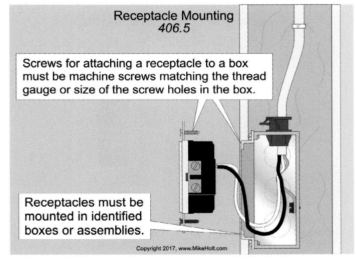

Receptacle Mounting
406.5

Screws for attaching a receptacle to a box must be machine screws matching the thread gauge or size of the screw holes in the box.

Receptacles must be mounted in identified boxes or assemblies.

Copyright 2017, www.MikeHolt.com

Figure 406–15

Author's Comment:

▪ The position of the ground terminal of a receptacle isn't specified in the *NEC*. The ground terminal can be up, down, or to the side. Proposals to specify the mounting position of the ground terminal have been rejected through many *Code* cycles. Figure 406–16

(A) Boxes Set Back. Receptacles in outlet boxes that are set back from the finished surface, as permitted by 314.20, must be installed so the mounting yoke of the receptacle is held rigidly to the finished surface or outlet box. Figure 406–17

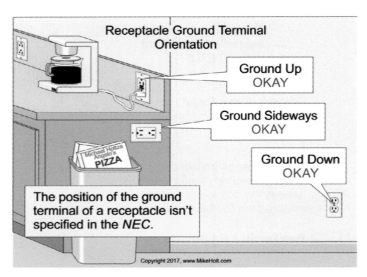

Figure 406–16

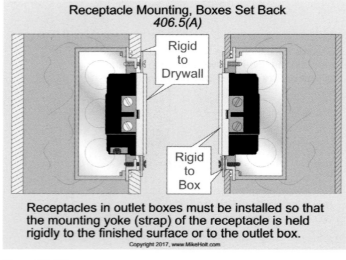

Figure 406–17

Author's Comment:

■ In walls or ceilings of noncombustible material, such as drywall, outlet boxes aren't permitted to be set back more than ¼ in. from the finished surface. In walls or ceilings of combustible material, outlet boxes must be flush with the finished surface [314.20]. There must not be any gaps more than ⅛ in. at the edge of the outlet box [314.21].

(B) Boxes Flush with the Surface. Receptacles mounted in outlet boxes that are flush with the finished surface must be installed so the mounting yoke of the receptacle is held rigidly against the outlet box or raised box cover.

(C) Receptacles Mounted on Covers. Receptacles supported by a cover must be held rigidly to the cover with at least two screws. Figure 406–18

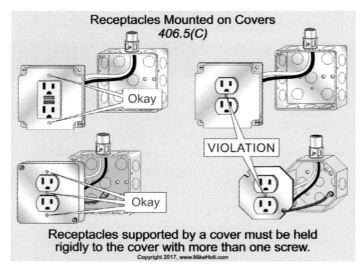

Figure 406–18

(D) Position of Receptacle Faces. Receptacles must be flush with, or project from, the faceplates.

(E) Receptacles in Countertop. Receptacle assemblies installed in countertop surfaces must be listed for countertop applications. Figure 406–19

Figure 406–19

Countertop receptacle assemblies that provide GFCI protection must be listed as GFCI receptacle assemblies for countertop surface application.

(F) Receptacles in Work Surfaces. Receptacle assemblies and GFCI assemblies listed for work surfaces or countertops can be installed in a work surface.

(G) Receptacle Orientation. Receptacles aren't permitted to be installed in a face-up position in countertop surfaces or work surfaces unless listed for countertop or work surface applications. Figure 406–20

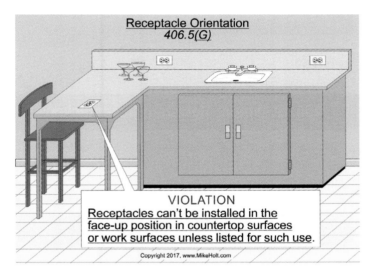

Figure 406–20

(H) Receptacles in Seating Areas and Similar Surfaces. Receptacles aren't permitted to be installed in a face-up position in seating areas or similar surfaces, unless the receptacle is:

(1) Part of a listed furniture power distribution unit,

(2) Part of a listed furnishing,

(3) Listed for use in countertops, or Figure 406–21

(4) Installed in a listed floor box.

(J) Voltage Between Devices. Receptacles aren't permitted to be in enclosures with other switches or receptacles if the voltage between the devices exceeds 300V, unless the devices are installed in enclosures equipped with barriers identified for the purpose, that are securely installed between adjacent devices. Figure 406–22

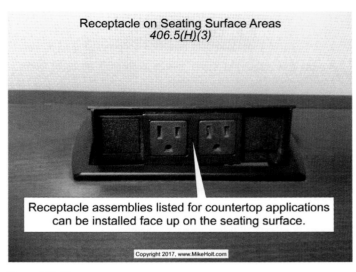

Figure 406–21

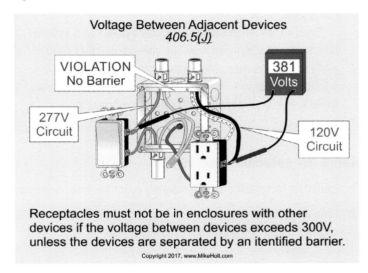

Figure 406–22

406.6 Receptacle Faceplates

A new rule requiring cover plates with USB ports or with night lights to be listed was added.

Analysis

NEW Faceplates by themselves don't need to be listed, but they must meet the construction requirements of this section. The thickness of the plate is regulated to ensure that full insertion of the attachment can be achieved, and the plate must completely cover the box and be seated against the wall surface. For a typical cover plate, that's about all the *NEC* is concerned with, which seems reasonable.

Even an object as simple as a cover plate can't escape new technology. You can now buy cover plates that contain night lights, and even more popular, face plates containing a USB charging port. These devices are now required to be listed to ensure the electrical safety of the product.

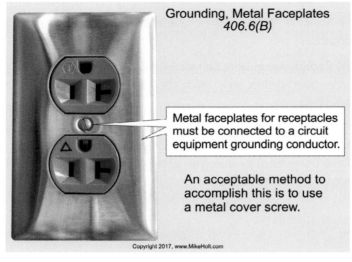

Grounding, Metal Faceplates
406.6(B)

Metal faceplates for receptacles must be connected to a circuit equipment grounding conductor.

An acceptable method to accomplish this is to use a metal cover screw.

Copyright 2017, www.MikeHolt.com

Figure 406–23

406.6 Receptacle Faceplates

Faceplates for receptacles must completely cover the outlet openings.

(B) Grounding. Metal faceplates for receptacles must be connected to the circuit equipment grounding conductor.

> **Author's Comment:**
>
> - The *NEC* doesn't specify how this is accomplished, but 517.13(B) Ex 1 for health care facilities permits the metal mounting screw(s) securing the faceplate to a metal outlet box or wiring device to be suitable for this purpose. Figure 406–23

(D) Receptacle Cover Plate with Integral Night Light and/or USB Charger. Cover plates that provide night light and/or Class 2 output connector(s) must be listed and constructed so that the night light and/or Class 2 circuitry is integral with the cover plate.

406.12 Tamper-Resistant Receptacles

The locations requiring tamper-resistant receptacles have been expanded, as have the types of receptacles requiring such protection.

Analysis

EXPANDED Next time you find yourself at a grocery store, hardware store, or just about any store short of a gas station, notice how many plastic receptacle inserts there are. Consumers want more protection than what a standard receptacle provides.

Tamper-resistant receptacles were introduced in the 2008 *Code* for dwelling units and this requirement was expanded in 2011 to include child care facilities, hotels, and motels. Not much changed in the 2014 *NEC*, but the 2017 edition is very different.

The logic is that if 125V receptacles are dangerous to children, then 250V receptacles are as well. The 2017 *Code* adds a requirement that 15A and 20A, 250V receptacles must be tamper resistant as well, although it seems likely that many of these receptacles will be the exception by being installed in a location where the receptacle is covered by an appliance or other piece of equipment. It's worth emphasizing that this rule is only for 15A and 20A receptacles, so those for ranges or dryers need not be tamper resistant.

Several locations where tamper-resistant receptacles will now be required have been added to the list of areas requiring protection. Preschools and elementary schools are now included. While it may seem that these areas already required tamper-resistant receptacles, since they meet the definition of "child care facilities," not all areas of a school needed to comply. The definition of a child care facility is a building or portion of a building where five or more children under the age of eight receive care, education, and so forth. This meant that some of the classrooms in a kindergarten through sixth-grade school met the definition but others didn't. The sixth-grade classroom doesn't need tamper-resistant protection, but the first-grade classroom does. The offices of the school staff don't need tamper-resistant protection, but lunch areas do.

One of the problems that needed to be addressed was that classrooms often change in terms of grade level. Yesterday this room housed fifth graders, today it houses second graders. To alleviate this problem, the entire school must now meet the requirements.

In addition, business offices, corridors, waiting rooms, and similar areas in medical and dental offices, and out-patient facilities now require tamper-resistant protection. They're also required in dormitories, waiting areas in areas described in article 518 (places of assembly), gymnasiums, skating rinks, and auditoriums.

Tamper-resistance expansion was added due to a report issued by the Consumer Product Safety Commission (CPSC) indicating that the most common areas for shocks due to inserting objects in receptacles is the home (already covered) followed by "unknown" and schools, then sports and recreation facilities and "other public property."

Do you get the feeling that in the near future all 15A and 20A receptacles will be tamper resistant? So do I...

406.12 Tamper-Resistant Receptacles

Nonlocking-type 15A and 20A, 125V and 250V receptacles in the following areas must be listed as tamper resistant:

Author's Comment:

■ On a tamper-resistant receptacle, inserting an object into one side of the receptacle doesn't open the internal tamper-resistant shutter. Simultaneous pressure from a two or three pronged plug is required for insertion. Figure 406–24

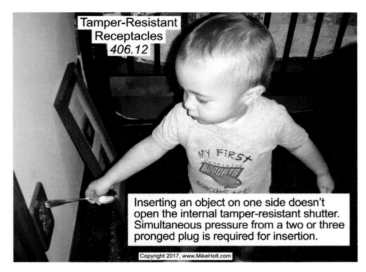

Figure 406–24

(1) Dwelling unit areas specified in 210.52 and 550.13 Figure 406–25

Figure 406–25

(2) Hotel and motel guest rooms and guest suites

(3) Child care facilities

Author's Comment:

- A child care facility is a building or portions thereof used for educational, supervision, or personal care services for five or more children seven years in age or less [406.2].

(4) Preschools and elementary education facilities

(5) Business offices, corridors, waiting rooms and the like in clinics, medical and dental offices, and outpatient facilities.

(6) Places of waiting transportation, gymnasiums, skating rinks, and auditoriums

(7) Dormitories

Note: Receptacle types covered by this requirement are identified as 5-15, 5-20, 6-15, and 6-20 in NEMA WD 6, *Wiring Devices—Dimensional Specifications*.

Ex to (1) through (7): Receptacles in the following locations aren't required to be tamper resistant:

(1) Receptacles located more than 5½ ft above the floor. Figure 406–26

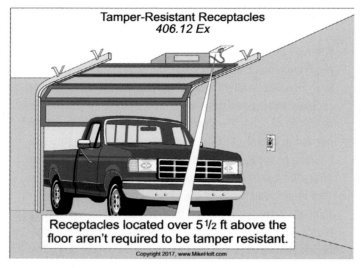

Figure 406–26

(2) Receptacles that are part of a luminaire or appliance.

(3) A receptacle located within dedicated space for an appliance that in normal use isn't easily moved from one place to another.

(4) Nongrounding receptacles used for replacements as permitted in 406.4(D)(2)(a).

SWITCHBOARDS, SWITCHGEAR, AND PANELBOARDS

Introduction to Article 408—Switchboards, Switchgear, and Panelboards

Article 408 covers the specific requirements for switchboards, switchgear, and panelboards that control power and lighting circuits. There's a tendency among some people in the industry to use the terms switchboard and switchgear interchangeably. Switchgear is manufactured and tested to more exacting standards and is configured differently than switchboards. For example, in switchgear there are physical barriers between breakers, and between the breakers and the bus. Switchgear is more durable and fault resistant, and is commonly selected for larger applications where low-voltage power circuit breakers and selective coordination are applied, such as computer data centers, manufacturing, and process facilities [Source NCCER].

As you study this article, remember some of these key points:

— One objective of Article 408 is that the installation prevents contact between current-carrying conductors and people or equipment.
— The circuit directory of a panelboard must clearly identify the purpose or use of each circuit that originates in the panelboard.
— You must understand the detailed grounding and overcurrent protection requirements for panelboards.

408.1 Scope

Article 408 covers the specific requirements for switchboards, switchgear, and panelboards that control power and lighting circuits. Figure 408–1

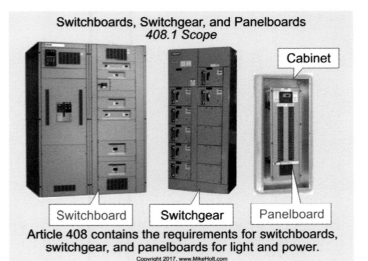

Switchboards, Switchgear, and Panelboards
408.1 Scope

Cabinet

Switchboard | Switchgear | Panelboard

Article 408 contains the requirements for switchboards, switchgear, and panelboards for light and power.

Copyright 2017, www.MikeHolt.com

Figure 408–1

408.4 Field Identification

The requirement for marking other than dwelling unit panels was expanded.

Analysis

EXPANDED

Every day there's an electrician who needs to de-energize and work on a panelboard. When it's necessary, figuring out how and where to shut the power off can become a job all on its own, especially in large commercial and industrial facilities.

The 2011 *NEC* added a requirement to mark the source of power for panelboards in other than dwelling units to let the electrician know how to shut the power off to a panel.

New to this edition of the *Code*, the manner in which the panelboard is marked is now addressed by specifying that

• • •

the label can't be handwritten. It also needs to withstand the environment involved, and it needs to be permanent. This correlates with the warning label requirements in 110.21(B).

408.4 Field Identification

(A) Circuit Directory or Circuit Identification. Circuits, and circuit modifications, must be legibly identified as to their clear, evident, and specific purpose. Spare positions that contain unused overcurrent protection devices must also be identified. Identification must include an approved amount of detail to allow each circuit to be distinguished from all others, and the identification must be on a circuit directory located on the face or inside of the door of the panelboard. See 110.22. Figure 408–2

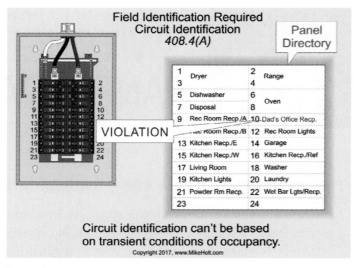

Figure 408–3

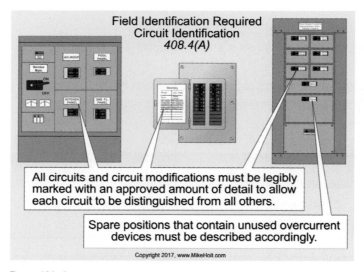

Figure 408–2

Circuit identification must not be based on transient conditions of occupancy, such as "Dad's Office Recp." Figure 408–3

(B) Source of Supply. Switchboards, switchgear, and panelboards supplied by a feeder, in other than one- or two-family dwellings, must be marked with a permanent, not handwritten label that withstands the environment indicating where the power supply originates. Figure 408–4

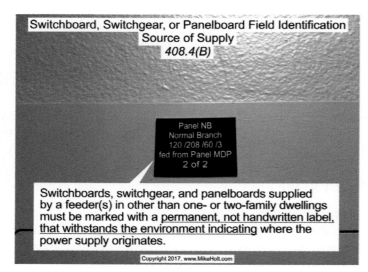

Figure 408–4

LUMINAIRES, LAMPHOLDERS, AND LAMPS

Introduction to Article 410—Luminaires, Lampholders, and Lamps

This article covers luminaires, lampholders, lamps, decorative lighting products, and lighting accessories for temporary seasonal and holiday use, including portable flexible lighting products, and the wiring and equipment of such products and lighting installations. Even though Article 410 is highly detailed, it's broken down into 16 parts. The first five are sequential, and apply to all luminaires, lampholders, and lamps:

- Part I. General
- Part II. Location
- Part III. Boxes and Covers
- Part IV. Supports
- Part V. Equipment Grounding Conductors

The first five parts contain mostly mechanical information, and aren't hard to follow or absorb. Part VI, Wiring, ends the sequence. The seventh, ninth, and tenth parts provide requirements for manufacturers to follow—use only equipment that conforms to these requirements. Part VIII provides requirements for installing lampholders. The rest of Article 410 addresses specific types of lighting.

Author's Comment:

- Article 411 addresses "Low-Voltage Lighting" which are lighting systems and their associated components that operate at no more than 30V alternating current, or 60V direct current.

Part I. General

410.1 Scope

This article covers luminaires, lampholders, lamps, decorative lighting products, lighting accessories for temporary seasonal and holiday use, portable flexible lighting products, and the wiring and equipment of such products and lighting installations. Figure 410–1

Author's Comment:

- Because of the many types and applications of luminaires, manufacturers' instructions are very important and helpful for proper installation. UL produces a pamphlet called the *Luminaire Marking Guide*, which provides information for properly installing common types of incandescent, fluorescent, and high-intensity discharge (HID) luminaires.

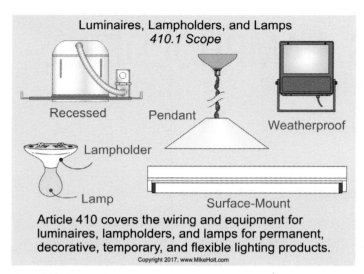

Luminaires, Lampholders, and Lamps
410.1 Scope

Recessed

Pendant

Weatherproof

Lampholder

Lamp

Surface-Mount

Article 410 covers the wiring and equipment for luminaires, lampholders, and lamps for permanent, decorative, temporary, and flexible lighting products.

Copyright 2017, www.MikeHolt.com

Figure 410–1

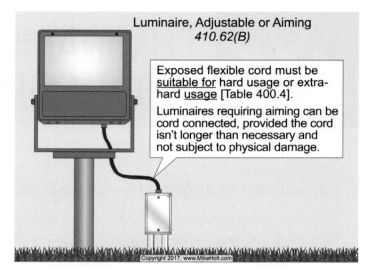

Luminaire, Adjustable or Aiming
410.62(B)

Exposed flexible cord must be suitable for hard usage or extra-hard usage [Table 400.4].

Luminaires requiring aiming can be cord connected, provided the cord isn't longer than necessary and not subject to physical damage.

Copyright 2017, www.MikeHolt.com

Figure 410–2

410.62 Cord-Connected Luminaires

The requirements for using a cord to install luminaires were clarified.

Analysis

CLARIFIED

It's a very common practice to install luminaires using a cord. Some aspects of the installation, such as how and where the cord is installed, weren't addressed in detail. This section now makes it clear what the requirements are if you use a cord to install luminaires.

410.62 Cord-Connected Luminaires

(B) Adjustable Luminaires. Luminaires that require adjusting or aiming after installation can be flexible cord connected, provided the exposed flexible cord is suitable for hard usage or extra-hard usage in accordance with Table 400.4. The flexible cord isn't permitted to be longer than necessary for luminaire adjustment, and it isn't permitted to be subject to strain or physical damage [400.14]. Figure 410–2

(C) Electric-Discharge and LED Luminaires. Cord-connected electric-discharge and LED luminaires must comply with (1), (2), and (3) as applicable.

(1) Cord-Connected Installation. A luminaire can be flexible cord connected if the luminaire is mounted directly below the outlet box, the flexible cord isn't subject to strain or physical damage, and the flexible cord is visible for its entire length except at terminations. Figure 410–3

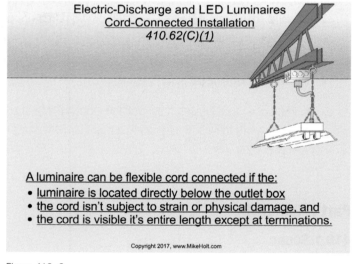

Electric-Discharge and LED Luminaires
Cord-Connected Installation
410.62(C)(1)

A luminaire can be flexible cord connected if the:
• luminaire is located directly below the outlet box
• the cord isn't subject to strain or physical damage, and
• the cord is visible it's entire length except at terminations.

Copyright 2017, www.MikeHolt.com

Figure 410–3

Author's Comment:

■ The *Code* doesn't require twist-lock receptacles for this application.

ARTICLE
411

LOW-VOLTAGE LIGHTING

Introduction to Article 411—Low-Voltage Lighting

Article 411 provides the requirements for lighting systems and their associated components operating at no more than 30V alternating current, or 60V direct current. They're often found in such applications as landscaping, kitchen over-the-counter lighting, commercial display lighting, and museums. Don't let the half-page size of Article 411 give you the impression that low-voltage lighting isn't something you need to be concerned about. These systems are limited in their voltage, but the current rating can be as high as 25A, which means they're still a potential source of fire. Installation of these systems is widespread and becoming more so.

Many of these systems now use LEDs, and 30V halogen lamps are also fairly common. Low-voltage lighting systems have an ungrounded secondary circuit supplied by an isolating transformer. These systems have restrictions that effect where they can be located, and have a maximum supply breaker of 25A.

411.1 Scope

The title of this article, as well as its scope, have been changed to more accurately describe the allowable voltages of these systems.

Analysis

CLARIFIED The title of the article and the scope of the article were revised to more accurately discuss the voltages that are applicable. A supply voltage of 30V ac or 60V dc has long been the practice for safety in a dry location, and 15V ac or 30V dc the standard safety practice in wet locations. Now with the 2017 change, it's an *NEC* requirement.

411.1 Scope

Article 411 covers the installation of low-voltage lighting systems that operate at a maximum of 30V ac or 60V dc in dry locations and a maximum of 15V ac or 30V dc in wet locations, as well as lighting equipment connected to a Class 2 power source. Figure 411–1

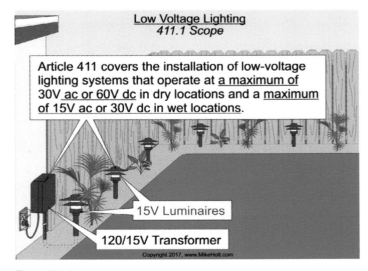

Low Voltage Lighting
411.1 Scope

Article 411 covers the installation of low-voltage lighting systems that operate at a maximum of 30V ac or 60V dc in dry locations and a maximum of 15V ac or 30V dc in wet locations.

15V Luminaires

120/15V Transformer

Copyright 2017, www.MikeHolt.com

Figure 411–1

ARTICLE
422 APPLIANCES

Introduction to Article 422—Appliances

Article 422 covers electric appliances used in any occupancy. The meat of this article is contained in Parts II and III. Parts IV and V are primarily for manufacturers, but you should examine appliances for compliance before installing them. If the appliance has a label from a recognized labeling authority (for example UL), it complies [90.7].

Part I. General

422.1 Scope

The scope of Article 422 includes appliances in any occupancy that are fastened in place, permanently connected, or cord-and-plug-connected. Figure 422–1

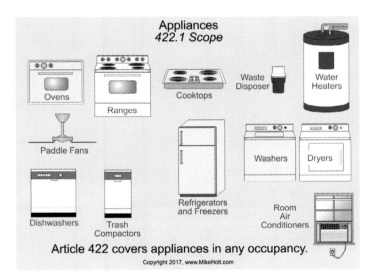

Figure 422–1

422.5 Ground-Fault Circuit-Interrupter (GFCI) Protection for Personnel

The rules for providing GFCI protection for specific appliances found throughout Article 422 have been relocated to this section, the voltage and current ratings for equipment requiring GFCIs have been specified, and the options for protection methods have been expanded.

Analysis

 EDITED GFCI requirements can be found scattered throughout the *Code* book, including Articles 210, 406, 422, 620, 680, and others. While this is necessary (GFCI rules for swimming pools should be in the swimming pool article), it can be frustrating when these rules are scattered throughout an individual article as well. In order to alleviate this, the GFCI rules that were found throughout Article 422 are now all located in this section, which results in the *NEC* being more user-friendly.

 CLARIFIED The voltage and current ratings of these appliances are now contained in this section as well. The equipment requiring GFCI protection in this article didn't have a specific voltage or current rating to specify when GFCI protection was required, so this change

● ● ●

actually doesn't expand any requirements, it reduces them. I've never seen a 480V, 100A vending machine, but if such a machine existed it would have required GFCI protection in 2014.

EDITED The methods used to provide GFCI protection have been expanded to provide flexibility in design. Previous editions of the *Code* required vending machines to have GFCI protection provided by the manufacturer either as part of the cord or part of the attachment plug. Couple that with a rule stating that the GFCI device had to be readily accessible and you've got the potential for a lot of problems, such as providing extra floor space around the machines and mischievous individuals testing and not resetting the GFCI device, which could result in not just warm soft drinks, but spoiled and contaminated food as well. In the 2017 *Code*, we can now provide GFCI protection in the cord, the attachment plug, the receptacle, the breaker, or anywhere upstream of the equipment, provided the device is readily accessible.

422.5 Ground-Fault Circuit-Interrupter (GFCI) Protection for Personnel

(A) General. The following appliances rated not over 250V and 60A, single- or three-phase, must be GFCI protected.

(1) Automotive vacuum machines provided for public use. Figure 422–2

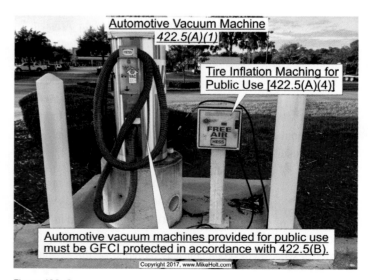

Figure 422–2

(2) Drinking water coolers, not drinking water dispensers. Figure 422–3

Figure 422–3

(3) High-pressure spray washing machines.

(4) Tire inflation machines provided for public use.

(5) Vending machines. Figure 422–4

Figure 422–4

(B) Type. The GFCI must be readily accessible, listed, and located in one or more of the following locations:

(1) A GFCI circuit breaker,

(2) A GFCI device or receptacle,

(3) GFCI integral with the attachment plug,

(4) GFCI within the supply cord not more than 12 in. from the attachment plug, or

(5) Factory installed GFCI within the appliance.

422.6 Listing Required

A new rule requires most appliances to be listed.

Analysis

NEW

Most people will agree that listed products are safe products, or at least safer than their unlisted equivalents. This has been universally agreed upon for well over 100 years. There's never been an article-wide rule to require appliances to be listed until now, but it only applies to appliances operating at 50V or more. This voltage threshold allows most Class 2 products to not be listed, which makes sense as the inherent design of a Class 2 power supply prohibits fatal electric shocks and fires.

422.6 Listing Required

Appliances rated to operate at 50V or more must be listed.

422.16 Flexible Cords

The cord requirements for dishwashers and trash compactors have been revised to reflect product standards.

Analysis

CLARIFIED

Believe it or not, installing a receptacle for a dishwasher in the space behind it is a violation of the product standard (UL 749). Electricians are installing the receptacle in the intended dishwasher location and inspectors are approving it because neither one owns the product standard and neither of them know it's a problem.

The problem comes when dishwasher installers come to install the appliance and refuse to do so because the listing instructions and the installation are in conflict. By requiring the receptacle to be adjacent to the space filled by the dishwasher this issue becomes moot.

Additionally, the maximum allowable cord length for dishwashers was increased from 4 ft to 6 ft 6 in. This is a much easier target to hit, and it doesn't make for any reduction in safety. As long as we're discussing cord length, the overall length of a cord for a range hood increased from 3 ft to 4 ft.

422.16 Flexible Cords

(A) General. Flexible cords are permitted to:

(1) Facilitate frequent interchange, or to prevent the transmission of noise and vibration [400.10(A)(6) and 400.10(A)(7)].

(2) Facilitate the removal of appliances fastened in place, where the fastening means and mechanical connections are specifically designed to permit ready removal [400.12(A)(8)].

Author's Comment:

■ Flexible cords aren't permitted to be used for the connection of water heaters, furnaces, and other appliances fastened in place, unless the appliances are specifically identified to be used with a flexible cord. Figure 422–5

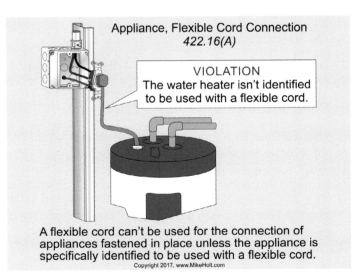

Figure 422–5

(B) Specific Appliances.

(1) In-Sink Waste Disposer. A flexible cord is permitted for an in-sink waste disposer if: Figure 422–6

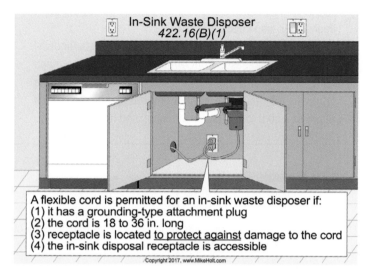

A flexible cord is permitted for an in-sink waste disposer if:
(1) it has a grounding-type attachment plug
(2) the cord is 18 to 36 in. long
(3) receptacle is located to protect against damage to the cord
(4) the in-sink disposal receptacle is accessible

Figure 422–6

(1) The flexible cord has a grounding-type attachment plug.

Ex: A listed in-sink waste disposer marked as protected by a system of double insulation isn't be required to be terminated with a grounding-type attachment plug.

(2) The flexible cord length is at least 18 in. in length and no longer than 3 ft.

(3) The receptacle must be located so as to protect against damage to the flexible cord.

(4) The receptacle is accessible.

(2) Dishwashers and Trash Compactors. A flexible cord is permitted for a dishwasher or trash compactor if:

(1) The flexible cord has a grounding-type attachment plug.

Ex: A listed dishwasher or trash compactor marked as protected by a system of double insulation isn't be required to be terminated with a grounding-type attachment plug.

(2) For a trash compactor, the flexible cord length is at least 3 ft in length and not longer than 4 ft, measured from the rear plane of the appliance. Figure 422–7

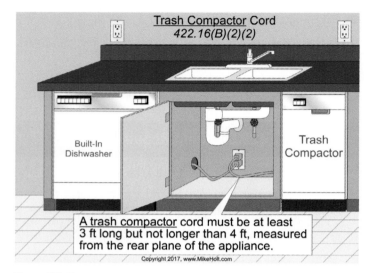

A trash compactor cord must be at least 3 ft long but not longer than 4 ft, measured from the rear plane of the appliance.

Figure 422–7

(3) For a built-in dishwasher, the length of the flexible cord is at least 3 ft and not longer than 6 ft 6 in., measured from the face of the attachment plug to the plane of the rear of the appliance. Figure 422–8

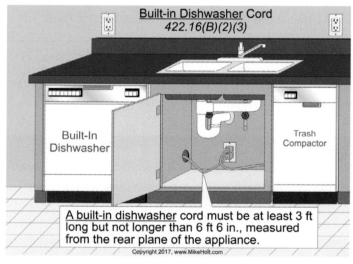

A built-in dishwasher cord must be at least 3 ft long but not longer than 6 ft 6 in., measured from the rear plane of the appliance.

Figure 422–8

(4) For a dishwasher or trash compactor, the receptacle must be located so as to protect against damage to the flexible cord.

(5) The receptacle for the trash compactor must be located in the space occupied by the trash compactor or in the space adjacent to the trash compactor.

(6) The receptacle for a built-in dishwasher must be located in the space adjacent to the space occupied by the dishwasher. Figure 422–9

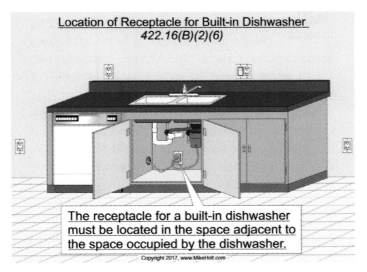

Figure 422–9

(3) Wall-Mounted Ovens and Counter-Mounted Cooking Units. Wall-mounted ovens and counter-mounted cooking units can be cord-and-plug-connected for ease in servicing or installation.

(4) Range Hoods. Range hoods can be cord-and-plug-connected if all of the following conditions are met: Figure 422–10

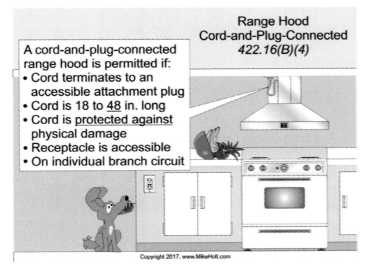

Figure 422–10

(1) The flexible cord for the range hood terminates with a grounding-type attachment plug.

Ex: A listed range hood marked as protected by a system of double insulation isn't be required to be terminated with a grounding-type attachment plug.

(2) The length of the flexible cord for the range hood isn't permitted to be less than 18 in. or longer than 48 in.

(3) The receptacle for the range hood must be located so as to protect against physical damage to the flexible cord.

(4) The range hood receptacle must be accessible.

(5) The range hood receptacle must be supplied by an individual branch circuit.

Author's Comment:

- An above the range microwave that contains a fan listed as a range hood must comply with this section, if it's cord-and-plug-connected.

422.18 Support of Ceiling Paddle Fans

This section was edited to include listed outlet box systems, locking supports, and mounting receptacles meeting 314.27(E) requirements.

Analysis

NEW When new technologies emerge, new *Code* rules soon follow. Sometimes the new technology is so unique that the new rule makes no sense unless you know exactly which product it addresses. This is certainly the case here.

A new product is available that can be mounted to a ceiling outlet box and allows a person to mount a luminaire or a paddle fan in about 10 seconds by pushing it onto the device called a "receptacle" (Article 100 change), then twisting and locking it into place. Language has been added to this rule to address this great new product.

422.18 Support of Ceiling Paddle Fans

Ceiling paddle fans must be supported independently of an outlet box or by one of the following:

(1) A listed outlet box or listed outlet box system must be marked as suitable for ceiling paddle fan support of not more than 70 lb. Outlet boxes for a ceiling paddle fan that weighs more than 35 lb must include the maximum weight to be supported in the required marking in accordance with 314.27(C). Figure 422–11

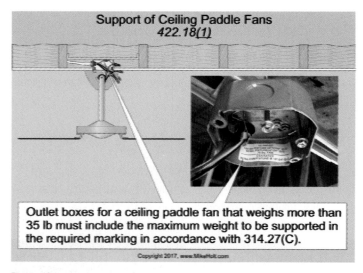

Support of Ceiling Paddle Fans
422.18(1)

Outlet boxes for a ceiling paddle fan that weighs more than 35 lb must include the maximum weight to be supported in the required marking in accordance with 314.27(C).

Copyright 2017, www.MikeHolt.com

Figure 422–11

(2) A listed outlet box system, a listed locking support and mounting receptacle, and a compatible factory installed attachment fitting designed for support, identified for the use and installed in accordance with 314.27(E).

422.21 Covering of Combustible Material at Outlet Boxes

The requirement for covering noncombustible finishes inside the fan canopy has been greatly reduced.

Analysis

REDUCED

In the 2014 *NEC* a new rule required combustible surfaces, such as a wood-covered ceiling inside a ceiling fan canopy to be covered by a noncombustible material. The change correlates with 410.23, which required the same thing for luminaires. It makes sense that the rules should be the same.

Section 422.21 now matches 410.23 by only requiring a combustible surface to be covered if it exceeds 180 sq. in. A round canopy would need to have a diameter of over 15 in. in order to exceed this, so most installations won't need to meet this requirement.

422.21 Covering of Combustible Material at Outlet Boxes

Any combustible ceiling finish that's exposed between the edge of a ceiling-suspended (paddle) fan canopy or fan and an outlet box that has a surface area of 180 sq. in. or more must be covered with noncombustible material. Figure 422–12

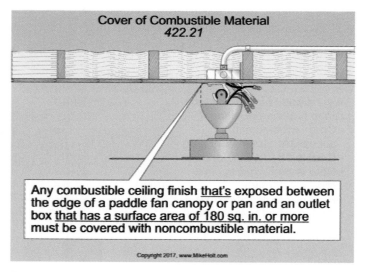

Cover of Combustible Material
422.21

Any combustible ceiling finish that's exposed between the edge of a paddle fan canopy or pan and an outlet box that has a surface area of 180 sq. in. or more must be covered with noncombustible material.

Copyright 2017, www.MikeHolt.com

Figure 422–12

422.31 Permanently Connected Appliance Disconnects

The disconnect rules for appliances are now all the same, regardless of VA or HP rating.

Analysis

CLARIFIED

Consistency in the *NEC* is certainly a good thing. When it comes to the disconnect requirements for appliances, the rules were different based on the ratings of the appliances. This wasn't consistent, but who's to say it was ever intended to be?

Larger equipment can have larger risks, so the rules were different. Now they're all the same, regardless of the VA or HP rating. A disconnecting means must be within sight of the appliance or it must be capable of being locked in the open position. This certainly makes for a consistent requirement, but it also decreases the old requirement substantially and without any technical justification, other than consistency within this *Code* section. I have feeling we haven't heard the end of this debate.

422.31 Permanently Connected Appliance Disconnects

(A) Appliances Rated at Not Over 300 VA or ⅛ Horsepower. For 300 VA or ⅛ horsepower or less appliances, a circuit breaker located within sight from the appliance, or is lockable with provisions for locking to remain in place whether the lock is installed or not in accordance with 110.25, can serve as the disconnect means.

(B) Appliances Rated Over 300 VA. For appliances rated over 300 VA, a switch or circuit breaker located within sight of the appliance, or is lockable with provisions for locking to remain in place whether the lock is installed or not in accordance with 110.25, can serve as the disconnect means. Figure 422–13

Author's Comment:

■ According to Article 100, "within sight" means that it's visible and not more than 50 ft from one to the other.

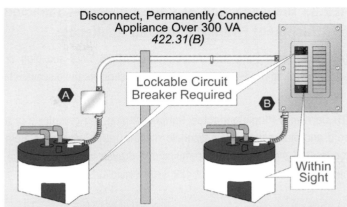

Figure 422–13

(C) Motor-Operated Appliances Rated Over ⅛ Horsepower. For motor-operated appliances rated over ⅛ horsepower, the disconnect must be located within sight from the motor-operated appliance or be lockable with provisions for locking to remain in place whether the lock is installed or not in accordance with 110.25.

Ex: An appliance containing a unit switch that complies with 422.34.

422.33 Disconnection of Cord-and-Plug-Connected or Attachment Fitting-Connected Appliances

The disconnect rules for appliances now include language that allows a cord connector or an attachment fitting to be used for appliance disconnects.

Analysis

EXPANDED

The disconnect rules for appliances now include language that allows an attachment fitting that's used for appliance connection to serve as the means of disconnect.

422.33 Disconnection of Cord-and-Plug-Connected or <u>Attachment Fitting-Connected Appliances</u>

(A) Attachment Plug and Attachment Fitting. Cord-and-plug or <u>attachment fitting-connected appliances</u> can serve as the disconnecting means.

(B) Cord-and-Plug-Connected Ranges. A plug and receptacle of a cord-and-plug-connected household electric range accessible from the front of the range by the removal of a drawer <u>meets</u> the disconnecting means requirements of 422.33(A). Figure 422–14

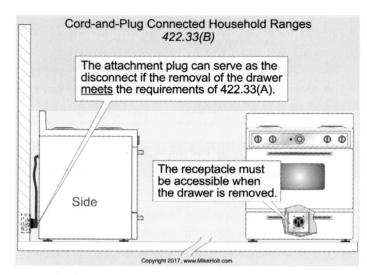

Figure 422–14

FIXED ELECTRIC SPACE-HEATING EQUIPMENT

Introduction to Article 424—Fixed Electric Space-Heating Equipment

Many people are surprised to see how many pages Article 424 has. This is a nine-part article on fixed electric space heaters. Why so much text for what seems to be a simple application? The answer is that Article 424 covers a variety of applications—heaters come in various configurations for various uses. Not all of these parts are for the electrician in the field—the requirements in Part IV are for manufacturers.

Fixed space heaters (wall-mounted, ceiling-mounted, or free-standing) are common in many utility buildings and other small structures, as well as in some larger structures. When used to heat floors, space-heating cables address the thermal layering problem typical of forced-air systems—so it's likely you'll encounter them. Duct heaters are very common in large office and educational buildings. These provide a distributed heating scheme. Locating the heater in the ductwork, but close to the occupied space, eliminates the waste of transporting heated air through sheet metal routed in unheated spaces, so it's likely you'll encounter those as well.

Part I. General

424.1 Scope

Article 424 contains the installation requirements for fixed electrical equipment used for space heating, such as heating cables, unit heaters, boilers, or central systems. Figure 424–1

> **Author's Comment:**
>
> - Wiring for fossil-fuel heating equipment, such as gas, oil, or coal central furnaces, must be installed in accordance with Article 422, specifically 422.12.

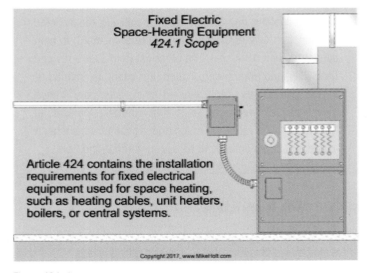

Figure 424–1

424.38 Area Restrictions

The allowable locations for space-heating cables have been extensively revised.

Analysis

CLARIFIED

The *NEC* used to prohibit space-heating cables from leaving the room in which they originated. This makes no sense at all, as there's no additional hazard created by such an installation. A floor heating cable that heats the toilet compartment of a bathroom wasn't permitted to leave that area and supply the rest of the bathroom... Such a rule is hardly justifiable. To stretch it a bit further, what would the danger be in heating both the bathroom and the hallway feeding it? No increased danger at all. New language now allows such installations.

EXPANDED

Section 424.38(B), which covers the prohibited locations of such cables, was greatly expanded as well. Installing such a cable in a closet has long been prohibited, yet 424.38(C) allows it in some applications. It's easy to see somebody wondering if it's allowed in a clothes closet by reading 424.38(B)(1) and then not looking any further thereby missing the specific allowance in 424.38(C). Now item (1) references (C) to help eliminate such confusion. The other list items were revised for clarity, and others were added. For example, instead of saying that cables aren't allowed over walls, now it says they aren't allowed over walls that intersect the ceiling. New items such as a prohibition under cabinetry have been added, but seem unlikely to be encountered in the field.

424.38 Area Restrictions

(A) Extend Beyond the Room or Area. Heating cables <u>are</u> permitted to extend beyond the room or area in which they originate.

(B) Uses Not Permitted. Heating cables aren't permitted to be installed:

(1) In closets.

(2) Over <u>the top of</u> walls.

(3) Over partitions that extend to the ceiling, unless they're isolated single runs of embedded cable.

(4) <u>Under or through walls.</u>

(5) Over cabinets whose clearance from the ceiling is less than the minimum horizontal dimension of the cabinet to the nearest cabinet edge that's open to the room or area.

(6) <u>In tub and shower walls.</u>

(7) <u>Under cabinets or similar built-ins having no clearance to the floor.</u>

424.39 Clearance from Other Objects and Openings

The rules for heating cables near lights have been clarified.

Analysis

CLARIFIED

Although it seems fairly obvious this rule was intended to apply to ceiling heating cables, the *Code* never quite said that. Now it does.

424.39 Clearance from Other Objects and Openings

Heating elements of <u>cables installed in ceilings</u> must be separated at least 8 in. from the edge of outlet boxes and junction boxes used for mounting surface luminaires, and 2 in. from recessed luminaires and their trims.

ARTICLE
430

MOTORS, MOTOR CIRCUITS, AND CONTROLLERS

Introduction to Article 430—Motors, Motor Circuits, and Controllers

Article 430 contains the specific rules for conductor sizing, overcurrent protection, control circuit conductors, controllers, and disconnecting means for electric motors. The installation requirements for motor control centers are covered in Part VIII, and air-conditioning and refrigeration equipment are covered in Article 440.

Article 430 is one of the longest articles in the *NEC*. It's also one of the most complex, but motors are also complex equipment. They're electrical and mechanical devices, but what makes motor applications complex is the fact that they're inductive loads with a high-current demand at start-up that's typically six, or more, times the running current. This makes overcurrent protection for motor applications necessarily different from the overcurrent protection employed for other types of equipment. So don't confuse general overcurrent protection with motor protection—you must calculate and apply them differently using the rules in Article 430.

You might be uncomfortable with the allowances for overcurrent protection found in this article, such as protecting a 10 AWG conductor with a 60A overcurrent protection device, but as you learn to understand how motor overcurrent protection works, you'll understand why these allowances aren't only safe, but necessary.

Part I. General

430.1 Scope

Article 430 covers motors, motor branch-circuit and feeder conductors and their protection, motor overload protection, motor control circuits, motor controllers, and motor control centers. This article is divided into many parts, the most important being: Figure 430–1

- General—Part I
- Conductor Size—Part II
- Overload Protection—Part III
- Branch Circuit Short-Circuit and Ground-Fault Protection—Part IV
- Feeder Short-Circuit and Ground-Fault Protection—Part V
- Motor Control Circuits—Part VI
- Motor Controllers—Part VII
- Motor Control Centers—Part VIII
- Disconnecting Means—Part IX

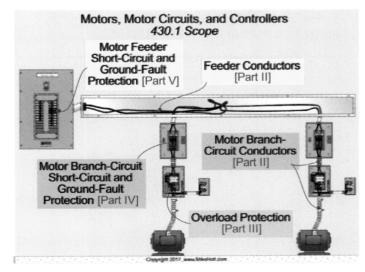

Figure 430–1

Note 1: Article 440 contains the installation requirements for electrically driven air-conditioning and refrigeration equipment [440.1]. Also see 110.26(E) for dedicated space requirements for motor control centers.

430.99 Available Fault Current

A new rule requiring motor control centers to be marked with the available fault current was added.

Analysis

NEW

Circuit breakers and fuses [110.9], and everything else [110.10], in an electrical installation must have an interrupting rating (breakers and fuses) or a short-circuit current rating (everything else).

In an oversimplified explanation, this rating is the amount of current these pieces of equipment can handle before they explode. If we're installing a premises wiring system, we need to know the available fault current to ensure that the equipment we're installing is properly rated.

For example, if the available fault current for a system is 15,000A, we'd better not have a 10,000A rated motor control center. If a fault were to occur, the motor control equipment could literally explode.

New to this edition of the *Code* is that if the motor is supplied by a motor control center (MCC) we should be able to go there and find out what the available fault current is because it now needs to be posted at the MCC.

430.99 Available Fault Current

The available short-circuit current at the motor control center and the date the short-circuit current calculation was performed must be documented and made available to those authorized to inspect the installation.

Introduction to Article 440—Air-Conditioning and Refrigeration Equipment

This article applies to electrically driven air-conditioning and refrigeration equipment. The rules in this article add to, or amend, the rules in Article 430 and other articles.

Each equipment manufacturer has the motor for a given air-conditioning unit built to its own specifications. Cooling and other characteristics are different from those of nonhermetic motors. For each motor, the manufacturer has worked out all of the details and supplied the correct protection, conductor sizing, and other information on the nameplate. So when wiring an air conditioner, trust the information on the nameplate and don't try to over-complicate the situation. The math for sizing the overcurrent protection and conductor minimum ampacity has already been done for you.

Part I. General

440.1 Scope

Article 440 applies to electrically driven air-conditioning and refrigeration equipment. Figure 440–1

Article 440 applies to electrically driven air-conditioning and refrigeration equipment.

Figure 440–1

440.9 Grounding and Bonding

A wire-type equipment grounding conductor is now required for some air-conditioning installations.

Analysis

NEW Electrical metallic tubing is permitted to be used as an equipment grounding conductor [250.118(4)]; research done by the Georgia Institute of Technology proves this wiring method serves this purpose.

The concern is that the installation must have all fittings installed and tightened properly [110.3(B) and 250.4(A)(3)], and the raceway must not be subject to severe physical damage [358.12(1)]. Experience has shown that when EMT is installed on rooftops workers often step on it thinking that it's impervious to damage. It isn't.

If EMT is used as the required circuit equipment grounding conductor, and it comes apart due to being stepped on, we have a recipe for disaster. If the raceway becomes energized due to a ground fault it remains energized. This rule

• • •

also applies to any other metal raceway types that are installed using non-threaded fittings. Such a disaster has happened before, resulting in death, and it will (unfortunately) probably happen again. With this new rule in effect, it's hoped that we can reduce this hazard for future generations.

440.9 Grounding and Bonding

 Scan this QR code for a video of Mike explaining this topic; it's a sample from the DVDs that accompany this textbook.

Where metal raceway is run exposed on a roof for air-conditioning and refrigeration equipment, an equipment grounding conductor of the wire type must be installed within the outdoor portions of metal raceways using non-threaded fittings. Figure 440–2

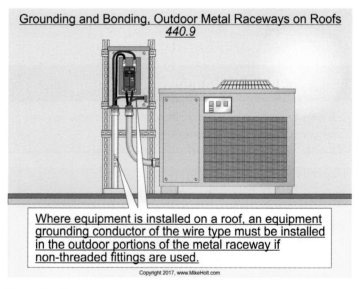

Grounding and Bonding, Outdoor Metal Raceways on Roofs
440.9

Where equipment is installed on a roof, an equipment grounding conductor of the wire type must be installed in the outdoor portions of the metal raceway if non-threaded fittings are used.

Copyright 2017, www.MikeHolt.com

Figure 440–2

440.10 Short-Circuit Current Rating

A new section was added with short-circuit current rating requirements.

Analysis

NEW Controllers of multimotor and combination-load equipment must have a short-circuit rating equal to or higher than the available short-circuit current. Equipment damage or injury is possible if a fault occurs that causes very high current levels and the equipment isn't rated to handle the amperage.

440.10 Short-Circuit Current Rating

(A) Installation. Motor controllers of multimotor and combination-load equipment must have a short-circuit rating equal to or higher than the available short-circuit current.

ARTICLE
445 GENERATORS

Introduction to Article 445—Generators

This article contains the electrical installation, and other requirements, for generators. These requirements include such things as where generators can be installed, nameplate markings, conductor ampacity, and disconnecting means.

Generators are basically motors that operate in reverse—they produce electricity when rotated, instead of rotating when supplied with electricity. Article 430, which covers motors, is the longest article in the *NEC*. Article 445, which covers generators, is one of the shortest. At first, this might not seem to make sense. But you don't need to size and protect conductors to a generator. You do need to size and protect them to a motor.

Generators need overload protection, and it's necessary to size the conductors that come from the generator. But these considerations are much more straightforward than the equivalent considerations for motors. Before you study Article 445, take a moment to read the definition of "Separately Derived System" in Article 100.

445.1 Scope

Article 445 contains the installation and other requirements for generators. Figure 445–1

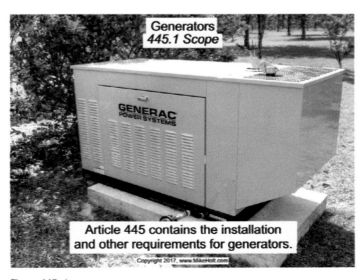

Figure 445–1

Author's Comment:

- Generators, associated wiring, and equipment must be installed in accordance with the following requirements depending on their use:
  - ◆ Article 695, Fire Pumps
  - ◆ Article 700, Emergency Systems
  - ◆ Article 701, Legally Required Standby Systems
  - ◆ Article 702, Optional Standby Systems

445.13 Ampacity of Conductors

An allowance has been added for conductors to be tapped on the load side of generator overcurrent protective devices.

Analysis

EXPANDED

Sometimes we discover that we've been doing things for years with no problems but it was never expressly allowed by the *NEC*. This is the case with tapping conductors from generators. Often several conductors are connected on the load side of the overcurrent protective device of a generator. This wasn't specifically allowed in the *Code*. An allowance has been added for these types of installations as long as they're done in accordance with 240.21(B).

445.13 Ampacity of Conductors

(A) General. The ampacity of the conductors from the generator winding output terminals to the first overcurrent protection device, typically on the generator, must have an ampacity of not less than 115 percent of the nameplate current rating of the generator. Figure 445–2

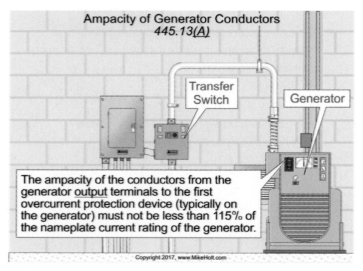

The ampacity of the conductors from the generator <u>output</u> terminals to the first overcurrent protection device (typically on the generator) must not be less than 115% of the nameplate current rating of the generator.

Copyright 2017, www.MikeHolt.com

Figure 445–2

Author's Comment:

■ Since the overcurrent protection device is typically part of the generator, this rule applies to the generator manufacturer, not the field installer.

■ Conductors from the load side of the generator overcurrent protection device to the transfer switch are sized in accordance with 240.4.

Example: *What size conductor is required from a 100A overcurrent protection device on a 20 kW, 120/240V single-phase generator to a 200A service rated transfer switch if the terminals are rated for 75°C conductor sizing?* Figure 445–3

Solution: *A 3 AWG conductor is required; Table 310.15(B)(16), rated 100A at 75°C [110.14(C)(1)(b)].*

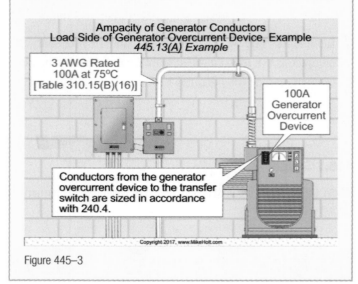

Ampacity of Generator Conductors
Load Side of Generator Overcurrent Device, Example
445.13(A) Example

3 AWG Rated
100A at 75°C
[Table 310.15(B)(16)]

100A
Generator
Overcurrent
Device

Conductors from the generator overcurrent device to the transfer switch are sized in accordance with 240.4.

Copyright 2017, www.MikeHolt.com

Figure 445–3

Generators that aren't a separately derived system must have the neutral conductor sized to carry the maximum unbalanced current as determined by 220.61, serve as part of the effective ground-fault current path, and be not smaller than required by 250.30. Figure 445–4

(B) Overcurrent Protection Provided. <u>Conductors can be tapped from the load side of the generator overcurrent protected device in accordance with 240.21(B).</u>

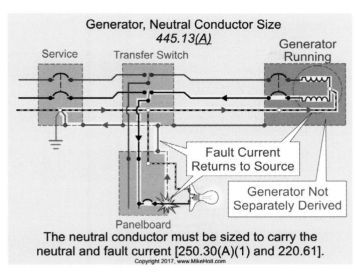

Generator, Neutral Conductor Size
445.13(A)

The neutral conductor must be sized to carry the
neutral and fault current [250.30(A)(1) and 220.61].

Copyright 2017, www.MikeHolt.com

Figure 445–4

445.18 Disconnecting Means and Shutdown of Prime Mover

The rules for a generator disconnecting means have been
clarified. And this time we mean it!

Analysis

CLARIFIED

The requirement for a generator disconnect
has been changed over and over during the
last few *Code* cycles. While that can be frustrating, writing a good rule is just as frustrating, and the *NEC*
is written by groups of people who are doing the best they
can—it just isn't that easy.

There are two separate issues that we're trying to deal
with when it comes to a generator disconnect; shutting off
the power and shutting off the actual engine of the generator. Most of the time we, as electricians, are more concerned
with just shutting off the power from the generator. This is
what 445.18(A) covers.

Sometimes, we need to actually shut the generator itself
off; this is what 445.18(B) discusses. It makes sense that
shutting off the generator itself can satisfy the rule; obviously the conductors will be de-energized if it isn't running.

If we want to use the generator shutoff as the required
conductor disconnect we can, but the switch must be

---

lockable in accordance with 110.25, meaning that the provisions for locking must remain in place whether the actual
lock is installed or not.

For a generator over 15kW, we need a way to shut it off
from outside of any building in which it might be contained.
This ensures that fire fighters can spray water on such a
building without being electrocuted.

445.18 Disconnecting Means and Shutdown of Prime Mover

(A) Disconnecting Means. Each fixed generator disconnect must be
lockable in the open position disconnect [110.25] that simultaneously
disconnects all its associated ungrounded conductors. Figure 445–5

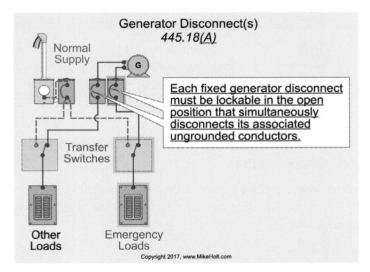

Generator Disconnect(s)
445.18(A)

Each fixed generator disconnect
must be lockable in the open
position that simultaneously
disconnects its associated
ungrounded conductors.

Copyright 2017, www.MikeHolt.com

Figure 445–5

(B) Shutdown of Prime Mover. Generators must have provisions to
shut down the prime mover, shutdown must comply with all of the
following:

(1) Be equipped with provisions to disable all prime mover start control circuits to render the prime mover incapable of starting.

(2) Initiate a shutdown mechanism that requires a mechanical reset.

The provisions to shut down the prime mover can satisfy the requirements of 445.18(A) where the shutdown is capable of being locked in the open position in accordance with 110.25. Generators with greater than 15 kW rating must be provided with an additional shutdown means located outside the equipment room or generator and comply with 445.18(B)(1) and (B)(2).

445.20 GFCI for Receptacles on 15 kW or Smaller Portable Generators

The rules for GFCI protection of generators are now separated into a list of bonded neutral generators and floating neutral generators.

Analysis

CLARIFIED

The requirements for bonded neutral and floating neutral generators are different, so they were separated in the 2017 *NEC*.

445.20 GFCI for Receptacles on 15 kW or Smaller Portable Generators

Receptacles on portable generators rated 15 kW or smaller must have GFCI protected integral to the generator or receptacle <u>as indicated in (A) or (B)</u>.

(A) Unbonded (Floating Neutral) Generators. Where the generator neutral conductor isn't bonded to the generator equipment grounding conductor within the generator, GFCI protection is required for all 15A and 20A, 125V receptacles. Figure 445–6

Ex: GFCI Protection isn't required for 125V receptacle(s) interlocked so that they aren't available for use when the 125/250V receptacle is in use.

(B) Bonded Neutral Generators. Where the generator neutral conductor is bonded to the generator equipment grounding conductor within the generator, GFCI protection is required for all 15A and 20A, 125V receptacles. Figure 445–7

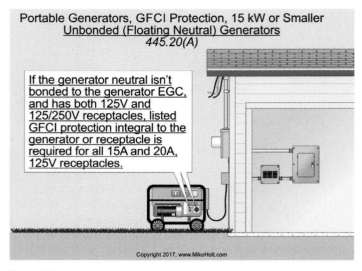

Figure 445–6

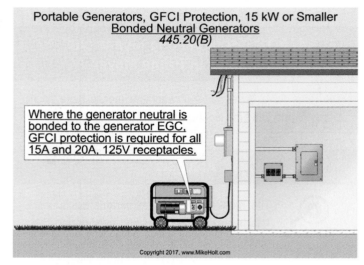

Figure 445–7

Note: See 590.6(A)(3) on GFCI protection requirements for 15 kW or smaller portable generators used for temporary power and lighting.

Ex. to (A) and (B): Where a generator is used for a portable application, a listed cord set or device incorporating listed GFCI protection is permitted if the generator was manufactured or remanufactured prior to January 1, 2015.

ARTICLE
480 STORAGE BATTERIES

Introduction to Article 480—Storage Batteries

The stationary battery is the heart of any uninterruptible power supply. Article 480 addresses stationary batteries for commercial and industrial grade power supplies, not the small, "point of use," UPS boxes.

Stationary batteries are also used in other applications, such as emergency power systems. Regardless of the application, if it uses stationary batteries, Article 480 applies.

Lead-acid stationary batteries fall into two general categories: flooded, and valve regulated (VRLA). These differ markedly in such ways as maintainability, total cost of ownership, and scalability. The *NEC* doesn't address these differences, as they're engineering issues and not fire safety or electrical safety matters [90.1].

The *Code* doesn't address such design issues as optimum tier height, distance between tiers, determination of charging voltage, or string configuration. Nor does it address battery testing, monitoring, or maintenance, which involve highly specialized areas of knowledge, and are required for optimizing operational efficiency. Standards other than the *NEC* address these topics.

What the *Code* does address, in Article 480, are issues related to preventing electrocution and the ignition of the gases that all stationary batteries (even "sealed" ones) emit.

480.1 Scope

Article 480 applies to stationary storage battery installations. Figure 480–1

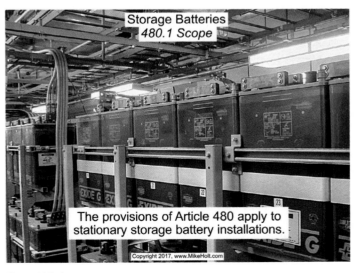

Figure 480–1

480.3 Listing Requirement

Most batteries must now be listed.

Analysis

NEW Listed products are those that have been tested to ensure their safety. Such testing not only includes how the product operates when working correctly, it also tests how they fail. Nobody but a qualified testing laboratory can do this. For well over 100 years the *NEC* has relied on product listing. In fact, I've heard an expert once describe electrical safety as a three-part system: We need product standards and testing to ensure product safety, we need a *Code* to establish the installation rules for products, and we need enforcement of the *NEC* and product standards. This change ensures that parts one and two of this concept are met leaving part three to the inspectors.

480.3 Listing Requirement

Storage batteries, other than lead-acid batteries, and battery management equipment must be listed.

480.4 Battery and Cell Terminations

The requirement to use anti-oxidizing compounds on terminations was clarified.

Analysis

CLARIFIED This section was revised to clarify that using an antioxidant compound can damage some equipment thereby causing an unsafe condition. The use of antioxidant products is only permitted if recommended by the battery manufacturer.

480.4 Battery and Cell Terminations

(A) Corrosion Prevention. Where connections between dissimilar metals occur, antioxidant material must be <u>used as recommended by the battery manufacturer</u>. Figure 480–2

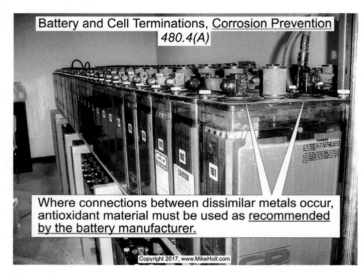

Figure 480–2

Note: The manufacturer's instructions may have guidance for acceptable materials.

(B) Intercell and Intertier Conductors and Connections. The ampacity of field-assembled intercell and intertier connectors and conductors must be sized so that the temperature rise under maximum load conditions and at maximum ambient temperature doesn't exceed the safe operating temperature of the conductor insulation.

Note: IEEE 1375, *Guide for the Overcurrent Protection of Stationary Battery Systems* provides guidance for overcurrent protection and associated cable sizing. Typical voltage-drop considerations for ac circuits might not be adequate for battery systems.

480.9 Battery Support Systems

The requirements for battery support systems have been decreased.

Analysis

CLARIFIED The 2014 *NEC* contained a whole host of requirements for battery support systems, most of which could be summed up in one sentence: Metal battery supports must be provided with nonconductive support members for the battery cells, or be constructed with a continuous insulating material. Paint alone isn't considered an insulating material. This change simplified the requirement.

Battery Support Systems
480.9

Battery support structures must be resistant to deteriorating action by the electrolyte. Metal structures must have nonconducting support members for the cells, or be constructed with a continuous insulating material.

Copyright 2017, www.MikeHolt.com   Ryan Arne

Figure 480–3

480.9 Battery Support Systems

The structure that supports the battery must be resistant to deteriorating action by the electrolyte. Metal structures must be provided with nonconducting support members for the cells, or be constructed with a continuous insulating material. Painting alone isn't considered as an insulating material. Figure 480–3

SPECIAL OCCUPANCIES

Introduction to Chapter 5—Special Occupancies

Chapter 5, which covers special occupancies, is the first of four *NEC* chapters that deals with special topics.

Chapters 6 and 7 cover special equipment, and special conditions, respectively. Remember, the first four chapters of the *Code* are sequential and form a foundation for each of the subsequent three chapters. Chapter 8 covers communications systems (twisted wire, antennas, and coaxial cable) and isn't subject to the requirements of Chapters 1 through 7 except where the requirements are specifically referenced in Chapter 8 [90.3].

What exactly is a "Special Occupancy?" It's a location where a facility, or its use, creates specific conditions that require additional measures to ensure the "practical safeguarding of people and property" purpose of the *NEC*, as put forth in Article 90.

The *Code* groups these special occupancies logically, as you might expect. Here are the general groupings:

- General environments that pose explosion or fire hazards. Articles 500 through 510.
- Specific types of environments that pose explosion or fire hazards. Articles 511 through 516—Examples include motor fuel dispensing facilities, aircraft hangars, and bulk storage plants.
- Facilities that pose evacuation difficulties. Articles 517 through 525—Examples include hospitals, theaters, and carnivals.
- Motion picture related facilities. Articles 530 and 540.
- Specific types of buildings. Articles 545 through 553—Examples include park trailers and floating buildings.
- Marinas, Boatyards, and Commercial and Noncommercial Docking Facilities, Article 555.
- Temporary installations. Article 590.

Many people struggle to understand the requirements for special occupancies, mostly because of the narrowness of application. However, if you study the illustrations and explanations here, you'll clearly understand them.

- **Article 500—Hazardous (Classified) Locations.** A hazardous (classified) location is an area where the possibility of fire or explosion exists due to the presence of flammable or combustible liquid-produced vapors, flammable gases, combustible dusts, or easily ignitable fibers/flyings.

- **Article 501—Class I Hazardous (Classified) Locations.** A Class I hazardous (classified) location is an area where flammable or combustible liquid-produced vapors or flammable gases may present the hazard of a fire or explosion.

- **Article 502—Class II Hazardous (Classified) Locations.** A Class II hazardous (classified) location is an area where the possibility of fire or explosion may exist due to the presence of combustible dust.

- **Article 503—Class III Hazardous (Classified) Locations.** Class III locations are hazardous because fire or explosion risks may exist due to easily ignitible fibers/flyings. These include materials such as cotton and rayon, which are found in textile mills and clothing manufacturing plants. They can also include establishments and industries such as sawmills and woodworking plants.

- **Article 511—Commercial Garages, Repair, and Storage.** These occupancies include locations used for service and repair operations in connection with self-propelled vehicles (including, but not limited to, passenger automobiles, buses, trucks, and tractors) in which flammable liquids or flammable gases are used for fuel or power.

- **Article 514—Motor Fuel Dispensing Facilities.** Article 514 covers gasoline dispensing and service stations where gasoline or other volatile liquids are transferred to the fuel tanks of self-propelled vehicles. Wiring and equipment in the area of service and repair rooms of service stations must comply with the installation requirements in Article 511.

- **Article 517—Health Care Facilities.** This article applies to electrical wiring in human health care facilities such as hospitals, nursing homes, limited-care facilities, clinics, medical and dental offices, and ambulatory care, whether permanent or movable. It doesn't apply to animal veterinary facilities.

- **Article 518—Assembly Occupancies.** Article 518 covers buildings or portions of buildings specifically designed or intended for the assembly of 100 or more persons.

- **Article 525—Carnivals, Circuses, Fairs, and Similar Events.** This article covers the installation of portable wiring and equipment for temporary carnivals, circuses, exhibitions, fairs, traveling attractions, and similar functions, including wiring in or on structures.

- **Article 547—Agricultural Buildings.** Article 547 covers agricultural buildings or those parts of buildings or adjacent areas where excessive dust or dust with water may accumulate, or where a corrosive atmosphere exists.

- **Article 550—Mobile Homes, Manufactured Homes, and Mobile Home Parks.** Article 550 covers electrical conductors and equipment within or on mobile and manufactured homes, conductors that connect mobile and manufactured homes to the electrical supply, and the installation of electrical wiring, luminaires, and electrical equipment in or on mobile and manufactured homes.

- **Article 555—Marinas, Boatyards, and Commercial and Noncommercial Docking Facilities.** This article covers the installation of wiring and equipment in the areas that comprise fixed or floating piers, wharves, docks, and other areas in marinas, boatyards, boat basins, boathouses, and similar locations used, or intended to be used, for repair, berthing, launching, storing, or fueling of small craft, and the mooring of floating buildings.

- **Article 590—Temporary Installations.** Article 590 covers temporary power and lighting for construction, remodeling, maintenance, repair, demolitions, and decorative lighting.

ARTICLE 500
HAZARDOUS (CLASSIFIED) LOCATIONS

Introduction to Article 500—Hazardous (Classified) Locations

A hazardous (classified) location is an area where the possibility of fire or explosion can be created by the presence of flammable or combustible gases or vapors, combustible dusts, or easily ignitable fibers/flyings. Electric arcs, sparks, and/or heated surfaces can serve as a source of ignition in such environments.

Article 500 provides a foundation for applying Article 501 (Class I Locations), Article 502 (Class II Locations), Article 503 (Class III Locations), and Article 504 (Intrinsically Safe Systems)—all of which immediately follow Article 500. This article also provides a foundation for applying Articles 510 through 516.

Before you apply any of the articles just mentioned, you must understand and apply Article 500 which is fairly long and detailed. You'll notice when studying this article that there are many Informational Notes that you should review. Although Informational Notes aren't *NEC* requirements [90.5(C)], they contain information that helps *Code* users better understand the related *NEC* rules.

A Fire Triangle (fuel, oxygen, and energy source) helps illustrate the concept of how combustion occurs. Figure 500–1

- *Fuel.* Flammable gases or vapors, combustible dusts, and easily ignitable fibers/flyings.
- *Oxygen.* Air and oxidizing atmospheres.
- *Ignition Source.* Electric arcs or sparks, heat-producing equipment such as luminaires and motors, failure of transformers, coils, or solenoids, as well as sparks caused by metal tools dropping on metal surfaces.

Many of the graphics contained in Chapter 5 use two shades of red to identify a Division location (darker red for Division 1 and lighter red to identify Division 2). In some cases, these color schemes are used as a background color to help you tell if the graphic applies to Division 1, Division 2, or both (split color background).

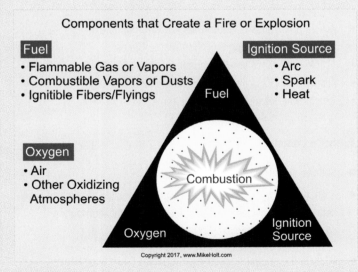

Components that Create a Fire or Explosion

Fuel
- Flammable Gas or Vapors
- Combustible Vapors or Dusts
- Ignitible Fibers/Flyings

Ignition Source
- Arc
- Spark
- Heat

Oxygen
- Air
- Other Oxidizing Atmospheres

Fuel

Combustion

Oxygen

Ignition Source

Copyright 2017, www.MikeHolt.com

Figure 500–1

500.1 Scope—Articles 500 Through 504

To prevent injury, death, or extensive damage to structures from fires or explosions, the *NEC* contains stringent requirements for equipment and its installation in hazardous (classified) locations where fire or explosion hazards may exist due to flammable gases, flammable liquid-produced vapors, combustible liquid-produced vapors, combustible dusts, or fibers/flyings. The specific requirements for electrical installations in hazardous (classified) locations are contained in: Figure 500–2

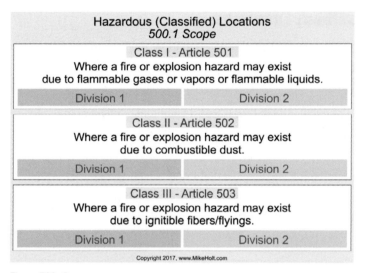

Hazardous (Classified) Locations
500.1 Scope

Class I - Article 501
Where a fire or explosion hazard may exist
due to flammable gases or vapors or flammable liquids.

| Division 1 | Division 2 |

Class II - Article 502
Where a fire or explosion hazard may exist
due to combustible dust.

| Division 1 | Division 2 |

Class III - Article 503
Where a fire or explosion hazard may exist
due to ignitible fibers/flyings.

| Division 1 | Division 2 |

Copyright 2017, www.MikeHolt.com

Figure 500–2

- Article 501. Class I—Flammable or Combustible Liquid-Produced Vapors or Flammable Gases
- Article 502. Class II—Combustible Dust
- Article 503. Class III—Easily Ignitible Fibers/Flyings
- Article 504. Intrinsically Safe Systems

Author's Comment:

- See the definition of "Structure" in Article 100.

- Locating electrical wiring and equipment outside a classified location provides the safest electrical installation and is often more cost-effective [500.5(A) Note].

- Many of the graphics contained in Chapter 5 use two shades of red to identify a Division location (darker red for Division 1 and lighter red to identify Division 2). In some cases, these color schemes are used as a background color to help you tell if the graphic applies to Division 1, Division 2, or both (split color background).

- The *NEC* doesn't classify specific hazardous (classified) locations, except as identified in Articles 511 through 517. Determining the classification of a specific hazardous area is the responsibility of those who understand the dangers of the products being used, such as the fire marshal, plant facility engineer, or insurance underwriter. It isn't the responsibility of the electrical designer, electrical contractor, or electrical inspector. Prior to performing any wiring in or near a hazardous (classified) location, contact the plant facility and design engineer to ensure that proper installation and materials are used. Be sure to review 500.4(B) for additional standards that might need to be consulted.

Other articles in Chapter 5 containing specific hazardous installation requirements include:

- Article 505. Class I, Zone 0, 1, and 2 Locations
- Article 511. Commercial Garages, Repair, and Storage
- Article 513. Aircraft Hangars
- Article 514. Motor Fuel Dispensing Facilities
- Article 515. Bulk Storage Plants
- Article 516. Spray Application, Dipping, and Coating Processes
- Article 517. Health Care Facilities

500.2 Definitions

Section 500.2 containing definitions was deleted, and the terms were relocated to Article 100.

Analysis

RELOCATED The *Code* defines terms in one of two locations—Article 100 or the xxx.2 section of an article. Article 100 is supposed to contain the definitions for terms that are used throughout the *NEC*, such as "ampacity," "dwelling unit," "outlet," and many others. Some terms are only used in one article, like "supply-side bonding jumper" that's only used in Article 250, so it's defined in 250.2. Section 500.2 has long included definitions that applied to Articles 500 through 516. In order to reduce confusion, the definitions contained in 500.2 have been relocated to Article 100 and include the text "[as applied to hazardous locations]."

CLASS I HAZARDOUS (CLASSIFIED) LOCATIONS

Introduction to Article 501—Class I Hazardous (Classified) Locations

If sufficient flammable or combustible gases, vapors, or liquids are, or may be, present to produce an explosive or ignitable mixture, you have a Class I location. Examples of such locations include some fuel storage areas, certain solvent storage areas, grain processing facilities (where hexane is used), plastic extrusion areas where oil removal is part of the process, refineries, and paint storage areas. Article 500 contained a general background on hazardous (classified) locations, and described the differences between Class I, II, and III locations and the differences between Division 1 and Division 2. Article 501 contains the actual Class I, Division 1 and Division 2 installation requirements, including wiring methods, seals, and specific equipment requirements.

Part I. General

501.1 Scope

Article 501 covers requirements for electrical and electronic equipment and wiring in Class I, Division 1 and Division 2 locations where flammable gases, flammable liquid-produced vapors, or flammable liquid-produced vapors may be present in the air and in quantities sufficient to produce explosive or ignitible mixtures [500.5(B)]. Figure 501–1

Requirements for Class I, Divisions 1 and 2 locations where flammable gases or vapors or flammable liquids may be present in quantities sufficient to produce explosive or ignitible mixtures.

Copyright 2017, www.MikeHolt.com

Figure 501–1

501.10 Wiring Methods

Type HDPE conduit is now acceptable under a Class 1, Division 1 location, and threadless intermediate metal conduit and rigid metal conduit fittings will now be permitted in Class I, Division 2 locations.

Analysis

REDUCED

Type HDPE conduit was added to the exception for 501.10(A)(1)(a) for areas under a Class I, Division 1 location if it meets the requirements of 514.8.

REDUCED

A Class I, Division 2 location is an area that doesn't contain an imminent threat of fire and/or explosion, so the safety requirements are substantially less than those in a Class I, Division 1 location where one spark can result in a catastrophe. Although this new allowance may seem strange at first glance, it really does make sense. When you consider that general-purpose enclosures are permitted in a Class I, Division 2 location, why would we need a threaded raceway system?

501.10 Wiring Methods

(A) Class I, Division 1.

(1) General. Only the following wiring methods are permitted within a Class I, Division 1 location.

(a) Threaded rigid metal conduit, or intermediate metal conduit, with explosionproof fittings. Figure 501–2

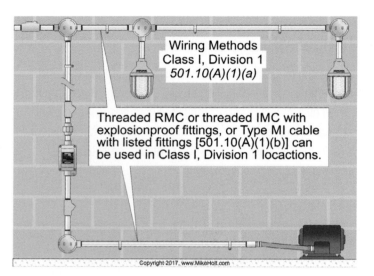

Wiring Methods
Class I, Division 1
501.10(A)(1)(a)

Threaded RMC or threaded IMC with explosionproof fittings, or Type MI cable with listed fittings [501.10(A)(1)(b)] can be used in Class I, Division 1 locactions.

Figure 501–2

Ex: PVC, RTRC, or HDPE conduit is permitted underground in accordance with 514.8.

(b) MI cable terminated with fittings listed for the location.

(c) In industrial establishments with restricted public access where only qualified persons will service the installation, MC-HL cable listed for use in Class I, Division 1 locations, with a gas/vaportight continuous corrugated metallic sheath, an overall jacket of suitable polymeric material, a separate equipment grounding conductor(s) sized in accordance with 250.122, based on the rating of the overcurrent protection device, and terminated with fittings listed for the application can be used. Such cable must comply with Part II of Article 330. Figure 501–3

Author's Comment:

- Article 100 defines a "Qualified Person" as one who has skills and knowledge related to the construction and operation of the equipment and has received safety training to recognize and avoid the hazards involved.

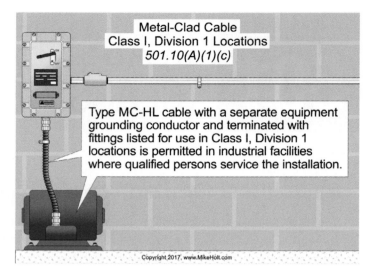

Metal-Clad Cable
Class I, Division 1 Locations
501.10(A)(1)(c)

Type MC-HL cable with a separate equipment grounding conductor and terminated with fittings listed for use in Class I, Division 1 locations is permitted in industrial facilities where qualified persons service the installation.

Figure 501–3

(d) In industrial establishments with restricted public access where only qualified persons will service the installation, ITC-HL cable terminated with fittings listed for the location.

(e) Types OFNP, OFCP, OFNR, OFCR, OFNG, OFCG, OFN, and OFC optical fiber cables can be installed in raceways [501.10(A)], and must be sealed in accordance with 501.15. Figure 501–4

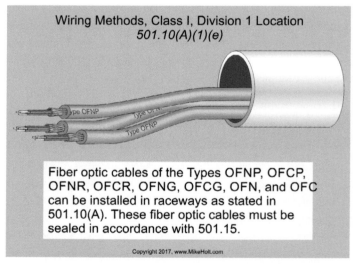

Wiring Methods, Class I, Division 1 Location
501.10(A)(1)(e)

Fiber optic cables of the Types OFNP, OFCP, OFNR, OFCR, OFNG, OFCG, OFN, and OFC can be installed in raceways as stated in 501.10(A). These fiber optic cables must be sealed in accordance with 501.15.

Figure 501–4

(2) Flexible Wiring. When necessary for vibration or movement, <u>one of</u> following are permitted to be used: Figure 501–5

(1) Flexible fittings,

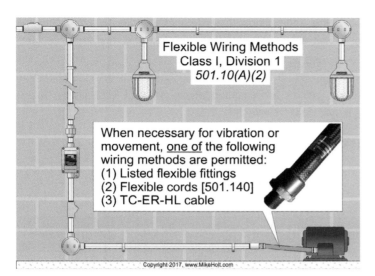

Figure 501–5

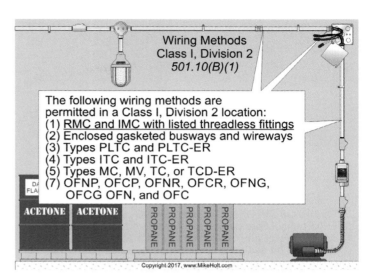

Figure 501–7

(2) Flexible cords in accordance with 501.140, or

(3) In industrial applications with restricted access, TC-ER-HL cable with listed fittings.

(3) Boxes and Fittings. Boxes and fittings must be approved by the authority having jurisdiction for Class I, Division 1 locations. Figure 501–6

Figure 501–6

(B) Class I, Division 2.

(1) General. All wiring methods included in Class 1, Division 1 locations [501.10(A)] and the following wiring methods are permitted within a Class I, Division 2 location. Figure 501–7

(1) Rigid and intermediate metal conduit with listed threadless fittings.

(2) Enclosed gasketed busways and enclosed gasketed wireways.

(3) Types PLTC and PLTC-ER cable terminated with listed fittings in accordance with Article 725.

(6) Where metallic conduit doesn't provide sufficient corrosion resistance, listed reinforced thermosetting resin conduit and Schedule 80 PVC conduit can be used, but only in industrial establishments where maintenance and supervision ensure that only qualified persons service the installation.

(7) Types OFNP, OFCP, OFNR, OFCR, OFNG, OFCG, OFN, and OFC optical fiber cables can be installed in cable trays or raceways [501.10(B)], and must be sealed in accordance with 501.15. Figure 501–8

(8) Cablebus

(2) Flexible Wiring. If flexibility is necessary, the following wiring methods are permitted: Figure 501–9

(1) Listed flexible metal fittings.

(2) Flexible metal conduit with listed fittings.

(3) Interlocked Type MC cable with listed fittings.

(4) Liquidtight flexible metal conduit with listed fittings.

(5) Liquidtight flexible nonmetallic conduit with listed fittings.

(6) Flexible cords listed for extra-hard usage, containing an equipment grounding conductor, and terminated with listed fittings.

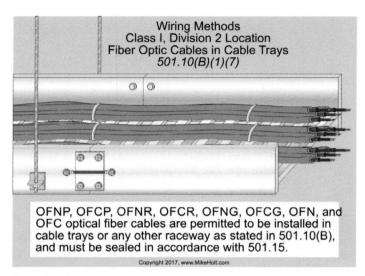

Figure 501-8

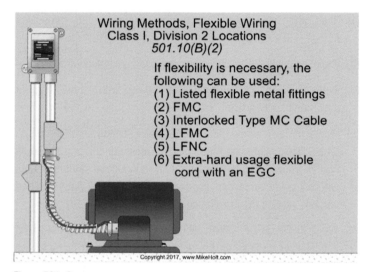

Figure 501-9

Author's Comment:

- See the definition of "Grounding Conductor, Equipment" in Article 100.

- If flexible cords are used, they must comply with 501.140.

(7) For elevator use, type EO, ETP, or ETT elevator cable can be used if the "Use" column of Table 400.4 allows it, and if terminated with listed fittings.

Note: See 501.30(B) for equipment grounding requirements where flexible conduit is used.

(4) Boxes and Fittings. General-purpose enclosures and fittings are permitted unless the enclosure contains make-and-break contacts for meters, instruments, and relays [501.105(B)(1)], switches, circuit breakers, or motor controllers [501.115(B)(1)], signaling, alarm, remote-control, and communications systems (twisted wire, antennas, and coaxial cable) [501.150(B)].

Author's Comment:

- See the definition of "Controller" in Article 100.

501.15 Raceway and Cable Seals

Clarifications for factory-sealed equipment were made, and provisions for sealing equipment in accordance with manufacturer's instructions were added.

Analysis

CLARIFIED In the previous *Code*, 501.15(A)(1) allowed factory sealed equipment to be installed without a field installed seal, provided the enclosure was marked "factory sealed." This was revised to clarify that equipment sealed at the factory might be marked "leads factory sealed," "seal not required," or similar language and not need a field installed raceway seal.

Sections 501.15(A)(1) and 501.15(D)(1) contain requirements for raceway seals and cable seals, respectively. Both require sealing fittings within 18 in. of explosionproof enclosures. New to this edition of the *NEC*, the sealing fitting can be installed further than 18 in. from the enclosure, if the manufacturer has such an allowance marked on the enclosure. This seems like a reasonable change, as the manufacturers of explosionproof equipment subject their products to a huge amount of testing, and they know better than anyone exactly what their equipment can handle and what it can't.

501.15 Raceway and Cable Seals

Note 1: Raceway and cable seals must be installed to: Figure 501–10

- Minimize the passage of gases and vapors from one portion of electrical equipment to another through the raceway or cable.

- Minimize the passage of flames from one portion of electrical equipment to another through the raceway or cable.

- Limit internal explosions to within the explosionproof enclosure.

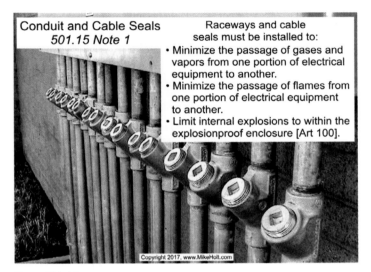

Figure 501–10

(A) Raceway Seal—Class I, Division 1. In Class I, Division 1 locations, raceway seals must be located as follows:

(1) Entering Enclosures. A raceway seal is required in each raceway that enters an explosionproof enclosure if either (1) or (2) apply:

(1) A raceway seal fitting must be installed in each raceway that enters an explosionproof enclosure that contains make-and-break contacts. A seal must also be provided where the enclosure contains equipment that operates at over 80 percent of the auto-ignition temperature of the gas or vapor in the area. Figure 501–11

Ex: A raceway seal isn't required if the make-and-break contacts are:

a. *Within a hermetically sealed chamber.*

b. *Immersed in oil in accordance with 501.115(B)(1)(2).*

c. *Contained within an enclosure that's identified for the location and marked as "Leads Factory Sealed," "Factory Sealed," "Seal not Required," or equivalent.*

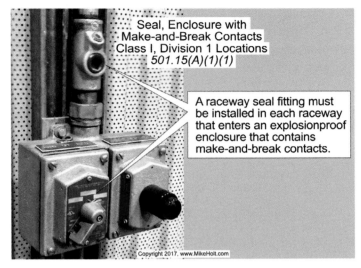

Figure 501–11

(2) A raceway seal fitting isn't required for trade size ½, ¾, 1, 1¼, or 1½ raceways that enter an explosionproof enclosure that doesn't contain any make-and-break contacts (junction and splice boxes). An example is an enclosure that only contains terminals, splices, or taps. However, a trade size 2 or larger raceway that enters any explosionproof enclosure must have a raceway seal fitting installed within 18 in. of the explosionproof enclosure [501.15(A)(1)(1)]. Figure 501–12

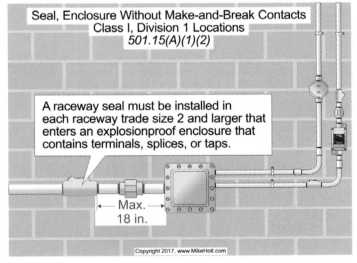

Figure 501–12

An enclosure identified for the location marked "Leads Factory Sealed," "Factory Sealed," "Seal not Required," or equivalent isn't considered to serve as a seal for another adjacent enclosure that requires a conduit seal.

The raceway seal fitting must be installed within 18 in. of the explosionproof enclosure or as required by enclosure markings. Figure 501–13

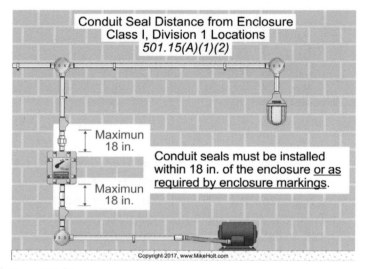

Figure 501–13

Only explosionproof unions, couplings, reducers, elbows, and capped elbows are permitted between the raceway seal and the explosionproof enclosure. Figure 501–14

Figure 501–14

(2) Pressurized Enclosures. A raceway seal fitting must be installed in each raceway that isn't pressurized where the raceway enters a pressurized enclosure. The raceway seal fitting must be installed within 18 in. of each raceway that terminates to the pressurized enclosure.

(3) Between Explosionproof Enclosures. A single raceway seal is permitted between two explosionproof enclosures containing make-and-break contacts if the raceway seal fitting is located not more than 18 in. from either explosionproof enclosure. Figure 501–15

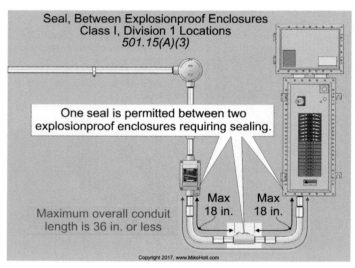

Figure 501–15

(4) Class I, Division 1, Boundary Seal. A raceway seal fitting must be installed in each raceway that leaves a Class I, Division 1 location within 10 ft of the Class I, Division 1 location on either side of the boundary. Figure 501–16

There must be no fitting, except for a listed explosionproof reducer installed at the raceway seal fitting, between the raceway seal fitting and the point at which the raceway leaves the Class I, Division 1 location. Figure 501–17

Ex 1: A raceway boundary seal fitting isn't required for a raceway that passes completely through the Class I, Division 1 area unbroken with no fittings installed within 1 ft of either side of the boundary. Figure 501–18

Ex 2: If the raceway boundary is below grade, the raceway seal can be located above grade, after the raceway emerges from below grade. Figure 501–19

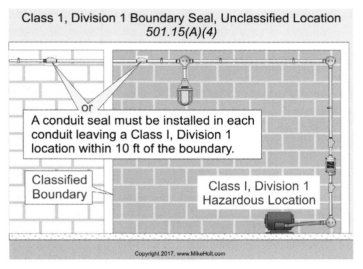

Figure 501–16

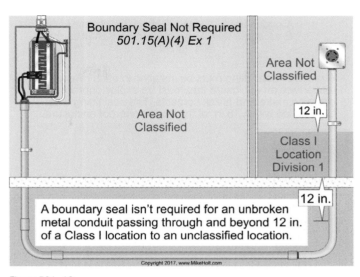

Figure 501–18

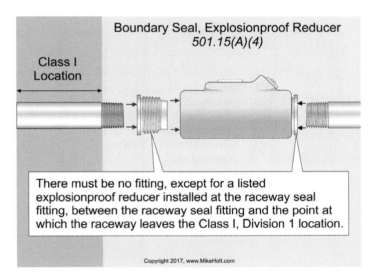

Figure 501–17

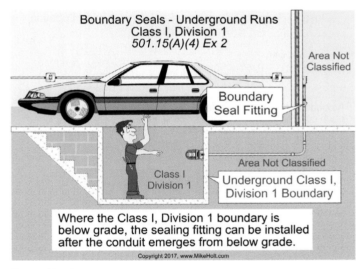

Figure 501–19

(B) Raceway Seal—Class I, Division 2. In Class I, Division 2 locations, raceway seals must be located as follows:

(1) Enclosures with Make-and-Break Contacts. A raceway seal fitting must be installed in each raceway that enters an enclosure that must be explosionproof and that contains make-and-break contacts. The seal fitting must be installed within 18 in. of the explosionproof enclosure. Figure 501–20

(2) Boundary Seal at Unclassified Location. A raceway seal fitting must be installed in each raceway leaving a Class I, Division 2 location. It can be installed on either side of the boundary within 10 ft of the Class I, Division 2 area. Figure 501–21

Except for listed explosionproof reducers installed at the raceway seal fitting, there must be no union, coupling, box, or fitting between the raceway seal fitting and the point at which the raceway leaves the Division 2 location.

Raceway boundary seals aren't required to be explosionproof, but must be identified for the purpose of minimizing the passage of gases permitted under normal operating conditions, and they must be accessible. See Figure 501–21

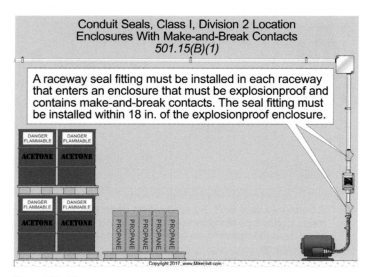

Figure 501–20

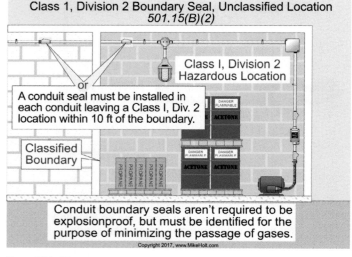

Figure 501–21

Author's Comment:

■ See the definition of "Accessible" as it relates to wiring methods in Article 100.

■ The raceway boundary seal at unclassified locations is used to minimize the passage of gases or vapors, not to contain explosions in the raceway system.

Ex 1: A raceway boundary seal fitting isn't required for a raceway that passes completely through the Class I, Division 2 area unbroken with no fittings installed within 1 ft of either side of the boundary.

Ex 2: A raceway boundary seal fitting isn't required for raceways that terminate in an unclassified location where the metal conduit transitions to cable trays, cablebus, ventilated busways, MI cable, or open wiring if:

(1) The unclassified location is located outdoors or the unclassified location is indoors and the conduit system is entirely in one room.

(2) The raceways must not terminate at an enclosure containing an ignition source in normal operation.

Ex 3: A boundary seal fitting isn't required for a raceway that passes from an enclosure or a room that's unclassified, as a result of pressurization, into a Class I, Division 2 location.

(C) Raceway Seals—Installation Requirements. If explosionproof sealing fittings are required in Class I, Division 1 and 2 locations, they must comply with the following: Figure 501–22

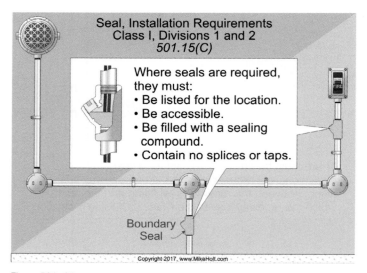

Figure 501–22

Ex: Boundary seals for Class 1 Division 2 locations that aren't required to be explosionproof [501.15(B)(2)] aren't required to comply with 501.15(C).

(1) Fittings. Raceway seal fittings must be listed for the specific sealing compounds and Class I location, and must be accessible.

(2) Compound. The raceway seal compound must be mixed and installed in accordance with manufacturer's instructions so it minimizes the passage of gases and/or vapors through the sealing fitting.

- The sealing compound must be from the same manufacturer as the raceway seal.

(3) Thickness of Compounds. Except for listed cable sealing fittings, the thickness of the raceway seal compound installed in completed seals, other than listed cable sealing fittings, aren't permitted to be less than the trade size of the seal fitting, but in no case less than ⅝ in.

(4) Splices and Taps. Splices and taps aren't permitted to be made within a raceway seal fitting.

(6) Number of Conductors or Optical Fiber Cables. The conductor or optical fiber tube cross-sectional area must not exceed 25 percent of the cross-sectional area of rigid metal conduit of the same trade size, unless the seal is specifically identified for a higher percentage fill. Figure 501–23

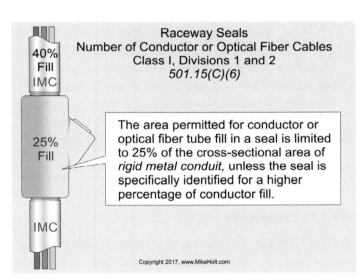

Raceway Seals
Number of Conductor or Optical Fiber Cables
Class I, Divisions 1 and 2
501.15(C)(6)

40% Fill IMC

25% Fill

The area permitted for conductor or optical fiber tube fill in a seal is limited to 25% of the cross-sectional area of *rigid metal conduit,* unless the seal is specifically identified for a higher percentage of conductor fill.

IMC

Copyright 2017, www.MikeHolt.com

Figure 501–23

- The cross-sectional area of intermediate metal conduit is approximately 7 percent greater than that of rigid metal conduit because the wall thickness of intermediate metal conduit is less than rigid metal conduit. If the cross-sectional area of intermediate metal conduit is used for conductor fill calculations, the 25 percent of "rigid metal conduit conductor fill" can be exceeded.

(D) Cable Seal—Class I, Division 1. In Class I, Division 1 locations, cable seals must be located as follows:

(1) Terminations. Type MC-HL cable is inherently gas/vaportight by the construction of the cable, termination fittings must permit the sealing compound to surround each individual insulated conductor to minimize the passage of gases or vapors.

Seals for cables entering enclosures must be installed within 18 in. of the enclosure or as required by the enclosure marking. Only explosionproof unions, couplings, reducers, elbows, and capped elbows can be installed between the sealing fitting and the enclosure. Figure 501–24

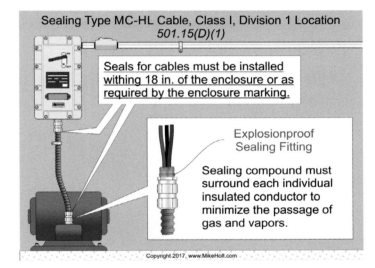

Sealing Type MC-HL Cable, Class I, Division 1 Location
501.15(D)(1)

Seals for cables must be installed withing 18 in. of the enclosure or as required by the enclosure marking.

Explosionproof Sealing Fitting

Sealing compound must surround each individual insulated conductor to minimize the passage of gas and vapors.

Copyright 2017, www.MikeHolt.com

Figure 501–24

Ex: The removal of shielding material or the separation of the twisted pairs isn't required within the raceway seal fitting. Figure 501–25

(2) Cables Capable of Transmitting Gases or Vapors in a Raceway. Raceways containing cables must be sealed after removing the jacket and any other coverings so that the sealing compound surrounds each individual insulated conductor or optical fiber tube in a manner so as to minimize the passage of gases and vapors.

Ex: The removal of shielding material or the separation of the twisted pairs isn't required within the raceway seal fitting. Figure 501–26

(3) Cables Not Capable of Transmitting Gases or Vapors in a Raceway. Each multiconductor cable installed within a raceway is considered to be a single conductor if the cable is incapable of transmitting gases or vapors through the cable core.

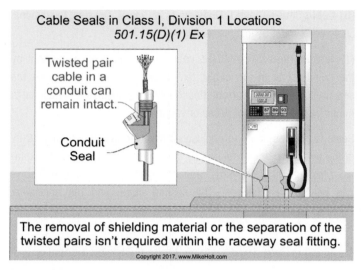

Cable Seals in Class I, Division 1 Locations
501.15(D)(1) Ex

Twisted pair cable in a conduit can remain intact.

Conduit Seal

The removal of shielding material or the separation of the twisted pairs isn't required within the raceway seal fitting.

Copyright 2017, www.MikeHolt.com

Figure 501–25

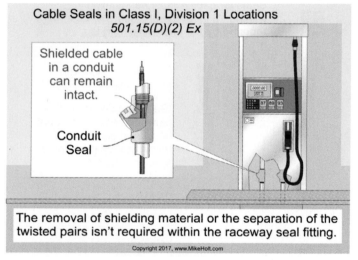

Cable Seals in Class I, Division 1 Locations
501.15(D)(2) Ex

Shielded cable in a conduit can remain intact.

Conduit Seal

The removal of shielding material or the separation of the twisted pairs isn't required within the raceway seal fitting.

Copyright 2017, www.MikeHolt.com

Figure 501–26

(E) Cable Seal—Class I, Division 2. In Class I, Division 2 locations, cable seals must be located as follows:

Ex: Seals aren't required in a Class 1 Division 2 location if the cable passes through the location and has an unbroken gas or vaportight sheath.

(1) Multiconductor Cable. Multiconductor or optical fiber cables that enter an explosionproof enclosure must be sealed after removing the jacket and any other coverings so that the sealing compound will surround each individual insulated conductor or optical fiber tube in a manner so as to minimize the passage of gases and vapors.

Multiconductor cables or optical fiber cables installed within a raceway must be sealed in accordance with 501.15(D)(2) or (3).

Ex 2: The removal of shielding material or the separation of the twisted pairs isn't required within the cable seal fitting.

(4) Cable Seal—Boundary. Cables without a gas/vaportight continuous sheath must be sealed at the boundary of the Class I, Division 2 location in a manner so as to minimize the passage of gases or vapors into an unclassified location.

501.115 Enclosures

The types of equipment not requiring a seal have been clarified.

Analysis

CLARIFIED Under the last edition of the *Code*, a switch, motor controller, or circuit breaker didn't require an explosionproof enclosure in a Class I, Division 2 location if contained in an explosionproof chamber marked "factory sealed." This allowance has been expanded to include "leads factory sealed," "seal not required," or other similar marking for equipment. Also, the switching mechanism can be contained in an identified enclosure, not only an explosionproof chamber.

501.115 Enclosures

(A) Class I, Division 1. Enclosures containing make-and-break contacts for switches, circuit breakers, motor controllers, and fuses, including pushbuttons, relays, and similar devices, must be identified as a complete assembly for use in a Class I, Division 1 location. Figure 501–27

(B) Class I, Division 2.

(1) Type Required. Enclosures containing make-and-break contacts for switches, circuit breakers, motor controllers, fuses, pushbuttons, relays, and other make-and-break contact devices must be identified for use in a Class I, Division 1 location in accordance with 501.105(A). Figure 501–28

Enclosures containing make-and-break contacts can be installed in a general-purpose enclosure if:

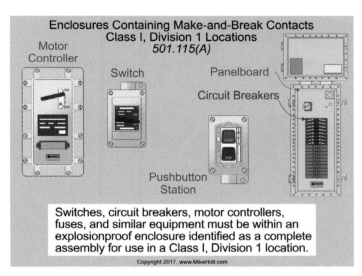

Figure 501–27

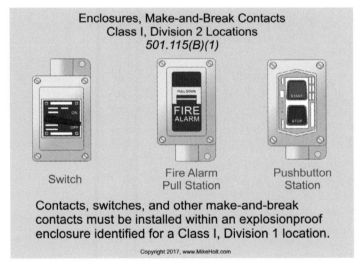

Figure 501–28

(1) The interruption of current occurs within a hermetically sealed chamber.

(2) The make-and-break contacts are oil-immersed.

(3) The interruption of current occurs within an enclosure that's identified for the location and marked "Leads Factory Sealed," "Factory Sealed," "Seal not Required," or equivalent.

501.145 Receptacles and Attachment Plugs

The allowance for using attachment plugs in Class I locations has been changed to allow only permitted flexible cords.

Analysis

CLARIFIED Certainly when one thinks of an attachment plug, they visualize it as being connected to a flexible cord. The code was revised because attachment plug must only be used with flexible cords.

501.145 Receptacles and Attachment Plugs

(A) Receptacles. Receptacles must be part of the premises wiring, unless they're part of a temporary portable assembly [501.140(A)(5)]. Figure 501–29

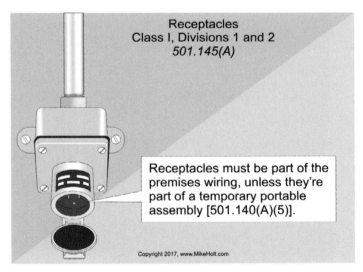

Figure 501–29

(B) Attachment Plugs. Attachment plugs must provide for the connection of an equipment grounding conductor of a permitted flexible cord and be identified for the class location. Figure 501–30

Author's Comment:

■ See the definitions of "Attachment Plug" and "Receptacle" in Article 100.

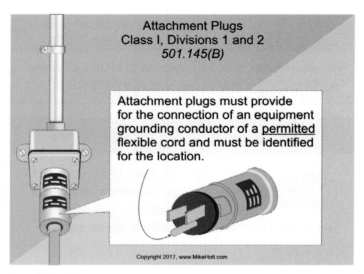

Attachment Plugs
Class I, Divisions 1 and 2
501.145(B)

Attachment plugs must provide for the connection of an equipment grounding conductor of a <u>permitted</u> flexible cord and must be identified for the location.

Copyright 2017, www.MikeHolt.com

Figure 501–30

■ Receptacles listed for Class I locations can be any of the following types:

◆ *Interlocked Switch Receptacle*. This receptacle contains a built-in rotary switch interlocked with the attachment plug. The switch must be off before the attachment plug can be inserted or removed.

◆ *Manual Interlocked Receptacle*. The attachment plug is inserted into the receptacle, and then it's rotated to operate the receptacle's switching contacts.

◆ *Delayed Action Receptacle*. This receptacle requires an attachment plug and receptacle constructed so that an electrical arc will be confined within the explosionproof chamber of the receptacle.

ARTICLE
511

COMMERCIAL GARAGES, REPAIR, AND STORAGE

Introduction to Article 511—Commercial Garages, Repair, and Storage

Article 511 covers locations used for the service and repair of vehicles that use volatile flammable liquids or flammable gases for fuel. If there's any fuel dispensing done in the building, then the requirements of Article 514 also apply. As long as there's no fuel dispensing taking place, the requirements are fairly straightforward.

First of all, it's essential to understand whether the facility is a major repair or minor repair garage. Pay careful attention to these definitions as you study this Article. The next factor that makes a difference in the classification of a location is the presence or absence of a below-floor pit. Finally, mechanical ventilation is critical and can change the classification of a location. Read this material carefully, review the illustrations, and you'll find that the Article 511 requirements aren't that difficult.

511.1 Scope

Article 511 applies to areas used for the service and repair operations of self-propelled vehicles including passenger automobiles, buses, trucks, tractors, and so on, in which volatile flammable liquids or flammable gases are used for fuel or power. Figure 511–1

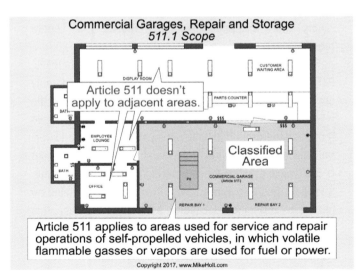

Commercial Garages, Repair and Storage
511.1 Scope

Article 511 doesn't apply to adjacent areas.

Classified Area

Article 511 applies to areas used for service and repair operations of self-propelled vehicles, in which volatile flammable gasses or vapors are used for fuel or power.

Copyright 2017, www.MikeHolt.com

Figure 511–1

Author's Comment:

- Installations within the scope of Article 511 include automobile service/repair centers, service/repair garages for commercial vehicles such as trucks and tractors, service/repair garages for fleet vehicles such as cars, buses, and trucks, and shops that service motorcycles and all-terrain vehicles (ATVs).

- This article doesn't apply to garages for diesel fueled or electric vehicle service garages.

511.3 Classification of Hazardous Areas

This section of the *NEC*, used to determine area classifications in commercial garages, has been turned into tables.

Analysis

EDITED While this section was written rather well, it's still very long and has multiple subsections. When this occurs in the *Code*, it's easy to find yourself reading the wrong requirement and creating problems for yourself. Consolidating this information in a table will improve the usability of the information tremendously.

511.3 Classification of Hazardous Areas

(A) Parking Garages. Parking or storage garages aren't required to be classified.

(B) Repair Garages, With Dispensing. Major and minor repair garages that dispense motor fuels must have the dispensing functions classified in accordance with Table 514.3(B)(1).

(C) Major and Minor Repair Garages. Where vehicles using Class I liquids or heavier-than-air gaseous fuels (such as LPG) are repaired, hazardous area classification is contained in Table 511.3(C).

(D) Major Repair Garages. Where vehicles using lighter-than-air gaseous fuels (such as hydrogen and natural gas) are repaired or stored, hazardous area classification guidance is found in Table 511.3(D).

(E) Modifications to Classification.

(1) Classification of Adjacent Areas. Areas adjacent to classified locations aren't classified if mechanically ventilated at a rate of four or more air changes per hour, or when walls or partitions effectively cut off the adjacent area. Figure 511–2

(2) Alcohol-Based Windshield Washer Fluid. Areas used for the storage, handling, or dispensing into motor vehicles of alcohol-based windshield washer fluid in repair garages are unclassified unless otherwise classified by a provision of 511.3.

Author's Comment:

- Windshield washer fluid isn't flammable.

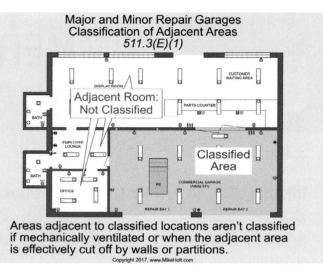

Major and Minor Repair Garages
Classification of Adjacent Areas
511.3(E)(1)

Areas adjacent to classified locations aren't classified if mechanically ventilated or when the adjacent area is effectively cut off by walls or partitions.

Copyright 2017, www.MikeHolt.com

Figure 511–2

511.8 Underground Wiring

A new section was added detailing the requirements for wiring beneath commercial garage floors.

Analysis

NEW The *Code* has always been silent on the issue of wiring beneath a commercial garage, until now. The new rule requires either threaded intermediate metal conduit or threaded rigid metal conduit, but in reality the exception almost removes the entire requirement.

The exception to the new rule allows for the use of HDPE, RTRC, or PVC conduit; since these are the most commonly encountered underground raceways, it nearly makes the whole discussion moot. The requirement is that the last two ft of the underground installation must be in threaded intermediate metal conduit or rigid metal conduit, which again is the typical practice when entering a hazardous location. Strangely, this rule applies even if the garage contains no hazardous (classified) locations. As is often the case, this new requirement will probably be revised, or at least revisited, in three years.

511.8 Underground Wiring

Wiring below a commercial garage must be installed in threaded rigid metal conduit or intermediate metal conduit.

Ex: PVC, Type RTRC conduit, and Type HDPE conduit can be installed below a commercial garage if buried under not less than 2 ft. of cover. Threaded rigid metal conduit or threaded intermediate metal conduit must be used for the last 2 ft of the underground run. An equipment grounding conductor in accordance with Article 250 is required within the raceway. Figure 511–3

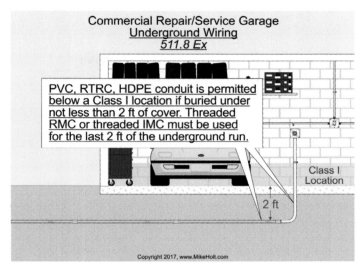

Figure 511–3

ARTICLE 514

MOTOR FUEL DISPENSING FACILITIES

Introduction to Article 514—Motor Fuel Dispensing Facilities

The portion of a facility where fuel is stored and dispensed into the fuel tanks of motor vehicles and marine craft, or into approved containers, must comply with Article 514.

What's most striking about this article is the large table that makes up about half of it. It doesn't provide any electrical requirements, list any electrical specifications, or address any electrical equipment. What this table does tell you is how to classify a motor fuel dispensing area based on the equipment contained therein. The rest of this article contains specific provisions, and refers to other articles that must be applied.

Author's Comment:

- Diesel fuel isn't a flammable liquid. Therefore, diesel dispensing equipment and associated wiring aren't required to comply with the hazardous (classified) location requirements of Article 514 [514.3(A)]. The other requirements in this article still apply, however.

514.1 Scope

This article applies to motor fuel dispensing facilities, marine/motor fuel dispensing facilities, motor fuel dispensing facilities located inside buildings, and fleet vehicle motor fuel dispensing facilities. Figure 514–1

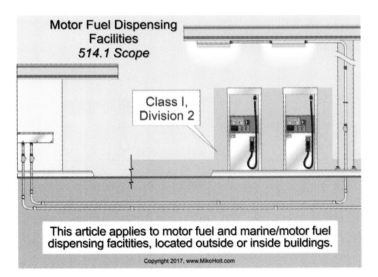

Figure 514–1

514.8 Underground Wiring

The allowance for underground nonmetallic raceways was expanded to permit HDPE conduit.

Analysis

CLARIFIED The common practice for wiring fuel dispensers is to use PVC conduit in the below-ground portion of the circuit and then transition to threaded intermediate metal conduit or rigid metal conduit for the last 10 ft of the conduit system. HDPE conduits are now also permitted in the below-ground portion meeting the requirements of the installation.

514.8 Underground Wiring

Wiring under a classified location must be installed in threaded rigid metal conduit or threaded intermediate metal conduit. Electrical conduits located below the surface of a Class I, Division 1 or 2 location, as identified in Table 514.3(B)(1) and Table 514.3(B)(2), must be sealed within 10 ft of the point of emergence above grade. Figure 514–2

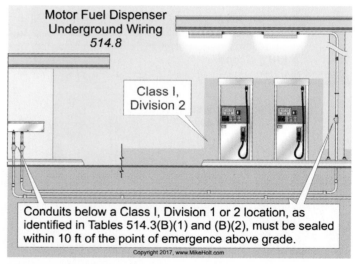

Figure 514–2

Except for listed explosionproof reducers at the raceway seal fitting, there must be no union, coupling, box, or fitting between the raceway seal fitting and the point of emergence above grade.

Ex 2: PVC, Type RTRC conduit, and Type HDPE conduit can be installed below a classified location if buried under not less than 2 ft of cover. Threaded rigid metal conduit or threaded intermediate metal conduit must be used for the last 2 ft of the underground run. An equipment grounding conductor in accordance with Article 250 is required within the raceway. Figure 514–3

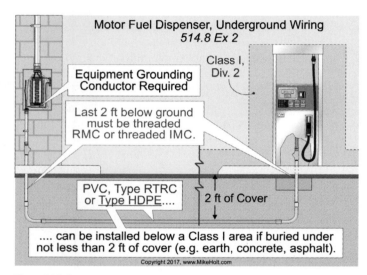

Figure 514–3

Author's Comment:

■ The underground area beneath dispensers isn't a classified location, because there isn't enough oxygen below ground to create ignition. There will be, however, a substantial amount of gasoline in the earth. Due to this, the *Code* makes requirements that act as though the underground area is classified, meaning that you must follow 514.8, even if you're just passing underneath the area without actually supplying equipment in the classified location.

514.9 Raceway Seal

The installation requirement for raceway seal fittings now matches 501.15 for boundary seals.

Analysis

 EDITED The boundary seal at a classified location ensures that gases and vapors don't migrate from the hazardous location to an unclassified location. If the gas or vapor migration were to occur, there could be catastrophic results, as the nonclassified location equipment could have a spark that would ignite the surrounding environment. Because of this concern, no fitting is permitted between the actual boundary of the classified location and the boundary seal, other than a listed explosionproof reducing bushing [501.15(A)(4) and (B)(2)].

Interestingly, previous editions of the *NEC* left out the allowance for the reducing bushing in this requirement, although it was almost certainly an oversight. If installing a reducing bushing at the boundary seal of a fuel dispenser (a very common practice) was a danger, I think we'd find a lot of gas stations blowing up.

514.9 Raceway Seal

(A) At Dispenser. A listed raceway seal must be installed in each raceway run that enters or leaves a dispenser. The raceway seal fitting <u>or listed explosionproof reducer at the seal</u> must be the first fitting after the raceway emerges from the earth's surface or concrete. Figure 514–4

(B) At Boundary. A raceway seal fitting that complies with 501.15 must be installed in each raceway run that leaves a Class I location and applies to both horizontal and vertical boundaries of the defined Class I location. Figure 514–5

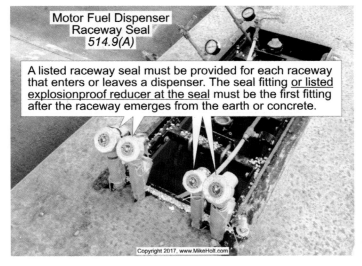

Figure 514–4

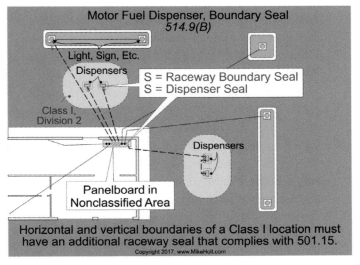

Figure 514–5

Author's Comment:

- If the boundary is beneath the ground, the sealing fitting can be installed after the raceway leaves the ground, but there must be no union, coupling, box, or fitting, other than listed explosionproof reducers at the sealing fitting in the raceway between the sealing fitting and the point at which the raceway leaves the earth's surface [501.15(A)(4) Ex 2].

514.11 Circuit Disconnects

The requirements for emergency electrical shutoff devices for fuel dispensers have been (somewhat) clarified and a new requirement was added for unattended dispensing facilities.

Analysis

CLARIFIED Shutting off the power to a fuel dispenser in the event of an emergency is certainly a requirement worth having in the *Code*, and it's almost certainly saved lives over the years.

People driving their cars into buildings and other objects are just unfortunate facts of life that often don't affect anything other than the driver's wallet. Driving into a bank of fuel dispensers, however, could be more interesting than an Independence Day fireworks display. We need to be able to shut the power off to all equipment in the area, and we need to be able do so quickly.

This isn't a new concept, and nearly all of the rules in the 2017 edition of the *NEC* were already in the 2014 edition, only now they're easier to find and less subject to debate. One new requirement is that, for unattended dispensing facilities, we need an emergency shutoff that's readily accessible to the patrons, and now we need an additional disconnect that's "readily accessible to each group of dispensing devices on an individual island." Considering the definition of "readily accessible," I'm not sure how this rule can be violated if you're satisfying the other rule for having a disconnect that's readily accessible to the patrons. The locations of the emergency shutoff and additional disconnect are in compliance with this rule as long as nobody needs to climb over or remove obstacles, use tools, or use a portable ladder to access them.

514.11 Circuit Disconnects

(A) Emergency Electrical Disconnects. Fuel dispensing systems must have a clearly identified emergency shutoff devices or disconnects installed at approved locations not less than 20 ft or more than 100 ft from the fuel dispensing devices that they serve. Figure 514–6

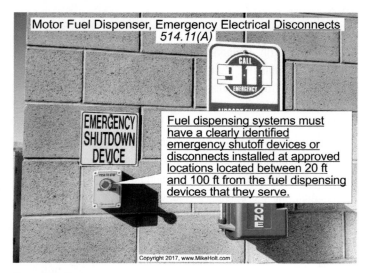

Figure 514–6

Emergency shutoff devices or disconnects must disconnect power to all dispensing devices; to all remote pumps serving the dispensing devices; to all associated power, control, and signal circuits; and to all other electrical equipment in the hazardous (classified) locations surrounding the fuel dispensing devices.

Author's Comment:

- See the definitions of "Accessible, Readily" and "Neutral Conductor" in Article 100.

(B) Attended Self-Service Stations. Attended self-service stations must have an emergency dispenser disconnect that's readily accessible to the attendant.

(C) Unattended Self-Service Stations. At unattended motor fuel dispensing facilities, the disconnects must be readily accessible to patrons and at least one additional disconnect must be readily accessible to each group of dispensing devices on an individual island.

ARTICLE
517

HEALTH CARE FACILITIES

Introduction to Article 517—Health Care Facilities

Health care facilities differ from other types of buildings in many important ways. Article 517 is primarily concerned with those parts of health care facilities where patients are examined and treated. Whether those facilities are permanent or movable, they still fall under this article. However, Article 517 wiring and protection requirements don't apply to business offices or waiting rooms. They don't apply to animal veterinary facilities either.

This article contains many specialized definitions that only apply to health care facilities. While you don't need to be able to quote these definitions, you should have a clear understanding of what the terms mean. As you study Parts II and III, keep in mind the special requirements of hospitals and why these requirements exist. The requirements in Parts II and III are highly detailed and not intuitively obvious. These are three of the main objectives of Article 517, Parts II and III:

- Maximize the physical and electromagnetic protection of wiring by requiring metal raceways.
- Minimize electrical hazards by keeping the voltage between patients' bodies and medical equipment low. This involves many specific steps, beginning with 517.11.
- Minimize the negative effects of power interruptions by establishing specific requirements for essential electrical systems.

Part IV addresses gas anesthesia stations. The primary objective of Part IV is to prevent ignition. Part V addresses X-ray installations and really has two main objectives:

- Provide adequate ampacity and overcurrent protection for the branch circuits.
- Address the safety issues inherent in high-voltage equipment installations.

Part VI provides requirements for low-voltage communications systems (twisted wire, antennas, and coaxial cable), such as fire alarms and intercoms. The primary objective there is to prevent compromising those systems with inductive couplings or other sources of interference. Part VII provides requirements for isolated power systems where the main objective is to keep them actually isolated.

Be aware that the *NEC* is just one of the standards that apply to health care locations, and there may be additional requirements from other standards and special requirements for sophisticated equipment.

Part I. General

517.1 Scope

Article 517 applies to electrical wiring in health care facilities, such as hospitals, nursing homes, limited care and supervisory care facilities, clinics, medical and dental offices, and ambulatory care facilities that provide services to human beings. Figure 517–1

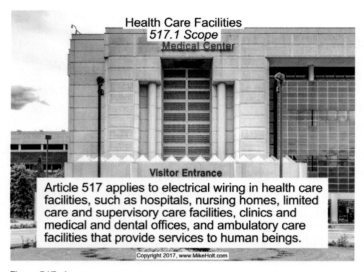

Figure 517–1

Author's Comment:

- This article doesn't apply to animal veterinary facilities.

517.2 Definitions

New definitions for "Governing Body" and "Medical Office (Dental Office)" have been added, and existing definitions for "Health Care Facility" and "Patient Care Space" have been clarified.

Analysis

NEW

Governing Body. The person or persons who have legal responsibility for the operation of a health care facility.

CLARIFIED

Health Care Facility. Most health care facilities are easily recognizable as such. When you drive by a hospital, there isn't much doubt as to what you're looking at. Mobile health care facilities are something you see every day although you may not realize it.

On large commercial construction sites where critical care is needed regularly, you can find mobile emergency care facilities (which are basically a trailer with medical facilities inside) on site to deal with the very real dangers of heat exhaustion, dehydration, heat stroke, and other medical concerns. Some other examples of mobile healthcare facilities covered by this rule are blood bank trailers, mobile radiology trailers, and mobile trauma trailers. What are the rules for the wiring in these mobile facilities? They're the same as in any other patient care space.

NEW

Medical Office (Dental Office). A new term, "Medical Office (Dental Office)" was added. These include the offices of your general care provider (doctor) and your dentist, as well an emergency clinic like an InstaCare facility (but not an emergency room). For most electricians, this is the extent of the health care wiring. An installation at a dental office or small doctor's office certainly has *Code* requirements that exceed those for other locations, but most of Article 517 really doesn't apply. Interestingly, this new definition doesn't seem to be used in the *NEC* yet so it doesn't appear to have any real value at this time.

CLARIFIED

Patient Care Space. The 2014 *Code* changed "patient care area" to "patient care space" in most locations in Article 517. Changes to this edition finish that job by using the terms correctly throughout the article, and changes in the definitions have been made for clarification. Most of the changes are in the form of Informational Notes which will help the governing body of the facility to determine the correct type of patient care space. The changes that aren't in the Notes simply clarify that caregivers aren't the only people who are considered. Other members of medical staff may not be caregivers, but could be injured due to a failure of equipment or system.

517.2 Definitions

Governing Body. The person(s) who have the overall legal responsibility for the operation of the health care facility.

Health Care Facilities. Buildings or portions of buildings, and mobile enclosures in which medical, dental, psychiatric, nursing, obstetrical, or surgical care are provided for humans.

Note: Examples of health care facilities include, but aren't limited to, hospitals, nursing homes, limited care facilities, supervisory care facilities, clinics, medical and dental offices, and ambulatory care facilities.

Hospital. A building or an area of a building used for medical, psychiatric, obstetrical, or surgical care on a 24-hour basis of four or more inpatients.

Invasive Procedure. Any procedure that penetrates the protective surfaces of a patient's body.

Nursing Home. A building or an area of a building used for the lodging, boarding, and nursing care, on a 24-hour basis, of four or more persons who, because of mental or physical incapacity, may be unable to provide for their own needs and safety without the assistance of another person.

Author's Comment:

- This includes nursing and convalescent homes, skilled nursing facilities, intermediate care facilities, and the infirmaries of homes for the aged.

Limited Care Facility. A building or an area of a building used for the housing, on a 24-hour basis, of four or more persons who are incapable of self-preservation because of age, physical limitations due to accident or illness, or limitations such as mental retardation/developmental disability, mental illness, or chemical dependency.

Medical Office (Dental Office). A building or part of building in which the following occur:

(1) Examinations and minor treatments or procedures are performed under the continuous supervision of a medical or dental professional;

(2) Only sedation or local anesthesia is involved and treatment or procedures don't render the patient incapable of self-preservation under emergency conditions; and

(3) Overnight stays for patients or 24-hour operation aren't provided.

Patient Bed Location. The location of an inpatient sleeping bed; or the bed or procedure table used in a critical care space.

Patient Care Space. Any space in a health care facility where patients are intended to be examined or treated. Figure 517–2

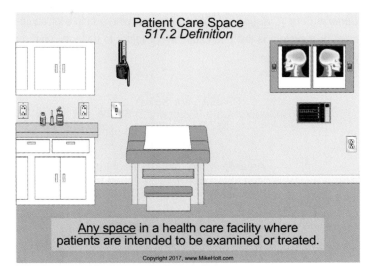

Figure 517–2

Note 1: The governing body of the facility designates patient care space in accordance with the type of patient care anticipated.

Note 2: Business offices, corridors, lounges, day rooms, dining rooms, or similar areas aren't classified as patient care space.

Basic Care (Category 3) Space. An area where failure of equipment or a system isn't likely to cause injury to the patients, staff, or visitors. Figure 517–3

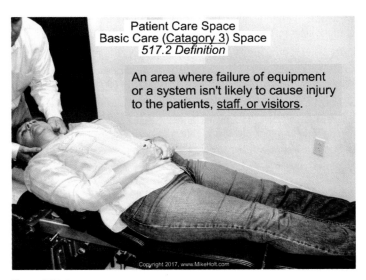

Figure 517–3

Note: Basic Care, Category 3 spaces, formerly known as basic care rooms (spaces) are typically where basic medical or dental care, treatment, or examinations are performed. Examples include, but aren't limited to, examination or treatment rooms in clinics, medical and dental offices, nursing homes, and limited care facilities.

General Care (Category 2) Space. An area where failure of equipment or a system is likely to cause minor injury to patients, staff, or visitors. Figure 517–4

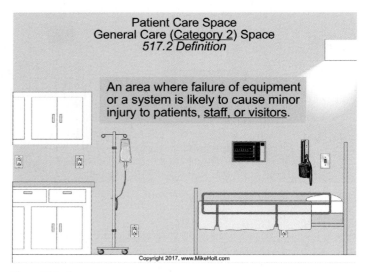

Figure 517–4

Note: General Care, Category 2 spaces were formerly known as general care rooms (spaces). Examples include, but aren't limited to patient bedrooms, in vitro fertilization rooms, procedural rooms, and similar rooms.

Critical Care (Category 1) Space. An area where failure of equipment or a system is likely to cause major injury or death to patients, staff, or visitors.

Note: Critical Care, Category 1 spaces, formerly known as critical care rooms (spaces) are typically where patients are intended to be subjected to invasive procedures and connected to line operated, patient care-related appliances. Examples include, but aren't limited to, special care patient rooms used for critical care, intensive care, and special care units such as angiography laboratories, cardiac catheterization laboratories, delivery rooms, operating rooms, post-anesthesia care units, trauma rooms, and other similar rooms.

Support (Category 4) Space. An area where failure of equipment or a system isn't likely to have a physical impact on patients, staff, or visitors.

Note: Support Category 4 spaces were formerly known as support rooms (spaces). Examples of these spaces include, but aren't limited to, anesthesia work rooms, sterile supply, laboratories, morgues, waiting rooms, utility rooms, and lounges.

Patient Care Vicinity. A space, within a location intended for the examination and treatment of patients, extending 6 ft beyond the normal location of the patient bed, chair, table, treadmill, or other device that supports the patient during examination and treatment and extending vertically to 7 ft 6 in. above the floor. Figure 517–5

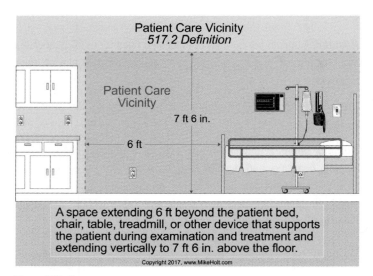

Figure 517–5

517.13 Grounding of Equipment in Patient Care Spaces

The title of this section was changed to match the rest of the article, some requirements for equipment grounding conductors (EGCs) in patient care spaces have been expanded while others are now reduced. Exception 2 of 517.13(B) was clarified and isolated ground receptacles are no longer a black hole in this rule.

Analysis

CLARIFIED

Metal Enclosures. In patient care spaces we need two equipment grounding conductors: one must be metal cable armor or a raceway type complying with 517.13(A); the other must be of the wire type installed inside the permitted wiring method in accordance with 517.13(B).

The rules for the wire-type equipment grounding conductor in 517.13(B) have been changed to add clarity. For example, in the previous version of the *NEC*, 517.13(B)(1)(2) required metal receptacle boxes to be connected to a wire-type equipment grounding conductor, but was silent on other metal enclosures! Now any metal enclosure housing electrical equipment must be connected to the equipment grounding conductor.

CLARIFIED

Luminaires. Exception 2 to 517.13(B) is one of the most misunderstood and misapplied allowances in the *Code*. In previous editions, luminaires above 7 ft 6 in., as well as switches outside the patient vicinity, only needed to comply with 517.13(A) and didn't need to satisfy 517.13(B). While that sounds great at first glance, it didn't do what most people thought it did.

In the 2014 *NEC*, after applying the exception, if you used a cable wiring method, you couldn't use traditional Type MC cable. Inspectors across the country regularly find themselves in situations where they must require thousands of feet of Type MC cable above the ceiling of a patient care space to be removed. Each time it's due to a misunderstanding of the exceptions in this section of the *Code*. The change to 517.13(B) Ex 2 will permit compliance by meeting the requirements of either 517.13(A) or (B). This means that typical MC cable can be used 7 ft 6 in. above a patient care space.

CLARIFIED

Isolated Ground Receptacles. Isolated ground (IG) receptacles have long been a problem in this section. How does a person satisfy these rules when using an IG receptacle? Up until now it was easy…you couldn't use an IG receptacle and still satisfy the letter of this section. Changes to the 2017 edition now remedy this problem by giving specific provisions for IG receptacles, but remember that their use is still quite limited by the requirements in 517.16.

517.13 Grounding of Equipment in Patient Care Spaces

Wiring in patient care <u>spaces</u> must comply with (A) and (B):

■ Patient care spaces include patient rooms as well as examining rooms, therapy areas, treatment rooms, and some patient corridors. They don't include business offices, corridors, lounges, day rooms, dining rooms, or similar areas not classified as patient care spaces [517.2].

(A) Wiring Methods. Branch circuit conductors serving patient care <u>spaces</u> must be contained in a metal raceway or cable having a metal sheath that qualifies as an equipment grounding conductor in accordance with 250.118. Figure 517–6

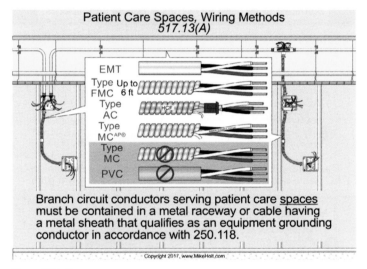

Figure 517–6

■ The metal sheath of traditional Type MC interlock cable isn't identified as an equipment grounding conductor [250.118(10)(a)], therefore this wiring method isn't permitted to be used for circuits in patient care spaces. Figure 517–7

■ The metal sheath of Type AC cable is identified as an equipment grounding conductor in 250.118(8) because it contains an internal bonding strip that's in direct contact with the metal sheath of the interlock cable. Figure 517–8 Part A

■ The metal sheath of Type MC^{AP} cable is identified as an equipment grounding conductor in 250.118(10)(a) because it contains an internal bonding strip that's in direct contact with the metal sheath of the interlock cable. Figure 517–8 Part B.

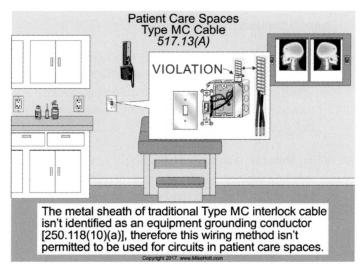

Figure 517–7

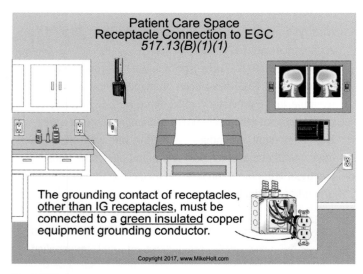

Figure 517–9

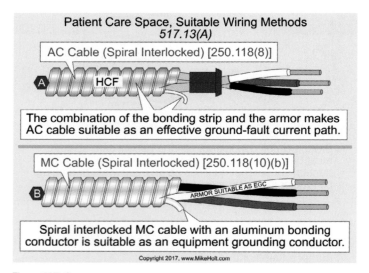

Figure 517–8

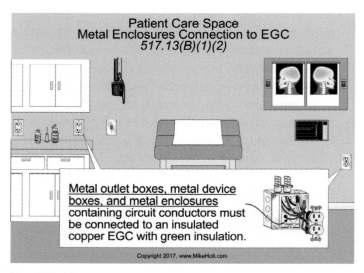

Figure 517–10

(B) Insulated Equipment Grounding Conductors and Insulated Bonding Jumpers.

(1) General. The following must be directly connected to an insulated copper equipment grounding conductor that has green insulation along its entire length and installed with the branch-circuit conductors in wiring methods as permitted in 517.13(A).

(1) The grounding contact of receptacles, other than isolated ground receptacles. Figure 517–9

(2) Metal enclosures containing circuit conductors. Figure 517–10

(3) Noncurrent-carrying conductive surfaces of fixed electrical equipment likely to become energized that are subject to personal contact, operating at over 100V. Figure 517–11

Ex 1: For other than isolated ground receptacles, an insulated equipment bonding jumper that directly connects to the equipment grounding conductor can connect the metal box and receptacle(s) to the equipment grounding conductor. Isolated ground receptacles must comply with the requirements contained in 517.16.

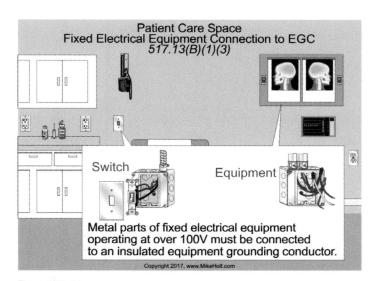

Figure 517–11

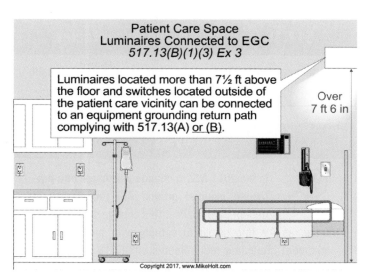

Figure 517–13

Ex 2: Metal faceplates for switches and receptacles can be connected to the equipment grounding conductor by the metal mounting screws that secure the faceplate to a metal outlet box or metal mounting yoke of switches [404.9(B)] and receptacles [406.4(C)]. Figure 517–12

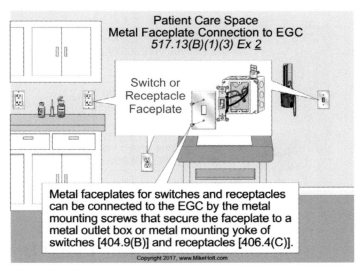

Figure 517–12

Ex 3: Luminaires located more than 7½ ft above the floor and switches located outside of the patient care vicinity are permitted to be connected to an equipment grounding return path complying with 517.13(A) or (B). Figure 517–13

(2) Sizing. Where metal receptacle boxes are used, the connection between the receptacle grounding terminal and the metal box must be copper wire sized no smaller than 12 AWG. Where receptacles and fixed electrical equipment are provided with overcurrent protection rated over 20A, equipment and bonding jumpers must be sized in accordance with 250.122, based on the rating of the overcurrent protection device. Figure 517–14

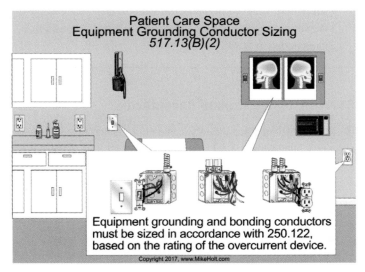

Figure 517–14

517.16 Isolated Ground Receptacles

The allowances for isolated ground receptacles in health care facilities now make sense.

Analysis

CLARIFIED

In the 2011 *NEC*, a change was made that prohibited isolated ground (IG) receptacles in patient care spaces. This change seemed warranted, as it's impossible to comply with the expanded equipment grounding requirements in 517.13 while using an IG receptacle. In fact, using an IG receptacle completely defeats the extra safety provided for in that section.

In the 2014 *Code*, IG receptacles were once again allowed in patient care spaces, but not in patient care vicinities. This change ensured that the patient reaped the safety benefits of 517.13, and allowed equipment such as computers (that aren't near the patient) to use an IG receptacle. The problem is that the language in 2014 said that the IG receptacle installation couldn't circumvent the safety afforded by 517.13…which is impossible.

A compromise has been achieved, IG receptacles can be used where they won't injure the patient, and they can be installed legally due to the removal of the preposterous language added in 2014.

517.16 Isolated Ground Receptacles

(A) Inside Patient Care Vicinity. Isolated <u>grounding</u> receptacles are permitted within the patient care space, but not within the patient care vicinity. Figure 517–15

Author's Comment:

- The patient care vicinity is a space extending 6 ft beyond the normal location of the patient bed, chair, table, treadmill, or other device that supports the patient during examination and treatment and extends vertically to 7 ft 6 in. above the floor [517.2 Definition].

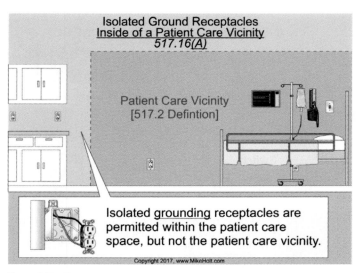

Figure 517–15

(B) Outside Patient Care Vicinity [as defined in 517.2]. Isolated grounding receptacle(s) within the patient care space [as defined in 517.2], but outside a patient care vicinity [as defined in 517.2] must comply with the following: Figure 517–16

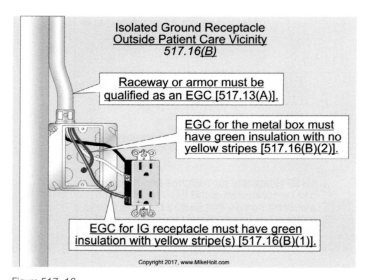

Figure 517–16

(1) The grounding terminal of isolated grounding receptacles in a patient care space must be connected to an insulated equipment grounding conductor in accordance with 250.146(D) in addition to the equipment grounding conductor paths required in 517.13(A). The equipment grounding conductor for the isolated grounding receptacle in the patient care space must have green insulation with one or more yellow stripes along its entire length.

(2) The insulated equipment grounding conductor required in 517.13(B)(1) must have green insulation with no yellow stripes and it isn't permitted to be connected to the grounding terminal of the isolated ground receptacle; the insulated equipment grounding conductor required by 517.13(B)(1) must be connected to the metal enclosure containing the receptacle as required by 517.13(B)(1)(2) and to conductive surfaces of fixed electrical equipment as required by 517.13(B)(1)(3).

Note 1: This type of installation is typically used where a reduction of electrical noise (electromagnetic interference) is necessary, and parallel grounding paths are to be avoided.

Note 2: Care should be taken in specifying a system containing isolated ground receptacles, because the grounding impedance is controlled only by the grounding wires and doesn't benefit from any conduit or building structure in parallel with the grounding path.

ARTICLE 525

CARNIVALS, CIRCUSES, FAIRS, AND SIMILAR EVENTS

Introduction to Article 525—Carnivals, Circuses, Fairs, and Similar Events

Article 525 covers the installation of portable wiring and equipment for carnivals, circuses, exhibitions, fairs, traveling attractions, and similar functions [525.1]. At first glance, a couple of questions arise, "Aren't these just like assembly occupancies?" and "Why do we need Article 525 if Article 518 covers the same thing?"

Yes, these locations are similar to assembly occupancies [Article 518], but they're not the same. In fact, there are two big differences:

- Article 525 applications are temporary, while Article 518 occupancies aren't.
- Article 518 doesn't cover amusement rides and attractions, while Article 525 does.

You may want to compare these two articles to see if you can spot other similarities and differences between them. Doing so will help you understand both articles better.

Part I. General Requirements

525.1 Scope

This article covers the installation of portable wiring and equipment for carnivals, circuses, exhibitions, fairs, traveling attractions, and similar functions. Figure 525–1

Figure 525–1

525.23 GFCI-Protected Receptacles and Equipment

GFCI devices that are part of portable cords must now be listed for portable use.

Analysis

NEW

It's long been recognized that GFCI protection is needed at carnivals, fairs, circuses, and similar events. Flexible cords are the typical method of wiring these events, and although they aren't allowed to be subject to physical damage, the real world shows that these cords often are. If the neutral in such a cord is damaged, the GFCI will no longer function...but it will fail in the closed (on) position, allowing for the potential of serious injury. GFCIs that are listed for portable use protect against the possibility of open neutrals and now they'll be required for these events if the equipment is supplied by a flexible cord.

525.23 GFCI-Protected Receptacles and Equipment

(A) GFCI Protection Required. GFCI protection is required for the following: Figure 525–2

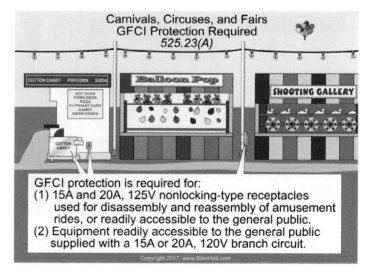

Carnivals, Circuses, and Fairs
GFCI Protection Required
525.23(A)

GFCI protection is required for:
(1) 15A and 20A, 125V nonlocking-type receptacles used for disassembly and reassembly of amusement rides, or readily accessible to the general public.
(2) Equipment readily accessible to the general public supplied with a 15A or 20A, 120V branch circuit.

Copyright 2017, www.MikeHolt.com

Figure 525–2

(1) 15A and 20A, 125V, nonlocking-type receptacles used for disassembly and reassembly of amusement rides and attractions, or readily accessible to the general public.

(2) Equipment readily accessible to the general public if it's supplied from a 15A or 20A, 120V branch circuit.

GFCI protection can be integral with the attachment plug, or located in the power-supply cord within 12 in. of the attachment plug, or listed cord set incorporating GFCI protection.

(B) GFCI Protection Not Required. GFCI protection isn't required for locking-type receptacles not accessible from grade level.

(C) GFCI protection Not Permitted. GFCI protection isn't permitted for egress lighting.

Author's Comment:

- The purpose of not permitting egress lighting to be GFCI protected is to ensure that exit lighting remains energized and stays illuminated.

(D) Receptacles Supplied by Portable Cords. Where GFCI protection is provided through the use of GFCI receptacles, and the branch circuits supplying the receptacles utilize flexible cord(s), the GFCI protection must be listed, labeled, and identified for portable use.

ARTICLE
547 AGRICULTURAL BUILDINGS

Introduction to Article 547—Agricultural Buildings

Two factors (dust and moisture) have a tremendous influence on the lifespan of agricultural equipment.

Dust gets into mechanisms and causes premature wear. But with electricity on the scene, dust adds two other dangers: fire and explosion. Dust from hay, grain, and fertilizer is highly flammable. Litter materials, such as straw, are also highly flammable. Excrement from farm animals may cause corrosive vapors that eat at mechanical equipment and wiring methods and can cause electrical equipment to fail. For these reasons, Article 547 includes requirements for dealing with dust and corrosion.

Another factor to consider in agricultural buildings is moisture, which causes corrosion. Water is present for many reasons, including wash down. Thus, this article has requirements for dealing with wet and damp environments, and also includes other rules. For example, you must install equipotential planes in all concrete floor confinement areas of livestock buildings containing metallic equipment accessible to animals and likely to become energized.

Livestock animals have a low tolerance to small voltage differences, which can cause loss of milk production and, at times, livestock fatality. As a result, the *NEC* contains specific requirements for an equipotential plane in buildings that house livestock.

547.1 Scope

Article 547 applies to agricultural buildings or to that part of a building or adjacent areas of similar nature as specified in (A) or (B). Figure 547–1

(A) Excessive Dust and Dust with Water. Buildings or areas where excessive dust and/or dust with water may accumulate, such as areas of poultry, livestock, and fish confinement systems where litter or feed dust may accumulate.

(B) Corrosive Atmosphere. Buildings or areas where a corrosive atmosphere exists, and where the following conditions exist:

(1) Poultry and animal excrement.

(2) Corrosive particles that may combine with water.

(3) Areas made damp or wet by periodic washing.

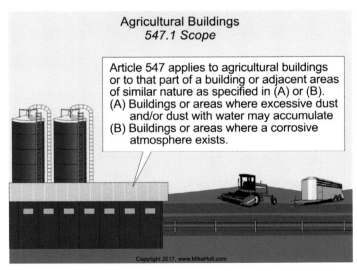

Figure 547–1

547.2 Definitions

The definition of equipotential plane was revised for accuracy.

Analysis

CLARIFIED

In previous editions of the *Code*, the definition of this term included a statement that the equipotential plane minimized voltages. Not only is that untrue, it's not possible. Installing rebar in concrete and connecting a conductor to it can't magically make neutral to earth (NEV) voltage go away. But it does reduce voltage differences between points in the equipotential plane and electrical equipment that's reachable from that plane. The rephrasing of this definition will help eliminate one of many misconceptions about grounding by removing it from the *NEC*.

547.2 Definitions

Equipotential Plane. An area where conductive elements are embedded in or placed under concrete, and bonded to the electrical system to minimize voltage differences within the plane. Figure 547–2

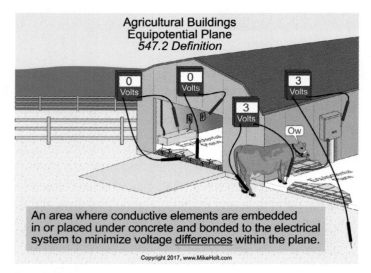

Agricultural Buildings
Equipotential Plane
547.2 Definition

An area where conductive elements are embedded in or placed under concrete and bonded to the electrical system to minimize voltage differences within the plane.

Copyright 2017, www.MikeHolt.com

Figure 547–2

MOBILE HOMES, MANUFACTURED HOMES, AND MOBILE HOME PARKS

Introduction to Article 550—Mobile Homes, Manufactured Homes, and Mobile Home Parks

Among dwelling types, mobile homes have the highest rate of fire. Article 550 addresses some of the causes of those fires with the intent of reducing these statistics.

This article recognizes that the same structures used for mobile or manufactured homes are also used for nondwelling purposes, such as construction offices or clinics [550.4(A)]. Thus, it excludes those structures from the 100A minimum service requirement.

According to the *NEC* there's a difference between a mobile home and a manufactured home, and Article 550 has different requirements for each. For example, you can't locate service equipment on a mobile home. However, you can install service equipment on a manufactured home (provided you meet seven conditions). Pay close attention to the definitions in 550.2 to help you understand the *Code* distinctions.

Mobile homes and manufactured homes aren't covered by the same building codes as a site-built home. They're covered instead by HUD standards. According to HUD, both are referred to as manufactured homes and the term "mobile home" hasn't been used for many years. This disparity between the *NEC* and industry practices can cause confusion, so read the *Code* carefully as you apply this article.

Part I. General

550.1 Scope

Article 550 covers electrical conductors and equipment installed within or on mobile and manufactured homes, conductors that connect mobile and manufactured homes to the electric supply, and the installation of electrical wiring, luminaires, and electrical equipment within or on mobile and manufactured homes. Figure 550–1

In addition, this article applies to electrical equipment related to the mobile home feeder/service-entrance conductors and service equipment as covered by Part III of this article.

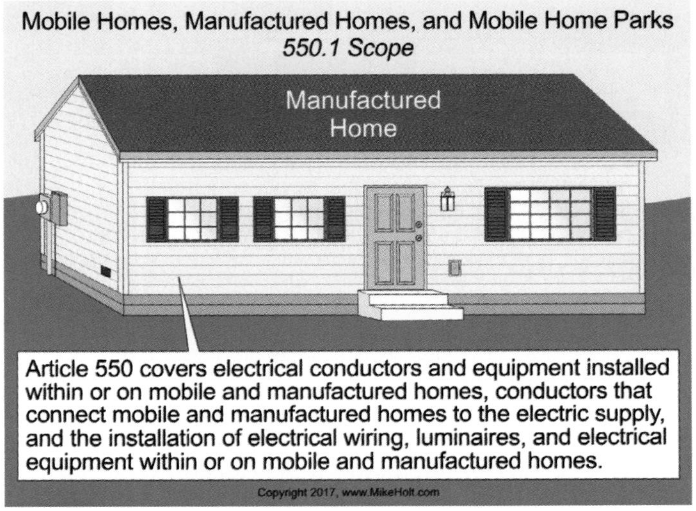

Mobile Homes, Manufactured Homes, and Mobile Home Parks
550.1 Scope

Manufactured Home

Article 550 covers electrical conductors and equipment installed within or on mobile and manufactured homes, conductors that connect mobile and manufactured homes to the electric supply, and the installation of electrical wiring, luminaires, and electrical equipment within or on mobile and manufactured homes.

Copyright 2017, www.MikeHolt.com

Figure 550–1

550.2 Definitions

The definition of a manufactured home was clarified.

Analysis

CLARIFIED

This change further clarifies that a manufactured home is still a manufactured home even when it isn't connected to utilities or air conditioning.

550.2 Definitions

Manufactured Home. A structure, in the travel mode, that's a minimum of 8 ft wide and 40 ft long built on a chassis and designed to be used as a dwelling unit with or without a permanent foundation. For the purpose of this article and unless otherwise indicated, the term "mobile home" includes manufactured homes <u>whether or not connected to the utilities, and includes the plumbing, heating, air conditioning, and electrical systems contained therein and excludes park trailers covered in 552.4</u>. Figure 550–2

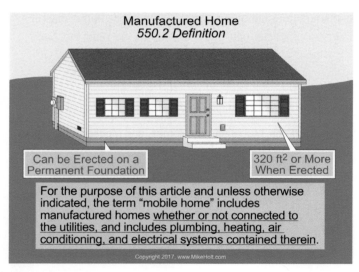

Manufactured Home
550.2 Definition

Can be Erected on a Permanent Foundation

320 ft² or More When Erected

For the purpose of this article and unless otherwise indicated, the term "mobile home" includes manufactured homes <u>whether or not connected to the utilities, and includes plumbing, heating, air conditioning, and electrical systems contained therein.</u>

Copyright 2017, www.MikeHolt.com

Figure 550–2

Author's Comment:

■ See Article 100 for the definition of "Dwelling Unit."

Mobile Home. A transportable structure built on a permanent chassis and designed to be used as a dwelling unit without a permanent foundation. In this article and unless otherwise indicated, the term "mobile home" includes manufactured homes.

Author's Comment:

■ One of the key differences between the *NEC* definitions of a manufactured home and a mobile home is that a manufactured home can be on or off a permanent foundation, while a mobile home isn't usually intended to be installed on a permanent foundation. Also, the *Code* states that a manufactured home is 8 ft or more wide and 40 ft or more long in the traveling mode. The *NEC* doesn't specify a minimum size for a mobile home.

550.13 Receptacle Outlets

Dishwashers in mobile and manufactured homes must now be GFCI protected.

Analysis

EXPANDED

GFCI protection for dwelling unit dishwashers was added as a requirement in the 2014 *Code*, but not to Article 550 for mobile and manufactured homes. This is typically the case, as most people forget that this article even exists. It appears that when rules for GFCIs in 210.8 or AFCIs in 210.12 are changed, it takes three years for the rules in this article to be changed to catch up. Language has now been added to make the requirements here the same as elsewhere in the *NEC*.

550.13 Receptacle Outlets

(B) GFCI-Protected Receptacles. 15A and 20A, 125V receptacles installed in the following locations must be GFCI protected:

(1) <u>Outdoors, including</u> compartments accessible from the outdoors. Figure 550–3

(2) Bathrooms.

(3) Kitchens, where receptacles are installed to serve countertop surfaces. Figure 550–4

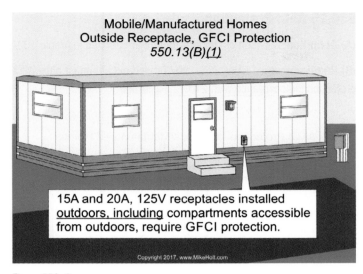

Figure 550–3

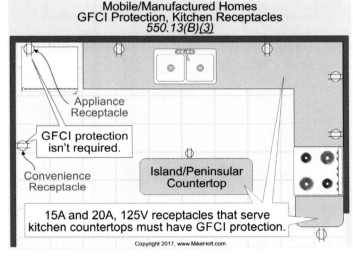

Figure 550–4

(4) Sinks where within 6 ft of the <u>outer edge of the</u> sink.

(5) <u>Dishwasher outlets</u>.

Note: See 422.5(A)(4) on GFCI protection requirements for dishwashers.

(E) Pipe Heating Cable Receptacle Outlet. Mobile and manufactured home pipe heat tape receptacle outlets must be located on the underside of the unit and

(1) Within 2 ft of the cold water inlet

(2) Connected to an interior GFCI-protected branch circuit, other than a small-appliance branch circuit

(3) On a circuit where all of the outlets are on the load side of the GFCI

(4) The pipe heating cable receptacle outlet isn't permitted to be considered as the required outdoor receptacle outlet specified in 550.13(D)(8). Figure 550–5

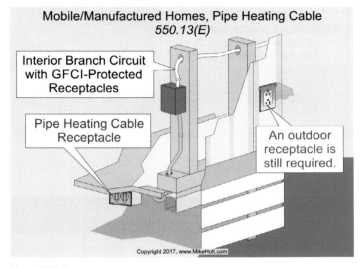

Figure 550–5

Author's Comment:

■ The purpose of connecting the pipe heating cable receptacle to an interior GFCI-protected circuit is to alert the occupants if the GFCI-protection device has opened and the pipe heating cable is no longer energized, and therefore no longer protecting the water pipes from freezing.

(F) Receptacle Outlets Not Permitted. Receptacle outlets aren't permitted in the following locations:

(1) Receptacle outlets aren't permitted to be installed within or directly over a bathtub or shower space. Figure 550–6

(2) A receptacle isn't permitted to be installed in a face-up position in any countertop.

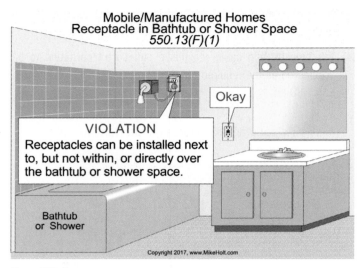

Mobile/Manufactured Homes
Receptacle in Bathtub or Shower Space
550.13(F)(1)

Okay

VIOLATION
Receptacles can be installed next to, but not within, or directly over the bathtub or shower space.

Bathtub or Shower

Copyright 2017, www.MikeHolt.com

Figure 550–6

550.25 AFCI Protection

The AFCI protection requirements for manufactured and mobile homes now mirror the rules for dwellings in 210.12.

Analysis

CLARIFIED

When thinking about AFCIs most people, myself included, think of dwelling units and Article 210. Due to this, the rules for manufactured and mobile homes are almost always three years behind the rules for dwelling units because very few people make public inputs (formerly known as *Code* change proposals) to Article 550.

In 2017 this requirement was changed to simply refer back to 210.12, meaning that every time 210.12 is revised, this section is automatically brought up to date.

There've been several proposals to do this over the years, and it seems that much of Article 550 could be deleted by passing them. As members of the Code Making Panels change, so too does their philosophy. Perhaps in a few years we won't have 11 subsections to 550.14…

550.25 AFCI Protection

(A) Definition. Arc-fault circuit interrupters are defined in Article 100.

(B) Requirements. 15A or 20A, 120V branch circuits must have AFCI protection in accordance with 210.12. Figure 550–7

AFCI Protection for Mobile/Manufactured Homes
550.25(B)

Porch

Bedroom 1 | Closet | Dining Room | Kitchen

Hallway

Bedroom 2 | Bath | Living Room

Laundry

120V branch circuits that supply 15A and 20A outlets must be protected by a listed combination AFCI breaker in accordance with 210.12.

Copyright 2017, www.MikeHolt.com

Figure 550–7

ARTICLE 555

MARINAS, BOATYARDS, AND COMMERCIAL AND NONCOMMERCIAL DOCKING FACILITIES

Introduction to Article 555—Marinas, Boatyards, and Commercial and Noncommercial Docking Facilities

Water levels aren't constant. Ocean tides rise and fall, while lakes and rivers vary in depth in response to rain. To provide power to a marina, boatyard, or docking facility, you must allow for these variations in water level between the point of use and the electric power source. Article 555 addresses this issue.

This article begins with the concept of the electrical datum plane. You might think of it as the border of a "demilitarized zone" for electrical equipment. Or, you can think of it as a line that marks the beginning of a "no man's land" where you simply don't place electrical equipment. Once you determine where this plane is, don't locate transformers, connections, or receptacles below that line.

555.1 Scope

The title of this article, its scope, and many of its provisions were changed to include residential installations.

Analysis

EXPANDED

It's not an exaggeration to say that marinas and boatyards are becoming a major problem in the electrical industry. People are swimming in these locations and they're being electrocuted or drowning due to electric shock and the subsequent inability to swim. This phenomenon is known as Electric Shock Drowning (ESD). A quick search on the Internet will find dozens of such stories.

Over the past few *Code* cycles we've seen added safety requirements for these locations as the risk of electrical hazards has become more and more apparent. While these changes certainly help, they were always inherently limited by the scope of this article, because single-family

dwelling installations were entirely exempt. One could even argue that townhouses and two-family dwellings, as well as apartment facilities weren't covered. This is no longer the case, as the scope has been expanded to include dwellings and end any argument whatsoever about the applicability to residential installations.

555.1 Scope

Article 555 covers the installation of wiring and equipment for fixed or floating piers, wharfs, docks, and other areas in marinas, boatyards, boat basins, boathouses, and similar occupancies, including <u>one-, two-, and multifamily dwellings, and residential condominiums.</u> Figure 555–1

Author's Comment:

- GFCI protection is required for outdoor 15A and 20A, 125V receptacles [210.8].

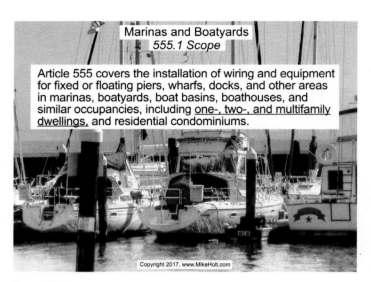

Marinas and Boatyards
555.1 Scope

Article 555 covers the installation of wiring and equipment for fixed or floating piers, wharfs, docks, and other areas in marinas, boatyards, boat basins, boathouses, and similar occupancies, including one-, two-, and multifamily dwellings, and residential condominiums.

Copyright 2017, www.MikeHolt.com

Figure 555–1

555.3 Ground-Fault Protection

The trip setting of the ground-fault protection device required in this section was reduced.

Analysis

CLARIFIED

This requirement was added to the *NEC* a few *Code* cycles ago to address the startling number of electrical injuries and deaths that have occurred around marinas and boatyards. The rule requires ground-fault protection, but not at personnel protection levels (4 to 6mA). Previous editions of the rule set the protection value at 100mA, and while that seems incredibly high, it would probably still prevent quite a few accidents. That value was lowered to 30mA in the 2017 edition of the *NEC* as a result of recommendations by the Fire Protection Research Foundation in their report titled *Assessment of Hazardous Voltage/Current in Marinas, Boatyards and Floating Buildings*. There can be no argument whatsoever that this change will increase safety, and with the number of tragedies we're seeing it's a welcome one.

Further changes were made to the language in this rule to clarify that it applies to all facilities within the scope of the article, including residential facilities.

555.3 Ground-Fault Protection

Scan this QR code for a video of Mike explaining this topic; it's a sample from the DVDs that accompany this textbook.

The overcurrent protection device(s) that supply marinas, boatyards, and commercial and noncommercial docking facilities must have ground-fault protection not exceeding 30 mA. Figure 555–2

Ground-Fault Protection
555.3

ON
60
OFF

PUSH TO TEST

The overcurrent device for the marina, boatyard, and commercial and non-commercial docking facilities must have ground-fault protection not exceeding 30 mA.

Copyright 2017, www.MikeHolt.com

Figure 555–2

555.24 Electric Shock Hazard Signage

A new section requires a warning sign at boat docks or marinas.

Analysis

NEW

This new requirement is intended to save lives. It comes from a recommendation made by the Fire Protection Research Foundation in their report titled *Assessment of Hazardous Voltage/Current in Marinas, Boatyards and Floating Buildings* to warn people of electrical hazards in the water. While this signage does nothing to remove the electrical hazard, it does the next best thing by letting people know to stay out of the water when near boat docks or marinas.

555.24 Electric Shock Hazard Signage

A permanent safety sign is required to give notice of electrical shock hazard risks to persons using or swimming near a boat dock or marina, and safety signs must meet all of the following requirements: Figure 555–3

(1) The sign must warn of the hazards using effective words, colors, or symbols or combination in accordance with 110.21(B)(1) and be of sufficient durability to withstand the environment.

(2) The signs must be clearly visible from all approaches to a marina or boatyard facility.

(3) The signs must state:

WARNING—POTENTIAL SHOCK HAZARD—
ELECTRICAL CURRENTS MAY BE PRESENT IN THE WATER

Electric Shock Hazard Sign
555.24

WARNING

POTENTIAL
SHOCK
HAZARD

ELECTRICAL CURRENT
MAY BE PRESENT
IN THE WATER

A permanent safety sign is required to give notice of electrical shock hazard risks to persons using or swimming near a boat dock or marina.

Copyright 2017, www.MikeHolt.com

Figure 555–3

ARTICLE
590 TEMPORARY INSTALLATIONS

Introduction to Article 590—Temporary Installations

It's a common misconception that temporary wiring represents a lower standard than that of other wiring. In truth, it merely meets a different standard. The same rules of workmanship, ampacity, and overcurrent protection apply to temporary installations as to others.

So, how is a temporary installation different? In one sense, it does represent a lower standard. For example, you can use Type NM cable rather than raceway-enclosed wiring without any limitations based on the type of construction, and you don't have to put splices in boxes. You must remove a temporary installation upon completion of the purpose for which it was installed. If the temporary installation is for holiday displays, it can't last more than 90 days.

Article 590 addresses the practicality and execution issues that are inherent in temporary installations, thereby making them less time consuming to install.

590.1 Scope

The requirements of Article 590 apply to temporary power and lighting installations, including power for construction, remodeling, maintenance, repair, demolition, and decorative lighting. Figure 590–1

This article also applies when temporary installations are necessary during emergencies or for tests and experiments [590.3(C)].

Author's Comment:

- Temporary wiring is only permitted for construction, remodeling, maintenance, repair, or demolition of buildings, structures, equipment, or similar activities or for emergencies and for tests, experiments, and developmental work. The temporary wiring must be removed immediately upon completion of construction or the purpose for which the wiring was installed [590.3].

- Temporary installations for trade shows must comply with Article 518, and temporary installations for carnivals, circuses, fairs, and similar events must be installed in accordance with Article 525, not Article 590.

Article 590 applies to temporary power and lighting installations, including power for construction, remodeling, maintenance, repair, demolition, and decorative lighting.

Figure 590–1

590.4 General

Changes to this section expand allowable wiring methods to include SE cable and revises rules relating to open splices on temporary wiring.

Analysis

CLARIFIED

Wiring Methods. Section 590.4(B), which covers feeders, and 590.4(C) for branch circuits were expanded to permit the use of SE cable. It seems rather odd that the 2014 *NEC* permitted Type NM cable for temporary wiring, but not Type SE cable. It was probably just an oversight, not only by the Code Making Panel but also by those that involved in the process of submitting input (proposals).

So in the 2017 *NEC*, SE cable is now allowed for temporary wiring for both feeders and branch circuits, and belowground raceways.

CLARIFIED

Open Splices. Open splices (splices outside of a box) have long been allowed on construction sites, but new changes to the 2017 *Code* now allow them anywhere! That's right, if you want to splice the cord feeding the holiday lighting at your house you can now do so since this rule no longer applies solely to construction sites. Open splices are allowed for nonmetallic cords or cables provided the equipment grounding conductor's continuity is maintained. If the cables are metallic, the metal sheath must be secured in a manner that ensures an effective ground-fault current path.

590.4 General

(A) Services. Services must be installed in accordance with Parts I through VIII of Article 230, as applicable.

(B) Feeders. Open conductors aren't permitted; however, cable assemblies, and hard usage and extra-hard usage cords, <u>and the following wiring methods are permitted:</u>

(1) Type NM and Type <u>SE cables</u>, exposed or concealed, can be used for temporary power in any building, without any height limitations based on the type of construction. Figure 590–2

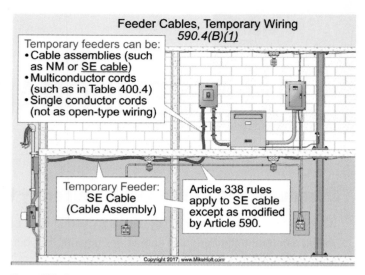

Feeder Cables, Temporary Wiring
590.4(B)(1)

Temporary feeders can be:
• Cable assemblies (such as NM or SE cable)
• Multiconductor cords (such as in Table 400.4)
• Single conductor cords (not as open-type wiring)

Temporary Feeder: SE Cable (Cable Assembly)

Article 338 rules apply to SE cable except as modified by Article 590.

Copyright 2017, www.MikeHolt.com

Figure 590–2

(2) Type SE cable is permitted to be installed within an underground raceway.

(C) Branch Circuits. Open conductors aren't permitted; however, cable assemblies, hard usage and extra-hard usage cords, <u>and the following wiring methods are permitted:</u>

(1) Type NM and Type <u>SE cables</u>, exposed or concealed, can be used for temporary power in any building, without any height limitations based on the type of construction. Figure 590–3

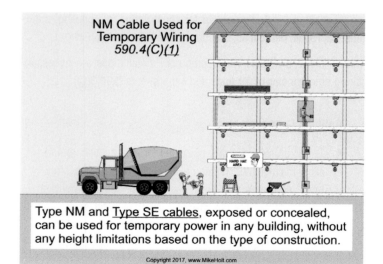

NM Cable Used for Temporary Wiring
590.4(C)(1)

HARD HAT AREA

Type NM and <u>Type SE cables</u>, exposed or concealed, can be used for temporary power in any building, without any height limitations based on the type of construction.

Copyright 2017, www.MikeHolt.com

Figure 590–3

(2) Type SE cable is permitted to be installed within an underground raceway.

(D) Receptacles.

(1) Receptacles on Lighting Circuit. On a construction site, receptacles aren't permitted to be placed on a branch circuit that supplies temporary lighting. Figure 590–4

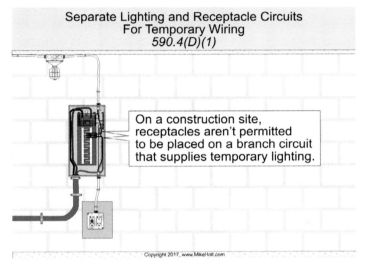

Figure 590–4

Author's Comment:

- This requirement is necessary so that illumination is maintained, even when the receptacle's GFCI-protection device opens.

(2) Receptacles in Wet Locations. 15A and 20A receptacles installed in a wet location must be within an enclosure that's weatherproof when an attachment plug is inserted. The outlet box hood must be listed for "extra-duty" use, and all nonlocking-type 15A and 20A, 125V and 250V receptacles in a wet location must be listed as weather resistant [406.9(B)(1)]. Figure 590–5

(E) Disconnecting Means. Ungrounded conductors of a multiwire branch circuit must have a disconnect at the power outlet or panelboard that opens all of the ungrounded conductors simultaneously. Individual single-pole circuit breakers with handle ties identified for the purpose, or a breaker with common internal trip, can be used for this application [240.15(B)(1)]. Figure 590–6

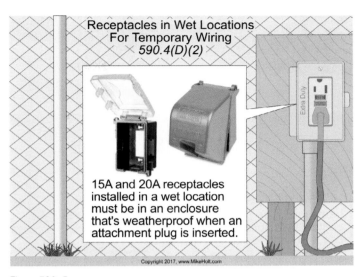

Figure 590–5

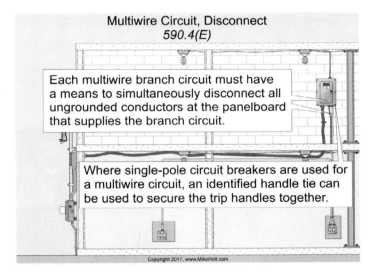

Figure 590–6

Author's Comment:

- See the definition of "Panelboard" in Article 100.

- For additional multiwire branch-circuit requirements, see 210.4 and 300.13(B).

(F) Lamp Protection. Lamps (bulbs) must be protected from accidental contact by a suitable luminaire or by the use of a lampholder with a guard. Figure 590–7

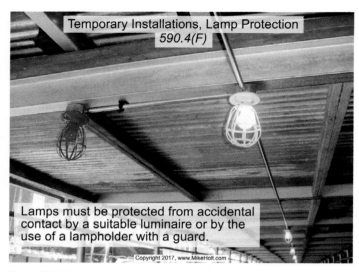

Figure 590–7

(G) Splices. A box isn't required for splices or junction connections where:

(1) The circuit conductors are from nonmetallic multiconductor cord or cable assemblies, provided that the equipment grounding continuity is maintained with or without the box. Figure 590–8

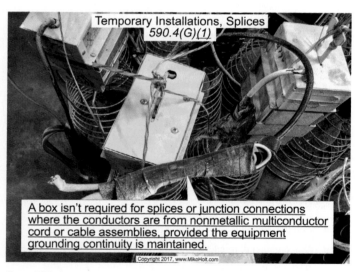

Figure 590–8

(2) The circuit conductors are from metal-sheathed cable assemblies terminated in listed fittings that mechanically secure the cable sheath maintaining effective electrical continuity.

(H) Protection from Accidental Damage. Cables and flexible cords must be protected from accidental damage and from sharp corners and projections. Protection must also be provided when cables and flexible cords pass through doorways or other pinch points.

(J) Support. Cable assemblies and flexible cords must be supported at intervals that ensure protection from physical damage. Support must be in the form of staples, cable ties, straps, or other similar means designed not to damage the cable or flexible cord assembly. Flexible cords, other than extension cords, aren't permitted on the floor or the ground when they're used as branch circuits or feeders. Figure 590–9

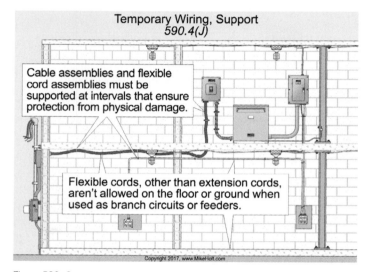

Figure 590–9

Author's Comment:

- The support requirement for temporary cables is determined by the authority having jurisdiction, based on the jobsite conditions [590.2(B)].

Vegetation isn't permitted to be used for the support of overhead branch circuit or feeder conductors. Figure 590–10

Ex: Vegetation can be used to support decorative lighting if strain-relief devices, tension take-up devices, or other means approved by the authority having jurisdiction are used to prevent damage to conductors from the movement of the live vegetation.

Vegetation-Supported Temporary Wiring
590.4(J)

Figure 590–10

590.6 Ground-fault Protection for Personnel

New allowances permit listed cord sets or devices with GFCI protection in addition to the required GFCI protection for personnel, and now permit "special purpose GFCIs" for receptacles.

Analysis

NEW

GFCI protection has been required for receptacles other than those rated 15A, 20A, and 30A, 125V for quite some time now. The only alternative to this has been the assured equipment grounding conductor program. New to the 2017 *NEC* is an allowance for "special purpose GFCIs."

Special purpose GFCIs are classified as Class C, D, or E, and they trip at 20mA instead of the 6mA of a Class A GFCI. Although special purpose GFCIs trip at a higher current value than Class A GFCIs, they still provide protection due to the speed at which they open the circuit during a ground fault.

Remember that the severity of an electric shock is dependent on two things: the amount of current and the length of time the victim is exposed to it. For example, 75mA for 0.50 seconds will typically send the victim into ventricular fibrillation. 20mA for a very short period of time is still considered safe.

590.6 Ground-fault Protection for Personnel

(A) Receptacle Outlets. Ground-fault protection for personnel is required for temporary wiring used for construction, remodeling, maintenance, repair, or demolition of buildings, structures, or equipment.

(1) Receptacles Not Part of Permanent Wiring. 15A, 20A, and 30A, 125V and 125/250V, single-phase receptacles that aren't part of the permanent wiring of the building or structure and that are in use by personnel must be GFCI protected. In addition to the required GFCI protection for personnel, listed cord sets or devices incorporating listed ground-fault circuit-interrupter protection for personnel identified for portable use are permitted. Figure 590–11

Receptacles Not Part of
Permanent Wiring
Temporary Power
590.6(A)(1)

15A, 20A, and 30A, 125V receptacles not part of permanent wiring used must be GFCI protected.

In addition the required GFCI protection, listed cord sets or adapters with listed GFCI protection are permitted.

Figure 590–11

(2) Receptacle Outlets Existing or Installed as Permanent Wiring. GFCI protection is required for all 15A, 20A, and 30A, 125V receptacle outlets that are installed or existing as part of the permanent wiring of the building.

Listed flexible cord sets or devices that incorporate listed GFCI protection can be used to meet this requirement. Figure 590–12

(3) Portable Generators. GFCI protection is required for all 15A, 20A, and 30A, 125/250V receptacles that are part of a portable generator rated not greater than 15 kW. Figure 590–13

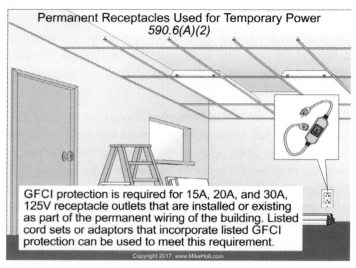

Permanent Receptacles Used for Temporary Power
590.6(A)(2)

GFCI protection is required for 15A, 20A, and 30A, 125V receptacle outlets that are installed or existing as part of the permanent wiring of the building. Listed cord sets or adaptors that incorporate listed GFCI protection can be used to meet this requirement.

Copyright 2017, www.MikeHolt.com

Figure 590–12

Portable Generator, 15 kW or Less
GFCI Protection of Receptacles
590.6(A)(3)

All 125V and 125/250V, single-phase, 15A, 20A, and 30A rated receptacles that are part of a 15 kW or smaller portable generator must be GFCI protected.

Copyright 2017, www.MikeHolt.com

Figure 590–13

(B) Other Receptacles. For temporary wiring installations, receptacles, other than those covered by 590.6(A)(1) through (A)(3) that supply temporary power used by personnel during construction, remodeling, maintenance, repair, or demolition of buildings, structures, equipment, or similar activities must be GFCI protected in accordance with 590.6(B)(1), (B)(2), or utilize the assured equipment grounding conductor program in accordance with 590.6(B)(3). Figure 590–14

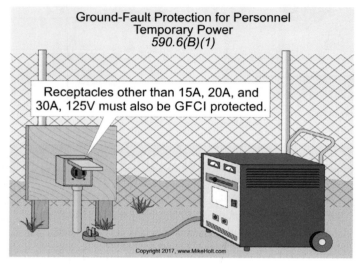

Ground-Fault Protection for Personnel
Temporary Power
590.6(B)(1)

Receptacles other than 15A, 20A, and 30A, 125V must also be GFCI protected.

Copyright 2017, www.MikeHolt.com

Figure 590–14

(1) GFCI Protection. Ground-fault circuit-interrupter (GFCI) protection for personnel.

(2) SPGFCI Protection. Special purpose ground-fault circuit-interrupter protection for personnel.

Introduction to Chapter 6—Special Equipment

Chapter 6, which covers special equipment, is the second of four *NEC* chapters that deal with special topics. Chapters 5 and 7 focus on special occupancies, and special conditions respectively. Remember, the first four chapters of the *Code* are sequential and form a foundation for each of the subsequent four. Chapter 8 covers communications systems (twisted wire, antennas, and coaxial cable) and isn't subject to the requirements of Chapters 1 through 7 except where the requirements are specifically referenced in Chapter 8. What exactly is "Special Equipment"? It's equipment that, by the nature of its use, construction, or by its unique nature creates a need for additional measures to ensure the "safeguarding of people and property" mission of the *NEC*, as stated in Article 90. The *Code* groups the articles in this chapter logically, as you might expect. Here are the general groupings:

- Prefabricated items that are assembled in the field. Articles 600 through 605. These are signs, manufactured wiring systems, and office furnishings.
- Lifting equipment. Articles 610 and 620. Cranes, hoists, elevators, dumbwaiters, wheelchair lifts, and escalators are included.
- Electric vehicle charging systems. Article 625.
- Electric welders. Article 630.
- Equipment for creating or processing information. Article 645 covers computers (information technology) and Article 646 pertains to portable (modular) data centers.
- X-ray equipment. Article 660.
- Process and production equipment. Articles 665 through 675. Induction heaters, electrolytic cells, electroplating, and irrigation machines are included.
- Swimming Pools, Spas, Hot Tubs, Fountains, and Similar Installations. Article 680.
- "New Energy" Technologies. Article 690 covers solar PV systems, Article 692 addresses fuel cells, and Article 694 pertains to small wind systems.
- Fire pumps. Article 695.

Author's Comment:

- The NFPA also produces a fire pump standard. It's NFPA 20, *Standard for the Installation of Stationary Pumps for Fire Protection.*

- **Article 600—Electric Signs and Outline Lighting.** This article covers the installation of conductors and equipment for electric signs and outline lighting as defined in Article 100. Electric signs and outline lighting include all products and installations that utilize neon tubing, such as signs, decorative elements, skeleton tubing, or art forms.

- **Article 604—Manufactured Wiring Systems.** Article 604 covers field-installed manufactured wiring systems used for branch circuits, remote-control circuits, signaling circuits, and communications circuits in accessible areas. The components of a listed manufactured wiring system can be assembled at the jobsite.

- **Article 620—Elevators, Escalators, and Moving Walks.** This article covers electrical equipment and wiring used in connection with elevators, dumbwaiters, escalators, moving walks, wheelchair lifts, and stairway chair lifts.

- **Article 625—Electric Vehicle Charging System.** An electrically-powered vehicle needs a dedicated charging circuit. And that's where Article 625 comes in. It provides the requirements for the electrical equipment needed to charge automotive-type electric and hybrid vehicles, including cars, bikes, and buses.

- **Article 640—Audio Signal Processing, Amplification, and Reproduction Equipment.** Article 640 covers equipment and wiring for audio signal generation, recording, processing, amplification and reproduction, distribution of sound, public address, speech input systems, temporary audio system installations, and electronic musical instruments such as electric organs, electric guitars, and electronic drums/percussion.

- **Article 645—Information Technology Equipment.** This article applies to equipment, power-supply wiring, equipment interconnecting wiring and grounding of information technology equipment and systems, including terminal units in an information technology equipment room.

- **Article 680—Swimming Pools, Spas, Hot Tubs, Fountains, and Similar Installations.** This article covers the installation of electric wiring and equipment that supplies swimming, wading, therapeutic and decorative pools, fountains, hot tubs, spas, and hydromassage bathtubs, whether permanently installed or storable.

- **Article 690—Solar Photovoltaic (PV) Systems.** Article 690 focuses on reducing the electrical hazards that may arise from installing and operating a solar PV system, to the point where it can be considered safe for property and people. The requirements of the *NEC* Chapters 1 through 4 apply to these installations, except as specifically modified by Article 690.

Author's Comment:

- The extent of Article 690 Solar PV systems is beyond the scope of this textbook and is included in a separate book, *Understanding NEC Requirements for Solar Photovoltaic Systems*. As the solar market continues to grow, the rules governing installations continue to evolve. Whether you're a designer, service contractor, installer, inspector, or instructor, you need to understand the *Code* requirements for solar installations. Mike's textbook and DVDs will give you the edge. His writing style, combined with the hundreds of instructional graphics, will help you better understand the *NEC* safety requirements and how they should be applied. The DVDs feature Mike and a panel of world-renowned solar experts who break down the rules and clarify their intent. To get your copy, visit www.MikeHolt.com/17Solar, or call 888.632.2633.

- **Article 695—Fire Pumps.** This article covers the electric power sources and interconnecting circuits for electric motor-driven fire pumps. It also covers switching and control equipment dedicated to fire pump drivers. Article 695 doesn't apply to sprinkler system pumps in one- and two-family dwellings or to pressure maintenance (jockey) pumps.

ARTICLE
600

ELECTRIC SIGNS AND OUTLINE LIGHTING

Introduction to Article 600—Electric Signs and Outline Lighting

One of the first things you'll notice when entering a strip mall is that there's a sign for every store. Every commercial occupancy needs a form of identification, and the standard method is the electric sign; thus, 600.5 requires a sign outlet for the entrance of each tenant location. Article 600 requires a disconnect within sight of a sign unless it can be locked in the open position.

Author's Comment:

- Article 100 defines an electric sign as any "fixed, stationary, or portable self-contained, electrically illuminated utilization equipment with words or symbols designed to convey information or attract attention."

Another requirement is height. Freestanding signs, such as those that might be erected in a parking lot, must be located at least 14 ft above vehicle areas unless they're protected from physical damage.

Neon art forms or decorative elements are subsets of electric signs and outline lighting. If installed and not attached to an enclosure or sign body, they're considered skeleton tubing for the purpose of applying the requirements of Article 600. However, if that neon tubing is attached to an enclosure or sign body, which may be a simple support frame, it's considered a sign or outline lighting subject to all of the provisions that apply to signs and outline lighting, such as 600.3, which requires the product to be listed.

600.1 Scope

Retrofit kits for signs are now covered by this article.

Analysis

CLARIFIED A retrofit kit is typically used to convert an incandescent or fluorescent luminaire into an LED luminaire. These retrofit kits have been discussed in Article 410 and even in Article 600, although the scope of 600 was silent on the issue. By including them in the scope of Article 600, it's clear that retrofit kits are covered in this article.

It's important to note that we're talking about retrofit kits. You can't just buy an LED driver, some wires, and an LED module to create your own LED light or electric sign. You need to use a listed retrofit kit, not just listed components [600.3].

600.1 Scope

Article 600 covers the installation of conductors, equipment, and field wiring for electric signs and outline lighting, <u>retrofit kits</u> including neon tubing for signs, decorative elements, skeleton tubing, or art forms. Figure 600–1

Figure 600–1

Author's Comment:

- Outline lighting is an arrangement of incandescent lamps or electric-discharge lighting to outline or call attention to certain features, such as the shape of a building or the decoration of a window [Article 100]. Figure 600–2

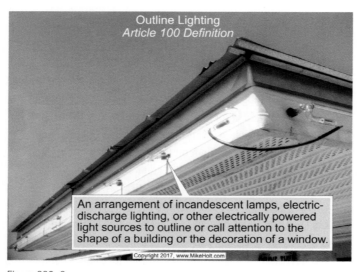

Figure 600–2

Note: Sign and outline lighting systems can include cold cathode neon tubing, high-intensity discharge lamps (HID), fluorescent or incandescent lamps, light emitting diodes (LEDs), and electroluminescent and inductance lighting.

600.2 Definitions

A new definition for "Photovoltaic (PV) Powered Sign" was added.

Analysis

NEW Yes, it says just what you think it should say, but definitions are important and they're necessary. A PV powered sign is one that's powered by a PV source, either as a stand-alone system or as an interactive system. A new section 600.34 was added as well, providing the requirements for these PV powered signs, which must also be listed in accordance with 600.3.

600.2 Definitions

Photovoltaic (PV) Powered Sign. A sign powered by an off-grid stand-alone, on-grid interactive, or non-grid interactive <u>Solar PV system</u>. Figure 600–3

Figure 600–3

Section Sign. A sign or outline lighting system that requires field-installed wiring between the subassemblies which can be physically joined or installed as separate remote parts of an overall sign. Figure 600–4

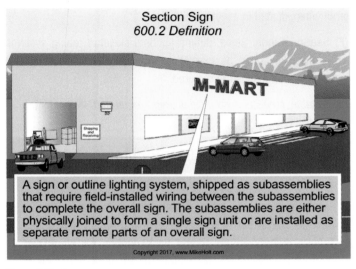

Figure 600–4

Skeleton Tubing. Neon tubing serving as a sign or outline lighting when not attached to an enclosure. Figure 600–5

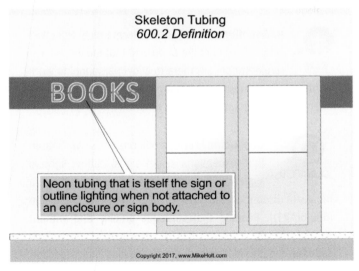

Figure 600–5

Analysis

EXPANDED Testing and subsequent listing of products ensures that a product is safe. This concept is well over 100 years old. It's such a well understood and accepted concept that not one single comment was made to reject this new requirement. In fact, many people probably thought it was already a *Code* rule, as a listing requirement for products, especially wiring methods, is something that we've just come to expect.

600.3 Listing

Fixed, mobile, or portable electric signs, section signs, outline lighting, PV powered signs, and retrofit kits, regardless of voltage, must be listed and installed in accordance with the installation instructions, except as permitted in (A) or (B). Figure 600–6

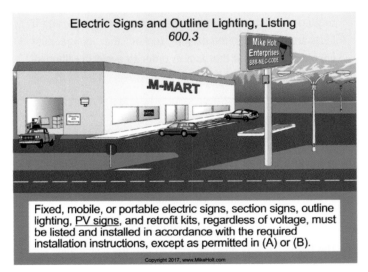

Figure 600–6

(A) Field-Installed Skeleton Tubing. Field-installed skeleton tubing isn't required to be listed.

(B) Outline Lighting. Field-installed outline lighting isn't required to be listed if it consists of listed luminaires wired in accordance with Chapter 3.

600.4 Markings

A requirement was added for signage to be listed, and marked with the manufacturer's information as well as input voltage and current. A section covering retrofitted signs was added.

Analysis

NEW

Electric signs come with their own unique hazards, including secondary conductors that operate at very high voltages. If someone finds themselves working on an electric sign, they need to know if the sign has been changed from its original installation so they can assess any new hazards that might not have existed before the retrofit. For example, if a facility maintenance worker replaced an LED lamp with a fluorescent lamp, it could result in an explosion.

This sign must notify service personnel that it's been retrofitted, it must contain the installer's name or logo, and if LEDs are installed at the existing sockets, the signage must specifically indicate that fact in order to avoid the dangerous situation described above.

600.4 Markings

(A) Signs and Outline Lighting Systems. Signs and outline lighting systems must be <u>listed and</u> marked with the manufacturer's name, trademark, or other means of identification.

(B) <u>Signs with a Retrofitted Illumination System.</u>

(1) <u>The retrofitted sign must be marked that the illumination system has been replaced.</u>

(2) <u>The marking must include the kit provider's and installer's name, logo, or unique identifier.</u>

(3) <u>Signs equipped with tubular light-emitting diode lamps powered by the existing sign sockets must have an additional warning label(s) alerting personnel during relamping that the sign has been modified and that fluorescent lamps aren't to be used.</u>

(D) Marking Visibility. The marking and listing labels required in 600.4(A) aren't required to be visible after installation, but must be visible during servicing.

(E) Durability. Marking must be permanent, durable, and weatherproof when located in a wet location.

(F) Section Signs. Signs, outline lighting, skeleton tubing systems and retrofit kits must be marked to indicate that field wiring and installation instructions are required.

Ex: Portable, cord-connected signs aren't required to be marked.

600.6 Disconnecting Means

Several changes have been made to the disconnect requirement for signs, including adding an Informational Note to express the intent of the rule, clarifying which conductors require disconnection, adding an exception for signs that contain a panelboard, indicating the location and type of warning sign in instances where the disconnect is remote, and adding an exception for the controller disconnect.

Analysis

NEW

Informational Note. A new Informational Note was added to remind the *Code* user that the disconnect requirements are there to allow personnel to work on the equipment without having to worry about someone energizing the circuit during that time.

CLARIFIED

Conductor. Previous editions of the *NEC* stated that (exceptions aside) signs, outline lighting systems, or skeleton tubing must have a means of disconnect that opened all of the wiring to the sign [600.6(A)(1)]. Reading that sentence quickly and without careful thought, it seems this is what several other *Code* sections require. A literal reading; however, indicated that the disconnect must open not only the ungrounded conductors, but the neutral and equipment grounding conductors as well! Now it's clear that the disconnect should open just the ungrounded conductors.

Signs Containing Panelboards. If a sign contains a panelboard, the panelboard itself can act as a disconnect of sorts, as it allows the worker to de-energize the circuit(s) on which he or she needs to work. This results in a safe situation if we're working on the branch circuits within the sign, but some workers might not realize that shutting off the breakers, or even a main breaker in the panelboard, doesn't shut off the panelboard itself. When this type of installation is encountered, a label must be placed to warn interested parties that the raceway feeding the panelboard contains energized conductors.

Warning signs. Like many other *Code* rules, the disconnecting means for a sign or outline lighting system must be within sight of the equipment [600.6(A)(2)]. If that condition isn't met, the disconnect must be lockable in accordance with 110.25.

Location Marking. New to this edition of the *NEC* is a requirement to tell workers where the sign disconnect is located if a disconnect isn't within sight of the sign. This seems like a reasonable requirement. The worker arrives to work on the sign and realizes it has no disconnect. Obviously there's a remote disconnect, but if the person doesn't know where it is, they might work on the sign while it's energized, defeating the entire purpose of the disconnect in the first place.

Controller Disconnect. A new exception allows the controller disconnect to be located remote from the controller [600.6(A)(3) Ex]. If this new exception is used, labels indicating the location of the disconnect are required, similar to the rule discussed above in 600.6(A)(2).

600.6 Disconnecting Means

Each circuit for a sign, outline lighting system, or skeleton tubing must be controlled by an externally-operable switch or circuit breaker that will open all ungrounded conductors. Figure 600–7

Where the circuit is a multiwire branch circuit, the switch or circuit breaker must open all ungrounded conductors of the circuit simultaneously in accordance with 210.4(B).

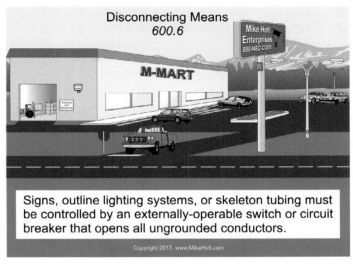

Signs, outline lighting systems, or skeleton tubing must be controlled by an externally-operable switch or circuit breaker that opens all ungrounded conductors.

Figure 600–7

Note: The location of the disconnect is intended to allow service or maintenance personnel local control of the disconnecting means.

(A) Location. The disconnect must be located in accordance with 600.6(A)(1), (A)(2), and (A)(3).

(1) At the Point of Entrance to a Sign. The disconnect must be located at the point where the conductors for a sign or outline lighting system enter a sign enclosure, sign body, or pole in accordance with 600.5(C)(3), and it must open all ungrounded conductors of the circuit. Figure 600–8

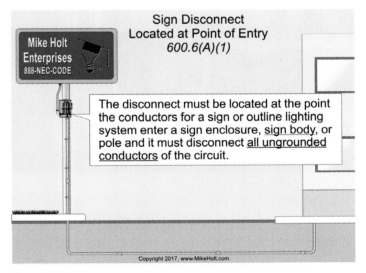

The disconnect must be located at the point the conductors for a sign or outline lighting system enter a sign enclosure, sign body, or pole and it must disconnect all ungrounded conductors of the circuit.

Figure 600–8

Ex 1: The disconnect isn't required for conductors that pass through a sign in a Chapter 3 raceway or metal-jacketed cable identified for the location.

Ex 2: A disconnect isn't required for circuits that supply an internal panelboard in a sign enclosure or sign body if the circuit conductors are enclosed in a Chapter 3 raceway or metal-jacketed cable identified for the location. A permanent field-applied warning label having sufficient durability to withstand the environment involved and comply with 110.21(B), and visible during servicing must be applied to the raceway or metal cable at or near the point of circuit conductor entry into the sign enclosure or sign body and read:

DANGER THIS RACEWAY CONTAINS
ENERGIZED CONDUCTORS

The warning label must identify the location of the disconnect for the energized circuit conductors. The disconnect must be capable of being locked in the open position lockable with provisions for locking to remain in place whether the lock is installed or not [110.25].

(2) Within Sight of the Sign. The disconnect must be within sight of the sign or outline lighting system it controls. Figure 600–9

Figure 600–9

If the disconnect is out of the line of sight from any section of the sign or outline lighting able to be energized, the disconnect must be lockable with provisions for locking to remain in place whether the lock is installed or not [110.25].

A permanent field-applied warning label, having sufficient durability to withstand the environment involved and complying with 110.21(B), that identifies the location of the disconnect is required on the sign at a location visible during servicing. Figure 600–10

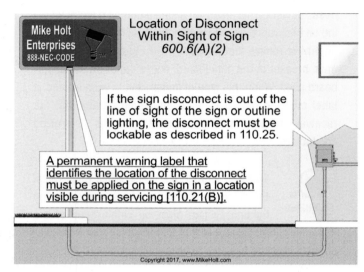

Figure 600–10

> **Author's Comment:**
>
> - According to Article 100, "within sight" means that it's visible and not more than 50 ft from one to the other.

(3) Within Sight of the Controller. Signs or outline lighting systems operated by electronic or electromechanical controllers located external to the sign or outline lighting system must have the disconnect installed in accordance with (1) through (3):

(1) Be located within sight of or in the same enclosure with the controller.

(2) Be capable of disconnecting the sign or outline lighting and the controller from all ungrounded supply conductors.

(3) Be lockable with provisions for locking to remain in place whether the lock is installed or not [110.25]. Figure 600–11

Ex: Where the disconnect isn't within sight of the controller, a permanent field-applied warning label having sufficient durability to withstand the environment involved and complying with 110.21(B), must be applied to the controller at a location visible during servicing identifying the location of the disconnect.

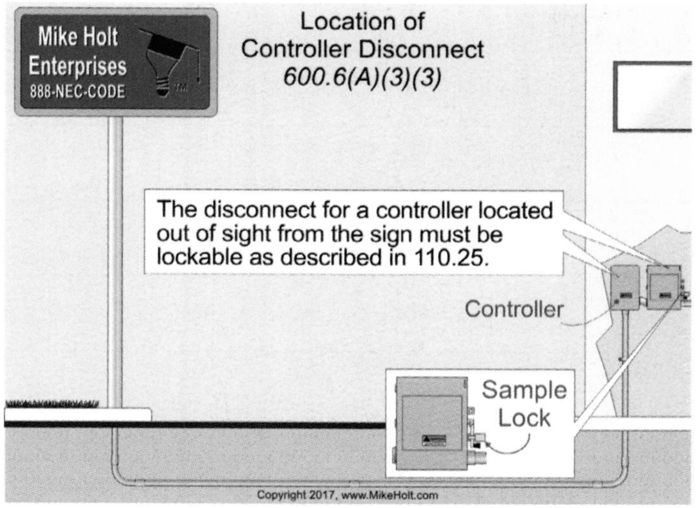

Location of
Controller Disconnect
600.6(A)(3)(3)

The disconnect for a controller located out of sight from the sign must be lockable as described in 110.25.

Controller

Sample
Lock

Copyright 2017, www.MikeHolt.com

Figure 600–11

600.24 Class 2 Power Sources

A clarification to requirements for the grounding and bonding of Class 2 power sources has been made.

Analysis

CLARIFIED

Previous editions of the *Code* required the metal parts of signs and outline lighting systems supplied from a Class 2 power source to be connected to an equipment grounding conductor. This makes no sense due to the fact that a Class 2 power source is ungrounded and there's no equipment grounding conductor for the required connection.

The 2017 *NEC* clarifies that it's the metal parts of the Class 2 power source that need to be connected to the circuit supplying power to the Class 2 power source.

600.24 Class 2 Power Sources

(A) Listing. Class 2 power supplies and power sources must be listed for use with electric signs and outline lighting systems or be a component in a listed sign.

(B) Grounding. Metal parts of the Class 2 power sources must be connected to the circuit equipment grounding conductor supplying the power source.

600.34 Photovoltaic (PV) Powered Sign

A new section was added to address the installation requirements for PV powered signs.

Analysis

NEW

As solar PV technology improves, more and more applications for where it can be used are popping up. One area that's seen huge growth in the use of PV is the sign industry. Whether it's a billboard or a traffic control sign, PV is finding its way into about every type of application. Rather than reinvent the wheel, this section gives you a few basic guidelines and points you to 690.

600.34 Photovoltaic (PV) Powered Sign

Field wiring of PV installation must be in accordance with Article 690 and sign installation instructions and the following:

(A) Equipment. PV components intended for use in PV powered sign systems must be listed for PV use.

(B) Wiring. Wiring external to the PV sign body must be:

(1) Listed, labeled, and suitable for photovoltaic applications

(2) Routed to closely follow the sign body or enclosure

(3) As short as possible and secured at intervals not exceeding 3 ft

(4) Protected where subject to physical damage

(C) Flexible Cords. Flexible cords must comply with Article 400, be identified as extra hard usage, rated for outdoor use, and water and sunlight resistant.

(D) Grounding. Grounding must comply with Article 690, Part V and 600.7.

(E) Disconnecting Means. The PV system disconnect must comply with Article 690, Part V, and 600.6.

(F) Battery Compartments. Battery compartments must require a tool to open.

MANUFACTURED WIRING SYSTEMS

Introduction to Article 604—Manufactured Wiring Systems

Article 604 applies to field-installed manufactured wiring systems, while Article 605 applies to relocatable partitions. In both cases, you're installing and/or assembling prewired components or subassemblies. These normally come with manufacturer's instructions, so *Code* compliance is almost automatic if you follow those instructions. However, you still need to:

- Compare the instructions against of Article 604 or Article 605, as appropriate.
- Use the proper connections.
- Apply the correct branch-circuit protection.
- Apply proper mechanical support to the electrical components, cords, and connectors.

The specific requirements contained in this article aren't difficult to understand, but you should be familiar with them before installing manufactured wiring systems or wired partitions.

604.1 Scope

Article 604 applies to field-installed manufactured wiring systems.
Figure 604–1

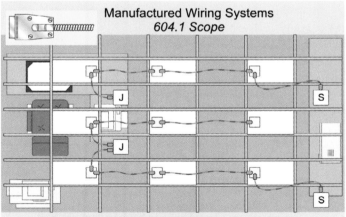

Manufactured Wiring Systems
604.1 Scope

Article 604 applies to field-installed wiring using preassembled components for circuits in accessible areas.

Copyright 2017, www.MikeHolt.com

Figure 604–1

604.6 Listing Requirements

Manufactured wiring systems must now be listed.

Analysis

NEW

Testing and subsequent listing of products ensures a product is safe. This is a concept that is well over 100 years old. In fact, it's such a well understood and accepted concept that not a single comment was made to reject this new requirement. In fact, many people probably thought this was already an *NEC* rule, as a listing requirement for products, especially wiring methods, is something that we've just come to expect. Although the wiring method used in the manufactured wiring system might have a listing requirement, the system itself didn't. When you look at the definition of manufactured wiring systems it tells us that this system can't be inspected without

• • •

it being destroyed. If that's the case, it really needs to be a listed product.

It's also worth noting that this article has been renumbered in an effort to create a parallel numbering system with the Chapter 3 wiring methods. Listing requirements are now located in 604.6, uses permitted and not permitted are in 604.10 and 604.12, and so forth.

604.6 Listing Requirements

Manufactured wiring systems and associated components must be listed.

ELEVATORS, ESCALATORS, AND MOVING WALKS

Introduction to Article 620—Elevators, Escalators, and Moving Walks

With the exception of dumbwaiters, the equipment covered by Article 620 moves people. Thus, a major concept in this article is that of keeping people separate from electrical power. That's why, for example, 620.3 requires live parts to be enclosed. This article consists of 10 parts:

- **Part I. General.** This part provides the scope of the article, definitions, and voltage limitations.

- **Part II. Conductors.** The single-line diagram of Figure 620.13 shown in the *NEC* illustrates how the requirements of Part II work together.

- **Part III. Wiring.** This addresses wiring methods and branch-circuit requirements for different equipment.

- **Part IV. Installation of Conductors.** Part IV covers conductor fill, supports, and related items.

- **Part V. Traveling Cables.** Installation, suspension, location, and protection of cables that move with the motion of the elevator or lift are all covered.

- **Part VI. Disconnecting Means and Control.** The requirements vary with the application.

- **Part VII. Overcurrent Protection.** While most of this part refers to Article 430, it does include additional requirements, such as providing selective coordination.

- **Part VIII. Machine and Control Rooms and Spaces.** The primary goal here is the prevention of unauthorized access.

- **Part IX. Equipment Grounding Conductor.** While most of this part refers to Article 250, it includes additional requirements as well. For example, 15A and 20A, 125V receptacles in certain locations must be GFCI protected.

- **Part X. Emergency and Standby Systems.** This deals with regenerative power and with the need for a disconnecting means that can disconnect an elevator from both the normal power system and the emergency or standby system.

Part I. General

620.1 Scope

Article 620 contains the requirements for the installation of electrical equipment and wiring in connection with elevators, escalators, and moving walks. Figure 620–1

Figure 620–1

620.16 Short-Circuit Current Rating

Elevator control panels must now be marked with the short-circuit current rating.

Analysis

NEW The short-circuit current rating of equipment is defined as "the available fault current at a nominal voltage to which equipment is able to be connected without sustaining damage exceeding defined acceptance criteria." In some instances, this literally means the amount of current it can handle without blowing up. When equipment is installed in violation of 110.10 (related to its short-circuit current rating), the results can be catastrophic and even deadly.

Section 110.10 contains a rule that applies to all equipment, and it requires (among other things) equipment to be installed in accordance with its short-circuit current rating.

That's all fine and dandy, but if you don't know the rating of the equipment you're dealing with you can't possibly know whether you're in compliance with this rule, and could be creating a future hazard in case of a fault. You need to know the rating of the equipment, and you need to know the available short-circuit current at the location of the wiring system you're installing. This new requirement will help to ensure safety by mandating that an elevator control panel be marked with its short-circuit current rating, which in turn allows the installer and inspector to ensure that it's *Code*-compliant.

620.16 Short-Circuit Current Rating

(A) Marking. Where an elevator control panel is installed, it must be marked with its short-circuit current rating, based on one of the following: Figure 620–2

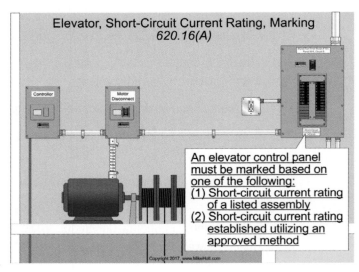

Figure 620–2

(1) Short-circuit current rating of a listed assembly

(2) Short-circuit current rating established utilizing an approved method such as UL 508A-2013, *Supplement SB*

(B) Installation. The elevator control panel can't be installed where the available short-circuit current exceeds the short-circuit current rating in accordance with 620.16(A).

620.23 Branch Circuit for Machine Room/Machinery Space

The circuiting requirements for lighting and receptacles in the equipment machine room/machinery space have been expanded.

Analysis

EXPANDED

Previous editions of the *NEC* stated that a separate branch circuit was required to supply the machine room/machinery space lighting and receptacle(s). Although it's a bit absurd, some people were reading this requirement as meaning that exactly one circuit was to be provided, no more, and no less.

Obviously providing two circuits is as safe (or safer) as an installation supplying only one, so it seems reasonable to allow this application. In fact, the change in this edition of the *Code* now requires two circuits; one for the lighting, and another for the receptacle(s) separate from any other circuits for additional loads! This prevents a service person using a receptacle from tripping the lighting circuit in the elevator pit or machine room and creating a dangerous situation.

Part III. Wiring

620.23 Branch Circuit for Machine Room/Machinery Space

(A) Separate Branch Circuits. Branch circuit(s) supplying lighting for machine rooms, control rooms, machinery spaces, and control spaces must be on a separate circuit than the circuit supplying receptacles. These circuits may not supply any other loads. The required lighting in these spaces isn't permitted to be connected to the load side of a GFCI for receptacles [620.85]. Figure 620–3

(B) Light Switch. The machine rooms and machinery space lighting switch must be located at the point of entrance to the machine room or machinery space. Figure 620–4

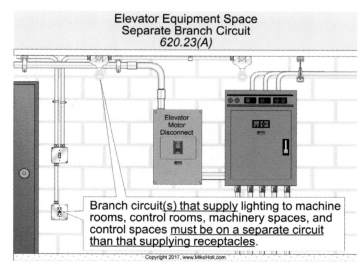

Figure 620–3

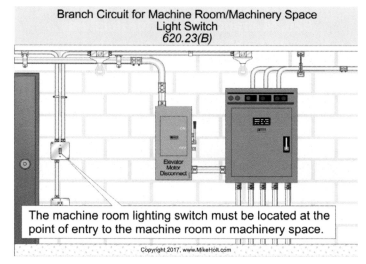

Figure 620–4

(C) Receptacle. At least one 15A or 20A, 125V duplex GFCI receptacle must be installed in each machine room or machinery space [620.85]. Figure 620–5

Note 1: See ASME A17.1/CSA B44, *Safety Code for Elevators and Escalators*, for illumination levels required for the machine room and machinery space.

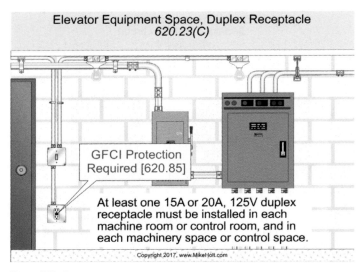

Figure 620–5

620.24 Branch Circuit for Hoistway Pit Lighting and Receptacles

The circuiting requirements for lighting and receptacles in a hoistway pit area have been expanded, and a new Informational Note was added.

Analysis

CLARIFIED

Separate Circuits. Previous editions of the *NEC* stated that a separate branch circuit was required to supply the hoistway pit lighting and receptacle(s). Although it's a bit absurd, some people were reading this requirement as meaning that exactly one circuit was to be provided, no more, and no less.

Obviously providing two circuits is as safe (or safer) as an installation supplying only one, so it seems reasonable to allow this application. In fact, the change in this edition of the *Code* now requires two circuits; one for the lighting, and another for the receptacle(s)! This prevents a service person using a receptacle from tripping the lighting circuit in the elevator pit or machine room and creating a dangerous situation.

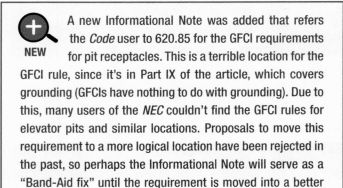

NEW

A new Informational Note was added that refers the *Code* user to 620.85 for the GFCI requirements for pit receptacles. This is a terrible location for the GFCI rule, since it's in Part IX of the article, which covers grounding (GFCIs have nothing to do with grounding). Due to this, many users of the *NEC* couldn't find the GFCI rules for elevator pits and similar locations. Proposals to move this requirement to a more logical location have been rejected in the past, so perhaps the Informational Note will serve as a "Band-Aid fix" until the requirement is moved into a better spot.

620.24 Branch Circuit for Hoistway Pit Lighting and Receptacles

(A) Separate Branch Circuits. Separate branch circuits must supply the hoistway pit lighting and receptacle(s), and the required lighting isn't permitted to be connected to the load side of a GFCI for receptacles [620.85].

(B) Light Switch. The lighting switch must be readily accessible from the pit access door. Figure 620–6

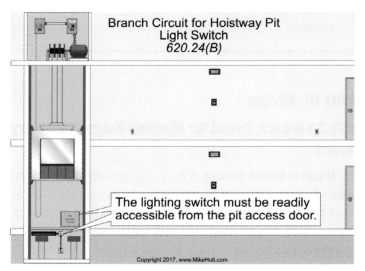

Figure 620–6

(C) Receptacle. At least one 15A or 20A, 125V duplex GFCI receptacle must be installed in a hoistway pit [620.85]. Figure 620–7

Note 2: See 620.85 for GFCI requirements for receptacles.

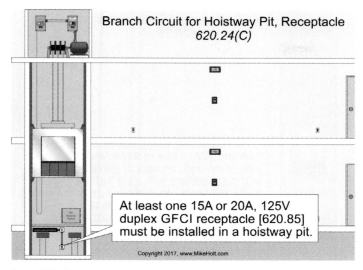

Branch Circuit for Hoistway Pit, Receptacle
620.24(C)

At least one 15A or 20A, 125V duplex GFCI receptacle [620.85] must be installed in a hoistway pit.

Copyright 2017, www.MikeHolt.com

Figure 620–7

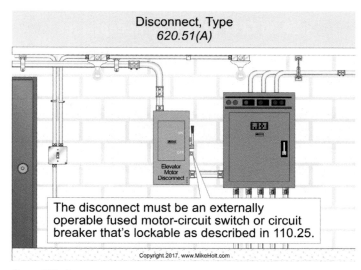

Disconnect, Type
620.51(A)

The disconnect must be an externally operable fused motor-circuit switch or circuit breaker that's lockable as described in 110.25.

Copyright 2017, www.MikeHolt.com

Figure 620–8

Note: See ASME A17.1/CSA B44, *Safety Code for Elevators and Escalators,* for additional information for the disconnect.

620.51 Disconnecting Means

The equipment that requires a disconnecting means is now clear.

Analysis

CLARIFIED

Previous editions of the *Code* stated that each "unit" needed a disconnect. This is a good requirement, but not a good sentence. What "units" is the *NEC* referencing? The intent of this rule was to provide a disconnect for each elevator, dumbwaiter, moving walk, platform lift, or stairway lift, but the *Code* didn't clearly indicate that fact. This change is probably going to be seen as a clarification and not a technical change, as again, it was the intent of the rule all along.

620.51 Disconnecting Means

A disconnect must be provided for each elevator, dumbwaiter, escalator, moving walk, platform lift, or stairway chairlift. The disconnect for the main power supply conductors must not disconnect the branch circuit required in 620.22, 620.23, and 620.24.

(A) Type. The disconnect must be an enclosed externally operable fused motor-circuit switch or circuit breaker that's lockable with provisions for locking to remain in place whether the lock is installed or not [110.25]. Figure 620–8

(B) Operation. If sprinklers are installed in hoistways, machine rooms, control rooms, machinery spaces, or control spaces; the disconnect can automatically open the power supply to the affected elevator(s) prior to the application of water.

(C) Location. The disconnect must be located so that it's only readily accessible to qualified persons. Figure 620–9

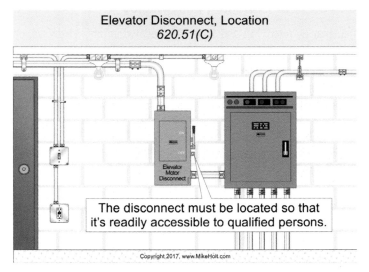

Elevator Disconnect, Location
620.51(C)

The disconnect must be located so that it's readily accessible to qualified persons.

Copyright 2017, www.MikeHolt.com

Figure 620–9

620.85 GFCI-Protected Receptacles

The receptacle GFCI rules for elevators and similar equipment were expanded.

Analysis

EXPANDED Many of the areas associated with elevators, escalators, and moving walks already require GFCI protection of receptacles, but there were still plenty of areas that didn't. New to the *NEC* is a requirement for GFCI protection of receptacles on the cars of elevators and dumbwaiters associated with wind turbine tower elevators, areas associated with platform and stairway lifts, and elevator control spaces and control rooms. Interesting, the change removed the rule for GFCI protection of receptacles for elevator cars that aren't associated with wind turbine towers.

GFCIs have a very good track record of preventing electrocution, so expanding the requirements to areas that are very similar to those already requiring protection is often a slam dunk in terms of *Code* changes.

620.85 GFCI-Protected Receptacles

Receptacles rated 15A and 20A, 125V located in pits, hoistways, on the cars of elevators and dumbwaiters associated with wind turbine tower elevators, on the platforms or in the runways and machinery spaces of platform lifts and stairway chairlifts, and in escalator and moving walk wellways must be of the GFCI type. Figure 620–10

Receptacles rated 15A and 20A, 125V receptacles installed in machine rooms, control spaces, and control rooms must be GFCI protected. Figure 620–11

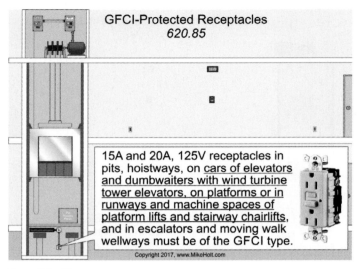

Figure 620–10

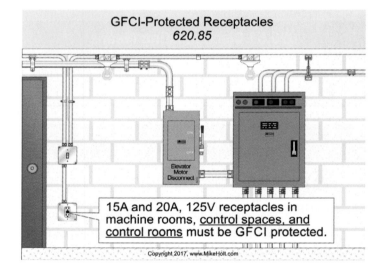

Figure 620–11

ARTICLE 625
ELECTRIC VEHICLE CHARGING SYSTEM

Introduction to Article 625—Electric Vehicle Charging System

Electric vehicles have been around for a long time. Anyone who's worked in a factory or warehouse has probably encountered an electric lift truck. And, of course, we're all familiar with golf carts. These and other off-road vehicles have charging requirements that are easily accommodated by small charging systems.

But today, a new challenge has emerged and is becoming increasingly common. That challenge is the electrically-powered passenger vehicle. Such a vehicle, especially an electric car or bus, weighs considerably more than a golf cart and just moving one takes a correspondingly larger motor. In fact, many designs use multiple drive motors.

And those motors are powered by batteries. Adding to the battery sizing requirement are other demands. For example, these vehicles:

- Must be able to travel at highway speeds over distances roughly comparable to those traveled by their internal combustion engine counterparts.

- Have loads you typically don't find on a golf cart, such as air conditioning, electric windows, stereo systems, windshield wipers, security systems, and window defrosters.

- Are expected to start in summer heat and in brutal winter cold.

So the battery system for an electrically-powered passenger vehicle is considerably larger than that for a golf cart or other typical off-road electric vehicle. Consequently, the charging system must be far more robust and able to deliver far more power than the charger for a golf cart.

The electrically-powered passenger vehicle needs a dedicated charging circuit. And that's where Article 625 comes in. It provides the requirements for the electrical equipment needed to charge automotive-type electric and hybrid vehicles, including cars, bikes, and buses.

This Article consists of three parts:

- **Part I. General.** This includes scope, definitions, voltages, and listing/labeling requirements.

- **Part II. Equipment Construction.** Most of this applies to the manufacturer, but there are a few requirements you need to know.

- **Part III. Installation.** This part covers overcurrent protection and the disconnecting means in addition to the different requirements for indoor and outdoor locations.

Part I. General

625.1 Scope

Article 625 covers the installation of equipment and devices related to listed electric vehicle conductive, inductive, or wireless power transfer charging equipment. Figure 625–1

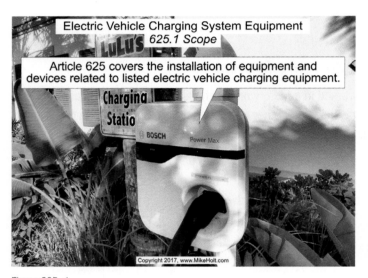

Electric Vehicle Charging System Equipment
625.1 Scope

Article 625 covers the installation of equipment and devices related to listed electric vehicle charging equipment.

Figure 625–1

625.2 Definitions

Definitions were added for Charge Power Converter, Fastened in Place, Fixed in Place, Output Cable To Primary Pad, Portable (as applied to electric vehicle charging system), Primary Pad, Wireless Power Transfer, and Wireless Power Transfer Equipment (WPTE).

Analysis

NEW Sometimes technology changes so fast that the *NEC* simply can't keep up with it. Electric vehicles and PV systems are changing so quickly that we could probably change the *Code* every year and still not keep up with these changing products.

WPTE is a technology that's anticipated to be available soon, and when it is it could prove quite interesting. WPTE is a pad on which an electric vehicle parks over to charge its battery. These products already exist on a much smaller

scale for cell phones. A new Part IV of this article has been created to cover these systems.

The one interesting issue related to the technology is whether there'll be any elevated electromagnetic fields (EMF) associated with this new product.

625.2 Definitions

Cable Management System. An apparatus designed to control and organize the output cable to the electric vehicle or to the primary pad.

Charger Power Converter. The device used to convert electricity to a high-frequency output for wireless power transfer.

Electric Vehicle. An on-road use automobile, bus, truck, van, neighborhood vehicle, and motorcycle primarily powered by an electric motor. Figure 625–2

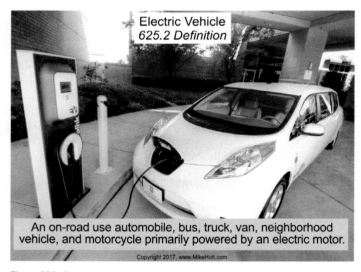

Electric Vehicle
625.2 Definition

An on-road use automobile, bus, truck, van, neighborhood vehicle, and motorcycle primarily powered by an electric motor.

Figure 625–2

Author's Comment:

■ Off-road self-propelled electric industrial trucks, hoists, lifts, transports, golf carts, airline ground support equipment, tractors, and boats aren't considered electric vehicles. Figure 625–3

Electric Vehicle Connector. A device that, when electrically coupled to an electric vehicle inlet, provides the electrical connection to the electric vehicle for the purpose of power transfer and information exchange. Figure 625–4

Figure 625–3

Figure 625–5

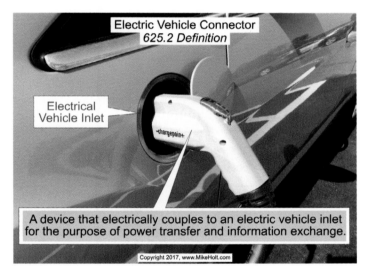

Figure 625–4

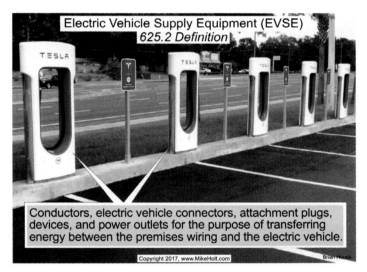

Figure 625–6

Electric Vehicle Inlet. The device on the electric vehicle into which the electric vehicle connector is electrically coupled for power transfer and information exchange. Figure 625–5

Author's Comment:

- The electric vehicle inlet is part of the electric vehicle and not part of the electric vehicle supply equipment.

Electric Vehicle Supply Equipment (EVSE). Conductors, electric vehicle connectors, attachment plugs, devices, and power outlets for the purpose of transferring energy between the premises wiring and the electric vehicle. Figure 625–6

Fastened in Place. Mounting means for EVSE in which the fastening means are designed to allow removal for relocation, interchangeability, maintenance, or repair without the use of a tool.

Fixed in Place. Mounting means for EVSE attached to a wall or surface with fasteners that require a tool to be removed.

Output Cable to the Electric Vehicle. An assembly consisting of a length of flexible EV cable and an electric vehicle connector (supplying power to the electric vehicle). Figure 625–7

Portable (as applied to EVSE). A device intended for indoor or outdoor use that can be carried from charging location to charging location and is designed to be transported in the vehicle when not in use.

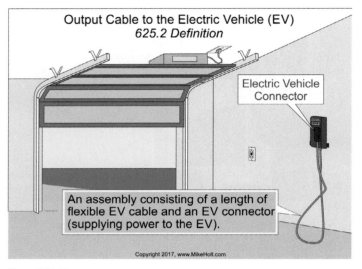

An assembly consisting of a length of flexible EV cable and an EV connector (supplying power to the EV).

Figure 625–7

Primary Pad. A device external to the EV that provides power via the contactless coupling and may include the charger power converter.

Wireless Power Transfer (WPT). The transfer of electrical energy from a power source to an electrical load via electric and magnetic fields or waves by a contactless inductive means between a primary and a secondary device.

Wireless Power Transfer Equipment (WPTE). Equipment consisting of a charger power converter and a primary pad. The two devices are either separate units or they're contained within a single enclosure.

625.5 Listed

The equipment required to be listed was clarified.

Analysis

CLARIFIED

The *NEC* used to require "all electrical materials, devices, fittings, and associated equipment related to electric vehicles" to be listed. That sounds fine, but not every single piece of electrical equipment can be listed because product standards don't exist for everything. By limiting the requirement to just the electric vehicle supply equipment (EVSE) and wireless power transfer equipment (WPTE) the rule isn't only easier to understand, but easier to comply with and easier to enforce.

625.5 Listed

Electric vehicle supply equipment (EVSE) and wireless powered transfer equipment (WPTE) must be listed. Figure 625–8

Electric vehicle supply equipment (EVSE) and wireless powered transfer equipment (WPTE) must be listed.

Figure 625–8

625.40 Electric Vehicle Branch Circuit

The circuiting requirement for electric vehicle charging systems has been relocated from 210.17 to 625.40.

Analysis

RELOCATED

While 210.17 was a functional location for this circuiting requirement, 625.40 is a better one.

625.40 Electric Vehicle Branch Circuit

Each outlet for charging electric vehicles must be supplied by an individual branch circuit that serves no other outlets. Figure 625–9

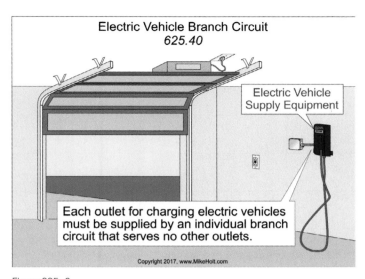

Figure 625–9

ARTICLE
630 WELDERS

Introduction to Article 630—Welders

Electric welding equipment does its job either by creating an electric arc between two surfaces or by heating a rod that melts from overcurrent. Either way results in a hefty momentary current draw. Welding machines come in many shapes and sizes. On the smaller end of the scale are portable welding units used for manual welding, such as in a fabrication shop. At the larger end of the scale are robotic welding machines the size of a house, used for making everything from automobile bodies to refrigerator panels. All of these must comply with Article 630.

The primary concern of Article 630 is adequately sizing the conductors and circuit protection to handle this type of load. Fortunately for the design engineer and the field electrician, this article requires certain information to be provided on the nameplate of the equipment. Article 630 explains how to use this information for the proper sizing of conductors and circuit protection.

Welding cable has requirements other conductors don't have. For example, it must be supported at not less than 6 in. intervals. Also, the insulation on these cables must be flame-retardant.

Part I. General

630.1 Scope

Article 630 covers electric arc welding, resistance welding apparatus, and other similar welding equipment connected to an electric supply system. Figure 630–1

Electric Welders
630.1 Scope

Article 630 covers electric arc welding, resistance welding apparatus, and other similar welding equipment connected to an electric supply system.

Copyright 2017, www.MikeHolt.com

Figure 630–1

630.6 Listing

A new requirement for the listing of welding and cutting equipment was added.

Analysis

NEW A safe electrical installation requires multiple components. It requires skilled electricians; knowledgeable inspectors; a practical, safe, and enforceable *Code*; and it requires product testing and listing. Welding equipment wasn't required to be listed under previous editions of the *NEC*, but that changed in 2017.

Testing laboratories are able to examine equipment in ways nobody else can. There are some pieces of equipment that don't need this kind of rigorous testing and examination, but welding and cutting equipment aren't among them. Requiring them to be listed should increase overall worker safety.

630.6 Listing

Welding and cutting power equipment must be listed.

AUDIO SIGNAL PROCESSING, AMPLIFICATION, AND REPRODUCTION EQUIPMENT

Introduction to Article 640—Audio Signal Processing, Amplification, and Reproduction Equipment

If you understand the three major goals of Article 640, you'll be able to better understand and apply the requirements. These three goals are to:

- Reduce the spread of fire and smoke.

- Comply with other articles.

- Prevent shock. This article includes several requirements, such as specifics in the mechanical execution of work, and requirements when audio equipment is located near bodies of water to reduce shock hazards peculiar to audio equipment installations.

In addition, Article 640 distinguishes between permanent and temporary audio installations. Part II provides requirements for permanent installations, and Part III provides requirements for portable and temporary installations.

Part I. General

640.1 Scope

(A) Covered. Article 640 covers equipment and wiring for permanent and temporary audio sound and public address system installations.
Figure 640–1

Note: Audio system locations include, but aren't limited to, restaurants, hotels, business offices, commercial and retail sales environments, churches, schools, auditoriums, theaters, stadiums, and outdoor events such as fairs, festivals, circuses, public events, and concerts.

(B) Not Covered. This article doesn't cover audio systems for fire and burglary alarms.

Audio Signal Processing, Amplification, and Reproduction Equipment
640.1(A) Scope

Article 640 covers equipment and wiring for permanent and temporary audio sound and public address system installations.
Copyright 2017, www.MikeHolt.com

Figure 640–1

640.3 Locations and Other Articles

The "requirements" for audio cables in ducts, plenums, and air-handling spaces are now really "requirements."

Analysis

CLARIFIED Section 640.3(B) used to say that *Code* users must "see 300.22…" as it relates to cables in plenum spaces. It didn't say you had to comply with it, just that you had to "see it." In all honesty though, it doesn't matter, since Article 300 applies to an Article 640 (audio system) installation unless specifically modified by that article [90.3].

Compare 640.3 to 725.3 for example, and you'll notice that only some of Article 300 applies to an Article 725 installation (remote-control, signaling, and power-limited circuits) because it specifically modifies the rules, whereas all of Article 300 applies to Article 640 because there's no such modification. In fact, as currently written, all of 640.3 could be deleted.

640.3 Locations and Other Articles

(A) Spread of Fire or Products of Combustion. Audio circuits installed through fire-resistant-rated walls, partitions, floors, or ceilings must be firestopped to limit the possible spread of fire or products of combustion in accordance with the specific instructions supplied by the manufacturer for the specific type of cable and construction material (drywall, brick, and so on), in accordance with 300.21. Figure 640–2

Author's Comment:

- Openings in fire-resistant walls, floors, and ceilings must be sealed so the possible spread of fire or products of combustion won't be substantially increased [300.21]. Although boxes aren't required for audio circuits, a box is required for an audio device located in a fire-rated assembly.

(B) Ducts and Plenum Spaces. Audio circuits installed in fabricated ducts must be in accordance with 300.22(B), and in accordance with 300.22(C) where installed in plenum spaces. Figure 640–3

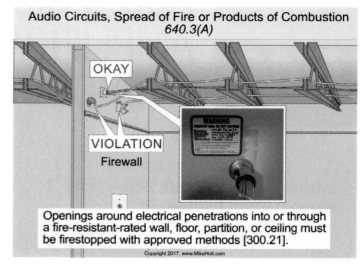

Figure 640–2

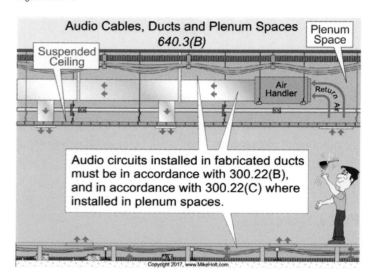

Figure 640–3

Ex 1: Class 2 and Class 3 plenum-rated cables installed in accordance with 725.135(B) and Table 725.154 can be installed in ducts specifically fabricated for environmental air.

Ex 2: Class 2 and Class 3 plenum-rated cables installed in accordance with 725.135(C) and Table 725.154 can be installed in plenum spaces.

(C) Cable Trays and Cable Tray Systems. Audio cables installed in cable trays and cable tray systems must be installed in accordance with Article 392.

Note: See Table 725.154(C) for the use of Class 2, Class 3, and PLTC cable in cable trays.

(D) Hazardous (Classified) Locations. Audio equipment in hazardous (classified) locations must be installed in accordance with Chapter 5.

640.22 Wiring of Equipment Racks and Enclosures

The fact that audio equipment should be both bonded and grounded was clarified.

Analysis

CLARIFIED

This section addresses the requirements for installed metal racks housing audio equipment. The audio industry has always been creative when it comes to bonding and grounding. Little hums and noises in audio systems are often traced to a poor equipment grounding conductor connection or improper wiring methods. The accepted industry practice to these issues is to simply disconnect the bonding and grounding conductors. This change makes it clear that these racks of equipment must be both bonded and grounded.

640.22 Wiring of Equipment Racks and Enclosures

Metal equipment racks and enclosures must be <u>bonded and</u> grounded. Bonding isn't required if the rack is connected to a technical power ground.

640.25 Loudspeakers in Fire-Resistance-Rated Partitions, Walls, and Ceilings

The rules for loudspeakers in fire-resistance-rated assemblies have been reduced.

Analysis

REDUCED

Few things are taken more seriously in the building codes than fire-resistance-rated assemblies, and for good reason. Consider a vertical exit enclosure (commonly known as a stair enclosure). In a very large building you won't be able to get out very quickly in the event of a fire. This is addressed by creating stair enclosures with either a one- or two-hour fire-resistance rating. Once an occupant(s) is in the stairway they're considered protected, and considered to be just as safe there as they would be if they were out of the building.

These stair enclosures are often the last line of defense against a building on fire, and they need to be treated with the utmost care. Fire-resistance-rated assemblies have a terrific track record...when done correctly. Unfortunately, we learned an awful lessen when the MGM Grand Hotel went up in flames in 1980. Eighty-seven people lost their lives, most due to smoke inhalation, and many of those victims were in the stairways where they should have been safe. What went wrong? There were multiple penetrations, like raceways, into the stairways that weren't protected by a listed through-penetration fire stop system.

The rule in 640.25 for speakers in fire-resistance-rated assemblies used to require the use of listed components. It now allows products to be used that aren't listed, only identified. This is a decrease in safety and there was no technical substantiation submitted for it.

640.25 Loudspeakers in Fire-Resistance-Rated Partitions, Walls, and Ceilings

Loudspeakers installed in fire-resistance-rated partitions, walls, or ceilings must be listed <u>and labeled for the purpose, or be identified as speaker assemblies for fire resistivity</u>, or be installed in an enclosure or recess that maintains the fire resistance rating.

ARTICLE 645
INFORMATION TECHNOLOGY EQUIPMENT

Introduction to Article 645—Information Technology Equipment

One of the unique things about Article 645 is the requirement for a shutoff switch readily accessible from the exit doors of information technology equipment rooms [645.10]. This requirement seems to be wrong on its face because it allows someone to shut power to the IT room off from a single point. So despite having a UPS and taking every precaution against a power outage, the IT system is still vulnerable to a shutdown from a readily accessible switch at the principal exit door(s).

What was the Code Making Panel thinking of when they added this requirement? They were thinking of fire and rescue teams. Having a means to shut down the power and disconnect the batteries before entering the IT room during a fire allows the rescue team to use fire hoses and other equipment without risking contact with energized equipment. Yes, there's loss of IT function during the shutdown, but if the room needs fire and rescue teams, that loss is the least of anyone's problems at that time. The shutdown allows the rescue of people and property. A breakaway lock can protect the IT room from inadvertent shutdown via this switch.

What about the rest of Article 645? The major goal is to reduce the spread of fire and smoke. The raised floors common in IT rooms pose additional challenges to achieving this goal, so this article devotes a fair percentage of its text to raised floor requirements. Fire-resistant walls, separate HVAC systems, and other requirements further help to achieve this goal.

645.1 Scope

Article 645 provides optional alternative wiring methods and materials to those methods and materials required in other chapters of this *Code* for information technology equipment and systems in an information technology equipment room. Figure 645–1

Note: An information technology equipment room is an enclosed area specifically designed to comply with the construction and fire protection provisions of NFPA 75, *Standard for the Fire Protection of Information Technology Equipment*.

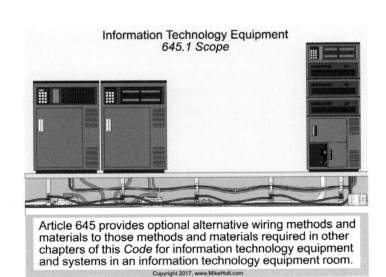

Information Technology Equipment
645.1 Scope

Article 645 provides optional alternative wiring methods and materials to those methods and materials required in other chapters of this *Code* for information technology equipment and systems in an information technology equipment room.

Copyright 2017, www.MikeHolt.com

Figure 645–1

645.3 Other Articles

> The wiring methods permitted in plenum spaces above information technology rooms are more clearly stated.

Analysis

EDITED This change isn't technical in nature, but it does improve the *NEC*. The previous *Code* simply stated that in ducts, plenums, and air-handling spaces you needed to follow "300.22, 725.135(B), 725.132(B)(2), 760.53(B), 760.135(B), 770.113(C), 800.113(C), and 820.113(C); and Table 725.154, Table 760.154, Table 760.154(a), Table 800.154(a), and Table 820.154(a)." Well that's quite a rule for the average user to swallow! Do you search out and then read each of the rules, since most people don't have them memorized? The changes to the 2017 edition of the *NEC* contain the same rules, but they actually tell you what they apply to so you don't need to search a dozen different sections only to find that 11 of them didn't apply to you.

645.3 Other Articles

Circuits and equipment must comply with 645.3(A) through (G), as applicable.

(A) Spread of Fire or Products of Combustion. Electrical circuits and equipment must be installed in such a way that the spread of fire or products of combustion won't be substantially increased. Openings into or through fire-rated walls, floors, and ceilings for electrical equipment must be firestopped using methods approved by the authority having jurisdiction to maintain the fire-resistance rating of the fire-rated assembly [300.21].

(B) Plenums. The following sections and tables apply to wiring and cabling in a plenum space above an information technology equipment room:

(1) Wiring in accordance with 300.22(C).

(2) Class 2 and Class 3 plenum rated cables in accordance with 725.135(C) and Table 725.154.

(3) Plenum-rated fire alarm cables in accordance with 760.53(B)(2), 760.135(C) and Table 725.154.

(4) Plenum-rated optical fiber cables in accordance with 770.113(C) and Table 770.154(a).

(5) Plenum-rated communications cables in accordance with 800.113(C) and Table 800.154(a), (b), and (c).

(6) Plenum-rated coaxial cables in accordance with 820.113(C) and Table 820.154(a).

(D) Classification of Data Circuits. Data circuits for information technology systems are classified as a Class 2 circuit [725.121(A)(4)] and must be installed in accordance with the requirements of Article 725 [725.1]. Class 2 circuit conductors installed in the same cable with communications circuits, are reclassified as communications circuits and the cable must be listed as communications cable [725.139(D)(1) and 800.133(A)(1)(c)].

645.4 Special Requirements

> The applicability of Article 645 has been clarified, again.

Analysis

CLARIFIED The requirements contained in Article 645 (Information Technology (IT) Equipment) are optional and always have been. You can install different wiring methods and cables because the area beneath the raised floor isn't treated as a plenum. You don't need plenum-rated cables below the raised floor because, if you follow the rules in 645.4, the space under the raised floor only handles the air in the IT room, and it isn't occupied.

That means the smoke from a nonplenum-rated cable won't travel throughout the building. It will be contained in the IT room, which, again, is unoccupied. The IT room requires an emergency switch [645.10] to shut off the power and the air-handling system to the room in the event of a fire, doubly ensuring safety.

645.4 Special Requirements

The alternative wiring methods to Chapter 3 and Parts I and III of Article 725 for signaling wiring and Parts I and V of Article 770 for optical fiber cabling are permitted where all of the following conditions are met:

(1) A disconnect that complies with 645.10 is provided.

(2) A dedicated heating/ventilating/air-conditioning (HVAC) system is provided for information technology equipment and is:

   a. Separated from other areas of the occupancy.

(3) Information technology and communications equipment in the information technology room is listed.

(4) The room is occupied and accessible only to persons needed for the maintenance and operation of information technology equipment.

(5) The information technology equipment room is separated from other occupancies by fire-resistant-rated walls, floors, and ceilings with protected openings.

(6) Only electrical equipment and wiring associated with the operation of the information technology room is installed in the room.

Note: This includes HVAC systems, communications systems (twisted wire, antennas, and coaxial cable) fire alarm systems, security systems, water detection systems, and other related protective equipment.

645.5 Supply Circuits and Interconnecting Cables

The permitted wiring methods under raised floors in IT equipment rooms are now contained in an even bigger list than before and a new Informational Note was added about securing and supporting.

Analysis

Wiring Methods. The wiring method list is 17 items long, and that's just in one of the subsections here. If you're installing wiring under the raised floor of an IT room, you can pretty much use any wiring method you wish. That's the whole idea of following this optional article. Oh yeah, you can't use Type NM Cable. Those guys are always left out of the party.

EDITED

NEW

Securing and Supporting. The wiring under the floor is no different than the wiring anywhere else in the building when it comes to securing and supporting, other than for cables that are part of listed IT equipment. An Informational Note was added to remind us of this fact, and it points to 300.11, which contains the general requirements for securing and supporting raceways and cables.

645.5 Supply Circuits and Interconnecting Cables

(A) Branch-Circuit Conductors. Branch-circuit conductors for information technology equipment must have an ampacity not less than 125 percent of the total connected load.

(B) Power-Supply Cords. Information technology equipment can be connected to a branch circuit by a power-supply cord meeting the following requirements:

(1) The power-supply cord is no longer than 15 ft. Figure 645–2

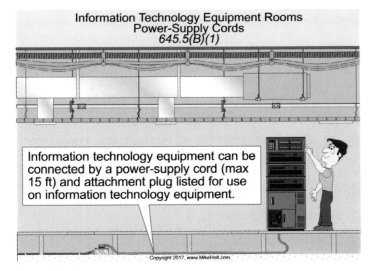

Figure 645–2

(2) The power-supply cord and attachment plug must be listed for use on information technology equipment.

(C) Interconnecting Cables. Cables listed for information technology equipment can be used to interconnect information technology equipment without the 15-foot cable length limitation contained in 645.5(B).

(D) Physical Damage. If exposed to physical damage, the supply circuits and interconnecting cables must be protected.

(E) Under Raised Floors. Where the area under the raised floor is accessible and openings minimize the entrance of debris beneath the floor, power cables, communication cables, connecting cables, inter-connecting cables, cord-and-plug connections, and receptacles associated with the information technology equipment can be installed under a raised floor. The installation requirement must comply with (1) through (3) as follows:

(1) Branch-Circuit Wiring Under Raised Floor. Figure 645–3

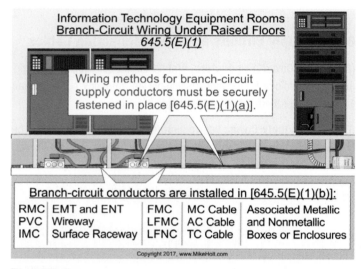

Figure 645–3

(a) Branch-circuit wiring under a raised floor must be securely fastened in place in accordance with 300.11.

(b) The following wiring methods are permitted under a raised floor:

(1) Rigid metal conduit

(2) Rigid nonmetallic conduit

(3) Intermediate metal conduit

(4) Electrical metallic tubing

(5) Electrical nonmetallic tubing

(6) Metal wireway

(7) Nonmetallic wireway

(8) Surface metal raceway with metal cover

(9) Surface nonmetallic raceway

(10) Flexible metal conduit

(11) Liquidtight flexible metal conduit

(12) Liquidtight flexible nonmetallic conduit

(13) Type MI cable

(14) Type MC cable

(15) Type AC cable

(16) Associated metallic and nonmetallic boxes or enclosures

(17) Type TC power and control tray cable

(2) Power-Supply Cords, Data Cables, and Cables and Conductors. Power-supply cords, interconnecting cables, cables and conductors are permitted under a raised floor as follows: Figure 645–4

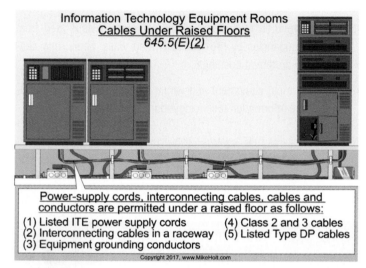

Figure 645–4

(1) Power-supply cords of listed information technology equipment in accordance with 645.5(B)

(2) Interconnecting cables enclosed within a raceway

(3) Equipment grounding conductors

(4) Plenum and nonplenum rated Class 2 and/or Class 3 cables and substitute cables in accordance with 725.154(A)

Note: Figure 725.154(A) contained in the *NEC* illustrates the cable substitution hierarchy for Class 2 and Class 3 cables.

(5) Listed Type DP cable

(3) Optical Fiber Cables. Plenum and nonplenum rated optical fiber cables. Figure 645–5

(F) Securing in Place Underfloor Raceway. Power-supply cables, communications cables, connecting, and interconnecting cables that are part of listed information technology equipment aren't required to be secured in place where installed under raised floors. Figure 645–6

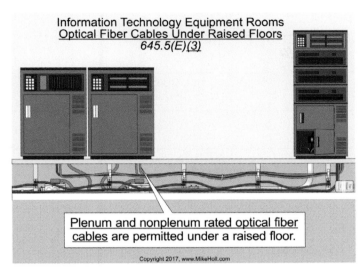

Figure 645–5

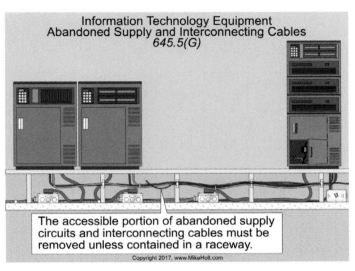

Figure 645–7

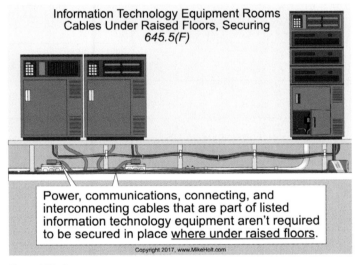

Figure 645–6

Note: Raceways and cables that aren't part of listed IT equipment must be secured and supported in accordance with 300.11.

(G) Abandoned Supply Circuits and Interconnecting Cables. The accessible portion of abandoned cables must be removed unless contained within a raceway. Figure 645–7

(H) Cables Identified for Future Use. Figure 645–8

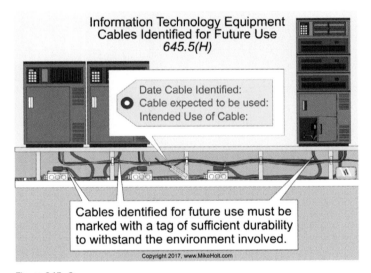

Figure 645–8

(1) Cables identified for future use must be marked with a tag of sufficient durability to withstand the environment involved.

(2) Cable tags must have the following information:

    a. Date cable was identified for future use

    b. Date of expected use

    c. Intended future use of the cable

ARTICLE 680

SWIMMING POOLS, SPAS, HOT TUBS, FOUNTAINS, AND SIMILAR INSTALLATIONS

Introduction to Article 680—Swimming Pools, Spas, Hot Tubs, Fountains, and Similar Installations

The requirements contained in Article 680 apply to the installation of electrical wiring and equipment for swimming pools, spas, hot tubs, fountains, and hydromassage bathtubs. The overriding concern of this article is to keep people and electricity separated.

Article 680 is divided into seven parts. The various parts apply to certain types of installations, so be careful to determine which parts of this article apply to what and where. For instance, Part I and Part II apply to spas and hot tubs installed outdoors, except as modified in Part IV. In contrast, hydromassage bathtubs are only covered by Part VII. Read the details of this article carefully so you'll be able to provide a safe installation.

- Part I. General.

- Part II. Permanently Installed Pools. Installations at permanently installed pools must comply with both Parts I and II of this article.

- Part III. Storable Swimming Pools, Storable Spas, and Storable Hot Tubs. Installations of storable pools, storable spas, and storable hot tubs must comply with Parts I and III of Article 680.

- Part IV. Spas and Hot Tubs. Spas and hot tubs must comply with Parts I and IV of this article; outdoor spas and hot tubs must also comply with Part II in accordance with 680.42.

- Part V. Fountains. Parts I and II apply to permanently installed fountains. If they have water in common with a pool, Part II also applies. Self-contained, portable fountains are covered by Article 422, Parts II and III.

- Part VI. Pools and Tubs for Therapeutic Use. Parts I and VI apply to pools and tubs for therapeutic use in health care facilities, gymnasiums, athletic training rooms and similar installations. If they're portable appliances, then Article 422, Parts II and III apply.

- Part VII. Hydromassage Bathtubs. Part VII applies to hydromassage bathtubs, but no other parts of Article 680 do.

Part I. General Requirements for Pools, Spas, Hot Tubs, and Fountains

Author's Comment:

- The requirements contained in Part I of Article 680 apply to permanently installed pools [680.20], storable pools [680.30], spas and hot tubs [680.42 and 680.43], and fountains [680.50].

680.1 Scope

The requirements contained in Article 680 apply to the installation of electric wiring and equipment for swimming pools, hot tubs, spas, fountains, and hydromassage bathtubs. Figure 680–1

The requirements contained in Article 680 apply to the installation of electric wiring and equipment for swimming pools, hot tubs, spas, fountains, and hydromassage bathtubs.

Figure 680–1

680.2 Definitions

A new definition for "electrically powered pool lift" was added, and the definition for storable pools (and other storable features) was revised.

Analysis

 NEW **Electrically Powered Pool Lift.** An electrically powered pool lift is something that's often found in newer nonresidential swimming pools. It allows people with disabilities, including those in wheelchairs, to use the swimming pool by lifting the occupant into the water. These lifts are so prevalent that a new part (Part VIII) was added to provide requirements for them.

 CLARIFIED **Storable Pools.** This definition was revised to clarify that storable pools are for aboveground use only. The previous *Code* edition stated that storable pools are constructed aboveground, but now it's clear they're only used aboveground.

680.2 Definitions

Dry-Niche Luminaire. A luminaire intended for installation in the floor or wall of a pool, spa, or fountain in a niche that's sealed against the entry of water.

Electrically Powered Pool Lift. An electrically powered lift that provides accessibility to and from a pool or spa for people with disabilities.

Forming Shell. A structure mounted in the wall of permanently installed pools, storable pools, outdoor spas, outdoor hot tubs, or fountains designed to support a wet-niche luminaire. Figure 680–2

Forming Shell
680.2 Definition

A structure designed to support a wet-niche luminaire.

Figure 680–2

Fountain. An ornamental pool, display pool, or reflection pool.

Hydromassage Bathtub. A permanently installed bathtub with a recirculating piping system designed to accept, circulate, and discharge water after each use. Figure 680–3

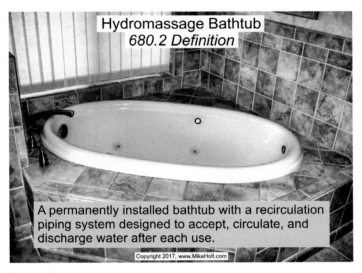

Figure 680–3

Low-Voltage Contact Limit. A voltage not exceeding the following values: Figure 680–4

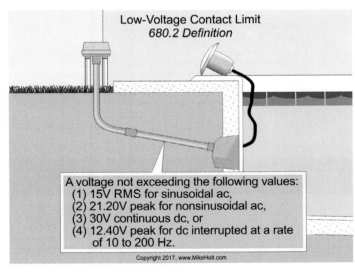

Figure 680–4

(1) 15V (RMS) for sinusoidal alternating current

(2) 21.20V peak for nonsinusoidal alternating current

(3) 30V for continuous direct current

(4) 12.40V peak for direct current that's interrupted at a rate of 10 to 200 Hz

Maximum Water Level. The highest level that water reaches before it spills out. Figure 680–5

Figure 680–5

Permanently Installed Swimming, Wading, Immersion, and Therapeutic Pools. Those constructed in the ground or partially in the ground, and all others capable of holding water in a depth greater than 42 in., and pools installed inside of a building, regardless of water depth, whether or not served by electrical circuits of any nature. Figure 680–6

Figure 680–6

Pool. Manufactured or field-constructed equipment designed to contain water on a permanent or semipermanent basis and used for swimming, wading, immersion, or other purposes.

Author's Comment:

■ The definition of a pool includes baptisteries (immersion pools), which must comply with the requirements of Article 680.

Spa or Hot Tub. A hydromassage pool or tub designed for recreational or therapeutic use typically not drained after each use. Figure 680–7

Figure 680–7

Storable Swimming Pool, or Storable/Portable Spas and Hot Tubs. Swimming, wading, or immersion pools intended to be stored when not in use, constructed on or above the ground and are capable of holding water to a maximum depth of 42 in., or a pool, spa, or hot tub constructed on or above the ground, with nonmetallic, molded polymeric walls or inflatable fabric walls regardless of dimension. Figure 680–8

Author's Comment:

■ Storable pools are sold as a complete package that consists of the pool walls, vinyl liner, plumbing kit, and pump/filter device. Underwriters Laboratories, Inc. (UL) requires the pump/filter units to have a minimum 25-ft cord to discourage the use of extension cords.

Wet-Niche Luminaire. A luminaire intended to be installed in a forming shell where the luminaire will be completely surrounded by water. Figure 680–9

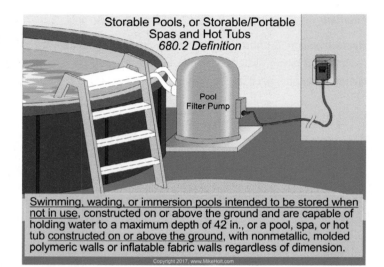

Figure 680–8

Figure 680–9

680.4 Approval of Equipment

A new rule requires electrical equipment associated with pools to be listed.

Analysis

NEW Swimming pools are constructed of a huge number of individual components that allow them to meet the needs of each installation. A previous oversight in the *Code* failed to require all of the electrical components of the pool, such as lights, pool cover motors, and other associated equipment, to be listed. I think we'll all feel much better knowing that everything electrical in nature associated with a pool will now be required to meet a listing standard. Thanks to the person who submitted this change, we'll all be safer.

680.4 Approval of Equipment

Electrical equipment installed in the water, walls, or decks of pools, fountains, and similar installations <u>must be listed</u>.

680.7 Grounding and Bonding Terminals

Grounding and bonding terminals now have specific location-driven requirements.

Analysis

NEW Swimming pools, spas, and hot tubs, along with their surrounding environments, are full of chemicals. The presence of these chemicals, combined with the inherent dampness of the locations, results in a highly corrosive environment. Because of the importance of the continuity of grounding and bonding connections we have this new section in the 2017 *NEC*.

This new rule has two independent requirements. First, all grounding and bonding terminals must be identified (see Article 100) for use in wet and corrosive environments; this applies to terminals installed in the field and by the manufacturer. These grounding and bonding terminals aren't required to be specifically listed for this application because such a product doesn't exist.

Terminals that are field-installed must be copper, copper alloy, or stainless steel and be listed for direct burial. It's worth noting that terminals, such as those commonly used on rebar, that are listed for direct burial are also listed for concrete encasement.

680.7 Grounding and Bonding Terminals

Grounding and bonding terminals must be identified for use in wet and corrosive environments and be listed for direct burial use. Figure 680–10

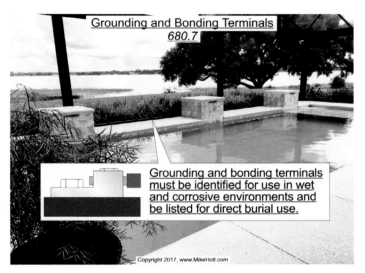

Grounding and bonding terminals must be identified for use in wet and corrosive environments and be listed for direct burial use.

Figure 680–10

680.11 Underground Wiring

This section number was changed and the cover (burial depth) requirements for pools and similar installations are now the same as other installations.

Analysis

CLARIFIED **Underground Depth.** In previous editions of the *Code*, Table 680.10 contained the minimum cover requirements for swimming pools and similar installations. This table has been the source of much confusion and many debates as it relates to its applicability. The solution was to simply apply the minimum cover for underground wiring for a pool or similar installation and use the requirements contained in Table 300.5.

The entire discussion about the distance away from the pool, which used to be 5 ft, was removed. Now wiring can be as close to the pool as you'd like, but wiring under the pool is only permitted for associated pool equipment.

• • •

Wiring Methods. The permitted wiring methods are now indicated. Most of the wiring methods one has come to expect for a pool are recognized, and Type MC cable (suitable for the location) is also permitted.

CLARIFIED

680.11 Underground Wiring

Underground pool wiring <u>must be installed in rigid metal conduit, intermediate metal conduit, rigid polyvinyl chloride conduit, reinforced thermosetting resin conduit, or Type MC cable listed for the location (sunlight-resistant or for direct burial)</u>. Wiring under a pool is only permitted if the wiring is necessary to supply pool equipment. Minimum cover depths for underground wiring must comply with the <u>cover requirements contained in Table 300.5.</u> Figure 680–11

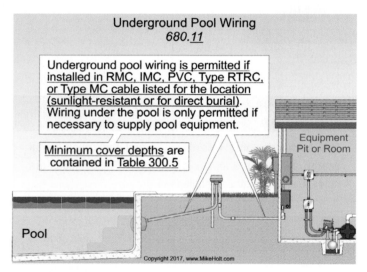

Underground Pool Wiring
680.11

Underground pool wiring is permitted if installed in RMC, IMC, PVC, Type RTRC, or Type MC cable listed for the location (sunlight-resistant or for direct burial). Wiring under the pool is only permitted if necessary to supply pool equipment.

Minimum cover depths are contained in Table 300.5

Equipment Pit or Room

Pool

Copyright 2017, www.MikeHolt.com

Figure 680–11

680.12 Equipment Rooms and Pits

The section number was changed and a reminder was added that pools and similar installations are in corrosive environments.

Analysis

Corrosive Environment. As discussed earlier in 680.7, the chemicals associated with swimming pools and similar installations create corrosive environments, particularly in indoor locations such as a pool equipment room. Section 300.6 is a general rule that requires all electrical equipment to be suitable for the environment in which it's installed.

CLARIFIED

Adding a reference to 300.6 in this section isn't really a technical change, because you have to comply with that rule regardless. Even though adding this text doesn't add any requirements, it might still serve as a worthwhile reminder to those installing and inspecting pools.

A new Informational Note was added as well, which, once again, reminds the *Code* user of the possibility of corrosion. It also provides a reference to an ANSI standard that gives guidance on ventilating locations such as pool chemical and equipment rooms. Storing pool chemicals in the same area as the electrical equipment is certainly a bad idea, but the *NEC* really can't regulate that, as it's not an installation issue and is therefore outside its scope [90.2].

NEW

680.12 Equipment Rooms and Pits

Permanently installed pool, storable pool, outdoor spa, outdoor hot tub, or fountain equipment isn't permitted to be located in rooms or pits that don't have drainage that prevents water accumulation during normal operation or filter maintenance.

<u>Equipment must be suitable for the corrosive environment in accordance with 300.6.</u> Figure 680–12

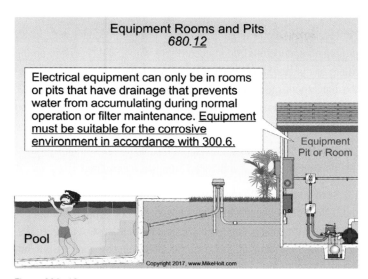

Equipment Rooms and Pits
680.12

Electrical equipment can only be in rooms or pits that have drainage that prevents water from accumulating during normal operation or filter maintenance. Equipment must be suitable for the corrosive environment in accordance with 300.6.

Equipment Pit or Room

Pool

Figure 680–12

Note: Chemicals such as chlorine cause severe corrosive and deteriorating effects on electrical connections, equipment, and enclosures. Ventilation of indoor spaces in accordance with ANSI/APSP-11, *Standard for Water Quality in Public Pools and Spas* can reduce the likelihood of the accumulation of corrosive vapors.

680.14 Corrosive Environment

A new section provides the requirements for equipment subject to corrosion.

Analysis

NEW As is the case with everything in Chapter 6, swimming pools and similar installations come with their own risks and therefore their own rules. Of particular concern are the effects of pool chemicals, such as chlorine, on electrical equipment. While 300.6 does an admiral job in requiring equipment to be suitable for the location, 680.14 might do an even better job by specifying exactly what can and can't be installed in these locations. 680.14(A) lists the locations of concern, while 680.14(B) tells us what can be installed in those areas.

680.14 Corrosive Environment

(A) Corrosive Environment. Areas where pool chemicals are stored; areas with circulation pumps, automatic chlorinators, and filters; and open areas under decks adjacent to or abutting the pool structure are considered to be a corrosive environment. Figure 680–13

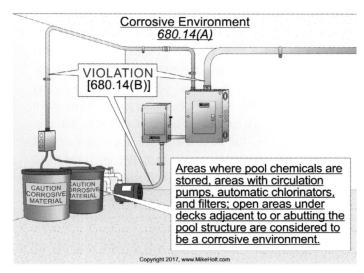

Corrosive Environment
680.14(A)

VIOLATION
[680.14(B)]

Areas where pool chemicals are stored, areas with circulation pumps, automatic chlorinators, and filters; open areas under decks adjacent to or abutting the pool structure are considered to be a corrosive environment.

CAUTION CORROSIVE MATERIAL

Figure 680–13

(B) Wiring Methods. Wiring methods (boxes and enclosures) in areas described in 680.14(A) must be listed and identified for use; rigid metal conduit, intermediate metal conduit, rigid polyvinyl chloride conduit, and reinforced thermosetting resin conduit are permitted in the corrosive environment areas specified in 680.14(A).

680.21 Motors

The allowable methods for wiring a pool motor have been greatly simplified.

Analysis

CLARIFIED The rules for how to wire a swimming pool motor in previous editions of the *NEC* were difficult to follow both for installers and inspectors. In this *Code* cycle numerous revisions were made that make it easier to understand and follow the rules for this section. The *NEC* now allows any wiring method contained in Chapter 3, such as RMC, IMC, PVC, and RTRC conduits, unless it's installed in a corrosive atmosphere and then must follow 680.14(B).

680.21 Motors

(A) Wiring Methods. The wiring to a pool-associated motor must comply with (A)(1) unless modified by (A)(2), (A)(3), (A)(4), or (A)(5).

(1) General. Where branch-circuit wiring for pool-associated motors is subject to physical damage or exposed to damp, wet, or corrosive locations, rigid metal conduit, intermediate metal conduit, rigid polyvinyl chloride conduit, and reinforced thermosetting resin conduit, or Type MC cable listed for the location must be used. Figure 680–14

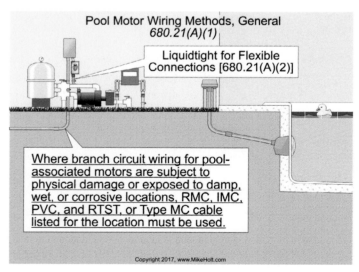

Figure 680–14

The wiring methods must contain an insulated copper equipment grounding conductor sized in accordance with 250.122, based on the rating of the circuit overcurrent protection device, but in no case can the equipment grounding conductor be sized smaller than 12 AWG. Wiring in dry and noncorrosive locations can be in any wiring method permitted in Chapter 3.

(2) Flexible Connections. Liquidtight flexible metal or liquidtight flexible nonmetallic conduit with listed fittings are permitted.

(3) Cord-and-Plug Connections. Cords for pool motors are permitted if the length doesn't exceed 3 ft and the cord contains a copper equipment grounding conductor, sized in accordance with 250.122, based on the rating of the overcurrent protection device, but not smaller than 12 AWG. Figure 680–15

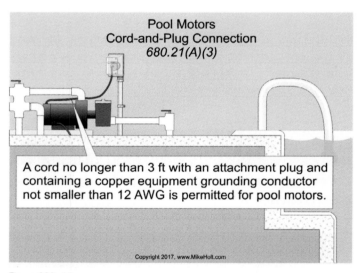

Figure 680–15

Author's Comment:

■ For outdoor spas and hot tubs, the flexible cord must be GFCI protected and it can be up to 15 ft long [680.42(A)(2)].

(C) GFCI Protection. GFCI protection is required for outlets supplying pool pump motors connected to single-phase, 120V through 240V branch circuits, whether by receptacle or by direct connection. Figure 680–16

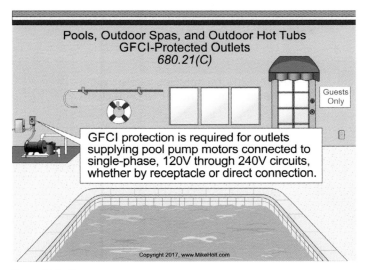

Figure 680–16

680.22 Lighting, Receptacles, and Equipment

The requirements for receptacles supplying circulation pumps were reduced, and new provisions for "low-voltage gas-fired" equipment were added.

Analysis

REDUCED

Receptacles for Pumps. Previous editions of the *NEC* required that receptacles used to supply power to a pump motor be at least 10 ft from the pool, be GFCI-protected, be of the grounding type, and be single receptacles. The 2017 *Code* now allows the receptacle to be within 6 ft of the pool, which correlates with most of the rules in Article 680, and they can be of the duplex type.

NEW

Low-Voltage Gas-Fired Equipment. New language was added to allow for low-voltage gas-fired equipment, such as luminaires, fireplaces, fire pits, and similar items. Reading the new text, you'll notice there aren't really any specific requirements for this equipment that don't already exist in Article 680, such as bonding the metal parts and utilizing power supplies that are listed. Although there aren't new requirements, it's still probably worth mentioning this equipment, because if the *NEC* doesn't mention it at all it could be construed as being prohibited.

680.22 Lighting, Receptacles, and Equipment

(A) Receptacles.

(1) Required Receptacle Location. At least one 15A or 20A, 125V receptacle must be located not less than 6 ft and not more than 20 ft from the inside wall of a permanently installed pool, outdoor spa, or outdoor hot tub. This receptacle must be located not more than 6½ ft above the floor, platform, or grade level serving the permanently installed pool, outdoor spa, or outdoor hot tub. Figure 680–17

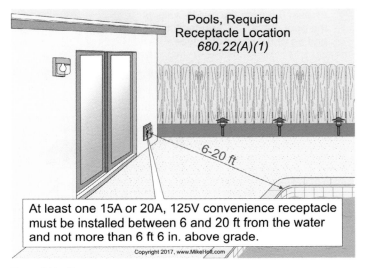

Figure 680–17

(2) Circulation System. Receptacles for permanently installed pool, outdoor spa, and outdoor hot tub motors, or other loads directly related to the circulation system must be located at least 6 ft from the inside walls of the pool, be GFCI protected, and be of the grounding type. Figure 680–18

(3) Other Receptacles. Receptacles not for motors or other loads directly related to the circulation system must be not less than 6 ft from the inside walls of a permanently installed pool, outdoor spa, or outdoor hot tub. Figure 680–19

(4) GFCI-Protected Receptacles. 15A and 20A, 125V receptacles located within 20 ft from the inside walls of a permanently installed pool, outdoor spa, or outdoor hot tub must be GFCI protected. Figure 680–20

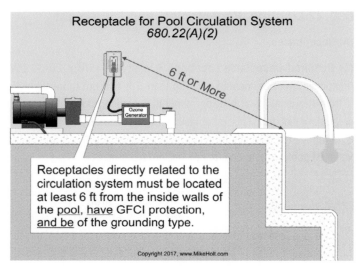

Receptacle for Pool Circulation System
680.22(A)(2)

6 ft or More

Receptacles directly related to the circulation system must be located at least 6 ft from the inside walls of the pool, have GFCI protection, and be of the grounding type.

Figure 680–18

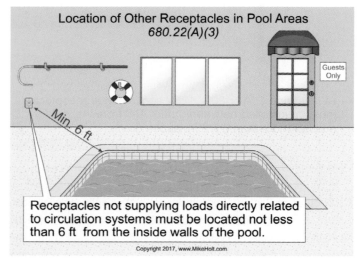

Location of Other Receptacles in Pool Areas
680.22(A)(3)

Guests Only

Min. 6 ft

Receptacles not supplying loads directly related to circulation systems must be located not less than 6 ft from the inside walls of the pool.

Figure 680–19

Author's Comment:

- Outdoor dwelling unit receptacles must be GFCI protected, regardless of the distance from a permanently installed pool, spa, or hot tub [210.8(A)(3)].

- 15A and 20A, 125V receptacles for nondwelling units located outdoors require GFCI protection [210.8(B)(4)].

(5) Measurements. The receptacle distance is measured as the shortest path an appliance flexible cord would follow without passing through a wall, doorway, or window.

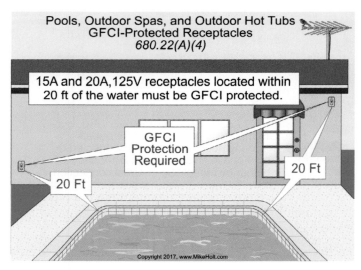

Pools, Outdoor Spas, and Outdoor Hot Tubs
GFCI-Protected Receptacles
680.22(A)(4)

15A and 20A, 125V receptacles located within 20 ft of the water must be GFCI protected.

GFCI Protection Required

20 Ft

20 Ft

Figure 680–20

(B) Luminaires and Ceiling Fans.

(1) New Outdoor Installations. Luminaires and ceiling fans installed above the water, or the area extending within 5 ft horizontally from the inside walls of a permanently installed pool, outdoor spa, or outdoor hot tub, isn't permitted to be less than 12 ft above the maximum water level.

(3) Existing Installations. Existing luminaires located less than 5 ft horizontally from the inside walls of a permanently installed pool, outdoor spa, or outdoor hot tub must be not less than 5 ft above the surface of the maximum water level, must be rigidly attached to the existing structure, and must be GFCI protected. Figure 680–21

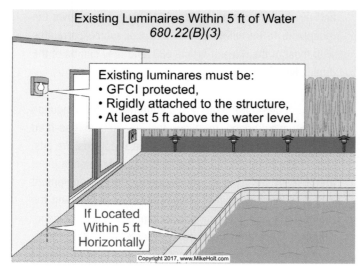

Existing Luminaires Within 5 ft of Water
680.22(B)(3)

Existing luminares must be:
• GFCI protected,
• Rigidly attached to the structure,
• At least 5 ft above the water level.

If Located Within 5 ft Horizontally

Figure 680–21

(4) Adjacent Areas. New luminaires installed between 5 ft and 10 ft horizontally from the inside walls of a permanently installed pool, outdoor spa, or outdoor hot tub must be GFCI protected, unless installed not less than 5 ft above the maximum water level and rigidly attached to the existing structure adjacent to or enclosing the permanently installed pool, outdoor spa, or outdoor hot tub.

(6) Low-Voltage Luminaires. Listed luminaires that don't require grounding, and that meet the low-voltage contact limit, can be less than 5 ft from the inside walls of the pool. Figure 680–22

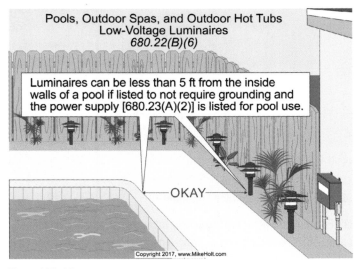

Figure 680–22

Author's Comment:

- The Low-Voltage Contact Limit is defined in 680.2.

(7) Low-Voltage Gas-Fired Luminaires, Fireplaces, Fire Pits, and Similar Equipment. Listed gas-fired luminaires, fireplaces, fire pits, and similar equipment using low-voltage ignitors supplied by listed transformers or power supplies that don't exceed the low-voltage contact limit can be located less than 5 feet from the inside walls of the pool. Metal parts of the equipment must be bonded in accordance with 680.26(B); metal gas piping must be bonded in accordance with 250.140(B) and 250.26(B)(7).

(C) Switching Devices. Circuit breakers, time clocks, pool light switches, and other switching devices must be located not less than 5 ft horizontally from the inside walls of a permanently installed pool, outdoor spa, or outdoor hot tub unless separated by a solid fence, wall, or other permanent barrier, unless the switching device is listed as being acceptable for use within 5 ft. Figure 680–23

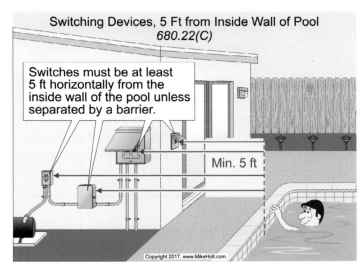

Figure 680–23

(D) Other Outlets. Other outlets aren't permitted to be located less than 10 ft from the inside walls of a permanently installed pool, outdoor spa, or outdoor hot tub. The receptacle distance is measured as the shortest path an appliance flexible cord would follow without passing through a wall, doorway, or window [680.22(A)(5)].

Note: Examples of other outlets may include remote-control, signaling, fire alarm, and communications circuits.

680.23 Underwater Luminaires

Some unenforceable language about GFCI protection has been removed, and the allowable wiring methods for underwater luminaires have been simplified.

Analysis

CLARIFIED

GFCI protection. The *Code* previously required GFCI protection for underwater luminaires to be installed in a manner that prevents shock hazard during relamping. It also required the physical location of the GFCI device (the test and reset buttons) be such that there's "no shock hazard…," but this is impossible. A GFCI will still allow you to get shocked, but in most cases it will keep the shock from being a fatal one. If you're talking about electricity there's always a shock hazard, and moving the GFCI device isn't going to change that fact.

• • •

Wiring Methods. Section 680.23(F)(1) was extensively revised to require corrosion-resistant wiring methods in areas where corrosion is a concern. This makes sense, and in actuality it was already required by 300.6. In areas where corrosion isn't a concern, any suitable wiring method can be used, and it must follow the wiring method rules in its applicable article. This is a significant simplification of the previous rule, making Article 680 better in 2017 than it was in 2014.

CLARIFIED

680.23 Underwater Luminaires

(A) General.

(2) Transformers and Power Supplies. Transformers and power supplies for underwater luminaires must be listed, <u>labeled, and identified</u> for swimming pool and spa use.

(3) GFCI Protection, <u>Lamping</u>, Relamping, <u>and Servicing</u>. Branch circuits that supply underwater luminaires operating at voltages greater than 15V for sinusoidal alternating current, 21.20V peak for nonsinusoidal alternating current, 30V for continuous direct current, and 12.40V peak for direct current interrupted at a rate of 10 to 200 Hz or less [680.2 Low-Voltage Contact Limit] must be GFCI protected. Figure 680–24

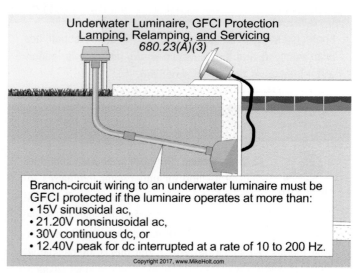

Underwater Luminaire, GFCI Protection
Lamping, Relamping, and Servicing
680.23(A)(3)

Branch-circuit wiring to an underwater luminaire must be GFCI protected if the luminaire operates at more than:
• 15V sinusoidal ac,
• 21.20V nonsinusoidal ac,
• 30V continuous dc, or
• 12.40V peak for dc interrupted at a rate of 10 to 200 Hz.

Copyright 2017, www.MikeHolt.com

Figure 680–24

(5) Wall-Mounted Luminaires. Underwater luminaires must be installed so that the top of the luminaire lens isn't less than 18 in. below the normal water level. Figure 680–25

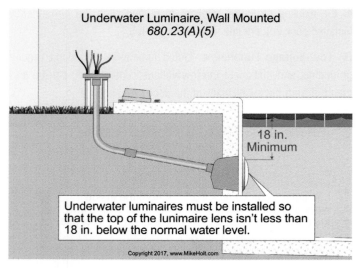

Underwater Luminaire, Wall Mounted
680.23(A)(5)

18 in.
Minimum

Underwater luminaires must be installed so that the top of the lunimaire lens isn't less than 18 in. below the normal water level.

Copyright 2017, www.MikeHolt.com

Figure 680–25

(B) Wet-Niche Underwater Luminaires.

(1) Forming Shells. Forming shells for wet-niche underwater luminaires must be equipped with provisions for raceway entries. Forming shells used with PVC conduit systems must include provisions for terminating an 8 AWG copper conductor.

(2) Wiring to the Forming Shell. The raceway that extends directly to the underwater pool wet-niche forming shell must comply with (a) or (b).

(a) Metal Raceway. Brass or corrosion-resistant rigid metal conduit approved by the authority having jurisdiction.

(b) Nonmetallic Raceway. A nonmetallic raceway to the forming shell must contain an 8 AWG insulated (solid or stranded) copper bonding jumper that terminates to the forming shell and junction box. Figure 680–26

The termination of the 8 AWG bonding jumper in the forming shell must be covered with a listed potting compound to protect the connection from the possible deteriorating effects of pool water.

(6) Servicing. The forming shell location and length of flexible cord in the forming shell must allow for personnel to place the removed luminaire on the deck or other dry location for maintenance. The luminaire maintenance location must be accessible without entering or going in the pool water. Figure 680–27

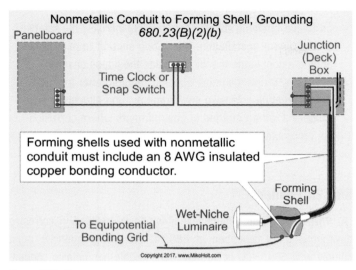

Figure 680–26

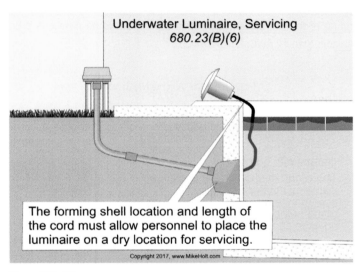

Figure 680–27

Author's Comment:

- While it may be necessary to enter the pool water, possibly with underwater breathing apparatus in some cases, the flexible cord must be long enough to allow the luminaire to be brought out and placed on a deck or other dry location where the relamping, maintenance, or inspection can take place without entering the pool water.

(F) Branch-Circuit Wiring.

(1) General. Where branch-circuit wiring for underwater luminaires is installed in corrosive environments as described in 680.14, the wiring methods must comply with 680.14(B) or be liquidtight flexible

nonmetallic conduit. The wiring methods must contain an insulated copper equipment grounding conductor sized in accordance with 250.122, based on the rating of the overcurrent protection device, but in no case can it be smaller than 12 AWG. Figure 680–28

In noncorrosive environments, any Chapter 3 wiring method is permitted.

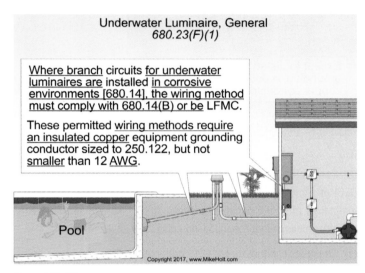

Figure 680–28

Ex: If connecting to transformers or power supplies for pool lights, liquidtight flexible metal conduit is permitted in individual lengths not exceeding 6 ft.

(2) Equipment Grounding Conductor. For other than listed low-voltage luminaires not requiring grounding, branch-circuit conductors for an underwater luminaire must contain an insulated copper equipment grounding conductor sized in accordance with Table 250.122, based on the rating of the overcurrent protection device, but not smaller than 12 AWG. Figure 680–29

The circuit equipment grounding conductor for the underwater luminaire isn't permitted to be spliced, except as permitted in (a) or (b).

(a) If more than one underwater luminaire is supplied by the same branch circuit, the circuit equipment grounding conductor can terminate at a listed pool junction box that meets the requirements of 680.24(A).

(b) The circuit equipment grounding conductor can terminate at the grounding terminal of a listed pool transformer that meets the requirements of 680.23(A)(2).

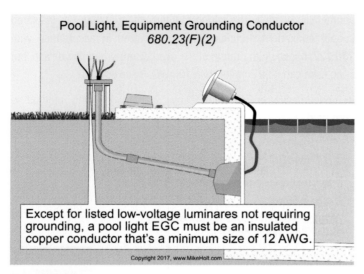

Pool Light, Equipment Grounding Conductor
680.23(F)(2)

Except for listed low-voltage luminares not requiring grounding, a pool light EGC must be an insulated copper conductor that's a minimum size of 12 AWG.

Copyright 2017, www.MikeHolt.com

Figure 680–29

(3) Conductors. The branch-circuit conductors on the load side of a GFCI or transformer that complies with 680.23(A)(8) for underwater luminaires must not occupy raceways or enclosures with other conductors unless one of the following conditions apply:

(1) The other conductors are GFCI protected.

(2) The conductor is an equipment grounding conductor as required by 680.23(B)(2)(b).

(3) The other conductors supply a feed-through type GFCI.

(4) The other conductors are GFCI protected within the panelboard.

680.25 Feeders

The wiring methods for feeders supplying pools and similar installations were changed into a reasonable requirement.

Analysis

CLARIFIED

Previous editions of this requirement were so unrealistically restrictive that many inspectors simply ignored them. The requirements were vague as to their applicability, and were the subject of many debates. If a person wanted to add a pool to an existing house, it often required remodeling a significant portion of the electrical system, assuming the environment was

corrosive, but it did absolutely nothing to increase the safety of the overall installation. This *Code* section implied that adding a pool made the wiring inside the house unsafe.

The *NEC* now contains specific requirements for feeders installed in corrosive environments, and allows for any Chapter 3 wiring method in environments where corrosion isn't a problem. What a welcome change!

680.25 Feeders

(A) Wiring Methods. Where feeder wiring is installed in corrosive environments as described in 680.14, the wiring methods must comply with 680.14(B) or be liquidtight flexible nonmetallic conduit. The wiring methods must contain an insulated copper equipment grounding conductor sized in accordance with 250.122, based on the rating of the overcurrent protection device, but in no case can it be smaller than 12 AWG. Figure 680–30

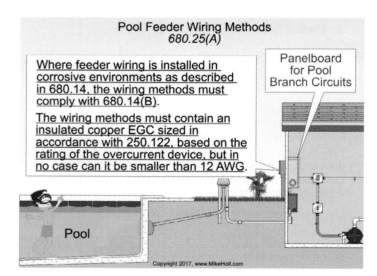

Pool Feeder Wiring Methods
680.25(A)

Where feeder wiring is installed in corrosive environments as described in 680.14, the wiring methods must comply with 680.14(B).

The wiring methods must contain an insulated copper EGC sized in accordance with 250.122, based on the rating of the overcurrent device, but in no case can it be smaller than 12 AWG.

Panelboard for Pool Branch Circuits

Pool

Copyright 2017, www.MikeHolt.com

Figure 680–30

In noncorrosive environments, any Chapter 3 wiring method is permitted.

680.26 Equipotential Bonding

Changes to the bonding requirements of perimeter surfaces (decking) were made for accuracy and logic.

Analysis

CLARIFIED

The perimeter surface around a pool must be bonded to the pool itself, the pool equipment, and the metal objects surrounding the pool, in accordance with 680.26. Previous editions of the *Code* stated that the perimeter surface was required to extend 3 ft from the outside edge of the pool, and a literal reading of that statement meant that you could never have a perimeter surface narrower than 3 ft. For example, an indoor pool next to a wall could be construed as noncompliant if the wall was within 3 ft of the pool. Changes to this edition clarify that you don't have to have 3 ft but you must bond everything as though you did. If you have a wall greater than 5 ft in height that's within 3 ft of the pool you only need to bond the perimeter surface on the pool side of the wall. This makes sense, especially if the wall in question is an exterior wall!

Author's Comment:

- The bonding requirements of this section don't apply to spas and hot tubs [680.42].

680.26 Equipotential Bonding

 Scan this QR code for a video of Mike explaining this topic; it's a sample from the DVDs that accompany this textbook.

(A) Performance. The required equipotential bonding is intended to reduce voltage gradients in the area around a permanently installed pool. Figure 680–31

(B) Bonded Parts. The parts of a permanently installed pool listed in (B)(1) through (B)(7) must be bonded together with a solid copper conductor not smaller than 8 AWG with listed pressure connectors, terminal bars, exothermic welding, or other listed means in accordance with 250.8(A). Figure 680–32

Equipotential bonding isn't required to extend to or be attached to any panelboard, service equipment, or grounding electrode.

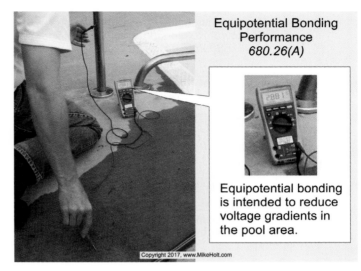

Figure 680–31

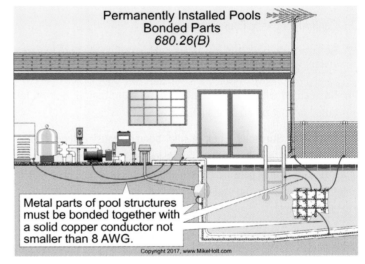

Figure 680–32

(1) Concrete Pool Shells.

(a) Structural Reinforcing Steel. Unencapsulated (bare) structural reinforcing steel bonded together by steel tie wires or the equivalent. Where structural reinforcing steel is encapsulated in a nonconductive compound, a copper conductor grid must be installed in accordance with 680.26(B)(1)(b). Figure 680–33

(b) Copper Conductor Grid. A copper conductor grid must comply with (b)(1) through (b)(4).

(1) Minimum 8 AWG bare solid copper conductors bonded to each other at all points of crossing in accordance with 250.8 or other approved means.

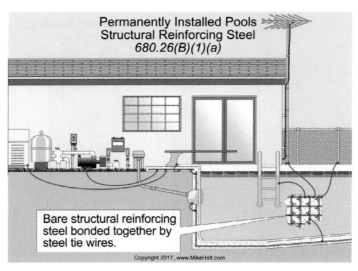

Figure 680–33

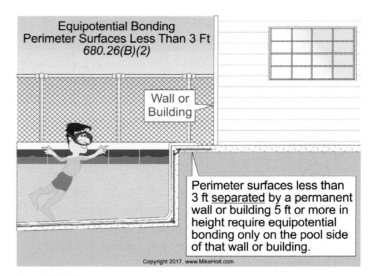

Figure 680–35

(2) Conform to the contour of the pool.

(3) Be arranged in a 12-in. by 12-in. network of conductors in a uniformly spaced perpendicular grid pattern with a tolerance of 4 in.

(4) Be secured within or under the pool no more than 6 in. from the outer contour of the pool shell.

(2) Perimeter Surfaces. Equipotential bonding must extend a minimum of 3 ft horizontally beyond the inside walls of a pool, where not separated from the pool by a permanent wall or building of 5 ft in height. Figure 680–34 and Figure 680–35

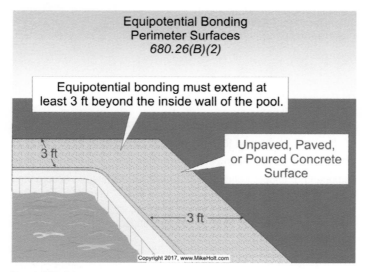

Figure 680–34

(a) Structural Reinforcing Steel. Structural reinforcing steel bonded together by steel tie wires or the equivalent in accordance with 680.26(B)(1)(a). Figure 680–36

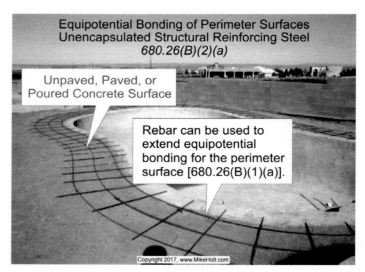

Figure 680–36

Author's Comment:

- The *NEC* doesn't provide any guidance on the installation requirements for structural reinforcing steel when used as a perimeter equipotential bonding method.

(b) Alternative Means. Where structural reinforcing steel isn't available (or is encapsulated in a nonconductive compound such as epoxy), equipotential bonding meeting all of the following requirements must be installed: Figure 680–37

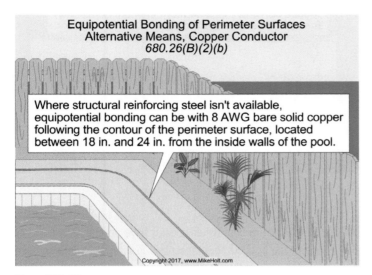

Figure 680–37

(1) The bonding conductor must be 8 AWG bare solid copper.

(2) The bonding conductor must follow the contour of the perimeter surface.

(3) Listed splicing devices must be used.

(4) The required conductor must be located between 18 in. and 24 in. from the inside walls of the pool.

(5) The bonding conductor must be secured in or under the deck or unpaved surface within 4 in. to 6 in. below the subgrade.

(3) Metallic Components. Metallic parts of the pool structure must be bonded to the equipotential grid.

(4) Underwater Metal Forming Shells. Metal forming shells must be bonded to the equipotential grid. Figure 680–38

(5) Metal Fittings. Metal fittings 4 in. and larger located within or attached to the pool structure, such as ladders and handrails, must be bonded to the equipotential grid. Figure 680–39

(6) Electrical Equipment. Metal parts of electrical equipment associated with the pool water circulating system, such as water heaters, pump motors, and metal parts of pool covers must be bonded to the equipotential grid. Figure 680–40

Figure 680–38

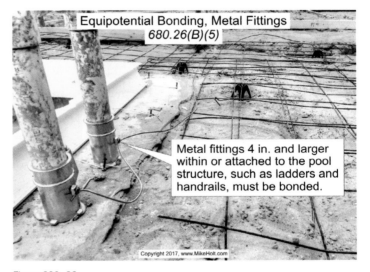

Figure 680–39

Ex: Metal parts of listed double-insulated equipment aren't required to be bonded.

(a) Double-Insulated Water-Pump Motors. If a double-insulated water-pump motor is installed, a solid 8 AWG copper bonding conductor must be provided for a replacement motor.

(7) Fixed Metal Parts. Fixed metal parts must be bonded to the equipotential grid, including but not limited to, metal-sheathed cables and raceways, metal piping, metal awnings, metal fences, and metal door and window frames. Figure 680–41

Ex 1: If separated from the pool structure by a permanent barrier that prevents contact by a person.

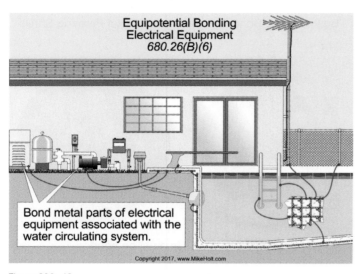

Figure 680–40

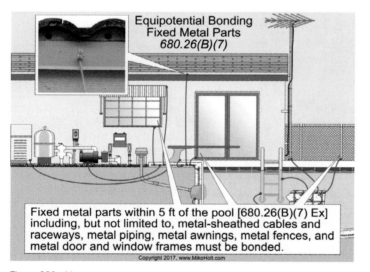

Figure 680–41

Ex 2: If located more than 5 ft horizontally from the inside walls of the pool structure. Figure 680–42

Ex 3: If located more than 12 ft measured vertically above the maximum water level.

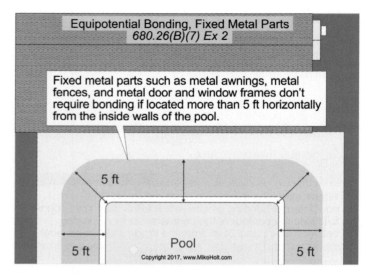

Figure 680–42

(C) Pool Water. If the pool water doesn't have an electrical connection to one of the bonded parts described in 680.26(B), an approved corrosion-resistant conductive surface that's at least 9 sq in. must be in contact with the water. The corrosion-resistance conductive surface must be bonded in accordance with 680.26(B), and be located in an area where it won't be dislodged or damaged during normal pool usage. Figure 680–43

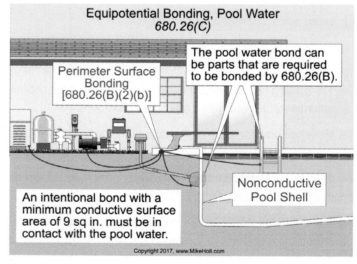

Figure 680–43

680.28 Gas-Fired Water Heaters

New GFCI provisions for gas-fired water heaters were added.

Analysis

NEW Most swimming pool equipment operates on a voltage high enough to kill you if there's a fault, and gas-fired water heaters are no exception. That being the case, it's a good idea to have it GFCI protected to prevent a problem before it happens. The electrical circuit for gas-fired water heaters has previously been an exception to the rules, but it isn't any longer. It's now required to be protected like all other pool equipment. This change didn't come with any documented incidents, but it's an excellent preventative measure.

680.28 Gas-Fired Water Heaters

Circuits serving gas-fired swimming pool and spa water heaters operating at voltages greater than 15V for sinusoidal alternating current, 21.20V peak for nonsinusoidal alternating current, 30V for continuous direct current, or 12.40V peak for direct current interrupted at a rate of 10 to 200 Hz [680.2 Low-Voltage Contact Limit], must be GFCI protected.

680.42 Outdoor Installations

The rules for the interior wiring supplying outdoor spas and hot tubs were simplified.

Analysis

CLARIFIED Hot tubs and spas certainly have their own dangers and deserve their own special electrical requirements, but does it really matter what the wiring method on the inside of a house is, if it's supplying a hot tub? I don't think so, and now Code Making Panel 17 doesn't either. This section now allows us to follow the rules in Chapter 3 to be compliant. Yet another great simplification in the 2017 *NEC*.

680.42 Outdoor Installations

(B) Equipotential Bonding. Equipotential bonding of perimeter surfaces in accordance with 680.26(B)(2) isn't required for outdoor spas and hot tubs if:

(1) The spa or hot tub is listed, <u>labeled, and identified</u> as a self-contained spa or hot tub for aboveground use. Figure 680–44

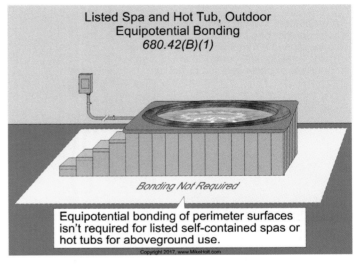

Figure 680–44

(2) The spa or hot tub is not identified as suitable for indoor use.

(3) The spa or hot tub is located on or above grade.

(4) If the top rim of the spa or hot tub is at least 28 in. above a perimeter surface located within 30 in. from the spa or hot tub. Figure 680–45

Figure 680–45

(C) Interior Dwelling Unit Wiring for Outdoor Spas or Hot Tubs. Any Chapter 3 wiring method is permitted in the interior of a dwelling unit for the connection to a motor disconnect and the motor, heating, and control loads that are part of a self-contained spa or hot tub or a packaged spa or hot tub equipment assembly. Figure 680–46

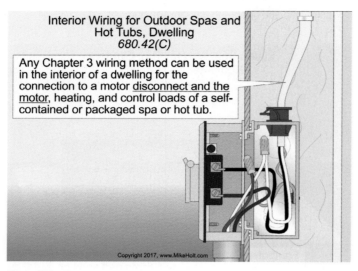

Interior Wiring for Outdoor Spas and Hot Tubs, Dwelling
680.42(C)

Any Chapter 3 wiring method can be used in the interior of a dwelling for the connection to a motor disconnect and the motor, heating, and control loads of a self-contained or packaged spa or hot tub.

Copyright 2017, www.MikeHolt.com

Figure 680–46

680.74 Equipotential Bonding

The rules for bonding hydromassage tubs have been reorganized and revised.

Analysis

REORGANIZED

There are a few sections in the *Code* that you know are going to be revised every three years like clockwork; one is 110.16 and the other is 680.74. Bonding a hydromassage tub is still a bit of a mystery. There've been no documented incidents of electrocution or even injury that I've been able to find, yet we're required to install an 8 AWG conductor in its vicinity, even when a double-insulated motor is installed.

New to this edition of the *NEC* we find ourselves needing to bond objects within 5 ft of the tub, unless they're small and unlikely to become energized. Several years ago it was very common to find fireplaces installed at the foot of a hydromassage tub. With these new requirements, the fireplace will need to be bonded.

680.74 Equipotential Bonding

(A) General. The following parts must be bonded together.

(1) Metal fittings within or attached to the hydromassage tub structure that are in contact with the circulating water.

(2) Metal parts of electrical equipment associated with the hydromassage tub water circulating system, including pump and blower motors.

(3) Metal-sheathed cables, metal raceways, and metal piping within 5 ft of the inside walls of the hydromassage tub and not separated from the tub area by a permanent barrier.

(4) Exposed metal surfaces within 5 ft of the inside walls of the hydromassage tub and not separated from the tub by a permanent barrier.

(5) Electrical devices not associated with the hydromassage tubs located within 5 ft from the hydromassage tub.

Ex 1: Small conductive surfaces not likely to become energized, such as air and water jets, supply valve assemblies, and drain fittings not connected to metallic piping, and towel bars, mirror frames, and similar nonelectrical equipment not connected to metal framing aren't required to be bonded.

Ex 2: Double-insulated motors and blowers aren't required to be bonded.

(B) Bonding Conductor. Metal parts required to be bonded by 680.74(A) must be bonded together using a solid copper conductor not smaller than 8 AWG. The bonding jumper isn't required to be extended or attached to any remote panelboard, service equipment, or any electrode. Figure 680–47

A bonding jumper long enough to terminate on a replacement nondouble-insulated pump or blower motor must be provided and it must terminate to the equipment grounding conductor of the branch circuit of the motor when a double-insulated circulating pump or blower motor is used. Figure 680–48

Hydromassage Bathtub, Bonding
680.74(B)

Metal parts required to be bonded by 680.74(A) must be bonded together using a solid copper conductor not smaller than 8 AWG. The bonding jumper isn't required to extended or attached to any remote panelboard, service equipment, or electrode.

Copyright 2017, www.MikeHolt.com

Figure 680–47

Hydromassage Bathtub, Bonding
680.74(B)

A bonding jumper long enough to terminate on a replacement nondouble-insulated pump or blower motor must be provided and it must terminate to the EGC of the branch circuit of the motor when a double-insulated circulating pump or blower motor is used.

Copyright 2017, www.MikeHolt.com

Figure 680–48

Part VIII. Electrically Powered Pool Lifts
680.80—680.85

A new Part VIII, covering electrically powered pool lifts, was added to this article.

Analysis

NEW Sections 680.80 through 680.85 are new additions to the 2017 *NEC*, and they apply to electrically powered pool lifts. Section 680.80 states that electrically powered pool lifts need to only comply with Part VIII of this article. Section 680.81 requires the lift to be listed, unless it's of a voltage lower than discussed in the three exceptions. Section 680.82 requires GFCI protection for the lift, unless, once again, the voltage is less than the low-voltage contact limit. Section 680.83 requires the lift to be bonded in accordance with 680.26. Section 680.84 requires switches be at least 5 ft from the wall of the pool, unless the voltages are lower than the low-voltage contact limit. Section 680.85 requires the lift to have a nameplate.

Introduction to Article 695—Fire Pumps

The general philosophy behind most *Code* requirements is to provide circuit overcurrent protection that will shut down equipment before allowing the supply conductors to overheat and become damaged from overload. Article 695 departs from this philosophy. The idea is that the fire pump motor must run no matter what; it supplies water to a facility's fire overcurrent protection piping, which in turn supplies water to the sprinkler system and fire hoses. This article contains many requirements to ensure that an uninterrupted supply of water is maintained.

Some of these requirements are obvious. For example, locating the pump where it's exposure to fire is minimized. It's important to ensure that the fire pump and its jockey (pressure maintenance) pump have a reliable source of power. Also, fire pump wiring must remain independent of all other wiring. Some of the requirements of Article 695 seem wrong at first glance, until you remember why that fire pump is there in the first place. For example, the disconnect must be lockable in the closed position. You would normally expect it to be lockable in the open position because other articles require that for the safety of maintenance personnel. But the fire pump runs to ensure the safety of an entire facility and everyone in it. For the same reason, fire pump power circuits can't have automatic overcurrent protection against overloads.

Remember, the fire pump must be kept in service, even if doing so damages or destroys the pump. It's better to run the pump until its windings melt, than to save the fire pump and lose the facility. The intent of this article is to allow enough time for building occupants to escape and, if possible, to save the facility.

695.1 Scope

(A) Covered. Article 695 covers the installation of: Figure 695–1

(1) Electric power sources and interconnecting circuits

(2) Switching and control equipment dedicated to fire pump drivers

(B) Not Covered. Article 695 doesn't cover:

(1) Performance, maintenance, and testing, and the internal wiring of the components of the system

(2) The installation of pressure maintenance (jockey or makeup) pumps

Figure 695–1

Note: Article 430 governs the installation of pressure maintenance (jockey or makeup) pumps, whether or not they're supplied by the fire pump.

(3) Transfer equipment upstream of the fire pump transfer switch(es)

Note: See NFPA 20, *Standard for the Installation of Stationary Pumps for Fire Protection,* for further information.

695.14 Control Wiring

The fire pump control wiring methods have been expanded.

Analysis

EXPANDED

Previous editions of the *Code* allowed the use of RMC, IMC, LFMC, Type MI cable, Type MC cable, and Type B LFNC. By specifying that only type B (gray color) could be used, it prohibited Type A (orange color). Type A LFNC has many restrictions in its use, including a 6-ft length limitation, in 356.12(3), so the likelihood of seeing it is still quite small. New to the 2017 *NEC* is the allowance to use EMT. If we can use LFNC, why couldn't we use EMT? We can now.

695.14 Control Wiring

(E) Wiring Methods. Control wiring must be in rigid metal conduit, intermediate metal conduit, liquidtight flexible metal conduit, <u>electrical metallic tubing</u>, liquidtight flexible nonmetallic <u>conduit, listed</u> Type MC cable with an impervious covering, or Type MI cable.

695.15 Surge Protection

Fire pump controllers must now have surge protection.

Analysis

NEW

Few people argue the advantages of having surge protection. In a commercial building, the computers probably all have surge protection, but the fire pump controller doesn't.

A study was conducted, commissioned by the NFPA Fire Protection Research Foundation, and it concluded that 12% of the fire pumps tested had damage due to surges. Surges can damage motor windings which shortens the life of motors, and controls are at even greater risk for damage from surges. It's not a good thing if a fire pump had to operate during a fire at full capacity and couldn't because of unnoticed damage. This requirement is pretty easy to justify from a safety perspective.

695.15 Surge Protection

<u>A listed surge protection device [Article 285] must be installed in or on the fire pump controller.</u>

CHAPTER 7

SPECIAL CONDITIONS

Introduction to Chapter 7—Special Conditions

Chapter 7, which covers special conditions, is the third of the *NEC* chapters that deal with special topics. Chapters 5 and 6 cover special occupancies, and special equipment, respectively. Remember, the first four chapters of the *Code* are sequential and form a foundation for each of the subsequent three chapters. Chapter 8 covers communications systems (twisted wire, antennas, and coaxial cable) and isn't subject to the requirements of Chapters 1 through 7 except where the requirements are specifically referenced there.

What exactly is a "Special Condition"? It's a situation that doesn't fall under the category of special occupancies or special equipment, but creates a need for additional measures to ensure the "safeguarding of people and property" mission of the *NEC*, as stated in 90.1(A).

The *Code* groups these logically, as you might expect. Here are the general groupings:

- *Power Systems.* Articles 700, 701, and 702. Article 700 addresses emergency systems, Article 701 applies to legally required standby systems, and Article 702 covers optional standby systems.

- *Interconnected Power Sources.* Article 705. This primarily has to do with generators or PV systems used for on-site power generation.

- *Low-Voltage, Limited Energy Systems.* Articles 725 through 770. Examples include control, signaling, instrumentation, fire alarm systems, and optical fiber installations.

- **Article 700—Emergency Systems.** The requirements of Article 700 apply only to the wiring methods for "Emergency Systems" that are essential for safety to human life and required by federal, state, municipal, or other regulatory codes. When normal power is lost, emergency systems must be capable of supplying emergency power in 10 seconds or less.

- **Article 701—Legally Required Standby Systems.** Legally required standby systems provide electrical power to aid in firefighting, rescue operations, control of health hazards, and similar operations, and are required by federal, state, municipal, or other regulatory codes. When normal power is lost, legally required standby systems must be capable of automatically supplying standby power in 60 seconds or less, instead of the 10 seconds or less required of emergency systems.

- **Article 702—Optional Standby Systems**. Optional standby systems are intended to protect public or private facilities or property where life safety doesn't depend on the performance of the system. These systems are typically installed to provide an alternate source of electrical power for such facilities as industrial and commercial buildings, farms, and residences, and to serve loads that, when stopped during any power outage, can cause discomfort, serious interruption of a process, or damage to a product or process. Optional standby systems are intended to supply on-site generated power to loads selected by the customer, either automatically or manually.

- **Article 725—Remote-Control, Signaling, and Power-Limited Circuits.** Article 725 contains the requirements for remote-control, signaling, and power-limited circuits that aren't an integral part of a device or appliance.

  - *Remote-Control Circuit.* A circuit that controls other circuits through a relay or solid-state device. For example, a circuit that controls the coil of a motor starter or lighting contactor is one type of remote-control circuit.

  - *Signaling Circuit.* A circuit that supplies energy to an appliance or device that gives a visual and/or audible signal. Circuits for doorbells, buzzers, code-calling systems, signal lights, annunciators, burglar alarms, and other indication or alarm devices are examples of signaling circuits.

- **Article 760—Fire Alarm Systems.** This article covers the installation of wiring and equipment for fire alarm systems. They include fire detection and alarm notification, voice communications, guard's tour, sprinkler waterflow, and sprinkler supervisory systems.

- **Article 770—Optical Fiber Cables and Raceways.** Article 770 covers the installation of optical fiber cables, which transmit signals using light for control, signaling, and communications. It also contains the installation requirements for raceways that contain optical fiber cables, and rules for composite cables (often called "hybrid" cables in the field) that combine optical fibers with current-carrying metallic conductors.

ARTICLE 700 EMERGENCY SYSTEMS

Introduction to Article 700—Emergency Systems

Emergency systems are legally required, often as a condition of an operating permit for a given facility. The authority having jurisdiction makes the determination as to whether such a system is necessary for a given facility and what it must entail. Sometimes, it simply provides power for exit lighting and exit signs upon loss of the main power or in the case of fire. Its purpose isn't to provide power for normal business operations, but rather to provide lighting and controls essential for human life safety.

The general goal is to keep the emergency operation as reliable as possible. The emergency system must be able to supply all emergency loads simultaneously. When the emergency supply also supplies power for other nonemergency loads, the emergency loads take priority over the others, and those other loads must be subject to automatic load pickup and load shedding to support the emergency loads if the emergency system doesn't have adequate capacity and rating for all loads simultaneously.

As you study Article 700, keep in mind that emergency systems are essentially lifelines for people. The entire article is based on keeping those lifelines from breaking.

Part I. General

700.1 Scope

Article 700 applies to the installation, operation, and maintenance of emergency power systems. These consist of circuits and equipment intended to supply illumination or power within 10 seconds [700.12] when the normal electrical supply is interrupted. Figure 700–1

Note 3: For specific locations where emergency lighting is required, see NFPA 101, *Life Safety Code*.

Author's Comment:

- Emergency power systems are generally installed where artificial illumination is required for safe exiting and for panic control in buildings subject to occupancy by large numbers of persons, such as hotels, theaters, sports arenas, health care facilities, and similar institutions.

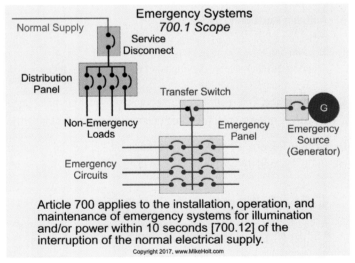

Article 700 applies to the installation, operation, and maintenance of emergency systems for illumination and/or power within 10 seconds [700.12] of the interruption of the normal electrical supply.

Copyright 2017, www.MikeHolt.com

Figure 700–1

700.3 Tests and Maintenance

The equipment that might require maintenance is no longer limited to just batteries.

Analysis

EXPANDED

Previous editions of the *Code* required batteries to be maintained, whether they were for starting a generator, turning on an exit sign, or anything else. This section has been expanded to include other emergency power equipment requiring maintenance like generators, transfer switches, and panels.

700.3 Tests and Maintenance

(A) Conduct or Witness Test. To ensure that the emergency power system meets or exceeds the original installation specifications, the authority having jurisdiction must conduct or witness an acceptance test of the emergency power system upon completion.

(B) Periodic Testing. Emergency power systems must be periodically tested to ensure that adequate maintenance has been performed and that the systems are in proper operating condition.

> **Author's Comment:**
>
> - Running the emergency power system under load is often considered an acceptable method of operational testing.

(C) Maintenance. Emergency system equipment must be maintained in accordance with manufacturer instructions and industry standards.

(D) Written Record. A written record must be kept of all required tests [700.4(A) and (B)] and maintenance [700.4(C)].

> **Author's Comment:**
>
> - The *NEC* doesn't specify the required record retention period.

700.5 Transfer Equipment

Transfer equipment must now be marked by the installer to indicate its short-circuit current rating.

Analysis

NEW

Transfer equipment is required by UL 1008 to be marked with its short-circuit current rating. At first glance this seems to be a rule with automatic compliance, but it does require some involvement from the installer. According to the Code Making Panel, transfer switches are typically marked with several different ratings that can vary based on the type(s) of overcurrent protection device(s) that are installed. If this is the case, the installer must determine which rating is applicable and indicate it on the equipment.

700.5 Transfer Equipment

(A) General. Transfer equipment must be automatic and be installed to prevent the inadvertent interconnection of normal and alternate sources of supply.

(C) Automatic Transfer Switches. Automatic transfer switches must be listed for emergency power system use. Figure 700–2

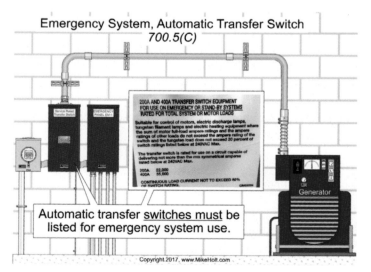

Figure 700–2

(D) Use. Transfer equipment must supply only emergency loads. Figure 700–3

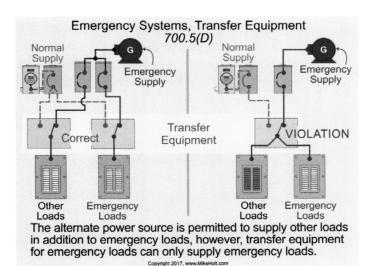

Figure 700–3

The alternate power source is permitted to supply other loads in addition to emergency loads, however, transfer equipment for emergency loads can only supply emergency loads.

Copyright 2017, www.MikeHolt.com

Author's Comment:

■ Multiple transfer switches are required where a single generator is used to supply both emergency loads and other loads.

(E) Documentation. The short-circuit current rating of the transfer equipment must be field marked on the exterior of the transfer equipment.

700.10 Wiring

This section was reorganized and raceways, cables, and receptacles, for emergency systems must now be marked. The exception regarding selective coordination for breakers feeding a common bus was turned into a permissive *Code* rule.

Analysis

REORGANIZED The *NEC* has long required certain components of an emergency system to be marked so as to be readily identifiable. These components were limited to boxes and enclosures, however.

New to this edition of the *Code* is that raceways and cables must also be marked. There are red cables and raceways that could, perhaps, meet this requirement, if marking the wiring method red is considered adequate by the AHJ. The *NEC* doesn't tell us what exactly the marking(s) must consist of, so there could be some growing pains with this rule. Receptacles are also required to be marked if connected to the emergency circuit, often a red receptacle with a metal faceplate marked "Emergency" will be sufficient.

What used to be an exception to 700.10(B)(5)(b) is now written as permissive text. Nothing technical changed, it's just strange to see an exception allow something that was already permitted. This change just makes the language a little better.

700.10 Wiring

(A) Identification. Emergency circuits must be permanently marked as components of an emergency circuit or system so they'll be readily identified by the following methods:

(1) Boxes and enclosures, including transfer switches, generators, and power panels for emergency circuits must be permanently marked as a component of an emergency circuit or system. Figure 700–4

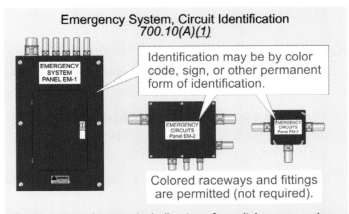

Identification may be by color code, sign, or other permanent form of identification.

Colored raceways and fittings are permitted (not required).

Boxes and enclosures, including transfer switches, generators, and power panels for emergency circuits must be permanently marked as a component of an emergency circuit or system.

Copyright 2017, www.MikeHolt.com

Figure 700–4

(2) Cable and raceway systems must be permanently marked, at intervals not exceeding 25 ft, as a component of the emergency circuit or system.

Receptacles supplied from the emergency system must have a distinctive color or marking on the receptacle or receptacle cover plate.

(B) Wiring. To ensure that a fault on the normal wiring circuits won't affect the performance of emergency wiring or equipment, all wiring to emergency loads must be kept entirely independent of all other wiring, except:

(1) Wiring in transfer equipment. Figure 700–5

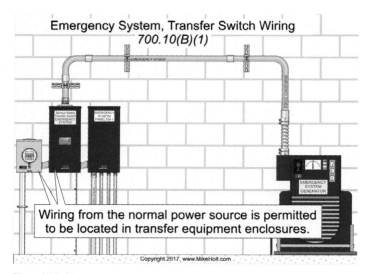

Emergency System, Transfer Switch Wiring 700.10(B)(1)

Wiring from the normal power source is permitted to be located in transfer equipment enclosures.

Copyright 2017, www.MikeHolt.com

Figure 700–5

(2) Luminaires supplied from two sources of power.

(3) A junction box attached to luminaires supplied from two sources of power.

(4) Wiring within a common junction box attached to unit equipment, containing only the branch circuit supplying the unit equipment and the emergency circuit supplied by the unit equipment.

(5) Wiring from an emergency source can supply emergency and other nonemergency loads as follows:

a. Separate vertical switchboard or switchgear sections or from individual disconnects mounted in separate enclosures must be used to separate emergency circuits from all other nonemergency circuits.

b. The common bus of separate sections of the switchgear, separate sections of the switchboard, or the individual enclosures must be either of the following:

i. Supplied by single or multiple feeders with overcurrent protection at the source.

ii. Supplied by single or multiple feeders with overcurrent protection, provided that the overcurrent protection that's common to an emergency system and any nonemergency system(s) is selectively coordinated with the next downstream overcurrent protective device in the nonemergency system(s).

c. Emergency circuits must not originate from the same vertical switchboard or switchgear section, panelboard enclosure, or individual disconnect enclosure as other circuits.

Author's Comment:

■ Separation of the circuits served by a generator source for emergency, legally required, and optional standby circuits may be accomplished by running feeders from a single generator to individual overcurrent protection devices or to a distribution switchboard that separates emergency circuits in different vertical sections from other loads.

(C) Wiring Design and Location. Emergency wiring circuits must be designed and located to minimize the hazards that might cause failure due to flooding, fire, icing, vandalism, and other adverse conditions.

700.12 General Requirements

The types of batteries permitted for emergency power have been revised.

Analysis

CLARIFIED In previous versions of the *NEC*, there were specific provisions in 700.12(A) based on the type of battery employed. The provisions have been removed, and the *Code* now simply requires the batteries to be a suitable type and have the capacity to do their job without the voltage falling to less than 87.50 percent of normal.

700.12 General Requirements

In the event of failure of the normal supply to the building, emergency power must be available within 10 seconds. Emergency equipment must be designed and located so as to minimize the hazards that might cause complete failure due to flooding, fires, icing, and vandalism. The emergency power supply must be any of the following:

(A) Storage Battery. Storage batteries must be of suitable rating and capacity to supply and maintain the total load for a period of at least 1½ hours, without the voltage applied to the load falling below 87½ percent of normal. Automotive-type batteries aren't permitted for this purpose.

(B) Generator Set.

(1) Prime Mover-Driven. A generator approved by the authority having jurisdiction and sized in accordance with 700.4 must have means to automatically start the prime mover when the normal service fails.

(2) Internal Combustion Engines as Prime Movers. If internal combustion engines are used as the prime mover, an on-site fuel supply must be provided for not less than two hours of full-demand operation of the system. Figure 700–6

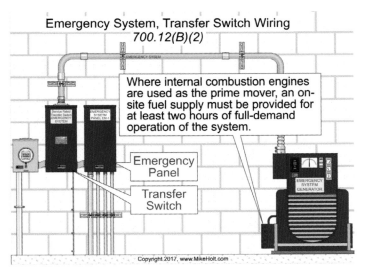

Emergency System, Transfer Switch Wiring
700.12(B)(2)

Where internal combustion engines are used as the prime mover, an on-site fuel supply must be provided for at least two hours of full-demand operation of the system.

Emergency Panel

Transfer Switch

Copyright 2017, www.MikeHolt.com

Figure 700–6

(6) Outdoor Generator Sets. If a generator located outdoors is equipped with a readily accessible disconnect located within sight of the building in accordance with 445.18, an additional disconnect isn't required on or at the building for the generator feeder conductors that serve or pass through the building. Figure 700–7

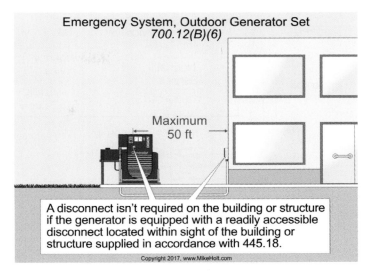

Emergency System, Outdoor Generator Set
700.12(B)(6)

Maximum 50 ft

A disconnect isn't required on the building or structure if the generator is equipped with a readily accessible disconnect located within sight of the building or structure supplied in accordance with 445.18.

Copyright 2017, www.MikeHolt.com

Figure 700–7

Ex: Where conditions of maintenance and supervision ensure that only qualified persons will monitor and service the installation and where documented safe switching procedures are established and maintained for disconnection, the generator disconnect isn't required to be located within sight of the building or structure served.

(C) Uninterruptible Power Supplies. Uninterruptible power supplies serving as the emergency power source must comply with the applicable requirements of 700.12(A) and (B).

(D) Separate Service. An additional service is permitted where approved by the authority having jurisdiction and the following: Figure 700–8

(2) The service conductors must be sufficiently remote electrically and physically from any other service conductors to minimize the possibility of simultaneous interruption of supply.

(F) Unit Equipment.

(1) Components of Unit Equipment. Individual unit equipment (an emergency lighting battery pack) must consist of the following: Figure 700–9

(1) A rechargeable battery

(2) A battery charging means

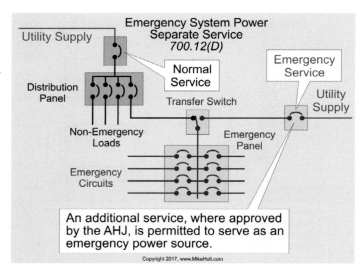

An additional service, where approved by the AHJ, is permitted to serve as an emergency power source.

Figure 700–8

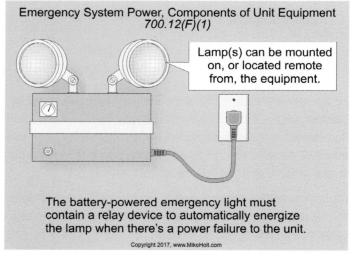

The battery-powered emergency light must contain a relay device to automatically energize the lamp when there's a power failure to the unit.

Figure 700–9

(3) Provisions for one or more lamps mounted on the equipment, or terminals for remote lamps, or both

(4) A relaying device arranged to energize the lamps automatically upon failure of the supply to the unit equipment

(2) Installation of Unit (Battery Pack) Equipment. The installation of battery pack equipment must meet the following:

(1) The batteries must be of suitable rating and capacity to supply and maintain the total lamp load:

(a) For a period of at least 1½ hours without the voltage falling below 87½ percent of normal battery voltage, or

(b) Supply not less than 60 percent of the initial emergency illumination for a period of at least 1½ hours.

(2) Emergency lighting battery pack equipment must be permanently fixed in place. Flexible cord-and-plug connection (a locking receptacle isn't required) is permitted for emergency lighting battery pack equipment designed for this purpose, provided the flexible cord doesn't exceed 3 ft in length.

(3) The branch-circuit wiring that supplies emergency lighting battery pack equipment must be the same branch-circuit wiring that supplies the normal lighting in the area, but the emergency lighting battery pack equipment must be connected ahead of any local switches. Figure 700–10

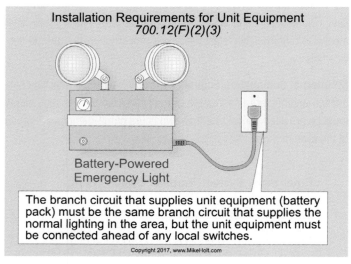

Figure 700–10

Ex: In a separate and uninterrupted area supplied by at least three normal lighting circuits that aren't part of a multiwire branch circuit, a separate branch circuit for unit equipment is allowed if it originates from the same panelboard as the normal lighting circuits and is provided with a lock-on feature.

Author's Comment:

■ There are two reasons why the emergency lighting battery packs must be connected ahead of the switch controlling the normal area lighting: (1) in the event of a power loss to the lighting circuit, the emergency battery lighting packs will activate and provide emergency lighting for people to exit the building, and (2) the emergency lighting battery packs won't turn on when the switch controlling normal lighting is turned off.

CAUTION: *Individual unit equipment must not be connected to the emergency circuit, because it won't operate when normal power is lost, since the equipment is being supplied by the emergency power system.*

(4) The branch circuit that feeds the emergency lighting battery pack equipment must be clearly identified at the distribution panel.

Author's Comment:

- Identification and marking must be in accordance with 110.22(A) and 408.4.

(6) Power for remote heads providing the exterior lighting of an exit door can be supplied by the unit equipment serving the area immediately inside the exit door.

700.25 Branch Circuit Emergency Lighting Transfer Switch

A new rule allows emergency lighting loads at a maximum of 20A that are supplied from branch circuits to be transferred to an emergency branch circuit using a listed Branch Circuit Emergency Lighting Transfer Switch(es) (BCELTS).

Analysis

NEW A new rule was added that allows emergency lighting loads at a maximum of 20 A that are supplied from branch circuits to be transferred using a listed Branch Circuit Emergency Lighting Transfer Switch (BCELTS) to an emergency branch circuit. The requirements of 700.5(C) that require transfer equipment to be mechanically held don't apply to a BCELTS.

700.25 Branch Circuit Emergency Lighting Transfer Switch

Emergency lighting supplied by branch circuits rated not greater than 20A can use a listed branch circuit emergency lighting transfer switch.

LEGALLY REQUIRED STANDBY SYSTEMS

Introduction to Article 701—Legally Required Standby Systems

In the hierarchy of electrical systems, Article 700 Emergency Systems receives first priority. Taking the number two spot is Legally Required Standby Systems, which fall under Article 701. Legally required standby systems must supply standby power in 60 seconds or less after a power loss, instead of the 10 seconds or less required for emergency power systems.

Article 700 basically applies to systems or equipment required to protect people who are in an emergency and trying to get out, while Article 701 basically applies to systems or equipment needed to aid the people responding to the emergency. For example, Article 700 lighting provides an exit path. But, Article 701 might control the elevator used by fire fighters to reach the applicable floor.

Part I. General

701.1 Scope

Article 701 applies to the installation, operation, and maintenance of legally required standby systems consisting of circuits and equipment intended to supply illumination or power when the normal electrical supply or system is interrupted. Figure 701–1

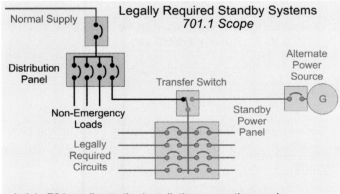

Legally Required Standby Systems
701.1 Scope

Article 701 applies to the installation, operation, and maintenance of legally required standby systems consisting of circuits and equipment intended to supply illumination or power when the normal electrical supply or system is interrupted.

Copyright 2017, www.MikeHolt.com

Figure 701–1

Author's Comment:

- Legally required standby systems provide electric power to aid in firefighting, rescue operations, control of health hazards, and similar operations.

701.3 Tests and Maintenance

The equipment that may require maintenance is no longer limited to just batteries.

Analysis

EXPANDED Previous editions of the *NEC* required that batteries be maintained, whether they were for starting a generator, turning on an exit sign, or anything else. Like section 700.3, this section has also been expanded to include other legally required equipment requiring maintenance like generators, panels and transfer equipment.

701.3 Tests and Maintenance

(A) Conduct or Witness Test. To ensure that the legally required standby system meets or exceeds the original installation specifications, the authority having jurisdiction must conduct or witness an acceptance test of the legally required system upon completion of the installation.

(B) Periodic Testing. Legally required standby systems must be periodically tested to ensure that adequate maintenance has been performed and that the systems are in proper operating condition.

> **Author's Comment:**
>
> ■ Running the legally required standby system to power the loads of the facility is often considered an acceptable method of operational testing.

(C) Maintenance. Legally required standby system equipment must be maintained in accordance with manufacturer instructions and industry standards.

(D) Written Record. A written record must be kept of all required tests and maintenance.

> **Author's Comment:**
>
> ■ The *NEC* doesn't specify the required record retention period.

701.5 Transfer Equipment

Transfer equipment must now be marked by the installer to indicate its short-circuit current rating.

Analysis

NEW Section 701.5(D), like 700.5(E) was added to require the installer to indicate the short-circuit current rating of transfer equipment. UL 1008 already requires the equipment to be marked with its short-circuit current rating but this rule still requires some involvement from the installer. According to the Code Making Panel, transfer switches are typically marked with several different ratings that can vary based on the type(s)

---

of overcurrent protection device(s) that are installed. If this is the case, the installer must determine which rating is applicable and indicate it on the equipment.

701.5 Transfer Equipment

(A) General. Transfer equipment must be automatic and be installed to prevent the inadvertent interconnection of normal and alternate sources of supply.

> **Author's Comment:**
>
> ■ Legally required standby systems and optional standby systems can be on the same transfer switch, but emergency power systems must have their own [700.6(D)].

(C) Automatic Transfer Switch. Automatic transfer switches must be listed for emergency use. Figure 701–2

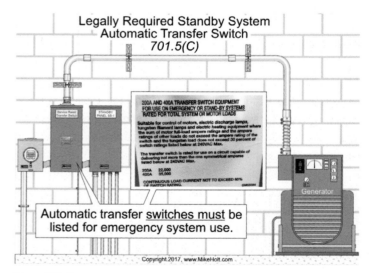

Figure 701–2

(D) Documentation. The short-circuit current rating of the transfer equipment must be field marked on the exterior of the transfer equipment.

OPTIONAL STANDBY SYSTEMS

Introduction to Article 702—Optional Standby Systems

Taking third priority after Emergency and Legally Required Systems, Optional Standby Systems protect public or private facilities or property where life safety doesn't depend on the performance of the system. These systems aren't required for rescue operations.

Suppose a glass plant loses power. Once glass hardens in the equipment—which it will do when process heat is lost—the plant is going to suffer a great deal of downtime and expense before it can resume operations. An optional standby system can prevent this loss.

You'll see these systems in facilities where loss of power can cause economic loss or business interruptions. Data centers can lose millions of dollars from a single minute of lost power. A chemical or pharmaceutical plant can lose an entire batch from a single momentary power glitch. In many cases, the lost revenue can't be recouped.

This article also applies to the installation of optional standby generators in homes, farms, small businesses, and many other applications where standby power isn't legally required.

Part I. General

702.1 Scope

The systems covered by Article 702 consist of those permanently installed, including prime movers, and those arranged for a connection to a premises wiring system from a portable alternate power supply. Figure 702–1

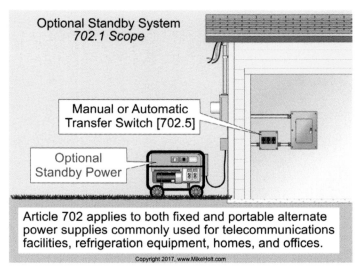

Figure 702–1

702.5 Transfer Equipment

Transfer equipment must now be marked by the installer to indicate its short-circuit current rating.

Analysis

NEW The change here was made to be consistent with the changes made in 700.5 and 701.5. Transfer equipment is required by UL 1008 to be marked with its short-circuit current rating, so at first glance that seems to be a rule with automatic compliance. According to the Code Making Panel, transfer switches are typically marked with several different ratings that can vary based on the type(s) of overcurrent protection device(s) that are installed. If this is the case, the installer must determine which rating is applicable and indicate it on the equipment.

702.5 Transfer Equipment

Transfer equipment is required for all fixed or portable optional standby systems. Figure 702–2

A transfer switch is required for all fixed or portable optional standby power systems.

Figure 702–2

Ex: Temporary connection of a portable generator without transfer equipment is permitted where conditions of maintenance and supervision ensure that only qualified persons will service the installation, and where the normal supply is physically isolated by a lockable disconnect or by the disconnection of the normal supply conductors.

The short-circuit current rating of the transfer equipment must be field marked on the exterior of the transfer equipment.

ARTICLE
725

REMOTE-CONTROL, SIGNALING, AND POWER-LIMITED CIRCUITS

Introduction to Article 725—Remote-Control, Signaling, and Power-Limited Circuits

Circuits that fall under Article 725 are remote-control, signaling, and power-limited circuits that aren't an integral part of a device or appliance. This article includes circuits for burglar alarms, access control, sound, nurse call, intercoms, some computer networks, some lighting dimmer controls, and some low-voltage industrial controls.

Let's take a quick look at the types of circuits:

- A remote-control circuit controls other circuits through a relay or solid-state device, such as a motion-activated security lighting circuit.
- A signaling circuit provides output that's a signal or indicator, such as a buzzer, flashing light, or annunciator.
- A power-limited circuit is a circuit supplied by a transformer or other electric power source that limits the amount of power to provide safety from electrical shock and/or fire ignition.

The purpose of Article 725 is to allow for the fact that these circuits "are characterized by usage and power limitations that differentiate them from electrical power circuits" [725.1 Note]. This article provides alternative requirements for minimum conductor sizes, overcurrent protection, insulation requirements, wiring methods, and materials.

Article 725 consists of four parts. Part I provides general information, Part II pertains to Class 1 circuits, Part III addresses Class 2 and Class 3 circuits, while Part IV focuses on listing requirements. The key to understanding and applying each of these parts is in knowing the voltage and energy levels of the circuits, the wiring method involved, and the purpose(s) of the circuit.

Part I. General

725.1 Scope

Article 725 contains the requirements for remote-control, signaling, and power-limited circuits that aren't an integral part of a device or utilization equipment. Figure 725–1

Note: These circuits have electrical power and voltage limitations that differentiate them from electrical power circuits. Alternative requirements are given with regard to minimum conductor sizes, overcurrent protection, insulation requirements, wiring methods, and materials.

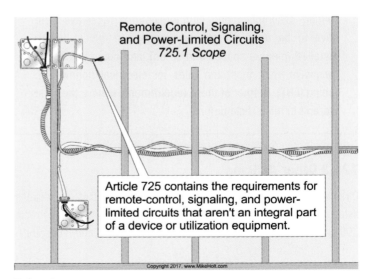

Remote Control, Signaling, and Power-Limited Circuits
725.1 Scope

Article 725 contains the requirements for remote-control, signaling, and power-limited circuits that aren't an integral part of a device or utilization equipment.

Copyright 2017, www.MikeHolt.com

Figure 725–1

Author's Comment:

- To understand when to apply the requirements of Article 725 for control, signaling, and power-limited circuits, you must understand the following Article 100 Definitions:
  - ◆ *Remote-Control Circuit.* Any electrical circuit that controls another circuit through a relay or equivalent device is a remote-control circuit. An example is the 120V circuit that operates the coil of a motor starter or lighting contactor, or the 24V circuit for a garage door opener.
  - ◆ *Signaling Circuit.* Any electrical circuit that energizes signaling equipment is a signaling circuit. Examples include doorbells, buzzers, signal lights, annunciators, burglar alarms, and other detection indication or alarm devices.

725.3 Other Articles

This article now contains provisions for cable routing assemblies and communications raceways.

Analysis

NEW Every three years the *Code* adds, removes, or relocates the rules for cable routing assemblies and for communications raceways. In the 2017, edition language was added here in 725.3. There really isn't anything interesting as far as the rules are concerned. Cable routing assemblies and communications raceways both have to be rated for the environment in which they're installed (plenum spaces and so on), and communications raceways must meet the rules for electrical nonmetallic tubing (ENT). Neither of these requirements is new, they just weren't in this article before.

725.3 Other Articles

Circuits and equipment must comply with the articles or sections listed in 725.3(A) through (N). Only those sections contained in Article 300 specifically referenced below apply to Class 1, 2, and 3 circuits.

Author's Comment:

- Boxes or other enclosures aren't required for Class 2 or Class 3 splices or terminations because Article 725 doesn't reference 300.15, which contains those requirements. Figure 725–2

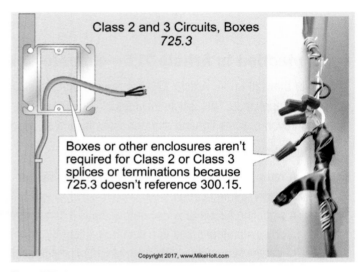

Class 2 and 3 Circuits, Boxes
725.3

Boxes or other enclosures aren't required for Class 2 or Class 3 splices or terminations because 725.3 doesn't reference 300.15.

Copyright 2017, www.MikeHolt.com

Figure 725–2

(A) Number and Size of Conductors in a Raceway. The number and size of conductors or cables within a raceway are limited in accordance with 300.17.

Author's Comment:

- Raceways must be large enough to permit the installation and removal of conductors without damaging conductor insulation.
- When all conductors within a raceway are the same size and insulation, the number of conductors permitted can be found in Annex C for the raceway type.

Example: How many 18 TFFN fixture wires can be installed in trade size ½ electrical metallic tubing? Figure 725–3

Solution: 22 THHN fixture wires can be installed in trade size ½ electrical metallic tubing [Annex C, Table C.1].

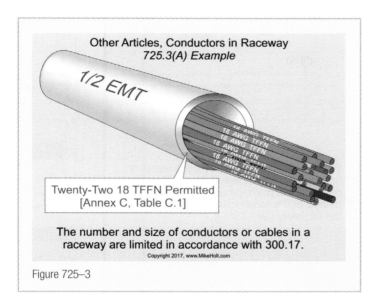

Figure 725–3

(B) Spread of Fire or Products of Combustion. Class 1, 2, and 3 circuits installed through fire-resistant-rated walls, partitions, floors, or ceilings must be firestopped to limit the possible spread of fire or products of combustion in accordance with the specific instructions supplied by the manufacturer for the specific type of cable and construction material (drywall, brick, and so on) [300.21]. Figure 725–4

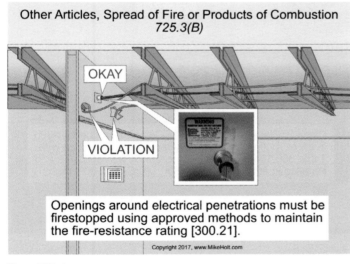

Figure 725–4

Author's Comment:

- Although boxes aren't typically required for Class 2 circuits, one is required for a Class 2 device located in a fire-rated assembly.

(C) Ducts and Plenum Spaces. Class 1, Class 2, and Class 3 circuits installed in ducts or plenums must comply with 300.22. Figure 725–5

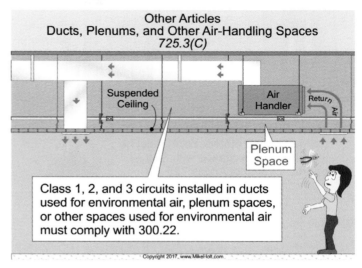

Figure 725–5

Ex. 1: Class 2 and Class 3 cables selected in accordance with Table 725.154 and installed in accordance with 725.135(B) and 300.22(B) Ex, are permitted to be installed in ducts specifically fabricated for environmental air.

Ex. 2: Class 2 and Class 3 cables selected in accordance with Table 725.154 and installed in accordance with 725.135(C) are permitted to be installed in plenum spaces.

(E) Cable Trays. Class 1, 2, and 3 circuits in cable trays must be installed in accordance with Article 392.

(F) Motor Control Circuits. Article 430, Part VI, where tapped from the load side of the motor branch-circuit, short-circuit, and ground-fault protective device(s) as specified in 430.72(A). Figure 725–6

(H) Raceways Exposed to Different Temperatures. If a raceway is subjected to different temperatures, and where condensation is known to be a problem, the raceway must be filled with a material approved by the authority having jurisdiction that will prevent the circulation of warm air to a colder section of the raceway. An explosion-proof seal isn't required for this purpose [300.7(A)]. Figure 725–7

Author's Comment:

- This raceway seal is one that's approved by the AHJ to prevent the circulation of warm air to a cooler section of the raceway, and isn't the same thing as an explosionproof seal.

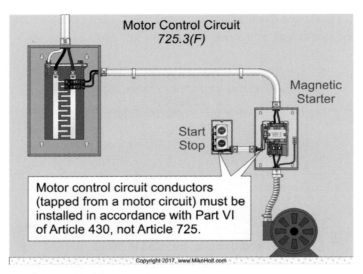

Figure 725–6

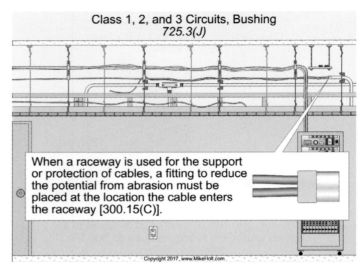

Figure 725–8

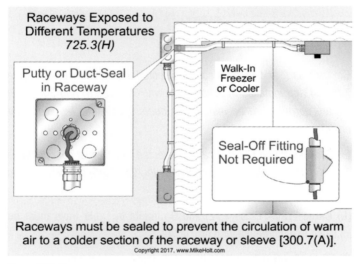

Figure 725–7

(J) Bushing. When a raceway is used for the support or overcurrent protection of cables, a fitting to reduce the potential for abrasion must be placed at the location the cables enter the raceway in accordance with 300.15(C). Figure 725–8

(L) Corrosive, Damp, or Wet Locations. Where installed in corrosive, damp, or wet locations, Class 2 and Class 3 cables must be identified for the location, in accordance with 110.11 and 310.10(G). Conductors and cables installed in underground raceways, or in raceways aboveground in wet locations, must also be identified for wet locations, in accordance with 300.5(B). Where corrosion may occur, the requirements of 300.6 must be used.

(M) Cable Routing Assemblies. Class 2, Class 3, and Type PLTC cables can be installed in cable routing assemblies selected in accordance with Table 800.154(c), listed in accordance with 800.182, and installed in accordance with 800.110(C) and 800.113. Figure 725–9

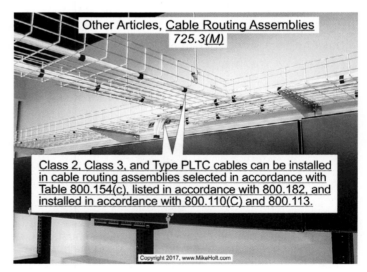

Figure 725–9

(N) Communications Raceways. Class 2, Class 3, and Type PLTC cables can be installed in communications raceways selected in accordance with Table 800.154(b), listed in accordance with 800.182, and installed in accordance with 800.113 and 362.24 through 362.56, where the requirements applicable to electrical nonmetallic tubing apply. Figure 725–10

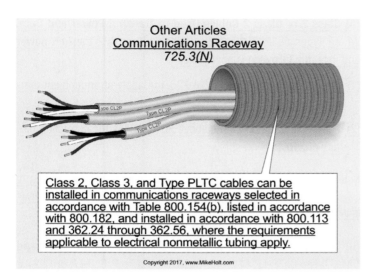

Figure 725–10

725.121 Power Sources for Class 2 and Class 3 Circuits

Some Class 2 power sources will require a label, effective January 1, 2018.

Analysis

NEW Class 2 power sources for IT equipment will need to have a label indicating the voltage and current at each output point in 2018. Although these are power-limited circuits and are therefore inherently safe, there's evidently some concern over using improper cables for this type of equipment.

According to the Code Making Panel, "Bundling of large numbers of Class 2 conductors from IT servers and other similar IT and industrial equipment can create safety issues with very small current levels so having the output ports identified with the current and voltage rating is critical so the installer can connect the proper cable types."

725.121 Power Sources for Class 2 and Class 3 Circuits

(A) Power Source. The power supply for a Class 2 or a Class 3 circuit must be:

(1) A listed Class 2 or Class 3 transformer. Figure 725–11

Figure 725–11

(2) A listed Class 2 or Class 3 power supply.

(3) Equipment listed as a Class 2 or Class 3 power source.

Ex 2: Where each circuit has an energy level at or below the limits established in Chapter 9, Table 11(A) and Table 11(B), the equipment isn't required to be listed as a Class 2 or Class 3 power transformer, power supply, or power source.

(4) Listed audio/video information technology equipment (computers), communications, and industrial equipment limited-power circuits.

(5) A dry cell battery rated 30V or less for a Class 2 circuit.

(C) Power Source for Audio and Industrial Equipment. Effective January 1, 2018—The power sources for limited power circuits in 725.121(A)(3) and limited power circuits for listed audio/video information technology (equipment) and listed industrial equipment in 725.121(A)(4) must have a label indicating the maximum voltage and current output for each connection point.

725.144 Transmission of Power and Data

A new section and table were added to address cables that transmit power and data.

Analysis

NEW Evidently there are concerns about overheating bundled cables that are transmitting data. Strange, I always thought Class 2 and Class 3 circuits were considered to be safe as it relates to fire [725.2]. However, there was a UL Fact Finding Report on large bundles of power and data on the same cables. It concluded that there was a potential danger of overheating and that typical wiring practices for LAN cable installations with currents below the previous *NEC* Class 2 tables, were overheating or melting. Who would have thought?

725.144 Transmission of Power and Data

Section 725.144 applies to Class 2 and Class 3 circuits that transmit power and data to a powered device. Parts I and III of Article 725, and 300.11, apply to Class 2 and Class 3 circuits that transmit power and data. Conductors that carry power for data circuits must be copper, and the current in the power circuit must not exceed the current limitation of the connectors.

Note 1: An example of cables that transmit power and data include closed-circuit TV cameras (CCTV).

Note 2: Connectors identified as 8P8C used with powered communications systems are typically rated at 1.30A maximum.

Table 725.144 Copper Conductor Ampacity in 4-Pair Class 2 or Class 3 Power/Data Cables with All Conductors Carrying Current

See *NEC* Table 725.144 for details.

(A) Class 2 or Class 3 Cables Used to Transmit Power and Data. Where Types CL3P, CL2P, CL3R, CL2R, CL3, or CL2 transmit power and data, the following is applicable:

(1) The ampacity ratings in Table 725.144 apply at an ambient temperature of 30°C (86°F).

(2) For ambient temperatures above 30°C (86°F), the correction factors of 310.15(B)(2) apply.

Note: One example of the use of Class 2 cables is a network of closed circuit TV cameras using 24 AWG, 60°C rated, Type CL2R, Category 5e local area network (LAN) cables.

(B) Class 2-LP or Class 3-LP Cables Used to Transmit Power and Data. Types CL3P-LP, CL2P-LP, CL3R-LP, CL2R-LP, CL3-LP, or CL2-LP can supply power to equipment at a current level up to the marked ampere limit located immediately following the suffix LP and can transmit data to the equipment. Class 2-LP and Class 3-LP cables must comply with the following, as applicable:

Note 1: The "(xxA)" following the suffix -LP indicates the ampacity of each conductor in a cable.

Note 2: An example of a Limited Power (LP) cable is Type CL2-LP (0.50A), 23 AWG; this cable can be used in any location where a Type CL2 could be used, and it's suitable to carry up to 0.50A per conductor, regardless of the number of cables in a bundle. If used in a 7-cable bundle, the same cable could carry up to 1.20A per conductor.

(1) Cables with the suffix "-LP" can be installed in bundles, raceways, cable trays, communications raceways, and cable routing assemblies.

(2) Cables with the suffix "-LP" and a marked ampere level must follow the substitution hierarchy of Table 725.154 and *NEC* Figure 725.145(A) for the cable type without the suffix "LP" and without the marked ampere level.

(3) System design is by qualified persons under engineering supervision.

725.179 Listing and Marking of Class 2 and Class 3 Cables

Text for Type LP (limited power) cables was added.

Analysis

NEW In order to address the growing concern over heat generated by cables transmitting data, a new cable type has been created called "Type LP" (limited power). These cables will end in the suffix "-LP", and will have their current rating indicated on the cable. This will allow them to be evaluated as they relate to the new rules found in 725.144.

725.179 Listing and Marking of Class 2 and Class 3 Cables

Class 2 and Class 3 cables, nonmetallic signaling raceways, and cable routing assemblies installed within buildings must be listed as being resistant to the spread of fire and other criteria in accordance with 725.179(A) through 725.179(I), and must be marked in accordance with 725.179(J). Figure 725–12

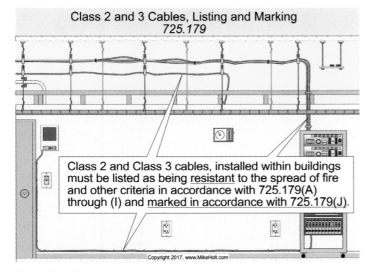

Class 2 and 3 Cables, Listing and Marking
725.179

Class 2 and Class 3 cables, installed within buildings must be listed as being resistant to the spread of fire and other criteria in accordance with 725.179(A) through (I) and marked in accordance with 725.179(J).

Copyright 2017, www.MikeHolt.com

Figure 725–12

(A) Types CL2P and CL3P. Listed Types CL2P and CL3P cable must be listed as suitable for use in plenum spaces. Figure 725–13

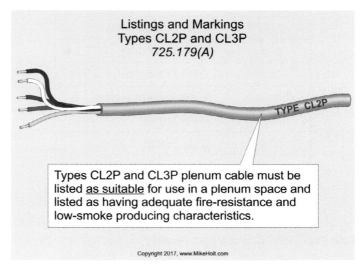

Listings and Markings
Types CL2P and CL3P
725.179(A)

TYPE CL2P

Types CL2P and CL3P plenum cable must be listed as suitable for use in a plenum space and listed as having adequate fire-resistance and low-smoke producing characteristics.

Copyright 2017, www.MikeHolt.com

Figure 725–13

(G) Cable Voltage Rating. Class 2 cables must have a voltage rating not less than 150V, and Class 3 cables must have a voltage rating not less than 300V.

(I) Limited Power (LP) Cables. Limited power (LP) cables must be listed as suitable for carrying power and data circuits up to a specified current for each conductor. The cables must be marked with the suffix "-LP" with the ampere limit located immediately following the suffix LP.

Note: The ampere limit located immediately following the suffix LP is the ampacity of each conductor in a cable. For example, Class 2 limited-power cables rated 1A would be marked CL2-LP (1.0A), CL2R-LP (1.0A), or CL2-LP (1.0A).

(J) Marking. Voltage ratings aren't permitted to be marked on the cables.

Note: Voltage markings on cables may suggest that the cables are suitable for Class 1 or electric power and light applications, which they aren't.

Table 725.179(J) Cable Marking	
CL3P	Class 3 plenum cable
CL2P	Class 2 plenum cable
CL3R	Class 3 riser cable
CL2R	Class 2 riser cable
PLTC	Power-limited tray cable
CL3	Class 3 cable
CL2	Class 2 cable
CL3X	Class 3 cable, limited use
CL2X	Class 2 cable, limited use

Note: Class 2 and Class 3 cable types are listed in descending order of fire resistance rating; Class 3 cables are listed above Class 2 cables because Class 3 cables can substitute for Class 2 cables.

ARTICLE
760 FIRE ALARM SYSTEMS

Introduction to Article 760—Fire Alarm Systems

Article 760 covers the installation of wiring and equipment for fire alarm systems, including circuits controlled and powered by the fire alarm. These include fire detection and alarm notification, guard's tour, sprinkler waterflow, and sprinkler supervisory systems. NFPA 72, *National Fire Alarm Code* provides other fire alarm system requirements.

Part I. General

760.1 Scope

Article 760 covers the installation of wiring and equipment for fire alarm systems, including circuits controlled and powered by the fire alarm system. Figure 760–1

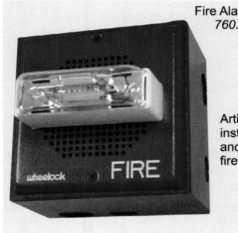

Fire Alarm Systems
760.1 Scope

Article 760 covers the installation of wiring and equipment for fire alarm systems.

Copyright 2017, www.MikeHolt.com

Figure 760–1

Author's Comment:

- Residential smoke alarm systems, including interconnecting wiring, aren't covered by Article 760, because they aren't powered by a fire alarm system as defined in NFPA 72.

Note 1: Fire alarm systems include fire detection and alarm notification, guard's tour, sprinkler waterflow, and sprinkler supervisory systems. Other circuits that might be controlled or powered by the fire alarm system include elevator capture, elevator shutdown, door release, smoke doors and damper control, fire doors and damper control, and fan shutdown.

NFPA 72, *National Fire Alarm and Signaling Code,* provides the requirements for the selection, installation, performance, use, testing, and maintenance of fire alarm systems.

Author's Comment:

- Building control circuits associated with the fire alarm system, such as elevator capture and fan shutdown, must comply with Article 725 [760.3(E)]. Article 760 applies if these components are powered and directly controlled by the fire alarm system.
- NFPA 101—*Life Safety Code* or the local building code specifies when and where a fire alarm system is required.

760.3 Other Articles

This article now contains provisions for cable routing assemblies and for communications raceways, and two new exceptions were added to address installing cables in ducts and plenum spaces.

Analysis

EDITED This section received a fair amount of editing, including moving the temperature correction factor to subsection (A) and clarifying the grouping and identification provisions. The changes weren't technical, but do make for a more easily understood requirement.

NEW Because of the complexity of modern fire alarm and smoke control systems, there are numerous devices that need to be installed in ducts and plenum spaces. New exceptions were added to allow just that.

760.3 Other Articles

Only those sections contained in Article 300 specifically referenced below apply to fire alarm systems.

(A) Spread of Fire or Products of Combustion. Fire alarm circuits installed through fire-resistant-rated walls, partitions, floors, or ceilings must be firestopped to limit the possible spread of fire or products of combustion in accordance with the instructions supplied by the manufacturer for the specific type of cable and construction material (drywall, brick, and so forth) [300.21]. Figure 760–2

(B) Ducts and Plenum Spaces. Power-limited and nonpower-limited fire alarm cables installed in ducts or plenum spaces must comply with 300.22. Figure 760–3

Ex. 1: Power-limited fire alarm cables selected in accordance with Table 760.154 and installed in accordance with 760.135(B) and 300.22(B) Ex, are permitted to be installed in ducts specifically fabricated for environmental air.

Ex. 2: Power-limited fire alarm cables selected in accordance with Table 760.154 and installed in accordance with 760.135(C) are permitted to be installed in plenum spaces.

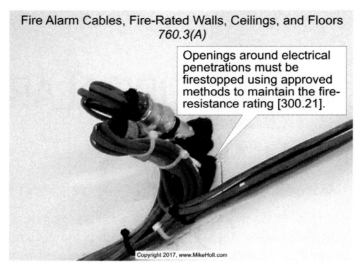

Fire Alarm Cables, Fire-Rated Walls, Ceilings, and Floors
760.3(A)

Openings around electrical penetrations must be firestopped using approved methods to maintain the fire-resistance rating [300.21].

Figure 760–2

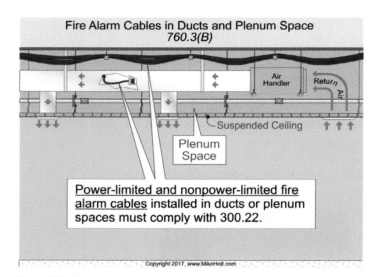

Fire Alarm Cables in Ducts and Plenum Space
760.3(B)

Power-limited and nonpower-limited fire alarm cables installed in ducts or plenum spaces must comply with 300.22.

Figure 760–3

(D) Corrosive, Damp, or Wet Locations. Fire alarm circuits installed in corrosive, damp, or wet locations must be identified for use in the operating environment [110.11], must be of materials suitable for the environment in which they're to be installed, and must be of a type suitable for the application [300.5(B), 300.6, 300.9, and 310.10(G)].

(E) Building Control Circuits. Class 1, 2, and 3 circuits used for building controls (elevator capture, fan shutdown, and so on), associated with the fire alarm system, but not controlled and powered by the fire alarm system, must be installed in accordance with Article 725 [760.1].

(F) Optical Fiber Cables. Optical fiber cables utilized for fire alarm circuits must be installed in accordance with Article 770.

(H) Raceways or Sleeves Exposed to Different Temperatures. If a raceway or sleeve is subjected to different temperatures, and where condensation is known to be a problem, the raceway or sleeve must be filled with a material approved by the authority having jurisdiction that will prevent the circulation of warm air to a colder section of the raceway. An explosionproof seal isn't required for this purpose [300.7(A)]. Figure 760–4

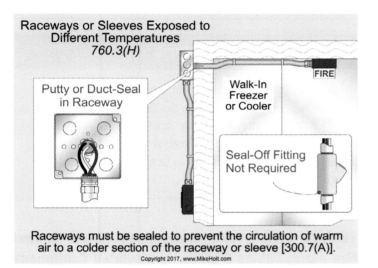

Figure 760–4

(J) Number and Size of Conductors in a Raceway. Raceways must be large enough to permit the installation and removal of conductors without damaging conductor insulation [300.17].

Author's Comment:

- When all conductors within a raceway are the same size and insulation, the number of conductors permitted can be found in Annex C for the raceway type.

Example: How many 18 TFFN fixture wires can be installed in trade size ½ electrical metallic tubing? Figure 760–5

Solution: Twenty-two 18 TFFN fixture wires can be installed in trade size ½ electrical metallic tubing conductors [Annex C, Table C.1].

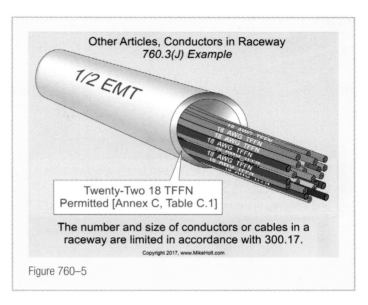

Figure 760–5

(K) Bushing. When a raceway is used for the support or protection of cables, a bushing to reduce the potential for abrasion must be placed at the location where the cables enter the raceway in accordance with 300.15(C). Figure 760–6

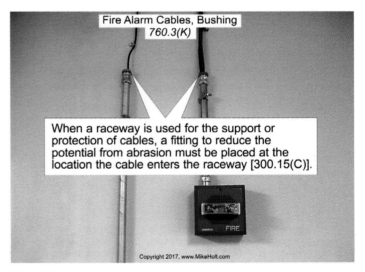

Figure 760–6

(L) Cable Routing Assemblies. Power-limited fire alarm cables can be installed in cable routing assemblies selected in accordance with Table 800.154(c), listed in accordance with 800.182, and installed in accordance with 800.110(C) and 800.113. Figure 760–7

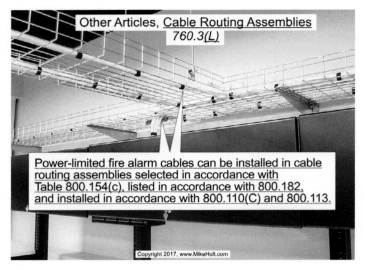

Figure 760–7

(M) Communications Raceways. Power-limited fire alarm cables can be installed in communications raceways selected in accordance with Table 800.154(b), listed in accordance with 800.182, and installed in accordance with 800.113 and 362.24 through 362.56, where the requirements applicable to electrical nonmetallic tubing apply. Figure 760–8

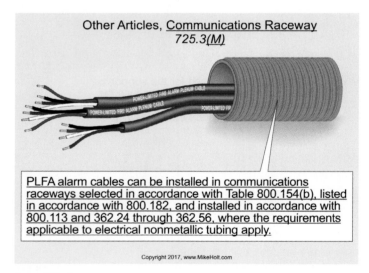

Figure 760–8

760.179 Listing and Marking of Power-Limited Fire Alarm Cables (PLFA) and Insulated Continuous Line-Type Fire Detectors

Power-limited fire alarm cables must now have a temperature rating of at least 60°C.

Analysis

NEW The voltage rating of power-limited fire alarm cables is specified in the *Code* so the installer and inspector know the limitations of the cable, whether it's marked with its voltage rating or not. The temperature rating of the cable has been added to this section for the same reason.

760.179 Listing and Marking of Power-Limited Fire Alarm Cables (PLFA) and Insulated Continuous Line-Type Fire Detectors

PLFA cable installed within buildings must be listed as being resistant to the spread of fire and other criteria in accordance with 760.179(A) through (H) and must be marked in accordance with 760.179 (I).

(C) Ratings. Fire alarm cable must have a voltage rating of not less than 300V and a temperature rating of no less than 60°C. Figure 760–9

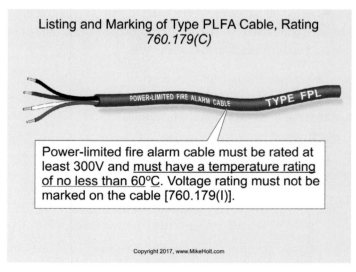

Figure 760–9

(D) Type FPLP. Type FPLP plenum cable is listed as being suitable for use in plenum space. Figure 760–10

(I) Marking. Cables must be marked in accordance with Table760.179(I). Voltage ratings aren't permitted to be marked on the cable.

Note: Voltage markings on cables may suggest that the cables are suitable for Class 1 or electric power and light applications, which they aren't.

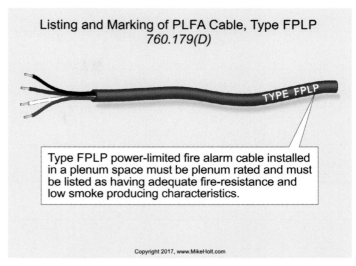

Figure 760–10

OPTICAL FIBER CABLES AND RACEWAYS

Introduction to Article 770—Optical Fiber Cables and Raceways

Article 770 provides the requirements for installing optical fiber cables and special raceways for optical fiber cables. It also contains the requirements for composite cables, often called "hybrid," that combine optical fibers with current-carrying conductors.

While we normally think of Article 300 in connection with wiring methods, you only need to use the Article 770 methods for optical fiber cables, except where it makes specific references to Article 300 [770.3]. For instance, in 770.113, reference is made to 300.22, which applies when installing optical fiber cables and optical fiber raceways in ducts and plenum spaces.

Article 90 states that the *NEC* isn't a design guide or installation manual. Thus, Article 770 doesn't deal with the performance of optical fiber systems. For example, it doesn't mention cable bending radii. It doesn't explain how to install and test cable safely either, but that doesn't mean you should look into an optical fiber cable, even if you can't see any light coming through it. Light used in these circuits usually isn't visible, but it can still damage your eyes.

Part I. General

770.1 Scope

Article 770 covers the installation of optical fiber cables, which transmit light for control, signaling, and communications. Figure 770–1

> **Author's Comment:**
>
> ■ The growth of high-tech applications and significant technological development of optical fibers and the equipment used to send and receive light pulses has increased the use of optical fibers. Since optical fiber cable isn't affected by electromagnetic interference, there's been a large growth in its uses in communications for voice, data transfer, data processing, and computer control of machines and processes.

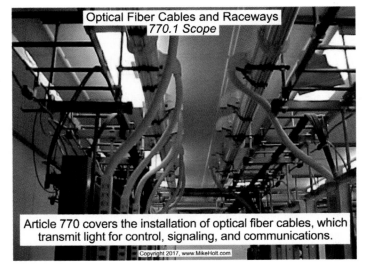

Optical Fiber Cables and Raceways
770.1 Scope

Article 770 covers the installation of optical fiber cables, which transmit light for control, signaling, and communications.

Copyright 2017, www.MikeHolt.com

Figure 770–1

770.2 Definitions

Many definitions have been relocated to Article 100.

Analysis

RELOCATED Most of the definitions in this article are for terms that are used in more places than just Article 770, so they've been relocated to Article 100 in accordance with the *NEC* style manual. Composite optical fiber cable, conductive optical fiber cable, innerduct, nonconductive optical fiber cable, and optical fiber cable were all relocated.

770.2 Definitions

Abandoned Optical Fiber Cable. A cable that isn't terminated to equipment and not identified for future use with a tag.

Exposed (to Accidental Contact). A conductive optical fiber cable that, in the case of failure of supports or insulation, the cable's non-current-carrying conductive members <u>might</u> contact an electrical circuit.

Note: See Article 100 for other definitions of Exposed (as applied to live parts) and Exposed (as applied to wiring methods).

Author's Comment:

- Section 770.25 requires the accessible portion of abandoned cables to be removed.

770.24 Mechanical Execution of Work

A new Informational Note was added to remind people about the effects paint, cleaners, and similar contaminants might have on cable jackets.

Analysis

NEW The effects that paint, plaster, cleaners, abrasives, corrosive residues, or other contaminants might have on cables are unknown. One thing that is known, however, is that the cables weren't tested with these items on them, and they probably don't add any benefit to the cables.

This new Informational Note is intended to remind *Code* users of this fact so discretion can be used when this situation arises. This note isn't saying that a trace amount of paint is going make your cable melt or otherwise fail, it just reminds us that it should be evaluated.

770.24 Mechanical Execution of Work

Equipment and cabling must be installed in a neat and workmanlike manner. Exposed cables must be supported by the structural components of the building so that the cable won't be damaged by normal building use. Such cables must be secured by straps, staples, hangers, cable ties, or similar fittings designed and installed in a manner that won't damage the cable, and be installed in accordance with 300.4(D) and 300.11. Figure 770–2

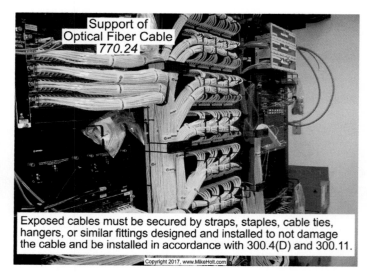

Support of Optical Fiber Cable 770.24

Exposed cables must be secured by straps, staples, cable ties, hangers, or similar fittings designed and installed to not damage the cable and be installed in accordance with 300.4(D) and 300.11.

Copyright 2017, www.MikeHolt.com

Figure 770–2

Communications raceways and cable assemblies must be securely fastened in place and the ceiling-support wires or ceiling grid aren't permitted to be used to support optical fiber raceways or cables [300.11]. Figure 770–3

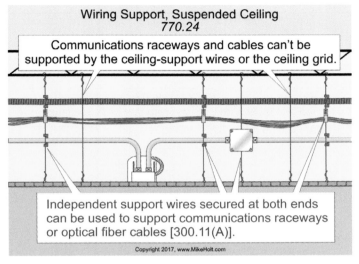

Wiring Support, Suspended Ceiling
770.24

Communications raceways and cables can't be supported by the ceiling-support wires or the ceiling grid.

Independent support wires secured at both ends can be used to support communications raceways or optical fiber cables [300.11(A)].

Copyright 2017, www.MikeHolt.com

Figure 770–3

Cables installed through or parallel to framing members or furring strips must be protected where they're likely to be penetrated by nails or screws by installing the wiring method so it isn't less than 1¼ in. from the nearest edge of the framing member or furring strips, or is protected by a ¹⁄₁₆ in. thick steel plate or the equivalent [300.4(D)].

Cable ties used to secure or support optical fiber cables in plenums must be listed for use in a plenum space. Figure 770–4

Note 1: Industry practices are described in ANSI/NECA/BICSI 568, *Standard for Installing Commercial Building Telecommunications Cabling* and ANSI/NECA/FOA 301, *Standard for Installing and Testing Fiber Optic Cables.* Figure 770–5

Note 3: Paint, plaster, cleaners, abrasives, corrosive residues, or other contaminants can result in an undetermined alteration of optical fiber cable properties.

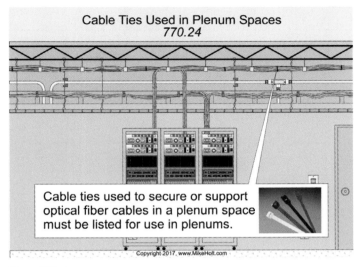

Cable Ties Used in Plenum Spaces
770.24

Cable ties used to secure or support optical fiber cables in a plenum space must be listed for use in plenums.

Copyright 2017, www.MikeHolt.com

Figure 770–4

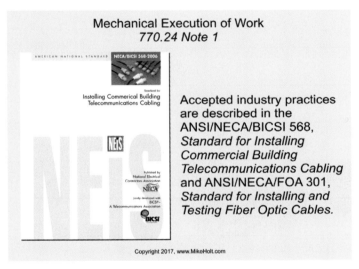

Mechanical Execution of Work
770.24 Note 1

Accepted industry practices are described in the ANSI/NECA/BICSI 568, *Standard for Installing Commercial Building Telecommunications Cabling* and ANSI/NECA/FOA 301, *Standard for Installing and Testing Fiber Optic Cables.*

Copyright 2017, www.MikeHolt.com

Figure 770–5

CHAPTER 8

COMMUNICATIONS SYSTEMS

Introduction to Chapter 8—Communications Systems

Chapter 8 of the *National Electrical Code* covers the wiring requirements for communications systems such as telephones, radio and TV antennas, satellite dishes, closed-circuit television (CCTV), and coaxial cable systems. Figure 1

Communications systems aren't subject to the general requirements contained in Chapters 1 through 4 or the special requirements of Chapters 5 through 7, except where a Chapter 8 rule specifically refers to one of those chapters [90.3]. Also, installations of communications equipment under the exclusive control of communications utilities located outdoors, or in building spaces used exclusively for such installations, are exempt from the *NEC* [90.2(B)(4)].

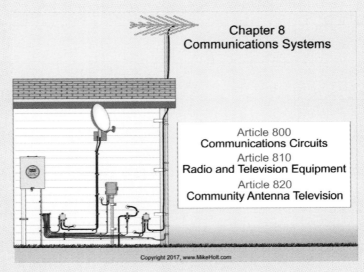

Figure 1

- **Article 800—Communications Circuits.** Article 800 covers the installation requirements for telephone wiring and for other related telecommunications purposes such as computer local area networks (LANs), and outside wiring for fire and burglar alarm systems connected to central stations.

- **Article 810—Radio and Television Equipment.** This article covers antenna systems for radio and television receiving equipment, amateur radio transmitting and receiving equipment, and certain features of transmitter safety. It also includes antennas such as multi-element, vertical rod and dish, and the wiring and cabling that connects them to the equipment.

- **Article 820—Community Antenna Television (CATV) and Radio Distribution Systems (Coaxial Cable).** Article 820 covers the installation of coaxial cables to distribute limited-energy high-frequency signals for television, cable TV, and closed-circuit television (CCTV), which is often used for security purposes. It also covers the premises wiring of satellite TV systems where the dish antenna is outside and covered by Article 810.

ARTICLE
800 COMMUNICATIONS CIRCUITS

Introduction to Article 800—Communications Circuits

This article has its roots in telephone technology. Consequently, it addresses telephone and related systems that use twisted-pair wiring. Here are a few key points to remember about Article 800:

- Don't attach incoming communications cables to the service-entrance power mast.
- Keep the grounding electrode conductor for the primary protector as straight and as short as possible.
- If you locate communications cables above a suspended ceiling, route and support them to allow access via ceiling panel removal.
- Keep these cables separated from lightning protection circuits.
- If you install communications cables in a Chapter 3 raceway, you must do so in conformance with the *NEC* requirements for the raceway system.
- Special labeling and marking provisions apply—follow them carefully.

Part I. General

800.1 Scope

This article covers communications circuits and equipment that extend voice, audio, video, interactive services, and outside wiring for fire alarms and burglar alarms from the communications utility to the customer's communications equipment up to and including equipment such as a telephone, fax machine or answering machine, and communications equipment [800.2 Communications Circuit]. Figure 800–1

Note: Communications circuits and equipment under the exclusive control of the communications utility are exempt from the *NEC* requirement, see 90.2(B)(4).

Author's Comment:

- The definition of "Communications Equipment" is contained in Article 100.

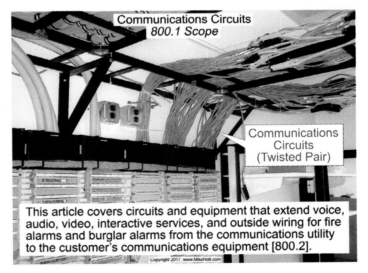

Communications Circuits
800.1 Scope

Communications Circuits (Twisted Pair)

This article covers circuits and equipment that extend voice, audio, video, interactive services, and outside wiring for fire alarms and burglar alarms from the communications utility to the customer's communications equipment [800.2].

Figure 800–1

800.2 Definitions

Some definitions were relocated to Article 100 and the definition of "point of entrance" was revised.

Analysis

CLARIFIED

The point of entrance is the point where a cable enters a building from a wall or floor. That's a pretty simple definition, certainly simpler than the one in previous editions of the *NEC*. Previous editions said that the point of entrance could be the real point of entrance, or it could be the point where a cable emerged from either IMC or RMC. This, in combination with 800.48, ultimately allowed for unlisted cables to be installed in buildings for a much greater length than intended, since the listing requirement only comes into play once you exceed 50 ft from the point of entrance. While that portion of the definition regarding RMC and IMC is now gone, the same rule still exists, since 800.48 allows you to encapsulate the cable in IMC or RMC and then measure 50 ft. So, what changed? Nothing really.

800.2 Definitions

Abandoned Communications Cable. A communications cable that isn't terminated to equipment and not identified for future use with a tag.

Author's Comment:

- Section 800.25 requires the accessible portion of abandoned communications cables to be removed.

Communications Circuit. The circuit that extends voice, audio, video, data, interactive services, and outside wiring for fire alarms and burglar alarms from the communications utility to the customer's communications equipment up to and including terminal equipment such as a telephone, fax machine, or answering machine.

Exposed (to Accidental Contact). A condition where failure of support or insulation can result in the circuit making contact with another circuit.

Point of Entrance. The point within a building at which the cable emerges from an external wall or concrete floor slab. Figure 800–2

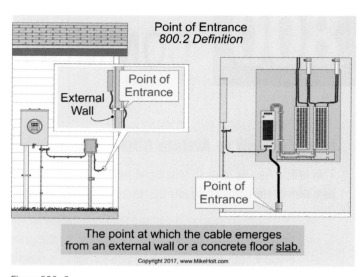

Figure 800–2

800.24 Mechanical Execution of Work

A new Informational Note was added to warn people about the effects paint, cleaners, and similar contaminants might have on cable jackets.

Analysis

NEW

The effects that paint, plaster, cleaners, abrasives, corrosive residues, or other contaminants might have on cables are unknown. One thing that is known, however, is that the cables weren't tested with those items on them, and they probably don't add any benefit to the cables. This new Informational Note is intended to remind *Code* users that discretion should be used if this situation arises. This note isn't saying that a trace amount of paint is going make your cable melt or otherwise fail, it just reminds us that it should be evaluated.

800.24 Mechanical Execution of Work

Equipment and communications cabling must be installed in a neat and workmanlike manner. Exposed communications cables must be supported by the structural components of the building so that the communications cable won't be damaged by normal building use. Cables must be secured with straps, staples, cable ties, hangers, or similar fittings designed and installed so as not to damage the communications cable. Figure 800–3

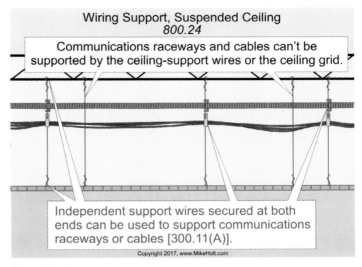

Wiring Support, Suspended Ceiling
800.24

Communications raceways and cables can't be supported by the ceiling-support wires or the ceiling grid.

Independent support wires secured at both ends can be used to support communications raceways or cables [300.11(A)].

Copyright 2017, www.MikeHolt.com

Figure 800–4

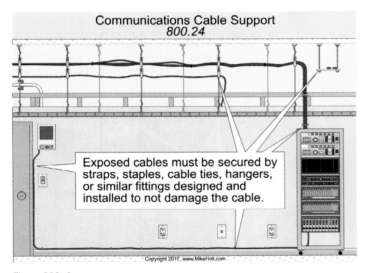

Communications Cable Support
800.24

Exposed cables must be secured by straps, staples, cable ties, hangers, or similar fittings designed and installed to not damage the cable.

Copyright 2017, www.MikeHolt.com

Figure 800–3

Communications raceways and communications cable assemblies must be securely fastened in place and ceiling-support wires or the ceiling grid aren't permitted to be used to support communications raceways or communications cables [300.11]. Figure 800–4

Author's Comment:

■ Raceways and cables can be supported by independent support wires attached to the suspended ceiling in accordance with 300.11(B).

Cables installed parallel to framing members or furring strips must be protected where they're likely to be penetrated by nails or screws, by installing the wiring method so it isn't less than 1¼ in. from the nearest edge of the framing member or furring strips, or is protected by a ¹⁄₁₆ in. thick steel plate or the equivalent [300.4(D)]. Figure 800–5

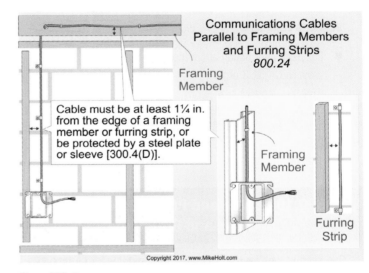

Communications Cables Parallel to Framing Members and Furring Strips
800.24

Framing Member

Cable must be at least 1¼ in. from the edge of a framing member or furring strip, or be protected by a steel plate or sleeve [300.4(D)].

Framing Member

Furring Strip

Copyright 2017, www.MikeHolt.com

Figure 800–5

Cable ties used to secure or support communications cables in plenums must be listed for use in plenum spaces. Figure 800–6

Note 1: Accepted industry practices are described in ANSI/NECA/BICSI 568, *Standard for Installing Commercial Building Telecommunications Cabling*, ANSI/ TIA 569, ANSI/TIA-568, *Commercial Building Telecommunications Infrastructure Standard*; ANSI/TIA-569-D, *Telecommunications Pathways and Spaces*; ANSI/ TIA-570-C, *Residential Telecommunications Infrastructure Standard*; ANSI/ TIA-1005-A, *Telecommunications Infrastructure Standard for Industrial Premises*; ANSI/TIA-1179, *Healthcare Facility Telecommunications Infrastructure Standard*; ANSI/TIA-4966, *Telecommunications Infrastructure Standard for Educational Facilities*; and other ANSI-approved installation standards.

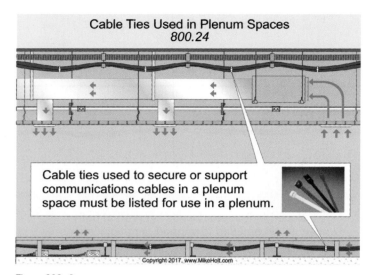

Cable Ties Used in Plenum Spaces
800.24

Cable ties used to secure or support communications cables in a plenum space must be listed for use in a plenum.

Copyright 2017, www.MikeHolt.com

Figure 800–6

Author's Comment:

■ For more information about these standards, visit www.NECA-NEIS.org.

Note 3: Paint, plaster, cleaners, abrasives, corrosive residues, or other contaminants may result in an undetermined alteration of communications wire and cable properties.

800.100 Cable and Primary Protector Bonding and Grounding

This section was revised to clarify that installing an intersystem bonding terminal is always okay.

Analysis

CLARIFIED

If you're installing communications equipment at a building, you must connect the primary protector and/or cable sheath to the metal parts of the electrical system. If the building has an intersystem bonding terminal this is easy to do; you just connect a bonding jumper to it and you're done [800.100(B)(1)]. If the building has no intersystem bonding terminal, you must follow the requirements of 800.100(B)(2).

The first sentence in that subsection was revised to clarify (sort of) that you can always install an intersystem bonding terminal, and if you do, you must comply with 250.94(A). Previous editions of the *NEC* said basically the same thing, just not quite as well.

800.100 Cable and Primary Protector Bonding and Grounding

The primary protector and the metallic member of cable sheaths must be bonded or grounded in accordance with 800(A) through (D). Figure 800–7

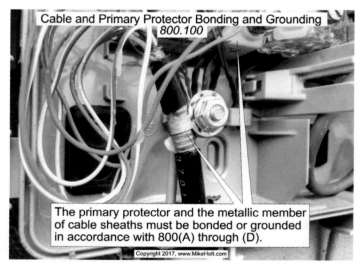

Cable and Primary Protector Bonding and Grounding
800.100

The primary protector and the metallic member of cable sheaths must be bonded or grounded in accordance with 800(A) through (D).

Copyright 2017, www.MikeHolt.com

Figure 800–7

(A) Bonding Conductor or Grounding Electrode Conductor.

(1) Insulation. The conductor must be listed and can be insulated, covered, or bare.

(2) Material. The conductor must be copper or other corrosion-resistant conductive material, stranded or solid.

(3) Size. The conductor isn't permitted to be smaller than 14 AWG with a current-carrying capacity of not less than the grounded metallic sheath member(s) or protected conductor(s) of the communications cable, but it's not required to be larger than 6 AWG.

(4) Length. The bonding conductor or grounding electrode conductor must be as short as practicable. For one- and two-family dwellings, the bonding conductor or grounding electrode conductor must not exceed 20 ft in length. Figure 800–8

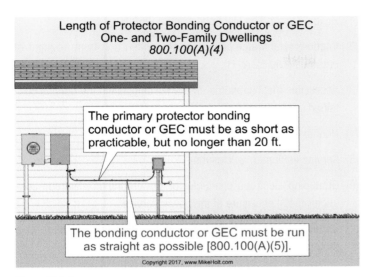

Figure 800–8

Note: Limiting the length of the bonding conductor or grounding electrode conductor helps limit induced voltage differences between the building's power and communications systems during lightning events.

Ex: If the bonding conductor or grounding electrode conductor is over 20 ft in length for one- and two-family dwellings, a separate rod not less than 5 ft long [800.100(B)(3)(2)] with fittings suitable for the application [800.100(C)] must be installed. The additional rod must be bonded to the power grounding electrode system with a minimum 6 AWG conductor [800.100(D)]. Figure 800–9

Figure 800–9

(5) Run in Straight Line. Run in as straight a line as practicable.

Author's Comment:

- Lightning doesn't like to travel around corners or through loops, which is why the grounding electrode conductor or bonding jumper must be run as straight as practicable.

(6) Physical Protection. The bonding conductor and grounding electrode conductor isn't permitted to be subject to physical damage. If installed in a metal raceway, both ends of the raceway must be bonded to the contained conductor or connected to the same terminal or electrode to which the bonding conductor or grounding electrode conductor is connected.

Author's Comment:

- Installing the bonding conductor or grounding electrode conductor in PVC conduit is a better practice.

(B) Electrode. The bonding conductor or grounding electrode conductor must be connected in accordance with (B)(1), (B)(2), or (B)(3):

(1) Buildings with an Intersystem Bonding Termination. The bonding conductor for the primary protector and the metallic sheath of communications cable must terminate to the intersystem bonding termination as required by 250.94. Figure 800–10

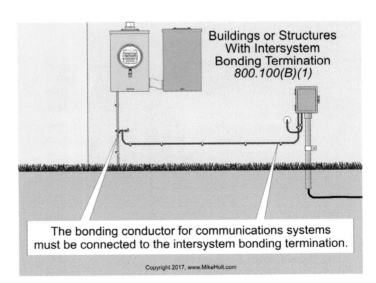

Figure 800–10

Author's Comment:

- According to the Article 100 definition, an "Intersystem Bonding Termination" is a device that provides a means to connect intersystem bonding conductors for communications systems to the grounding electrode system. Figure 800–11

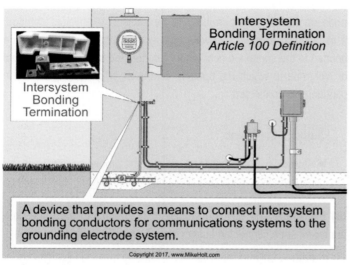

Figure 800–11

(2) Building Without Intersystem Bonding Termination. The bonding conductor or grounding electrode conductor must terminate to the nearest accessible: Figure 800–12

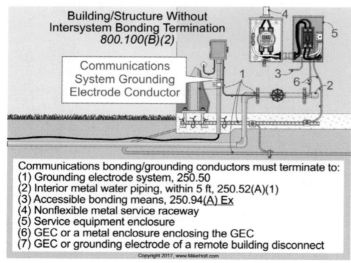

Figure 800–12

(1) Building grounding electrode system [250.50].

(2) Interior metal water piping system, within 5 ft from its point of entrance [250.52(A)(1)].

(3) Accessible means external to the building, using the options contained in 250.94(A) Ex.

(4) Nonflexible metallic service raceway.

(5) Service equipment enclosure.

(6) Grounding electrode conductor or the grounding electrode conductor metal enclosure of the power service.

(7) Grounding electrode conductor or the grounding electrode of a remote building disconnect [250.32].

The intersystem bonding termination must be mounted on the fixed part of an enclosure so that it won't interfere with the opening of an enclosure door. A bonding device isn't permitted to be mounted on a door or cover even if the door or cover is nonremovable.

(3) In Buildings Without Intersystem Bonding Termination or Grounding Means. The grounding electrode conductor must connect to:

(1) Any individual grounding electrodes described in 250.52(A)(1), (A)(2), (A)(3), or (A)(4).

(2) Any individual grounding electrode described in 250.52(A)(7) and (A)(8), or to a rod not less than 5 ft long and ½ in. diameter located not less than 6 ft from electrodes of other systems. Figure 800–13

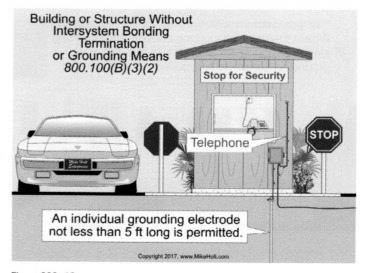

Figure 800–13

Author's Comment:

- The reason communications rods only need to be 5 ft long is because that's the length the telephone company used before the *NEC* contained requirements for communications systems. Telephone company rods were only 5 ft long because that's the length that would fit in their equipment trailers.

(C) Electrode Connection. Terminations at the grounding electrode must be by exothermic welding, listed lugs, listed pressure connectors, or listed clamps. Grounding fittings that are concrete-encased or buried in the earth must be listed for direct burial [250.70].

(D) Bonding of Electrodes. If a separate grounding electrode, such as a rod, is installed for a communications system, it must be bonded to the building's power grounding electrode system with a minimum 6 AWG conductor. Figure 800–14

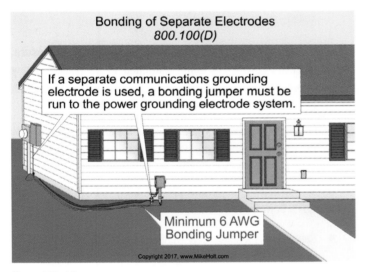

Figure 800–14

Note 2: Bonding of electrodes helps reduce induced voltage difference between the power and communications systems during lightning events. Figure 800–15

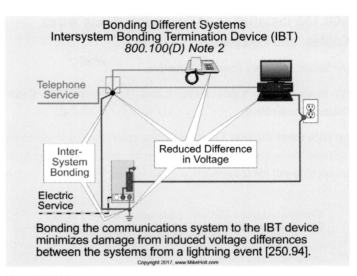

Figure 800–15

800.133 Installation of Communications Wires, Cables, and Equipment

The types of circuits that can share a raceway or other enclosure with communications cables were increased.

Analysis

EXPANDED Separation of communications cables from conductors of light and power is a serious safety concern. It has nothing to do with the performance of the cables, as that goes well beyond the "practical safeguarding" intention discussed in 90.1. Communications cables must be separated from conductors of lighting and power so they don't become energized to levels they aren't capable of handling. Furthermore, even if the cables could handle 120V without melting, what about the equipment to which they're connected? You could have a very dangerous situation on your hands if you energized communications cables to 120V.

There's no danger in having communications cable and coaxial cable in the same raceway, nor is there danger in sharing a raceway with a Class 2 or Class 3 remote-control, signaling, or limited-energy circuit [Article 725], and there's no real danger in sharing with a power-limited fire alarm circuit [Article 760]. Changes to this edition of the *Code* reflect those two types of circuits in a much clearer manner than before.

800.133 Installation of Communications Wires, Cables, and Equipment

(A) Separation from Power Conductors.

(1) In Raceways, Cable Trays, Boxes, Enclosures, and Cable Routing Assemblies.

(a) With Other Circuits. Communications cables can be in the same raceway, cable tray, cable routing assembly, box, or enclosure with cables of any of the following: Figure 800–16

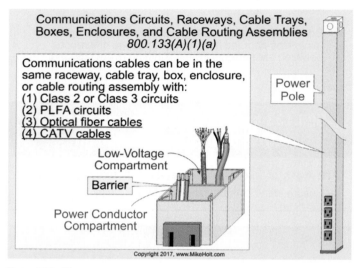

Figure 800–16

(1) Class 2 and Class 3 circuits in accordance with Article 645 or Parts I and III of Article 725.

(2) Power-limited fire alarm circuits in accordance with Parts I and III of Article 760.

(3) Optical fiber cables in accordance with Parts I and V of Article 770.

(4) Coaxial cables in accordance with Parts I and V of Article 820.

(b) Class 2 and Class 3 Circuits. Class 2 or Class 3 conductors can be within the same cable with communications conductors, if the cable is communications rated in accordance with Article 800 [725.139(D)(1)]. Figure 800–17

Author's Comment:

■ A common application of this requirement is when a single cable is used for both voice communications and data.

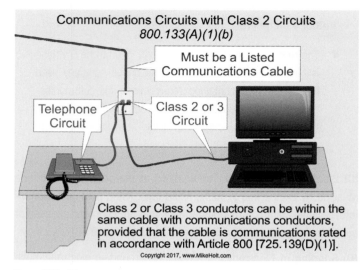

Figure 800–17

■ Listed Class 2 cables have a voltage rating of not less than 150V [725.179(G)], whereas communications cables have a voltage rating of at least 300V [800.179].

(c) With Power Conductors in Same Raceway or Enclosure. Communications conductors aren't permitted to be placed in any raceway, compartment, outlet box, junction box, or similar fitting with conductors of electric power or Class 1 circuits.

Ex 1: Communications circuits can be within the same enclosure with conductors of electric power and Class 1 circuits where separated by a permanent barrier or listed divider.

Author's Comment:

■ Separation is required to prevent a fire or shock hazard that can occur from a short between the communications circuits and the higher-voltage circuits.

Ex 2: Communications conductors can be mixed with power conductors if the power circuit conductors are only introduced to supply power to communications equipment. The power circuit conductors must maintain a minimum ½ in. separation from the communications circuit conductors.

(2) Other Applications. Communications circuits must maintain 2 in. of separation from electric power or Class 1 circuit conductors.

Ex 1: Separation isn't required if electric power or Class 1 circuit conductors are within a raceway or in metal-sheathed, metal-clad, nonmetallic-sheathed, or underground feeder cables, or if communications cables are within a raceway. Figure 800–18

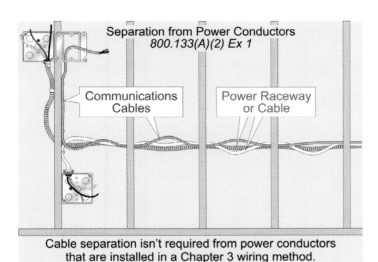

Separation from Power Conductors
800.133(A)(2) Ex 1

Communications Cables

Power Raceway or Cable

Cable separation isn't required from power conductors that are installed in a Chapter 3 wiring method.

Copyright 2017, www.MikeHolt.com

Figure 800–18

(B) Support of Communications Cables. Communications cables aren't permitted to be strapped, taped, or attached to the exterior of any raceway as a means of support. Figure 800–19

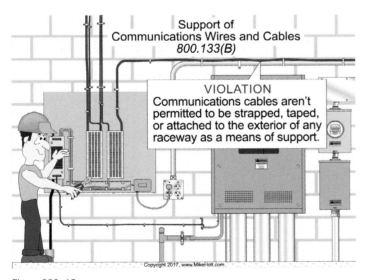

Support of Communications Wires and Cables
800.133(B)

VIOLATION
Communications cables aren't permitted to be strapped, taped, or attached to the exterior of any raceway as a means of support.

Copyright 2017, www.MikeHolt.com

Figure 800–19

Ex: Aerial spans of communications cable can be attached to the exterior of a raceway mast. Figure 800–20

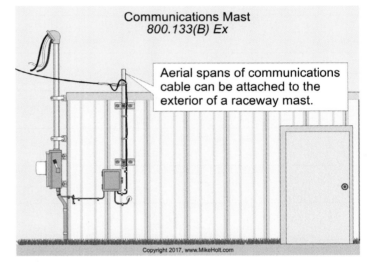

Communications Mast
800.133(B) Ex

Aerial spans of communications cable can be attached to the exterior of a raceway mast.

Copyright 2017, www.MikeHolt.com

Figure 800–20

Introduction to Article 810—Radio and Television Satellite Equipment

This article covers transmitter and receiver (antenna) equipment—and the wiring and cabling associated with that equipment. Here are a few key points to remember about Article 810:

- Avoid contact with conductors of other systems.
- Don't attach antennas or other equipment to the service-entrance power mast.
- Keep the bonding conductor or grounding electrode conductor as straight as practicable, and protect it from physical damage.
- If the mast isn't bonded properly, you risk flashovers and possible electrocution.
- Keep in mind that the purpose of bonding is to prevent a difference of voltage between metallic objects and other conductive items, such as swimming pools.
- Clearances are critical, and Article 810 contains detailed clearance requirements. For example, it provides separate clearance requirements for indoor and outdoor locations.

Part I. General

810.1 Scope

Article 810 contains the installation requirements for the wiring of television and radio receiving equipment, such as digital satellite receiving equipment for television signals and amateur/citizen band radio equipment antennas. Figure 810–1

Author's Comment:

- Article 810 covers:
  - ◆ Antennas that receive local television signals.
  - ◆ Satellite antennas, which are often referred to as satellite dishes.
  - ◆ Roof-mounted antennas for AM/FM/XM radio reception.
  - ◆ Amateur radio transmitting and receiving equipment, including HAM radio equipment (a noncommercial [amateur] communications system).

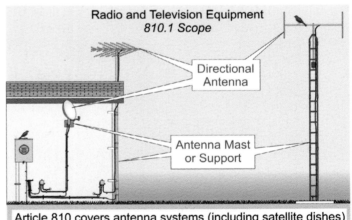

Article 810 covers antenna systems (including satellite dishes) for radio and television receiving equipment, and amateur and citizen band radio transmitting and receiving equipment.

Copyright 2017, www.MikeHolt.com

Figure 810–1

810.15 Metal Antenna Supports—Grounding

The requirement to ground antennas was reduced.

Analysis

CLARIFIED The general requirement found in this section is for masts and metal support structures for antennas to be bonded to the metal parts of the electrical system, which are grounded to earth. This is typically done by connecting the antenna to the intersystem bonding terminal described in 250.94, should one exist.

NEW New to this edition of the *NEC* we find an allowance to omit this connection if the antenna is in the "zone of protection" that's established when a lightning protection system is installed in accordance with NFPA 780.

810.15 Metal Antenna Supports—Grounding

Outdoor masts and metal structures that support antennas must be grounded in accordance with 810.21 <u>unless the antenna and its related supporting mast or structure are within a zone of protection defined by a 150-ft radius rolling sphere.</u> Figure 810–2

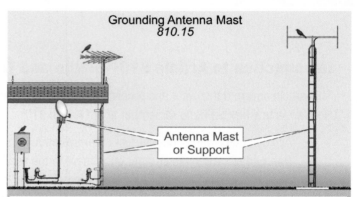

Grounding Antenna Mast
810.15

Antenna Mast or Support

Outdoor masts and metal structures that support antennas must be grounded/bonded in accordance with 810.21 <u>unless the antenna and its related supporting mast or structure are within a zone of protection defined by a 150-ft radius rolling sphere.</u>

Copyright 2017, www.MikeHolt.com

Figure 810–2

Note: See NFPA 780, *Standard for the Installation of Lightning Protection Systems*, 4.8.3.1 for the application of the term "rolling sphere."

ARTICLE 820

COMMUNITY ANTENNA TELEVISION (CATV) AND RADIO DISTRIBUTION SYSTEMS (COAXIAL CABLE)

Introduction to Article 820—Community Antenna Television (CATV) and Radio Distribution Systems (Coaxial Cable)

This article focuses on the distribution of television and radio signals within a facility or on a property via cable, rather than their transmission or reception via antenna. These signals are limited energy, but they're high frequency.

- As with Article 800, you must determine the "point of entrance" for these circuits.
- Ground the incoming coaxial cable as close as practicable to the point of entrance.
- If coaxial cables are located above a suspended ceiling, route and support them to allow access via ceiling panel removal.
- Clearances are critical, and Article 820 contains detailed clearance requirements. For example, it requires at least 6 ft of clearance between coaxial cable and lightning conductors.
- If the building or structure has an intersystem bonding termination, the bonding conductor must be connected to it.
- If you use a separate grounding electrode, you must run a bonding jumper to the power grounding system.

Author's Comment:

- For Articles 800, 810, and 820, the difference between a "bonding conductor" and a "grounding electrode conductor" is where they terminate. The bonding conductor terminates at the intersystem bonding termination; the grounding electrode connects to the power grounding electrode system [250.50].

Part I. General

820.1 Scope

Article 820 covers the installation of coaxial cables for distributing high-frequency signals. Figure 820–1

Note: The *NEC* installation requirements don't apply to communications utility equipment, such as coaxial cables located outdoors or in building spaces under the exclusive control of the communications utility [90.2(B)(4)]. Figure 820–2

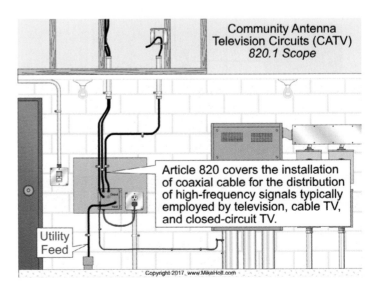

Community Antenna
Television Circuits (CATV)
820.1 Scope

Article 820 covers the installation of coaxial cable for the distribution of high-frequency signals typically employed by television, cable TV, and closed-circuit TV.

Utility Feed

Copyright 2017, www.MikeHolt.com

Figure 820–1

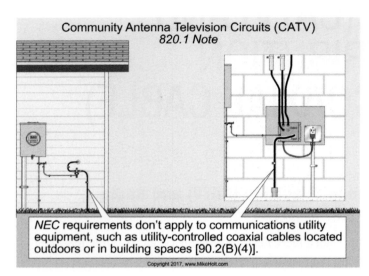

Community Antenna Television Circuits (CATV)
820.1 Note

NEC requirements don't apply to communications utility equipment, such as utility-controlled coaxial cables located outdoors or in building spaces [90.2(B)(4)].

Figure 820–2

Author's Comment:

- Coaxial cables that connect antennas to television and radio receiving equipment [810.3] and community television systems [810.4] must be installed in accordance with this article. Figure 820–3

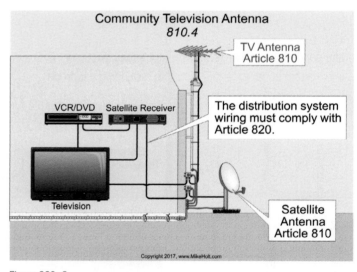

Community Television Antenna
810.4

TV Antenna
Article 810

VCR/DVD   Satellite Receiver

The distribution system wiring must comply with Article 820.

Television

Satellite Antenna
Article 810

Figure 820–3

820.2 Definitions

The definition of "point of entrance" was revised to be consistent with similar sections of the *NEC*.

Analysis

CLARIFIED The point of entrance is the point where a cable enters a building from a wall or floor. That's a pretty simple definition, certainly simpler than previous editions of the *Code*. Previous editions said that the point of entrance could be the real point of entrance, or it could be the point where a cable emerged from either IMC or RMC. This, in combination with 820.48, ultimately allowed for unlisted cables to be installed in buildings for a much greater length than intended, since the listing requirement only comes into play once you exceed 50 ft from the point of entrance. While that portion of the definition regarding RMC and IMC is now gone, the same rule still exists, since 820.48 allows you to encapsulate the cable in IMC or RMC and then measure 50 ft. So, what changed? Nothing really.

820.2 Definitions

Abandoned Coaxial Cable. A cable that isn't terminated to equipment and not identified for future use with a tag.

Point of Entrance. The point within a building where the coaxial cable emerges from an external wall or concrete floor slab. Figure 820–4

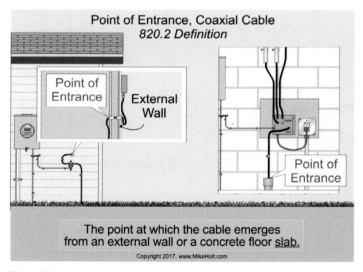

Point of Entrance, Coaxial Cable
820.2 Definition

Point of Entrance

External Wall

Point of Entrance

The point at which the cable emerges from an external wall or a concrete floor slab.

Figure 820–4

Author's Comment:

- See 820.48 for extending the point of entrance for unlisted cables.

820.24 Mechanical Execution of Work

A new Informational Note was added to warn people about the effect paint, cleaners, and similar contaminants might have on cable jackets.

Analysis

NEW The effects that paint, plaster, cleaners, abrasives, corrosive residues, or other contaminants might have on cables are unknown. One thing that is known, however, is that the cables weren't tested with those items on them, and they probably don't add any benefit to the cables. This new Informational Note is intended to remind *Code* users of this fact and the need to use discretion should this situation arise. This note isn't saying that a trace amount of paint is going make your cable melt or otherwise fail, it just reminds us that it should be evaluated.

820.24 Mechanical Execution of Work

Equipment and coaxial cabling must be installed in a neat and workmanlike manner. Exposed coaxial cables must be supported by the structural components of the building so that the coaxial cable won't be damaged by normal building use. Coaxial cables must be secured by straps, staples, cable ties, hangers, or similar fittings designed and installed so as not to damage the coaxial cable. Figure 820–5

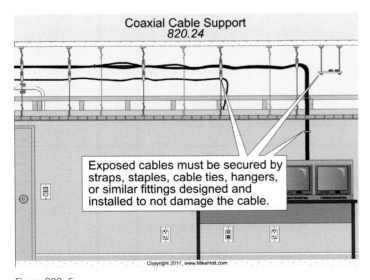

Figure 820–5

Coaxial cables installed through or parallel to framing members or furring strips must be protected where they're likely to be penetrated by nails or screws, by installing the coaxial cables so they aren't less than 1¼ in. from the nearest edge of the framing member or furring strips, or by protecting the coaxial cable with a ¹⁄₁₆ in. thick steel plate or the equivalent [300.4(D)]. Figure 820–6

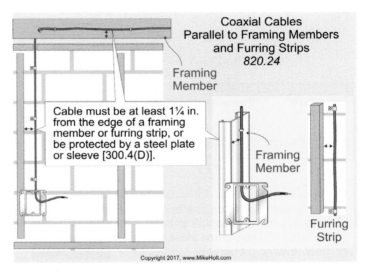

Figure 820–6

Raceways that contain coaxial cables must be securely fastened in place. Ceiling-support wires or the ceiling grid aren't permitted to be used to support raceways or coaxial cables [300.11]. Figure 820–7

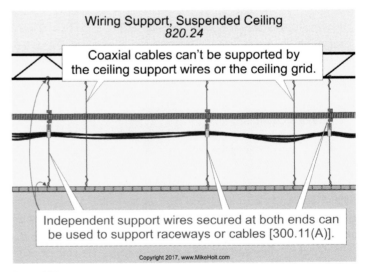

Figure 820–7

Author's Comment:

- Raceways and coaxial cables can be supported by independent support wires attached to the suspended ceiling in accordance with 300.11(B).

Cable ties used to secure or support coaxial cables in plenums must be listed for use in plenum spaces. Figure 820–8

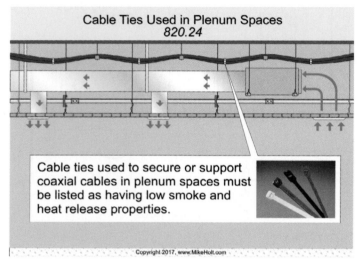

Cable Ties Used in Plenum Spaces
820.24

Cable ties used to secure or support coaxial cables in plenum spaces must be listed as having low smoke and heat release properties.

Copyright 2017, www.MikeHolt.com

Figure 820–8

Note 1: Accepted industry practices are described in ANSI/NECA/BICSI 568, *Standard for Installing Commercial Building Telecommunications Cabling*, ANSI/TIA/EIA 568-B, *Part 1, General Requirements Commercial Building Telecommunications Cabling Standard*, ANSI/TIA 569-B, *Commercial Building Standard for Telecommunications Pathways and Spaces*, ANSI/TIA 570-B, *Residential Telecommunications Infrastructure*, and other ANSI-approved standards. Figure 820–9

Author's Comment:

- For more information about these standards, visit www. NECA-NEIS.org.

Note 2: See 4.3.11.2.6.5 and 4.3.11.5.5.6 of NFPA 90A, *Standard for the Installation of Air-Conditioning and Ventilating Systems*, for discrete combustible components installed in accordance with 300.22(C).

Note 3: Paint, plaster, cleaners, abrasives, corrosive residues, or other contaminants may result in an undetermined alteration of coaxial cable properties.

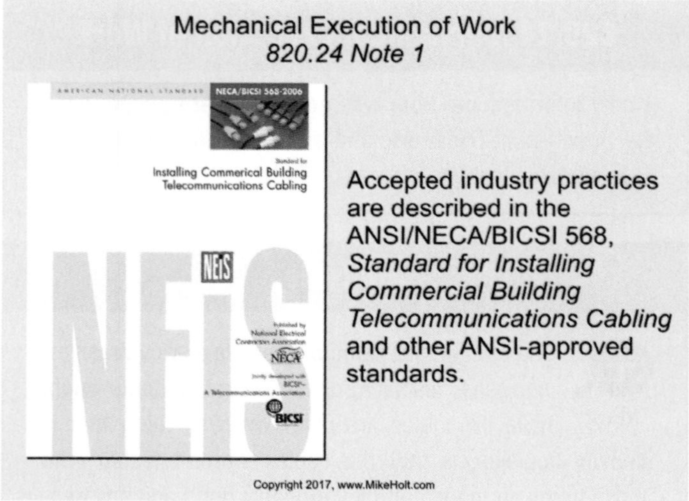

Mechanical Execution of Work
820.24 Note 1

Installing Commercial Building
Telecommunications Cabling

NEIS

Accepted industry practices are described in the ANSI/NECA/BICSI 568, *Standard for Installing Commercial Building Telecommunications Cabling* and other ANSI-approved standards.

Copyright 2017, www.MikeHolt.com

Figure 820–9

820.100 Bonding and Grounding Methods

This section was revised to clarify that installing an intersystem bonding terminal is always okay.

Analysis

CLARIFIED

If you're installing coaxial cable at a building you must connect the cable shield to the metal parts of the electrical system. If the building has an intersystem bonding terminal this is easy to do; you just connect a bonding jumper to it and you're done [820.100(B)(1)]. If the building has no intersystem bonding terminal you must follow the requirements of 820.100(B)(2).

The first sentence in that subsection was revised to clarify (sort of) that you can always install an intersystem bonding terminal, and if you do you must comply with 250.94(A). Previous editions of the *NEC* basically said the same thing, just not quite as well.

820.100 Bonding and Grounding Methods

The outer conductive shield of a coaxial cable must be bonded or grounded in accordance with the following:

Ex: For systems using coaxial cable completely contained within the building (they don't exit the building) and isolated from outside cable systems, the shield can be grounded by a connection to an equipment grounding conductor as described in 250.118. This connection can be made through a grounded receptacle using a dedicated bonding jumper and a permanently connected listed device.

Use of a cord and plug for the connection to an equipment grounding conductor isn't permitted.

(A) Bonding Conductor or Grounding Electrode Conductor.

(1) Insulation. The bonding conductor or grounding electrode conductor must be listed and can be insulated, covered, or bare.

(2) Material. The bonding conductor or grounding electrode conductor must be copper or other corrosion-resistant conductive material, stranded or solid.

(3) Size. The bonding conductor or grounding electrode conductor isn't permitted to be smaller than 14 AWG with a current-carrying capacity of not less than the outer sheath of the coaxial cable, but not required to be larger than 6 AWG.

(4) Length. The bonding conductor or grounding electrode conductor must be as short as practicable. For one- and two-family dwellings, the bonding conductor or grounding electrode conductor must not exceed 20 ft. Figure 820–10

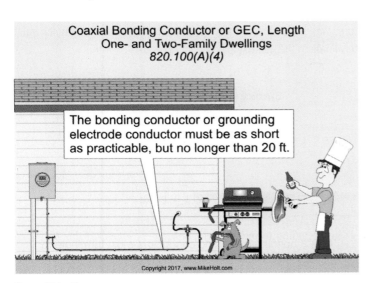

Coaxial Bonding Conductor or GEC, Length
One- and Two-Family Dwellings
820.100(A)(4)

The bonding conductor or grounding electrode conductor must be as short as practicable, but no longer than 20 ft.

Copyright 2017, www.MikeHolt.com

Figure 820–10

Note: Limiting the length of the bonding conductor or grounding electrode conductor at other than dwelling units will help to reduce voltage differences between the building's power and CATV systems during lightning events.

Ex: If it's not practicable to limit the coaxial bonding conductor or grounding electrode conductor to 20 ft in length for one- and two-family dwellings, a separate rod not less than 8 ft long [250.52(A)(5)],

with fittings suitable for the application [250.70] must be installed. The additional rod must be bonded to the power grounding electrode system with a minimum 6 AWG conductor [820.100(D)]. Figure 820–11

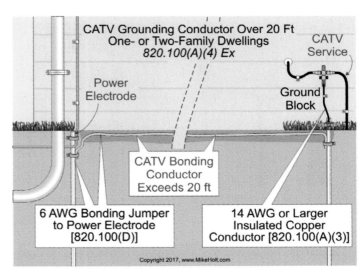

CATV Grounding Conductor Over 20 Ft
One- or Two-Family Dwellings
820.100(A)(4) Ex

CATV Service

Power Electrode

Ground Block

CATV Bonding Conductor Exceeds 20 ft

6 AWG Bonding Jumper to Power Electrode [820.100(D)]

14 AWG or Larger Insulated Copper Conductor [820.100(A)(3)]

Copyright 2017, www.MikeHolt.com

Figure 820–11

(5) Run in Straight Line. The bonding conductor or grounding electrode conductor to the electrode must be run in as straight a line as practicable.

Author's Comment:

- Lightning doesn't like to travel around corners or through loops, which is why the bonding conductor or grounding electrode conductor must be run as straight as practicable.

(6) Physical Protection. The bonding conductor or grounding electrode conductor must be mechanically protected where subject to physical damage, and where installed in a metal raceway both ends of the raceway must be bonded to the bonding conductor or grounding electrode conductor. Figure 820–12

Author's Comment:

- Installing the bonding conductor in PVC conduit is a better practice.

(B) Electrode. The bonding conductor or grounding electrode conductor must be connected in accordance with (B)(1), (B)(2), or (B)(3).

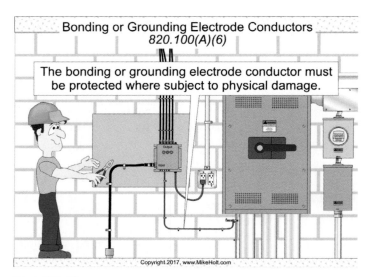

Figure 820–12

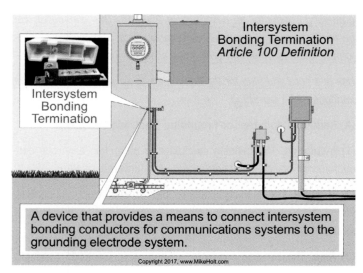

Figure 820–14

(1) Buildings With an Intersystem Bonding Termination. The bonding conductor or grounding electrode conductor for the CATV system must terminate to the intersystem bonding termination as required by 250.94. Figure 820–13

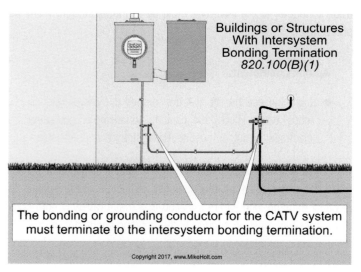

Figure 820–13

Author's Comment:

■ According to the Article 100 definition, an "Intersystem Bonding Termination" is a device that provides a means to connect bonding conductors for communications systems to the grounding electrode system, in accordance with 250.94. Figure 820–14

■ Bonding all systems to the intersystem bonding termination helps reduce induced voltage differences between the power and the radio and television systems during lightning events.

(2) In Buildings With Grounding Means. If an intersystem bonding termination is established, 250.94(A) applies. If not, at existing structures, the bonding conductor or grounding electrode conductor must terminate to the nearest accessible: Figure 820–15

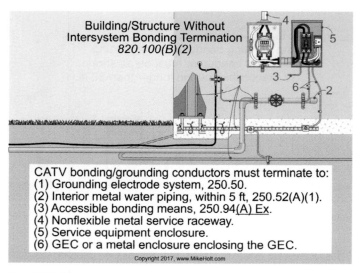

Figure 820–15

(1) Building grounding electrode system [250.50].

(2) Interior metal water piping system, within 5 ft from its point of entrance [250.52(A)(1)].

(3) Accessible means external to the building, using the options contained in 250.94(A) Ex.

(4) Nonflexible metallic service raceway of the power service.

(5) Service equipment enclosure.

(6) Grounding electrode conductor or the grounding electrode conductor metal enclosure.

(7) The grounding electrode conductor or the grounding electrode of a remote building disconnect [250.32].

The intersystem bonding termination must be mounted on the fixed part of an enclosure so that it won't interfere with the opening of an enclosure door. A bonding device isn't permitted to be mounted on a door or cover even if the door or cover is nonremovable.

(3) In Buildings Without Intersystem Bonding Termination or Grounding Means. The bonding conductor or grounding electrode conductor must connect to:

(1) Any one of the individual grounding electrodes described in 250.52(A)(1), (A)(2), (A)(3), (A)(4), or

(2) Any individual grounding electrodes described in 250.52(A)(5), 250.52(A)(7), and (A)(8). Figure 820–16

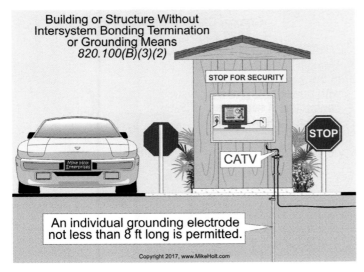

Figure 820–16

(C) Electrode Connection. Terminations to the grounding electrode must be by exothermic welding, listed lugs, listed pressure connectors, or clamps. Grounding fittings that are concrete-encased or buried in the earth must be listed for direct burial [250.70].

(D) Bonding of Electrodes. If a separate grounding electrode, such as a rod, is installed for the CATV system, it must be bonded to the building's power grounding electrode system with a minimum 6 AWG conductor. Figure 820–17

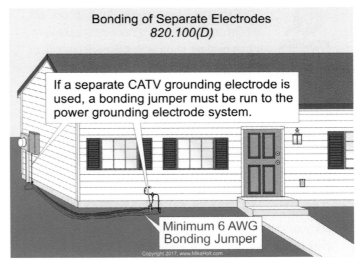

Figure 820–17

Note 2: Bonding all systems to the intersystem bonding termination helps reduce induced voltage between the power and CATV system during lightning events. Figure 820–18

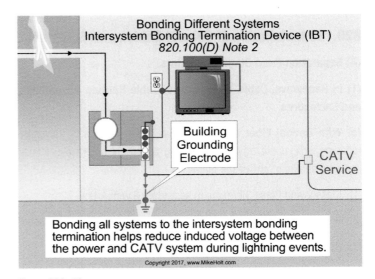

Figure 820–18

820.133 Installation of Coaxial Cables and Equipment

The types of circuits that can share a raceway or other enclosure with coaxial cable were increased.

Analysis

EXPANDED

Separation of coaxial cables from conductors of light and power is a serious safety concern. It has nothing to do with the performance of the cables, as that goes well beyond the "practical safeguarding" intention discussed in 90.1. Coaxial cables must be separated from conductors of lighting and power so they don't become energized to levels they aren't capable of handling. Furthermore, even if the cables could handle 120V without melting, what about the equipment to which they're connected? You could have a very dangerous situation on your hands if you energized coaxial cable to 120V.

There's no danger in having coaxial cable and twisted pair (communications cable) in the same raceway, nor is there danger in sharing a raceway with a Class 2 or Class 3 remote-control, signaling, or limited-energy circuit [Article 725], and there's no real danger in sharing with a power-limited fire alarm circuit [Article 760]. Changes to this edition of the *Code* reflect those two types of circuits in a much clearer manner than before.

820.133 Installation of Coaxial Cables and Equipment

(A) Separation From Other Conductors.

(1) In Raceways, Cable Trays, Boxes, Cable Routing Assemblies, and Enclosures.

(a) With Optical Fiber Cables. Coaxial cables can be in the same raceway, box, cable tray, cable routing assembly or enclosure with jacketed cables of any of the following: Figure 820–19

(1) Class 2 and Class 3 circuits in accordance with Article 725

(2) Power-limited fire alarm systems in accordance with Article 760

(3) Optical fiber cables in accordance with Article 770

(4) Communications circuits in accordance with Article 800

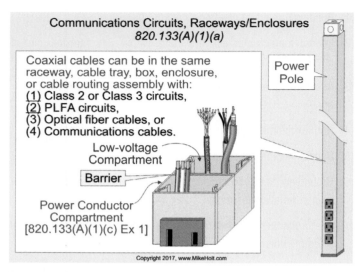

Figure 820–19

(b) Electric Light, Power, Class 1, Nonpower-Limited Fire Alarm, and Medium-Power Network-Powered Broadband Communications Circuits. Coaxial cables aren't permitted to be placed in any raceway, compartment, outlet box, junction box, or other enclosures with conductors of electric light, power, Class 1, nonpower-limited fire alarm, or medium-power network-powered broadband communications circuits.

Ex 1: Coaxial cables are permitted in the same enclosure with conductors of electric power and Class 1 circuits, where separated by a permanent barrier or listed divider. Figure 820–20

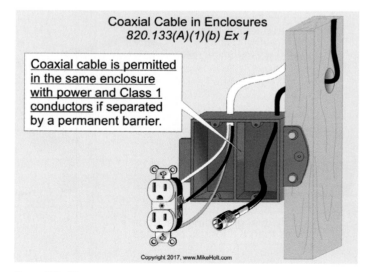

Figure 820–20

- Separation is required to prevent a fire or shock hazard that can occur from a short between the higher-voltage circuits and the coaxial cable.

Ex 2: Coaxial cables can be mixed in enclosures other than raceways or cables with power conductors if the power circuit conductors are only introduced to supply power to coaxial cable system distribution equipment. The power circuit conductors must be separated at least ¼ in. from the coaxial cables.

(2) Other Applications. Coaxial cables must maintain 2 in. of separation from electric power or Class 1 circuit conductors.

Ex 1: Separation isn't required if electric power or conductors are within a raceway or in metal-sheathed, metal-clad, nonmetallic-sheathed, or underground feeder cables, or if coaxial cables are within a raceway. Figure 820–21

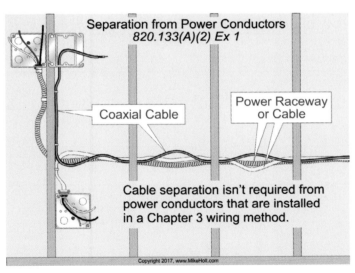

Figure 820–21

(B) Support of Cables. Coaxial cables aren't permitted to be strapped, taped, or attached to the exterior of any raceway as a means of support. Figure 820–22

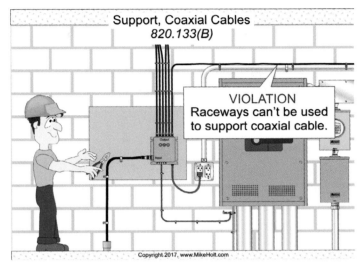

Figure 820–22

Ex: Overhead (aerial) spans of coaxial cables can be attached to a raceway-type mast intended for the attachment and support of such conductors. Figure 820–23

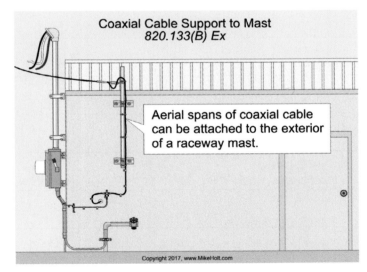

Figure 820–23

FINAL EXAM

Please use the 2017 *Code* book to answer the following questions.

CHAPTER 1— GENERAL RULES

1. A(n) _____ that performs field evaluations of electrical or other equipment is known as a "Field Evaluation Body (FEB)."

    (a) part of an organization
    (b) organization
    (c) a or b
    (d) none of these

2. When protecting equipment against damage from the weather during construction, minimum _____ provisions provided in NFPA 5000 *Building Construction and Safety Code*, the *International Building Code (IBC)*, and the *International Residential Code for One- and Two-Family Dwellings (IRC)* can be referenced for additional information.

    (a) safety
    (b) flood
    (c) weather
    (d) none of these

3. In other than dwelling units, in addition to requirements for field or factory marking of equipment to warn qualified persons of potential electric arc-flash hazards, a permanent label shall be field or factory applied to service equipment rated _____ or more.

    (a) 600A
    (b) 1,000A
    (c) 1,200A
    (d) 1,600

4. *NFPA 70E, Standard for Electrical Safety in the Workplace*, provides guidance, such as determining severity of potential exposure, planning safe work practices, arc-flash labeling, and selecting _____.

    (a) personal protective equipment
    (b) coordinated overcurrent protective devices
    (c) a and b
    (d) none of these

5. Reconditioned equipment shall be marked with the name, trademark, or other descriptive marking by which the _____ responsible for reconditioning the electrical equipment can be identified, along with the date of the reconditioning.

    (a) name of the individual
    (b) approving authority
    (c) organization
    (d) listing agency

6. NFPA 70E, *Standard for Electrical Safety in the Workplace*, provides guidance for working space about electrical equipment, such as determining severity of potential exposure, planning safe work practices, arc-flash labeling, and selecting personal protective equipment.

    (a) True
    (b) False

7. All switchboards, switchgear, panelboards, and motor control centers shall be located in dedicated spaces and protected from damage, and outdoor installations shall be _____.

(a) installed in identified enclosures
(b) protected from accidental contact by unauthorized personnel or by vehicular traffic
(c) protected from accidental spillage or leakage from piping systems
(d) all of these

CHAPTER 2—WIRING AND PROTECTION

8. For the application of GFCI protection for personnel, when determining distance from receptacles for sinks [210.8(A)(7) and 210.8(B)(5)] and bathtubs or shower stalls [210.8(A)(9)], the distance shall be measured as the _____ path the cord of an appliance connected to the receptacle would follow without piercing a floor, wall, ceiling, or fixed barrier, or passing through a door, doorway, or window.

(a) longest
(b) shortest
(c) most direct
(d) none of these

9. In other than dwelling units, all single-phase receptacles rated 150 volts-to-ground or less, 50A or less and three-phase receptacles rated 150 volts-to-ground or less, 100A or less installed in _____ shall have GFCI protection for personnel.

(a) rooftops
(b) kitchens
(c) bathrooms
(d) all of these

10. GFCI protection shall be provided for lighting outlets not exceeding 125V installed in crawl spaces.

(a) True
(b) False

11. The 120V, 20A branch circuit required for a garage isn't permitted to supply readily accessible outdoor receptacle outlets.

(a) True
(b) False

12. 120V, single-phase, 15A and 20A branch circuits supplying outlets and devices installed in guest _____ of hotels and motels shall be protected by any of the means described in 210.12(A)(1) through (6).

(a) rooms
(b) suites
(c) a and b
(d) none of these

13. For one- and two-family dwellings, at least one receptacle outlet shall be installed in each _____.

(a) separate unfinished portion of a basement
(b) attached or detached garage with electric power
(c) accessory building with electric power
(d) all of these

14. The receptacle outlet required for indoor electrical service equipment shall not be required to be installed for _____.

(a) multifamily occupancies
(b) assembly occupancies
(c) one- and two-family dwellings
(d) equipment pits

15. Each meeting room of not more than _____ sq ft in other than dwelling units shall have outlets for nonlocking-type, 125V, 15A or 20A receptacles installed in accordance with 210.71(B).

(a) 500
(b) 1,000
(c) 1,500
(d) 2,000

16. For the purposes of 210.71, examples of rooms that aren't meeting rooms include _____.

(a) auditoriums
(b) schoolrooms
(c) coffee shops
(d) all of these

17. Where a portion of a feeder is connected at both its supply and load ends to separately installed pressure connections in accordance with 110.14(C)(2), it shall be permitted to have an allowable ampacity _____ the sum of the continuous load plus the noncontinuous load.

    (a) not less than
    (b) equal to
    (c) not greater than
    (d) none of these

18. Raceways entering from outside must be sealed with a product identified for use with the _____ insulation.

    (a) conductor
    (b) cable
    (c) a or b
    (d) none of these

19. Conductors other than service conductors shall not be installed in the same _____ in which the service conductors are installed.

    (a) service raceway
    (b) service cable
    (c) enclosure
    (d) a or b

20. Load management control conductors having _____ protection shall be permitted within raceways containing service conductors.

    (a) GFCI
    (b) AFCI
    (c) overcurrent
    (d) GFPE

21. Overhead service conductors or service equipment can be supported to hardwood trees.

    (a) True
    (b) False

22. Where exposed to the weather, raceways enclosing service-entrance conductors shall be _____ for use in wet locations and arranged to drain.

    (a) approved
    (b) listed
    (c) a or b
    (d) none of these

23. The service disconnecting means rated 1,000V or less shall be marked to identify it as being suitable for use as service equipment and shall be _____.

    (a) weatherproof
    (b) listed or field labeled
    (c) approved
    (d) acceptable

24. Meter sockets supplied by and under the exclusive control of an electric utility shall not be required to be _____ in accordance with 230.66.

    (a) approved
    (b) rated
    (c) listed
    (d) all of these

25. Switches containing fuses and circuit breakers shall be readily accessible and installed so the center of the grip of the operating handle of the switch or circuit breaker, when in its highest position, is not more than _____ above the floor or working platform.

    (a) 2 ft
    (b) 4 ft 6 in.
    (c) 5 ft
    (d) 6 ft 7 in.

26. NFPA 780, *Standard for the Installation of Lightning Protection Systems* provides information on the installation of _____ for lightning protection systems [250.4(B)(1)].

    (a) grounding
    (b) bonding
    (c) a and b
    (d) none of these

27. The building or structure grounding electrode system shall be used as the _____ electrode for the separately derived system.

    (a) grounding
    (b) bonding
    (c) grounded
    (d) bonded

28. The common grounding electrode conductor installed for multiple separately derived systems shall be permitted to be the metal structural frame of the building or structure that complies with 250.68(C)(2) or is connected to the grounding electrode system by a conductor not smaller than _____.

    (a) 3/0 AWG copper
    (b) 250 kcmil aluminum
    (c) a or b
    (d) none of these

29. Metal in-ground support structures permitted as grounding electrodes include, but aren't limited to, pilings, casings, and other _____.

    (a) water piping
    (b) gas piping
    (c) structural metal
    (d) none of these

30. When a ground ring is used as a grounding electrode, it shall be installed at a depth below the earth's surface of not less than _____.

    (a) 18 in.
    (b) 24 in.
    (c) 30 in.
    (d) 8 ft

31. A(n) _____ AWG or larger copper or aluminum grounding electrode conductor exposed to physical damage shall be protected in rigid metal conduit, IMC, PVC conduit, reinforced thermosetting resin conduit Type XW (RTRC-XW), EMT, or cable armor.

    (a) 10
    (b) 8
    (c) 6
    (d) 4

32. If a building or structure is supplied by a service or feeder with _____ or more disconnecting means in separate enclosures, the grounding electrode connections shall be made in accordance with 250.64(D)(1), 250.64(D)(2), or 250.64(D)(3).

    (a) one
    (b) two
    (c) three
    (d) four

33. Bonding jumper(s) from grounding electrode(s) shall be permitted to be connected to an aluminum or copper busbar not less than _____ and of sufficient length to accommodate the number of terminations necessary for the installation in accordance with 250.64(F).

    (a) ⅛ in. thick x 1 in. wide
    (b) ⅛ in. thick x 2 in. wide
    (c) ¼ in. thick x 1 in. wide
    (d) ¼ in. thick x 2 in. wide

34. Interior metal water piping that's electrically continuous with a metal underground water pipe electrode and is located more than _____ ft from the point of entrance to the building shall not be used as a conductor to interconnect electrodes of the grounding electrode system.

    (a) 2
    (b) 4
    (c) 5
    (d) 6

35. Metal components in a run of an underground nonmetallic raceway and isolated from possible contact by a minimum cover of _____ in. to all parts of the metal components shall not be required to be connected to the grounded system conductor, supply-side bonding jumper, or grounding electrode conductor.

    (a) 6
    (b) 12
    (c) 18
    (d) 24

36. Communications system bonding termination connections to an aluminum or copper busbar must not be less than ¼ in. thick x 2 in. wide and be of sufficient length to accommodate at least _____ terminations for communications systems in addition to other connections.

    (a) two
    (b) three
    (c) four
    (d) five

37. Equipment bonding jumpers shall be of copper, aluminum, copper-clad aluminum, or other corrosion-resistant material.

    (a) True
    (b) False

38. The bonding jumper used to bond the metal water piping system shall be sized in accordance with _____, except as permitted in 250.104(A)(2) and 250.104(A)(3).

    (a) Table 250.102(C)(1)
    (b) Table 250.122
    (c) Table 310.15(B)(16)
    (d) Table 310.15(B)(6)

39. Metal gas piping installed in or attached to a building shall be considered bonded when one or more grounding electrodes are used, if the grounding electrode conductor or bonding jumper to the grounding electrode is of sufficient size.

    (a) True
    (b) False

40. Metal water piping systems and structural metal that's interconnected to form a building frame shall be bonded to separately derived systems in accordance with 250.104(D)(1) through 250.104(D)(3).

    (a) True
    (b) False

41. If exposed structural metal that's interconnected to form the building frame exists in the area served by the separately derived system, it shall be bonded to the grounded conductor of each separately derived system and each bonding jumper shall be sized in accordance with Table 250.102(C)(1) based on the largest ungrounded conductor of the service.

    (a) True
    (b) False

42. Where circuit conductors are installed in parallel in multiple raceways or cables and include an EGC of the wire type, the equipment grounding conductor must be installed in parallel in each raceway or cable, sized in compliance with 250.122 based on the overcurrent protective device for the feeder or branch circuit.

    (a) True
    (b) False

43. Except as provided in 250.122(F)(2)(b) for raceway or cable tray installations, the equipment grounding conductor in each multiconductor cable shall be sized in accordance with 250.122 based on the _____.

    (a) largest circuit conductor
    (b) overcurrent protective device for the feeder or branch circuit
    (c) smallest branch circuit conductor
    (d) overcurrent protective device for the service

CHAPTER 3— WIRING METHODS AND MATERIALS

44. For locations not specifically identified in Table 300.5, a lesser cover depth than required in Column 5 shall be permitted where specified in the installation instructions of a(n) _____ low-voltage lighting system.

    (a) approved
    (b) labeled
    (c) listed
    (d) none of these

45. For locations not specifically identified in Table 300.5, a cover depth of _____ in. shall be permitted for pool, spa, and fountain lighting, installed in a nonmetallic raceway, limited to not more than 30V where part of a listed low-voltage lighting system.

    (a) 6
    (b) 12
    (c) 18
    (d) 24

46. Where raceways or cables are exposed to direct sunlight on or above rooftops, raceways or cables shall be installed a minimum of _____ in. above the roof to the bottom of the raceway or cable.

    (a) ¼
    (b) ½
    (c) ⅞
    (d) 1⅛

47. The wiring space within enclosures for switches and overcurrent devices shall be permitted for other wiring and equipment subject to limitations for specific equipment as provided in _____.

    (a) 312.8(A)
    (b) 312.8(B)
    (c) a and b
    (d) none of these

48. _____ drainage openings not smaller than ⅛ in. and not larger than ¼ in. in diameter shall be permitted to be installed in the field in boxes or conduit bodies listed for use in damp or wet locations.

    (a) Listed
    (b) Approved
    (c) Labeled
    (d) Identified

49. When calculating box fill, each space within a box installed with a barrier shall be calculated separately.

    (a) True
    (b) False

50. Outlet boxes required in 314.27 shall be permitted to support _____ locking, support, and mounting receptacles used in combination with compatible attachment fittings.

    (a) identified
    (b) listed
    (c) approved
    (d) labeled

51. Unless otherwise specified, the applicable product standards evaluate the fill markings covered in 314.28(A)(3), based on conductors with Type _____ insulation.

    (a) THHW
    (b) RHW
    (c) THHN
    (d) XHHW

52. Type MC cable shall be supported and secured by staples; cable ties _____ for securement and support; straps, hangers, or similar fittings; or other approved means designed and installed so as not to damage the cable.

    (a) listed
    (b) identified
    (c) a and b
    (d) none of these

53. Nonmetallic-sheathed cable shall be permitted to be unsupported where the cable is _____.

    (a) fished between access points through concealed spaces in finished buildings or structures and supporting is impracticable
    (b) not more than 4½ ft from the last point of cable support to the point of connection to a luminaire or other piece of electrical equipment and the cable and point of connection are within an accessible ceiling in one-, two-, or multifamily dwellings
    (c) a and b
    (d) none of these

54. Type TC-ER cable used for interior wiring in one- and two-family dwelling units that's suitable for pulling through structural members is marked "TC-ER-JP."

    (a) True
    (b) False

55. For interior installations of Type SE cable with ungrounded conductor sizes _____ AWG and smaller, where installed in thermal insulation, the ampacity shall be in accordance with the conductor's temperature rating.

(a) 14
(b) 12
(c) 10
(d) 8

CHAPTER 4—EQUIPMENT FOR GENERAL USE

56. Flexible cord sets and power-supply cords shall not be used as a substitute for _____ wiring.

(a) temporary
(b) fixed
(c) overhead
(d) none of these

57. Flexible cord sets and power-supply cords shall not be used where they _____.

(a) run through holes in walls, ceilings, or floors
(b) run through doorways, windows, or similar openings
(c) attached to building surfaces, unless permitted by 368.56(B)
(d) all of these

58. Flexible cord sets and power-supply cords shall not be permitted above suspended or dropped ceilings even if contained within an enclosure for use in "other spaces used for environmental air."

(a) True
(b) False

59. All nonlocking-type, 125V, 15A and 20A receptacles that are controlled by _____, or that incorporate control features that remove power from the receptacle for the purpose of energy management or building automation, shall be permanently marked with the word "controlled."

(a) wall switches
(b) remote control
(c) wireless communication
(d) an automatic control device

60. Where attachment to an equipment grounding conductor doesn't exist in the receptacle enclosure, a non-grounding-type receptacle shall be permitted to be replaced with a GFCI-type receptacle; however, some equipment or appliance manufacturers require that the _____ to the equipment or appliance includes an equipment grounding conductor.

(a) feeder
(b) branch circuit
(c) small-appliance circuit
(d) none of these

61. Listed tamper-resistant receptacles shall be provided where replacements are made at receptacle outlets that are required to be tamper-resistant elsewhere in this *Code* except where a non-grounding receptacle is replaced with _____ receptacle.

(a) an isolated
(b) a GFCI-type
(c) another non-grounding
(d) any of these

62. Nonlocking-type 125V and 250V, 15A and 20A receptacles installed in _____ shall be listed as tamper resistant.

(a) guest rooms and guest suites of hotels and motels
(b) child care facilities
(c) preschools and elementary education facilities
(d) all of these

63. Nonlocking-type 15A and 20A, 125V and 250V receptacles in a dwelling unit shall be listed as tamper resistant except _____.

(a) receptacles located more than 5½ ft above the floor
(b) receptacles that are part of a luminaire or appliance
(c) a receptacle located within the dedicated space for an appliance that, in normal use, isn't easily moved from one place to another
(d) all of these

64. _____ rated 250V or less and 60A or less, single- or 3-phase, shall be provided with GFCI protection for personnel.

(a) Tire inflation machines provided for public use
(b) Vending machines
(c) a and b
(d) none of these

65. The GFCI required for appliances shall be readily accessible, listed, and located _____.

    (a) within the branch circuit overcurrent device
    (b) in a device or outlet within the supply circuit
    (c) in an integral part of the attachment plug
    (d) any of these

66. All appliances operating at _____ volts or more shall be listed.

    (a) 20V
    (b) 30V
    (c) 50V
    (d) 60V

67. The receptacle for a built-in dishwasher shall be located _____ occupied by the dishwasher.

    (a) in the space
    (b) adjacent to the space
    (c) a or b
    (d) none of these

68. For permanently connected motor-operated appliances with motors rated over _____, a switch or circuit breaker located within sight from the motor-operated appliance, or be capable of being locked in the open position in compliance with 110.25, can serve as the appliance disconnect.

    (a) ⅛ hp
    (b) ¼ hp
    (c) 15A
    (d) b and c

69. Where multimotor and combination-load equipment for air-conditioning and refrigeration is installed outdoors on a roof, a(n) _____ conductor of the wire type shall be installed in outdoor portions of metallic raceway systems that use non-threaded fittings.

    (a) equipment grounding
    (b) grounding
    (c) equipment bonding
    (d) bonding

70. Receptacle outlets that are a part of a _____ kW or smaller portable generator shall have listed ground-fault circuit-interrupter protection (GFCI) for personnel integral to the generator or receptacle.

    (a) 10
    (b) 15
    (c) 20
    (d) 25

71. GFCI protection for 15 kW or smaller portable generators shall not be required where the 125V receptacle outlets(s) is interlocked such that it isn't available for use when any 125/250V receptacle(s) is in use.

    (a) True
    (b) False

72. If the 15 kW or smaller portable generator was manufactured or remanufactured prior to _____, listed cord sets or devices incorporating listed GFCI protection for personnel identified for portable use shall be permitted.

    (a) January 1, 2012
    (b) January 1, 2013
    (c) January 1, 2014
    (d) January 1, 2015

CHAPTER 5—SPECIAL OCCUPANCIES

73. _____ for fuel dispensing systems shall disconnect power to all dispensing devices; to all remote pumps serving the dispensing devices; to all associated power, control, and signal circuits; and to all other electrical equipment in the hazardous (classified) locations surrounding the fuel dispensing devices.

    (a) Emergency shutoff devices
    (b) Electrical disconnects
    (c) a or b
    (d) none of these

74. The patient care space of a health care facility known as a "_____" is a space in which failure of equipment or a system isn't likely to have a physical impact on patient care.

(a) Critical Care (Category 1)
(b) General Care (Category 2) Space
(c) Basic Care (Category 3) Space
(d) Support (Category 4) Space

75. In patient care spaces, luminaires more than _____ ft above the floor and switches located outside of the patient care vicinity shall be permitted to be connected to an equipment grounding return path complying with 517.13(A) or (B).

(a) 7
(b) 7½
(c) 7¾
(d) 8

76. In health care facilities, isolated ground receptacles are typically installed where a reduction of electrical noise (electromagnetic interference) is necessary, and _____ grounding paths are to be avoided.

(a) series
(b) parallel
(c) series-parallel
(d) none of these

77. The purpose of the equipotential plane in agricultural buildings or adjacent areas is to minimize voltage differences within the plane, as well as between planes, grounded equipment, and the earth.

(a) True
(b) False

78. Permanent safety signs shall be installed to give notice of electrical shock hazard risks to persons using or swimming near a boat dock or marina and shall _____.

(a) comply with 110.21(B)(1) and be of sufficient durability to withstand the environment
(b) be clearly visible from all approaches to a marina or boatyard facility
(c) state, "WARNING—POTENTIAL SHOCK HAZARD—ELECTRICAL CURRENTS MAY BE PRESENT IN THE WATER"
(d) all of these

79. Receptacles rated other than 125V, single-phase, 15A, 20A, and 30A for temporary installations shall be protected by a(n) _____.

(a) GFCI protection for personnel
(b) SPGFCI protection for personnel
(c) written assured equipment grounding conductor program
(d) any of these

CHAPTER 6—SPECIAL EQUIPMENT

80. The location of the sign and outline lighting system feeder or branch circuit disconnect is intended to allow _____ personnel complete and local control of the disconnecting means.

(a) service
(b) maintenance
(c) a or b
(d) none of these

81. Where the disconnecting means is out of the line of sight from any section of a sign or outline lighting able to be energized, the disconnecting means shall be _____ in the open position in accordance with 110.25.

(a) secured
(b) bolted
(c) lockable
(d) none of these

82. Interconnecting cables under raised floors that support information technology equipment shall be listed Type _____ cable having adequate fire-resistant characteristics suitable for use under raised floors of an information technology equipment room.

(a) RF
(b) Type UF
(c) LS
(d) DP

83. An electrically powered lift that provides accessibility to and from a pool or spa for people with disabilities is known as an "electrically powered _____ lift."

(a) spa
(b) disability
(c) pool
(d) tub

84. When installed for swimming pools, grounding and bonding terminals shall be _____ for direct burial use.

    (a) identified
    (b) labeled
    (c) listed
    (d) approved

85. Underground wiring shall not be permitted under a pool unless this wiring is necessary to supply pool equipment permitted by Article 680, and the _____ cover depths shall be as given in Table 300.5.

    (a) maximum
    (b) permissible
    (c) minimum
    (d) any of these

86. Adequate ventilation of indoor spaces such as _____ rooms is addressed by ANSI/APSP-11, *Standard for Water Quality in Public Pools and Spas*, and can reduce the likelihood of the accumulation of corrosive vapors on electrical pool equipment.

    (a) equipment
    (b) storage
    (c) a and b
    (d) none of these

87. Wiring methods in the areas described in 680.14(A) shall be _____ for use in such areas.

    (a) listed
    (b) labeled
    (c) identified
    (d) a and c

88. For permanently installed pools, a GFCI shall be installed in the branch circuit supplying luminaires operating at more than the low-voltage _____.

    (a) setting
    (b) listing
    (c) contact limit
    (d) none of these

89. Wiring methods installed in corrosive environments as described in 680.14 shall contain an insulated copper equipment grounding conductor sized in accordance with Table 250.122, but not smaller than 12 AWG.

    (a) True
    (b) False

90. For equipotential bonding, the perimeter surface to be bonded shall be considered to extend for _____ ft horizontally beyond the inside walls of the pool and shall include unpaved surfaces and other types of paving.

    (a) 3
    (b) 5
    (c) 10
    (d) 12

91. Where installed for hydromassage bathtubs _____ shall be bonded together.

    (a) all exposed metal surfaces that are within 5 ft of the inside walls of the tub and not separated from the tub area by a permanent barrier
    (b) electrical devices and controls that aren't associated with the hydromassage tubs and that are located within 5 ft from such units
    (c) a and b
    (d) none of these

92. The 8 AWG solid bonding jumper required for equipotential bonding in the area of hydromassage bathtubs shall not be required to be extended to any _____.

    (a) remote panelboard
    (b) service equipment
    (c) electrode
    (d) any of these

93. A(n) _____ surge protection device shall be installed in or on the fire pump controller.

    (a) listed
    (b) labeled
    (c) identified
    (d) approved

CHAPTER 7—SPECIAL CONDITIONS

94. If wiring from an emergency source is used to supply emergency and other loads, then _____ switchgear sections or _____ switchboard sections, with or without a common bus, or individual disconnects mounted in separate enclosures shall be used to separate emergency loads from all other loads.

    (a) separate vertical
    (b) separate horizontal
    (c) combined vertical and horizontal
    (d) none of these

95. One example of the use of cables for Class 2 or Class 3 circuits that transmit power and data is the connection of closed-circuit TV cameras (CCTV).

    (a) True
    (b) False

96. Where Types CL3P, CL2P, CL3R, CL2R, CL3, or CL2 transmit power and data, _____.

    (a) the ampacity ratings in Table 725.144 shall apply at an ambient temperature of 30°C (86°F)
    (b) for ambient temperatures above 30°C (86°F), the correction factors of 310.15(B)(2) shall apply
    (c) a or b
    (d) none of these

97. When using Table 725.144, bundle sizes over _____ cables, or conductor sizes smaller than 26 AWG, ampacities shall be permitted to be determined by qualified personnel under engineering supervision.

    (a) 129
    (b) 178
    (c) 187
    (d) 192

98. Table 725.144 only lists four conductor sizes because the conductor sizes in data cables in wide-spread use are typically 22 to 26 AWG.

    (a) True
    (b) False

99. A Type CL2- LP(0.50), 23 AWG could be used in any location where a Type CL2 could be used; however, the LP cable would be suitable for carrying up to 0.50A per conductor, regardless of the number of cables in a bundle.

    (a) True
    (b) False

100. Paint, plaster, cleaners, abrasives, corrosive residues, or other contaminants may result in an undetermined alteration of optical fiber cable _____.

    (a) usefulness
    (b) voltage
    (c) properties
    (d) none of these

ABOUT THE AUTHOR

Mike Holt—Author

Founder and President,
Mike Holt Enterprises
Groveland, FL
www.MikeHolt.com

Mike Holt's electrical career has spanned all aspects of the trade from being an apprentice to becoming a contractor and inspector. His teaching career began in 1974 when he became an exam preparation instructor at a local community school. He was so successful that his students encouraged him to open his own training school dedicated to helping the electrical industry. In 1975, Mike opened his school while also running a full-service electrical contracting firm. His school became so successful that by 1980 he stopped electrical contracting to completely devote his time to electrical training at a national level. Today, Mike Holt Enterprises is a leading training and publishing company for the industry, specializing in helping electrical professionals take their careers to the next level.

A part of Mike's story that impacts the way he designs training programs is his own educational journey. As a young man he was unable to complete the requirements for his high school diploma due to life circumstances. Realizing that success depends on one's education, Mike immediately attained his GED. Then ten years later he attended the University of Miami's Graduate School for a Master's degree in Business Administration. Because of this experience, he understands the needs of his students, and strongly encourages and motivates them to continue their own education. He's never lost sight of how hard it can be for students who are intimidated by the complexity of the *NEC*, by school, or by their own feelings about learning. His ultimate goal has always been about increasing electrical safety and improving lives—his commitment and vision continue to guide him to this day.

Mike has written hundreds of books, and created DVDs, online programs, MP3s, and other training materials that have made a huge impact on the industry. He's mastered the art of explaining complicated concepts in a simple but direct style. His ability to simplify

technical concepts and his one-of-a-kind presentation style explain his unique position as one of the premier speakers and *Code* experts in the United States. In addition to Mike's extensive list of companies around the world for whom he's provided training, and materials he's produced, Mike has written articles that have been seen in numerous industry magazines including, *Electrical Construction & Maintenance* (EC&M), *CEE News, Electrical Design and Installation* (EDI), *Electrical Contractor* (EC), *International Association of Electrical Inspectors* (IAEI News), *The Electrical Distributor* (TED), *Power Quality* (PQ) *Magazine,* and *Solar Pro Magazine*.

Mike resides in Central Florida, is the father of seven children, has five grandchildren, and enjoys many outside interests and activities. His commitment to pushing boundaries and setting high standards has also extended into his personal life. He's an 8-time National Barefoot Waterskiing Champion, has set many world records in that sport, and has competed in three World Barefoot Waterskiing Tournaments. In 2015, he started a new career in competitive mountain bike racing and continues to find ways to motivate himself mentally and physically.

What distinguishes Mike is his commitment to living a balanced lifestyle; placing God first, family, career, and self.

Special Acknowledgments

My Family. First, I want to thank God for my godly wife who's always by my side and my children, Belynda, Melissa, Autumn, Steven, Michael, Meghan, and Brittney.

My Staff. A personal thank you goes to my team at Mike Holt Enterprises for all the work they do to help me with my mission of changing people's lives through education.

The National Fire Protection Association. A special thank you must be given to the staff at the National Fire Protection Association (NFPA), publishers of the *NEC*—in particular, Jeff Sargent for his assistance in answering my many *Code* questions over the years. Jeff, you're a "first class" guy, and I admire your dedication and commitment to helping others understand the *NEC*. Other former NFPA staff members I would like to thank include John Caloggero, Joe Ross, and Dick Murray for their help in the past.

ABOUT THE ILLUSTRATOR

Mike Culbreath—Illustrator

Mike Culbreath
Graphic Illustrator
Alden, MI
www.MikeHolt.com

Mike Culbreath devoted his career to the electrical industry and worked his way up from apprentice to master electrician. He started in the electrical field doing residential and light commercial construction, and later did service work and custom electrical installations. While working as a journeyman electrician, he suffered a serious on-the-job knee injury. As part of his rehabilitation, Mike completed courses at Mike Holt Enterprises, and then passed the exam to receive his Master Electrician's license. In 1986, with a keen interest in continuing education for electricians, he joined the staff to update material and began illustrating Mike Holt's textbooks and magazine articles.

Mike started with simple hand-drawn diagrams and cut-and-paste graphics. When frustrated by the limitations of that style of illustrating, he took a company computer home to learn how to operate some basic computer graphic software. Upon realizing that computer graphics offered increased flexibility for creating illustrations, Mike took every computer graphics class and seminar he could to help develop his computer graphic skills. He's now worked as an illustrator and editor with the company for over 30 years and, as Mike Holt has proudly acknowledged, has helped to transform his words and visions into lifelike graphics.

Originally from south Florida, Mike now lives in northern lower Michigan where he enjoys hiking, kayaking, photography, gardening, and cooking; but his real passion is his horses. Mike loves spending time with his children (Dawn and Mac) and his grandchildren Jonah, Kieley, and Scarlet.

Special Acknowledgments—I would like to thank Eric Stromberg, an electrical engineer and super geek (and I mean that in the most complimentary manner because I think this guy is brilliant), for helping me keep our graphics as technically correct as possible. I would also like to thank all of our students for the wonderful feedback they provide that helps us improve our graphics.

I also want to give a special thank you to Cathleen Kwas for making me look good with her outstanding layout design and typesetting skills; to Toni Culbreath who proofreads all of my material; and to Dawn Babbitt who assists me in the production and editing of our graphics. I would also like to acknowledge Belynda Holt Pinto, our Director of Operations, Brian House for his input (another really brilliant guy), and the rest of the outstanding staff at Mike Holt Enterprises, for all the hard work they do to help produce and distribute these outstanding products.

And last but not least, I need to give a special thank you to Mike Holt for not firing me over 30 years ago when I "borrowed" one of his computers and took it home to begin the process of learning how to do computer illustrations. He gave me the opportunity and time needed to develop my computer graphic skills. He's been an amazing friend and mentor ever since I met him as a student many years ago. Thanks for believing in me and allowing me to be part of the Mike Holt Enterprises family.

ABOUT THE MIKE HOLT TEAM

Technical Writing Team

There are many people who played a role in the production of this textbook—first and foremost is the technical team. Their efforts are reflected in the quality and organization of the information contained in this textbook, and in its technical accuracy, completeness, and usability.

Daniel Brian House

Brian House played a key role by assisting in the re-writing and editing of this textbook, coordinating the content and the illustrations, and assuring the technical accuracy and flow of the information presented. Brian is a permanent addition to the technical writing team at Mike Holt Enterprises, and also served as a member of the Video team for the DVDs that accompany this textbook

Ryan Jackson

Ryan Jackson created the first draft text for the introduction and analysis for all of the *Code* changes in this edition. His knowledge of the *Code* is paramount, and his research and perseverance created the back-bone of this textbook. Ryan is an electrical inspector, as well as being certified in building, plumbing, and mechanical inspection, and building and electrical plan review for commercial and residential occupancies. He's a highly sought-after seminar instructor who teaches in several states, and loves helping students increase their understanding of the *Code*.

When Ryan isn't working, he can often be found in his garage turning wood on his lathe, or in the kitchen where he enjoys wine making. Ryan married his high school sweetheart, Sharie, and they have two beautiful children together: Kaitlynn and Aaron.

Editorial and Production Team

A special thanks goes to **Toni Culbreath** for her outstanding contribution to this project. She worked tirelessly to proofread and edit this publication. Her attention to detail and dedication is irreplaceable.

Many thanks to **Cathleen Kwas** who did the design, layout, and production of this textbook. Her desire to create the best possible product for our customers is greatly appreciated.

Also, thanks to **Paula Birchfield** who was the Production Coordinator of this product. She helped keep everything flowing and tied up all of the loose ends.

Thanks to **Bruce Marcho** for doing such an excellent job recording, editing, and producing our DVDs. Bruce has played a vital role in the production of our products for over 25 years.

DVD Team Members

The following special people provided technical advice in the development of this textbook as they served on the video team along with author Mike Holt and graphic illustrator Mike Culbreath.

Bruce Angeloszek
Electrical Contractor/Owner
Beacon Falls, CT

Bruce Angeloszek holds a State of Connecticut Unlimited Electrical Contracting License, and a State Electrical Inspector's license. He's the proud owner of CT Electrical Services, which has been operating since 1994 and he's personally involved on every project. His company represents the proven skills and expertise in all electrical areas including, Generac Generators, solar PV systems, and battery back-up and solar PV hybrid systems.

Bruce has a passion for the *NEC* and attends as many seminars and classes as possible. He's been following Mike Holt's career since the 1990s and contributes much of his electrical knowledge and success to Mike Holt Enterprises. Bruce knows that the more *Code*-educated you are, the more you prosper in the electrical industry.

Bruce has been married to his lovely wife Lee for 27 years and has two children. When not working, he takes long biking rides through many of the scenic parts of New England.

"My customers' needs are very important to me. Intelligence, safety, ethics, and accountability are key components to my business."

David Harsche
Master Electrician
Tampa, FL

David Harsche is from Beachwood, New Jersey and is committed to serving the Electrical Industry. He worked his way up from an apprentice to a Journeyman/Foreman electrician during the four years he worked in the commercial, industrial, and residential fields of the trade. He became a Master Electrician during his fifth year and was promoted to superintendent during his sixth. David moved to Tampa, Florida where he worked for several years as a project manager and managed multimillion-dollar electrical projects. He later worked as a Hillsborough County Electrical Inspector.

David had successfully started, marketed, and now manages Team Electric in Tampa, Florida. He's been self-employed for several years with a focus on lighting design, electrical investigation, and commercial and residential electrical work. He recently competed in the NFPA *National Electrical Code* Championship and placed second. David replaced Dick Widera (whom he believes is an amazing man) as the Secretary of the IAEI Suncoast Division.

"I want to thank God, my wife Renee, and my daughter Katlin; without them I wouldn't be where I am at today."

Michael Holt, Jr.
Electrical Contractor/Owner
Groveland, FL

Michael Holt, Jr. is the son of Mike Holt, and has been exposed to the electrical trade his entire life. He's a Florida State Certified Electrical Contractor, and has owned his own electrical service and repair business in Central Florida since 2008. Michael's company does wiring, troubleshooting, and reconfigurations for low-voltage systems, as well as building premises wiring for both residential and commercial customers. It's a business that prides itself on providing outstanding professional customer service, while incorporating safety and quality in all of the work it does. In fact, customer service and loyalty are the cornerstones of Michael's business model that have helped him build his reputation and can be attributed for much of his company's success.

He's embarked on a life journey to not only improve his personal life, but to also affect the lives of others by way of mentorship to the young professionals of the world. His hobbies include jet skiing, motocross racing, and stand-up comedy, both as a performer and a member of the audience. Michael is very much a people person and is very active in his community. He has a daughter, Haylee, whom he absolutely adores.

Daniel Brian House

Mike Holt Enterprises
Leesburg, FL
www.MikeHolt.com

Brian House is a high-energy entrepreneur with a passion for doing business the right way. He's a licensed unlimited electrical contractor having worked throughout the southeast United States since the 1990s. From single family homes to industrial manufacturing he's enjoyed experiencing all aspects of the trade. Whether it was service work, designing energy-efficient lighting retrofits, biomass powered generators or installing solar PV systems, Brian has first-hand experience with the ups and downs of electrical contracting and a vision for its future.

Since 2000, Brian has enjoyed teaching at seminars and apprenticeship classes. He joined the Mike Holt video teams in 2010 and in 2014 joined the Mike Holt staff as the technical director. He continues to teach seminars and is actively involved in developing and teaching apprenticeship classes.

Brian and his wife Carissa have shared the joy of four children and many foster children during 19 years of marriage. When not mentoring youth at work or church, he can be found racing mountain bikes with his kids or fly fishing on Florida's Intracoastal Waterway.

Eric Stromberg

Electrical Engineer/Instructor
Los Alamos, NM

Eric Stromberg is a professional engineer with a long background in the electrical industry. He started as an apprentice electrician and worked his way up to being a journeyman. After graduating from the University of Houston with a degree in Electrical Engineering, he worked in the life safety field, installing life safety systems in high-rise buildings. He then went to work for Dow Chemical where he engineered major industrial systems in several countries, in addition to managing an electrical engineering department and electrical inspection department.

Eric also served on the electrical advisory board to the Texas department of licensing and regulation for eight years, as well as the exam board for electrician licensing. He's taught exam review courses for the Professional Engineering exam, was a certified continuing education instructor for electrician licensing, and taught electrical courses at a local college. Eric currently teaches *Code* classes, in New Mexico, for electrician licensing.

Eric's oldest daughter, Ainsley, teaches for an international school in Zurich, Switzerland where she lives with her husband Nathan. His son Austin served in the Air Force, is a pilot and the owner of an aerial photography business, and is graduating this year with a degree in Aviation logistics. His youngest daughter, Brieanna, is a singer/songwriter in Austin, Texas.

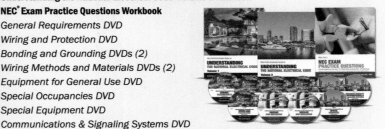
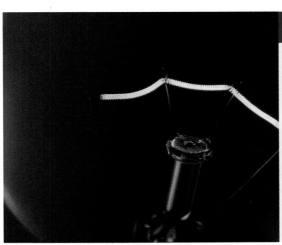

Save 25% On These Best-Selling Libraries

Understanding the NEC® Complete Training Library

This library makes it easy to learn the Code. Your package includes the following best-selling textbooks and DVDs:

Understanding the National Electrical Code® Volume 1 Textbook
Understanding the National Electrical Code® Volume 2 Textbook
NEC® Exam Practice Questions Workbook
General Requirements DVD
Wiring and Protection DVD
Bonding and Grounding DVDs (2)
Wiring Methods and Materials DVDs (2)
Equipment for General Use DVD
Special Occupancies DVD
Special Equipment DVD
Communications & Signaling Systems DVD

Product Code: 17DECODVD   List Price: $599.00   Now only $449.25

Electrical Theory DVD Training Package

Understanding electrical theory is critical for anyone who works with electricity. The topics in this textbook will help you understand what electricity is, how it's produced and how it's used. You'll learn everything from a brief study of matter to how to perform basic electrical calculations critical for everyday use.

Library includes:

Electrical Theory Textbook
Electrical Fundamentals and Basic Electricity DVD
Electrical Circuits, Systems, and Protection DVD
Alternating Current, Motors, Generators, and Transformers DVD

Product Code: ETLIBD   List Price: $299.00   Now only $224.25

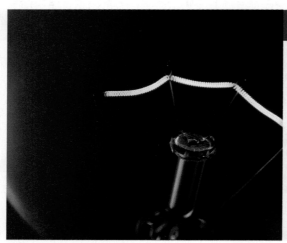

Bonding and Grounding DVD Training Package

Grounding and Bonding is the least understood and most important article in the NEC®. This program focuses on Article 250 but also addresses grounding rules throughout the Code Book. The textbook and DVDs are informative and practical, and include in one single place, all articles that relate to bonding and grounding. The full-color illustrations help break down the concepts and make them easier to understand. This is a great resource for everyone that really needs to understand bonding and grounding. Order your copy today.

Library includes:

Bonding and Grounding Textbook
Bonding and Grounding DVDs (2)

Product Code: 17NCDVD2   List Price: $210.00   Now only $157.50

Call Now 888.NEC.CODE (632.2633)

& mention discount code: B17BK25

Mike Holt Enterprises

All prices and availability are subject to change